WESTMINSTER ABBEY
AND ITS ESTATES IN
THE MIDDLE AGES

WESTMINSTER ABBEY
AND ITS ESTATES IN THE MIDDLE AGES

BY

BARBARA HARVEY

OXFORD
AT THE CLARENDON PRESS
1977

Oxford University Press, Walton Street, Oxford OX2 6DP

OXFORD LONDON GLASGOW NEW YORK
TORONTO MELBOURNE WELLINGTON CAPE TOWN
IBADAN NAIROBI DAR ES SALAAM LUSAKA ADDIS ABABA
KUALA LUMPUR SINGAPORE JAKARTA HONG KONG TOKYO
DELHI BOMBAY CALCUTTA MADRAS KARACHI

© *Oxford University Press 1977*

British Library Cataloguing in Publication Data

Harvey, Barbara
  Westminster Abbey and its estates in the Middle Ages
  Bibl. – Index.
  ISBN 0-19-822449-4
  1. Title
  333.3'22'0942132   HD610.L/
  Church lands – England – Westminster,
  London – History

*Printed in Great Britain
at the University Press, Oxford
by Vivian Ridler
Printer to the University*

PREFACE

THIS book is a study neither of the religious and domestic history of the monks of Westminster nor of the economic history of their estates. It is an attempt to capture the view of their estates that the monks had from Westminster over some five hundred years, and to weigh the consequences for their tenants of the thoughts provoked by it. The theme of the book will, I hope, explain what may at first appear surprising omissions. Thus the foundation of anniversaries and chantries is recounted, since by these the Abbey's possessions were greatly augmented, but nothing is said of the consequences for monastic life at Westminster of the liturgical obligations undertaken by the monks in return for the new benefactions. A chapter is devoted to the role of the manorial demesnes in the monastic economy, but none to the economic development of the demesnes themselves. The monks, it is suggested, were exigent landlords in the thirteenth and fourteenth centuries, but ineffectual in the fifteenth; little or no attempt, however, has been made to describe the administrative developments, whether in the Abbey's precinct or in the manors, that were concomitants of this change.

The material used in this study has been collected over a period of more than twenty years. I thank the Dean and Chapter of Westminster for the opportunity afforded me of exploring the Abbey's rich archive, in the uniquely beautiful surroundings of the Muniment Room, over so many years. For the generous facilities which I have enjoyed in the Muniment Room, I am also deeply indebted to Mr. L. E. Tanner, formerly Librarian and Keeper of the Muniments, to Mr. H. M. Nixon, the present Librarian, and to Mr. N. H. MacMichael, Keeper of the Muniments. Lord Petre has allowed me to use records relating to some of the Abbey's former possessions in Gloucestershire and Warwickshire now forming part of the Petre family archives and deposited in the Gloucestershire Records Office. I am grateful to the staff of that repository for facilitating my work there. Further, I gladly acknowledge the help which I have received at the Essex Record Office, the Hertfordshire Record Office, the Bodleian Library, the British Library, and the Public Record Office. The Dean and Chapter of St. Paul's have permitted me to use the ministers' accounts for the manor of Stevenage now in the library of St. Paul's Cathedral. Mr. J. S. G. Simmons, Librarian of the Codrington Library, enabled me to use the list of burials in the Abbey which is now in All Souls College MS. 126. Through the kindness of Mr. Michael Maclagan, Portcullis Pursuivant, I have been able to transcribe two other lists of burials, now in the library of the College of Arms. For help with the list of burials in Appendix II, I am, again, indebted to Mr. MacMichael; his additions and corrections to this list far exceed those specifically recorded in the text. In proof the book benefited greatly from Mrs. Susan Hall's expertise. For the care and consideration of the officers of the Clarendon Press I am indeed grateful.

Finally, I have to thank, although I cannot hope to do so adequately, the friends and mentors whose advice and encouragement have so greatly assisted the writing of this book: Professor M. McKisack, Professor V. H. Galbraith, Sir Richard Southern, Dr. P. Chaplais, Lady de Villiers, Miss L. M. Brown, Miss J. E. Bridge, Miss N. V. Dunbar, Mrs. S. Raban, Dr. H. M. Chew, Dr. P. R. Hyams, Miss S. M. G. Reynolds, and Mrs. S. J. Loach. To Sir Richard Southern, who read the whole of the work in typescript and offered many suggestions for its improvement, I am especially indebted.

Barbara Harvey

December 1976

CONTENTS

List of Tables   *page* ix

List of Maps   ix

Abbreviations   x

Abbots of Westminster   xii

Introduction   1

I. The Foundation of Westminster Abbey   20

II. Income and its Sources   26

III. Subinfeudation and the Division of Goods   70

IV. Free Tenants on the Demesne Manors   101

V. The Manorial Demesnes   127

VI. Purchases of Property   164

VII. Customary Land to 1348: the Size of Holdings   203

VIII. Customary Land to 1348: Rents and Services   216

IX. Customary Land from 1348 to *c.* 1390   244

X. From Villeinage to Customary Tenure, *c.* 1390 to
   c. 1490   268

XI. The Land Transactions of the Abbey's Tenants   294

Conclusion   331

Appendices
   I. The Demesne Manors of Westminster Abbey,
      to 1540   335
   II. Burials, Confraternity, Perpetual Anniversaries
       and Chantries, and other forms of Spiritual
       Benefit   367

III. Appropriated Churches   *page* 402

IV. Major Purchases of Property   413

V. The Acreage of Demesne Land and of Customary Land in the Demesne Manors, *c.* 1300 to *c.* 1330   428

VI. Holdings in the Demesne Manors of Westminster Abbey, to 1348, Classified by Tenure   431

VII. Holdings of Customary Land in the Demesne Manors of Westminster Abbey, to 1348, Classified by Arable Acreage   434

VIII. The Extended Value of the Annual Dues for Virgated Holdings of Customary Land in the Demesne Manors of Westminster Abbey in the Early Fourteenth Century   438

IX. Customary and Contractual Rents per Arable Acre in the Demesne Manors of Westminster Abbey in the Early Fourteenth Century   443

Glossary   448

Bibliography   452

Index   475

LIST OF TABLES

I. The Finances of the Major Royal Foundations   *page* 34

II. The Annual Income of Westminster Abbey from Parish Churches according to the Taxation of Pope Nicholas IV, 1291   50

III. The Annual Income of Westminster Abbey from Churches in 1535   53

IV. The Annual Value of the Goods of Westminster Abbey according to the Taxation of Pope Nicholas IV, 1291   58

V. The Net Annual Income of Westminster Abbey in 1535   62

VI. The Net Annual Income of Westminster Abbey, 1086–1535   63

VII. Teamlands, Plough-Teams, and Population in the Demesne Manors of Westminster Abbey in 1086, as recorded in Domesday Book   123

VIII. The Average Annual Value of the Receipts of Grain and Malt entered in the Annual Account of the Steward of the Abbot's Household, 29 September 1362–29 September 1369   137

IX. The Average Annual Value of the Grain and Malt received by the Conventual Granger, 1350–1370   147

X. The Annual Dues owed by a Tenant in Villeinage of a Virgate of Customary Land at Teddington in the Early Thirteenth and Early Fourteenth Centuries   220

XI. The Number of Admittances to Customary Land and of Transfers *inter vivos* recorded in the Manors of Islip and Launton in the Later Middle Ages   324

LIST OF MAPS

I. The Demesne Manors of Westminster Abbey in 1086   471

II. The Principal Estates of Westminster Abbey in 1535   472–3

III. Churches Appropriated to Westminster Abbey by 1540   474

ABBREVIATIONS

B.I.H.R.	*Bulletin of the Institute of Historical Research*
Cal. Ch. R.	*Calendar of Charter Rolls* (H.M.S.O., 1903–)
Cal. Cl. R.	*Calendar of Close Rolls* (H.M.S.O., 1892–)
Cal. Fine R.	*Calendar of Fine Rolls* (H.M.S.O., 1911–)
Cal. Fines, London and Midd.	*A Calendar to the Feet of Fines for London and Middlesex*, vol. i, *Richard I to Richard III*, ed. W. J. Hardy and W. Page (London, 1892–3)
Cal. Inq. post mortem	*Calendar of Inquisitions post mortem* (H.M.S.O., 1904–)
Cal. Liberate R.	*Calendar of Liberate Rolls* (H.M.S.O., 1916–)
Cal. Papal Letters	*Entries in the Papal Registers relating to Great Britain and Ireland*, ed. W. H. Bliss, C. Johnson, and J. A. Twemlow: *Calendar of Papal Letters* (H.M.S.O., 1893–)
Cal. Pat. R.	*Calendar of Patent Rolls* (H.M.S.O., 1901–)
Camden	Camden, W., *Reges, Reginae, Nobiles et Alii in Ecclesia Collegiata B. Petri Westmonasterii Sepulti usque ad Annum Reparatae Salutis 1600* (London, 1600)
C.R.R.	*Curia Regis Rolls* (H.M.S.O., 1922–)
C.U.L.	Cambridge University Library
Customary	*Customary of the Benedictine Monasteries of Saint Augustine, Canterbury, and Saint Peter, Westminster*, ed. E. Maunde Thompson (2 vols., Henry Bradshaw Soc., xxiii, xxviii, 1902, 1904)
D.B.	*Domesday Book* (2 vols., 1783)
D.N.B.	*Dictionary of National Biography*
Dugdale, *Mon. Ang.*	W. Dugdale, *Monasticon Anglicanum*, ed. J. Caley H. Ellis, and B. Bandinel (6 vols., London, 1817–30)
Essex Fines	*Feet of Fines for Essex*, ed. R. E. G. Kirk, E. F. Kirk, P. H. Reaney, M. Fitch, *et al.* (4 vols., Essex Archaeological Soc., 1899–1964)
Flete	*The History of Westminster Abbey by John Flete*, ed. J. Armitage Robinson (Cambridge, 1909)
Foedera	*Foedera, conventiones, literae et cujuscunque generis acta publica, etc.*, ed. T. Rymer (20 vols., London, 1704–35)

G.E.C.	G. E. Cokayne, *The Complete Peerage*, ed. V. Gibbs, H. A. Doubleday, *et al.* (London, 1910–)
Gilbert Crispin	J. Armitage Robinson, *Gilbert Crispin, abbot of Westminster* (Cambridge, 1911)
Harmer	F. E. Harmer, *Anglo-Saxon Writs* (Manchester, 1952)
Knights of Edward I	C. Moor, *Knights of Edward I* (5 vols., Harleian Soc., lxxx–lxxxiv, 1929–32)
Letters and Papers, Henry VIII	*Calendar of Letters and Papers, Foreign and Domestic, Henry VIII*, ed. J. S. Brewer, J. Gairdner, and R. H. Brodie (H.M.S.O., 1864–1932)
Liber Niger Quaternus	Westminster Abbey Muniments, Book No. 1
Monks	E. H. Pearce, *The Monks of Westminster* (Cambridge, 1916)
P.R.S.	Pipe Roll Society
Regesta	*Regesta Regum Anglo-Normannorum, 1066–1154*, ed. H. W. C. Davis, R. J. Whitwell, R. H. C. Davis, and H. A. Cronne (4 vols., Oxford, 1913–69)
Sawyer	P. H. Sawyer, *Anglo-Saxon Charters: An Annotated List and Bibliography* (London, 1968)
Surrey Fines	*Pedes Finium; or Fines relating to the County of Surrey levied in the King's Court from the seventh year of Richard I to the end of the Reign of Henry VII* (Surrey Archaeological Soc., extra vol. i, 1894)
T.P.N.	*Taxatio ecclesiastica Angliae et Walliae auctoritate P. Nicholai IV, c. A.D. 1291*, ed. S. Ayscough and J. Caley (Record Commission, 1802)
T.R.E.	*Tempore Regis Edwardi*
V.C.H.	*Victoria History of the Counties of England*
V.E.	*Valor Ecclesiasticus temp. Henrici VIII, auctoritate Regia Institutus*, ed. J. Caley, and J. Hunter (6 vols., Record Commission, 1810–34)
Walter de Wenlok	*Documents Illustrating the Rule of Walter de Wenlok, abbot of Westminster, 1283–1307*, ed. B. F. Harvey (Camden, 4th. ser., ii, 1965)
W.A.M.	Westminster Abbey Muniment(s)
—— Reg. Bk.	—— —— ——, Register Book
W.D.	Westminster Domesday (a cartulary, now W.A.M. Bk. no. 11)

ABBOTS OF WESTMINSTER[1]

958–993/7	Wulsin
–997–c.1020	Alfwy
c.1020–49	Wulnoth
c.1049–c.1071	Edwin
c.1071–c.1075	Geoffrey
1076–c.1085	Vitalis
c.1085–1117/18	Gilbert Crispin
1121–c.1136	Herbert
1138–c.1157	Gervase de Blois
1158–73	Laurence
1175–90	Walter of Winchester
1191–1200	William Postard
1200–14	Ralph de Arundel
1214–22	William de Humez
1222–46	Richard de Berking
1246–58	Richard de Crokesley
1258	Philip de Lewesham
1258–83	Richard de Ware
1283–1307	Walter de Wenlok
1308–15	Richard de Kedyngton
1315–33	William de Curtlington
1333–44	Thomas de Henle
1344–9	Simon de Bircheston
1349–62	Simon de Langham
1362–86	Nicholas de Litlington
1386–1420	William Colchester
1420–40	Richard Harwden
1440–62	Edmund Kyrton
1463–9	George Norwich
1469–74	Thomas Millyng
1474–98	John Estney
1498–1500	George Fascet
1500–32	John Islip
1533–40	William Benson

[1] For whom see *Heads of Religious Houses, England and Wales, 940–1216*, ed. D. Knowles, C. N. L. Brooke, and V. C. M. London (Cambridge, 1972), pp. 76–7; and *Monks*, p. 193.

Introduction

(i) *Themes*

THE subject matter of this book is the history of one of England's great estates—how that estate was put together in the tenth and eleventh centuries, how most of the vast acquisitions of this period were kept together over the next five hundred years, and how, during that time, they were made to supply the changing needs, in cash and kind, of their owners, the monks of Westminster. Around the year 1300, the whole comprised not less than 38,000 acres. This figure, however, relates only to the demesne manors of the monks, and, in these manors, only to the home farms, the demesnes in the narrower sense of the word, and to the land of the customary tenants; it takes no account of the fees, outside the demesne manors and within them, which the abbot and convent of Westminster granted earlier, on a generous, even improvident, scale. With these added, the figure would be, on a conservative estimate, twice as large;[1] almost certainly, around the year 1100, when the process of erosion was already under way, the monks had possessed in demesne considerably more than 60,000 acres.

At any one time, the several parts of the estate, the demesne manors, the subinfeudated portion, and, within the former, the demesnes and the tenant-land, provided the livelihood of thousands of men and women, some of whom acquired, as tenants, rights in the land that in the end rivalled, if they did not supersede, those of the monks of Westminster themselves.

[1] Historians have been understandably shy of estimating the acreage of medieval estates. In the mid-thirteenth century the bishop of Ely had c. 70,000 acres, of which c. 20,000 were demesne land and c. 20,000 held in villeinage; but the figure of c. 70,000 acres includes all tenant-land in the demesne manors and not only that held on customary terms. At the end of the century, when the net income of the abbot and convent of Westminster was c. £1,640 per annum, that of the bishop of Ely was c. £2,550 per annum. See E. Miller, *The Abbey and Bishopric of Ely* (Cambridge, 1951), pp. 82–3, 87, 94; and below, pp. 57 ff. It has been suggested that the minimum requirement for membership of the English landed aristocracy at the end of the eighteenth century was an estate of c. 5,000 acres, and at the end of the nineteenth century, one of c. 10,000 acres (G. E. Mingay, *English Landed Society in the Eighteenth Century* (London, 1963), p. 19; F. M. L. Thompson, *English Landed Society in the Nineteenth Century* (London, 1963), p. 27.

But the whole existed for the support of a community that may never have numbered more than about eighty monks and declined in the end to fewer than thirty—for them, for their servants and dependants, and for the upkeep of their splendid but costly buildings.

As the possessors of so large an estate, the abbot and convent of Westminster were in a position greatly to influence social conditions in the regions where their principal holdings lay; these were the West Midlands and the Home Counties. Of course, in periods when most people probably made do with fewer than ten acres, one need not possess 50,000 or 60,000 to be powerful; 1,000 would do, or even 200 or 300. But in the traditional societies of the kind that peopled medieval England, a special importance and significance attaches to the truly great landowner. He epitomizes the values of those societies—their acceptance of extremes of wealth and poverty, their capacity for waste, their cult of hierarchy. Possessed, as a rule, of political authority in addition to landed wealth, he can do much more than other human agencies to ensure the continuance of the *status quo*; when change occurs, he has better opportunities than others of moderating its pace. All this was true of the monks of Westminster in their day. I have been concerned in particular to trace the role of the monks in the economic life of their times. How, in general, is this to be conceived?

The authentic history of the monastic foundation at Westminster begins in the tenth century and ends with the Dissolution of the monastery in 1540. Although throughout this long period the English economy was characterized by widespread poverty and by a scarcity of large surpluses, it also experienced profound changes that were in sum of an improving kind. At the heart of these developments was the growth of a system of exchanges centred on towns but affecting, in the end, every branch of activity in town and countryside alike. From the late twelfth century to the early fourteenth, the development of this system was accompanied by, and helped to promote, a more or less rapid rise in prices; but from the end of the fourteenth century until the beginning of the sixteenth, prices of the main items of consumption were probably, in general, stable or sagging. Each of these periods witnessed a qualitative change in the behaviour of the monks of Westminster as landowners.

When prices began to rise rapidly, towards the end of the twelfth century, perhaps as much as one-third (reckoning by value) of the estate which the abbot and convent of Westminster had received at the hands of their tenth- and eleventh-century founders was in the hands of the perpetual tenants who, in many cases, already enjoyed the main profits of the soil and whose share of the latter could only grow larger as long as the rise in prices continued. On the other hand, the mode of life at Westminster reflected clearly the rise in standards of living that characterized the aristocracy, to which the monks corporately belonged; only an expansion of resources could sustain it in the new economic situation.

Very quickly, under the pressure of these circumstances, the monks put off one conception of their role as landowners and of the ways in which their estate should be made to serve their needs and adopted another. Manors were used less readily and less frequently as the currency of rewards and favours, the better to serve the end, now considered to be of overwhelming importance, of yielding an income in cash or kind. Wherever possible, they were withdrawn from the hands of the farmers to whom it had been customary to entrust them in the eleventh and twelfth centuries; some of those in the hands of perpetual farmers were repurchased. On the manorial demesnes, the monks assumed direct responsibility for large-scale production for the market. On tenant-land, customary dues were exploited with a new vigour and rewarding attention to detail. Despite the inflationary trend of the period and the heritable nature of very nearly all tenancies, rents were kept at, or raised to, a level that would often have been beyond the reach of the monks in a free market for land. In this way an income was extracted from the customary land of the estate that was almost commensurate with the extent of this land in proportion to that of the estate as a whole. Around the year 1300, when the abbot of Westminster had rather more than 7,000 acres of customary land in his portion and rather less than 6,000 acres of demesne land of all kinds, he probably derived nearly half his annual income from the former.[1] It was a state of affairs that some

[1] Below, p. 139, where it is suggested that domanial income accounted for not more than half the whole. The free tenures of the estate now yielded only a small income; the Abbey's income from rents and from seignorial dues came, in overwhelming degree, from customary land.

other landlords, to whom custom had become an impediment to the successful exploitation of tenant-land, might well have envied.

The monks owed the degree of success which they enjoyed in the exploitation of customary land in the thirteenth century to the dependent status of their tenants, nearly all of whom held in villeinage. When, therefore, in the mid-fourteenth century, the demand for land fell sharply and discontent with the old conditions of tenure became explicit among their tenants, the monks fought hard for the principle that only those who would hold in villeinage could still be admitted to heritable tenancies. Many of the tenants of this period, however, were unwilling to hold on these terms; in any case, the inheritance patterns which had formerly provided a succession of tenants were now disrupted. Accordingly, and probably for the first time in the recent history of the estate, a considerable area of tenant-land was held contractually, for terms of limited duration.

The customary conditions of tenure repelled tenants in this period, not only on account of their explicit association with villeinage, but also because they were still the means of imposing on the land an uneconomically heavy burden of rent. Labour services were often an important issue in the ensuing disputes. The monks, though of no mind to use all the services that were still nominally owing to them, seem to have found the idea of permanent commutation a singularly difficult one to accept; and the very practice of assessing villein rents largely in terms of labour services and their cash equivalents made it hard for even well-intentioned parties to agree on the just rent for customary land in the circumstances of the later fourteenth century. Should the assessment have regard to the fall in the demand for land or to the rise in the cost of labour? Rents were in fact raised on several manors of the estate in the years after 1348.

From *c.* 1390, however, the monks' treatment of their estate and their tenants betrays a change of outlook. As the demesnes were put on lease—and some were already on lease before this date—the abbot and convent ceased to be intimately concerned, as producers, with labour problems. In their role of large-scale consumers of agrarian produce, they were gradually reassured by the relatively low levels at which grain prices

settled towards the end of the century; in any case, the corn
rents owed by some of the lessees of their demesnes gave them
a hedge against inflation, should it come. But the fundamental
change was their recognition, slow but unmistakable in the
sources of this period, that most of the inhabitants of their
manors were not of villein status but free. By the mid-fifteenth
century, only those who could be shown to be of servile
parentage, the *nativi de sanguine*, were unfree; these were
probably a small group. But it would, of course, be more
appropriate to say that a revolution in concepts of status in
English society at large now compelled the monks of Westminster to exploit their tenant-land along different lines from
those followed by their thirteenth- and fourteenth-century
predecessors. The change need not have gone further than the
lowering of rents to an economic level. The monks, however,
carried into this period their old inability or reluctance to
think in business-like terms of what the land would bear and
the tenant could afford to pay. By the end of the fifteenth
century, the rents paid by their customary tenants often represented considerably less than the economic rent for the land in
question. As often as not, the abbot and convent relied for the
collection of these rents on the latter-day farmers of their
demesnes, tenants who were themselves enjoying generous
terms by 1500. The monks were keeping, as we should say, a low
profile; few of their tenants any longer had reason to hate
them; few perhaps ever saw them.

Throughout the long period which has been so cursorily
surveyed, nearly all the tenants of the Abbey's customary land,
the main subjects of these changes in policy and outlook on
the part of the monks of Westminster, were peasants. This term,
however, is in need of elucidation before it can be useful in a
description of medieval husbandry arrangements. It is used
here, not in the technical sense of one who is the proprietor of
the land that he farms, but more generally, to denote a farmer
who, whatever his legal status, works his own land, with or
without assistance from others. We are concerned, therefore,
with the agrarian base of the Abbey's estate.

If, in the Middle Ages, great landowners, and among them
the monks of Westminster, were at times committed to agrarian
production to an extent that makes modern conceptions of

economic growth seem not wholly irrelevant to their enterprises, in the case of peasants, it is necessary to ask how far they
participated in an organized produce market at all. In fact the
very use of money rents instead of labour services or renders in
kind implies a regular traffic in peasant surpluses. Although the
state of the sources makes it impossible to trace the use of these
rents on the Abbey's estates before the thirteenth century, their
use elsewhere is clearly attested at a much earlier date; very
likely the tenants whom the monks of Westminster acquired
when the monastery was first endowed in the tenth and eleventh
centuries were already meeting some of their obligations in
this way. But it is unlikely that, at this date, the peasants on the
Abbey's estates or on any others were often caught up in any
market except that of their own village. It was probably in the
twelfth century that their surpluses, individually small but
cumulatively quite large, became important to the urban
market in agrarian produce. In the late Middle Ages, peasants,
now working not only their own holdings but often the manorial
demesnes as well, became the main producers of corn, and
probably of wool. It seems appropriate to call these the two
most significant stages in the development of peasant production
in medieval England.

The first of these changes left most of the tenants of Westminster Abbey, as it had almost certainly found them, subsistence farmers. Moreover, many of them were subsistence
farmers in the meagrest sense of these words: their holdings
were the means of only the barest of livelihoods, if as much.
Nearly 50 per cent of the tenants whose holdings are recorded
in the early thirteenth century held fewer than ten acres of
arable land; a century later, a little over 50 per cent did so, and
where other means of livelihood were available in addition to
arable land, the proportion was much higher; thus in the semi-
urbanized manor of Ashwell, in the early fourteenth century,
about 73 per cent of a large body of customary tenants held
fewer than ten acres each. These, then, were Lilliputian producers who can have had only tiny surpluses to market. By
the end of the fourteenth century, on the other hand, though
not long before that date, the majority of the Abbey's tenants
were probably subsistence farmers in a rather different sense—
their holdings normally provided them with a competent

livelihood, well above the bread-line; and in the course of the fifteenth century, the Abbey's estates, in common with so many others, numbered among their tenants some who, though still peasants in the sense defined above, were nevertheless commercial farmers whose main concern was production for the market. In what ways, if at all, are the policies which the monks of Westminster pursued as landlords related to these changes in production at the base of society on their estates?

The trends in landholding described in the previous paragraph are in fact so commonplace, so apt to occur in so many different social settings and against backgrounds of such diverse tenurial conditions that their main explanation must lie outside the lord–tenant relationship. Population trends, inheritance customs, the presence or absence of rural industries, the scope and intensity of the landholder's own desires as a consumer—these, in the long run, were the main determinants of the scale of peasant husbandry in the Middle Ages; in the long run the conditions of landholding imposed by landlords on their tenants had only a permissive or inhibiting effect within limits decided by these other factors.

Thus, in the present case, the high rents demanded by the monks of Westminster in the early Middle Ages were among several factors tending to keep peasant farming on this estate in that period at a level that was not very often higher than that of bare subsistence; equally, their hostility to the fragmentation of holdings beyond a certain point helped to stave off the collapse of that line. For most of the fifteenth century, by contrast, tenurial conditions on the Abbey's estates were tolerant of an enlargement of holdings and expansion of the scale of peasant production, the main explanation of which must be sought elsewhere. In between these two periods lies another, coinciding roughly with the second half of the fourteenth century, when the monks' influence as landlords on the enterprises of their tenants was, on a superficial view, more fateful than ever before or after: though land was abundant, they refused to allow it to be cheap, thus denying to their tenants for several decades the full benefits, and, in some cases, any of the benefits, of the new balance between land and people; and even at the end of the century, few perhaps of the peasant holdings on the estate were really large. Yet a period when family labour, the great stand-by of peasant husbandry, was scarce and hired labour prohibitively expensive for the small farmer was not likely to be one of rapid adaptation to a new and enlarged scale of husbandry, had the monks of Westminster been as free with their land as Prince Nekhlyudov with his. Even in this period we must look elsewhere for the main regulator of the pace of change.

In fact, in the medieval agrarian economy change was at nearly all times so slow as almost to require another vocabulary than the vocabulary of change for its description; the historian is lucky if he can trace its outlines in less than a secular time-span. The terrain, the weather, harvest—the physical environment never ceased to be dominant, and, in consequence, the *status quo* itself, independent, it seems, of human agency, had a quite extraordinary capacity to stifle influences that would, in other circumstances, make for change, and, indeed, for rapid change. The relations of the monks of Westminster with their tenants, like those of any landlord of the period, belong in this context of things as they were; there, it may be suggested, they are of great intrinsic interest and importance. The impression which I retain from my study of the monks of Westminster and their tenants is how closely the latter depended on the former in the short run but how little this dependence affected the scale and direction of long-term change in rural society on the monastic estate. I can only hope that I have not distorted the facts.

(ii) *Sources*

An attempt to penetrate the secrets of a monastic estate-office depends for its success on the existence of some at least of the central records of the community in question, in addition to the manorial records that are so obviously needed in such an inquiry. From the latter alone the historian may hope to reconstruct the outlines of policy; without the former, he will never understand the springs of action.

The fact that the pre-Reformation community at Westminster was so quickly succeeded by a collegiate body having virtually identical endowments ensured a high survival-rate in the case of each of these categories of records at the Abbey. There can be very few ecclesiastical muniment rooms the contents of which do as much to facilitate a study of the kind attempted in this book as do those preserved in the Muniment Room at Westminster Abbey.[1] Anyone who explores this superb collection must salute the memory of Richard Widmore, by whom it was first put in order; and he will find Widmore's own *History* of the Abbey still indispensable.[2] Despite the excellence of the sources, some lacunae should be noted.

Although a handful of *ministers' accounts* survives from earlier decades, nothing like an unbroken series of such accounts begins to be available until the 1270s, and in the case of a few manors of considerable importance in the monastic economy, the trickle never becomes a flood. Only a few accounts for Denham, for example, survive from the entire Middle Ages; yet after its recovery in demesne in 1292, Denham was a favourite place of residence of the abbots of Westminster and of cardinal importance to the abbatial economy. With the notable exception of the rolls for Launton, no long run of *court rolls* is extant for a period earlier than the second half of the fourteenth century. Even in the fifteenth century, the survival-rate of ministers' accounts is much higher than that of court rolls. Towards the end of this century, the former begin to be supplemented by the Abbey's *Registers,* or *Lease-Books*; from 1485 more or less every demise of a manor or manorial demesne belonging to the estate is recorded in these sources.

From the early thirteenth century until the Dissolution— that is, for about half the entire life-span of the monastic foundation at Westminster—the Abbey's goods were formally divided between the abbot, on the one hand, and the prior and convent, on the other. The *abbatial records*—the central records relating to the abbot's household and treasury—are most numerous for the abbacies of Walter de Wenlok (1283–1307), Nicholas de Litlington (1362–86), and William Colchester (1386–1420). From the abbacies of Wenlok and Litlington there survive *day-accounts*, recording not only the minutiae of

---

[1] However, some records relating to the monastic community and its estates have strayed from this repository; the most important of these are noted in the Bibliography (below, pp. 452 ff.).

[2] R. Widmore, *An History of the Church of St. Peter, Westminster, commonly called Westminster Abbey, chiefly from Manuscript Authorities* (London, 1751); also, Widmore, *An Enquiry into the Time of the First Foundation of Westminster Abbey* (London, 1743). The generosity of Professor C. R. Cheney put me in seisin of a copy of both these works.

consumption in the household, but also the household's itinerary. In reckoning income, we depend, in the case of Wenlok, on the *accounts of the abbot's receiver*, or *treasurer*; in that of Litlington, on the *accounts of the steward*, or *clerk, of the household*, who now handled the major part of his revenues, and the *accounts of the abbot's steward*, or *receiver, in the Western Parts*.¹ The last-named officials served Colchester, too, and some of their accounts for this period have survived; but the development of private coffers, with a spending power that was clearly large, though now incalculable, makes it unwise for us to rely any longer on their accounts for a comprehensive record of the abbot's income.

Many of the *records relating to the life of the prior and convent and to their estates* are already well known from the use which E. H. Pearce made of them in *The Monks of Westminster*.² It was in particular the survival of some 6,000 *obedientiaries' accounts* that made possible the compilation of this unique work, a biographical register of the late-medieval community at Westminster, on which all other studies of the monastery's history in that period must largely depend. One of the features of monastic life at Westminster recorded in these accounts, and that assisted Pearce, was the late-medieval custom of allotting to each professed monk, who is therefore named in the rolls, a share in the surplus income of the major royal foundations— those, in particular, of Eleanor of Castile, Richard II and Anne of Bohemia, and Henry V. For the present study, the custom, which deflected into the hands of the monks, severally, an income that amounted in sum to between £200 and £300 per annum, has another significance: it helps to show in how large a measure the financial problems of the late-medieval community of monks were internally generated—a product less of fortuitous changes in the yield of their manors than of the way in which they chose to spend that yield once it reached their central coffers. And, by recording many purchases of property on the part of the monks of Westminster, the obedientiaries' accounts also help us to piece together the details of the monks' own attack on these problems, for it was by augmenting their already wide estates that the monks of Westminster tried, from time to time, to make up real or imagined short-falls in

---

¹ The name given to the abbot's manors in Glos., Warwicks., and Worcs.
² Cambridge, 1916.

income. The *accounts of the conventual treasurers*, who administered
the revenues of the monastery other than those assigned to the
obedientiaries, are still more useful in this respect, for most of
the purchases made in the fourteenth century, the period of the
greatest acquisitions, were paid for out of their funds. From the
end of the thirteenth century these accounts are also indispensable sources for estimating the total income of the prior and
convent: from then until the sixteenth century, if this source is
lacking, so too is our capacity to estimate monastic income. In
the early sixteenth century, however, the most reliable account
of both abbatial and conventual income is that contained in
the *Valor Ecclesiasticus*.[1] The lease-books confirm the substantial
accuracy of the valuation of the goods of Westminster Abbey
contained in this source.

Charters and other deeds, the most numerous of all the records
surviving from the medieval period at Westminster, are in a
category of their own. With the exception of the royal charters,
real or putative, conveying or confirming to the Abbey the
lands and privileges that the monastic community was granted
by its royal patrons, or would like to have been granted, these
are of local reference and often of a very small-scale reference
at that—the record of the acquisition or alienation of perhaps
a few acres or roods of land. Hundreds of those that now survive
in the Muniment Room were executed elsewhere but at the
Abbey and had no reference to the monks of Westminster when
they were made: subsequently, however, the monks acquired
the land in question and, with it, the relevant archive. But many
other charters preserved at Westminster were executed by, or
on behalf of, the monks of Westminster, or in their favour.
Evidence in every period of the monks' acquisition or alienation
of property, or of both these processes, these charters are
particularly important sources for the twelfth century at
Westminster, the spendthrift century, when property that it
would later require years of calculation to recover, was too
lightly alienated. The monks of Westminster were, moreover,
great compilers of *cartularies*.[2] By far the most useful of these

---

[1] *Valor Ecclesiasticus temp. Henrici VIII auctoritate Regia Institutus*, ed. J. Caley and
J. Hunter (6 vols., Record Commission, 1810–34).
[2] For the full list, see G. R. C. Davis, *Medieval Cartularies of Great Britain* (London,
1958), pp. 116–17.

works are the so-called 'Westminster Domesday' and the 'Liber Niger Quaternus'. The former, though compiled mainly in the fourteenth century, has additions extending to the mid-fifteenth. The latter is a renewal, made between *c.* 1474 and *c.* 1485, of an earlier cartulary of the same name. (John Flete, who put together his *History of Westminster Abbey* probably between *c.* 1420 and *c.* 1440, used the original, which he calls the 'niger papirus'.)[1] Both these cartularies contain many items in addition to charters. A summary of the *Taxation of Pope Nicholas IV* in the Liber Niger Quaternus[2] has been particularly useful in this study.

The last source to be noticed in this survey is the abovementioned *History of Westminster Abbey* by John Flete,[3] the most useful, as it is the most objective and 'scientific' of the studies on the monastery—themselves few in number—that were ever written by monks of Westminster. Flete entered the monastery in 1420 or 1421 and was ordained priest in 1422 or 1423.[4] Since at this time it was the practice of the community at Westminster to have the newly professed ordained at the earliest opportunity—that is, as soon as they reached the canonical age of twenty-four—it appears that he had been born at the very end of the previous century. His career conforms to a pattern that was probably common enough in Black Monk houses: he held more or less every office open to a monk, including the priorate, but never the highest office of all. He was perhaps a little young to become abbot when Richard Harwden died, in 1440; a little old on Edmund Kyrton's death, in 1462; or perhaps his gifts were so patently those of a good second-incommand that he was not considered seriously on either occasion.

In the preface to the *History*[5] Flete declares the purpose of the work: it is to relate the foundation, dedication, and history of the house and to set out its privileges, from A.D. 184, the supposed date of the first foundation at Westminster, until 1443. This was to be done from chronicles and other original

---

[1] *Flete*, p. 136. I have not used the version of the Liber Niger Quaternus which is now College of Arms, London, Young MS. 72.

[2] Fos. 140ᵛ–142ᵛ; see below, p. 50 (Table II, note).

[3] *The History of Westminster Abbey by John Flete*, ed. J. Armitage Robinson (Cambridge, 1909).

[4] *Monks*, pp. 137–8.   [5] *Flete*, pp. 33–4.

sources, the testimony of which Flete believed to be the only safe defence of his monastery against its enemies and detractors. Further, Flete wanted to make known the identity of the abbots of Westminster, the pastors who had overseen the flock at Westminster in what he describes as its ceaseless work in the field of the Lord.

As Armitage Robinson, Flete's editor, pointed out,[1] the *History* has four main parts. The story of the foundation and miraculous dedication of the Abbey is followed by copious extracts from papal bulls and royal charters, the evidence of its privileges, and these by lists of the Abbey's relics and indulgences; lives of the abbots, prefaced by a brief recapitulation of the account of the foundation, conclude the work.

The latest papal letter cited by Flete in the second section of his work is a letter of Innocent III, written in 1199;[2] the latest royal charter, one of Richard I's for the Abbey.[3] He has put before his readers all the evidence needed to demonstrate the antiquity of the Abbey's status as the coronation church of the kings of England and repository of the royal regalia and to show that the decision of papal judges-delegate in 1222, affirming the monastery's exempt status and subjection *nullo mediante* to Rome—a decision cited in full—was implicit in papal and royal grants from an early date and abundantly confirmed down to the eve of the hearing. This was perhaps the main purpose of this part of the *History*. But the preface to the work seems to show that these chapters are, even so, unfinished, for here Flete not only gives the year 1443 and the twenty-second regnal year of Henry VI[4] as, in a general sense, the term of his treatment of the Abbey's liberties: he says explicitly that among the sources whence the dignity and freedom of the Church are to be derived are charters of the kings of England, down to the twenty-second year of Henry VI.[5] Further, among the proofs of the Abbey's exempt status which the preface reviews in summary form is the right, belonging to the abbot of Westminster, in consequence

---

[1] Ibid., p. 1.

[2] Ibid., pp. 49–50. For this letter see *The Letters of Pope Innocent III (1198–1216) concerning England and Wales*, ed. C. R. and M. G. Cheney (Oxford, 1967), no. 113.

[3] *Flete*, p. 55; the charter is now W. A. M. Charters xlv.

[4] The twenty-second regnal year of Henry VI ran from 1 Sept. 1443 to 31 Aug. 1444; see, on this point, below, p. 14.

[5] *Flete*, p. 34.

of the Abbey's exempt status, of expelling penitents from the church at the beginning of Lent and reconciling them on Maundy Thursday.[1] There is, however, no reference to this privilege in the body of the work. Thus Flete's chapters on the Abbey's privileges are unfinished.

So too, and much more evidently, are the lives of the abbots, which make up the fourth and longest part of the *History*. The last abbot to have his shepherding of the monastic flock in the field of the Lord related by John Flete was Nicholas de Litlington, who died in 1386; the abbacies of William Colchester and Richard Harwden are unrecorded. What, then, is the significance of the date 1443, and why was the *History* left unfinished? How was it, indeed, that in the early fifteenth century, a time when the Abbey seems to have been at peace with the whole world, the monks of Westminster commissioned this propagandist study of their rights and privileges?

The year 1443 has no significance in the Abbey's history other than that derived from its appearance in Flete's preface.[2] It was, no doubt, the year in which he happened to write this part of the *History*; presumably he was writing in the last four months of the year, for only those months belonged to the twenty-second regnal year of Henry VI. For Flete himself it was a busy year and the forerunner of others that were to be even busier.[3] At the beginning of it, he was chamberlain. By the end, he was also warden of Queen Eleanor's manors. Before the end of 1444, he had added the offices of abbot's receiver and sacrist to these others; a year later he was also warden of Henry V's manors and keeper of the New Work. The rest of his life, until, in 1456, he became prior, was spent in a whirl of administrative activity that can have left little or no time for the painstaking scrutiny of Abbey muniments that underlies the

---

[1] *Flete*, p. 34. Flete here cites a now lost portion of the Abbey's thirteenth-century *Customary*. Note also, in his notices of Abbots Ware and Curtlington, references to material on the Hospital of St. James at Westminster which the reader is to find 'supra' (ibid., pp. 115, 123). Since the Abbey claimed rights of visitation at the Hospital by virtue of acts of Clement III, it is likely that the references are to passages which Flete intended to insert in the section on privileges, but no such entries are found there; see Liber Niger Quaternus, 137.

[2] Cf. V. H. Galbraith, 'A visitation of Westminster in 1444', *English Historical Rev.* 37 (1922), 85, where it is suggested that Flete chose 1443 as the term of his work from a desire to avoid narrating the suspension of Abbot Kyrton from office, in 1444.   [3] See, for what follows, *Monks*, pp. 137–8.

History. We must conclude that most of this work was put together before 1443; in this year Flete, realizing, perhaps, how thick and fast other responsibilities were coming his way, made a fair copy of what he had done and added a preface in which he set a term to his work that he now had little hope of achieving. It was in his early years as a monk that he was the monastery's historian; this probably explains why he spent perhaps as many as thirteen or fourteen years after ordination without the burden of any other office; his first known office was that of almoner, which he held in or about the year 1436.

Most of the *History of Westminster Abbey* was, then, composed in the 1420s or 1430s. From what quarter came the assault on the monastery's freedom and privileges that it was intended to ward off? Flete had in mind a verbal assault: *sinistre assertiones* were the enemy's weapon.[1] The attack may have been no more than a figment of his imagination, an excuse for writing on the part of one who would have written in any case, and the same may be true of Br. Richard of Cirencester, who struck much the same note of apprehension in the course of his *Speculum Historiale*, written at Westminster towards the end of the previous century.[2] More probably, both writers express the lasting sense of insecurity that possessed the monks of Westminster in consequence of events at the end of Edward III's reign and during that of his successor. The most dramatic of these events was the murder of Richard Hawley in 1378, in the choir of the church, during mass;[3] but in the long run the quarrel with the canons of the chapel of St. Stephen in the Palace of Westminster, which began in the same decade, was more vexatious to the monks. Although the settlement of this dispute in 1394 was, on the whole, favourable to the latter, it could not erase the unhappy memory of this challenge to cherished rights of jurisdiction in the parish of St. Margaret's; St. Stephen's was a royal chapel, and at critical points in the struggle the king, the Abbey's patron, had not been found on the side of the angels.[4] This

[1] *Flete*, p. 63.
[2] *Ricardi de Cirencestria Speculum Historiale de Gestis Regum Angliae*, ed. J. E. B. Mayor (Rolls Series, 1863–9); see, in particular, ibid. ii. 249–50, where the attack of *moderni* on the privilege of sanctuary in the Abbey is deplored. The *Speculum Historiale* was one of Flete's sources for the early history of the Abbey.
[3] For Hawley, see below, p. 378 and n.
[4] *V.C.H. London* i. 567–8. For the settlement of 1394, see W. A. M. 18451.

quarrel was, no doubt, in Flete's mind when he referred, in his preface, to the right of the abbot of Westminster, as ordinary, to custody of clerks convicted before a royal judge in the Palace of Westminster.[1]

It is the long final section of Flete's work, devoted to the lives of the abbots of Westminster, that is useful in a study of the monastery's material fortunes. Flete's standard life covers half a dozen or so topics: details of election or appointment are followed by a recital of the property and privileges obtained for the house by the abbot in question, by the liturgical and other details of his anniversary, the date of his death (sometimes given inaccurately), the place of burial, and the epitaph on the tomb. In most cases the greater part, though not the whole, of the information which Flete imparts came from sources that are readily identifiable, still extant, and such as he might have been expected to use; he uses, for example, the Abbey's cartularies, the *Customary* compiled under Richard de Ware,[2] and the *Flores Historiarum*, itself a Westminster chronicle from 1265 to 1327.[3] The use of pipe, memoranda, and originalia rolls and *recorda communia* shows more ingenuity;[4] these he must have scrutinized in the Treasuries of the Exchequer, then housed in the monastic precincts and in the Tower of London, or in the Treasury of Receipt in the Palace of Westminster. For his accounts of Simon de Langham and Nicholas de Litlington, Flete was able to draw, additionally, on what was evidently a still vivid tradition at Westminster about these abbots, but from Edwin's death in *c.* 1071 until Langham's election in 1349 he relies principally on sources of the kind described above. Although the biographies so compiled are exceedingly useful, they contain little information, and in some cases none, that a present-day historian could not easily put together for himself; their usefulness consists, not in the information imparted, but in the order of priorities revealed in them: the present study is not

---

[1] *Flete*, p. 34.

[2] *Customary of the Benedictine Monasteries of Saint Augustine, Canterbury, and Saint Peter, Westminster*, ed. E. Maunde Thompson (2 vols., Henry Bradshaw Soc. xxiii, xxviii, 1902–4).

[3] A. Gransden, 'The Continuations of the *Flores Historiarum* from 1265 to 1327', *Mediaeval Studies* (Toronto) 36 (1974), 472 ff. Flete, however, uses *Flores* for the period before 1265 (*Flete*, pp. 101, 103, 108).

[4] Ibid., pp. 116, 127–8, 134, 138.

more interested in the income and endowments of Westminster Abbey than were, so it seems, John Flete and his contemporaries.

For the period down to *c.* 1071, it is different: some of the sources on which Flete relied here can no longer be identified. It was, for example, in no source to our knowledge extant today that he learnt that a church had been founded at Westminster in the second century A.D., in the time of Lucius, king of the Britons, converted to pagan uses under Diocletian, and restored by Ambrosius Aurelianus towards the end of the fifth century.[1] We cannot trace to an earlier source the names of the seven abbots who preceded Wulsin, whom St. Dunstan appointed,[2] or the circumstance that Abbot Wulnoth was ordained abbot 'mediante Cnutone Anglorum rege', which king relied greatly on Wulnoth's counsel.[3]

These early lives have a didactic purpose, among others. The reader is meant to notice that the early abbots of Westminster were Englishmen, and he is to contrast this state of affairs with that obtaining in the late eleventh century and the early twelfth, when foreign abbots were so often intruded by the king. For this theme, simple as it is, and light as Flete's touch is in developing it, we need postulate no source other than his own inventiveness; the very juxtaposition of the English names of the abbots of Westminster down to 1066 and the foreign names of those that followed was probably enough to suggest the contrast that Flete is trying to bring out. Similarly with the lives of the pre-Conquest abbots considered as a whole and the history of the church at Westminster from the second century to the fifth, Flete himself is much the most likely source of the information to be found here but in no other work. Is this conclusion, however, compatible with his claim to have found the latter history 'in quodam libro vetustissimo chronicarum' and the names of Wulsin's seven predecessors in 'munimenta vetustissimorum librorum'?[4] Flete is in general so scrupulous in the

---

[1] Ibid., pp. 34–5, 63, 76–7. The inspiration for this story was the claim of Glastonbury Abbey to have been founded at that time. On the Glastonbury legend, see J. Armitage Robinson, *Somerset Historical Essays* (London, 1921), pp. 1 ff., where it is pointed out that disputes about the precedence of abbots at General Councils lent this story topical significance in the early fifteenth century. This point may have been in Flete's mind when he wrote.

[2] The seven were Siward, Ordbritht, Alfwy, Alfgar, Adymer, Alfnod, and Alfric (*Flete*, p. 78).

[3] Ibid., p. 81.

[4] Ibid., pp. 34, 78.

use of his sources as to make it seem improbable, on first consideration, that he would have fabricated this claim. Yet its vagueness contrasts oddly with his usual, precise way of naming his source—'in libro Consuetudinarii iv^a parte, capitulo viii°, titulo Coquinarii; ex Speculo Regali de gestis regum Angliae, libro iv° capitulo xxv in fine'; and so on.[1] And, although Richard of Cirencester wrote at length on the early history of the Abbey, he did not know of a church at Westminster before the time of Saebert of Essex, that is, before the seventh century, and he did not name Wulsin's predecessors.[2] This surely suggests that the 'vetustissimi libri' had been put together since his time. Nor, it seems, did Cirencester know that Canute relied greatly on the counsel of Abbot Wulnoth; yet he records the fact that Canute was a benefactor to the Abbey.[3] We must conclude that Flete, though so painstakingly faithful to his sources from the late eleventh century onwards, felt free to embroider and invent some parts of the earlier history of the Abbey. To this extent, and despite his general sobriety, he belonged to the exotic tradition of historiography at Westminster founded long ago by Sulcard and Osbert of Clare.[4]

Readers need to be warned not only of the nature and scope of an historian's sources but also of the way in which they have been used. Inevitably, a study of the present kind, concerned with long-term trends in the getting and spending of wealth and with the exploitation of the assets from which that wealth was derived, trenches on the domain of quantitative history— or, to speak more precisely, on a domain that would belong to quantitative history were the period in question the nineteenth or twentieth century and not the eleventh to the sixteenth. Every medievalist knows that it is exceedingly difficult and as a rule impossible to extract from medieval records quantitative

[1] *Flete*, pp. 65, 76.

[2] *Speculum Historiale* i. 92–6; ibid. ii. 94–5. Cirencester follows the twelfth-century tradition that Saebert was himself the founder of the first church at Westminster; for this, see *Flete*, p. 9. He adds the detail that the foundation was on the site of a temple of Apollo, and this fact Flete wove into his own narrative.

[3] *Speculum Historiale* ii. 185.

[4] For Sulcard, see below, pp. 20 ff.; and for Osbert of Clare, *Letters of Osbert of Clare, prior of Westminster*, ed. E. W. Williamson (Oxford, 1929), *passim*, and P. Chaplais, 'The Original Charters of Herbert and Gervase, abbots of Westminster (1121–1157)', *A Medieval Miscellany for Doris Mary Stenton*, ed. P. M. Barnes and C. F. Slade (Pipe Roll Soc., N.S. xxxvi), pp. 89 ff.

data that would satisfy the canons of criticism applied to such evidence in that later period. Certainly, this study contains no such data. It does, however, include many figures. These have been put together as carefully as possible; nevertheless, they embody guess-work, in measure that will, it is hoped, be plain in the individual case. Another person, working over the same material, might have arrived—perhaps one day will arrive—at different conclusions. For the figures, as for the argument of the book as a whole, I can claim only that the balance of probabilities seemed to favour them.

I

The Foundation of Westminster Abbey

THE first account of the origins of Westminster Abbey was
written by a monk of the house named Sulcard, while Vitalis
was abbot, that is, between 1076 and c. 1085.[1] Sulcard claimed
for the Abbey the distinction of foundation during the lifetime
of Aethelbert of Kent and consecration at the hands of St.
Peter, the Prince of the Apostles.

The occasion of the foundation was Aethelbert's desire to
honour St. Peter in London, as he had already honoured St.
Paul, by the dedication of a church there. Aethelbert himself,
however, was not the founder of the new church, nor, in the end
was this built within the confines of the city, for, before the king
had taken steps to fulfil his wish, a rich citizen of London and
his wife, both nameless in Sulcard's account but later identified
at Westminster with Aethelbert's nephew, Saebert, king of the
East Saxons, and his wife, obtained his permission to build a
church in honour of St. Peter on an island in the Thames
2 miles distant from the city. The site was Thorney Island, but
the church took a new name at her consecration, and this was
occidentale monasterium, so called from the prevailing wind or the
situation west of the city—Sulcard perhaps did not know which
was the more likely explanation. It is not said that this first
church at Westminster was a monastic foundation.

The consecration day was chosen and christians were summoned from all quarters. Darkness fell, however, while Mellitus,
the consecrating bishop, was still half a mile from the church;
besides, the waters of the Thames were high and Thorney
inaccessible without a boat. Accordingly, Mellitus slept that
night on the far side of the river. During the night St. Peter
appeared on the river bank. The Apostle persuaded a fisherman

---

[1] B. W. Scholz, 'Sulcard of Westminster, "Prologus de Construccione Westmonasterii"', *Traditio* 20 (1964), 59 ff.

to take him to the island, where, on landing, he struck the ground twice, producing a spring of water in each place. Attended by the heavenly choir, he came to the church, now radiant with a light that illuminated the whole island, and consecrated it. Returning to the shore, he told a stupified fisherman his name and the purpose of his appearing and instructed him to warn Mellitus the next morning that he would find the church already consecrated when he arrived. Then, having promised the man a large haul and forbidden him ever to fish on Sundays, for this was a Sunday, St. Peter returned to heaven. The fisherman duly carried his message to Mellitus, who did indeed find the signs of consecration on the walls of the church, but he preached there and celebrated mass. When, much later, the founder and his wife died, they were buried in the church.

Sulcard did not believe that the church so founded had flourished for long: neglected by Aethelbert's successors, it had been restored by a king named Offa, who gave it land in Blechenham.[1] Offa intended to establish a monastic community at Westminster; but having relinquished worldly cares, he died a monk at Rome before this work was finished. This detail shows that the king to whom the story referred was not Offa the Great, although he, too, was later honoured at Westminster as a benefactor,[2] but the Offa who was king of Essex at the beginning of the eighth century. John Flete, the fifteenth-century historian of the Abbey, understood the reference in this sense.[3]

It is not impossible that Offa of Essex should have booked land at Blechenham to the Church, for Blechenham was in Middlesex, itself long a part of the East Saxon kingdom by the early eighth century. Moreover, the foundation of a church by a king outside but near his chief city is occasionally mentioned in continental Europe during the Dark Ages.[4] But only sources associated with Westminster refer to the existence of a church

---

[1] Ibid., pp. 85–6. [2] *Sawyer*, 124.

[3] *Flete*, p. 43. Cf. ibid., p. 63, and C. N. L. Brooke, *London 800–1216: The Shaping of a City* (London, 1975), p. 295.

[4] See in general E. Ewig, 'Résidence et capitale pendant le haut Moyen Age', *Revue historique* 230 (1963), 25 ff. (I owe this reference to Professor P. R. L. Brown.) It is to be noted, however, that the monks of Westminster never claimed that their church had possessed lands in Essex itself before the tenth century; all their early claims related to lands in Middlesex and Hertfordshire. For Blechenham, in Hendon, see *V.C.H.* Midd., v. 16.

on this site before the time of St. Dunstan. That no *monastery* existed here in the time of Aethelbert is clear from Bede's failure to mention such a foundation. To all these early traditions, the words in which Flete disingenuously dismissed the seven shadowy abbots—figments in all probability of his own imagination—who ruled at Westminster between the time of Offa of Essex and that of St. Dunstan seem applicable: 'mallem igitur ista sub dubio relinquere quam aliquid mendaciter et sine causa fingere.'[1]

The first biographers of St. Dunstan did not think of the establishment of the regular life at Westminster as one of his noteworthy achievements; indeed, they are silent about it.[2] William of Malmesbury, however, says that Westminster was a small monastery, intended to house twelve monks.[3] The circumstances of the foundation and its early history are recorded in greater detail in the so-called Telligraphus of Aethelred II for Westminster Abbey than in Sulcard's *Prologus*. In the form in which it survives, this charter[4] is certainly spurious; it may have been composed in the early twelfth century by Westminster's leading forger, Osbert of Clare, some of whose mannerisms it seems to betray.[5] But Aethelred II soon became of such poor repute that a forger would be unlikely to father on this king a charter that he was composing *ab initio*; nor is it likely that such a charter would impose the common burdens on the Abbey, as the Telligraphus does. Behind this document there may lie an authentic charter of Aethelred's reign; if so, the former may preserve traditions about the foundation that go back to the lifetime of some of the monks whom St. Dunstan himself admitted to the monastery.

Dunstan, we are told in this source, was given the church at Westminster by King Edgar in return for 120 mancuses of gold,[6] and with the lands he obtained the king's permission

---

[1] *Flete*, p. 78; and see above, p. 17.

[2] *Memorials of St. Dunstan, Archbishop of Canterbury*, ed. W. Stubbs (Rolls Series, 1874), pp. 1 ff.

[3] *Gesta Pontificum Anglorum*, ed. N. E. S. A. Hamilton (Rolls Series, 1870), p. 178.

[4] B. Thorpe, *Diplomatarium Anglicum Aevi Saxonici* (London, 1865), pp. 296–8; *Sawyer*, 894.

[5] For Osbert's work, see *Medieval Miscellany for Doris Mary Stenton*, ed. Barnes and Slade, pp. 91 ff.

[6] Sulcard says that Dunstan gave Edgar a gold ewer worth 50 shekels in return for the *facultas* of restoring the church (*Traditio* 20 (1964), 86).

to establish the Benedictine observance on the site. This, however, was not the full extent of his outlay on Westminster: in purchases of land from private persons and from the king (who is here said to have sold Dunstan 5 hides at Westminster itself) he spent 390 mancuses of gold and £152 in silver— that is, reckoning thirty silver pennies to the mancus, a little over £200. That Dunstan spent so much is not hard to believe if, as his biographer Osbern says, he was entrusted with the disposal of the wealth which the lady Elfgifu left to God,[1] but Edgar's part in the transactions is singularly interesting. If there had indeed been an earlier monastery at Westminster, the site, so it appears, had been absorbed into the royal demesne, whence Edgar now released it; *secularium prioratus* at Westminster had taken this special form. By the twelfth century it was evidently believed at Westminster that much land had been lost to the church in this way, for Edgar's charter for the Abbey, which was written at this time, puts into the king's mouth a general renunciation of the gains of the royal demesne.[2]

The probable date of St. Dunstan's foundation at Westminster is 959.[3] Sulcard found nothing to say about the monastery between Edgar's death in 975 and the beginning of the reign of Edward the Confessor. Harold Harefoot, however, was buried in the Abbey, though he died as far away as Oxford,[4] and the church attracted a number of benefactions in these years. Two of these are attested by sources which seem to be independent of the Abbey. One was a bequest of land at Kelvedon, in Essex, by Leofwine, Wulfstan's son;[5] the other, the bequest of an estate at Brickendon, in Hertfordshire, by Aelfhelm Polga, who had been one of Edgar's ministers and who was a benefactor of Ramsey Abbey and Ely as well.[6] The score of estates which the monks possessed by 1042 must have been mainly the acquisition of these

---

[1] *Memorials of St. Dunstan*, pp. 87–9.   [2] *Sawyer*, 774.
[3] Ibid. 670. Dunstan was bishop of London 959–60.   [4] Below, p. 372.
[5] *Sawyer*, 1522. This, however, was not the main estate which the Abbey later possessed at Kelvedon, for which see below, p. 342. Further, the Abbey is never known to have possessed the land at *Mearcyncg seollan* which was bequeathed by Leofwine.
[6] *Sawyer*, 1487; for the identity of the testator as Aelfhelm Polga, see D. Whitelock, *Anglo-Saxon Wills* (Cambridge, 1930), p. 134.

years; Dunstan had obtained only a handful for his church. At this date the Abbey's possessions were worth perhaps *c.* £80 per annum by Domesday reckoning.[1] Edward the Confessor's biographer describes the Abbey at this time as a poor and insignificant monastery, where a small community eked out the slender endowments given to it for the service of Christ.[2] In comparison with other English monasteries of this period, it was in fact neither poor nor rich.

This monastery Edward chose as his place of burial. Moreover, to provide a fit setting for his tomb, Edward rebuilt the church, and his gifts transformed the Abbey into one of the richest monasteries in the kingdom.[3] By Sulcard's time, it was believed at Westminster that the Confessor intended to make a pilgrimage to Rome, but, abandoning this idea on account of the dangers to the realm from his absence, decided to honour St. Peter another way, by restoring the church that was dedicated to him at Westminster.[4] It is unlikely that Edward claimed for his monks a special position *vis-à-vis* the bishop of London, or that he commended them to the see of Rome, although, later, the Abbey traced its privilege of exemption to this period and, indeed, to the reign of Edgar.[5] If the Confessor did confer a special ecclesiastical status on the monastery, the act was not effectual for long. Sulcard, writing in the 1070s or 1080s, had so little thought of using the story of the church's consecration at the hands of St. Peter to demonstrate its exemption from the authority of the ordinary that he puts into the mouth of the Saint an

---

[1] The probable possessions of the Abbey in 1042, with the value *T.R.E.*, if this is given in Domesday Book, were: in Essex: Fanton (£3), Ham (£1), Kelvedon (£5); in Herts.: Aldenham (£8), Datchworth and Watton (£4), Titeburst (13*s.*); in Midd.: Hampstead (£5), Hanwell (£7), Hendon (£12), Paddington, Shepperton (£7), Sunbury (£7), Westminster (£12); in Surr.: Morden (£6); in Suss.: Chollington in Eastbourne, Parham. See also below, pp. 341 ff.

[2] *The Life of King Edward who rests at Westminster*, ed. F. Barlow (London, 1962), p. 44.

[3] For these gifts see below, p. 27 and n.   [4] *Traditio* 20 (1964), 90–1.

[5] *Sawyer*, 774, 1011, 1039–41, 1043. In the early twelfth century, it was believed at Westminster that the Abbey's privileges had been controverted between Bishop Robert of Jumièges and Abbot Wulnoth (d. 1049). For this tradition, see ibid. 1011, and a spurious bull of Paschal II, now *Papsturkunden in England*, ed. W. Holtzmann (Berlin and Göttingen, 1930–52), i. 9. For exemption at Westminster and elsewhere, see D. Knowles, 'The Growth of Exemption', *Downside Review* 50 (1932), 201–31, 396–436. Robert of Jumièges held the see of London in 1050–1.

explicit injunction that Mellitus is to exercise episcopal functions there.[1] Sulcard wrote this story ingenuously, to promote the cult of St. Peter in his monastery; for him its significance was devotional, not legal. The Abbey became the *filius specialis* of St. Peter in the twelfth century, just at the time when the king's rights over the church emerged clearly as those of patron, neither more nor less.

The Confessor's choice of Westminster as his burial place was a personal one, which did not necessarily extend to his family or to his immediate successors on the throne of England. After the Battle of Hastings, Harold's body was brought to Waltham Abbey, and Waltham, which he had favoured in his lifetime, might well have been his chosen burial place had he died full of years and honour. William the Conqueror was buried at Caen.[2]

What the Abbey won and never lost at the death of Edward the Confessor was the status of being the coronation church of the English kings. Since 1066 they have all been crowned there, excepting only those who have not been crowned at all; Henry III, who was crowned in haste at Gloucester on his father's death, underwent a second coronation at Westminster, so strong was the Abbey's claim to authenticate the king's title in this way. The custom was started by Harold[3] and William the Conqueror, each of whom had reason to associate his inauguration rites as closely as possible with the shrine of the Confessor. Thus Edward was the founder of the Abbey's greatness in a double sense: he raised the church to the front rank of English monasteries in respect of its wealth and numbers; and, perhaps without any design on his part, his decision to be buried there ensured that the Abbey became the coronation church of the kings of England. In comparison with all this, even St. Dunstan's foundation belongs to the pre-history of the Abbey.

---

[1] *Traditio* 20 (1964), 84. St. Peter instructed the fisherman to tell Mellitus to exercise *ministerium . . . episcopale* in the church.

[2] For royal burials at Westminster, see below, pp. 28–9.

[3] Since Harold was present at Edward the Confessor's death-bed and crowned the next day, the conclusion is inescapable that he was crowned at Westminster; see F. Barlow, *Edward the Confessor* (London, 1970), pp. 249 ff.

II

Income and its Sources

THE income of Westminster Abbey was not derived exclusively from real property. In overwhelming degree, however, it came from that source. In 1535 the monks had a net income of not less than *c*. £2,800 per annum, and the monastery was then, in wealth, second only to Glastonbury Abbey among English religious houses.[1] We shall first consider the principal ways in which this astonishing wealth was acquired, and one or two potentially lucrative aspects of the monks' life which brought them surprisingly little in the way of an income; next, their income at different points in the Middle Ages, and finally how rich or poor they were, given the standards of living which they affected. One relevant topic, the monks' own purchase of property, is reserved for a later chapter. The main concern will be with net income, that is, with the expendable surplus that came into the hands of the monks each year after deduction of the necessary and inescapable expenses of administering the assets from which the income was derived.[2]

(i) *The Confessor's Foundation; Royal Anniversaries and Chantries*

Edward the Confessor intended his burial place to be one of the principal monasteries in the kingdom, and it must be assumed that he was ready to spend whatever was necessary to achieve this end. Since, however, his choice lighted on a house that was already moderately wealthy, his outlay was not

---

[1] Below, p. 63, where the actual figure suggested is £2,827 per annum. For the net income of other religious houses according to *V.E.*, see D. Knowles, *The Religious Orders in England*, vol. iii: *The Tudor Age* (Cambridge, 1959), pp. 473–4; here, however, the rating is according to *gross* income, and the figure given for *net* income at Westminster is smaller than that given above.

[2] For the significance of 'net income' in 1086, see below, p. 55.

inordinately large. At perhaps not a great deal more than £270 per annum, the value of the gifts from Edward which had already taken effect on the day when he was alive and dead made up about 63 per cent of the total value of the monks' possessions then.[1] In prospect his benefactions were far greater than these figures suggest, for the monks were to receive Martinsley wapentake in Rutland when Queen Edith died, and they had almost certainly been given Islip, the Confessor's birth-place, although this manor was not yet in their possession.[2] So far as the distribution of the Abbey's estates is concerned, Edward's gifts were supremely important, for, by making over the manors of Pershore and Deerhurst to the monks, he introduced them to an entirely new focus of influence in the West Midlands, and in Hampshire, Oxfordshire, and Rutland they had no foothold before he gave them one.

After the Norman Conquest, the Abbey suffered one great disappointment. This was in Rutland, where William apparently took Martinsley wapentake into his own hands on the death of Queen Edith.[3] Islip, moreover, eluded their grasp until the beginning of the thirteenth century. But William's desire to afforest their manor at Windsor was a stroke of good fortune that left the monks, in the end, almost as well off as they would have been had the Confessor's full intentions been carried out. William, nervous of carrying out the afforestation at the expense of the Abbey, gave in exchange for Windsor lands that were probably many times more valuable. It was this profitable transaction, whereby the Abbey acquired manors in Battersea and Wandsworth,

---

[1] Many gifts were later fathered on Edward by the monks of Westminster. Of the estates which they held at his death, it is safe to say that the following were in fact given by Edward: Easthampstead and Windsor (Berks.), Deerhurst (Glos.), Eversley (Hants), Ashwell, Stevenage, and Wheathampstead (Herts.), Staines (Middx.), Deene and Sudborough (Northants.), Launton (Oxon.), Perton (Staffs.), and Pershore (Worcs.). The total value of the monks' possessions in 1066, excluding the very few for which no value is given, was *c.* £430 per annum. Neither figure takes account of renders of honey at Deerhurst and Pershore. See Appendix I (below, pp. 337 ff.).

[2] *Harmer*, no. 94; see also ibid., pp. 323–4 and 514–15; *V.C.H. Rutland* i. 139–40; *V.C.H. Oxon.* vi. 208. Martinsley wapentake was worth £142 per annum *T.R.E.* and Islip £7 per annum.

[3] *V.C.H. Rutland* i. 139–40. For the Abbey's long struggle to obtain manorial and other rights in Rutland, see below, pp. 47 and 356–7.

Feering and Ockendon,[1] that carried it into the top flight of monastic wealth, as we find this recorded in Domesday Book. The monastery had a net income of *c.* £515 per annum and could support a community of some eighty monks; this, we know, was about the size of the community which Gilbert Crispin ruled at Westminster or of that for which he thought it sensible to provide.[2]

Because Edward the Confessor was buried at Westminster, it was inevitable, despite the slow progress of his cult, that the post-conquest kings should wish to be crowned there. This circumstance brought the monastery great honour but scarcely any material gains, except whatever are implied in the possession of the coronation regalia; the monks made good their claim to the regalia in the twelfth century. From William the Conqueror's time, only those kings who were buried in the Abbey, or whose consorts were buried there, proved notable benefactors to it. Accordingly, the years down to 1216 were lean, for none of the Norman or Angevin kings chose to lie there, and neither the burial of Henry I's queen, Matilda, in the Abbey nor the canonization of Edward the Confessor in 1161 uncovered the springs of royal generosity again. Matilda herself gave the monks some property near their wharf in the city of London, and Henry I allowed them one halfpenny a day from the farm of London, to provide a candle at her tomb.[3]

The turning-point in the Abbey's fortunes came in the reign of Henry III, when the young king adopted Edward the Confessor as his patron saint and, in 1245, chose the Abbey as his own place of burial. Down to the Dissolution of the monastery, and the dismantling of the Confessor's shrine, nearly all Henry's successors on the throne and not a few of the royal consorts chose to lie near the saint in the church which Henry so gloriously restored; their choice was not only

---

[1] It is possible that Benfleet (Essex) and Pyrford (Surr.) were acquired as part of the same transaction. For references see below, pp. 340 ff.

[2] *Customary*, p. 149. For the figure of *c.* £515 per annum see below, pp. 55–6 and n. For the wealth of other religious houses in 1086, see D. Knowles, *The Monastic Order in England* (2nd edn., Cambridge, 1963), pp. 702–3; these figures, however, are for gross income.

[3] *Gilbert Crispin*, pp. 155–6. For Matilda's anniversary at Westminster, see below, p. 388 (no. 3).

of extreme importance in making the Abbey a place of national resort, but, over the centuries, a source of considerable material gain to the monks. Besides paying modestly for the commemoration of his mother, Isabella of Angoulême, and one or two minor members of the royal family in the Abbey, Henry III proposed to endow his own and his wife's anniversary there with the gift of lands worth nearly £100 per annum; and in 1265 the monks obtained from Henry the grant of the lands of the rebel, Richard de Culworth.[1] In the end, however, this property eluded them, and throughout the Middle Ages Henry's anniversary, that of the monastery's third founder, was supported by nothing more substantial than the revenues of the church of Feering; in 1249, before Henry's larger designs had fallen through, Innocent IV permitted the appropriation of this church for the purpose.[2] Subsequently, however, four of the kings and queens who were buried in the Abbey chose to have their principal commemoration there and paid generously for the privilege, or their relatives and executors made the choice on their behalf. They were Eleanor of Castile, Richard II, for himself and Anne of Bohemia, Henry V, and Henry VII; and to their names must be added that of Henry VII's mother, the Lady Margaret Beaufort, Countess of Richmond, who, not content with her share in the prayers to be offered in Henry's chapel, endowed a foundation of her own at Westminster with lands worth *c.* £90 per annum by the reckoning of the *Valor Ecclesiasticus*.[3]

At the centre of every such foundation was a provision for the liturgical commemoration of the founder—yearly, on the anniversary of the death, and, as a rule, week by week as well; and for Henry V and Henry VII daily masses were endowed in addition to the anniversaries. Every foundation provided as well for a reward to the monks for their labour in saying the many masses and prayers. But down to the time when Henry VII incorporated an educational foundation in his chantry, the scale of the endowments was determined mainly

---

[1] Below, p. 391 (no. 25 and n.); see also ibid. (nos. 21–2) and p. 392 (no. 30).
[2] Below, p. 406.
[3] For these foundations see below, pp. 393 ff. (nos. 38, 55, 58, 62–3), and for their value in 1535, Table I (below, p. 34).

by the founder's intentions concerning the third essential feature of the anniversary, the distribution of alms. Was this to be limited only by the number of the poor who should present themselves at the monastery on the right day and at the right time? If so, a very large endowment was needed; but if not, much less would do. Thus on the anniversaries of Eleanor of Castile and Richard II and Anne of Bohemia, the monks were to give 1*d*. for victuals to every poor person who should come to the Abbey before the third hour, and for each of these foundations they were promised lands worth £200 per annum.[1] But Henry V's executors limited the distribution to doles of 10*d*. per annum for each of twenty-four select poor and a general distribution of £20 on the anniversary; and his foundation was to comprise lands worth only £100 per annum.[2]

Henry VII's foundation eclipsed them all, providing as it did for a chantry staffed by three monks who had graduated at Oxford or Cambridge, for the better education of the monks of Westminster from whose ranks the chantry priests were to be drawn, and for many lesser commemorations of Henry annually at other churches in the kingdom. To pay for all these extra charges on their income, the monks were given or enabled to buy property of the gross value of *c*. £800 per annum.[3]

The royal benefactors of Westminster Abbey, other than Edward the Confessor, had in common the prudent habit of making over to the monks property that had only recently come into their hands or had never lodged there at all, and Edward himself followed this practice as far as he could. In granting Pershore and Deerhurst to the Abbey, Edward was giving away property which he had acquired as recently as 1056, on the death of Earl Odda, whose ancestor, Aelfhere, had taken the manors from the minsters in these places.[4] These manors accounted for nearly one-half the total value of the Confessor's gifts to the Abbey. Such of the endowments of

---

[1] Below, p. 393 (no. 38), and p. 397 (no. 55). There was also to be, in each case, a weekly distribution of alms.

[2] Below, p. 398 (no. 58).

[3] *Cal. Cl. R.*, *Henry VII* ii. 389; and see below, p. 399 (no. 62 and n.). For the income of Henry VII's foundation in 1535, see Table I (below, p. 34).

[4] C. S. Taylor, 'Deerhurst, Pershore and Westminster', *Trans. Bristol and Gloucs. Archaeological Soc.* 25 (1902), 230 ff.

Richard II's foundation as were not taken from alien priories came, with scarcely an exception, from the estate of Richard Scrope,[1] and the Abbey was given no lands for Henry V's anniversary, but an allowance from the Exchequer instead, until 1445, when two manors of the alien priories, at Offord Cluny and Letcombe Regis, became available.[2] Sixty years later, the possessions of the College of St. Martin-le-Grand and other religious houses, private chapels, and chantries contributed largely to the endowment of Henry VII's chantry.[3]

The endowment of Eleanor of Castile's anniversary shows how inroads on the royal demesne were avoided at a time when church lands were not so conveniently available for underwriting the cost of royal anniversaries. Eleanor died in November 1290, but already, four years before the event, the abbot and convent of Westminster were purchasing land for her anniversary with money which she had put at their disposal.[4] Of these early purchases, however, only the land bought from Edward I's servant, Simon de Ellesworth, in Turweston became a permanent part of Eleanor's foundation. Until very recently this property had belonged to the Scovill family; the monks paid Simon de Ellesworth £133. 6s. 8d. for it.[5] Knowle, Birdbrook, and Westerham, three other manors destined for the foundation, were already in Eleanor's or Edward I's hands. Knowle had belonged to Sir William de Ardern, whose misfortune it was, first, to be implicated in the civil war of Henry III's reign on the losing side, and, subsequently, in 1276, to die, leaving as his heir a brother, an idiot who became a royal ward. Edward I had custody of Knowle and of Ardern's other lands for the three remaining years of his brother's life, and in 1284 he and Eleanor purchased it from the surviving member of the family; she was Amice de Ardern, the wife of John le Lou.[6] Birdbrook had belonged to Sir Gilbert Pecche, whose debts to the king

---

[1] *Cal. Ch. R.* v. 375 ff. For the exception, Stokenchurch, see *V.C.H. Bucks.* iii. 98.

[2] *Foedera* xi. 89–93.

[3] *V.E.* i. 411–12. In 1535 the net value—i.e. the gross value, excluding local reprises—of the possessions of St. Martin-le-Grand, the largest contributor, in the hands of the Abbey was *c.* £320 per annum; but see also below, p. 399 (no. 62 and n.).

[4] W.A.M. 23627–8; *Monks*, p. 15.   [5] Below, p. 416 (no. 9).

[6] *Cal. Fine R.* i. 72, 118; *Cal. Pat. R., 1281–92*, pp. 174–5. For William de Ardern see *Knights of Edward I* i. 18–19.

Eleanor was granted in 1280; Gilbert's surrender of this and other properties followed in 1283.[1] Four years earlier, Sir Robert de Camville surrendered the manor of Westerham into the queen's hands in order to obtain his freedom from imprisonment on what was probably a trumped-up charge of neglecting military service owing to the king in Wales.[2] The claims of Robert de Camville's heirs pursued the monks well into the reign of Edward III.[3]

Denham was a more difficult case to manage, since, as far as we know, neither Robert de Fileby nor John and Joan de Bohun, who had interests in the manor, were in serious financial difficulties. Yet Abbot Wenlok and his monks dearly coveted this property, which had been given to their church by one of Edward the Confessor's thegns but fee-farmed by their predecessors towards the end of the twelfth century for £15 per annum;[4] they must be regarded as the real instigators of Edward's designs upon it. It is possible that the king took the manor in hand on the grounds that the fee-farm rent owing for the manor from Robert de Fileby was in arrears, as, indeed, it was, but only to the extent of £6. 13s. 4d.[5] At all events, the manor was in Eleanor's hands before her death, and in 1292 Edward I restored it to the demesne of the Abbey.[6] For the monks, who did not enter formally into possession of Turweston, Knowle, Birdbrook, or Westerham until a little later, it was the first-fruits of Eleanor's foundation. The protests of the Bohun family continued for some fifty years, but unavailingly.[7]

---

[1] *Cal. Cl. R.*, *1279–88*, p. 28; cf. ibid., pp. 70, 80; P. Morant, *History and Antiquities of the County of Essex* (London, 1768), ii. 344. For Gilbert Pecche, see *Knights of Edward I*, iv. 23.

[2] For Robert de Camville, see ibid. i. 178. The story, told from the Camville viewpoint, is in W.A.M. 5144; see also *Cal. Cl. R.*, *1279–88*, p. 80. Robert de Camville was allowed to retain a life-interest in the manor, but he died within the year (ibid.; and P.R.O., C.P. 25 (i), 284/21/90). (For the last reference and the second in the following note, I am grateful to Mr. N. H. MacMichael.)

[3] W.A.M. 5144; G. Wrottesley, *Pedigrees from the Plea Rolls, collected from the Pleadings in the Various Courts of Law, A.D. 1200 to 1500* (n.d.), p. 5.

[4] Below, p. 338. In 1284 John de Fileby, the tenant in fee, granted a life-interest in the manor to Robert de Fileby, who in 1286 transferred his rights to Joan de Bohun. When Edward I took the manor in hand, a farmer named Ralph de Broghton was in possession (*Cal. Cl. R.*, *1288–96*, p. 224).

[5] *V.C.H. Bucks.* iii. 257.   [6] Below, pp. 338–9.

[7] *Cal. Cl. R.*, *1337–9*, p. 510.

This dependence on windfall properties meant that the endowment of royal anniversaries could be a slow process. If, on the one hand, all the lands needed for Eleanor of Castile's had been found by 1295,[1] Henry V's foundation, on the other, was not endowed until 1445.[2] That of Richard II and Anne of Bohemia never possessed endowments on the scale intended by its founder.[3] Moreover, the distribution of alms and the due performance of the liturgy laid heavy charges on each foundation. Henry VII estimated that his would spend *c.* £580 per annum in this way.[4] As Table I shows, the monks enjoyed only a small surplus from Queen Eleanor's foundation in its early years.

Nevertheless, these funds became exceedingly important to monastic finances at Westminster, and, in the long run, they had profound effects on the life of the community there. Since the endowments were exempt from both royal custody during vacancies and royal subsidies, they provided the novelty of a tax-free income; they were thus worth more than the bare figures of income would suggest. More important, owing to the decision, taken virtually in principle at the end of Walter de Wenlok's abbacy, that the surplus income of such foundations belonged to the convent, if it so wished, for pittances,[5] this money was the key-stone of the wage-system at Westminster, and into the wage-fund were poured, in due course, sums that equalled the entire income of less favoured houses elsewhere. As time went on, alms-giving was allowed to consume a smaller and smaller proportion of the income of Queen Eleanor's foundation, the monks' own wages, more and more of it; and the pittances of the brethren recovered more

---

[1] *Cal. Ch. R.* ii. 461.

[2] Above, p. 31; see also below, p. 398 and n.

[3] W.A.M. 23970 ff.; and see Table I. The best years for this foundation were those between 1395 and 1399, when it received £200 per annum from the Exchequer.

[4] *Cal. Cl. R., Henry VII* ii, p. 149. The estimate includes the cost of educating the monk-priests of the chantry at Oxford. If *V.E.* (i. 411–12, 418–20) is to be believed, the monks managed to pare their expenditure on these items to *c.* £368 per annum; but they also spent *c.* £170 per annum from the income of the fund on the collegiate establishment of St. Martin-le-Grand.

[5] *Walter de Wenlok*, p. 19. This decision, made in respect of Queen Eleanor's foundation, was applied, with few modifications, to similar cases in the future. The surplus issues of Denham, which always went to the abbot, were excluded from its scope.

TABLE I. *The Finances of the Major Royal Foundations*

| | c. 1300 Annual | | | c. 1400 Annual | | | 1535 Annual | | |
	Income	Expenditure (£)	Surplus	Income	Expenditure (£)	Surplus	Income	Expenditure (£)	Surplus
Eleanor of Castile	176	148	28	248	62	186	212	68	144
Richard II and Anne of Bohemia				168	59	109	162	70	92
Henry V							75	25	50
Margaret, Countess of Richmond							90	47	43
Henry VII							766	538	228
Total	176	148	28	416	121	295	1,305	748	557

Sources: W.A.M. 13313–19, 23631 (cf. W.A.M. 23632–6); W.A.M. 23727–43, 23970–83; *T.P.N.*, 46; *V.E.* i. 410–24.

Notes

(i) 'Income' is the net income reaching the central coffers of the Abbey in respect of the royal foundations; thus it is normally the issues of the manors with which they were endowed, but after the deduction of local manorial expenses. In 1535 it is the income recorded in *V.E.*, less the so-called reprises, in so far as these represented local administrative charges or rent charges. With the exception of one item, the figures for the foundation of Eleanor of Castile in *c.* 1300 have been derived from the accounts of that foundation for 1301–4, the earliest to survive. The exception is the Abbey's income from Denham, which escaped notice in these accounts, since it was assigned to the abbot's portion. The sum of £42. 18s. 10d. per annum has been allowed for this manor. The figure, which is almost certainly too low, has been arrived at by adding together the amount which the abbot distributed in alms for the queen's soul from the issues of Denham (£30. 6s. 8d. per annum) and the value of the manor according to *T.P.N.* (£12. 12s. 2d. per annum). The fee-farm rent of £15 per annum, which the monks were already receiving from Denham before 1291, has been excluded from consideration.

Both in the case of Eleanor's foundation and that of Richard II and Anne of Bohemia, the figure for *c.* 1400 is the average net income for the years (respectively 10 and 7) between Sept. 1395 and Sept. 1405 for which accounts survive, together with, in the case of Eleanor's foundation, the appropriate allowance for Denham.

By 1535, the monks had assigned some of the lands originally acquired for these two foundations to other uses. Since the purpose of the table is to show the wealth which the royal foundations brought to the Abbey, it takes no account of these changes. Thus the figure for the foundation of Richard II and Anne of Bohemia at this date includes the Abbey's income from Hodford and Cowhouse, although these manors were now in fact assigned to the abbot's portion.

(ii) 'Expenditure' is the cost of the specific obligations undertaken by the monks as conditions of receiving the benefactions, other than the pittances which they themselves received, in accordance with the wishes of the donors. The main items as a rule were alms for the poor and candles for the tomb, but their obligations in respect of Henry VII's chantry were much more extensive—more extensive in fact than is apparent from *V.E.*, for this source fails to show that the monks of Westminster spent *c.* £170 per annum from the income of the foundation on the support of the collegiate body which continued in existence at St. Martin-le-Grand, despite the appropriation of that church to the Abbey.

(iii) It follows that 'Surplus' was not entirely at the monks' disposal, for even when the net issues of the manors forming the endowments of these foundations reached the monastery, some administrative costs had still to be met, but normally much of the surplus shown in the table was indeed at the monks' disposal; it was from this money that their pittances were paid. In *c.* 1300 and again in *c.* 1400 *c.* £13 per annum of the whole was enjoyed by the abbot; in 1535 the whole of the surplus went in effect to the convent, although book-keeping practices tend to conceal this fact.

Around the year 1400, much of the 'surplus' attributed in the table to the foundation of Richard II and Anne of Bohemia was in fact consumed by the expenses consequent on the acquisition of landed endowments in place of the annual allowance from the Exchequer with which the foundation began in 1394.

quickly than the alms of the poor from the slump in income
experienced by the foundation of Richard II and Anne of
Bohemia after 1399.[1] This cynical disregard of the right order
of priorities is a theme of cardinal importance in the history
of the late-medieval Abbey. The surplus income of the royal
foundations represented between 1 and 2 per cent of the total
net income of the Abbey at the end of the thirteenth century,
c. 12 per cent at the end of the fourteenth, and *c.* 20 per cent
in 1535.[2]

Finally, the royal anniversaries, haphazardly endowed as
they were, had some small effect on the geographical distribution of the Abbey's estates. John Islip's monks in the early
sixteenth century were rich, as Vitalis's had been in the late
eleventh, in the regions where the royal gifts had come thickest,
and these were still the Home Counties and the West Midlands;
but it is also the case that the Abbey had more possessions
further afield at the later date—in Warwickshire and Lincolnshire, for example, and even in Yorkshire—and this was owing
to the circumstance that property had been given or purchased in these parts for the royal anniversaries.

(ii) *Other Gifts*

The value of the lands which Westminster Abbey had
acquired at the hands of private donors amounted to £38 per
annum by Domesday reckoning at the death of Edward the
Confessor and to £55. 10*s.* per annum in 1086, and these
figures probably represent respectively 9 and 11 per cent of
the value of the demesne estate at the dates in question.[3]
They are an imperfect guide to the extent of private giving
in the early years of St. Dunstan's and the Confessor's foundation, since not a few of the benefactors who attempted to give

---

[1] W.A.M. 23976 ff. In 1404–5, £32. 13*s.* 4*d.* was spent on pittances for the
brethren, but there is no record of the payment of 1*d.* a week per person to 140 poor
persons, in accordance with the terms of the foundation (W.A.M. 23983; and see
below, p. 397, no. 55).

[2] For the total net income of the Abbey at these dates, see Table VI (below,
p. 63).

[3] The new acquisitions between the death of Edward the Confessor and 1086
were Kelvedon Hatch and Paglesham (Essex) and Tooting (Surr.), for which see
below, pp. 343, 359. Tooting, however, was in the hands of a tenant in 1086.
The figures in the text exclude the gifts of St. Dunstan, which were valued at
£30–40 per annum in 1086.

land to the monks at this time were unable to carry through their purpose. Not all these losses to the monastery are attributable to the political vicissitudes of the period, although some, of course, are; several arose from the circumstance that the would-be donor did not possess an interest in his land such that he could alienate it to the Church. Aelfhelm Polga's bequest of land at Brickendon is a case in point. Aelfhelm was one of King Edgar's thegns, and rich enough to be a benefactor to Ramsey Abbey and Ely Abbey as well.[1] He made his will towards the end of the tenth century or early in the eleventh, and a copy of it came into the possession of the monks of Westminster. About 1060, however, Earl Harold gave Brickendon to Waltham Abbey, and this grant Edward the Confessor confirmed. The king's readiness to do this must mean that the testator had not possessed a devisable interest in the estate.

Most of the Abbey's benefactors before the Conquest were men of substance. Occasionally gifts at the hands of donors who were apparently free men, neither more nor less, are mentioned, but as a rule, although the gifts might be small, the donors were of some importance. Leofcild, who bequeathed Moulsham to the monastery, may have been sheriff of Essex for some years during the Confessor's reign, and Ailric, son of Mariete, who gave the monks the only land in Lincolnshire that they were to possess for many years to come, had a considerable estate and rights of sake and soke.[2] As far as we know, the pre-Conquest monastery attracted no benefactor from the country north of Lincolnshire or west of Buckinghamshire.

The underlying purpose of these early gifts is usually described in general terms as that of benefiting the donor's soul, but from the early twelfth century, as the relationship between the monks of Westminster and their benefactors became more formalized, so the return which the latter could expect for their gifts was expressed more precisely. The first specific privilege mentioned is burial in the Abbey or within its precincts. This, in the Middle Ages, was never a preserve of rank

[1] For Aelfhelm and Brickendon, see Whitelock, *Anglo-Saxon Wills*, p. 31; *V.C.H. Herts.* iii. 410.

[2] *Harmer*, no. 84; see also ibid., pp. 564–5, and *The Lincolnshire Domesday and the Lindsey Survey*, ed. C. W. Foster, T. Longley, and F. M. Stenton (Lincoln Record Soc., xix), pp. 13, 59, 196, 229.

or professional distinction, although it is true to say that certain parts of the Abbey church were available only to those who could show either qualification, or both; the monks were in general readier to confer the right of burial than others to accept it. In the fourteenth century, for example, it was a real scoop for the monastery when William 'de Palacio' asked for burial there, for he was keeper of the Palace of Westminster, where the Abbey's claims to spiritual jurisdiction were jealously contested, and probably dean of St. Stephen's chapel there; William was buried near the holy water stoup by the cloister door.[1] Whoever showed the keener spirit, the supplicant for the right of burial or the monks in offering this, a gift or legacy usually marked the request, and it was in this way that the monks of Westminster acquired one addition of the utmost importance to their estate after the Norman Conquest. This was the manor of Eye, on the very door-step of the monastery, in present-day Pimlico and Mayfair. They were given this property by Geoffrey de Mandeville I, whose first wife was buried in the Abbey cloister and who wished himself for burial there.[2]

A burial did not always occasion an addition to the monastery's endowed income and perhaps rather rarely did so in the later Middle Ages. In this period the monks' hopes were pinned mainly on the offerings at the funeral mass and on the payments customarily made by the deceased's relatives and executors for the hearse and candles which were perquisites of the sacrist after the funeral. In 1395, after John de Waltham's funeral, they received £40 for these items;[3] in 1430, when Lewis Robsart was buried, only £10.[4] In the case of humbler people, the monks seem now to have received a small fee for the privilege of burial in their church. Thus in 1445–6 they received 13s. 4d. for the burial of Mr. John Russell.[5]

About the time of Geoffrey de Mandeville's death, in c. 1100, the institution of confraternity is first mentioned at Westminster. Between 1107 and 1115, the three daughters of Deorman gave the monks property in London for their souls,

[1] Below, p. 379 and n.
[2] Below, p. 372; and for Eye, see below, p. 350. Geoffrey de Mandeville I also gave land at Tilbury to the Abbey for the soul of Athelaise (*Gilbert Crispin*, p. 127).
[3] Below, p. 380 n. [4] Below, p. 382 and n. [5] Ibid., and n.

for burial and for confraternity,[1] and it need not be doubted
that William the chamberlain's gift of 3 hides in Kingsbury
obtained for him the benefits of confraternity at about this
time, or a little earlier, although the so-called Telligraphus
of William I which records this fact is a patent forgery of a
later age.[2]

Most of our knowledge of confraternity at Westminster is
derived from the thirteenth-century *Customary* of the Abbey.[3]
The *confrater*, who, it was anticipated, might need to be addressed in French instead of Latin—but not, it seems, in English—
shared with the monks in all the spiritual benefits of their
alliance with other churches. When he died, his obsequies
would include a mass to be sung by every priest in the community and his name would be enrolled in the Abbey's martyrology and entered in the next mortuary brief that went out for
a monk. But the *Customary* did not envisage burial within the
precincts as a normal part of confraternity.

An anniversary, regularly celebrated every year, cost more.
The institution is first mentioned at Westminster in the twelfth
century, but most of the foundations of this period—themselves
few in number—commemorated abbots of the house or, in
one case, the prior. Prior Robert de Molesham's, for which
£5 per annum was assigned from the revenues of St. Mary's
altar, perhaps honoured the prime part he played in for-
warding the cult of the Virgin at Westminster.[4] In the
thirteenth century, a wider range of persons, both inside and
outside the monastery, was commemorated in this way. Early
in the century, Br. Richard le Gras endowed an anniversary
for himself, his father, William le Gras, and their kindred,[5]
and later a brewer of Stratford endowed an anniversary for
himself and Br. John le Fundur with a croft in Feering and as

---

[1] Below, p. 386 and n.

[2] Ibid. William the chamberlain's gift, which was probably of land at Chalkhill in Kingsbury, was also made for the clothing of a friend named Hubert
as a monk of Westminster, and it may have had the further purpose of ending an
old dispute about this land. The latter had been pledged by one of the Abbey's
men for a debt *T.R.E.*; the wording of the entry about it in *D.B.* (i. 128b), where
William is said to hold 'sub abbate S. Petri', is very likely explained by the fact
that Kingsbury was in dispute between William and the monks. See also below,
p. 349.

[3] *Customary* ii. 232 ff.

[4] Below, pp. 388–9 (no. 8).

[5] Below, p. 389 (no. 14).

much rent as £10 would buy.[1] But the monks occasionally celebrated an anniversary mass that was not endowed and not intended, by those who requested it, to form part of a regular observance, year after year. On these occasions they received small *ad hoc* payments for their services, and the offerings.

Chantries at Westminster were a fashion mainly of the fourteenth century. They made a much greater demand than any of these other forms of association on the liturgical resources of the monastery and necessitated correspondingly larger endowments. In 1285, in one of the earliest of these arrangements which we know of at the Abbey, the royal clerk, Geoffrey de Aspale, provided for the services of the two chaplains who were to celebrate daily in the Abbey for his soul and the souls of his kindred with the gift of the manor of Halliford.[2] Halliford, like Denham, was a part of the ancient endowment of the Abbey which had been fee-farmed by the monks in the twelfth century; Aspale evidently purchased the manor from the farmer of the day, the impecunious Robert de Crevequer, in order to restore it to the demesne of the church.[3] Some fifty years later, Sir John de Shorditch was promised two monk-chaplains for his chantry, in return for endowments that he had the king's licence to amortize at a value not exceeding £13. 6s. 8d. per annum—and mortmain valuations commonly represented much less than the true annual value of the land in question.[4] In the 1360s or 1370s, Simon de Langham reckoned that his monastery would need an income of £26. 13s. 4d. per annum for his and his parents' chantry; this was to be staffed by four monks.[5]

By the end of the Middle Ages there were thus four principal ways in which benefactors might be linked with the Abbey and claim the intercessions of the monks. In addition, men and women might have the so-called spiritual benefits of the monastery—that is, a regular share in the prayers of the monks,

---

[1] Below, p. 392 (no. 27).

[2] Below, p. 393 (no. 36). On chantries see in general K. L. Wood-Legh, *Perpetual Chantries in Britain* (Cambridge, 1965), *passim*.

[3] Crevequer had been a rebel in the civil war of Henry III's reign (*Cal. Inq. Misc.* i. 809). For Halliford see below, pp. 351–2.

[4] Below, p. 395 (no. 44 and n.); see also below, p. 179.

[5] Below, p. 396 (no. 51).

but one that nevertheless fell short of the full privileges of the *confrater*; and in the later Middle Ages there occur specific grants of some of the privileges formerly understood to be part of confraternity, such, for example, as the right to have one's name enrolled, on decease, in the Abbey's martyrology.[1] The names of those who are known to have made use of any of these forms of association with the monastery are listed in Appendix II.[2] It is certain, from the loss of the Abbey's martyrology, that the list of *confratres* is incomplete, and the same is true of the list of burials. But when every allowance has been made for the deficiencies of the evidence, the late eleventh century and the twelfth remain a bleak period for the monks of Westminster. The interest which the Confessor's thegns showed in the Abbey was not maintained for long by the Anglo-Norman baronage after the Conquest; these men, it seems, rarely thought of the Abbey when they thought of their religion. Even later, when Westminster had become the centre of the English government, the seat of parliament, and, for a brief period, the site of a wool staple as well, the Abbey failed to consolidate a place for itself in the religious life of the clerks and men of affairs who now peopled the town. Accordingly, the monks did not succeed in coaxing out of their middle-class neighbours here or in the City of London, the benefactions that they no longer received from the landholding aristocracy. Briefly, in the thirteenth century, it seemed that they might manage to do this, but in the long run they failed. Although by the end of the Middle Ages, the list of the anniversaries and chantries to which the monks were committed was a long one—perhaps embarrassingly long, to a community declining in numbers—many of the persons commemorated belonged in their lifetime to the monastic family; they were abbots, monks, their relatives and friends, or servants of the Abbey. Indifference on the part of others extended not only to the specific religious benefits that laity of means could obtain at the Abbey, but also to successive building projects there. Private contributions to the building fund in the later

---

[1] Below, pp. 371–2, 400–1.

[2] Below, pp. 372 ff. Of the anniversaries kept at the Abbey, only the perpetual ones are noted here; the sacrist's rolls suggest that the others were not a numerous category.

Middle Ages were, as far as we know, few in number and for
the most part small. From Richard Whittington, for example,
only one donation, of £6. 13s. 4d., is recorded.[1] It does not seem
likely that the situation was different in the thirteenth century.

These facts are not surprising, given the character of the
Abbey as the coronation church and place of sepulture of the
kings of England. Nothing grows under a big tree, and over
the centuries the great shade cast by royal patronage at
Westminster kept private benefactions small. It is impossible
to say how much of their income the monks in fact owed to
such gifts, for most of these lost their identity through absorp-
tion in the general funds of the monastery or in an estate that
was the care of a local bailiff or reeve; but the proportion was
certainly small at all times. If an order of precedence were
to be established among benefactors who were not of royal
blood, the name of Simon de Langham would certainly head
the list. In addition to the endowment of his chantry, Langham
gave £400 to the fabric fund and left the monks all the debts
owing to him at his death (c. £975), beside his books, plate,
and vestments.[2] To Nicholas de Litlington, Langham's well-
born successor as abbot of Westminster, the monks owed
some of the most valuable additions to their store of plate that
they ever received. In 1378, Litlington gave to the refectory
forty-eight silver dishes, two chargers, and twenty-four salts,
weighing £104 in all, and to the misericord, twenty-four
dishes, twelve salts, and two chargers, weighing £40—all
with his initials and a coronet superimposed, together with
rents worth £6. 13s. 4d. per annum for their upkeep.[3] Besides
relieving the monotony of refectory life, Litlington thus notably

---

[1] W.A.M. 23471. For the accounts of the new work from the mid-fourteenth
century onwards, see W.A.M. 23452A ff. For the situation in the thirteenth century,
see *History of the King's Works*, ed. H. M. Colvin (London, 1963–   ), i. 135. Whittington and Br. Richard Harwden were Henry V's commissioners in the expenditure of £666. 13s. 4d. per annum which that king assigned to the new work at
Westminster (R. B. Rackham, 'The Nave of Westminster', in *Proceedings of the
British Academy* 4 (1909–10), 45–6).   [2] W.A.M. 9225*.

[3] *Flete*, pp. 135–6; *Monks*, p. 86. It was a condition of Litlington's gifts that a
prayer be said for his soul and the souls of all the faithful departed daily in the
refectory. The monks had been obliged to sell much of their plate immediately
after the Black Death of 1348–9; see below, p. 66. Litlington also gave the Abbey
vestments and the missal that now bears his name. He was almost certainly a
member of the Despenser family, but his exact parentage remains a mystery. For
his anniversary, see below, p. 395 (no. 48).

augmented the moveable wealth of the monastery. Until the fourteenth century, however, Geoffrey de Mandeville easily led the field, on account of the exceptionally desirable site of the property which he gave in Eye and the beginnings, in his foundation at Hurley, of the Abbey's small empire of dependent houses.[1]

(iii) *The Shrine and the Relics*

The relative scarcity of private benefactors at Westminster reflects the failure of Edward the Confessor's shrine to achieve the status of a major centre of pilgrimage. This episode belongs mainly to the history of saints and their relics, but for the monks of Westminster its material consequences were grievous, and to this extent the story is part of our present theme.

Edward the Confessor was canonized by Alexander III in 1161,[2] in the first act of canonization by the first pope to enjoy an effective monopoly of the process. The first translation, which was in effect the removal of the Confessor's body from a tomb below the ground to a shrine above it, followed some two and a half years later, but all the evidence suggests that the cult hung fire for very nearly a century longer. The turning-point seemed perhaps to have come in 1236, when Gregory IX recommended the observance of the feast of St. Edward to the whole English Church.[3] It was one thing, however, for the pope to declare a *festum feriandum*; quite another to bring about the observance of the rule, and the feast of the Translation of St. Edward was never popular in England. None of the surviving lists of *festa ferianda* issued by the bishops of the thirteenth century and later periods for the guidance of their subjects includes it.[4] As for St. Edward's other feast, the Deposition on 5 January, not even its liturgical

---

[1] For Eye, see above, p. 38, and for the foundation of Hurley Priory, *Gilbert Crispin*, pp. 32–3.   [2] Barlow, *Edward the Confessor*, pp. 323–4.

[3] *Les Régistres de Grégoire IX*, ed. L. Auvray *et al.* (Bibliothèque des Écoles françaises d'Athènes et de Rome (4 vols., Paris, 1896–1955), ii. 3330; see also *Councils and Synods, with other Documents relating to the English Church, II. A.D. 1205–1313*, ed. F. M. Powicke and C. R. Cheney (Oxford, 1964), i. 243). The monks of Westminster also possessed a mandate of Innocent IV of 1248 enjoining the regular observance of the feast of St. Edward on the Church in England (W.D., 406). Both translations, in 1163 and 1269, were on 13 Oct.

[4] For a conspectus of these lists, see C. R. Cheney, 'Rules for the observance of feast-days in medieval England', *B.I.H.R.* 34 (1961), 117 ff.

observance by the religious was common. Very few artistic representations of St. Edward or of the legends associated with him have survived, except in the Abbey itself or in places having a connection with the church or with the royal court.[1] By the second half of the fourteenth century it was the feast of Relics and the patronal festival of St. Peter, not that of St. Edward, that the public crier proclaimed in the city of London on behalf of the monks of Westminster.[2]

The collection of relics that the monks of Henry III's church put together for the edification of their visitors seems in a sense to have anticipated that the future would not be with St. Edward himself, for the *pièce de résistance* was not any relic of that saint but the Precious Blood of Christ, obtained for them by Henry from the Patriarch of Jerusalem in 1247.[3] Next came the girdle of the Virgin, itself, however, the gift of the Confessor.[4] Less tangible than the relics and the shrine, where they were principally exhibited, was the mystique of kingship enveloping pilgrims in a church that was the coronation church of the kings of England and, for not a few, their place of sepulture as well.

All amounted, it seems, to very little in popular esteem. The aggregate of offerings made in the Abbey church is first recorded in 1317–18, when it was £36. 3s. 7½d.,[5] a paltry figure, one may say, for a church with these unique associations; but the offerings received by the monks of Westminster at this time came to them on the ebb-tide of Edward II's popularity. The boom in the next reign—offerings amounted to very nearly £120 in 1372–3[6]—reflects the better success of Edward's son in winning and keeping his subject's affection.

[1] The evidence is summarized in L. E. Tanner, 'Some representations of St. Edward the Confessor in Westminster Abbey and elsewhere', *Jnl. British Archaeological Assoc.*, 3rd ser., 15 (1952), 1 ff.

[2] W.A.M. 19626, 19630. In each of these years (1359 and 1365) the monks paid the crier 2s. for his pains. The feast of Relics at Westminster was on 16 July. See also *Flete*, p. 105.

[3] For the patriarch's testimony to the authenticity of this relic, see W.D., 394ᵛ, and for the relics of St. Edward in the fourteenth century, *Flete*, p. 19.

[4] Ibid., pp. 69–70.

[5] W.A.M. 19618. The sacrist, whose accounts supply the figures in this paragraph, had charge of the shrine, the relics and every altar and image in the church, with the exception of those in the Lady Chapel; but in the fourteenth and fifteenth centuries relics seem rarely to have been shown in the Lady Chapel.

[6] W.A.M. 19633.

No less eloquently does the decline after Richard II's assumption of his majority, to a figure even lower than that of 1317–18, speak of that king's estrangement from his people.[1] From these straits not even Henry V's devotion to the Confessor and decision himself to be buried at Westminster could rescue the monks; in Henry VI's reign the sacrist of Westminster often accounted for less than £10 per annum in offerings.[2] Later, only Henry VII's funeral, in the half-finished splendour of the new Lady Chapel, momentarily swelled the sacrist's takings. This occasion brought in £158. 18s.; but there had always been such windfalls at royal funerals and coronations.[3]

(iv) *Parish Churches*

The church of St. Margaret of Antioch, immediately adjacent to the Abbey, provided the nucleus of the monastery's income from tithe and glebe-land. As defined by papal judges-delegate in 1222, the parish of St. Margaret's extended, in present-day terms, on the north to Oxford Street and on the west to the Serpentine and the Westbourne stream; on the south and east the boundary was the Thames, to a point south of Waterloo Bridge. The parish included all the land between Whitehall and the Thames, except the church of St. Martin-in-the-Fields and St. Martin's own precinct, and it also included the vills of Paddington, Knightsbridge, and Westbourne.[4] The rationale of this arrangement is probably to be found in the fact that these vills formed part of the ancient endowment of the Abbey, their inhabitants having been at one time dependent on the monks for the sacraments; most probably they were comprised in the estate of 13½ hides at Westminster attributed to the Abbey in Domesday Book.

[1] W.A.M. 19637 ff. The figure in 1397–8, the last full year of the reign for which the sacrist's account survives, was £23. 8s. ¾d. (W.A.M. 19657).

[2] The accounts for the reign are W.A.M. 19663 ff.

[3] W.A.M. 19765. The same account shows that the sum of £20 was taken in offerings at the funeral of Henry's mother, Margaret, Countess of Richmond, who also died in 1509.

[4] D. Wilkins, *Concilia Magnae Britanniae et Hiberniae* (London, 1737), i. 598–9; A. M. Burke, *Indexes to the Ancient Testamentary Records of Westminster* (London, 1913), pp. v–vi; see also M. B. Honeybourne, 'The sanctuary boundaries and environs of Westminster Abbey and the college of St. Martin-le-Grand', *Jnl. British Archaeological Assoc.*, n.s. 38 (1932), 316 ff.; G. Saunders, 'Results of an inquiry concerning the situation and extent of Westminster, at various periods', *Archaeologia* 26 (1836), 223 ff., where, however, Plan II is not entirely correct.

In the fourteenth century, tradition at Westminster honoured the Confessor as the founder of a church dedicated to St. Margaret and standing hard by his monastery at Westminster, but it also affirmed that there had been an earlier church, on a site now included in that of the Abbey, and, indeed, that this 'church' was in the nave of the monastic church.[1] A dedication to St. Margaret of Antioch is unlikely before the end of the eleventh century; the tradition that the Abbey's parish was served by a church other than the Abbey itself from an earlier period than this was probably the way in which the monks of late-medieval Westminster made sense of a baffling episode in the history of their monastery. Dunstan's monks may in fact have served the laity in their own monastic church not only at festivals—a practice which Sulcard describes[2]—but regularly. When exactly the first church dedicated to St. Margaret was built at Westminster we do not know, but the work was evidently done near enough in time to the refoundation of the monastery by the Confessor to be remembered at Westminster as the Confessor's own doing.

St. Margaret's, whenever it was built, relieved the monastic church of what would otherwise have been a distracting concourse of people. By the twelfth century the legal position of the monks was that of rector. The Taxation of Pope Nicholas IV valued the rectory at £20 per annum and the vicarage, which was not yet appropriated, at £8,[3] sums that appear at first sight a small income for the mother church of a parish now including the permanent seat of the English government within its bounds. Personal tithes, however, must have made up a large part of the revenues of St. Margaret's from an early period, and these were always difficult to assess and collect. The sum of £28 per annum may not be far short of the true value of the rectory and vicarage together at that date. Early in the fourteenth century the monks themselves valued the vicarage of St. Margaret's at £8. 13s. 4d. per annum.[4]

---

[1] Liber Niger Quaternus, 76ᵛ; see also H. F. Westlake, *St. Margaret's, Westminster: the Church of the House of Commons* (London, 1914), pp. 3–4.

[2] *Traditio* 20 (1964), 88–9. Sulcard here recounts the miraculous cure of a cripple by St. Peter in the Abbey on the feast of St. Peter in Chains, when, as he says, '*ex consuetudine deuocionis erga patronum suum conuenire solet multorum frequencia*'.

[3] Below, p. 408.　　　　　　　　　　　　　　　[4] Ibid., and n.

Soon after the Norman Conquest, the monks received one of the few donations of tithe that ever came their way at the hands of a lay benefactor. The donor was William the Conqueror, the tithes those of Rutland, and William's motive that of compensating the Abbey for the disappointment of its claim to the vast estate which Edward the Confessor had promised them in Rutland on the death of Queen Edith.[1] It took the monks a century and a half to obtain the benefit of this donation, and even then all that came into their possession were the rectorial tithes of the church of Oakham.[2] Elsewhere it seems to have depended on their own initiative whether or not they obtained a share of the revenues of the churches on their estates.

Two different situations are betrayed in the final list of their pensions and portions. In the one, they were securely in possession of the advowson of the church in question; it was only a matter of persuading an incumbent whom they had chosen to concede them a share of the tithes. In the other, the advowson eluded the monks, but after a struggle ending in the grant of a pension or portion by their successful rival. In the century after the Confessor's death the abbot and convent did not press their claims hard outside the diocese of London. There, however, they established a claim to pensions in nineteen churches, one or two representing, no doubt, a sizeable proportion of the income of the church in question when first agreed between the monks and their incumbent. All these pensions, amounting to £21. 13s. 4d. per annum, Gilbert Foliot confirmed to the Abbey when he was bishop of London (1163–87).[3]

[1] See above, p. 27.

[2] Below, p. 404. Of the rectorial tithes, sheaves to the value of £2 per annum now went to the incumbent of Oakham.

[3] *The Letters and Charters of Gilbert Foliot*, ed. A. Morey and C. N. L. Brooke (Cambridge, 1967), no. 462. The churches in question were: St. Martin-in-the-Fields; St. Clement Danes; St. Dunstan-in-the-West; St. Bride's, Fleet Street; St. Martin-by-Ludgate; St. Alban, Wood Street; St. Agnes; St. Clement, Candlewick Street; St. James-in-Vintry; St. Laurence near the Bridge; St. Matthew, Friday Street; St. Margaret, Bridge Street; St. Magnus the Martyr—all in London or Westminster; and, elsewhere, the churches of Feering, Hendon, Kelvedon, Little Tey, North Ockendon, and Sawbridgeworth. The pension from Sawbridgeworth, entered in this source as being of £15 per annum, was in fact only of £5 per annum; see Liber Niger Quaternus, 141. Gilbert Foliot also confirmed the tithes of White Roding (Essex) to the monks. From *Papsturkunden in England* i. 70,

Soon after this, in parishes where they possessed the advowson, the monks ceased to be content with what were virtually
allowances from the incumbents of their churches and adopted
the more ambitious policy of trying to appropriate the whole
income of the benefice. To this policy Clement III gave a
modified blessing in 1189, in an open-ended privilege permitting them to appropriate the tithes of the churches of which
they were the patrons, when vacancies should occur, for the
support of the brethren, their guests, and the poor, provided
only that vicarages were ordained and synodals paid.[1] The
resort to the papacy, and, indeed, the very appeal to Gilbert
Foliot for his confirmation of the *status quo* in the diocese of
London, betray the need which the monastery felt in the
second half of the twelfth century to place the diversion of
parish revenues to its own funds on a firmer legal base. They
are tributes to the success already achieved by the English
bishops in driving home the lesson that monastic claimants
to tithe must be able to show proof of title. The tide of ecclesiastical reform was against the monks, and a century after the
issue of Clement III's bull there were probably not more
than nine churches, in addition to St. Margaret's itself, where
the Abbey had the major portion of the tithes.

Their first successes[2] were at Battersea and Wandsworth,
in the diocese of Winchester, and at South Benfleet, in the
diocese of London. Richard of Ilchester (1174–88) allowed the
monks to appropriate the tithes of Battersea and Wandsworth,
provided they assigned a vicarage, and Richard fitz Neal
(1189–98), Foliot's successor, did the same for them at South
Benfleet. At South Benfleet, however, the vicar was assigned,
not only a stipend of £2. 13s. 4d. per annum, the offerings
and the small tithes, but a share of the rectorial tithes as well—
a fact which may account for the relatively low value of the
rectory here (£6. 13s. 4d. per annum) in 1291. The church

it appears that the monks explicitly claimed the tithes or a portion of these in
nearly thirty places outside London by the mid-twelfth century; the majority of
these were situated in Rutland or helped to make up the vast manor of Pershore.

[1] *Papsturkunden in England* i. 261. For the change on the part of monasteries in
general from an appetite for pensions to one for the major share of the income of
the benefices, see C. R. Cheney, *From Becket to Langton: English Church Government,
1170–1213* (Manchester, 1956), p. 133.

[2] For the appropriations mentioned in this paragraph, see below, pp. 404 ff.

at Staines, valuable on account of its dependent chapels, was probably appropriated before the end of the century; at Oakham the monks advanced from a pension of £20 per annum to the possession of nearly all the rectorial tithes, and so to the partial fulfilment of William I's intentions for them in Rutland, in 1231; five years later, Honorius III's mandate for the appropriation of Ashwell was put into effect, notwithstanding the opposition of Robert Grosseteste; and a mandate of Innocent IV, issued in 1249, assisted the monks to an apparently trouble-free appropriation of the church of Feering for the anniversary of Henry III and Eleanor of Provence. At Wheathampstead, on the other hand, they were unable to obtain more than half the rectorial tithes, and in 1258 they were driven to a formal renunciation of their claim to the tithes of Hendon, a set-back not to be reversed for more than two centuries.

Ten years later, the English Church received, in the canons of the Council of London, an authoritative ruling on the circumstances in which religious might appropriate the revenues of parish churches: they were to be allowed to do this only in cases of real poverty or for other legitimate cause.[1] Ottobuono's ambiguous words left more than one door open, but at the very least they meant that monks who applied for a licence to appropriate must be able to show a pretext, whether in a recent occasion of impoverishment or in the assumption of new and expensive duties, making it imperative to augment their income. As a matter of fact, no such pretext occurred in the life of the monks of Westminster until the monastery was damaged by fire in 1298, and perhaps mainly for this reason the second half of the thirteenth century added little or nothing to their income from tithes. Thus although the Taxation of Pope Nicholas IV was not made until 1291, what we find in its valuations of the Abbey's churches is a record of gains made for the most part between *c.* 1180 and *c.* 1250.

The value of the Abbey's total income from parish churches according to this source was £273 per annum, of which sum 77 per cent came from the rectories. However, pensions worth *c.* £10 per annum, which Gilbert Foliot had confirmed to the

---

[1] *Councils and Synods,* ed. Powicke and Cheney, ii. 770.

monks, were omitted from the Taxation,[1] and it is clear that
some of the Abbey's rectories were undervalued there. The
church at Staines, for example, was valued at £46. 13s. 4d.
per annum. But in 1282–3 this church yielded the monks a
net income of £18. 3s. 0d. from sales of corn, together with

TABLE II. *The Annual Income of Westminster Abbey from Parish*
Churches According to the Taxation of Pope Nicholas IV, 1291

(£)

(i)	(ii)	(iii)	(iv)
Appropriated Churches	*Portions*	*Pensions*	*Total*
210*	51	12	273

Sources: T.P.N., *passim*; Liber Niger Quaternus, 140ᵛ–142ᵛ.†

* *T.P.N.*, in common with other sources of the period, uses the name 'rectory of
Oakham' to describe the manor and the appropriated church of Oakham, considering these as a single entity; this 'rectory' it values at £70 per annum. In
Table II, an income of £46 per annum has been allowed for the appropriated
church, the rectory in the strict sense. This sum takes account of the relative values
of spiritualities and temporalities at Oakham in 1535 (£47: £25). It is, however,
likely that spiritualities were relatively more important at the earlier date; if so,
the sum of £46 per annum underestimates the Abbey's income in 1291 from the
appropriated rectory here. The total in this column also allows for vicars' portions
at St. Martin-in-the-Fields, London, and at Feering which are mentioned
in Liber Niger Quaternus, 140ᵛ–142ᵛ, but not in *T.P.N.*; to this extent Table II
departs from the evidence of *T.P.N.* For the portions in question, see below,
pp. 406, 408, and nn.
    † This summary of the entries relating to the Abbey's goods in *T.P.N.* was made
between 1301 and 1335. It therefore includes an income from Morden church
which the monks did not enjoy before the appropriation of that church in 1301.

142 quarters of barley for the monks' brewing; and this was a
year when the best barley from the demesne of this manor
fetched 6s. 8d. per quarter.[2] In the early fourteenth century the
monks valued the church at Teddington at £8 per annum,

    [1] The pensions omitted in 1291 were those from St. Clement Danes, St. Dun-
stan-in-the-West, St. Alban, Wood Street, St. Agnes, St. Clement, Candlewick
Street, St. James-in-Vintry, St. Laurence near the Bridge—all in London; and
those from North Ockendon and Kelvedon (Essex).
    [2] W.A.M. 16908; below, p. 409 and n. Sales of tithe-corn brought in a gross
sum of £34. 2s. 7½d. at Staines this year, but the costs of collection amounted to
£15. 19s. 7½d. The manor of Staines belonged to the abbot's portion, the rectory
to the convent. The abbot was responsible for collecting the tithes. In 1306–7
he handed over £33. 6s. 8d. in cash and paid the tithe-collector's stipend of
£6. 13s. 4d.; but we do not know how much tithe-corn was delivered to the
monastery this year; see *Walter de Wenlok*, pp. 130, 207.

although it was valued at no more than £6 in 1291.[1] We should no doubt attribute an income from churches considerably in excess of £273 per annum to the monks of Westminster in 1291, but another figure could only be guess-work. The figure of £273 itself represents *c.* 17 per cent of the whole income of the monastery at the end of the thirteenth century and *c.* 24 per cent of the income of the prior and convent, to whose portion all rectories, portions and pensions were assigned at this date.[2]

The fire of 1298 at Westminster left the church and chapter-house unscathed but damaged the domestic buildings and the cloister, and on the morrow of it the monks apparently devised a programme for the appropriation of four churches—Morden, Longdon in Worcestershire, Sawbridgeworth, and Kelvedon. Morden fell easily at the next vacancy, in 1301, through a direct application to John de Pontissara,[3] but the papal mandate on which the monks relied in the other three cases was not forthcoming for thirty years, and even so it required a further act of Clement VI to circumvent the hostility of the bishop of London, in whose diocese both churches lay, to the appropriation of Sawbridgeworth and Kelvedon.[4] When the matter of these two churches was finally brought to an end, in 1356, John of Reading noted in his chronicle that it had been in suspense at the curia since the time of John XXII; in fact Br. Alexander de Pershore and Br. Reginald de Hadham first raised there the possibility of appropriating Kelvedon church in the very year of the fire.[5]

The Abbey itself carried through only two more appropriations, in each case by papal mandate. The church at Aldenham was appropriated in 1391, when the monks undertook to keep the anniversary of Richard II's coronation, on St. Swithun's day;[6] and nearly ninety years later, in 1477, they

---

[1] Below, p. 410. For the assessment of spiritualities in general in 1291, see R. Graham, *English Ecclesiastical Studies* (London, 1929), pp. 282 ff.

[2] For the Abbey's income in *c.* 1300, see Table VI (below, p. 63).

[3] Below, p. 411.

[4] For the appropriations of Longdon, Sawbridgeworth, and Kelvedon, see below, pp. 412, 409, 407.

[5] *Chronica Johannis de Reading et Anonymi Cantuariensis, 1346–67*, ed. J. Tait (Manchester, 1914), p. 116 (*s.a.* 1352); and see W.A.M. 9243–5.

[6] Below, p. 403. From 1397 the expenses of Abbot Colchester's anniversary were also met from the revenues of this church.

obtained the rectory of Hendon, on the grounds of poverty
and the decay of their buildings.[1] This rectory, the latest that
the Abbey acquired on its own initiative, was the only one
ever to be absorbed into the abbot's portion—this despite the
agreement which Abbot Berking made with his monks and
which was reaffirmed by their successors in 1252, to the effect
that the fruits of future appropriations should be divided
between the abbot and the convent.[2]

The delay characteristic of schemes to appropriate churches
at Westminster was paralleled in the purchase of land, for in
this sphere of economic enterprise, too, the monks sometimes
had to wait years before the prey fell into their toils.[3] The
costs of appropriation, on the other hand, were much smaller
than those of land-purchase, since nothing was given in respect
of the capital value of the newly acquired asset: all the expenses were incidental to the proceedings at the curia, in
Chancery, or before the diocesan. Not even the sum of £120
which the monks paid to cameral merchants in respect of
Sawbridgeworth and Kelvedon in 1353–4, the last, no doubt,
of many disbursements in this cause, made the transaction
other than a highly profitable one for them; these churches
were worth £73. 6s. 8d. per annum according to the Taxation
of Pope Nicholas IV, and probably considerably more than
this sum in reality.[4]

Nevertheless, at the end of the fifteenth century, the monks of
Westminster had relatively little to show for three centuries
of application to the business of appropriating tithes, which
Clement III's bull had seemed so greatly to facilitate. In
fewer than one church in four of which they owned the advowson did they have the rectorial tithes, and in most of the
remainder they could claim, apart from the advowson, only
a pension or portion that had not altered since the thirteenth
century, if as much as that. It was owing to the foundations
of the Countess of Richmond and Henry VII that the value
of Westminster Abbey's income from tithe and glebe-land
reached the level recorded in the *Valor Ecclesiasticus*.

When the *Valor* was made, the monks were drawing *c.* £907

---

[1] Below, p. 407.
[2] *Walter de Wenlok*, pp. 226, 229.   [3] Below, pp. 172–3.
[4] W.A.M. 19549; below, pp. 409, 407.

per annum from churches.[1] This figure, however, includes their income from some non-parochial churches given by Henry VII for his anniversary. From parish churches, whether the rectory was wholly appropriated to their use or liable only for a pension or portion, they derived £595 per annum.[2] This, on the face of it, is an impressive figure, marking an improvement on their achievements as appropriators two or three centuries earlier.

TABLE III. *The Annual Income of Westminster Abbey from Churches in 1535*

(£)

(i)		(ii)	(iii)
*Appropriated Churches**		*Pensions and Portions*	*Total*
Parish	*Other*		
539	312	56	907
	851		

Source: *V.E.* i. 410 ff.; and see below, pp. 403 ff.

* Omitting Dodford (diocese of Lincoln) and St. Botulph's, Aldersgate (London), for which no values are given in *V.E.*, and for which it is hard even to guess at a figure. However, for reasons given below (p. 402), a few other appropriated parish churches may be overvalued in this Table.
Of the monks' total income as appropriators of the collegiate church of St. Martin-le-Grand (London), the sum of *c.* £73 per annum came from parish churches and has been included under this head.

But from the churches already appropriated by 1291 and which had supplied them with an income of at least £210 per annum at that date, and probably considerably more than this sum, they now drew only £181 per annum, if as much. What is known of the purchasing power of money in the 1290s and the 1530s suggests that the real income of the monastery from tithes in these churches had declined by a significant margin in the meantime, and figures for individual churches point the lesson

[1] The figure represents *c.* 32 per cent of the Abbey's net income in 1535, for which see Table V (below, p. 62). But the two figures are not strictly comparable, since some of the income from churches was earmarked for inescapable expenditure in connection with the royal anniversaries, and such income has been excluded from the figure given in Table V. A more apt comparison is that between the Abbey's income from churches and the clear value (£3,470 per annum) of the Abbey according to *V.E.*; the former is *c.* 26 per cent of the latter.
[2] i.e. 17 per cent of the clear value of 1535, and 21 per cent of the net income of that date.

more sharply; these show, moreover, that some of the Abbey's recent acquisitions had suffered the same fate as the rectories which had been in its possession before 1291. The rectory of Wandsworth, for example, was valued at £6. 13s. 4d. per annum in 1535 and that of Battersea at £6 per annum; yet in 1291 the former had been assessed at £20 per annum and the latter at £17. 13s. 4d. per annum.[1] Aldenham rectory, worth £8. 6s. 2d. per annum when the *Valor* was made, had been valued at £38. 13s. 4d. per annum at the time of the appropriation in 1391.[2]

It is easy to account for these figures. Nearly all the Abbey's rectories were at farm in 1535; its current income from this source was determined, therefore, by the rental value of the tithes and glebes in question when they had first been leased, and this, in most cases, was more than a century earlier; as in the case of their demesnes, so in that of their rectories, the monks rarely altered the terms of leases in this long period, except, on occasion, to lengthen the term of years.[3] Yet when the initial leases were made, trends in agriculture were such as to encourage a severely pessimistic forecast of the future yield of praedial tithes, the main perquisite of rectors. To this extent the monks of Westminster on the eve of the Dissolution were in the common situation of parish rectors throughout England at this time, for it was not only the monastic appropriator whose tithes were now commonly at farm and not only his that were at farm for antiquated rents.[4]

Another problem the monks shared only with rectors whose churches lay, as many of theirs did, if not in or near London itself, then in other centres of population where livelihood came only in part from husbandry. Here, we know, tithes provoked acute controversy at the end of the Middle Ages, and, largely on account of the place of personal tithes in the parishioner's obligation, proved singularly difficult to collect.[5] The church of St. Margaret's, Westminster, is no exception to these remarks. The rectory and vicarage were valued together

[1] Below, pp. 411–12. [2] Below, p. 403. [3] Below, pp. 154 ff.
[4] See in general A. G. Dickens, *The English Reformation* (London, 1964), pp. 46–7; P. Heath, *The English Parish Clergy on the Eve of the Reformation* (London, 1969), pp. 148 ff.
[5] J. A. F. Thomson, 'Tithe disputes in later medieval London', *English Historical Review* 78 (1963), 1 ff.

in the *Valor Ecclesiasticus* at £24 per annum and currently yielded approximately this amount each year;[1] but it is difficult to believe that the tithable income of early Tudor Westminster amounted to no more than £240 per annum, taking one year with another.

(v) *The Income of Westminster Abbey*

What income did the monks amass in these various ways and by their own purchases of land? The starting-point of such a computation must be the value of the Abbey's estates in 1086. The date is dictated by the making of the Domesday Survey in that year, but it is in any case appropriate to attempt an estimate of the monastery's income at the end of William I's reign. By then the foundation period was at an end. What the monks were ever to lose of all the wealth that the Confessor and his thegns tried to give them had already slipped from their grasp, and they were to receive few additions to their endowments for 150 years after the Conqueror's death. Yet William's own grants to Westminster Abbey must certainly be included in any assessment of the wealth of the house in the early Middle Ages. The figure for 1086 can be compared with that for the income of the monastery at four later dates: *c.* 1175, *c.* 1300, *c.* 1400, and 1535. All these estimates are shown in Table VI,[2] but each, like the Domesday figure itself, needs some explanation.

Two figures can be derived from Domesday Book for the landed wealth of the Abbey in 1086. One relates to the whole estate, including those parts said to be in the hands of tenants and valued separately from the demesne manors of the monks. This, the gross value of the lands, amounted to *c.* £620 per annum, and, since it is likely that most of the tenants who are named in the Survey held of the Abbey in fee, this is probably a figure for the estate with its subinfeudated portions included; these were mainly to be found in Worcestershire.[3] The net value of the estate in 1086, excluding such lands of the tenants as are valued separately, was *c.* £511 per annum, and of the

---

[1] Below, p. 408 and n. In 1542–3, however, in the first year of the existence of the see of Westminster, income from St. Margaret's amounted to £34. 15*s.* 10*d.* per annum (P.R.O., S.C. 6, Henry VIII/2414/A8, A 20ᵛ).

[2] Below, p. 63.   [3] On the Domesday tenants, see below, pp. 71 ff.

two figures, this is the significant one;[1] the subinfeudated portion of their estate contributed little to the income of the monks year by year at this date. With the manor of Launton, which is not valued in Domesday Book, the estate was worth perhaps *c.* £515 per annum.

Some ninety years after the making of Domesday Book, the lands of Westminster Abbey came into royal custody on the death of Abbot Laurence, and this is the first vacancy at Westminster for which any form of account survives. Laurence died on 11 April 1173, and his successor, Walter of Winchester, was elected in July 1175; thus the vacancy lasted about two years and three months. The account that is entered in the Pipe Roll is that of the keepers of the Abbey's lands in Essex and Hertfordshire from 24 June 1173 until the end of the vacancy, a period of at least two years, or—to use the vocabulary of manorial rents—eight quarter-days.[2] Their receipts in that period amounted to £435. 6s. 10d., of which the sum of £408. 15s. 4d. came *de firmis maneriorum*, the rest from *perquisitiones*, a word probably denoting fluctuating sources of income other than manorial farms and rents.[3] If we can assume that these receipts reflect with fair accuracy the monastery's own income from these lands in normal times, it follows that the Abbey possessed an income of *c.* £218 per annum from its lands in Essex and Hertfordshire in *c.* 1175. For two reasons, however, we must suspect that this figure errs on the side of generosity. In the first place, the king may have retained custody of the Abbey's lands beyond the date of Walter of Winchester's appointment; thus the keepers may have been accounting for a period that was a little longer than two years. And, secondly, in a vacancy at this date, it would be surprising if none of the

---

[1] For a figure higher than £515 but lower than £620, see Knowles, *Monastic Order in England*, p. 702.

[2] *Pipe Roll, 21 Henry II* (P.R.S. xxii), pp. 79–80. These lands were initially granted to an episcopal keeper, who was probably Roger of Worcester, but, on or about 24 June 1173, Clement Decanus and Gilbert de Hendon took them over. Their account was rendered in 1175. It is not an easy one to interpret. The interpretation given in the text above rests on the assumption—which seems to be warranted—that the references to receipts from the farms of the manors *de iii annis* is to be understood as a reference to receipts stretching into three Exchequer years but not covering a period of three entire years.

[3] For the possible meanings of *firme maneriorum* and *perquisitiones*, see P. D. A. Harvey, 'The Pipe Rolls and the Adoption of Demesne Farming in England', *Economic History Rev.*, 2nd ser., 27 (1974), 347–50.

keepers' income had been gained at the expense of the capital value of the lands in custody; some, for example, probably came from extraordinary tallages that the monks themselves would not imitate.

If the lands in Essex and Hertfordshire yielded *c.* £218 per annum at this date, what was the Abbey's estate as a whole worth? In 1086 these two counties provided 29·5 per cent of the Abbey's net income.[1] If their share at the end of the twelfth century was approximately the same, the Abbey's total net income at that date was *c.* £739 per annum. The contribution of Essex and Hertfordshire may in fact have been rather larger at the end of the twelfth century than at the earlier date, since the Abbey's possessions in these counties had been less seriously affected than some others elsewhere by subinfeudation.[2] This is another reason why we should regard our figure as the maximum that is likely.

When the Taxation of Pope Nicholas IV was made, more than a century later, the lands of Westminster Abbey were divided between the abbot and convent, and this arrangement was already of long standing.[3] Moreover, conventual revenues were divided between, on the one hand, half a dozen important obediences, and, on the other, the funds of the conventual treasurers. The monks made a summary of this vital record of their temporal and spiritual goods, in which they noted how the income attributed to them in it was apportioned between abbot, prior, treasurers, and obedientiaries. The gist of this summary is set out in Table IV.[4]

Pope Nicholas IV's assessors set out to record the *verus valor* of the goods of the English Church, but it seems clear that they were in general content to record rental values.[5] They went to work, however, in a period when many of the possessions of the Church were not on lease but in hand and subject to the direct exploitation of their owners. The first opportunity of checking the accuracy of their work in the case of Westminster Abbey is provided by the accounts of the conventual treasurers for the years 1297–8 and 1304–5.[6]

---

[1] £152: £515.   [2] Below, pp. 72 ff.   [3] Below, pp. 85 ff.
[4] Below, p. 58.   [5] Graham, *English Ecclesiastical Studies*, pp. 271 ff.
[6] W.A.M. 19838, 19841. The account for 1297–8 runs from 29 Sept. to 29 Sept., that for 1304–5 from 24 June to 24 June. The treasurers' account for the period 25 Nov. 1307 to 29 Sept. 1308, which also survives, is too much damaged to be

At this date, the treasurers accounted, not only for their own manors and churches, but also for those of the pittancer. In these two years their cash receipts averaged *c.* £542 per annum.[1] To this sum must be added the value of the liveries of corn which the convent received from its manors and churches at this time, most of which came from the treasurers' portion and the churches assigned to the pittancer; this probably amounted on average to not less than *c.* £165 per annum.[2] Of the grand total of £707 per annum, *c.* 22 per cent belonged in fact to the

TABLE IV. *The Annual Value of the Goods of Westminster Abbey according to the Taxation of Pope Nicholas IV, 1291*

(£)

(i)	(ii)	(iii)	(iv)	(v)
Abbot	Prior	Conventual Treasurers	Obedientiaries	Total
271	7	509	507	1,294

Sources: *T.P.N., passim;* W.A.M. Liber Niger Quaternus, 140ᵛ–142ᵛ.*

* For this summary of the entries relating to the Abbey's goods in *T.P.N.* see Table II, nn. (above, p. 50). For the Abbey's taxable income in the early fourteenth century, see also Bodleian Library, Oxford, Dodsworth MS. 76, fo. 108.

pittancer;[3] the income of the conventual treasurers at this time was, therefore, *c.* £551 per annum.

This figure is *c.* 8 per cent higher than the assessment of the treasurers' goods according to the Taxation of Pope Nicholas IV. On the other hand, the inference to be drawn from the assessment in the Taxation that approximately equal proportions of the monastery's income were assigned, on the one hand, to the obedientiaries and reserved, on the other, to

useful in this context; it is, however, the source of some figures in Chapter V (below, p. 145).

[1] £506 in 1297–8, and £577 in 1304–5. Accounting arrears and extraordinary receipts of all kinds have been excluded from consideration; the latter include the sum of £60 received in 1304–5 in respect of lands of which the prior and convent had been granted the usufruct by Edward I until a loan of £666. 13s. 4d. to the king should have been repaid; see *Cal. Cl. R., 1302–1307*, p. 26.

[2] See below, p. 145. Perhaps 20 per cent of the corn liveries came from churches assigned to the obedientiaries, but most of the latter's contribution was supplied by the pittancer's churches at Oakham and South Benfleet.

[3] An inference from the assessments of 1291: on this occasion the goods of the pittancer were assessed at £140 per annum, the treasurers' at £509 per annum. £140: (£140+£509) = *c.* 22 per cent.

the treasurers is probably correct; this balance persisted throughout the monastery's later history and is reflected in the *Valor Ecclesiasticus*.[1] We can perhaps estimate the actual income of the obedientiaries by applying the same percentage correction to the figure for their income derived from the Taxation and shown in Table IV; if so, their income was *c.* £548 per annum.[2] The whole income of the convent, excluding the surplus of the royal foundations, thus amounted to *c.* £1,099 per annum at the end of the thirteenth century. With the convent's share of that surplus and the prior's small portion added, it was *c.* £1,121 per annum.

In the case of the abbot's portion of lands, the Taxation was guilty of a much larger margin of error. At this time the abbot had a central treasury, which received virtually all the surplus revenues of his manors, and in effect the same system operated during periods of royal custody, for then very nearly the whole issues of the temporalities came into the hands of the keeper. Between September 1306 and September 1309—that is, during the last fifteen months of Walter de Wenlok's abbacy and the first twenty-one months of the ensuing vacancy—the net receipts, first of the abbot's receiver and then of the keeper, were, on average, £439 per annum.[3] This figure, however, undervalues the abbot's portion. Although Wenlok's household received small liveries in kind from the manors, the cash value of these was not entered by the receiver in his account. Moreover, the keeper who took over at Wenlok's death did not have the issues of the manor of Denham, and during his first two years in charge—1307–9—demesne husbandry was hampered by the running down of livestock and sale of seed corn which occurred at the beginning of the vacancy. The abbot's net income at the end of the thirteenth century was probably not less than *c.* £520 per annum.[4] This sum, however, exceeds the

[1] Below, pp. 61–2. The reference at both dates is to the income of the convent excluding the prior's portion and the surplus of the royal foundations.

[2] £507 × 108 per cent.

[3] *Walter de Wenlok*, pp. 199 ff.; P.R.O., S.C. 6/1109/4. John de Foxle, the keeper appointed in 1307, had been steward of Abbot Wenlok's lands.

[4] A very rough estimate, based on the assumption that normally, at this time, net income from the sale of demesne produce might attain but not exceed the sum of *c.* £260 per annum, but taking into account the fact that the abbot's cash income from rents fell and his wage bill rose above the levels obtaining during a vacancy when domanial production was in full swing. For the figure of *c.* £260 per

valuation of the abbot's portion according to the Taxation of Pope Nicholas IV by *c.* 92 per cent. The different situation of the two estates must chiefly explain why the abbot's portion was so seriously undervalued in comparison to that of the convent: a high proportion of his temporal goods, but none of theirs, lay in the diocese of Worcester. The income of Westminster Abbey from all sources was thus probably *c.* £1,641 per annum or more at this time.

Almost a century later, on the death of Nicholas de Litlington, in 1386, the monks of Westminster agreed to pay the king a farm of £533. 6*s.* 8*d.* per annum, or *pro rata* for a shorter period, for the temporalities of the monastery during the vacancy, and the same farm was agreed between the monks and the Exchequer on William Colchester's death in 1420.[1] We do not know whether this sum was intended to represent the *verus valor* of the abbot's portion at the end of the fourteenth century, the value according to the extent—a much less realistic thing—or a compromise between the two. Whatever the case, his net income from the lands that were liable for custody can hardly have been less than £533 per annum at this time, and he had, in addition, *c.* £13 per annum from Denham.[2] With the final figure of £546 per annum; we may compare the annual receipts of the abbot's two principal financial officers in this period, the steward of his household and the receiver in the Western Parts. Their joint receipts at the turn of the century now averaged *c.* £450 per annum.[3] It is, however,

annum, see below, pp. 138–9. In one respect, the income returned by the keeper during the vacancy was abnormally high: the run-down of livestock at the beginning of the vacancy made possible the sale of agistment and hay on an unusually large scale—the keeper made *c.* £100 in each of these years from such sales. The idea of a 'normal year' in domanial husbandry is, of course, itself an abstraction.

[1] *Cal. Fine R.* x. 167; xiv. 354.

[2] The cash render of this manor was now *c.* £58 per annum. But, although the payments in question were now in fact made by the abbot from his central coffers and not direct from the issues of Denham, we must, in the present context, deduct from the sum of *c.* £58 per annum the sums of, respectively, £30. 6*s.* 8*d.* per annum owing for the alms of Queen Eleanor and £15 per annum owing to the convent for the old farm of the manor; the abbot incurred these expenses by reason of his tenure of the manor of Denham. See W.A.M. 24545–6.

[3] W.A.M. 24542, 24545–6 (the accounts of the steward of the household for, respectively, 1390–1, 1400–1, and 1401–2); W.A.M. 24411–18 (the accounts of the steward of the Western Parts for seven years between 1399 and 1408). A comparison of Colchester's income with Abbot Litlington's is also to the point. In the 1360s, Litlington had *c.* £600 per annum (below, p. 139 and n.). But the

clear from their accounts that these officials had by no means exclusive control of abbatial funds; not a little of the abbot's income now went into his private coffers, of which, it seems, no account was kept.

The conventual treasurers now had a cash income of *c.* £580 per annum, but their manors were sending liveries of corn worth on average *c.* £220 per annum to the monastic granger;[1] their total income was therefore *c.* £800 per annum. How much should be allowed in respect of the obedientiaries at this date? By the end of the fourteenth century the obedientiary system at the Abbey was already set in a mould that was to persist until the Dissolution, and quite probably conventual revenues were divided between the obedientiaries on the one hand and the treasurers on the other in approximately the proportions recorded in 1535; the *Valor Ecclesiasticus* shows that the treasurers

relatively frugal way of life revealed in the accounts of Colchester's household makes the hypothesis of a fall in the abbot's income since the mid-fourteenth century seem plausible.

1 Estimates based on the surviving treasurers' accounts (nine) and accounts of the monastic granger (eight) for the period 29 Sept. 1395–29 Sept. 1405 (W.A.M. 19880–90, 19201–14). The liveries received by the granger have been valued in accordance with the average prices given by Thorold Rogers for the decades 1391–1400 and 1401–10 (J. E. Thorold Rogers, *A History of Agriculture and Prices in England from the Year after the Oxford Parliament (1259) to the Commencement of the Continental War (1793)* (Oxford, 1866–1902), i. 245; iv. 292. A very little of this corn came from manors and churches that were not assigned to the treasurers, but the amounts in question were too small to be significant in the present context. The liveries represent about one-third of the corn consumed in the monastery, whether in bread, ale, or fodder, in this period. The treasurers now frequently purchased corn at prices lower than those extracted by Rogers. Each year, however, a considerable proportion of their purchases was made from the Abbey's obedientiaries, at what were probably preferential prices; it has therefore seemed appropriate to use, not these prices, but Rogers's in valuing the liveries.

The following figures can be abstracted from dockets made at the audit of ministers' accounts in the 1390s (Essex Record Office, D/DM/M 156–9):

Annual value of the manors assigned to the conventual treasurers or administered by them on behalf of other obedientiaries: in 1391–2 (excluding Downe, Surr.), *c.* £992; in 1392–3, *c.* £979; in 1393–4, *c.* £889.

Annual value of the rectories assigned to, respectively, the conventual treasurers and the warden of the churches: in 1391–2, *c.* £267; in 1392–3, *c.* £229; in 1393–4, *c.* £254.

Annual value of the manors of Queen Eleanor's foundation: 1391–2, *c.* £230; 1392–3, *c.* £239.

None of these figures, however, is exactly comparable to any given in the text above. That for Queen Eleanor's foundation is comparable to the figure for the income of the foundation given in Table I (above, p. 34).

See also Essex Record Office, D/DM/M 153–5.

then had *c.* 51 per cent of the whole income of the convent, excluding the prior's portion and the surplus of the royal foundations, and the obedientiaries *c.* 49 per cent.[1] If these figures are also true of the years around 1400, they suggest that the obedientiaries of that period had an income of *c.* £769 per annum. The new foundation of Richard II and Anne of Bohemia,

TABLE V. *The Net Annual Income of Westminster Abbey in 1535*

		(£)		
(i)	(ii)	(iii)	(iv)	(v)
Abbot	*Prior*	*Conventual Treasurers*	*Obedientiaries**	*Total*
664	55	785	1,323	2,827
		2,108		

Source: *V.E.* i. 410 ff.

* In reckoning the income of the obedientiaries, I have deducted some expenses incurred by the monks, in keeping royal anniversaries and maintaining a collegiate establishment at St. Martin-le-Grand, which *V.E.* disallows or ignores, and to this extent the figures in this table depart from the evidence of *V.E.* These expenses are referred to in the text. Of the obedientiaries' total income of £1,323 per annum, *c.* £557 per annum was the surplus of the royal foundations after deduction of these expenses and the reprises allowed in *V.E.*; the whole of this surplus was now enjoyed by the convent. Thus the obedientiaries other than the wardens of the royal foundations had a net income of *c.* £766 per annum. See also Table I, n. (above, p. 34).

together with Eleanor of Castile's, yielded a surplus of *c.* £295 per annum, of which all but *c.* £13 went to the convent.[2] The entire income of the monastery was *c.* £2,407 per annum.[3]

By 1535, when the *Valor Ecclesiasticus* was made, nearly all the demesnes belonging to the Abbey, and many of its manors, were on lease. In general, the *Valor* gives a fair account of the gross income of Westminster Abbey, and, in particular, it records receipts from rents and farms with a high degree of accuracy.[4] The gross income of the monastery recorded in this source was nearly £4,000 per annum, the so-called 'clear

---

[1] £785: £1,548; £763: £1,548. See Table V and n.

[2] See Table I and n. (above, p. 34).

[3] Cf. the valuation of the Abbey's goods made on the occasion of the appropriation of Aldenham rectory in 1391; the figure was £2,000 per annum (*Cal. Papal Letters* iv. 430).

[4] For the valuations of the Abbey's main properties in 1535, see below, pp. 337 ff.

value' £3,470 per annum. In calculating 'clear value', however, Henry VIII's commissioners excluded much of the expenditure necessarily incurred in keeping the royal anniversaries and the costs to the monks of Westminster of maintaining a collegiate establishment at the church of St. Martin-le-Grand, of which they were appropriators.[1] If this expenditure is taken into account, the net income of the house falls to £2,827 per annum; it was, even so, *c.* 17 per cent higher than at the end of the fourteenth century.

TABLE VI. *The Net Annual Income of Westminster Abbey, 1086–1535*

(£)

	(i)	(ii)	(iii)	(iv)	(v)
	1086	*c.* 1175	*c.* 1300	*c.* 1400	1535
Abbot			520	546	664
Prior			7	10	55
Convent			1,114	1,851	2,108
Total	515	739	1,641	2,407	2,827

Of the five estimates of monastic income at Westminster, now shown together in Table VI, the first stands apart from the rest, for the Domesday Survey, from which it is derived, was made, not only generations before the monks of Westminster kept any accounts or made extents, but in an age that was, as a whole, unversed in these arts and had little or no technical skill of the kind to bring to the task of appraising the value of land. In common with the *Valor Ecclesiasticus*, moreover, Domesday Book ignores receipts from the most important incidents of feudal tenure in its valuations. Despite these limitations, and others that have already been mentioned, these figures probably reflect changes in the income of Westminster Abbey over a period of four and a half centuries with a fair degree of accuracy. Even the figure for 1086 has this to recommend it, that the limitations of the juries making the assessments were those of the monks themselves in the exploitation of the land.[2]

[1] For the latter costs see below, p. 399, n. 1.
[2] On the Domesday procedure in general see, however, V. H. Galbraith, *Domesday Book: Its Place in Administrative History* (Clarendon Press, Oxford, 1974), pp. 42–3.

It need not be asked of a monastery having an unbroken existence for five centuries and a half whether its monks normally lived within their income, for no religious community could survive for any length of time if it did otherwise; soon rather than late, the number of the monks, their mode of life, and their income—the variables in the situation—had to reach equilibrium. There were, however, two periods when the resources of the monks of Westminster were strained to the limit. The first was probably just beginning when Abbot Laurence died in 1173 and in its most dangerous phase when Richard de Berking was elected in 1222. It was in this period that the formal division of the monastic estates between the abbot and the convent was finally carried through;[1] the monks no doubt found that two administrative structures were considerably more expensive to maintain than one. At much the same time, the newly affirmed need for papal confirmation added a costly refinement to election procedures;[2] new liturgical fashions impelled the monks, under Abbot William de Humez, to begin a Lady Chapel at their own expense,[3] and the common life, leaving behind the sparing habits that had contented Gilbert Crispin and his monks, issued in the comfortable round of meat-days and pittances described in the Abbey's thirteenth-century Customary; and all took place against a background of rising prices and without the assistance of large additions to the eleventh-century endowments. Yet, as the figures show, the monks of Westminster weathered the storm; indeed, they emerged at the end of the thirteenth century with an income that was in actual terms 122 per cent higher than a century earlier. The rise in real terms was of course much smaller, but what is known of the thirteenth-century price-rise suggests that this, too, may have been considerable. How was this achieved?

Perhaps the least important factor was the renewal of royal favour in the reign of Henry III. A patron who took a lively

---

[1] Below, pp. 85 ff.

[2] Below, p. 89 and n. We should note, among the difficulties of this period, the exceptionally heavy costs to the Abbey (£1,000) of the election of William Postard to the abbacy in 1191. Flete says that this sum was paid for Postard's 'confirmation'; it was very likely the cost to the monks of having an abbot of their own choice instead of William Longchamp's brother (*Flete*, p. 98; *Chronicles of the Reigns of Stephen, Henry II and Richard I*, ed. R. Howlett (4 vols., Rolls Series, 1884–9), iii. 420).

[3] *History of the King's Works*, ed. Colvin, i. 131–2.

interest in his monastery could be, indeed, an expensive blessing, and from time to time the monks of Westminster may have been tempted to see Henry III in this light. But Henry gave them the gothic church that they would certainly have coveted for themselves in due course, thus averting financial embarrassment many times more acute than any occasioned by the building of the Lady Chapel. By setting a fashion for royal burials in the Abbey that continued steady over nearly two centuries, he assured the monks of several enviable additions to their endowment income. The main fruits of these were still in the future in 1300, but small gains were already in hand then.

More important was the policy of land-purchase initiated by Richard de Berking and continued by his three immediate successors. Between Berking's election in 1222 and Walter de Wenlok's death in 1307 half a dozen major properties and many other small ones were purchased by the monks.[1] Royal favour may have told here, too, for the abbot and convent of Westminster probably owed some of their purchasing power to the circumstance that Richard de Berking had a profitable career in the royal service. Henry III, we are told, preferring him to all the magnates of the realm, made him his special counsellor and the chief baron of the Exchequer.[2] In Berking's day, perhaps, the abbot's coffers were replenished with the fruits of office. At all events, John Flete noted later that Berking helped with the costs of the appropriations carried through during his abbacy: the churches of Oakham and Ashwell were acquired partly or wholly 'sumptibus suis'.[3]

But the thirteenth-century rise in income reflects mainly the great gains that accrued to the monks of Westminster when they took most of their demesne manors in hand, as they did in the opening decades of the century, instead of leaving them in the hands of farmers.[4] The gains did not consist wholly, and perhaps not mainly, in the profits which now came their way as producers on their home farms: they were derived largely

[1] Below, pp. 414 ff.   [2] *Flete*, p. 103.

[3] Ibid. Flete errs in saying that the church of Battersea was also acquired during Berking's abbacy. After the division of goods between the abbot of Westminster and the convent, all the fruits of appropriated churches went to the latter; hence the significance, to Flete, of Berking's outlay.

[4] Below, pp. 131 ff.

from the manorial tenant-land, the rents of which the new arrangement brought under the monks' unchallenged control for what must have been in many cases the first time since the foundation of the Abbey.

The second difficult period occurred in the mid-fourteenth century. John of Reading, who lived through it, was inclined to blame the favouritism and extravagance of Abbot Simon de Bircheston (1344–9), but a more likely explanation is the strain imposed on the Abbey's resources by the new work on the buildings and the cloister, which had been damaged in the fire of 1298; once again the monks had begun to build at their own expense, and with what result Flete tells us when he says that they owed debts amounting to £1,600 at Bircheston's death.[1] To these problems were immediately added the far greater ones presented by the fall in land values after the Black Death. It was at this juncture in their fortunes that the monks, perhaps for the first and last time in their history, sold a vast amount of plate and jewels to relieve their ordinary revenues.[2]

This time the margin of recovery was smaller. Yet it is a remarkable fact that the actual income of the Abbey rose by as much as 47 per cent between the beginning and the end of the fourteenth century. Once again, wealth at the abbot's command helped to save the day. Simon de Langham's family was probably not a rich one, but Langham acquired riches, first as treasurer of the realm, then as bishop and archbishop, and finally as cardinal.[3] His gifts and those of his successor, Nicholas de Litlington, who was one of the very few well-born abbots ever to preside at Westminster and who continued to command great resources after taking the habit, must have seemed providential to the hard-pressed community, who were thus enabled to resume the purchase of real property on an ambitious scale.[4] How well the monks did in a material sense— and perhaps in some other ways as well—is reflected in the size

---

[1] *Chronica Johannis de Reading et Anonymi Cantuariensis, 1346–1367*, p. 108; *Flete*, p. 131; W. R. Lethaby, *Westminster Abbey and the Kings' Craftsmen. A Study of Mediaeval Building* (London, 1906), pp. 200–2.

[2] See Liber Niger Quaternus, 80, where the sale of jewels worth £315. 13*s.* 8*d.* is recorded in 1349.

[3] For Langham, see A. B. Emden, *Biographical Register of the University of Oxford to A.D. 1500* (3 vols., Oxford, 1957–9), ii. 1095–7; and for his gifts to the monastery see also above, p. 42.

[4] Below, pp. 164 ff.

of the community at this time. The Abbey was able to maintain as many monks at the end of the fourteenth century as it had supported at the beginning. Indeed, its numbers may have been slightly higher in a normal year at the later date: there were fifty-seven professed monks in 1399, but only fifty in 1307.[1]

Throughout the fourteenth century the rents of the tenant-land of the estate were a main component of the Abbey's income, and *a fortiori* this is true of the period enclosed by our last two figures, those for, respectively, *c.* 1400 and 1535. It was, however, in this last period that the monks finally came to terms with the realities of landlordism in the late medieval world. This meant, above all, the watering down of the political element in the lord–tenant relationship that helped to keep rents uneconomically high even when the demand for land fell catastrophically in the second half of the fourteenth century.[2] Acre for acre the rental value of their estate fell in the fifteenth century, and since there was little increase, if any, in the number of the acres until the endowment of Henry VII's anniversary and that of his mother's began at the end of the century, their income was almost certainly sagging for much of this final period. As though to exacerbate the situation, in 1440 the pope provided Edmund Kyrton, a man lamentably lacking in worldly wisdom and, indeed, in plain common sense, to the abbacy,[3] and in 1463 the monks themselves chose, as Kyrton's successor, George Norwich, a man of much the same stamp. When Norwich retired four years later, he left debts amounting to nearly £3,000.[4] Not surprisingly, six years later the monks of Westminster were able to convince Sixtus IV that they were poor; they were given the rectory of Hendon to help them in their necessity.[5] But for the bounty of Henry VII and the Countess of Richmond, the early Tudor inflation would have hit them hard; as it was, their actual income was probably *c.* 11 per cent higher in 1535 than it had been when Henry VII and his mother first

---

[1] There were 55 professed monks in the house in Dec. 1305 and Dec. 1306; 50 in Dec. 1307; 58 at Michaelmas in 1398, 57 in 1399, and 54 in 1400 (W.A.M. 19882–3, 23733; *Walter de Wenlok*, pp. 198, 203, 212); but it is hazardous to rely, as we must, in the early fourteenth century, on isolated figures.

[2] Below, pp. 244 ff.

[3] *Monks*, p. 130. For Kyrton, see also *English Historical Rev.*, 37 (1922), 83–8.

[4] Widmore, *History of the Church of St. Peter, Westminster*, p. 193.

[5] Above, pp. 51–2.

turned their thoughts to the Abbey. Given their own shrinking numbers, the rise in income was enough to tide the monks over.

How do these trends in wealth compare with those experienced by other members of the aristocracy of medieval England? First, the position of the monks of Westminster in that body, itself no monolithic or unchanging institution, must be established. Although the abbot of Westminster, as a tenant-in-chief, royal counsellor, and, later, a prelate summoned by writ to parliament, was inevitably drawn into the way of life of the social élite of his time, his monks never rose higher than enjoyment of a middle-class standard of living— with, of course, the difference provided by the austerities that remained *de rigueur* to the end, even in the richest Black Monk houses. As a great landowner, however, the whole monastic community belonged, with the abbot, to an élite, and, on a superficial view, was very highly placed in it. For most of the fourteenth century, an income of 1,000 marks (= £666. 13s. 4d.) per annum from land was considered to be the minimum qualification for the aspiring earl;[1] yet the abbot and convent of Westminster began this century with an income more than twice that in amount and ended it with one that was nearly fourfold. In the present context, however, the minimum is an *ignis fatuus*, compounded of values according to the extent and beyond the reprises that defy analysis. We can place the abbot and convent of Westminster in the landowning class of their times only by considering the actual incomes of real persons and corporations. Though probably well placed at all times among religious houses and in the end, as we have seen, second only to Glastonbury Abbey in the country as a whole, Westminster Abbey could not challenge the wealth of the richest episcopal sees or that of the higher nobility. In 1086, when the archbishop of Canterbury had £1,246 per annum and the bishop of Winchester and his monks £1,325, the Abbey had only £515.[2] At the end of the thirteenth century, when the archbishop had £2,616 per annum and the bishop of Ely £2,550,

---

[1] G. A. Holmes, *The Estates of the Higher Nobility in Fourteenth-Century England* (Cambridge, 1957), p. 4.

[2] F. R. H. Du Boulay, *The Lordship of Canterbury. An Essay on Medieval Society* (London, 1966), p. 243; R. Lennard, *Rural England, 1086–1135. A Study of Social and Agrarian Conditions* (Oxford, 1959), pp. 77–8; above, pp. 55–6.

the Abbey had £1,641.[1] Towards the end of the fourteenth century it had much more—£2,407 per annum in *c.* 1400—but there were probably several earls in this period possessed of more than £3,000 per annum from land.[2] For all their acres, we should place the abbot and convent of Westminster at all times in the second rank of the great landowners of medieval England.

Did the wealth of the company that they kept there move in the same direction as theirs, at roughly the same pace and under the influence of like decisions on the part of its owners? In the present state of knowledge it is impossible to say, but certainly, among the class of great landowners considered as a whole, some significantly different performances come to light. Thus between 1086 and the 1170s, the Abbey's income— its actual income, not, of course, its real income—rose by 43 per cent but that of the archbishopric of Canterbury by only 10·5 per cent;[3] between the 1170s and the end of the thirteenth century, the Abbey's income rose by 122 per cent, but that of the bishopric of Ely by perhaps as much as 177 per cent.[4] Perhaps it was in the fourteenth century that the monks of Westminster outdid all their ecclesiastical contemporaries—or were there other landowners in this period, who, unassisted by the care- fully planned marriages that so often boosted lay fortunes in the hour of need, achieved, as the monks did, a rise in income of nearly 50 per cent between 1300 and 1400?[5]

[1] Du Boulay, loc. cit.; Miller, *Abbey and Bishopric of Ely*, p. 94; above, p. 60.

[2] Holmes, op. cit., p. 5; above, p. 62.

[3] Westminster: from £515 per annum to £739 per annum; Canterbury: from £1,246 per annum to £1,377 per annum. See above, pp. 56–7; and Du Boulay, *Lordship of Canterbury*, p. 243. The figure for the archbishopric is the average for the years 1170 and 1172; the archbishop's income in 1168 was £1,596 (= 28 per cent higher than the Domesday figure).

[4] Westminster: from £739 per annum to £1,641 per annum; Ely: from £920 per annum to £2,550 per annum. See above, pp. 57–60; and Miller, *Abbey and Bishopric of Ely*, p. 94.

[5] From £1,641 per annum to £2,407 per annum (above, pp. 60–2).

III

Subinfeudation and the Division of Goods

THE lands of Westminster Abbey fell into two distinct geographical parts, and this division is shown clearly in the Domesday enumeration of the manors: a substantial number of these was situated in Worcestershire and Gloucestershire, but many lay in counties near London. The Abbey's possessions were already more widely dispersed than was the case with the general run of monastic estates in medieval England, and later benefactions enhanced the difference. Another feature, however, they shared with more or less every estate of consequence, lay or ecclesiastical, throughout the Middle Ages. This was the general mode of their exploitation: some of the manors were held in demesne and exploited by the monks themselves; the rest were granted in fee to tenants who held by a variety of tenures and for a variety of services. This arrangement had legal and economic consequences of the first importance.

In the first place, when legal concepts relating to estates in land were clarified in the twelfth century, the monks emerged as the legal owners, under the king, of the freehold of their demesne manors but not of the freehold elsewhere on their estate. And, secondly, although they never ceased to appropriate a significant proportion of the profits of the soil in demesne manors for themselves, the main profit from the subinfeudated portion of the estate found its way into other men's pockets; indeed, in the later Middle Ages the monks' share here was so small as to seem scarcely worth preserving at all. The abbot and convent of Westminster would never have been short of income had they kept all their manors in demesne, whatever troubles of a different order such a course of action might have brought upon them. As it was, a dangerously large number of the manors on their fee was effectively outside their control by the thirteenth century. How did this come about?

(i) *The Domesday Tenancies*

Domesday Book names twenty-five mesne tenants on the Abbey's fee, and in a few places it records the existence of such tenants without naming them; among the unnamed tenants is, for example, a knight holding four hides of land at Battersea.[1] Some of the tenants named are obscure now and may well have been so at the time, but the list as a whole has a familiar ring: Roger de Lacy, Urse the sheriff, Geoffrey de Mandeville, Gilbert fitz Turold—these names belong in any roll-call of Anglo-Norman feudalism. One in two[2] of the persons named was a tenant-in-chief of the Crown, although these men did not always hold in chief in the counties where they held mesne tenancies of the monks of Westminster. In all, the lands of the Abbey's tenants account for *c.* 17 per cent of the gross annual value of its estate as this is recorded in the Survey: *c.* £106 of a total of *c.* £620. But since in a few places the tenancies, though destined in some cases, at least, and perhaps in all, to lead to the permanent alienation of the land in question from the Abbey, were still nominally part of the demesne manor and valued with it, this estimate underrates the extent to which the monks' possessions had been or were being eroded by such arrangements.

Nearly all the land in question was situated in Worcestershire or Gloucestershire, and here we are meant to understand that it no longer formed part of the demesne of the Church. At Deerhurst the *dominicum manerii* consisted of the chief manor and the berewicks still held in demesne by the monks; this was valued at £26 per annum, the lands of the *homines* at £14 per annum.[3] Similarly, in Pershore and its many members, the

[1] *D.B.* i. 32. The following mesne tenants are named: in Surr.: Odbert; in Midd.: [William] Baynard, Ralph Peverel, William the chamberlain (who also held of the Abbey in Essex); in Herts.: Geoffrey de Mandeville, Peter the sheriff; in Glos.: Reinbald; in Glos. and Worcs.: Walter Ponther, Girard the chamberlain, William fitz Baderon, Baldwin, Thurstin fitz Rou, Gilbert fitz Turold, Elfrid; in Worcs.: the king, Urse the sheriff, a priest named William, Drogo fitz Ponz, Roger de Lacy, Artur, William fitz Corbuz, Alured de Merleberg, and a priest named Leofnoth, who held a salt-pan in Droitwich; in Essex: Roger 'de Ramis', Ralph Baynard.

[2] Possibly an unusually large proportion even for an estate of this size in this period. On the significance of mesne tenants who were themselves of baronial status, see S. Harvey, 'The knight and the knight's fee in England', *Past and Present* 49 (Nov. 1970), 10 ff.

[3] *D.B.* i. 166; and see below, p. 344 and n. 6.

extensive lands of the Abbey's tenants were not part of the monk's demesne.[1] Moreover, nearly all the land occupied by the Abbey's tenants in 1086 was already in the hands of tenants in 1066. One of the rare exceptions, Walter Ponther's hide in Besford, was 'waste' in 1086 and had been so *T.R.E.*[2]

If the Domesday tenants on the Abbey's fee had predecessors *T.R.E.*, their arrival had nevertheless resulted in a thorough disturbance of the pre-Conquest pattern of tenancies. It is true that Alured de Merleberg, a Norman follower of the Confessor, not only retained his estate at Severn Stoke but enlarged it.[3] Similarly, the English Elfrid retained his much smaller holding at Moreton-in-Marsh.[4] And locally the pre-Conquest division of the land might still obtain. Thus at Eckington, Urse the sheriff now held Dunning's 3 hides and 3 virgates of land, and Thurstin fitz Rou held Brictric's 3 hides.[5] But the Domesday mesne tenancies were on the whole larger than the holdings of the pre-Conquest period—at Powick, for example, the lands of eight tenants *T.R.E.* were now in the hands of only four men[6]— and the identity of some of the pre-Conquest estates extending into more than one manor had been lost. One of the casualties was the estate of Brictric. This extended far beyond the limits of the Abbey's lands, but here it included land in Hasfield, in Deerhurst, and in Eckington and Longdon, in Pershore. The first two properties went to Thurstin fitz Rou, the third to Urse the sheriff.[7]

Not one of the charters which the monks of Westminster granted to their Domesday tenants in these western manors— if, indeed, the early enfeoffments were made by charter—has survived. We know, however, that nearly all the lands in question were lost to the Abbey's demesne for ever. It seems likely that these tenants already held by a fully heritable title in 1086.

Nearer home the Domesday picture is different. The mesne tenancies here were in sum and individually small. Odbert's manor at Tooting was assessed at 4 hides;[8] Geoffrey de Mandeville held 2½ hides at Ayot, 3 virgates at Titeburst, and a virgate and a mill at Ashwell;[9] at Feering, Roger 'de Ramis' had to be

[1] *D.B.* i. 174ᵇ–175. [2] Ibid. i. 174ᵇ. [3] Ibid. i. 175.
[4] Ibid. i. 166. [5] Ibid. i. 174ᵇ. [6] Ibid.
[7] Ibid. i. 166, 174ᵇ. [8] Ibid. i. 32. [9] Ibid. i. 135–135ᵇ.

content with a mere 85 acres.[1] Moreover, in this part of the fee, the land of the Abbey's tenants is often described in terms which indicate that it was still part of the monks' demesne. The whole manor of Ashwell, including Geoffrey de Mandeville's virgate and the half-hide which Peter the sheriff held there 'jacuit et jacet in dominio aecclesiae Sancti Petri Westmon';[2] Ralph Peverel's hide at Hampstead was land of the *villani*;[3] and the Domesday valuation of the monks' manor at Battersea includes the 4 hides of their unnamed knight.[4] From the status of their lands as part of the Abbey's demesne, we may perhaps infer that these tenants had only a life-interest in their lands. The case of the immortal Baynard, in Westminster, suggests that there may have been a correlation between tenancies on the demesne and tenancies for a limited term. Baynard, whose charter of enfeoffment, despite anachronisms in the extant copy, certainly records an authentic transaction, had only a life-interest in his land.[5] Although the latter is valued separately from the chief manor in Westminster, Domesday says of it: 'Haec terra jacuit et jacet in aecclesia Sancti Petri.'[6]

These contrasts between the situation in the West Midlands, on the one hand, and the Home Counties, on the other, suggest at first sight that the factor of distance, a familiar one in the context of the administration of medieval estates, had been at work, inhibiting grants, and particularly heritable grants, on the inlying manors of the estate, but reconciling the monks to their necessity elsewhere. On closer inspection, however, the evidence suggests that antiquity of title may have been the cardinally important factor in bringing about the Domesday pattern of tenures on the fee of Westminster Abbey. For the distant manors that the Abbey possessed in 1086 were also among its latest acquisitions. Pershore and Deerhurst, where the mesne tenancies fell thickest, had been given to the monks by Edward the Confessor, and many of the thegnlands recorded here *T.R.E.* probably go back to the period when the monks of Pershore Abbey and Deerhurst Minster were in possession of these manors. After the Conquest, the monks of Westminster were not

---

[1] Ibid. ii. 14^b.   [2] Ibid. i. 135.   [3] Ibid. i. 128.   [4] Ibid. i. 32.
[5] *Gilbert Crispin*, p. 38, a reference showing that this fee was in Tothill, in Westminster. On the life-tenancies of this period, see J. C. Holt, 'Politics and property in early medieval England', *Past and Present* 57 (Nov. 1972), 33-4.
[6] *D.B.* i. 128.

able and perhaps never tried to prevent the takeover of such land effected in these parts by Urse, by Thurstin fitz Rou, and by their companions. The aggression of the Norman baronage against monastic lands in Worcestershire extended beyond the limits of the Westminster fee.[1] In all probability the most that the monks could do was to regularize their relationship with the newcomers by accepting their homage and what service they could get. Everything known about these men suggests that the main initiative in their arrival on the Abbey's fee would have been their own. One, at least, of these who succeeded to the place that they carved out for themselves seems later to have had a qualm of conscience about his situation. This was Robert *dispensator*, who purchased Comberton, in Pershore, from Gilbert fitz Turold, its Domesday tenant, but later surrendered it 'pro anima sua'.[2]

The history of the manors nearer home, in southern and eastern England, was different. Many of these properties had been in the Abbey's hands since the time of Edgar and Dunstan, and very sparing were the monks here with thegnlands before the Conquest and with fees after it. On none of the lands in Bedfordshire, Buckinghamshire, Hertfordshire, Middlesex, Surrey, or Sussex that they claimed to have held since Dunstan's time or from an earlier period was there a fee larger than Baynard's 3 hides at Westminster. By contrast, at Battersea, a recent acquisition, the monks had been obliged to tolerate losses and disseisins affecting $7\frac{1}{2}$ hides once belonging to the manor.[3] At Ayot they did well even to have it recorded that Geoffrey de Mandeville held $2\frac{1}{2}$ hides of them, for their claim to that manor rested on uncertain foundations and was soon to fail altogether.[4] Where they had been securely in possession for many years, they had shown a marked hostility to subtenancies.

(ii) *Enfeoffment for Knight Service*

One question remains. What is the connection, if any, between the creation or recognition of these fees by the monks of Westminster after the Norman Conquest and the imposition on their monastery of a *servitium debitum* of knights for the feudal host?

---

[1] For examples, see *V.C.H. Worcs.* i. 240–1; see also *Regesta* ii. 903.
[2] *Gilbert Crispin*, p. 146.   [3] *D.B.* i. 32.
[4] *Harmer*, pp. 310–11; *V.C.H. Herts.* iii. 59.

In the mid-twelfth century the *servitium debitum* of Westminster Abbey was almost certainly of fifteen knights.[1] We have no grounds other than those which suggest that quotas were in general defined early in the Anglo-Norman period for taking this figure back into the reign of William I, but the uncertainty extends only to the fixing of the Abbey's quota; beyond all reasonable doubt, the monks were already burdened with military obligations then. For a time after the Conquest, they apparently discharged some of their obligation or, quite probably, the whole of it, by employing household knights, quartered in houses adjacent to the Abbey.[2] These men would have been useful to them, and particularly to the abbot, in other ways too, since the duties of a knight to his lord extended far beyond the specifically knightly obligation of military service. It is perhaps an indication of the importance which the monks attached to the personal attendance of their knights from time to time at Westminster that, even when they began to enfeoff knights with land, some of the estates which they chose for the purpose were near the Abbey. William Baynard's fee was a stone's throw away, in Tothill; Battersea, only two or three miles away.

How many of the mesne tenancies recorded in 1086 were burdened, as these were, with an obligation to perform knight service? In his *carta* in 1166, the abbot of Westminster returned several enfeoffments for fractions of a knight's service.[3] Thus Wakelin held in Surrey for the service of one-third of a knight, and Richard de Reimes in Essex for the service of half a knight; Walter de Clifford and William Haket each held a hide in Worcestershire for the service of one-fifth of a knight. There is of course nothing remarkable in the mere existence of obligations reckoned in fractions of the service of a single knight. But it is noteworthy that some of the fractions appearing in the abbot's *carta* cannot be put with others to form a whole. There are not three other fifths to add to those of Walter de Clifford and William Haket; no other thirds complement Wakelin's. Further, Wakelin's service of the third of a knight can hardly have been intended to be reckoned as the third part of the normal period of service for a whole knight, for a period of 40

---

[1] H. M. Chew, *The English Ecclesiastical Tenants-in-Chief and Knight Service* (Oxford, 1932), p. 5 and n.   [2] *D.B.* i. 128.
[3] *The Red Book of the Exchequer*, ed. H. Hall (Rolls Ser., 1896), i. 188–9.

days is not divisible into three. It appears, therefore, that when these fractional obligations were agreed, the monks of Westminster already expected scutage rather than bodily service on the part of their knights; the arrangements belong, perhaps, not to the first, but to the second generation of Anglo-Norman feudalism. Some may represent a reduction of heavier obligations dating from this earlier period that proved in the end too expensive for the tenant to discharge, given the size of the fee in question. Wakelin of Surrey may have been successor to the unnamed knight who held 4 hides at Battersea in 1086; and 4 hides were a relatively generous provision for a whole knight's service in the Domesday period.[1] On the other hand, it is not impossible that in this early period Roger 'de Ramis', presumably the ancestor of Richard de Reimes, should have owed a whole knight's service in return for his tiny holding at Feering, although, if he did so, he would have made nothing out of the arrangement himself. In fact he paid the monks 10s. per annum in lieu of service;[2] and it is not until 1166 that the service due from this fee is recorded as that of half a knight.

It seems likely that most of the Abbey's mesne tenancies in Worcestershire and Gloucestershire carried a burden of knight service by 1086, although not necessarily one that was to persist unchanged into the later Anglo-Norman period and beyond. The main reason for reaching this conclusion is the reappearance of these Domesday tenancies among the fees held for knight service which the abbot recognized in his return in 1166. The lands of Urse the sheriff, for example, made up the greater part of the estate which William de Beauchamp held in 1166 for the service of seven knights,[3] Walter Ponther's lands were absorbed into the fee for which Hugh le Poher then owed the service of three knights;[4] and Thurstin fitz Rou's into Henry de

---

[1] *Past and Present* 49 (Nov. 1970), 15. Wakelin's fee is to be identified with that held by Robert de la Dune in Wandsworth, in Battersea, for the service of one-third of a knight in the mid-thirteenth century (*Book of Fees* ii. 688).

[2] *D.B.* ii. 14b.

[3] *Red Book of the Exchequer* i. 188. For William de Beauchamp I's lands on the Abbey's fee, see *V.C.H. Worcs.* i. 327–8; and for Urse's, ibid., pp. 300–4. Urse was William's maternal grandfather.

[4] *Red Book of the Exchequer* i. 188. Walter Ponther's lands on the Abbey's fee were in Todenham, in Deerhurst, and in Besford, Powick, Pirton, and Peopleton, in Pershore. For the descent of the lands in Pershore, see *V.C.H. Worcs.* iv. 20 and n., 148, 181, 187.

Newmarket's fee, owing the service of two knights.[1] Indeed, the only mesne tenancies recorded in these parts in 1086 which cannot plausibly be fitted into one or other of the fees returned in 1166 are those occupied at the earlier date by tenants too humble to be named, such, for example, as the 2 hides of two Frenchmen at Defford.[2] That Alured de Merleberg owed service for his lands at Severn Stoke is very likely indeed. In 1086 Alured held 15 hides here.[3] Soon after the making of Domesday Book, however, the demesne manor at Severn Stoke came into the king's hands, where it remained.[4] From the fact that the king was returned in 1166 as owing the service of one knight to the Abbey for this fee, it is clear that the estate was burdened with knight service when it came into his hands.[5]

(iii) *The Fee-Farms*

By the end of the twelfth century, the subinfeudated part of the Abbey's estate was far more extensive than it had been in 1086. What proportion of the estate was affected cannot be expressed in current values, because, of course, no valuations survive from this period, but those of Domesday Book will serve well enough to establish the order of magnitude. The manors which passed out of the demesne between 1086 and c. 1200 were valued at more than £150 per annum in the Survey, and this figure represents c. 29 per cent of the value (c. £515 per annum) of the Abbey's whole demesne estate at the time.[6] Some thirty manors were affected. A few of these were situated in the Western Parts. Most, however, were much nearer the Abbey. The list includes, for example, Ham, Moulsham, and Paglesham in Essex, Chelsea, Halliford, and Shepperton, and part of Hendon in Middlesex, Denham and Cippenham in East Burnham in Buckinghamshire. The monks, it seems, had overcome their reluctance to grant fees in this part of their estate.

---

[1] *Red Book of the Exchequer* i. 188. These fees were in Hasfield, in Deerhurst, and Eckington, in Pershore; for the descent, see J. H. Round, *Studies in Peerage and Family History* (London, 1907), p. 194.

[2] *D.B.* i. 174ᵇ. [3] Ibid. i. 175.

[4] B.L. Cotton MS. Vespasian B. xxiv, fo. 6, cited in *V.C.H. Worcs.* iv. 192–3. Only 12 hides are here said to be in the king's hands. It is, however, relevant that 3¾ hides of Alured's 15 were in the hands of tenants in 1086.

[5] *Red Book of the Exchequer* i. 188. For a similar case, see *V.C.H. Worcs.* i. 257.

[6] For the details, see Appendix I (below, pp. 337 ff.); and for the figure, £515 per annum, above, p. 56.

In the creation of these newer fees, knight service was of small importance. The majority of the tenants owed the monks, not knight service, but a render in cash or kind; they were fee-farmers, not military tenants, and their ancestors are found, therefore, not among the feudal magnates who took over the Abbey's mesne tenancies in the reign of William I, but among the far more elusive farmers and lessees who had the care of so many of the demesne manors of the estate at that time and subsequently.

Even in the eleventh century, the monks of Westminster had kept some of their demesne manors out of the hands of the farmer or lessee. Domesday Book implies that, although the manor of Deerhurst and all its members had been at farm in the reign of Edward the Confessor, it was now in hand: 'Totum manerium *T.R.E.* dabat de firma xlj libras et viij sextaria mellis ad mensuram regis. Modo valet xl libras.'[1] At Pershore, too, the render which betrays the presence of a farmer seems to have been a thing of the past in 1086, and at Hussingtree, one of the members of this enormous manor, there is an explicit reference in the Survey to a keeper or bailiff, who had a hide of land as his reward.[2] Wick, by Pershore, having been farmed by Gilbert Crispin to Robert *dispensator*, was later solemnly restored to the church by Robert's wife and his brother.[3] From a charter of King Stephen we learn that the Abbey's manors of Paddington, Fanton, and Claygate were then in the hands of a monk-warden.[4]

Farmers and lessees, then, did not monopolize the demesne manors of the early medieval estate, nor is it possible to rationalize their presence or absence in terms of the distance of the manors in question from the monastery. In 1086, Morden, in Surrey, and Kelvedon, in Essex, were certainly at farm, for each rendered to the monks a sum (or perhaps the equivalent in kind) in excess of its Domesday value.[5] Hendon and Chelsea were at farm in the lifetime of Gilbert Crispin, who was already abbot when the Survey was made,[6] and considerably

---

[1] *D.B.* i. 166; cf. Lennard, *Rural England, 1086–1135*, p. 125.　　[2] Ibid. i. 174ᵇ-5.
[3] *Gilbert Crispin*, p. 146. Robert himself had surrendered Wick before he died; his wife and brother made the formal, public surrender at the high altar in the presence of witnesses. For Robert *dispensator* see also above, p. 74.
[4] *Regesta* iii. 936.　　　　　　　　　　[5] Below, pp. 358, 342, and nn.
[6] Below, pp. 352, 350.

later than this, William de Eynesford III received Benfleet for his life, in return for a farm of £24 per annum.[1]

If some of the decisions that the monks made about their estates in the eleventh and twelfth centuries were, to our way of thinking, anomalous, that is so because we exaggerate their freedom of choice. The typical farmer or lessee of this period was not a prudent farm-manager-cum-rent-collector, carefully chosen by the monks to look after such of their estates as were inconveniently distant from Westminster. He was a servant of the Abbey, skilled perhaps in quite different employments, but expecting nevertheless to be rewarded with a manor or two; he was a prelate or a magnate having servants of his own whom he would gladly install in another man's property; or a grasping royal official with ample opportunity to spot the under-exploited properties in his territory. All these types are represented among the farmers of Westminster Abbey. Alger, to whom Gervase de Blois and his monks fee-farmed Ham, was probably one of the Abbey's clerks.[2] A little earlier in the century, William de Buckland, who was sheriff of Berkshire and the son of a sheriff, had the farm of Cippenham, in East Burnham, Tetworth and Tonge, and Chelsea.[3] In 1189–90, Hugh de Nonant, bishop of Coventry, received a lease of the manor of Perton, in Staffordshire, for his life,[4] and some ten or twenty years later Claygate was demised to Geoffrey fitz Peter, earl of Essex.[5]

In the early Middle Ages, the Abbey's farms and leases comprised the whole manorial estate, tenant-land as well as demesne; this, at least, is true of every such arrangement known to us in detail. But since the deeds which conveyed them are usually of a laconic brevity, and other sources of information under this head virtually non-existent, we do not know how much liberty of action farmers and lessees enjoyed. If they had only a life-interest in the property, they probably needed the monks' permission for major changes, whether on the demesne

[1] W.D., 602ᵛ. William surrendered the farm in or before the first year of Richard I. See also below, p. 340.

[2] *B.I.H.R.* 40 (1967), 135. Alger's grandfather, Puncelinus, held the manor previously.

[3] *Gilbert Crispin*, p. 154. Chelsea was to revert to the monks on William's death; he had fee-farms of the other properties.

[4] Below, p. 357, n. [5] Below, p. 358.

or on the tenant-land. Thus the rents and services of the tenants of the manor would still have been regulated by the monks of Westminster. Heritable leases, however, naturally weakened the landlord's authority, and the monks would have had little or no power of intervention where perpetual fees were well established.

More is known about the rents paid by farmers. In the early twelfth century, food farms were still in regular use at the Abbey. A document which was probably drawn up during the vacancy after Gilbert Crispin's death (1117/18–21) describes the several components of a week's farm: 6 coombs of grain for bread, 20 pecks of malt, and 10 of grout,[1] 3 coombs of oats, £3. 7s. for the kitchen, and 13s. 4d. for the servants; in the case of the distant manors, however, a week's farm was commuted into the payment of £8. 10s.[2] In fact food renders were already being superseded by money rents on the inlying manors of the estate. William de Buckland held Chelsea for £4 per annum and geld, when the king took geld;[3] and Abbot Herbert (1121–36) demised Ockendon for a money rent.[4] Hendon, which Herbert's predecessor, Gilbert Crispin, demised to a tenant named Gunter and his heir for a week's farm per annum, his successor, Gervase de Blois, farmed to Gilbert de Hendon for £20 per annum for all services.[5] Here the monks had second thoughts about the wisdom of surrendering a food render, and later in the century their tenant at Hendon was required to pay a week's farm and £13 per annum as well. But it is unlikely that more than a handful of the manors that were still at farm or on lease in the early thirteenth century owed food renders; of the manors then assigned to the portion of the prior and convent, only Hendon and Kelvedon did so.[6]

In the same period, manorial values, where they were not kept low by heritable tenancies, rose well above their Domesday level. By the end of the twelfth century, this is only to be expected,

---

[1] A cheap kind of ale.   [2] *Gilbert Crispin*, p. 41.

[3] Ibid., p. 154. Cf. Miller, *Abbey and Bishopric of Ely*, p. 40, where it is suggested that food renders may already have been a declining part of the revenues of the Abbey of Ely at the end of the eleventh century.

[4] W.D., 446ᵛ. The lease, made in 1125, was to Henry fitz Wlured, for his life and that of his heir. Henry was to pay £10 per annum, and his heir £11 per annum; but see below, p. 81 and n.

[5] *B.I.H.R.* 40 (1967), 135–6.   [6] *Walter de Wenlok*, pp. 215 ff.

although even so, the scale of the rise is sometimes arresting; in some cases, values rose between 1086 and the end of Herbert's abbacy, in 1136. Powick, valued at £20 per annum in 1086, was farmed by Herbert to the monks of Great Malvern Priory for £24 per annum.[1] William de Eynesford's farm of £24 per annum for Benfleet was four times the Domesday value.[2] And the rent of £15 per annum which Walter of Winchester asked for Denham towards the end of the twelfth century represented more than twice the value of this manor in 1086.[3] Where, on the other hand, farmers early succeeded in obtaining fully heritable tenancies, rents were already in some cases absurdly low by 1200. The manor of Chelsea was still at farm for £4 per annum; the farm of Moulsham, £9 per annum, was identical with the value of the manor *T.R.E.* and £3 lower than the figure for 1086; at £10 per annum, the farm of Ockendon was identical with the Domesday valuation of this manor.[4]

How was it that the monks of Westminster allowed the affliction of heritable farms to get such a hold on their demesnes? We can probably dismiss the notion that they were for a long time unaware of the dangers of the practice; they can be discovered too early attempting to recover grants in fee, or spelling out their reversionary rights in manors that were farmed on a temporary basis, for this to be a convincing explanation of the lamentable inroads which their estate had suffered by *c.* 1200.

Under Gervase de Blois, who installed Dameta, his mother, as tenant in fee at Chelsea, sheer corruption played its part,[5] but far more important over the twelfth century as a whole was the expectation men had that the lords of great estates would reward some of their servants and well-wishers with estates in land; always, the demands which patronage made on the Abbey's demesne were in competition with its role in providing

---

[1] Below, p. 363. [2] Below, p. 340. [3] Below, pp. 338–9 and n.

[4] For the farm of Moulsham, see below, p. 343, and for the farms of Chelsea and Ockendon, *Walter de Wenlok*, p. 215. It is clear from the latter reference that the provision (for which see above, p. 80, n.) in Abbot Herbert's farm of Ockendon, that the rent should rise to £11 per annum when the heir of Henry fitz Wlured entered, did not take effect.

[5] For a more generous view, see H. G. Richardson and G. O. Sayles, *The Governance of Mediaeval England from the Conquest to Magna Carta* (Edinburgh, 1963), pp. 415–16 and n. The suggestion made here that the manor of Chelsea was identical with that part of Eye known as La Neyte is erroneous. For the pall worth £5 and the *gersuma* of £2 paid by Dameta, see *Flete*, p. 89.

the livelihood of the abbot and convent of Westminster themselves. In the later Middle Ages the monks might have solved
some of their problems without prejudice to their own long-
term needs by parting with the coveted manors for terms of
years, but the term of years had no very respectable place in
the feudal nexus of relationships to which these twelfth-century
arrangements belong; a sheriff or a bishop, perhaps even a
monastic servant such as Alger the clerk, would have regarded
the offer as a disparaging one, and it is unlikely that it ever
occurred to the monks to make it.[1]

They did, however, use life-grants, and some of their difficulties arose from the weakening, as the twelfth century drew to its
close, of the principle that such grants were indeed for a limited
duration. Hugh de Nonant had only a life-grant of Perton, but
the manor is never again found among the demesne possessions
of the Abbey. Such an outcome to a life-grant was, no doubt,
assisted by the development of tenancies for life into free tenements that occurred at this time; and this development had
other consequences that made life-tenancies less attractive to
lords than had been the case in the past. Once he had been
recognized as the possessor of a free tenement—and this happened between the age of Glanvil and that of Bracton—the
tenant for life could use novel disseisin against his lord, who
may also have found himself less than adequately protected
against his tenant in the matter of waste.[2] For landlords the
grant of a life-tenancy was now perhaps scarcely less imprudent
than a grant in fee.

By *c.* 1200, as we have seen, manors which together had
probably provided between one-quarter and one-third of the
income of the monks of Westminster in 1086 were in the grip of
tenants holding in fee.[3] But it is not of course the case that the
monks had yet sacrificed one-quarter to one-third of their
potential income from land, for each one of these feoffees paid
a farm, and in several cases the farm had been fixed recently;
it was not yet uneconomically low. Between 1086 and the 1170s,
the actual income of the Abbey rose by 43 per cent from £515

[1] See in general A. W. B. Simpson, *An Introduction to the History of the Land Law*
(Oxford, 1961), pp. 68 ff.

[2] F. Pollock and F. W. Maitland, *History of English Law before the Time of
Edward I* (2nd edn., 2 vols., Cambridge, 1968), ii. 6 ff.; Simpson, op. cit., pp. 66 ff.

[3] Above, p. 77.

per annum to £739 per annum.[1] Further, a manor at farm owed the abbot hospitality in addition to the farm itself—a duty fearsome enough to the tenant and sufficiently valuable to the monks to provoke much expensive litigation between the parties concerned around the year 1200.[2] And fee-farms, no less than knights' fees, were liable for the feudal incidents of escheat, wardship, and marriage. The worst of the losses of income lay in the future, when the price-rise would have gone much further than was the case now. At the end of the thirteenth century, the annual sum which the monks could expect to receive as tenants in demesne of Deerhurst, for example, was at least twice the sum of the rent which they were entitled to receive from their fee-farmer there.[3] The year 1200 provides the *terminus ad quem* of the present discussion of fee-farms because the grants were more or less at an end by this date. It needed only a few small alienations by Ralph de Arundel (1200–14) to bring down the convent's wrath on that prelate.[4]

Among the factors discouraging the grant of new farms after this date were developments in the land law. One of these changes, the elevation of life-tenancies into free tenements protected by the real actions of the royal courts, has already been mentioned.[5] Another was the degree of success now enjoyed by the tenant in fee in his struggle for freedom of alienation;[6] the monks knew that in these circumstances the tenants in demesne of the subinfeudated part of the Abbey's estate could become remote, unfamiliar figures, with whom they would have only formal, mainly legal, contacts, and these of a very occasional kind.

Of greater immediate importance, perhaps, was the new attention to the canon law on alienation that papal visitation, occurring at Westminster for the first time during the abbacy of Ralph de Arundel, may have inculcated there. From time to

---

[1] Above, p. 69 and n.

[2] For an example, see F. M. Stenton, *The First Century of English Feudalism, 1066–1166* (2nd edn., Oxford, 1961), pp. 267–9. Hospice rights are mentioned at Deerhurst, Denham, Hendon, Longdon, Ockendon, Powick, and Sudborough; for references, see *Walter de Wenlok*, p. 8 n.

[3] Below, p. 197.   [4] Below, p. 84 and n.

[5] Above, p. 82.

[6] J. M. W. Bean, *The Decline of English Feudalism, 1215–1540* (Oxford, 1968), pp. 40 ff.; D. W. Sutherland, *The Assize of Novel Disseisin* (Oxford, 1973), pp. 86 ff. For the situation on the Abbey's fee, see more particularly, below, pp. 311 ff.

time, much earlier than this, the alienation of the goods of the monastery had excited condemnation at Westminster. On these occasions, the emphasis had been on the enormity of the practice when carried through without the consent of the convent, as had been the case, for example, during the ruinous vacancy preceding the election of Abbot Herbert in 1121.[1] If the charters which explicitly associate the convent of Westminster in the grant of some of the fee-farms of Gervase de Blois are to be believed, the monks of that period were not opposed root and branch to the practice.[2] Nor did the papacy try to uphold at Westminster the full rigours of the prohibition of all alienations, howsoever made, that was found in Gratian: as late as 1199, Innocent III required of Abbot William Postard only that he should not alienate the monastery's possessions without the consent of his chapter.[3] This was probably the lesson that Nicholas of Tusculum, the legate, tried to drive home when he visited the Abbey in 1213, and the times were sufficiently hard at Westminster to make the matter a pressing one. Nicholas spent eighteen days there on his arrival in England, and some three months later, presumably after consultation with the pope, Ralph de Arundel was deposed from the abbacy.[4] 'Magna controversia et contentio' between the abbot and the convent had been a feature of Arundel's rule, as Flete tells us. That his offence touched the old issue of alienations is made virtually certain by litigation on the part of his successor, William de Humez, to recover properties alienated by Abbot Ralph without the consent of the chapter.[5]

The most persuasive of all the arguments against continuing the practice of granting fee-farms was the gathering crisis that

---

[1] *Regesta* ii. 1252; cf. *B.I.H.R.* 40 (1967), 128.

[2] *B.I.H.R.* 40 (1967), 138 ff.

[3] *Letters of Pope Innocent III concerning England and Wales*, ed. C. R. and M. G. Cheney, no. 113; cf. Gratian, *Decreti Secunda Pars*, C. XII, q. ii, cap. 18–19. See also H. G. Richardson, 'The coronation in medieval England', *Traditio* 16 (1960), 151 ff.   [4] *Flete*, p. 100.

[5] *C.R.R.* viii. 212, 265; ibid. x. 187. The properties in dispute in these cases were: 40 acres with appurtenances in Pershore, 40 acres with appurtenances in Feering, and 1 carucate of land with appurtenances in Wheathampstead. Neither the alienation at Pershore nor that at Feering is mentioned in the list of fee-farms *temp.* Abbot Ralph which W.D., 129, purports to give. Monastic property alienated by a prelate without the consent of his convent could be recovered only when the abbacy in question was over, and by litigation; see Sutherland, *Assize of Novel Disseisin*, p. 112.

now threatened the finances of the abbot and convent of Westminster. If the full cost to the Abbey of its fee-farms was not yet apparent, this period was nevertheless in general an exceedingly difficult one for the finances of the monks of Westminster.[1] There could be no further erosion of the demesne when resources were as severely strained as theirs were now.

(iv) *The Division of Goods between the Abbot and Convent*

By a decision on the part of Gilbert Crispin to which we owe our only knowledge of the size of the early medieval community at Westminster, an income sufficient for the clothing of eighty monks was assigned to the monastic chamber there; the sum of £70 per annum was considered sufficient for the purpose, and it came partly from the Abbey's properties in London.[2] Not much later than this, and perhaps even in Crispin's own lifetime, other sums, amounting to nearly £60 per annum, were assigned for the alms and pittances of the monks, their fuel, the support of their servants, and the Maundy.[3] Thus an obedientiary system began to take shape within a generation of the foundation of the Confessor's church. Some words in a letter reputedly of Innocent II to Gervase de Blois suggest that Gervase may have tried to overthrow his predecessors' arrangements. Gervase is here ordered to place lands and rents in the hands of his monks; and the injunction, also in this letter, that the abbot should administer internal and external affairs on their advice underlines the connection between the development of separate portions and the movement, which the Abbey experienced in common with so many other houses, to formalize the role of the convent in the monastic administration.[4] But at the end of the twelfth century, only a very small endowment had been set aside for the monks' food, the major item of domestic expenditure. This was the sum of £8 per annum from the issues of Parham assigned to that purpose during the abbacy of William Postard; yet the kitchener needed *in toto*

[1] Above, p. 64.
[2] *Gilbert Crispin*, p. 41. (*Cillentuna* in this list was Chollington, in Suss., for which see below, p. 359.) See also *Customary* ii. 149; by this date, however, the chamberlain had an income of £88 per annum.
[3] *Gilbert Crispin*, p. 41.
[4] *Papsturkunden in England* i. 24. The letter was almost certainly altered, if not composed in its entirety, by Osbert of Clare; see *B.I.H.R.* 40 (1967), 127–9.

£146 per annum.[1] Moreover, if the abbot had already learnt to live with an independently minded convent, or, to a large extent, apart from it, he had not yet formally recognized any of its so-called rights in the written texts that were characteristic of ecclesiastical privileges, and by now not only of these.

For these reasons, the perpetual grant of manors and rents which Abbot William de Humez made to his monks for their kitchen, in a charter invoking on anyone who should infringe its terms anathemas of a kind hitherto reserved for the monastery's enemies in the world, was a turning-point in relations between the abbot and convent of Westminster. This document marks the true division of goods, as the monks themselves recognized when they put it at the beginning of the sections devoted to these themes in their two principal cartularies.[2] Humez granted the monks and their successors, for the kitchen, lands then yielding an income of *c.* £150 per annum, with the proviso that the allowance of 8*s.* a day, which the kitchen had received hitherto from the general coffers of the Abbey,[3] would be resumed if the lands in question should subsequently be lost to the monks. His successor, Richard de Berking, went further. In 1225, he conceded to the monks formal rights in the administration of the lands and income assigned to their maintenance; the abbot would, for example, appoint as obedientiaries those whom the convent wished to have and dismiss them when asked to do so.[4] Further, the convent now assumed responsibility for all monastic expenditure, with the exception of the items that were specifically charged to the abbot's funds in the indenture setting out the new arrangements. To this end, he added to the convent's existing share of the monastic lands five manors which the monks always referred to subsequently as their 'principal' manors; these were Battersea and Wandsworth, Feering, Stevenage, Aldenham, and Wheathampstead.

From this time onwards the abbot of Westminster, on the one hand, and the prior and convent, on the other, had no revenues

---

[1] i.e. 8*s.* a day; see *Walter de Wenlok*, p. 216; and for the assignment on the issues of Parham, see below, p. 359.

[2] *Walter de Wenlok*, pp. 215–16, and references given there.

[3] With the exception of the assignment of £8 per annum on the issues of Parham mentioned above.

[4] *Walter de Wenlok*, pp. 217–22. This agreement is dated 11 Nov. 1225. A supplementary agreement was made before 3 Feb. 1226 (ibid., pp. 222–4).

in common; lands were assigned either to the abbot's portion or to the convent's, and in so far as the compositions which Berking's successors sealed with their monks related to the material wealth of the house and not to constitutional matters, they were concerned with points of detail—here, with the transfer of a rent from the abbot to the convent; there, with spelling out the abbot's responsibility for a particular type of expenditure.[1] After 1225, the convent had its separate portion, and the obedientiaries who administered it enjoyed great freedom of action—hence the eagerness of the prior and convent to control their appointment and dismissal.

We do not know what prompted Gilbert Crispin to make the first assignment of revenues to the convent of Westminster, or why he singled out the chamber on the occasion. The impulse behind the changes of the early thirteenth century is unmistakable: it was the determination of the prior and convent to have what they called a 'certain portion',[2] and to enjoy the enhanced liberty of action that this would give them. The possibility of persuading the king to relinquish his claim to custody over such a portion during vacancies seems to have been only a secondary consideration, although Berking and his monks, when making the agreement of 1225, must have been aware that other monasteries had found this advantage in similar arrangements. In fact the king did not allow the prior and convent of Westminster to keep their portion during a vacancy until 1252; on Berking's death in 1246, the whole monastic estate went into custody in the usual way.[3]

When the division of goods was made in 1225, the abbot of Westminster was more or less a stranger to the common life of the monastery. Part of his time was spent itinerating at a distance from Westminster; even when at Westminster, he sometimes preferred La Neyte, the manor house on the estate in Eye that Berking purchased,[4] to his lodgings within the precinct; when in the precinct, he assisted rather infrequently in choir and refectory. This way of life, though a target in the Black Monk world at large for papal and capitular reformers, was apparently accepted without question in the monastery

---

[1] Ibid., pp. 225 ff.   [2] Ibid., p. 222.
[3] *Cal. Pat. R., 1232–47*, p. 494; cf. ibid., *1247–58*, p. 150; *Flete*, p. 110.
[4] Below, p. 414 (no. 1).

itself. But evidently it was still hoped to minimize the practice of employing other monks, even if they were obedientiaries, at a distance from the house; it is only in this way that we can explain why all the Abbey's possessions in the West Midlands were assigned to the abbot and none to the convent; the convent was given the lion's share of the properties in the Home Counties. Thus the abbot took Pershore and Deerhurst and all the members of these manors; the convent, all the manors in Essex and Hertfordshire. At the end of the thirteenth century, as we have seen, the abbot's portion probably yielded a net income of *c.* £520 per annum, a sum representing *c.* 32 per cent of the whole income of the monastery at the time.[1]

On this portion the compositions laid three major charges.[2] First, the abbot was to be responsible to the king for military service and scutage, the main items in the forinsic service of the Abbey's lands. At the time, this was almost certainly the most expensive duty assigned to the abbot, and he was given, in compensation, all the monastery's knights' fees and thus its income from the incidents of military tenure. He was to entertain all the most important and expensive guests—the king, and legates, archbishops, and papal nuncios travelling with twelve horses or more—and to bear the whole cost of litigation about the Abbey's possessions and privileges, whether in church courts or in lay ones. Over and above these extraordinary expenses and the many lesser items of monastic expenditure for which the abbot assumed responsibility in 1225 or at subsequent revisions of the compositions, his portion bore the running costs of an elaborate household; Walter de Wenlok, at the end of the thirteenth century, had a *meignee* of some forty to fifty persons, all entitled to eat in his household if they were in the vicinity, all receiving his livery.[3]

The abbot's portion was not capable of sustaining for long all the charges that were laid upon it early in the thirteenth century. His difficulties arose partly, as did those of the monas-

---

[1] Above, p. 59; and see Table VI (above, p. 63). Cf. Knowles, *Monastic Order in England*, p. 436 n., where it is suggested that the abbot in a house where revenues were divided may normally have had 'about a fourth part'.

[2] *Walter de Wenlok*, pp. 219–20, 228, 230, 234–5.

[3] Ibid., pp. 246–8. Of the forty-six persons listed here who were entitled to receive Wenlok's livery, twenty-one were menial servants who would normally have been resident in the household.

tic community as a whole, from the crippling effects exerted by fee-farms on manorial values as the century advanced. They are explained in part by the high cost of papal confirmation to newly elected abbots, and, before this new burden was placed on the monastery, by the astonishing cost—£1,000, if Flete is correct—of the vacancy preceding the election of William Postard in 1191.[1] In part they were made inevitable by the secular mode of life now thought appropriate for the abbot of Westminster. It must also be remembered that Richard de Berking and his monks had none but the most rudimentary accounts to assist their calculations of what each party could expect to receive from the manors assigned to it in 1225; there was an element of hit and miss in the whole affair.

The difficulties showed themselves at the end of the century in the bitter disputes, many of them about money, that divided Walter de Wenlok from his monks in the last years of his abbacy,[2] and later, when the fires of controversy were exhausted, in the quiet setting aside of several clauses in the compositions. In the second half of the fourteenth century, the convent paid, for example, the cost of lawsuits relating to its own lands and shared fully in the defence of the Abbey's privileges; it contributed to the procurations of papal envoys; and it was even willing to help the abbot with the small amount of military service that the king still demanded.[3] Wenlok's monks would have contested all three points. The abbot, for his part, economized over servants and retainers, fees and robes; he had to do

---

[1] *Flete*, p. 98; Flete notes that the debt was paid over a period of seven years. For the probable explanation of this episode, see above, p. 64 n. The first abbot-elect of Westminster to be asked for a stipulated sum as common service at his confirmation was probably Philip de Lewesham, in 1258; the amount then was £400. From 1334 the sum was 2,000 florins (a sum equivalent, in the early fourteenth century, to c. £333); see W. E. Lunt, *Financial Relations of the Papacy with England, to 1327* (Cambridge, Mass., 1939), pp. 677 ff.; idem, *Financial Relations of the Papacy with England, 1327–1534* (Cambridge, Mass., 1962), pp. 825 ff. Common service, however, was by no means the only item of expense on these occasions.

[2] *Walter de Wenlok*, pp. 17 ff.

[3] W.A.M. 19847 ff. It is clear, however, from the charges against George Norwich in 1467, on the occasion of his suspension from office, that the composition laying on the abbot responsibility for the defence at law of all the monastery's lands and privileges was still in theory valid; the monks now said that they wished the arrangement to be waived for the future. See Widmore, *History of the Church of St. Peter, Westminster*, p. 195.

this, since, with only *c.* £546 per annum, he was relatively poor, as poverty was understood in the world of the high aristocracy to which he half belonged.[1]

Although carrying through a separation of portions, the composition of 1225 affirmed the need for the abbot and the prior and convent to make important decisions jointly: the abbot might not alienate any of his goods, nor the prior and convent any of theirs, without the consent of the other party.[2] The deputies of the legate Ottobuono, who visited the house in 1268, evidently considered that the chief danger lay in independent action by the prior and convent, for the statutes resulting from their visitation forbade the prior and convent to negotiate large loans or long leases, to alienate property or to make any agreement whatsoever under the common seal without the consent of the abbot.[3] It would require a more thorough scrutiny of the evidence than that underlying these pages to determine the fate of these rules in any period of the monastery's history, but the signs are that the monks of Westminster slowly learnt to obey them—the rules in question became part of the institutional framework of their estates administration in the later Middle Ages. Thus when the manorial demesnes were once again put on lease in the fourteenth and fifteenth centuries, the seal seems to have been used correctly. For example, there has come to light no conventual lease that was sealed when the abbot is known to have been incapable, through absence, of giving his assent to an act in chapter, or during a vacancy.[4] As to the abbots of the late Middle Ages, probably only Edmund Kyrton and George Norwich flouted the rules, and neither was allowed to die in

---

[1] £546 per annum, the figure for *c.* 1400, represents *c.* 23 per cent of the Abbey's total net income at that date, for which see Table VI (above, p. 63). For the fourteenth-century economies, compare Litlington's and Colchester's expenditure on menial and other servants and on retainers with that of Wenlok (W.A.M. 24510 ff.; *Walter de Wenlok*, pp. 159 ff.). Litlington's income, however, was larger than Colchester's; see above, p. 60 and n.

[2] *Walter de Wenlok*, pp. 221–2.

[3] W.D., 28–9; see also B.L. Cotton MS. Faustina A. III, 210 ff., and A. H. Sweet, 'A papal visitation of Westminster in 1269', *Anglican Theological Review* 5 (1922), 29–34.

[4] For leases made from 1485, see W.A.M. Reg. Bks. i–ii, *passim*. Before 1485, some leases were entered in the cartulary known as Liber Niger Quaternus, but in this period we depend principally on the survival of the original indentures. On the use of the seal in Chapter, see also below, p. 153.

office: each was forced either to delegate his powers or to resign the abbacy itself.[1]

(v) *The Abbot's role after* c. *1225*

Despite the division of goods, the abbot continued greatly to influence the affairs of the monastery. The very opposition that he encountered from his constitutionally minded monks in the thirteenth century serves only to drive home the point: they opposed because there was a force to be opposed. Some of the strength of the opposition at this time is explained by the fact that the abbot—paradoxically, in view of his own mode of life— was an agent of reform to his monks: in so far as papal and capitular decrees for the reform of the common life had any success at all in the monastery, it was through the insistence of the abbot. Thus Wenlok opposed the application of the surplus from Queen Eleanor's manors to the wage-fund of the monks until within a week of his death.[2]

In the secular sphere, the abbot's influence was now felt principally in three ways. First, even after the division of goods, he had oversight of the entire expenditure of the monastery.[3] The obedientiaries' accounts suggest that, unless, exceptionally, the abbot happened to be overseas, no major new item of expenditure was undertaken without his consent; and his presence at the yearly audit of these accounts, which is attested many times over, ensured that the rules were kept. With the consent of the senior monks, he could initiate payments from conventual funds, and payments of this kind *e precepto abbatis*, though never individually large, occur not infrequently in the accounts. Of greater importance than these formalities of procedure was the influence of his way of life on theirs. A pre- late who had himself left the common life so far behind could hardly persuade his monks of the singular value for them of its old simplicities, and Wenlok is the last abbot who is known even to have made the attempt.

Next, on the abbot depended the defence of the monastery's rights and privileges in a society that was at times notably hostile to these. Much more than the costs of litigation was

---

[1] *Monks*, pp. 129–30, 141–2.   [2] *Walter de Wenlok*, p. 238 n.
[3] The following remarks are based to a large extent, though not exclusively, on the accounts of the conventual treasurers (W.A.M. 19838 ff.).

involved in this responsibility. Whoever paid the lawyers' fees and all other expenses incurred in litigation, it was the abbot who monitored the operation. When, in Richard II's reign, the canons of St. Stephen's Chapel in the Palace of Westminster challenged the Abbey's monopoly of jurisdiction in the monastic precinct, it was the strenuous exertion of Abbot Litlington that won for his monks, if not exactly victory, then at least an honorable compromise.[1] Inevitably, however, by the end of the fourteenth century, his relatively straitened circumstances made him less effective than he had been formerly, for an effective role depended on having constant access to the best professional advice and on a wide range of friendships in the world outside the cloister, both expensive advantages in late-medieval England, and advantages that probably none of the fifteenth-century abbots possessed in sufficient measure.

In land-purchase, too, the fifteenth-century abbots did less for the monastery than their predecessors. Indeed, they were able to do virtually nothing: between the end of the fourteenth century and the endowment of the anniversaries of Henry VII and his mother early in the sixteenth, not a single large property came into the possession of the monks of Westminster by purchase. In the thirteenth and fourteenth centuries, however, the list of their acquisitions is an impressive one,[2] and to appreciate how important the abbot's role was in these we have only to read Flete's account of the matter. In Flete's eyes, the history of the monastery was made up largely of the deeds of its abbots, and among these none was more glorious than the purchases of property with which Berking and his successors had enriched their monks. He was not the first of the brethren to think along these lines. The services of this kind that Berking himself had rendered to the monastery were recorded for all to see in barbarous Latin on his tombstone in the Lady Chapel:

> Ricardus Berkyng prior et post inclitus abbas:
> Henrici regis prudens fuit iste minister.
> hujus erat prima laus Insula rebus opima:
> altera laus aeque Thorp, census Ocham decimaeque:
> tertia Mortonae Castrum simili ratione;
> et regis quarta de multis commoda charta.

[1] *Flete*, p. 136; *V.C.H. London* i. 567–8; and see above, p. 15.
[2] Below, pp. 414 ff.

Clementis festo mundo migravit ab isto,
M domini C bis XL sextoque sub anno.
cui detur venia per te, pia virgo Maria.[1]

What the monks thought admirable about this abbacy of twenty-four years was the purchase by Berking of La Neyte and Castlemorton and the appropriation in his time of the church of Oakham with Barleythorpe.

Under Berking, as later under Langham and Litlington, the abbot's part in land-purchase probably included the provision of some of the necessary capital from private sources.[2] Other abbots contributed perhaps initiative, the technical skills that their counsellors and retainers were well qualified to give, and a very useful standing with the king and his officials who had, after 1279, to license the transactions.

On all these counts—by what they did in these fields of action and by what in the end they were unable to do—the abbots of Westminster continued greatly to influence the Abbey's material fortunes, even though so much of their old power may seem to have passed to the obedientiaries in the thirteenth century. Towards the end of the Middle Ages, they began, indeed, to assume control of some of the major obediences themselves. John Estney, George Fascet, and John Islip all held the offices of sacrist and warden of the new work concurrently with that of abbot.[3] If the history of a monastery which began in the eleventh century with little more than £500 per annum and ended, in the sixteenth, with nearly £3,000 per annum can be considered a tragic theme, the abbot has a better claim than anyone else to be regarded as the hero of the following pages.

Even so, his influence on the day-to-day and week-by-week administration of the goods of the prior and convent, which comprised, in all probability, never less than two-thirds of the whole goods of the Abbey, was often small in the fourteenth

---

[1] *Flete*, p. 106. For the *commoda charta*, see *Cal. Ch. R.* i. 208–9, and for the acquisition of La Neyte, Castlemorton, and of the rectory of Oakham with Barleythorpe, below, pp. 414–15 (nos. 1 and 3) and p. 404.

[2] Above, p. 66.

[3] *Monks*, pp. 197, 209. William Benson, Islip's successor, was at different times during his abbacy warden of the new work and of St. Mary's chapel, and cellarer (ibid., pp. 196, 201, 209). For this trend in monastic administration generally, see D. Knowles, *The Religious Orders in England*, ii (Cambridge, 1955), 328–30.

and fifteenth centuries. It becomes clear, in piecing together
the history of this estate, that, if the abbot's formal approval
was normally asked in cases where the law prescribed this, he
and his monks saw nothing strange in proceeding up to that
point independently of each other. Around 1300, for example,
they were reaching somewhat different judgements on the
wisdom of commuting labour services into money rents, and
later the terms on which the abbot demised his manorial
demesnes were different from those favoured by the prior and
convent in the case of theirs.[1] At this level of the monastic
administration, the right hand often did not know what the
left was doing. Yet it was the cumulative force of these smaller
decisions that so often carried the action forward, into a situation which could only be resolved by the sagacity and determination of the abbot.

(vi) *The Abbots*

What sort of men were they on whom these burdens were
placed? The monks of Westminster began to enjoy the unques-
tioned right of free election early in the thirteenth century,
about the time of the division of goods. The strength of royal
influence on elections between the Norman Conquest and the
1220s, by which John Flete was impressed in the fifteenth
century,[2] is attested by the fact that only two abbots of this
period were promoted *e gremio*, and Abbot Herbert, one of the
exceptions, was almost certainly the choice of Henry I.[3] But
from Richard de Berking's election in 1222 until 1533, when
William Benson was brought from Peterborough to preside over
the last years at Westminster, the king rarely attempted to do
more than grant the licence to elect and his formal assent to the
free choice of the monks when this had been made; now the
monks of Westminster could rarely blame anyone but them-

---

[1] Below, pp. 153 ff., 233–4 ff.

[2] Above, p. 17. Flete uses phrases such as 'creatus est', 'successit', 'introductus
. . . ordinatus est', by which he means to imply the absence of a free election, of
all the post-Conquest abbots down to and including Walter of Winchester (1175–
90), with the exception of Laurence, whose mode of appointment he leaves without
comment.

[3] On Herbert, see *Flete*, p. 87, and *Monks*, p. 41. See also *Letters of Osbert of
Clare*, ed. Williamson, pp. 2–4. William Postard (1191–1200) was also elected *e
gremio*, but see above, p. 64 n.

selves if each successive abbot was not, in St. Benedict's words, that person of their number fitted by excellence of life and teaching for the task.[1]

To the earlier period of effective royal influence on elections belong the only two abbots, in a long line, who attained distinction as writers, teachers, or preachers. Of these two, Gilbert Crispin (1085–1117/18) and Laurence (1158–73), the former was the more important figure, by far, in the intellectual life of his times and was able to do far more than Laurence to foster the intellectual resources of the monastery. Gilbert Crispin's best known work was his *Disputatio Judei et Christiani*.[2] In this dialogue with a Jew of Mainz, settled in London, he grappled with fundamental objections to the central doctrine of the christian faith, the Incarnation, which his friend and master, St. Anselm, perhaps under the direct influence of this debate, reflected upon later in the *Cur Deus Homo*. As late as thirty years after his death, Gilbert Crispin's opinion on a theological point was quoted with respect at the Council of Rheims.[3] His abbacy is the only period in which a mood of intellectual excitement can be sensed in the cloister at Westminster. But Henry II's choice of Laurence, formerly prior of Durham, as abbot of Westminster in 1158 suggests that there were still remnants of this former distinction at the Abbey, and, moreover, that public preaching may still have been a feature of life in the church and chapter-house there, as it had been a generation earlier, in the time of Osbert of Clare, for Laurence was a theologian and prolific writer of sermons.[4] As far as we know, only two of the freely elected abbots of Westminster, Simon de Langham and Thomas Millyng, had studied theology;[5] none is known to have made the smallest contribution to any branch of

---

[1] *S. Benedicti Regula Monasteriorum*, ed. C. Butler (2nd edn., Freiburg-im-Breisgau, 1927), cap. lxiv.

[2] On Gilbert Crispin, see *Gilbert Crispin, passim*, and R. W. Southern, *Saint Anselm and his Biographer: A Study of Monastic Life and Thought, 1059–c. 1130* (Cambridge, 1963), pp. 88–91, 205–6, and references given there.

[3] *Gilbert Crispin*, pp. 51–2.

[4] *Symeonis Monachi Opera Omnia*, ed. T. Arnold (2 vols., Rolls Ser., 1882–5), ii. 330; *Letters of Osbert of Clare*, ed. Williamson, p. 56.

[5] Millyng graduated in Theology; Langham's university career is less well documented, but his library suggests a serious interest in this field of study; see B. F. Harvey, 'The Monks of Westminster and the University of Oxford', *The Reign of Richard II: Essays in Honour of May McKisack*, ed. F. R. H. Du Boulay and C. M. Barron (London, 1971), p. 114 n.; ibid., p. 129.

thought or learning, although Langham, the most distinguished among them, put together a notable library in the course of a long life that took him, in the end, far from Westminster.[1] In the fourteenth and fifteenth centuries, when the Abbey was sending monks to the university, the abbots, more often than not, had missed this experience.

From the early thirteenth century, the monks of Westminster looked, as a rule, for those pre-eminently practical qualities in their abbots that we have seen the latter in fact needed—administrative capacity and adroitness in public relations. Not surprisingly, since these are qualities that grow with use, length of profession mattered; the hint in the Rule, that the monk fitted for the abbacy by excellence of life and teaching might prove to be the most junior in the house, fell, most probably, on deaf ears.[2] Most of the abbots whose *curriculum vitae* can be recovered were in their forties at the time of their election and had been professed some twenty years or more. William Colchester was probably about forty-eight-years old and had been a monk for more then twenty-five years when elected, in 1386;[3] Richard Harwden was about forty-six-years old and a monk of more than twenty-two years' standing when he was chosen to succeed Colchester in 1420.[4] Although John Islip (1500–32) was only thirty-six-years old when elected, he had, even so, been a monk for twenty years, for he had entered the monastery, after the custom of the period, at the age of fifteen.[5] From Thomas de Henle (1333–44) to Richard Harwden (1420–40), every abbot, with the exception of Langham, had been arch-deacon, treasurer, or warden of the new work[6]—that is to say, he had held one of the more demanding of the monastic offices. Earlier, when details of the *cursus honorum* at Westminster are lacking, the same character of a man of affairs is some-times reflected in the abbot's public life. Richard de Berking

[1] Emden, *Biographical Register of the University of Oxford to A.D. 1500* ii. 1095–7.
[2] *S. Benedicti Regula*, ed. Butler, cap. lxiv.
[3] *Monks*, p. 103. The ages of Colchester and Harwden have been inferred from the well attested fact that, in this period, monks of Westminster were normally ordained as soon as they reached the minimum canonical age—i.e. twenty-four. Colchester said his first mass in 1361–2.
[4] Ibid., p. 126. Harwden had probably said his first mass in 1398.
[5] Ibid., p. 167.
[6] Ibid., pp. 193 ff. Langham is exceptional in another respect, too: of the six abbots of this period, he alone had studied at Oxford.

(1222–46) was a baron of the Exchequer,[1] and Richard de Ware (1258–83), Treasurer;[2] Richard de Crokesley (1246–58) is mentioned for the last time in public life as a royal nominee to the Committee of Twenty-Four at the parliament of Oxford in 1258.[3] Surprisingly, however, few of the priors of Westminster were promoted to the abbacy—in the thirteenth century, only Berking and Philip de Lewesham, and in the fourteenth, only Langham and Nicholas de Litlington.[4] Not until the second half of the fifteenth century did promotion from the one office to the other become usual.

Despite these preoccupations of the monks in making their choice, or on account of them, social rank was a secondary consideration. Nicholas de Litlington, who was not only well born, but also able to command considerable wealth, even after his profession as a monk, and this in a period when the monastery was feeling the pinch, had to wait his turn to become prior, let alone abbot. Though professed more than sixteen years, and therefore of a respectable seniority, he saw Simon de Langham preferred for the priorship in the spring of 1349, and Benedict de Chertseye promoted to the same office later in that extraordinary year, when Langham became abbot. Litlington was made prior only on the demotion of Benedict de Chertseye, who disgraced himself by making the pilgrimage to Rome in 1350, the Jubilee Year, without the abbot's leave.[5] But from the late twelfth century, the community probably attracted so few well born recruits that the modest social origin of its abbots has no particular significance, except as confirmation of the former fact. Several abbots were of middle-class origin—a circumstance that they probably had in common with many of their monks. Ralph de Arundel was a Londoner;[6] Walter de

---

[1] Above, p. 65.

[2] T. F. Tout, *Chapters in the Administrative History of Mediaeval England* (6 vols., Manchester, 1920–33), vi. 19.

[3] *Documents of the Baronial Movement of Reform and Rebellion, 1258–1267*, selected by R. E. [sic] Treharne, ed. I. J. Sanders (Oxford, 1973), p. 100. Crokesley died on 17 July 1258 (*Monks*, p. 50); see also *Flores Historiarum* ii. 320–1.

[4] *Monks*, pp. 193–4. Lewesham died before the confirmation of his election. Of the fifteenth- and early-sixteenth-century abbots, Millyng, Estney, Fascet, and Islip had all been priors.

[5] Ibid., pp. 85, 89, 92. For Litlington's parentage, see above, p. 42 n.

[6] *The Historical Works of Ralph of Diceto, dean of London*, ed. W. Stubbs (2 vols., Rolls Ser., 1876), ii. 172.

Wenlok, the son of an apothecary of Wenlock, in Shropshire;[1] William Colchester's parents were in fact citizens of Colchester.[2]

Two abbots, if Flete is to be believed, were of outstanding excellence. Thomas de Henle's claim to spiritual distinction does not rest on Flete's own words, but on his epitaph; this, however, would now be lost had not Flete recorded it.[3]

> Hic abbas Thomas Henle jacet, aspicito, mas.
> Petre, pater Romae, memor esto sui, rogo, Thomae.
> fratres jure regens, sacram vitam, scio, degens:
> verax sermone fuit et plenus ratione,
> auxilians vere genti quam vidit egere.
> quos sanctos scivit monachos, hos semper adivit;
> atque sibi tales monachos fecit speciales.
> rex et magnates laudant ejus bonitates.
> nunc jacet orbatus Thomas sub marmore tectus.
> sit, precor, electus et cum sanctis sociatus.
> Octobris fato decessit mense grabato,
> anno milleno ter centeno, scio pleno
> corde, quadragesimo quarto, sepelitur in imo.

Although scarcely more is known about Henle than is contained in Flete's pages, one or two facts about his promotion to the abbacy recorded elsewhere suggest that he may indeed have been chosen for perfection of life. Since he fell below the educational standard normally expected of a Black Monk prelate at this time, a papal dispensation was needed before he could be blessed, and the king dispensed him from residence at Westminster for a period of seven years, so that he might devote himself to study; the duty of representing the Abbey in the world and even pastoral duties could wait.[4]

Simon de Langham is more directly commended by Flete, but his zeal for holiness is perhaps a little more in question than Henle's. Flete says that Langham's monks wept at his departure for the see of Ely as St. Martin's disciples mourned for him.[5] Langham, it is true, proved himself to be an excellent man of business in a period of financial crisis for the Abbey; the monks may have been moved by the prospect, opened by his departure, of renewed poverty. Yet Flete clearly believed that Langham had

---

[1] *Monks*, p. 60.   [2] Ibid., p. 103.   [3] *Flete*, pp. 126–7.

[4] *Cal. Papal Letters* ii. 410; *Cal. Pat. R.*, *1334–8*, pp. 116, 238.

[5] *Flete*, p. 132. Flete's source was W.A.M. 9225*. For Langham, see also *Chronica Johannis de Reading et Anonymi Cantuariensis, 1346–67*, ed. Tait, pp. 108–9.

effected reforms of a higher order than this. He had eradicated 'insolentias, abusiones, singularitates, superfluitates et malitias', and restored a much-needed norm of discipline, previously undermined by self-willed actions.[1] This is high praise, and we have only to read on to discover how it was earned, for Flete next describes how Langham ended singularity in the misericord—by which is meant the use of this institution mainly by individuals in special circumstances—by regularizing its use by all the brethren for the recreation of meat-eating. Langham in fact allowed his monks the benefits of *Summi Magistri*, which had finally given papal blessing to the use of the misericord by able-bodied monks.[2] Here, then, was not another saint, but an abbot whose balanced judgement and realistic appraisal of situations brought a new degree of peace to the house—the prelate who stabilized observance at a level that all could reach and all would accept. Had Flete's *History* been finished, it would perhaps have praised also the moral excellence of a later abbot, William Colchester. It is impossible to study Colchester's mode of life without concluding that here was a prelate singularly free, for his time and situation, of a taste for ease or luxury, a man sensitive to the needs of the poor and fertile in schemes to relieve them.[3]

If we are looking for moral excellence or spiritual insight, the roll of honour is short. But so too is the list of the abbots who were evidently failures or whose rule provoked such storms at Westminster that we must suspect a proud and inflexible spirit on their part, matching the contumacy of the monks whom they were called to rule. The shortcomings of Geoffrey of Jumièges (*c.* 1071–*c.* 1075), Gervase de Blois (1138–57), and Ralph de Arundel (1200–14) led, in the end, to their deposition from office;[4] Edmund Kyrton (1440–62) was forced to resign, and George Norwich (1463–9) sent into retirement, both having shown themselves to be foolish and extravagant men, lamentably

---

[1] 'voluntarii usus'; see *Flete*, p. 130.

[2] D. Knowles, *The Religious Orders in England*, i (Cambridge, 1948), 282.

[3] See, in particular, the regular relief, in the form of small pensions, given by Colchester to the deserving poor of his demesne manors (W.A.M. 24410–18). For Colchester, see also E. H. Pearce, *William de Colchester, abbot of Westminster* (S.P.C.K., London, 1915), and *Monks*, pp. 103–5.

[4] *Flete*, pp. 84, 100; *Symeonis Monachi Opera Omnia*, ed. Arnold, ii. 330; see also above, p. 84.

deficient in business capacity.[1] At the time of Walter de Wenlok's death in 1307, the indiscipline of the community was a
matter of common knowledge outside the cloister, and Wenlok
was locked in a quarrel with the prior, Reginald de Hadham,
in which a number of senior monks and the major part of the
community as a whole took Hadham's side.[2] Kyrton, however,
was provided to the abbacy against the wishes of the *major et
sanior pars* of the community, which had just given its voice to
another candidate,[3] and Geoffrey of Jumièges and Gervase de
Blois were appointed by the king;[4] only three of these six were
the choice of the monks themselves.

The truth is probably that in a long line of elective abbots
the really good and the really bad are exceptional; mediocrity
tends to prevail. Most of the abbots who presided at Westminster
after 1200 resembled their monks in nothing so much as their
utter lack of real distinction of any kind. Was it perhaps because they were too much gifted, too colourful, that so few
priors of Westminster ever became abbots? It almost seems
likely. Distinguished or mediocre, most of the abbots who
presided at Westminster after the beginning of the thirteenth
century are, like so many other prelates of the post-Gregorian
period, more easily pictured in the office or counting-house than
in church or chapel, at prayer.

[1] *Monks*, pp. 130, 141–2. In 1444, Kyrton was suspended from office until the
next meeting of the General Chapter (*English Historical Rev.* 37 (1922), 87).

[2] *Walter de Wenlok*, pp. 17 ff.

[3] The election of Nicholas Ashby, then prior of Westminster, was quashed by
the pope; on this episode, see *Cal. Papal Letters* ix. 128; *Cal. Cl. R., 1435–41,*
pp. 432–3; *Cal. Pat. R., 1436–41*, pp. 395, 397.

[4] *Flete*, pp. 84, 88.

IV

Free Tenants on the Demesne Manors

(i) *The Population Recorded in 1086*

THE great majority of the persons enumerated on the lands of
Westminster Abbey in 1086 were classified by the Domesday
commissioners as villans, or placed in the more dependent
categories of the bordar, cottar, and *servus*. Except in the five
places where burgesses are recorded—these were Ashwell,
Cricklade, Droitwich, Pershore, and Staines[1]—the number of
those who could claim to be of freer status than a villan was
exceedingly small. The villans represented *c.* 44 per cent of the
enumerated population of the estate considered as a whole,
excluding the burgesses and a few others who clearly do not
belong among the peasantry;[2] they came well ahead of the
bordars (representing *c.* 31 per cent of the whole[3]) and would
still have been ahead if bordars and cottars, who seem in
general to have had common characteristics in Domesday
England,[4] were to be counted together as a single class; the
figure for bordars and cottars together is *c.* 40 per cent.[5] Freemen and sokemen represent, by contrast, a mere 3·5 per cent
of the whole.[6]

---

[1] Domesday Book attributes the church at Cricklade, many burgesses there,
and the third penny of the vill to Westminster Abbey, but it also attributes the
third penny to the king (*V.C.H. Wilts.* ii. 115, 127). The Abbey's connection with
Cricklade seems quickly to have lapsed. On Ashwell, see H. C. Darby and E. M. J.
Campbell, *The Domesday Geography of South-East England* (Cambridge, 1962), pp.
88–9; and on Droitwich, where the abbot of Westminster was only one of several
lords having burgesses, Darby and I. B. Terrett, *The Domesday Geography of Midland
England* (2nd edn., Cambridge, 1971), pp. 263–5.

[2] i.e. excluding, of those listed in the final column of Table VII (see pp. 123–6),
the Frenchmen, burgesses, knights, and (with more hesitation), the priests. The
exact figures are 616: 1,412.   [3] 433: 1,412.

[4] R. Lennard, 'The economic position of the bordars and cottars of Domesday
Book', *Economic Journal* 61 (1951), 342–71.

[5] 568: 1,412.

[6] 50: 1,412. (The ranks of the free include the radman of Peopleton.)

This pattern, however, was not universal, and exceptions to it were particularly common in Worcestershire and Essex. In half the members of the huge manor of Pershore, although not in Pershore itself, and in more than half the manors in Essex,[1] the bordars and cottars were more numerous than the villans. What does this different pattern signify? We can hardly be in doubt, given the extent to which bordars and cottars were demesne-oriented people over the estate as a whole. The bordar's importance in the demesne economy is strikingly demonstrated at Staines.[2] There was land for twenty-four ploughs in this manor, and evidently the whole of it had been opened up, for there were thirteen ploughs on the demesne and eleven in the hands of the villans. In fact more than half a large cultivable area, and perhaps much more than half, was held in demesne. The importance of the eight cottars and twelve *servi* in the demesne economy must have been eclipsed by that of the exceptionally numerous bordars: fifty-eight of these are mentioned, most of them holding, it appears, only a very few acres;[3] these assuredly were the characteristic demesne workers of Staines. There were, moreover, thirteen manors on the Abbey's estate where a demesne existed—this we know, since demesne plough-teams are mentioned—but where no one standing lower on the ladder of dependence than a bordar is recorded;[4] it looks as though the bordars bore the brunt of demesne demands for labour here, too.

It seems likely, therefore, that demesne needs were pressing with special severity on the Abbey's tenants in Worcestershire and Essex in 1086. The demesnes in the manors the population

---

[1] Excluding Feering, where six of the bordars were under the sokemen. Bures, moreover, has been excluded altogether from consideration.

[2] *D.B.* i. 128–8ᵇ. See, more generally, Lennard, *Rural England, 1086–1135*, pp. 342 ff.

[3] Thirty-six bordars had *in toto* 3 hides; four had *in toto* 40 acres; ten had 5 acres each; and eight had *in toto* 1 virgate. It is, however, relevant to consider the size of the virgate at Staines; this was of *c.* 10 acres. If we may assume that the four bordars with 40 acres had more or less equal shares, each had the arable holding, if not the other facilities, of a virgater; and the ten bordars, each with 5 acres, had those of a half-virgater.

[4] In Bucks.: Denham, E. Burnham; in Essex: Benfleet, Fanton, Paglesham, Wennington; in Lincs.: Doddington; in Northants.: Deene and Sudborough; in Staffs.: Perton; in Surr.: Claygate; in Worcs.: Birlingham and Hussingtree. If the plough-teams mentioned at Ham and Ingatestone were on the demesne the number of manors to which the remark in the text applies is fifteen.

of which was characterized by a preponderance of bordars or cottars were perhaps particularly large in relation to the area of tenant-land. If so, they must have been worked to a large extent by the plough-teams of the tenants, for demesne plough-teams were not outstandingly numerous in any of the manors; but there is nothing inherently improbable in this. Whatever the precise details of the situation, it is clear that the monks of Westminster were making the weight of their authority as landlords felt in both these regions.

In Worcestershire we can only take note that this was the situation in 1086; how it had come about we do not know. In Essex, however, there is every indication that the condition of the Abbey's peasantry had worsened since the Norman Conquest. The monks had twelve manors here in demesne in 1086,[1] and in eight of these bordars were more numerous than villans. Moreover, with three exceptions,[2] the smaller of the two manors in Fanton, Ingatestone, and Wennington, these manors now had a larger number of bordars than in 1066. This could have resulted as well from an upgrading of cottars and *servi* as from a downgrading of villans, and at the Abbey's other manor in Fanton, indeed, both trends are in evidence. There were six villans, one bordar, and four *servi* here in 1066, but in 1086, one villan, nine bordars, and, it seems, no *servi*.[3] But at Ockendon the number of villans had declined in a period when the number of *servi* had remained constant;[4] here and at Moulsham[5] a depression of the villans had helped to bring about the Domesday situation. Further, manorial values suggest a strenuous exercise of lordship in this county, for in all the Abbey's demesne manors in Essex, Ingatestone and the smaller manor in Fanton only excepted, the value of the manor had risen since 1066.[6] And although freemen and sokemen were characteristic of Essex society as a whole in 1086, of all the Abbey's manors in this county, only Feering could boast of possessing either.

---

[1] The Abbey's small property at Bures has been excluded from the reckoning.

[2] Excluding, again, Feering, where, however, the number of the villans also fell between 1066 and 1086.

[3] *D.B.* ii. 14. [4] Ibid. ii. 15.

[5] There were eight villans at Moulsham *T.R.E.*, and four bordars; in 1086, three villans and twenty-one bordars; two *servi* are noted in 1086, but none *T.R.E.* (ibid.). [6] Below, pp. 340 ff.

(ii) *The Situation in* c. *1225*

In due course the situation of 1086 was altered almost beyond recognition, and the most striking of all the changes that transformed it was the rise of a class of free tenants on the Abbey's estates. The reference here is not to the tenants who held the manors subinfeudated for knight service or for fee-farm rents, but to those within the confines of the demesne manors whom the monks came to recognize as free. The origins of this development are to be placed sometime between the end of the eleventh century and *c.* 1225, and probably early rather than late in this period, but on some manors free tenure did not attain its maximum extent until after *c.* 1225.

The pivotal date, *c.* 1225, is derived from the earliest surviving custumal of the Abbey's manors.[1] All the manors surveyed in this document were assigned to the convent at the division of goods completed in that year, early in the abbacy of Richard de Berking, and it is likely that the custumal itself was put together soon after the conclusion of these arrangements. Such a date is consistent with the entry which records that at Ashwell a certain Master William paid 2*s.* per annum as increment of rent by arrangement with Abbot Humez; Humez, Berking's predecessor, died in 1222. The division of goods was in itself a notable event in the history of the estate, since there is every sign that, once possessed of their several portions, the abbot and convent differed to a degree in some of the policies that they applied there. Further, some of the manors surveyed in the custumal had probably not long been out of the hands of the farmers to whom so many of the Abbey's properties were entrusted in the twelfth century. We are thus shown tenurial conditions at an important juncture in the history of the estate.

Eleven manors are dealt with in more or less detail in this document—in Surrey, Battersea and Wandsworth, and Morden; in Middlesex, Greenford, Knightsbridge and Paddington, and Teddington; in Essex, Feering; in Hertfordshire, Aldenham, Ashwell, Stevenage, and Wheathampstead; in Oxfordshire, Launton. Not all are treated in the same way. In most cases an

---

[1] B.L. Add. Ch. 8139. W.A.M. 9287 another copy of this custumal, has the entries in a slightly different order and now lacks nearly the whole of the entries for Knightsbridge and Paddington.

attempt is made to list both the free and the customary tenants, with their rents and services, and these lists seem to be up to date, for some of the tenants mentioned in them appear in Abbey charters of the early thirteenth century. At Feering, however, and at Knightsbridge and Paddington, the free tenants are omitted, although such tenants existed there at this time;[1] and at Ashwell, Stevenage, and Wheathampstead not even the customary tenants are listed: we are told the total area of land in their hands and the rents and services of a standard holding, but neither the names of the individual tenants nor the size of their holdings. At Launton the list of tenants is selective: it names only those whose rents did not conform to the standard assessment for a virgate.

These anomalies are probably explained by the circumstances in which the custumal was made. The prior and convent of Westminster, newly possessed of their separate portion, wished to have a comprehensive custumal of their manors; but they did not exert themselves to the extent of making a detailed survey of each manor for the purpose: they put together what they found in the existing monastic archive relating to the places in question. Happily for them, detailed, up-to-date custumals existed for the majority of their manors, made perhaps when these were recovered from the hands of farmers; but at Feering and at Knightsbridge and Paddington the existing material did not cover the free tenants, and at Ashwell, Stevenage, and Wheathampstead it was very sketchy indeed, amounting as it did to little more than a statement of custom in general terms. Thus the custumal is a patchwork—here as detailed and precise a document as could have been found in the archives of any estate at this time; in other places, brief or manifestly incomplete.

About 11 per cent[2] of the total number of tenants named in this source are described as free; they were *libere tenentes*. But

[1] For references later in the century, see W.D., 110 ff., 246ᵛ–247. Some of the free tenements of the manor or manors—usage varied at this time—of Knightsbridge and Paddington were situated in the vill of Westbourne. The custumal does record the existence of some customary tenants at Knightsbridge and Paddington who also held a little free land; see below, p. 115 n. The failure to mention free tenants at Launton is consistent with other evidence pointing to the absence of free tenure here for the greater part of the Middle Ages (*V.C.H. Oxon.* vi. 237).

[2] 39: 348. The latter figure includes the seventeen tenants who are named at Launton. For further details of the holdings enumerated in the custumal of *c.* 1225, see below, pp. 432, 435.

clearly, in view of the omissions of which the custumal is guilty, this figure underestimates the numerical importance of free tenants on the manors in question. In any case, an over-all percentage would be of little use, since free tenants were unequally distributed among the manors. Morden, for example, had only three, in a total tenant-population of twenty-one, but at Ashwell, where free tenants occupied one-third of the entire extent of tenant-land, they were almost certainly a numerous body.[1] Similarly, in the case of the abbot's manors, which do not come fully into view until the second half of the thirteenth century, some had a large number of free tenants, others, very few. But it is more important to us to know that such a class was now in existence than to be able to measure the phenomenon precisely. On this point the custumal is emphatic: there were free tenants and customary tenants, and rarely, it seems, did membership of the two classes overlap, for only a handful of the tenants enumerated in this source held both freely and by customary tenure. The idea of freedom inhered not only in the tenure—in the homage, fealty, and service of the Abbey's free tenants—but in the land that was held on these terms. The custumal refers both to *acre libere* and to *terra consuetudinaria*.

In the thirteenth century, free tenants, so called, were free, not in the relative sense that is true of freemen and sokemen in the Domesday period, but as the condition was understood from the reign of Henry II onwards: they were the legal owners of the freehold of their lands and qualified to sue in respect of these in the royal courts. Yet even if there is no exact comparison between freedom at the end of the eleventh century and freedom at the end of the twelfth, the virtual absence of freemen on this estate in 1086 does make the recognition of such a class in the ensuing period more interesting than it would otherwise be. Evidently, when Henry II and his successors offered the protection of the royal courts to free tenants, many of the inhabitants of the fee of Westminster Abbey who qualified for this great boon were descendants of men who had been classified in 1086 as villans. How was it that some of the villans of that earlier period were able to take the road that led eventually to freedom, when others were not?

---

[1] There were 12½ virgates of free land at Ashwell, and 25½ virgates of customary land. The virgate in this manor was probably of *c.* 40 acres.

(iii) *The Development of Free Tenure*[1]

The explanation is partly, no doubt, that the villans of 1086 were not as uniform a class as the use of a single word to categorize them all would suggest: some were much freer, in eleventh-century terms, than others, and their successors contrived in due course to be free, as freedom was understood in the twelfth century. But the problem is not entirely one of terminology. The developed class of free tenants on this estate probably included not a few who themselves or whose ancestors were once truly in a state of dependence aptly described as the condition of being a villein; some men really did escape from dependence into freedom in the twelfth and thirteenth centuries. The story of their liberation has two aspects. One is the success of certain tenants in extricating themselves from the burden of regular praedial service, the distinctive burden of customary or villein tenure. The other is the readiness of the monks of Westminster to recognize some, though not all, who achieved this as *libere tenentes*; for no one on this estate or on any other could enfranchise his own tenure—everything depended in the last resort on the readiness of the landlord to concur in the development by accepting the homage or fealty of the aspiring free man.

Even on the Abbey's demesne manors, free tenants occasionally held for military service. At Longdon, for example, a field called 'Baxternydyng' was held by this service in the late fourteenth century,[2] and a messuage and half-virgate held for military service is mentioned at Islip in the same period.[3] Most free tenants, however, held in return for services that resemble those of the socager, but, perhaps on account of a lingering

[1] A topic that has, in general, attracted less attention than its concomitant, the development of villeinage. For some illuminating remarks see M. M. Postan, *Essays on Medieval Agriculture and General Problems of the Medieval Economy* (Cambridge, 1973), pp. 285–9; and, on freedom, not necessarily in a tenurial context, J. Scammell, 'Freedom and marriage in medieval England', *Economic History Rev.*, 2nd ser., 27 (1974), 523–37. On the manors of Westminster Abbey, however, the distinction between freedom and villeinage was almost certainly of greater practical importance to peasants than is suggested of this distinction in general in Professor Postan's essay.

[2] W.A.M. 21127. Walter Hunte is here said to hold by military service, but to render 6s. 8d. per annum, suit of court, heriot, and relief.

[3] W.A.M. 14863. It may be relevant that both Longdon and Islip were out of the demesne of the Abbey for a period in the early Middle Ages; see below, pp. 362, 356.

element of uncertainty in their dues, the word socage is rarely used of these tenements in Abbey sources. The Abbey's free tenants normally owed a relief, equivalent to a year's rent, on taking up their land, a heriot on death or when the land was alienated, suit of court, and a fixed money rent. Renders in kind were not uncommon, and tallage, though a rare component of free rents, is not unheard of; Algar de Bruges, for example, who was a free tenant at Bridges, in Battersea, in the second half of the thirteenth century, owed this due, and Thomas Lowys owed it at Pyrford in the early fourteenth century.[1] The one element that seems never to be found among the obligations of free tenure was that of regular praedial service. Harvest works, occasional carrying service, ploughing boons, the work of supervising mowers and reapers, even mowing and reaping in person, providing the service was precisely defined—all these were common demands upon free tenants; but week-work, the distinctively base form of labour service, was never, to our knowledge, asked of such men.

This privilege was far from being of merely theoretical interest, a feature of the tenure that would have helped the royal courts to identify it as free had the matter come into their purview; in many places the customary tenants must have noticed it frequently and enviously, for the burden of week-work on them was not finally lifted until the second half of the fourteenth century.[2] The villeins of Islip, for example, were still heavily burdened with this kind of service when Abbot Wenlok enfranchised the half-virgate of one of their number, the elder William de Throp. William's son had rendered the abbot 'praiseworthy service', and the enfranchisement of the family holding was his reward.[3] As a half-virgater holding in villeinage, the elder Throp had owed two and a half days' work a week and various other forms of bodily service, among them regular carrying services; the cash value of his annual dues according to the extent was 11s. 8½d. per annum.[4] Now, as a tenant in fee,

---

[1] W.A.M. 27494, 27469. Lowys, who held a messuage and 14 acres of land in the vill of Woodham, owed a fixed tallage of 1s. 6d. per annum. However, against his name in the extent where this fact is recorded the word *nativus* is written. 'Bruges' = Bridges.

[2] Below, pp. 225 ff., 256 ff.   [3] W.D., 273.

[4] Below, p. 440. (The details of customary rents at Islip in the early fourteenth century are also true of the late thirteenth century.)

he was to render 6s. 6¼d. per annum, three-weekly suit of court, heriot, and relief. Since most of the customaries of Islip performed week-work for part of the year and some for the whole of it, William de Throp's exemption, in a manor where there were few other free tenants, must have been conspicuous.

In the early Middle Ages a tenant who threw off the burden of regular labour services did not become thereby a freeholder. Unless he could persuade his lord to receive his homage or fealty as a free tenant, he entered the somewhat ambiguous territory of the gavelman or molman—the rent-payer who was more free than an *operarius* or *custumarius* but not so free as a free man. On the Westminster fee, at Staines, a class of gavelmen who were distinct from the free tenants yet not one with the customaries is mentioned down to the mid-fourteenth century.[1] As a rule, however, we should not envisage escape from praedial service and the landlord's recognition of the free status of the man who achieved this as separate stages in the ascent to freedom: the landlord was apt to be involved from the beginning, offering freedom from service and the status of a free tenant as parts of one and the same bargain. His motive, if it was not simply that of rewarding favoured servants, as Abbot Wenlok rewarded William de Throp at Islip, was usually a fiscal one: there was money to be made, for it is safe to assume that most newly enfranchised tenants bought their freedom: they paid a premium for the enfranchisement of their tenure. The grant of free tenure was in fact one way in which a landlord could capitalize his resources. Well aware of this, the legislators of the Black Monk Order forbade monastic prelates to enfranchise customary land unless to do so was evidently to the utility of the church, and their chapters gave express consent.[2]

In the twelfth century the monks of Westminster were no better at resisting the temptation to enfranchise small tenancies on their demesne manors than at fending off fee-farmers from their larger properties; and here, as we have seen, their record was poor.[3] And although some whose lands they enfranchised had to be content initially with a life-grant, many, in the end,

---

[1] W.A.M. 16872, 16930–1; see also below, p. 112.

[2] *Documents Illustrating the Activities of the General and Provincial Chapters of the English Black Monks, 1215–1540*, ed. W. A. Pantin (Camden, 3rd ser., xlv, xlvii, liv), i. 66; cf. *Walter de Wenlok*, pp. 221–2.

[3] Above, pp. 77 ff.

won through to heritable interests in their land. From the heirs and successors of these men, the monks could expect to receive only fixed rents, however inflationary the age. Yet the monks were not equally vulnerable to this temptation in all types of property; the aspiring free man was more likely to realize his hopes in some circumstances than in others. Most of those who attained recognition as free tenants on the monastic estate did so in one or other of three situations.

In the first place, the tenants of large holdings had a better than average chance of winning their way through to freedom. We know the size of twenty-six of the free holdings enumerated in the custumal of *c.* 1225, and twelve of these were larger than the typical villein holding of the manors to which they belonged.[1] Further, of the eighteen holdings half a hide or more in extent that are listed in this source, exactly half were held freely. Many of these holdings were probably of the manorial type, with a tiny demesne and tenant-land of their own. Why, then, should extent of holding have helped the free man so much?

Several factors played their part. First, the larger the holding, the greater the economic security that it afforded and the better the tenant's chances of avoiding the voluntary act of commendation to a lord that was one of the roots of dependence everywhere in medieval society. Moreover, the scale of operations of such a tenant made it easier for him than it was for other men to find the cash for a money rent once he had entered the nexus of dependence. And finally, once within this nexus, the tenant of a large holding benefited from the sheer difficulty

[1] The holdings were those of Geoffrey fitz Pentecost (more than 1¾ hides), Adam de Deorhurste (3 virgates), Robert *marescallus* (1 hide, 3 acres), and a tenant named Peter (1½ virgates), at Battersea and Wandsworth; John Ducet (1½ virgates), and Richard Winneledun' (2½ virgates) at Morden; Peter Hut (3 virgates), Walter West (2½ virgates, a croft, and 2 acres), and Walter Baldewine (3 virgates), at Teddington; Thomas Picot (2 virgates), at Aldenham; Roger de Aula (half a hide and 15 acres) and William Horsendune (half a hide), at Greenford. At Battersea and Wandsworth, Robert *marescallus* and Peter probably held some customary land as well. The size of Thomas Picot's holding at Aldenham is recorded in W.D., 187. For the other holdings, see B.L. Add. Ch. 8139; and for the size of customary holdings in *c.* 1225, below, p. 435. It is not intended, by the emphasis placed in the above account on size of holding in the initial winning of freedom, to suggest that free tenants were a homogeneous economic group or class in early-medieval England, or to deny that the freedom of a holding was often demonstrated, over the years, in its becoming, not merely smaller than it had once been, but small in an absolute sense; see, on these points, Lennard, *Rural England, 1086–1135*, pp. 348 ff.

encountered by any landlord in assessing such a holding for labour services. The basic unit of assessment was usually the half-virgate or virgate holding, and this was certainly the case on the manors of Westminster Abbey.[1] But if 1 virgate owed 5 days' work a week, as many such holdings may have done in the early days of villeinage, what was to be the obligation of 2- or 3-virgate holdings? Was the tenant of 2 virgates, like the inhabitants of Ishmaelia, to work a ten-day week? As long as landlords insisted on treating every large holding as a single farm, manned by a single household—and this seems to have been their usual practice in the twelfth century—and not as the complex of demesne land and tenant-land that it may often have been, the problem of assessing an appropriate quota of service was singularly difficult. From the beginning, therefore, the tenant of such a holding was likely to be mainly a rent-payer; he had a better chance than many other people of escaping the net of praedial service.

Urban institutions provided a different form of encouragement for the development of free tenure. Outside Westminster itself, there was not a single place on the Abbey's fee that a visitor from Italy or the Low Countries would have classified with conviction as a town, but urban life, as that institution is to be understood in medieval England, was not lacking. In many places on the fee, there existed that combination of urban and rural institutions, of market and burgage tenures with fields and meadows, in one and the same setting, that was so common in the English countryside as a whole. At Ashwell, Pershore, and Staines, as we have seen, Domesday references to burgesses prefigure the growth of such towns,[2] and later, Denham, Hendon, and Stevenage, to name only three, developed into this hybrid kind of settlement. Each was the Casterbridge of its region, a town that was, in Thomas Hardy's phrase, 'the complement of the rural life around; not its urban opposite'.[3]

[1] Below, pp. 203 ff. The virgate was more commonly used than the half-virgate for this purpose. [2] Above, p. 101.

[3] *The Life and Death of the Mayor of Casterbridge*, cap. ix. For an account of small towns, including Pershore, in the later Middle Ages that emphasizes, in contrast to the text above, their economic differentiation from the surrounding country-side, see R. H. Hilton, *The English Peasantry in the Later Middle Ages* (Oxford, 1975), pp. 76–94.

Such a setting was at once favourable and hostile to the growth of freedom in the surrounding countryside. The money rents and premiums associated with free tenure were easily supported by townsmen, who often, indeed, lacked sufficient scope for investment within the town itself. Thus it is usual to find a fringe of small freeholdings around the walls and suburbs of towns, much of it owned, though not necessarily cultivated, by the townsmen themselves. On the other hand, the lords of manors in the neighbourhood of towns were often notably reluctant to commute the labour services owing from their villein holdings; the townsman's constant need for labour and readiness to pay well for it made dependence on wage labour a frightening prospect to the rural employer, and it is to this circumstance that we must attribute the paradox that labour services tended to persist longest in those regions where economic life was most highly developed.[1] In general, however, the forces encouraging the growth of free tenure in and about urban settlements were stronger than the forces of reaction.

On the Westminster estates, the case of Staines illustrates these contradictions to perfection, and the net gains that accrued, in the end, to freedom in such a setting. This manor, part town, part village, belonged to the abbot's portion of lands, and the abbot continued to exact week-work from the tenants of standard virgate and half-virgate holdings until the Black Death made it virtually impossible to continue the practice.[2] These holdings, however, accounted for only a very small part of the fields of Staines: most of the land here was free land, and by the fourteenth century the great majority of the abbot's tenants were freeholders, not villeins. In 1353, the abbot had two customary tenants at Staines, twenty-seven gavelmen, and forty-one free tenants;[3] before the Black Death, there were more customaries, but still, even then, a heavy preponderance of freeholders.[4] The market and shops of Staines, though

[1] See E. A. Kosminsky, *Studies in the Agrarian History of England in the Thirteenth Century* (Oxford, 1956), pp. 168, 187, where the relative importance of labour rent in eastern England is noticed. Kosminsky concluded from his study of the Hundred Rolls that this is a source tending to give 'an unduly low estimate of the money and produce rent of villeins and an unduly high estimate of their labour rent' (ibid., p. 167). In fact, works other than week-work may be seriously underestimated here.   [2] Below, p. 227 n.   [3] W.A.M. 16786.

[4] The tenemental situation of this period has to be pieced together from ministers' accounts, see W.A.M. 16907 ff. For Staines, see also *V.C.H. Midd.* iii. 22.

perhaps the immediate source of livelihood for only a minority of the population, exercised a dominant influence over the social structure of the entire community there.

Finally, the monks were tolerant of freedom in the context of colonization; in fact most of the tenants who ever held agricultural land by one of the free tenures in the demesne manors probably owed their good fortune to a colonizing situation. In this respect, the estates of Westminster Abbey were not, of course, unusual: assarting and freedom quite commonly advanced together in the early Middle Ages, and this for reasons which are easily discovered. A landlord who refrained from imposing the burdens of villein tenure on new lands in the twelfth and thirteenth centuries suited himself as much as his tenants. The extent of his demesnes may now have been more or less settled, and the services that should maintain it more or less apportioned between the virgates already in existence. He did not always need the extra services that an extension of villeinage would have provided; indeed, the wisdom of relying whole-heartedly on customary services for demesne needs was already in question. Further, a heavy burden of rent and services, such as villein holdings often bore, might make the work of colonization, expensive as it could be, impracticable; it would also repel many new settlers. Long-term as well as short-term considerations seemed to point to free tenures, or at least to the cash option instead of labour rent, if villein tenure was insisted upon.

These considerations evidently weighed both with the monks of Westminster and with their fee-farm tenants, for free holdings became extensive on the colonizing manors of the Abbey's fee in the twelfth and thirteenth centuries, whether these manors were then in demesne or in the hands of such farmers. It is recorded of sixteen manors on the Abbey's fee in Domesday Book that the number of ploughs in existence fell below the number that could be employed,[1] but this circumstance, where

[1] The manors were: Easthampstead (Berks.); Denham (Bucks.); Fanton (Essex); Aldenham, Ashwell, Stevenage, and Wheathampstead (Herts.); Greenford, Hampstead, Hendon, Sunbury, and Westminster (Midd.); Sudborough (Northants.); Pyrford and Tooting (Surr.); Parham (Suss.). In twelve manors the combined total of the demesne ploughs and those of the tenants was the same as the recorded plough-capacity; in thirty manors (excluding Bures, Cricklade, and Droitwich, and counting Deerhurst and its berewicks as a single manor) plough-capacity or the number of ploughs is not recorded. See Table VII (below, pp. 123–6).

it is noted, probably indicates no more than a failure on the part of the monks and their tenants to cultivate the full extent of the lands that were quickly and demonstrably cultivable.[1] The area of woodland noted in the Domesday descriptions is a better indication of long-term opportunities for colonization, and some of the Abbey's manors were generously endowed in this respect—there was wood at Wheathampstead for 400 swine, at Aldenham, for 800, and at Hendon, for 1,000;[2] at Deerhurst, a wood 2 leagues long and half a league in breadth;[3] at Longdon, a wood 3 leagues long and 2 in breadth.[4] On all these manors, and on some others beside, colonization took place subsequently on a large scale, with consequences for tenurial arrangements. At Aldenham and Pyrford, *c.* 30 per cent of the tenant-land was held freely in the early fourteenth century;[5] at Ashwell the proportion was *c.* 43 per cent;[6] at Hendon, *c.* 54 per cent;[7] and at Wheathampstead it was as high as *c.* 87 per cent.[8] The share of the free tenants at Hendon would still exceed one-third of the whole if half a dozen large

[1] The most important recent contribution to the large literature on the Domesday teamland is J. S. Moore, 'The Domesday Teamland: A Reconsideration', *Trans. Royal Historical Soc.* 5th ser., 14 (1964), 109–30.

[2] *D.B.* i. 128[b], 135.

[3] Ibid. i. 166. In the berewicks of Deerhurst—Hardwicke, Bourton-on-the-Hill, Todenham, and Sutton-under-Brailes—there was a wood 1 league long and half a league in breadth.

[4] Ibid. i. 174[b].

[5] For Aldenham, see C.U.L. MS. Kk 5. 29, fos. 63[v] ff. (an extent of 1315), and for Pyrford, W.A.M. 27469 (an extent of 1330). All the figures given in the text above rest to some extent on conjecture, and this element is largest in the case of Ashwell. For the tenurial structure in the manors mentioned above, see also below, pp. 432–3.

[6] C.U.L. MS. Kk 5. 29, fos. 83[v] ff. (an extent of 1315); and see previous note.

[7] C.U.L. MS. Kk 5. 29, fos. 53 ff. (printed in *Trans. London and Middlesex Archaeological Soc.*, N.S., 6 (1929–32), 580–630). This extent suggests that in 1321 more than 1,300 field-acres were in the hands of free tenants at Hendon, but probably not much more than 1,050 to 1,100 acres in the hands of the customaries. Six large holdings, however, absorbed *c.* 720 of the free acres. The manor of Hodford, included in this extent as one of the free holdings of the chief manor of Hendon, has been excluded from all these calculations; for this manor, see below, p. 352; and for the tenurial structure of Hendon, below, p. 432. A few free holdings in Hendon were described in terms of the carucate, not the acre, in 1321. It has been assumed in this note that the carucate here was of 120 acres.

[8] C.U.L. MS. Kk 5. 29, fos. 69[v]–78[v] (an extent of 1315). The figure for Wheathampstead given in the text relates also to Kinsbourne; the latter, though already a separate manorial unit for certain purposes, was surveyed with Wheathampstead in 1315.

holdings, none of them perhaps of the peasant type, were to be excluded from the reckoning.[1]

(iv) *The Identity of the Early Free Tenants*

So much for the characteristic environments of free tenure. Who first exploited them we do not know, but the custumal which the monks of Westminster made early in Berking's abbacy probably records the names of some successors of these pioneers who were not remoter than the second or third generation. Certainly, men were alive then whose grandfathers had seen Henry II, in extending the availability of royal justice to all free tenants, formulate the vital juridical principle for lack of which every local breakthrough on this and all other estates might have been in vain.

About forty tenants of free land are enumerated in this source.[2] Unhappily for the historian, all held their land in manors situated relatively near the Abbey, in Middlesex, Surrey, or Hertfordshire; the entire sample comes from economically 'advanced' areas, and this circumstance may have done much to determine what sort of men they were. About half the number are no more than names today, but a little information can be pieced together about the rest, mainly with the assistance of the Abbey's cartularies and charters, where they appear, some many times over, as parties to land transactions or as witnesses.

A few were, it seems, local figures and no more. If mentioned as witnesses, it is in respect of transactions relating to the manor

---

[1] See above, p. 114 n.

[2] At Battersea, Geoffrey fitz Pentecost' (who also appears at Wandsworth), Stephen, Adam de Deorhurste, Peter, Walter Brun', Robert *marescallus*, Alice, wife of Gilbert, Cecily, wife of Adam, Walter Woderove; at Wandsworth, Robert de la Dune, John de Elverding', Richard de Heyford, William Herevi, Walkelin, Sumer, John *carpentarius*, Walter *heres*, Gilbert fitz Ailmar; at Morden, John Ducet, Richard de Winneledun' and William Wattun'; at Teddington, Peter Hut, Walter West, John fitz Walter, Walter Baldewine, Geoffrey de B[er]kinges; at Aldenham, Thomas Picot, Ralph fitz Adam, Thomas *de camera*, John Douraunt, Ralph Testard, Robert *ad boscum*, and William and John de Idufestre; at Greenford, Walter, *quondam miles*, Roger *de aula*, and William de Horsendune. In addition, a knight holding land by Penge, in Battersea, is recorded but not named, and the name of one of the free tenants in Battersea is now illegible. At Knightsbridge and Paddington, Richard *forestarius* and a few other tenants held small acreages of land in addition to their main customary holdings. Certainly in the case of Richard's holding, and probably in the other cases, too, this land was free.

where they held their own free tenements; the inference is that
they were the kind of person whom parties to such transactions
liked to employ as witnesses of the act of livery of seisin and of
the charter itself. Thomas Picot, for example, witnesses charters
transferring property in Aldenham, where he himself held two
virgates of the monks in fee,[1] and William Herevi, a free tenant
at Wandsworth, may be identical with the man of that name
who later attested charters relating to property in Battersea
and Wandsworth.[2] Walter, the quondam knight of Greenford,
may well have been unknown outside that place. A victim of
the Angevin price-rise, or an old man who had hung up his
arms? We do not know; but if Walter was in fact a small landholder who could no longer afford to live as a knight, he fits
very well into the landscape of Angevin England.[3]

Others were of greater consequence. Two, Walkelin, who
held free land at Wandsworth, and Stephen, a tenant at
Bridges, in Battersea, were apparently too well known to the
monks to need any other name in their custumal, although
each, presumably, had a second name. Walkelin may have
been Walkelin de Matham, but, even so, we know nothing about
him except that he also held land in Wheathampstead.[4] Another
tenant, Sumer, needed, it appears, no forename to be readily
identified; it is simply noted that for the *terra Sumer* in Wandsworth a rent of 5*s*. 6*d*. per annum was owing. The Sumer
family—Henry, Ralph, and Richard are mentioned at this
date—is much in evidence in Abbey deeds of Berking's time.
The owner of the *terra Sumer* in Wandsworth was probably
Henry, who held, in addition to free land in that vill, one of the
mills there.[5] These were not his only assets: he also held land
of the monks at Charing, between Westminster and the City of
London,[6] and his frequent appearance as a witness of charters
relating to a variety of places on the Abbey's fee marks him out
as, in all likelihood, an important lay official of the monastery.[7]
Geoffrey de Berkinges, a free tenant at Teddington, is styled

---

[1] W.A.M. 4483, 4485. A man of the same name occurs in witness-lists *temp.*
Edward I.
[2] W.D., 165ᵛ, 167–167ᵛ.   [3] *Past and Present* 49 (Nov. 1970), 30 ff.
[4] W.D., 207ᵛ.
[5] W.A.M. 1767. For Ralph and Richard, see W.D., 101–2, 106ᵛ–107.
[6] W.A.M. 17143 A.
[7] W.A.M. 17324–8, 17330–1, etc.

magister in other sources;[1] he must have been a clerk. John Ducet, a free tenant at Morden, evidently belonged to the family of Nicholas Ducet, who had been sheriff of the City of London towards the end of the twelfth century, for Nicholas, we know, purchased two and a half virgates of land in Morden of one Richard de Sakespeye.[2] Although it is made clear by other references that Robert de la Dune's interests were centred on Wandsworth, they were not confined there; it is known, for example, that he held property in Kingston.[3]

Few of these men were certainly peasants. Some undoubtedly belonged to the tiny middle class of Angevin England—they were business men, clerks, or administrators. Scarcely anything is known about the role of such men in the actual creation of free tenures on the monastic fee in the twelfth century, yet nothing would be less surprising than to discover that they had been present on the field from the beginning, among the shock troops of the movement. For if anyone could afford the necessary capital outlay, the certain sum of money, as the charters of enfeoffment put it, that oiled the wheels of so many grants in fee, it was a merchant or trader; and no one better deserved a grant with or without this preliminary than one of the Abbey's own servants or officials. So, although it is tempting to think of the free tenants of the Abbey's manors, the principal *dramatis personae* of this chapter, as peasants, for, after all, in these centuries most people *were* peasants, the temptation is perhaps one to be often resisted.

(v) *The Charters*

The use of charters by the monks of Westminster in their enfeoffments can be traced to the abbacy of Gilbert Crispin,[4] and quite probably the practice was even older than this. The early charters, however, relate to considerable properties. That

---

[1] W.A.M. 16218, 16237.

[2] W.D., 170ᵛ–171; and for Nicholas, see S. Reynolds, 'The Rulers of London in the Twelfth Century', *History* 57 (1972), 355. John Ducet, however, held only 1½ virgates in Morden.

[3] W.A.M. 1890. In this grant to Robert of a messuage in Kingston, he is said to be 'of Wandsworth'. His garden in Wandsworth adjoined the manorial court there (W.D., 580). For the property known as Downe, in Wandsworth, see below, p. 358.

[4] *Gilbert Crispin*, pp. 138, 154.

in which Gervase de Blois and his monks enfeoffed Robert their marshal with 3 virgates of land in Wheathampstead is the earliest surviving example of the usage in connection with an estate humble enough to be reckoned in virgates, and the monks' anxiety to place on record the fact that Robert was henceforth to pay the geld owing from this land may explain why a charter was used;[1] further, since the virgate at Wheathampstead was of 80 acres, Robert the marshal was possessed of a considerable property. By the end of the century, as their cartularies show, the monks were using charters for all kinds of grant, and we can assume that nearly all the free tenants mentioned in the custumal of *c.* 1225 would have possessed this evidence of their status.

By the thirteenth century, most of the Abbey's free tenants, though not all,[2] held heritably, and, accordingly, most of the charters granted to the free tenants specified heritability. The right of alienation was a different matter, and charters of the time of Richard de Berking show the monks entering a positive challenge, as many other landlords did at this time,[3] to the capacity of under-tenants to alienate their land freely. Some charters of this period contain a clause forbidding alienations by the feoffee without their licence. For example, a charter of Abbot Richard de Berking and his monks, granting a messuage and acre of land in Staines to William, son of Robert de Stanes, contained a clause forbidding alienation on William's part, except with their licence.[4] A charter of Richard de Berking and his monks, relating to land in Eye, required the grantee, not only to seek a licence before alienating, but also to give the monks the first refusal of the land, if alienated.[5] This difference

---

[1] *B.I.H.R.* 40 (1967), 141. In the same charter, Robert was granted the land in Wheathampstead formerly held by Richard de Osumull'.

[2] Free tenants holding for life are mentioned at Battersea, Fanton, and Hendon in the early fourteenth century (C.U.L. MS. Kk 5. 29, fos. 46, 56ᵛ, 118ᵛ).

[3] See, in general, for the period *c.* 1250 to *c.* 1300, Sutherland, *Assize of Novel Disseisin*, pp. 86 ff. A landlord's concern in such cases was to prevent alienations that prejudiced his own rights.

[4] W.D., 133ᵛ–134. For a similar requirement in a charter of Abbot Walter de Wenlok and his monks, relating to a tenement in Hampstead, see ibid., 119ᵛ.

[5] Ibid., 101. The charter confirmed to Laurence, son of William le Petit, one half-virgate of land which his father held of the Abbey, and another which his father held of William de Herlane, with all liberties and free customs held by the latter, except those pertaining to La Neyte. For Laurence, and for La Neyte, see also below, p. 414, no. 1.

in wording, however, was probably not significant, for, as long as sales required licences, the monks, as the source of the licence, were inevitably placed in a privileged position as against all other potential purchasers. At least one charter survives from Berking's abbacy which granted land to the beneficiary to be held by himself and any assignee he chose 'exceptis viris religiosis'.[1] This fear of unfettered alienation can be traced in some of the acts of Berking's successors. Richard de Ware used the formula 'heirs and assigns' without qualification in some of his charters, thus conferring explicitly a fee simple interest, as this was now generally understood;[2] in others, he still did not mention the right to assign. In a grant at Feering, Ware forbade alienation to religious or to the Jews.[3] No doubt with the intention of preventing alienation, Abbot Wenlok granted the Throps their half-virgate at Islip in fee tail: the grant was to William and Matilda, his wife, and to their son, William, and the heirs of William the younger's body.[4]

By now, however, all the Abbey's free tenants, except the tenants in tail, were probably free to alienate without fear of harassment from the monks, unless the prospective purchaser turned out to be one of the Abbey's own villeins; villeins might not hold free land without surrendering their charters of enfeoffment and accepting the status of tenant at will on the land in question.[5] On an estate where the great majority of the inhabitants were of unfree status down to the fourteenth century, this was in fact a grievous limitation on the tenant in fee's right to alienate, and a strict enforcement of this rule is no doubt one of the reasons underlying the separateness of the free and villein landholding groups on the Abbey's manors. Not only at the beginning of the thirteenth century, when the procedure of subinfeudation may conceal the true state of affairs from us, but also later, when alienation was by substitution, and all came to light, the identities of the two tenurial groups rarely overlapped. At Aldenham, for example, in 1315, only seven tenants held both free land and customary land, although 128 held

---

[1] W.D., 202–202ᵛ (the grant of an acre in Aldenham to Simon, chaplain, of Aldenham).
[2] For an example at Battersea, see ibid., 168.
[3] Ibid., 257ᵛ.
[4] Ibid., 273; and see above, pp. 108–9.
[5] Below, p. 312.

one or the other.[1] At Pyrford, in 1330, only six, in a tenant-population numbering 162, held by both tenures.[2]

(vi) *The Policy of Repurchase*

Well before the monks of Westminster brought themselves to accept the alienability of free tenures, they were deeply committed to a policy of repurchasing these tenures wherever possible and thus redeeming some of the principal mistakes of their twelfth-century predecessors. Indeed, the fact that, in the early thirteenth century, many of their free tenants were not able to alienate their fees at will assisted the execution of this policy. Some of the freeholds mentioned in the custumal of *c.* 1225 were soon in hand again. During Ware's abbacy, for example, the monks recovered a free holding at Aldenham comprising 28½ acres of arable and 5 acres of woodland that a tenant named Robert *de bosco* held in *c.* 1225; they purchased this property from William, son of Robert's son, Walter.[3] At Stevenage, a corrody consisting of 6 quarters of wheat, 2 quarters of barley, and 1 quarter of oats per annum, together with 4 cartloads of brushwood and 4*s.* for clothing per annum was the price at which a palmer named Osbert sold a virgate and 5 acres of land, together with a messuage, houses, a croft, and a garden, to the prior and convent in the vacancy preceding Ware's election in 1258.[4] At Morden, the repurchase of freeholds was already under way when Berking was elected.[5] Everywhere on the demesne manors this policy complemented the recovery of the fee-farmed portion of the estate which began at about this time.[6] There are thus two senses in which Berking's early years are a term in the growth of free tenures on the Abbey's estates: the custumal in which they are enumerated, however imperfectly, for the first time was, as it happens, made then; and the creation of such tenures was, as a matter of fact, more or less over when this document was put together.

---

[1] Below, p. 432.

[2] Ibid. A late-fourteenth-century reference to the fishery opposite the bond tenements in Woodham, in Pyrford, suggests that the villeins in at least one of the vills of this manor were segregated, as to their dwellings, from other people (W.A.M. 27421).

[3] W.A.M. 4507; W.D., 192ᵛ. The charter says that William received £2. 6*s.*

[4] Ibid., 213ᵛ–214. Osbert was allowed to keep the houses, croft, and the garden for his life. The virgate in question is described as one-time customary land.

[5] Ibid., 170–1.   [6] Below, pp. 166 ff.

Time had not stood still on the lands which had been en-franchised under Berking's predecessors, in preparation for the moment when the monks of Westminster should possess them-selves of the freehold once again. Many of the Abbey's free tenants were tempted, as were the monks, to capitalize their resources by making grants in fee, and the restrictions which the Abbey imposed on their freedom to alienate, though in some cases severe, did not prevent a slow morcellement of tenures in consequence. The monks often found therefore, on repurchasing fees in the thirteenth century, that they had acquired much less than the whole of the property in question in demesne; much of it was still in the hands of tenants in fee, who would for the future owe them homage but whose services they had not prescribed and could not change. In 1260, for example, the abbot and convent acquired from Alice de Berking the homage and service of four men who had been free tenants on her small fee in Battersea and Wandsworth.[1] In 1285, John, called *le marescal*, quitclaimed his small estate in Wheathampstead to the monks, who acquired with it the rents of John's thirty-four tenants,[2] and at about this time they acquired with William de Ware's lands in Ashford the rents and services of his twenty-six tenants there.[3]

Paradoxically, therefore, the number of the Abbey's free tenants mounted as the policy of repurchasing freeholds gathered momentum. At Aldenham, for example, eight free tenants are recorded in *c.* 1225, but twenty-one towards the end of the century; at Battersea and Wandsworth, twenty in *c.* 1225, but fifty in 1268.[4] Every purchase, however, brought the monks at least a small piece of land in demesne; thus over the estate as a whole the extent of the free tenements was now shrinking.

This fact only makes the extent of free land still in existence in the early fourteenth century the more impressive. In nearly one in three of the manors then in demesne,[5] if not in more, the

---

[1] W.D., 164ᵛ–165. The tenants in question were William de Bruges, John de Bruges, Hugh le Kuv[er] (alias Cappere), and Geoffrey Sakespeye. These names appear among those of the monks' free tenants at Battersea and Wandsworth in 1268, and it is from the custumal of this date that we learn that Alice de Berking's small estate lay partly in Wandsworth, partly in Bridges (i.e. Bruges) (W.A.M. 27494).

[2] W.D., 205ᵛ–206. [3] Ibid., 145ᵛ–146. [4] Below, p. 432.

[5] 14: 44 (counting Deerhurst and Hardwicke, Wheathampstead and Kins-bourne, and Battersea and Wandsworth as, severally, single manors).

greater part of the tenant-land was, almost certainly, held by one or other of the forms of free tenure, and on the manors of the prior and convent considered as a whole the area of the free land rivalled, if it did not exceed, the area of customary land.[1] To some extent, the present generation of monks could attribute this—to them—lamentable fact to the wastefulness of the fee-farm tenants who had formerly been in possession of so much of their estate. Of the manors where free tenures now in all probability still preponderated, Castlemorton, Denham, Deerhurst and Hardwicke, Feering, and Hendon had all been for long periods in the hands of fee-farmers. Yet there was blame to be apportioned nearer home: even in manors which never left the demesne, the monks of the early Middle Ages had signally failed to keep the perpetual tenant at bay.

[1] For the acreage of customary land in some of these manors, see below, pp. 428–30; in some, however, the extent of both customary land and free land is a matter of guess-work, if, indeed, even guess-work is possible. The acreage of the free tenancies probably exceeded that of the customary tenancies in the following manors at this date: on the abbot's portion, at Castlemorton, Denham, Deerhurst and Hardwicke, Eye, Laleham, Longdon, Staines, and Yeoveney; on the convent's portion, at South Benfleet, Fanton, Feering, Hendon, Stevenage, and Wheathampstead and Kinsbourne. Westminster itself has been excluded from consideration.

TABLE VII. *Teamlands, Plough-teams, and Population in the Demesne Manors of Westminster Abbey in 1086, as recorded in Domesday Book*[1]

County and Manor	Team-lands	Plough-teams Demesne	Other	Freemen	Sokemen	Villans	Bordars	Cottars	Servi	Others
Berks.										
Easthampstead	8		5			14				
Bucks.										
Denham	12	2	7			15	3			
East Burnham	6	1	5			6	1			
Essex										
Benfleet		2	5			15	12			
Bures[2]						1				
Fanton (i)		1[3]	1			1	9			
(ii)		Nil					1			
Feering		4	12½[4]		12	27	30[5]		11	
Ham		1					5			
Ingatestone		1	1			1	1			
Kelvedon		2	4			18	7		3	
Kelvedon [Hatch]		2	1			1	10		2	
Moulsham		3	4			3	21		2	
Ockendon		2	4			7	8		4	
Paglesham		1	1				11			
Wennington		½	½			2	1			
Glos.										
Deerhurst		3	10			20	8		6	
—— Berewicks of[6]		13	21			45	27		37	
Hants										
Eversley			3			10	4			

Table VII (cont.)

County and Manor	Team-lands	Plough-teams Demesne	Plough-teams Other	Freemen	Sokemen	Villans	Bordars	Cottars	Servi	Others
Herts.										
Aldenham	6	1	3			8		5	2	reeve
Ashwell	12	2	5			16	9	9	4	priest; 14 burgesses
Datchworth	3	1	2			6		2		
Holwell[7]	6	2	4			11	4		3	
Stevenage	10	2	7			16	8		4	
Tewin	1½									
Titeburst								2		
Watton	2	1	1				4	2		
Wheathampstead	10	3	5			15	12	9		priest
Lincs.										
Doddington	4	1	4			14	6			priest
Thorpe	6		7½		30					
Midd.										
Cowley	1	1	1			2		1		
Greenford	7	1	5	1[8]		9	7	3	6	
Hampstead	3½	1	1½[9]			1	5		1	
Hanwell	5	1	4			5	6	4	2	
Hendon	16	3	8			26	12	6	1	priest
Shepperton	7	1	6			17		5	2	priest
Staines[10]	24	13	11			16	58	8	12	46 burgesses
Sunbury	6	1	4			10	5	5	1	priest
Westminster	13	6	6			19		43		knights and other homines[11]
Northants.										
Deene	8	2	6			17	6			
Sudborough	8	1	6		5	12	2			priest; 2 smiths

Staffs.									
Perton	6	1	1	5	13	2		8	knight
Surr.									
Battersea	2	3		14	45	17			
Claygate		1		1	3	2		1	
Morden		3		4	8		5	3	
Pyrford	13	1		6	37	14			
Tooting	1½	1		½	2				
Suss.									
Parham	4	1		2	8		5		
Wilts.									
Cricklade									many burgesses
Worcs.									
Pershore					10			11	*ancilla*; 28 burgesses
Besford[12]	5	1½		7					
Birlingham		2		4	3	4			
Bricklehampton				6	10	10			
Defford				8[13]	8	10			2 Frenchmen, with 4 *bovarii*
Droitwich								4	3 priests; 31 burgesses; *ancilla*; 6 *coliberti*
Eckington		2		2	6	6	2	4	
Hussingtree[14]		1		6	12	17		6	priest; 2 *ancille*
Longdon		3		6	10	9			
Pensham		2		4	3	4		4	
Peopleton				4	1	10			
Powick		2		14[15]	16		2	4	radman; Frenchman; priest; *ancilla*; Frenchman; 2 *bovarii*; 3 *coliberti*
Snodsbury		2		11	6		16	4	
Wick		1		12	9	25		1	2 French serjeants[16]

Notes to Table VII

¹ The Abbey's manor at Launton (Oxon.) is not described in *D.B.*

² The Abbey had 50 acres here, and an Englishman held them (*D.B.* ii. 14).

³ One plough-team *T.R.E.* and in 1086; but 'possunt adhuc fieri ii. caruce in dominio' (ibid.).

⁴ Of which 2½ belonged to the sokemen (ibid. 14ᵇ).

⁵ Of whom six were under the sokemen (ibid.).

⁶ Hardwicke, Bourton-on-the-Hill, Todenham, and Sutton-under-Brailes; the last-named is now in Warwicks.

⁷ In 1086 Holwell was in Beds.

⁸ 'Quidam franc'.

⁹ Including half a team on the hide of villans' lands which Ralph Peverel held.

¹⁰ With four berewicks; for their identity see below, p. 354 n.

¹¹ There were twenty-five 'domus militum abbatis et aliorum hominum' in this manor (*D.B.* i. 128).

¹² This manor, though in demesne, was held by a priest named William, who had *homines* under him (ibid. 174ᵇ).

¹³ Two of these belonged to the Frenchmen (ibid.).

¹⁴ The description of Hussingtree is puzzling. In this manor assessed at 6 hides, eleven villans had four ploughs, but the warden of the manor ('qui hanc terram custodit') had 1 hide, and on this land there was one plough in demesne and one villan and six bordars had two ploughs (ibid.).

¹⁵ One of which belonged to the priest.

¹⁶ *Servientes*.

V

The Manorial Demesnes

(i) *Extent and Definition*

AT the beginning of the fourteenth century, the abbot and
convent of Westminster possessed more than 14,500 acres of
arable demesne land—the abbot *c.* 4,835 acres and the prior
and convent *c.* 9,680 acres.[1] The acreage of demesne meadow,
pasture, and woodland is more difficult to estimate and is,
indeed, precisely recorded only in a group of manors assigned
to the conventual treasurers or administered by them on behalf
of other obedientiaries.[2] Here it was equivalent to *c.* 20 per cent
of the total acreage of the arable demesnes. If the same proportion was true of the estate as a whole, the abbot and convent
had *c.* 2,910 acres of such land in demesne at this time—the
abbot *c.* 970 acres, and the prior and convent, *c.* 1,940 acres.
Much of this land, however, was still subject to rights of
common.

With the acreage of demesne land it is useful to compare that
of the Abbey's customary land, the other part of the estate that
was still effectively under the control of the monks. Around the

---

[1] For the details, which, however, contain a large element of guess-work see
Appendix V (below, pp. 428–30). With the exception of Oakham, in manors where
the rectory was appropriated, the figures in the appendix and in the text above
relate to both the manorial demesne and the rectorial glebe, the latter having
been, to all intents and purposes, absorbed in the former. For these manors, see
below, p. 428 n. The demesne at Islip has been counted among the abbatial
demesnes, despite the fact that this manor was temporarily alienated between
1299 and 1318. It is of interest that in 1308–9 the keeper of the abbot's portion
during vacancy had 2,331 acres under crops, and in 1309–10, 2,112 acres. Denham, however, was not in custody; nor was Islip; and tillage in general was still
suffering from a run-down of livestock at the opening of the vacancy in 1307.
See P.R.O., S.C. 6/1109/4.

[2] Aldenham, Ashford, Ashwell, Battersea and Wandsworth, South Benfleet and
Fanton, Feering, Hampstead, Hendon, Kelvedon, Knightsbridge, Morden,
Stevenage, Teddington, and Wheathampstead and Kinsbourne. Even in these
manors, however, it is in doubt whether woodland is fully recorded.

year 1300, the abbot's manors almost certainly included more
than *c.* 7,000 acres of customary land.[1] The proportion of
arable demesne land to customary land on the manors of his
portion where an estimate can be attempted was 51 per cent.
On the corresponding manors of the prior and convent, the
proportion was as high as 71 per cent. Each of these figures,
however, underestimates the relative extent of the demesnes,
since many of the Abbey's demesnes at this date, if not all, were
measured by the royal perch of 16½ feet, but on tenant-land
customary measures persisted; customary acres were in general
smaller than 'royal' acres, and this is probably true of those in
use on the Abbey's estates. The estate as a whole comprised
not less than 38,000 acres—assorted acres—of demesne (whether
arable, meadow, pasture, or woodland) and customary land.[2]

So much is probably true of the two portions, each considered
as a whole, but the extent of the demesnes and their acreage
in relation to that of the tenant-land varied greatly from manor
to manor. The abbot's demesnes were, on the whole, small. In
only five of his manors—Bourton-on-the-Hill, Denham, Hardwicke, Todenham, and Islip—was there a demesne exceeding
300 acres; only at Hardwicke was the figure of 500 acres
exceeded. Yet, if the abbatial demesnes were small, the area of
customary land in these manors was sometimes smaller. This is
true, for example, of Staines and Yeoveney, if only the arable
demesne is taken into account; but we know that the abbot
had extensive meadows in these manors, in addition to the
arable.[3] At Sutton-under-Brailes, on the other hand, the area
of customary land was more than three times as large as that
of the arable demesne,[4] and the demesne of *c.* 120 acres at
Pyrford must have weighed lightly in the minds of the abbot

---

[1] 4,830 acres, excluding Castlemorton, Denham, Eye and Longdon, and
Deerhurst, Hardwicke, Pensham, Pershore and Wick, for which the figures are not
known. In the first four named of these manors, the acreage of customary land was
probably small, in the others, probably extensive; but in the group of manors
considered as a whole, the arable demesne was probably more extensive, in
proportion to customary land, than in the manors which yield the percentage
mentioned in the text.

[2] Of which, if the above estimates are approximately correct, *c.* 21,000 acres
(= 55 per cent) were customary land.

[3] W.A.M. 16822 ff., 16907 ff. However, the precise acreage of the demesne
meadows here is not known.

[4] 755 acres: 200 acres.

and his officials as an asset against more than 1,000 acres of customary land.

The prior and convent had more large demesnes. Largest of all was that at Feering, comprising, with the glebe, *c.* 725 acres of arable and *c.* 105 acres of meadow and pasture. The average size of the arable demesnes in the five so-called principal manors of the prior and convent—Aldenham, Battersea and Wandsworth, Feering, Stevenage, and Wheathampstead—was as much as 552 acres. If, however, the well-balanced manor was one with a preponderance of tenant-land—and this was so for a number of reasons—it must be said that the abbot of Westminster had reason to envy the prior and convent, for, despite the great extent of the demesnes in their portion considered as a whole, within each manor the due proportions had more often been maintained, and this notwithstanding some extensive grants in fee in earlier centuries. Of the five principal manors, it was only at Feering that the area of the demesne exceeded that of the customary land. At Hendon the latter far exceeded the former, despite earlier grants on an exceptionally generous, not to say improvident, scale.[1]

We have been concerned so far with the nominal demesne of the Abbey's manors; that is to say, not with the acres that were in fact exploited directly by the abbot and convent at the beginning of the fourteenth century, but with the whole area of the land in each manor that was deemed to be their *dominicum*, whether or not it was in hand or on lease for the time being. This we have distinguished rather sharply from the manorial tenant-land, and there is abundant evidence to show that by the end of the thirteenth century the monks of Westminster themselves thought of their demesne in this way, as *sui generis* among their possessions. To Abbot Wenlok's monks or to William de Curtlington's the manorial demesnes were assets having their own pattern of loss and gain and in need, from time to time, of policy decisions that might properly differ in principle from those applied in the exploitation of tenant-land.

The earlier the period, the more blurred does this distinction between demesne and tenant-land become. To Gilbert Crispin's monks or Herbert's, and even to Laurence's or William Postard's, demesne and tenant-land might be together on lease or

---

[1] For these grants see above, pp. 114–15.

together in hand; together they might produce a food farm or a money rent. But the notion that these two parts of the manorial estate were readily separable or that the one rather than the other should supply them with this or that kind of income lay in the future. Only in one context was the distinction between the two always to be taken into account. This was the fiscal context: tenant-land, but not, as a rule, the demesne land of a tenant-in-chief, was liable for the royal geld—the principle was established by the late eleventh century and may have been of greater antiquity than this.[1] This, however, no more fostered a view of demesne and tenant-land as different kinds of property than late-medieval distinctions between the chattels that were to be assessed for the tax on moveables and those that were exempt fostered a view of these as different kinds of possession, to be used or enjoyed in different ways. Perhaps not until Richard de Berking and his monks conducted their great appraisal of monastic resources early in the thirteenth century was it appreciated that demesne land and tenant-land might be exploited in fundamentally different ways.

When this happened, most of the demesnes may already have reached the limits that we have been able to identify in the early fourteenth century. It follows, if this is so, that twelfth-century farmers and fee-farmers had in some cases the major part in the decision where to draw the line. But Berking himself was not inactive. Part of his assarts at Islip and Castlemorton[2] may have been taken into the demesne; and it is certain that by the purchase of La Neyte, in Eye, he acquired, not only a new house, but fields and meadows which were kept in demesne.[3] These were perhaps the last years of large-scale expansion. Towards the end of the thirteenth century, when for the first time we may hope to find additions to the demesnes betrayed if not explicitly recorded in the ministers' accounts of the manors where they were made, the gains were few in number and on a small scale.

The Abbey's demesnes, in common with others belonging to great landowners, passed through three distinct administrative

---

[1] R. S. Hoyt, *The Royal Demesne in English Constitutional History: 1066–1272* (New York, 1950), pp. 52–8.

[2] For which see *Flete*, pp. 103–4, and *V.C.H. Oxon.* vi. 212.

[3] W.A.M. 26850 ff., and for the purchase of La Neyte, see below, p. 414 (no. 1).

phases in the Middle Ages. In the first, which lasted until the early thirteenth century, many were on lease or at farm, and a high proportion of these eventually passed from the monks' possession into that of tenants holding in fee. Soon after 1200, however, the demesnes which had escaped the inroads of the perpetual tenant were taken in hand, to be exploited directly by the abbot, the prior, or one of the obedientiaries. The monks' confidence in this policy perceptibly weakened in the early fourteenth century, but it was not until the 1360s or 1370s that the policy of leasing gathered real momentum again. The third period, opening then, is distinguished from the earlier period of leasing by the fact that it was now usual, as it had not been then, to demise only the home farms of each manor—the demesne in the limited sense of the word; the leases and farms of the twelfth century extended to the tenant-land and in some cases to the whole complex of manorial rights as well.

In a broad sense this chronology is common to both the abbot's portion of lands and to that of the prior and convent. Inevitably, however, in each period the calls which the abbot made upon his demesnes differed somewhat from those made by his monks on theirs, for the abbot, who resided in his manors for much of the year, could live off his demesnes, if he chose, in a quite literal sense that was never true of the prior and convent in respect of theirs. It is not intended in this chapter to describe the domanial economy of each or either portion in detail at any point in the Middle Ages—that large theme must be reserved for a later occasion. Two more limited tasks will be attempted, and the first of these is to discover, so far as the sources permit, the income in cash and kind that the abbot and convent received from their respective demesnes when these were in hand in the thirteenth and fourteenth centuries—that is, the role of the demesnes in the monastic economy of the period. What were these *c.* 17,500 acres of land worth to the monks of Westminster in the period when the attention of the abbot and his monks was focused on them as never before or after?

(ii) *The Demesnes in Hand*

The Abbot's Portion

The abbot of Westminster's withdrawal from the common life of his monastery probably began within a few years of the

dedication of the Confessor's church. It owed little to the separation of the abbot's goods from those of the convent—this was
not effected until the thirteenth century—but a great deal to
the duties which fell on the abbot, willy-nilly, in the feudalized
society of Anglo-Norman England. The knights who were living
in houses near the Abbey when the Domesday Survey was made
needed a focus of activity away from the field of campaign,
and they no doubt found this, more often than not, in the
precinct of the abbot's chamber at Westminster.[1] By the end
of his abbacy, Gilbert Crispin had a steward and a chamberlain
and, most significant of all, for the fact implies that he occasionally said the office in private, a chaplain.[2] Rodbert,
capellanus, attested a grant by Crispin's successor, Herbert,[3] and
there is no reason to doubt that by this time the abbot was often
absent from the office; quite probably it was now his normal
practice to eat and sleep apart from his monks. It was no acci-
dent that the names of most of the priors of Westminster, on
whom devolved the duties of the abbot in absence, are known
from this time.

Although monastic affairs and, occasionally, the business of
the realm took the abbot outside his regular circuit, the focal
points of his itinerary were always the Abbey's own manors.
After the separation of goods in 1225 the conventual manors
were formally closed to him, except for brief visits of correction,
but he kept the rights of hospice which his predecessors had
won for themselves and their successors at the manors which
were at fee-farm.[4]

It was not only the greater ease of provisioning the household
by this means that first encouraged the abbot to make a regular
circuit of manors: the necessity of showing himself to the
Abbey's tenants and farmers pointed the same way, for in the
twelfth century a landlord who stayed at home was as little
master of his lands as a king of France who never went south
of the Loire. The taking in hand of the demesnes early in the
thirteenth century added a third cogent reason for a peripatetic
mode of life, namely the need to oversee the work of bailiffs and

---

[1] For these knights, see *D.B.* i. 128, and for the situation of the abbot's chamber
in the Anglo-Norman abbey, J. Armitage Robinson, *The Abbot's House at Westminster*
(Cambridge, 1911), pp. 3–4.

[2] *Gilbert Crispin*, pp. 154–5.

[3] W.D., 124.

[4] *Walter de Wenlok*, pp. 8, 219, 227–8, 231.

reeves. Wenlok's letters reveal an abbot who took his own decisions about matters such as seed-corn and labour services —a man at home, it seems, with many of the details of the running of a farm.[1]

In Wenlok's time, although each of the abbot's demesne manors could accommodate his household for a few nights, only a few had facilities that consistently tempted him to prolong his stay. These were La Neyte, Pyrford, and Denham—none of the three more than two days' journey from Westminster—Sutton-under-Brailes, in the Western Parts, and Islip, the link between the western and the eastern manors.[2] Any of these manors might see the abbot for a month or even longer at a time; on the other hand, some of his visits were so brief as to make it clear that their purpose was the transaction of particular items of business.

In the course of the fourteenth century, the abbot, turning away from the hustle and bustle of so much travelling, adopted a more leisured way of life that took him regularly to fewer manors, and Islip, despite William de Curtlington's outlay on a new house there,[3] became merely a resting-place for the household on its way to Sutton-under-Brailes. Litlington's views on these matters are betrayed in the cellars that he laid down at the beginning of his abbacy, in 1362–3. He bought two pipes of wine for his house at Westminster, two for Sutton-under-Brailes, three for Pyrford, and one for Denham.[4] Of the manors that Litlington is known to have visited regularly, only La Neyte is missing from this list. William Colchester, his successor, seems to have preferred Birlingham to Sutton-under-Brailes; and later, extensive alterations to the manor house here helped to consume Edmund Kyrton's extravagant years as abbot.[5] Thus until the mid-fifteenth century, and perhaps for longer than this, the abbot continued to show himself even in the distant parts of his estate. John Islip, however, may rarely have moved further afield than Hendon and Wandsworth (both manors that were now part of the abbot's portion).[6] At the time

[1] Ibid., *passim*.
[2] Ibid., pp. 35 ff. Wenlok also stayed frequently at Birchetts Green, near Hurley.
[3] *Flete*, p. 122.   [4] W.A.M. 24510.
[5] W.A.M. 24445; and for glimpses of Colchester's itinerary, see W.A.M. 24410 ff.
[6] For fragments of Islip's itinerary, see W.A.M. 33320, 33324.

of the Dissolution, in 1540, the abbot of Westminster, once a familiar figure to many of the Abbey's tenants, in all parts of the estate, was probably to most of them now a stranger.

Until the abbacy of Richard de Ware (1258–83), we do not know how the abbot's household was provisioned, except on the occasion of his visits to manors where he was entitled to receive hospitality from the Abbey's fee-farm tenants, and even in Ware's time the evidence is scrappy. It suggests that in his later years—and it is only about these that anything can be said —Ware relied much on his demesnes for the provision of grain. Thus the day-account for his household shows that he drew on the demesne granaries at Laleham, Pyrford, Islip, Todenham, Bourton-on-the-Hill, and Pershore in the closing weeks of 1275; in addition, some of the pigs, poultry, and cheese consumed in the household came from demesne stores.[1] In 1279–80, the demesne at Islip supplied Ware's household with more than 200 quarters of wheat, and with 124 quarters of oats and 151 quarters of malt beside.[2] That year corn sales at Islip, a manor with an arable demesne of nearly 500 acres, brought in less than £2. 10s.[3]

In the household ordinances of Walter de Wenlok, who succeeded Ware, it was assumed that the household drew on manorial issues in this way: the steward was empowered to requisition wheat, malt, oats, wood, and charcoal from manorial reeves and bailiffs, and any other goods, provided only that essential manorial stocks were not depleted.[4] But there would have been little point in requiring the steward and the local officials to set a price on liveries in kind to the household unless the abbot's manors and the household itself had economies that were essentially of the cash kind. Yet the ordinances prescribe this practice: all corn and malt coming to the household from the manors was to be 'mis en certein pris solom la vente del pais'.[5]

In fact Wenlok's household, at least in his later years, depended in large measure on the market for stores of every kind. The system of accounting prescribed in the ordinances was

---

[1] W.A.M. 24489.   [2] W.A.M. 14777.
[3] Ibid. The exact sum was £2. 9s. 5¾d.
[4] *Walter de Wenlok*, p. 242.
[5] Ibid. The rule applied also to all manorial produce that could be sold.

strictly enforced between 1295 and 1297; in these years, therefore, we are well placed to discover the degree of dependence
of the household on domanial supplies. This was in some cases
small. Thus the limit of Todenham's contribution in 1295–6
was twelve pigs worth £1. 16s.; that of Bourton-on-the-Hill's,
five oxen worth £2. 2s. 8d.; and in the same year 45 quarters of
barley were sold at Eye, but none sent to the abbot's household.[1]
In Wenlok's later years, his marshal regularly purchased oats
for his horses.[2] If the abbot wanted fresh beef or mutton, he
would probably buy it from a butcher; from the demesnes he
was likely to receive only the not very succulent rejects of a
husbandry designed to produce plough-oxen, milch cows, and
wool-bearing wethers and ewes. The demesnes did, however,
produce pigs for the household and contributed much under
this head to the Martinmas slaughter of livestock that was a
feature of its economy now and for a long time to come. Thus
in 1286, on 10 November, the steward put the carcases of three
oxen, a cow, and thirty pigs from the Western Parts into his
larder at Islip, and eighteen days later fifty-three pigs from
Laleham and Yeoveney were slaughtered and put in store at
Pyrford.[3]

Fourteenth-century abbots of Westminster did not match
Wenlok's confidence in the capacity of the market to supply
the essential needs of his household at reasonable cost, but we
are not in a position to estimate the extent of their dependence
on domanial supplies until the 1360's, when Nicholas de
Litlington was abbot. Even then exact figures elude us, for the
steward of the abbot's household, the official who was ulti-
mately responsible for its entire provisioning, kept two distinct
accounts and did not repeat in the one details already recorded
in the other. His most important transactions were recorded in
his main account, rendered at Michaelmas each year, but the
details of his very considerable petty-cash expenditure were

---

[1] W.A.M. 25924, 8247, 26860. The much larger surplus rye crop at Eye was
also sold this year, but, since the abbot's household used little rye, this sale has no
significance in the present context.

[2] *Walter de Wenlok*, pp. 107, 109, 114; cf. ibid., pp. 196–7. For the use of demesne
produce, see ibid., pp. 134, 136. Many details of arrangements in Wenlok's time
are preserved in the day-accounts of his household (W.A.M. 9251–2, 24490–
502). For the day-account for 1289–90, see *Walter de Wenlok*, pp. 164 ff.

[3] W.A.M. 24490.

entered in a day-account. From the 1360s there survive four of his annual accounts—those for 1362–3, 1364–5, 1367–8 and 1368–9—but no day-accounts.[1] Nevertheless, these four accounts are enough to show that Litlington's household economy rested on very different foundations from those of Wenlok's.

The day when the abbot's demesnes would rear cattle and sheep specifically for his table was still in the future. Under these heads, Litlington, like Wenlok, took from the demesnes merely what was deemed unsuitable for other uses; thus in 1368 or 1369, seven cows, described dauntingly as 'cronate et valde debiles',[2] were supplied to the household from the manor of Denham. Pigs, however, were reared for the abbot's table in large numbers; so, too, was a considerable amount of poultry, and renders in kind from the abbot's tenants were another source of poultry supplies. In the four years mentioned above, the steward's annual account recorded liveries of livestock from the demesnes that were probably worth, on average, c. £22 per annum.[3] It is safe to assume that a substantial, if not the major, part of the household's supply of meat now came from these sources.

As for grain, always a more important item in the household budget than meat, the abbot was now heavily dependent on domanial supplies. Table VIII shows the average annual value of the receipts of grain and malt from all sources which the steward entered in the four annual accounts surviving from the 1360s; the prices used for this purpose are the averages for these years in Thorold Rogers's *History of Agriculture and Prices in England.* According to this mode of reckoning, demesne liveries of grain to the household were worth more than £90 per annum and represented c. 76 per cent of the total grain receipts which the steward acknowledged from all sources in these accounts. What percentage of the household's entire grain supplies was provided by the manorial demesnes we cannot know—the steward's

---

[1] W.A.M. 24510–13. The steward's day-account for the years 1371–3 does, however, survive; so, too, his annual accounts for these years. See P.R.O., S.C. 6/1261/6; W.A.M. 25414–16*. I have preferred to base the remarks in the text on the practice of the 1360s rather than on that of the better documented 1370s on account of the need to get as close as possible to the period when all the demesnes were still in hand; even in the 1360s that period was already slipping into the past.

[2] W.A.M. 24513. The cows were valued at 8s. each.

[3] A rough estimate, using the prices for livestock in Rogers, *History of Agriculture and Prices in England* i. 361–3.

day-accounts where further liveries were, no doubt, recorded, have not survived—but this figure, too, was almost certainly a high one. In any case, it is enough to know that the demesnes were now supplying the household with grain worth more than £90 per annum to realize their great importance in the provisioning of Litlington's household.

TABLE VIII. *The Average Annual Value of the Receipts of Grain and Malt entered in the Annual Account of the Steward of the Abbot's Household, 29 September 1362–29 September 1369**

	Liveries from Demesnes	Purchases	From Other Sources†	Total
Pounds (£)	94	23‡	7	124
Percentage	76	18	6	100

* Average of four years, derived from the accounts for 1362–3, 1364–5, 1367–8 and 1368–9 (W.A.M. 25410–13). The grain and malt have been valued according to the prices in Rogers, *History of Agriculture and Prices in England* i. 232–3. The steward's accounts themselves value the grain and malt received each year, but, since the value of the livery in kind is not always clearly distinguished from the cash livery of the manor in question, it has not been possible to use the steward's own prices in compiling the figures in the Table. It is clear, however, that the steward bought corn and malt, and valued the liveries of corn and malt that he received from the abbot's manors, at prices that were in general lower than those extracted by Rogers for these years. In using Rogers's data, it is necessary to remember that he enters prices under the calendar year of the opening Michaelmas of the account in question; thus his prices for the year 1362 are extracted from accounts running from Mich. 1362 to Mich. 1363.

† Mainly presents and so-called loans of grain from the conventual granger. It may be doubted whether many of the loans were repaid.

‡ The value according to Rogers's prices. In fact the steward spent *c.* £20 per annum on purchases of corn and malt in these years.

The move towards self-sufficiency on the part of the fourteenth-century abbots of Westminster altered the role of the manorial demesnes in the overall economy of the abbot's portion. The demesnes were important to Walter de Wenlok as a source of cash income—an income earned principally by the sale of wool and of corn. How much did Wenlok make in each of these ways? His gross receipts from wool sales amounted to *c.* £68 in 1305–6 and *c.* £77 in the following year,[1] but unhappily we have no means of isolating sales of corn from other items of income until 1308–9, the first full year of account of the vacancy after Wenlok's death; unlike the officials in

[1] *Walter de Wenlok*, pp. 196, 200.

charge of abbatial finances during Wenlok's lifetime, the keeper
during vacancy rendered an account which makes this possible.
The keeper, whose charge excluded Denham, accounted for
gross receipts of £133 from the sale of corn in the course of this
year, and he spent nearly as much (£115) on the purchase of
corn for seed, for fodder, and for liveries to demesne workers.[1]
Both figures, however, were out of the ordinary. That for
receipts, which relates to the corn harvested on the abbatial
demesnes in 1308, was much lower than it would have been,
but for the keeper's failure to cultivate a wheat crop that year;[2]
and his outlay on the purchase of corn reflects the fact that the
abbatial granaries were empty when he took them over at
the end of December 1307—nearly all the corn needed on the
demesnes for seed, fodder, or livery during the remainder of
the manorial year had to be purchased. The figure which the
keeper returned in respect of corn sales the next year, before
he relinquished custody on 25 April 1310, is a better guide to
Wenlok's own scale of production in a typical year towards the
end of his abbacy; this sum was £254.[3] In the same period
(29 September 1309 to 25 April 1310), the keeper spent £13
on the purchase of corn for domanial needs. If we double this
figure, we shall probably be more in danger of exaggerating
than of minimizing the keeper's likely outlay on this item had
his custody of the abbatial demesnes continued for the full
manorial year.

The keeper's expenditure on corn was necessary to maintain
the acreage under seed on the demesnes and the labour force
which cultivated the latter. It seems appropriate, therefore, to
deduct the figure of £26 from that of £254:[4]

$$£254 - £26 = £228.$$

[1] P.R.O., S.C. 6/1109/4. The actual figures are £132. 15s. ¾d., and £115. 1s. 10½d.
Of the latter sum, £7. 13s. 4d. was the price of half the crop of 44 acres of wheat
and 4 acres of mesline sown in accordance with a champarty arrangement at
Yeoveney.

[2] Presumably the run-down of livestock at the beginning of the vacancy made it
impossible to do the fallow-ploughing that was necessary for a wheat crop.

[3] P.R.O., S.C. 6/1109/4. The keeper had no corn in hand when he relinquished
custody; i.e. gross receipts from sales of corn would have been no higher than
£254, had the demesnes been in custody for the entire manorial year.

[4] It will not escape notice that the sum of £254 relates to the acreage cultivated
and harvested in 1308–9, whereas the sum of £26 is an extrapolated figure for
outlay in 1309–10. But, as pointed out in the text, each figure is probably the best
(in the sense of the most typical) of its kind that is available.

Even this figure is still a gross one, which exaggerates net annual income from wainage on the abbatial demesnes in the period in question. To arrive at the net figure, we should have to deduct many other items of expenditure that go unrecorded in the surviving records, and a sum for overheads. The same is true, *mutatis mutandis*, of the figures relating to sales of wool in 1305–6 and 1306–7, given above: these are gross figures, which take no account of the costs of producing the wool in question. From year to year, moreover, the profits of domanial husbandry fluctuated, as prices fluctuated. Yet although this scanty evidence is so imperfect and the figures derived from it so conjectural, we may perhaps conclude that at the beginning of the fourteenth century, when the manorial demesnes were exploited mainly with a view to cash profits, they provided not more than half the total net income of the abbot of Westminster —his net income at this date was probably c. £520 per annum.[1]

Abbot Litlington, in his early years, had a net income of c. £600 per annum;[2] the face value of his income was thus higher than that of Wenlok's, its real value possibly lower. In estimating the proportion of this income that Litlington received in kind, we must take into account, not only liveries of corn and livestock, but also valuable liveries of hay from the demesnes to the household. Eye, a Thames-side manor with ample meadows, was particularly important as a source of hay. As we have seen, the liveries of corn and livestock for which the steward accounted in his annual account were worth c. £116 per annum,[3] and there would have been, in addition, further liveries recorded in

[1] For this figure, see above, p. 59. The estimate of domanial income given in the text takes into account the fact that an abbot of this period, unlike the keeper of his manors during vacancy, had an income from the demesne at Denham. Demesne land of all kinds made up rather less than half the whole acreage of the abbot's estate at this time; see above, pp. 127–8.

[2] A calculation based on the accounts of the steward of the household for the years 1362–3, 1364–5 and 1367–9 (W.A.M. 25410–13). In these years the steward was the sole receiver, and the whole of the abbot's income, whether received in kind or in cash, was valued in his annual account; later, in the course of the 1370s, he lost this position, as a considerable part of the abbot's income was deflected into the private coffers of the abbot. The rise in the abbot's income from c. £520 per annum to c. £600 per annum between the beginning of the fourteenth century and the 1360s is explained mainly, though not entirely, by the fact that Litlington enjoyed an income from the manor of Islip; Wenlok sacrificed this for the time being in 1299, in the exchange that restored Deerhurst to his demesne. See below, pp. 173–4, 196–7 and n.

[3] c. £94 in corn; c. £22 in livestock; see above, pp. 136–7.

detail only in his day-account. At least 20 per cent of his income was received under this form and not in cash.

How much more the demesnes contributed, in the form of cash, we do not know. By now, however, wool was certainly the main cash crop. Litlington's gross receipts from the sale of wool were £82 in 1362–3 and £153 in 1364–5.[1] Arable husbandry, by contrast, was now of minor importance as a source of cash income—a change that is explained not only by the deflection of its products away from the market and into the household, but also by the leasing of demesne land; this policy Simon de Langham and Nicholas de Litlington carried further than their predecessors of the early fourteenth century.[2] The manorial accounts of the period reflect this new state of affairs. At Eye, for example, sales of corn brought in no more than *c.* £6 per annum gross[3] in the first ten years of Litlington's abbacy; in the last ten years of Wenlok's abbacy, the corresponding figure is *c.* £16 per annum.[4] And at Hardwicke, where the abbot had a demesne of *c.* 760 acres, the gross receipts from corn sales were only *c.* £18. 10*s*. in 1371–2 and *c.* £13 the following year.[5]

The Portion of the Prior and Convent

The domestic economy of the convent of Westminster is first outlined in the early twelfth century, in a document plausibly assigned by Armitage Robinson, its editor, to the vacancy following the death of Abbot Gilbert Crispin in 1117 or 1118.[6] These early arrangements belong, therefore, to the period before the division of goods, when the abbot of Westminster and his monks drew upon common funds. But any domestic record

---

[1] W.A.M. 24510–11. No wool sales are recorded in the accounts of the steward of the household in 1367–8 or in 1368–9. None may have been made in these years; but it is more likely that the proceeds were accounted for locally by bailiffs and reeves and help to swell the steward's receipts from these officials.

[2] Below, pp. 149 ff.

[3] i.e. with no deduction made for the costs of tillage.

[4] W.A.M. 26862 ff., 26918 ff. The figures relate to, respectively, the decade beginning at Michaelmas 1362 and that ending at Michaelmas 1307. The earlier of the two figures is the average of eight years in that period; the later, the average of seven years. Fictitious sales, into the abbot's household, which are entered in some of the accounts in the decade 1362–72, have been excluded from consideration.

[5] W.A.M. 8443–4. The exact figure in 1371–2 was £18. 9*s*. 9½*d*.; in 1372–3, £12. 19*s*. 5¾*d*.

[6] *Gilbert Crispin*, p. 41; cf. ibid., pp. 44–5. For the date of Gilbert Crispin's death, see now Knowles, Brooke, and London, *Heads of Religious Houses, England and Wales, 940–1216*, p. 77.

of this period is necessarily concerned mainly with the needs of the convent, since the lion's share of monastic revenues was devoted to the upkeep of the eighty or so monks who formed the early-twelfth-century community; in a vacancy, moreover, only the needs of the convent need be considered.

The monastic economy of this period was, it seems, a mainly cash economy. The monks reckoned their basic needs in terms of a composite bundle of goods and money. Each week they needed 6 coombs of wheat, 20 pecks of malt, 10 of grout, and 3 coombs of oats, and the sum of £3. 7s. for the kitchen. Together with a contribution of 13s. 4d. to the upkeep of the monastic servants, these liveries in cash and kind constituted the so-called farm of the monks for a week, and we are to understand that, in the course of the year, the inlying manors of the Abbey supplied one or more such farms, according to size. Distant manors, however, did not send supplies in kind: for them a week's farm was a comprehensive cash payment of £8. 10s. Further, the other needs of the monks—their alms, pittances, fuel, clothing, the Maundy distribution, and the needs of their servants over and above the provision made for these in a week's farm, were all reckoned in cash terms. For alms and pittances, for example, the sum of £32 was needed each year, and this came from Benfleet, Fanton, Paglesham, Wennington, and Comberton; the chamberlain's annual allowance of £70 for the clothing of the monks came from the London properties, among others. Here is a picture of a community that had passed far beyond the stage of self-sufficiency: it purchased, not only cloth—for this even St. Dunstan's monks were no doubt dependent on bought supplies—but fuel and, to a certain extent, food and drink, the basic items of housekeeping.

A century and more later, the needs of the monks of Westminster were not precisely those of Gilbert Crispin's time. Numbers in the community had fallen sharply. As far as food, drink, and clothing were concerned, however, this fall was almost certainly more than offset by a rise in the number of servants, officials, and corrodians. No less important to those concerned in the Abbey's domestic arrangements was the refusal of the modern monk to be content with the simple, meatless diet of his predecessors. Moreover, no religious house in London or its environs could hope to buy fish cheaply. And the monks of Westminster were fastidious in these matters; when, for example, the pittancer provided them with the dish of fish to which they were entitled from the issues of the church of Oakham, it was his duty to choose the fish from the best that could be bought on the day in question.[1] Still, however, for both the monks and their army of dependents, bread and ale were the staple foods. It was the ease or difficulty of obtaining from other sources the vast quantities of grain consumed yearly under these heads that the prior and convent had chiefly in mind when they decided what should now be done with the produce of their demesnes. We find them in some periods a little ahead of the abbot—more dependent on the market in the middle decades of the thirteenth century than he perhaps was at that time, yet quicker than he to fall back on domanial supplies at the end of the century.

When the prior and convent acquired their separate portion, in 1225, it was apparently agreed that $2\frac{1}{2}$ quarters of wheat were required daily, and 3 quarters of barley and 6 of oats every other day, for the bread and ale of the monks themselves, their corrodians and guests, and all other persons entitled to receive liveries in this form. Annually, therefore, the prior and convent needed $912\frac{1}{2}$ quarters of wheat, $547\frac{1}{2}$ quarters of barley, and 1,095 quarters of oats.[2] These rations are not recorded in any of the surviving compositions of that period; we learn of them from Ware's *Customary*, which derives them explicitly from the 'prima assignacio segregatae porcionis conventus'. They were evidently agreed at that time, but never set down in writing. The *Customary* also records the financial arrangements considered necessary in the circumstances. It was assumed that wheat could be bought for 5s. per quarter, barley for 3s., and oats for 2s., and, accordingly, to the internal cellarer, the official responsible for laying in the stores of grain needed for bread and ale,[3] was assigned an income that would enable him to purchase $912\frac{1}{2}$ quarters of wheat, $547\frac{1}{2}$ quarters of barley, and 1,095 quarters of oats at these prices; the necessary sum was £419. 15s.

It is likely, though not certain, that, in estimating the amount

---

[1] *Customary* ii. 76. [2] Ibid., pp. 102–3.
[3] Ibid., p. 71. The external cellarer had oversight of the convent's manors and was in a more general sense responsible for provisioning the monastery.

of grain needed day by day and week by week, Abbot Berking and his monks assumed the existence of a community numbering eighty monks, the number on which, long ago, Gilbert Crispin had based his assignment to the chamber.[1] If so, the cellarer could have made do with less than the above-mentioned sum in the first half of the thirteenth century, when the community was much smaller than in Crispin's time; but in the long run this antiquated mode of reckoning provided a very useful protection against a rise in corn prices.

These details, perhaps, do not matter very much. The significant feature of the arrangement described in the *Customary* is the underlying assumption that everything could and indeed should properly be expressed in cash terms. It does not of course follow that the cellarer did in fact purchase all his grain in Abbot Berking's time, or in Ware's, but the presumption is that he acquired most of it in this way.

If so, a considerable change occurred in the closing decades of the thirteenth century. To perceive it, however, it is necessary to make use of a document from a later period, the account of the monastic granger for the year 1348–9;[2] with the exception of Ware's *Customary*, this is the earliest surviving record of the amount of grain required by the prior and convent of Westminster in the course of a single year. The administrative arrangements outlined in the *Customary* were now superseded: the granger was the universal provider of grain for bread and ale in the monastery, and manorial officials sent liveries of corn to his granary in the precincts. If, however, there was a need to purchase corn, the transaction was carried through by the conventual treasurers, who had taken over most of the financial functions of the internal and external cellarers of Ware's time. In the course of the year 1348–9, the granger received the following grain:[3]

				Malt		
Wheat	*Barley*	*Drage*	*Oats*	*Barley*	*Drage*	*Oats*
603	456	169	182	143	440	7

[1] Ibid., p. 102. Unfortunately, there is a hiatus in the text of the *Customary* at the material point, but the number *quater viginti* occurring immediately before this probably refers to the number of monks for whom the cellarer was, in theory, to cater. For Abbot Crispin's assignment to the chamber, see above, p. 85.

[2] W.A.M. 19155.

[3] The figures are correct to the nearest quarter and exclude the remainder of the previous year.

Thus the granger received *c*. 600 quarters of wheat, *c*. 810 quarters of other grains, and *c*. 590 quarters of malt. According to the rates of increment recorded in the brew-house this year, this volume of malt represents in sum *c*. 530 quarters of the grains from which it was made.[1] We may therefore summarize the figures by saying that in 1348–9 the granger received *c*. 600 quarters of wheat and *c*. 1,340 quarters of other grains, either before or after malting. The wheat was destined for the Abbey's bakery, the other grains mainly for the brew-house; a little of the oats, however, was used for fodder.

The year 1348–9 was abnormal by any standards, since twenty-six monks—perhaps half, or more than half, the entire complement—died in the early summer of 1349, when the Black Death struck the monastery, and no doubt the servants and dependents of the Abbey did not escape the plague. Moreover, later accounts show both that the amount of corn coming into the granary was not constant from year to year, and that the relative proportions of the different grains comprised in the whole changed with changing prices; more drage, for example, was obtained for the brew-house, and less barley, in years when barley was dear. Nevertheless, these figures, recording as they do the grain which the granger thought it prudent to lay in before the catastrophe, which he could not have predicted, occurred, are a useful guide to the needs of the monastery at any time in the first half of the fourteenth century; throughout this period, numbers were probably much as they were in 1348 and the opening months of 1349. We shall probably not exaggerate the needs of the community around the year 1300 if we assume that they were of this order of magnitude. How then did the prior and convent obtain these necessary stores of grain at the beginning of the fourteenth century?

We know only what can be inferred from the very few accounts of the conventual treasurers to survive from this

---

[1] The rates of increment in respect of the increase of volume in malting which are recorded in the granger's accounts fluctuate widely from year to year. Thus in the first five years for which such accounts survive (1348–50, 1351–3, 1354–5) they were, in the case of barley, respectively, *c*. 1 quarter in 7; *c*. 1 in 4; *c*. 1 in 3.5; *c*. 1 in 6; and *c*. 1 in 22. In 1348–9 the rate for drage was *c*. 1 in 11; that for oats, *c*. 1 in 21. See W.A.M. 19155 ff.

period. In 1304–5 and 1307–8, the following purchases of grain and malt, in quarters, are recorded:[1]

	Wheat	Barley	Drage or Mesline	Oats	Malt
1304–5	144	364	15	876	102
1307–8	138	458	2	274	184

In 1304–5, the total cost of the purchases was £258; in 1307–8 it was £262.[2] Unhappily, the second of the two accounts in question does not cover a complete year: it runs from 25 November 1307 to 20 September 1308, and this fact may explain why purchases in 1307–8 were more than 400 quarters down on the total for 1304–5. But the near identity of the amount spent on grain and malt in each of these years suggests a more cogent reason for these fluctuations, namely that the prior and convent adjusted their purchases to the state of the market, buying up to but not beyond a certain figure. The average purchases of the two years were: *c.* 140 quarters of wheat, *c.* 990 quarters of other grains, and *c.* 140 quarters of malt. If, as seems likely, the malt was, in both years, barley malt,[3] the last item represents perhaps 124 quarters of grain.[4] If, therefore, these figures are typical of their period, the prior and convent must have obtained at least *c.* 460 quarters of wheat each year from their manorial demesnes or their rectories, and perhaps *c.* 230 quarters of cheaper grains. At the prices obtaining in the first decade of the fourteenth century, such liveries were probably worth not less than *c.* £165 per annum.[5] The demesnes and rectories supplied nearly 40 per cent, reckoning by value, of all the grain consumed by the prior and convent, their servants

---

[1] W.A.M. 19841–2. The exact periods covered by these accounts are: 24 June 1304–24 June 1305; 25 Nov. 1307–29 Sept. 1308. The account for 29 Sept. 1297–29 Sept. 1298 is extant but in too poor a condition at the material points to be useful (W.A.M. 19838).

[2] £258. 6s. 1½d., and £262. 0s. 5¼d.

[3] The malt purchased in 1304–5 was certainly barley malt, and the price paid suggests that the same is true of the purchases of 1307–8.

[4] A rough estimate, based on the average of the increments for barley in malting recorded in the five earliest extant granger's accounts.

[5] A rough estimate, using the average prices for the decade in Rogers, *History of Agriculture and Prices in England* i. 245. I have assumed that, of the grains other than wheat, *c.* 40 per cent was barley, *c.* 40 per cent drage, and *c.* 20 per cent oats— figures which almost certainly underestimate the livery of barley and overestimate that of oats.

and dependents at this time. For wheat, always the dearest of the grains, the monks now relied principally on their own manors and churches; indeed, it may have been their practice to buy this grain only towards the end of the year, as demesne supplies gave out—hence the fact that the treasurers bought a considerable amount of barley and oats between 29 September 1303 and 24 June 1304, as we know from their account for this period, but only six quarters of wheat.[1]

The trend towards self-sufficiency was much accentuated in the first half of the fourteenth century, until, in the 1350s and 1360s, the prior and convent were buying a mere 20 per cent or less of their grain. Table IX, showing this state of affairs, is derived from the granger's accounts, which now begin to survive in good numbers; his average grain receipts in each of the decades 1350–60 and 1360–70 have been valued in accordance with Thorold Rogers's annual prices for grain in these years. As in the case of the figures relating to the abbot's household given earlier,[2] so in this, the cash figures in the Table have no absolute validity, for the price of grain in the markets available to the monks of Westminster in this period was often different from and, indeed, in the case of the convent's purchases, considerably higher than that obtaining in the markets supplying Rogers with his data;[3] the percentages, however, probably reflect with fair accuracy the relative importance of the several sources of grain drawn upon by the monks of Westminster at this time.

The prior and convent of Westminster possessed, in their appropriated churches, a source of income not shared by the abbot, who resigned all such property to them after the division of goods in 1225, and in the 1350s and 1360s their churches sent considerable quantities of grain to the granaries at Westminster; some of this was tithe corn, the rest the produce of the rectory farms. Because the granger did not always distinguish the livery received from a church, on the one hand, from

---

[1] W.A.M. 19840. This account, covering a nine-month period, records the purchase of 271 quarters, 1 bushel of barley, and 537 quarters, 2 bushels of oats.

[2] Above, p. 137.

[3] See, more particularly, Table IX, n. By contrast, the abbot of Westminster purchased corn at prices that were in general a little lower than Rogers's prices in this period; see Table VIII, n. (above, p. 137). But the abbot made most of his purchases in his own manors and probably at preferential prices.

that of the demesne of the manor in question, on the other, we do not know the exact proportions of each in this period, but orders of magnitude are sufficiently clear. Together, the two kinds of livery made up very nearly 70 per cent of total grain

TABLE IX. *The Average Annual Value of the Grain and Malt received by the Conventual Granger, 1350–1370**

	Liveries from Demesnes and Churches	Corn Rents	Purchases†	From Other Sources‡	Total
1350–60					
Pounds (£)	197	18	57	19	291
Percentage	68	6	20	6	100
1360–70					
Pounds (£)	292	51	61	18	422
Percentage	69	12	15	4	100

* The decades run, in each case, from Michaelmas to Michaelmas, and in each case the figures are the averages for six years: 1351–3, 1354–7, and 1358–9; 1363–5 and 1366–70. They are derived from W.A.M. 19157 ff. Values are according to the prices in Rogers, *History of Agriculture and Prices in England* i. 232–3. Very similar figures are obtained by the use of the decennial averages, ibid. i. 245.

† To facilitate comparison with the figures in other columns, purchases have been valued according to Rogers's prices. In fact the conventual treasurers, who were responsible for buying grain, spent *c.* £110 per annum on corn and malt in the decade 1350–60 (= average of six years: 1350–2, 1353–4, 1356–8, and 1359–60) and *c.* £92 per annum in the next decade (= average of eight years: 1360–5, 1366–7, and 1368–70). In the decade 1350–60, however, purchases were particularly large in three years for which the granger's accounts do not survive, viz., 1350–1 (£361), 1357–8 (£151), and 1359–60 (£137), and in neither decade is there an exact correspondence in date between the treasurers' and the granger's accounts that are still extant. Nevertheless, it is clear that the prior and convent of Westminster paid in general higher prices for their purchases of grain than the prices extracted by Rogers in this period. See W.A.M. 19846 ff.

‡ Many of the items comprised under this head in the Table were transfers of grain from other obedientiaries, who may themselves have acquired it by purchase or as livery.

receipts in each decade; the manorial demesnes probably supplied between 40 and 50 per cent of the latter. Although, therefore, the prior and convent now obtained a high proportion of their necessary grain supplies from their own possessions, as did the abbot of Westminster, manorial demesnes were less important to them than to him in this context: in the 1360s, Abbot

Litlington's demesnes supplied between 70 and 80 per cent of the grain consumed by his household.[1]

Nearly all the liveries of grain received from the manorial demesnes of the convent's portion came from the manors assigned to the treasurers or administered by these officials on behalf of other obedientiaries.[2] In the case of these manors, the arable demesnes probably provided very little in the way of a cash income by the end of the thirteenth century; wool was the main crop, as it was later to be on the abbot's demesnes as well.[3] The ministers' accounts for Feering illustrate the unimportance of corn as a cash crop on these manors at this time. Gross receipts from the sale of corn here amounted on average to less than £10[4] per annum in the first decade of the fourteenth century; yet tillage averaged 438 acres per annum in the same period.[5]

To the other obedientiaries the demesnes supplied cash rather than kind down to the very end of the period when they were in hand. Even on these manors, however, the Abbey's income from the rents of the tenant-land often rivalled and sometimes exceeded the profits of husbandry. This seems to have been the case at Westerham, for example, and at Knowle, two of the manors assigned to the anniversary of Eleanor of Castile.[6] Almost certainly, the manorial demesnes provided less than half the income of *c.* £563 per annum possessed by these officials around the year 1300.[7]

(iii) *The Demesnes on Lease Again*

The Chronology of Leasing

The difficulty of making large-scale husbandry pay in the Middle Ages has become a commonplace among historians of

---

[1] Above, p. 136.   [2] For these manors, see below, pp. 337 ff.
[3] Above, p. 140.   [4] £9. 15s. 1½d.
[5] Average of nine years in the decade Michaelmas 1300–Michaelmas 1310; see W.A.M. 25603–22.

[6] An impressionistic judgement, based on W.A.M. 26393 ff. (accounts for Westerham) and W.A.M. 27699 ff. (accounts for Knowle). Demesne enterprise at Westerham included a vaccary of some forty to fifty cows that was at farm in some years during this period. At Knowle, in 1302–3, the monks capitalized some of their resources in the sale of 414 oaks for £90 (W.A.M. 27701).

[7] For the income of the obedientiaries in question see above, p. 59, but, to the figure of *c.* £548 per annum shown there, add *c.* £15 per annum from the royal foundations.

the period, but when exactly did landlords themselves become aware of this truth? Illumination can hardly have dawned before the introduction of an efficient system of account, and this seems to have been delayed on nearly all estates until the second half of the thirteenth century; until this time manorial accounts, where they existed at all, were probably too simple, too much concerned with the financial position of the accounting official *vis-à-vis* his lord, to shed light on profit and loss on the part of the enterprise as a whole. In the late thirteenth century it proved not enough to have an account for each manor: a profit calculation, showing the net return of each property and how it was made up, was essential if a landlord was to discover the true state of affairs on his estate. The abbot of Westminster began to require such information of some of his accountants and auditors towards the end of the thirteenth century; the prior and convent, of theirs, probably not until a decade or more later. Evidently the lessons so learnt struck home, for quite soon both the abbot and the convent began to put the less profitable or least accessible of their demesne acres on lease. Thus, early in the fourteenth century, the abbot experimented with the policy of leasing the entire demesne at Pinvin and that at Staines and the greater part of the arable demesne at Laleham;[1] at Sutton-under-Brailes, he was so sure of the need for retrenchment that he demised some acres of demesne land to tenants on secure, customary terms.[2] The prior and convent, for their part, leased the demesne lands at Pattiswick, in the manor of Feering, from 1304,[3] and by 1339–40, the greater part of their demesne at Ashford was on lease.[4]

The early fourteenth century was not a period when the signs of the economic times were easy to read, and evidently the abbot and convent of Westminster did not feel sure that they had interpreted these correctly, for the bolder of these early experiments in leasing demesne land were for the most part

[1] The lease at Pinvin, which is first mentioned in 1306–7 but may have been made before this date, came to an end in 1318; that at Staines, though made for a five-year term, was in fact in operation for only a year; the demesne at Laleham was on lease between 1302 and 1305. See W.A.M. 22093 ff., 27113–14; *Walter de Wenlok*, p. 111 n.
[2] Glos. Records Office, D 1099/M48.   [3] W.A.M. 25612 ff.
[4] W.A.M. 26729 ff.

short-lived. Decisions after 1350 can at first have been no easier. On the one hand, the unprecedented scarcity of labour further undermined the precarious economics of large-scale production; on the other, the high corn prices of the 1350s and 1360s, if a temptation to landlords to stay in the field as producers, disinclined them, as consumers, to do without demesne liveries. The fate of the demesnes of the five so-called principal manors of the prior and convent, from each of which the latter were accustomed to receive liveries of corn on a large scale, suggests uncertainty of mind at Westminster about the best course of action in these and the ensuing decades. The manor of Aldenham—the tenant-land as well as the demesne—was demised to Walter de Aldebury as early as 1352–3, and after Aldebury, who did not see out his term of twenty years, another lessee, John Dytton, is mentioned.[1] But both demesne and tenant-land at Aldenham were in hand again by 1371–2.[2] From *c.* 1370 the demesne at Feering was now on lease, now in hand, until the policy of leasing finally triumphed here in the first decade of the fifteenth century.[3] The demesne at Stevenage was still in hand in 1375;[4] those at Battersea and Wandsworth and Wheathampstead, in the 1390s.[5] The prior and convent were cultivating part of their large demesne at Ashwell in the first decade of the fifteenth century.[6] The demesne at Denham, belonging to the abbot's portion of lands, was not demised until the 1430s.[7] Other reasons, namely their continued esteem for wool as a cash crop, and the demand for mutton in the abbot's household, encouraged the monks to keep some demesne pastures in hand even later than this. At Bourton-on-the-Hill, for example, the abbot of Westminster continued to need the

[1] W.A.M. 19849 ff.; and for Aldebury and Dytton, see below, p. 152. The demise to Dytton, which was also for twenty years, was made in 1360–1.

[2] W.A.M. 26094; cf. W.A.M. 19866. For liveries of corn from Aldenham to the monastery in the period after 1371–2, see W.A.M. 19171 ff.

[3] W.A.M. 25695 ff.

[4] P.R.O., S.C. 6/872/6.

[5] For Battersea and Wandsworth, see the liveries of corn from that manor recorded in the accounts of the conventual granger in this period (W.A.M. 19201 ff.). However, the demesne at Downe, in Wandsworth, was on lease from 1396 (W.A.M. 27583 ff.). For Wheathampstead, see W.A.M. 8929–30.

[6] W.A.M. 26293. In 1410–11, probably the last year in which a demesne was cultivated, 75 acres were sown.

[7] W.A.M. 3411–12; and for the chronology of leasing on the abbot's demesnes, see *Economic History Rev.*, 2nd ser., 22 (1969), 17 ff.

services of a master shepherd until *c.* 1450; and at Eye he was still grazing his own sheep at that date.[1]

Yet it was the arguments in favour of leasing that prevailed at Westminster after 1350: every decade that passed saw more and more of the Abbey's demesnes put on lease. Moreover, it was now usually a case of all or nothing: the demesne was demised in its entirety, not little by little, here an acre, there an acre, in the piecemeal fashion characteristic of the first half of the century. About 1370, early in the abbacy of Nicholas de Litlington, it becomes apparent that a new period is opening in the history of these properties. On the Abbey's estates, as, it seems, was the case universally, the new policy of leasing lasted as long as the Middle Ages themselves, and indeed far beyond that term—nothing has ever induced landowners operating on the scale of Westminster Abbey to return whole-heartedly to the practice of cultivating large arable farms themselves, and the collegiate body that succeeded to the possessions of the monks of Westminster after 1540 has been no exception to this rule. The remainder of this chapter will be devoted to an account of the main features of the new arrangements on the monastic estate; this is its second major topic.

Some of these arrangements can be explained only by reference to earlier periods in the history of the estate—to that immediately preceding, when the abbot and convent discovered the enormous costs and small rewards of demesne husbandry, or to the early Middle Ages, when the estate suffered so grievously from the inroads of the perpetual tenant. But the late-medieval monks of Westminster were not always glancing over their shoulders at the past; the pressure of contemporary events is also reflected in the new arrangements: these were devised in a period when an unprecedented abundance of land and scarcity of labour made the little store of economic wisdom inherited by the current generation of monks from their predecessors obsolescent.

The Lessees

Most of the lessees to whom the abbot of Westminster demised his demesnes in the later Middle Ages were peasants—a term

[1] W.A.M. 24448, 26969 ff.

to be understood in the present context as denoting a self-employed farmer who took part in the working of his own land; many were the reeves and rent-collectors of the manors where the demesnes were situated. Not infrequently, the lease passed from father to son, and the family's hold on the farm was secured for long periods of time. Richard and Thomas Stowte, each in turn rent-collector, are mentioned as lessees of the demesne at Sutton-under-Brailes between 1442 and 1497, and the Curry family farmed the demesne at Chaceley for about fifty years in this century.[1] Not every lessee, however, was a peasant; one exception to the rule is John Monemouth, a merchant of Gloucester, to whom the demesne at Hardwicke was demised in 1373.[2]

The demesnes of the prior and convent more often passed into the hands of capitalists such as Monemouth, who had not made their money in land and did not depend for an income mainly on the success of their investments in husbandry. In the fourteenth century the type is represented by members of the professional classes. Thus Walter de Aldebury, who obtained the lease of the manor of Aldenham in the middle of the century, was a royal clerk, and so was his successor, John Dytton.[3] Later, citizens of London made their appearance. Thomas Pernell, for example, who took a lease of the demesne and rectory of Paddington in 1489, was a butcher of London, and James Ewell, lessee of Downe, in 1517, a haberdasher of London.[4] In 1519, the demesne and rectory of South Benfleet were demised to William Cowper, a merchant of the Staple, jointly with Robert Markham, who is described as a gentleman of London.[5] Yet on the convent's portion, too, many of the lessees of this period were peasants.

The Form and Content of the Leases

Every surviving lease of a demesne which has been noticed in this period at Westminster Abbey was in the chirograph form that conferred a common law interest in the land, and each part once bore, if it does not still do so, the common seal

[1] *Economic History Rev.*, 2nd ser., 22 (1969), 20–1.
[2] Ibid. Monemouth's wife was a tenant jointly with him.
[3] *Cal. Pat. R., 1358–61*, p. 147; ibid., *1361–4*, p. 346; *Cal. Cl. R., 1354–60*, p. 352; and see above, p. 150.
[4] W.A.M. Reg. Bk. i. 39ᵛ–40; ibid. ii. 111.   [5] Ibid. 139–139ᵛ.

of the Abbey and the seal of the lessee. We owe our virtually complete information about the indentures made after 1485 to the monks' practice of copying them into registers, for these books have survived.[1] At first, in the fourteenth century, the indentures were dated either locally, at the manor to which they related, or at Westminster. By the end of the fifteenth century all were dated in Chapter at Westminster. This does not mean, however, that every lessee now attended at Westminster; nor should we envisage the taking of the common seal to the manors in the fourteenth century, in cases of that period where indentures were dated there. In both periods the seal of the lessee was, almost certainly, applied locally, in advance of the application of the common seal in Chapter.[2]

In the fourteenth and early fifteenth centuries, most of the Abbey's lessees received some livestock and implements at the inception of their lease. Unless the arrangement was of the champarty type—and by the fifteenth century this form was uncommon—no large provision of livestock was made: draught beasts were provided, with perhaps a few cows and pigs, and nearly always some poultry and seed-corn. When John Clerk, the rector, took over the demesne at Launton in 1386, he received, in addition to seed-corn, livestock valued at £11. 7s. 8d.[3] On the other hand, even this level of expenditure would have been beyond the means of many farmers. Thomas de Parham, who was granted a twenty years' lease of the demesne at Morden in 1358–9, but apparently on the understanding that he purchase the existing stock from the Abbey, was still paying off his debt of £16. 19s. 8¼d. three years later.[4]

However, in this respect, too, the practice of the abbot and that of the convent eventually diverged. By the end of the

[1] W.A.M. Reg. Bks. i ff., of which i and ii cover the period down to the Dissolution. For a fourteenth-century example of a lease, see W.A.M. 15175, the lease of the demesne at Islip, in 1395, to John Derby, chaplain of St. Edward the Confessor's chapel at Islip, for twelve years.

[2] For an example of sealing in two stages, but of a different kind of document, see the ordination of the vicarage of Aldenham in 1399; the seal of the abbot and convent was applied in Chapter at Westminster on 30 Nov.; that of the vicar (who was already in possession of a portion in this church) at Aldenham the same day (W.A.M. Bk. iii. 8–10).

[3] W.A.M. 15383. No values are given for the poultry which Clerk received. The demesne at Launton in the early fourteenth century comprised *c.* 330 acres of arable.

[4] W.A.M. 19854, 19857.

fifteenth century, the stock and land lease had all but disappeared from the abbot's lands; only the lessee at Pensham
was still provided with stock.[1] But on the convent's lands the
demesnes at Battersea and Wandsworth, South Benfleet,
Westerham, Hendon, and Steventon, and several others beside,
were leased with livestock and implements down to the Dissolution.[2] Those who benefited by this arrangement were not
all lessees of the peasant type; thus William Cowper and Robert
Markham, the two Londoners to whom the demesne at South
Benfleet was demised in 1519, received livestock valued at
£23. 16s. 8d. on this occasion.[3]

The vast majority of leases in this period were for terms of
years, not for lives or a life. At first prudence must have favoured
the term of years, and a short term at that, but, whatever the
monks' own inclination in this matter, after 1285 their liberty
of action was restricted by the Statute of Westminster II.
Chapter 41 of this statute forbade religious to alienate the lands
given to them by their founders; if alienation took place, the
alienee would forfeit the property in question to the donor who
had given it to the monks in the first place.[4] Leases for lives
came under this ban, and the king exercised his power to dispense from the rule sparingly. The monks of Westminster
seldom obtained licences for such leases. One of their successful
applications, however, was made in 1373, on the occasion of the
demise of the demesne at Hardwicke to John and Elizabeth
Monemouth for their joint and several lives.[5] Earlier, in 1316,
Edward II licensed a demise of Knowle, in Warwickshire, to
Ralph de Perham for his life.[6]

Of the term of years in Abbey leases of this period, it is true
on the whole to say, the later the date, the longer the term.
The demesne at Claygate for example, was demised for terms of,

---

[1] *Economic History Rev.*, 2nd ser., 22 (1969), 21.

[2] W.A.M. Reg. Bk. ii, *passim*.

[3] Ibid. 139ᵛ. A new demise of this demesne to William Cowper and his wife in
1524 included livestock to the same value (ibid. 205ᵛ).

[4] 13 Edward I, cap. 41. See also *Councils and Synods*, ed. Powicke and Cheney,
ii. 965; and on life-tenancies and the term of years, Simpson, *Introduction to the
History of the Land Law*, pp. 66 ff.

[5] *Cal. Pat. R., 1370–4*, p. 366.

[6] Ibid., *1313–17*, p. 435; see also ibid., *1327–30*, p. 198. The terms of this lease
provided for an increase of rent from £46. 13s. 4d. per annum to £52 per annum
after the first ten years.

respectively, five and three years in the 1350s, but by the 1480s the term here was nine years, and by the Dissolution, twenty-four.[1] At Aldenham, which was demised for twenty years in the mid-fourteenth century, Humphrey Coningsby, a serjeant at law, was, in 1504, granted a thirty-year term,[2] and in the same decade John Mannyng, described as a yeoman of Westminster, obtained a thirty-one-year lease at Launton, where terms of seven or thirteen years had been usual a century and a half earlier.[3]

Aldenham, Claygate, and Launton were all assigned to the prior and convent, and Claygate, in particular, where the term lengthened considerably after the beginning of the sixteenth century, is typical of the conventual demesnes as a whole. It was, however, only in these last decades that any of the convent's lessees was allowed a term as long as thirty years. The longest of all that are noted in the lease-books of this period is the sixty-year term which William Porter, a clerk in Chancery, was allowed in respect of the conventual manor of Morden and the rectory of Morden in 1511.[4]

On the abbot's demesnes, by contrast, a thirty-year term was in no way unusual, even in the mid-fifteenth century, and not a few lessees were allowed longer than this. Leases for years determinable on lives gave some tenants a measure of dynastic security, without violation of the law prohibiting demises of monastic property for lives. In 1427 the demesne at Hardwicke, long since recovered from the Monemouths, was demised for forty years, determinable on the lives of John Solas, Joan, his wife, and John and Thomas, their sons;[5] and later, in 1453, that at Longdon, in Worcestershire, was demised for forty years, determinable on the lives of John Holdy, his wife, and their two sons.[6] The different geographical situation of, respectively, the abbot's demesnes and those of the convent may explain

---

[1] W.A.M. 19849, 19852; W.A.M. Reg. Bk. i. 12ᵛ; ibid. ii. 225, 254.
[2] Ibid. 191ᵛ. The demise to Coningsby included the rectory as well as the demesne. For the earlier leases of Aldenham, see above, p. 150.
[3] W.A.M. Reg. Bk. ii. 225ᵛ; cf. W.A.M. 15369 ff.
[4] W.A.M. Reg. Bk. ii. 212.
[5] W.A.M. 8466; and for the stock received by John Solas on this occasion, see W.A.M. 8467. On leases for years determinable on lives see *The Agrarian History of England and Wales*, vol. iv, *1500–1640*, ed. J. Thirsk (Cambridge, 1967), pp. 320–1.
[6] W.A.M. 21030; see also *Economic History Rev.*, 2nd ser., 22 (1969), 24.

these differences in terms; each party may have followed the custom of the region.

The right to assign the lease to another, which is so clearly implied in a long term, if conferred on a sole lessee, is mentioned explicitly in leases made towards the end of the fifteenth century; then it is sometimes hedged about with the proviso that the assignee must make his own indenture with the monks; in some leases a space of two months was allowed.[1] On the other hand, the practice was not forbidden in earlier leases, as, for example, subleasing so often was; quite probably it was tolerated long before it begins to be regularly mentioned. The requirement that assignees enter into agreements with them suggests that the monks were alive to the importance of securing for themselves the advantage of a rise in rents, should one occur; but even in the early sixteenth century rents were so seldom raised on a change of tenancy that this seems a remote possibility.[2]

Although arrangements for crop-sharing eventually became rare on these estates, in the fourteenth century both the abbot and the convent required some of their lessees to pay the whole or a proportion of their annual dues in kind. For example, John Clerk, who had a demise of the manor of Kelvedon in the 1350s, owed 20 quarters of wheat per annum, beside a money rent of £13. 6s. 8d.,[3] and corn renders accounted for nearly the entire rent asked of the lessee of the demesne at Islip forty years later, in 1395.[4] This is only to be expected, given the importance of corn liveries to both the abbot and the convent earlier in the century, while the demesnes were still in hand.

Within a few years, however, the demesne at Islip was on lease for a money rent,[5] and, in the course of the century, corn renders became unusual anywhere on the abbot's portion of lands. They persisted on several conventual manors throughout the fifteenth century, and early in the sixteenth century they

---

[1] e.g. W.A.M. Reg. Bk. i. 30 (Hardwicke, 1488); ibid. i. 40 (Paddington, manor and rectory, 1489). In the case of the rectory of Longdon, in 1485, only one month was allowed for the making of the new indenture (ibid. i. 6).

[2] Below, pp. 158 ff.

[3] W.A.M. 19849. The demise to Clerk was for his life.

[4] W.A.M. 15175. This indenture is dated 19 Jan. 1396, but the twelve-year lease which it records ran from 29 Sept. 1395.

[5] W.A.M. 14831.

were introduced more widely here. In 1518, the annual rent of the manor of Halliford was set at £11. 6s. 8d. and 21 quarters of good, clean corn in season;[1] and in 1511 a rent of £13. 6s. 8d. and 10 quarters of oats per annum was asked of the incoming tenant at Down,[2] in Northolt. At the Dissolution, the lessees of the demesnes in two of the five principal manors of the prior and convent, Battersea and Wandsworth, and Stevenage, still owed corn rents.[3]

Whatever their form, annual dues on the Abbey's demesnes show divergent trends in the second half of the fourteenth century: in some places they moved upwards from the level agreed initially after the Black Death of 1348–9; in others, down. This is very likely owing in part to difficulty experienced by the monks and their lessees in discovering, in a period when so many of the familiar landmarks of the agrarian scene were removed, what burden the farms in question would bear; but it also reflects real local differences in the fortunes of husbandry at this time.

In the fifteenth century, it is much easier both to discern a prevailing trend in Abbey rents and to account for the exceptional movements which did not conform to it. By 1450 many of the rents of the Westminster demesnes were lower than they had been in the second half of the fourteenth century, and some had been sagging continuously for several decades. In some cases the 1420s or 1430s witnessed the substitution of a noticeably lower rent than that which had been demanded during the last fifty or sixty years. The rent of the demesne at Launton, for example, fell to £6 and then to £4 per annum in the 1420s, from the £12 per annum which the lessee here had paid in the first decade of the century;[4] the rent of the demesne

---

[1] W.A.M. Reg. Bk. ii. 116–116ᵛ. [2] Ibid. 28–28ᵛ.

[3] Ibid. 280ᵛ, 284ᵛ–285. The lessee at Stevenage owed 24 quarters of good, clean, seasonable malt per annum; at Battersea and Wandsworth, the lessee owed £24. 13s. 4d. and 8 quarters of oats and 2 quarters of barley per annum. At Wheathampstead, another of the principal manors, the lessee of the mill and of the Abbey's portion of the tithes owed £10 and 40 quarters of good, seasonable corn per annum (ibid. 88ᵛ).

[4] W.A.M. 15396 ff. In 1408–9, the eleventh year of a thirteen-year term, the prior and convent remitted £2 per annum of the rent of £12 per annum. The lease at £12 per annum included the mill, earlier demised separately @ £1. 6s. 8d. per annum. The mill is not mentioned in references to the lease of the demesne in the 1420s, but the leases of the demesne in this decade included a virgate of tenant-land which had not previously been demised with the demesne.

at Deerhurst was reduced from £7. 13*s*. 4*d*. to £5. 13*s*. 4*d*. per annum in 1419 or 1420.[1]

In the second half of the century, a few rents were raised. Thus by the late 1470s, the lessee at Denham owed £15, a boar, two cart-loads of hay, and 2 quarters of oats per annum, for a demesne which his predecessors had held for £12 per annum in the first half of the century.[2] At Eye, the rent rose from £13. 6*s*. 8*d*. per annum to £21, a boar, and 6 cart-loads of hay per annum after 1460; not all this rise can be accounted for by the inclusion of additional meadowland and pasture in the lease, although this was a feature of the period.[3]

Most of the demesnes where rents rose were situated, as in the case of Denham, in or near a small town or, as at Eye, near the metropolis itself, and the group as a whole weighs light in the balance against the many demesnes where rents remained for a century and more at the level to which they fell after 1400. In the 1530s, the lessee at Launton was still paying the rent of £4 per annum which had been introduced in the 1420s,[4] and at Paddington, the rent of £19 per annum which Thomas Kempe, described as a gentleman, agreed to pay in 1514 was less, by the margin of 6*s*. 8*d*. per annum, than the rent paid by Edmund Bybbesworth here in 1422–3.[5]

As to entry fines, which could have been used to correct the level of the recurring annual dues, we can do no more than note the almost unbroken silence of the Abbey's records on the subject. From the fourteenth century until 1540, only a handful of payments which are described as fines or which there is reason to think may have been fines have come to light in the context of the leasing of the demesnes, and none of these amounted to as much as a year's rent of the land in question.[6]

---

[1] W.A.M. 8455 ff. The rent for this demesne had recently been raised by a very similar margin. See also *Economic History Rev.*, 2nd ser., 22 (1969), 23.

[2] W.A.M. 3408, 3411, 3414, 3419. The earlier leases, moreover, included some livestock.

[3] W.A.M. 26983 ff.

[4] See below, p. 356, n. 5, and for the sixteenth-century accounts, see W.A.M. 15413 ff.

[5] W.A.M. 19918, where a payment of £9. 13*s*. 4*d*. from Bybbesworth for half a year is mentioned; see also W.A.M. Reg. Bk. ii. 63.

[6] For fines in the case of the abbot's portion, see *Economic History Rev.*, 2nd ser., 22 (1969), 22. I am indebted to Mr. Stephen Knighton, of Magdalene College, Cambridge, for the information that some entry fines and sealing fees are recorded, after 1540, in the Act Book of the Dean and Chapter of Westminster. The sums

Yet the very silence of the sources is impressive, since it extends not only to the surviving leases—the mention of fines in indentures of leases was in general rare[1]—but also to the central records of the Abbey where we should expect such payments to be entered, if the monks received them at all. And although many lessees were required to execute a bond to cover the prompt payment of their rent and the fulfilment of other covenants in the lease, no bond that has come to light mentions the payment of a fine; after 1485, however, when the surviving series of lease-books begins, virtually every bond that was made has been preserved. It is thus exceedingly likely that the whole burden of the rent owed by the monks' lessees consisted in the payments and services set out in their indentures. As a rule these included the duty of entertaining monastic officials when they came to hold courts or inspect the property, and nothing that we know about the standard of living of monks of Westminster in the later Middle Ages suggests that this would have entailed only trifling expenditure; but the annual dues were the main burden.

So far we have considered these in terms of the cash, corn or livestock in which they were assessed and paid, but what mattered to the monks and to their lessees, and what in every period holds the chief interest for the historian, is the real level of rents, measured in terms of changing prices. Too little is known at present about price movements in the later Middle Ages and early sixteenth century for this to be readily ascertained. It seems clear, however, that, as corn prices fell towards the end of the fourteenth century, several decades in advance of a general fall in rents on the Abbey's demesnes, the real level of cash rents—and cash already preponderated in these rents— rose. The reduction of the 1420s and 1430s tardily adjusted the balance in favour of the tenant, and for several decades to come there is little reason to doubt that the mainly sagging rents on the Abbey's demesnes matched generally sagging prices in the

involved, however, were on the whole modest. Of twenty-three fines paid for rural properties between 1543 and 1556, five were equivalent to less than the annual rent, and six others equivalent to less than two years' rent; two others exceeded the latter level by a narrow margin. In four cases the lease for which the fine was paid was not entered in the Abbey's Register Book, and the rent is therefore unrecorded.

[1] See, for the early sixteenth century, *Agrarian History of England and Wales* iv. 318.

wider market. Finally, the greater use of corn rents after 1500 gave the monks a slightly more flexible income as it began to seem likely that prices were moving decisively upwards again;[1] but by the 1530s, the lessees of the Abbey's demesnes, holding, as most of them did, for relatively long terms and at rents which had been fixed many decades ago, must have felt the advantage of their situation.

The System in Operation

At nearly every point in this description of the Abbey's demesne leases, differences in practice between the abbot's portion and that of his monks have come to light. Without question, the most telling of these relates to the identity of the lessees: lessees of the capitalist type, whether of middle-class or gentry origins, are more in evidence on the convent's demesnes than on those of the abbot, and this, it may be suggested, was so for two reasons. First, the convent's demesnes, nearly all of which were situated in the Home Counties, were inevitably attractive to a type of lessee whose other interests were apt to be focused on London or its environs; and, in the second place, the prior and convent, who, more often than the abbot, had looked to their demesnes for a cash income before they were put on lease, were naturally more eager in this period to deal with lessees of assured resources, whose capacity to pay substantial cash rents year in, year out, was never in doubt.

Both in the case of the abbot's demesnes, however, and in that of the convent's, the overriding impression of this period, and especially of the fifteenth century, is of an undemanding exercise of lordship. This was a period when first the abbot and in due course the prior and convent divested themselves of the capacity to effect changes in the rents of their demesnes for many years at a time; this is the significance of the ever lengthening terms of years that distinguish their late-medieval leases. Often, but particularly on the abbot's estates, a generously conceived demesne lease was the perquisite of the local rent-collector or bailiff, the factotum on whom the organization of the monastic estate at the manorial level chiefly depended;

---

[1] For the difficult problem of price movements at the end of the fifteenth century and early in the sixteenth, see R. B. Outhwaite, *Inflation in Tudor and Early Stuart England* (London, 1969), pp. 9 ff.

once again, as in the twelfth century, the needs of patronage were consuming domanial resources.

For a long time the high costs and low profits of agrarian enterprise, both well-attested features of the century after the Black Death, make sense of the monks' decision to use their demesnes in this way; many times, no doubt, they were faced with Hobson's choice. Towards the end of the fifteenth century, however, it becomes less certain that the demands which the monks of Westminster made upon the lessees of their demesnes, unexacting as these were, reflected the real strength of the demand for this type of property, or, indeed, that either the abbot or his monks were thinking in these terms at all. The early sixteenth century, when, so it appears, prices were at last losing their late-medieval stability, was the very period in which the long terms of years, already a feature of the abbot's leases, began to be copied by the prior and convent in theirs. In the last years of the monastery's existence, it can hardly be doubted that the main profits of husbandry on its demesnes were appropriated, not by the monks themselves, but by their lessees. On the manors near London, a traffic in leases developed, with the result that the actual length of demesne tenancies here was often far different from the term of years mentioned in the leases giving rise to them. James Ewell, for example, kept the demesne at Down for only one year, from 1517 to 1518, although he had a forty-one-year term, and his successor, to whom Ewell almost certainly assigned his lease, himself saw out fewer than eight years of a similar term.[1] One would give much to know how the consideration that passed between the two parties in such a deal compared with the rent that each in turn agreed to pay the monks of Westminster, but here the sources fail us. Lessees of the peasant type, by contrast, normally saw out their terms, even in the early sixteenth century; or they surrendered the lease, only to obtain a renewal which should include other

---

[1] W.A.M. Reg. Bk. ii. 111, 118–118ᵛ. Ewell's successor was Thomas Galle; each is described as a haberdasher of London. In 1526 Down was leased to Richard Rogers, a fuller of London, who is described as an executor of the will of Richard Inkman, gentleman (ibid. 229ᵛ). Since executors were normally allowed the remainder of the term of an Abbey lease, on the decease of the lessee, with the proviso that they enter into a new indenture with the monks, it seems likely that Inkman had himself obtained a lease of this demesne since 1518. If so, however, the monks failed to enter the indenture in their Registers.

members of the family. Since these men and women paid little in the way of a fine, if anything at all, their position is comparable to the enviable one of copyholders by inheritance.

All in all, it may seem that the monks of Westminster were about to repeat on their demesne land the mistakes that had cost them so dear three centuries earlier, when in manor upon manor the advantage of rising land values was enjoyed, not by themselves, but by their fee-farmers.[1] In fact the legal impediments to such folly were very much greater in the later period than they had been earlier, and the degree of risk to the monastic possessions correspondingly smaller. Since the twelfth century, as we have seen, changes in the land law had made it exceedingly difficult for the monks to grant any other term but a term of years.[2] But the lessee holding for years, however long his term, was denied the real actions of the royal courts;[3] though he might in practice enjoy so many of the advantages of a heritable interest in the property which he held on lease, he could never hope to establish a perpetual interest at law. Every miscalculation that the monks made under this head was capable of annulment, given only time and the will to effect a change.

Moreover, the law now much assisted the monks in enjoyment of the benefits of the other covenants in their leases. If, in this period, a tenant did not pay his rent promptly, he could be distrained; if he broke other parts of the agreement, he would forfeit the substantial sum named in the bond which he had been obliged to seal at the commencement of his lease; and in many deeds the right of re-entry was reserved for the monks in the case of these and other delinquencies.

The higher the status of the lessee, the more likely were these safeguards to be ineffective. They failed, for example, in the case of John Cassy, a well-connected lessee of the demesne at Deerhurst at the end of the fifteenth century, who withheld his rent for many years. Of Cassy, the abbot complained that no remedy could be obtained against him in the ordinary course of the law 'by cause of his grete myght', kynne and alyaunce'.[4]

---

[1] Above, pp. 77 ff.   [2] Above, pp. 82 ff.

[3] S. F. C. Milsom, *Historical Foundations of the Common Law* (London, 1969), pp. 127–8.

[4] W.A.M. 32850 A. For Cassy, see *Trans. of the Bristol and Gloucestershire Archaeological Soc.* 11 (1886–7), 4.

But there were in fact few men like Cassy among the Abbey's lessees in this period. The humbler men whom the abbot and convent preferred seem normally to have honoured their obligations, or so we may infer from the scarcity of references to large arrears of rent or serious dilapidations. This was one of the advantages of entrusting the demesnes to such people.

Beside the law itself, the late-medieval monks of Westminster often had reason to bless the crystal-clear definitions of its embodiment, the conveyance. Was the lessee to have the rents as well as the demesne, and, if so, the rents of free tenants with those of the customaries? Did the meadows and pastures go with the arable, and was he to have the profits of the courts? Could he call on the customary tenants for their labour services and was the Abbey still to have the use of the manor house? When a deputation of monks came to hold the courts, was it to be regaled with ale, or with wine? It was all now specified in the indenture. As with every definition of tenurial obligations, there is a sense in which the particularity of these leases marks the limitation of seignorial power: the abbot of Westminster, who had once been permitted by custom to billet his entire household on his tenants,[1] now had to specify in writing whether or not his deputies were to be given a drink of ale. But, given the circumstances which told so strongly in favour of the tenant and against the landlord for the greater part of the fifteenth century, a close definition of obligations served the purposes of the abbot and convent exceedingly well; it helped them to hold a difficult line.

In short, down to the end of the fifteenth century, the monks probably did as well on their demesnes as any landlord of the period could—they played a poor hand with some little skill. Nor is it really surprising that their practice of granting long leases at relatively low rents survived into the early sixteenth century, when the economic conditions which had brought it to birth were waning. Having acted in this way for the best part of a century, the monks required a bigger stimulus than any provided by the slow beginnings of the Tudor inflation before they would change their practice. In any case, society now expected them to dispose of their demesnes in this way; not for them the short term and the rack rent.

[1] Above, p. 83 and n.

VI

Purchases of Property

The Thirteenth and Fourteenth Centuries

(i) *Chronology and Scope of the Purchases*

JOHN FLETE, the fifteenth-century historian of Westminster Abbey, knew of no purchases of property by the monks of Westminster that were worthy of record before the thirteenth century. Then, however, his account of Richard de Berking is devoted largely to the acquisitions which enabled that abbot to augment the monastery's income by *c.* £200 per annum.[1] Berking ruled the house from 1222 until 1246, and from this time until Nicholas de Litlington's abbacy (1362–86), Flete constantly returns to this theme of the acquisition of real property.

Although Flete's list of purchases is by no means complete, his chronology is in a broad sense correct: the thirteenth and fourteenth centuries were the period when the monks of Westminster actively purchased real property, and the acquisitions began, as he implied, with the election of Richard de Berking and were more or less at an end at the death of Nicholas de Litlington.[2] But the first half of the fourteenth century, though not barren of achievement in this very materialistic sphere of monastic life, was much less productive than the preceding age or the following. Two particularly active periods of land-purchase can be distinguished in the centuries covered by Flete's *History*, the one extending from Berking's succession to the death of Walter de Wenlok in 1307, the other from Simon

---

[1] *Flete*, pp. 103–5. The figure occurs in Matthew Paris, *Chronica Majora* (ed. H. R. Luard, 7 vols., Rolls Series, 1872–83), iv. 154. Flete's source, however, was *Flores Historiarum*; see *Flores Historiarum*, ed. Luard (Rolls Series, 1890), ii. 314. Flete believed that Berking's acquisitions included the rectory of the church of Battersea, but this was appropriated during the abbacy of Walter of Winchester (1175–90); see below, p. 411.

[2] For details, see Appendix IV (below, pp. 413 ff.).

de Langham's election in 1349 to the death of Litlington. In each case, it was only through the acquisition of new sources of income that the monks of Westminster could hope to maintain their standard of living and scale of activities, for both in the early thirteenth century and in the mid-fourteenth their income was seriously inadequate for their real or presumed needs.[1]

Given the need, where were the monks to begin? The subinfeudated portion of the estate was always at the centre of their calculations. This comprised, in addition to the manors held of them in return for military service or for a fee-farm render, hundreds of small fee simples in the manors which were still in demesne.[2] Further, several of the main offices in the monastery were burdened with a perpetual and lucrative serjeanty, the holder of which drew ample rewards in return for services which, if not of a wholly ceremonial kind, could nevertheless be performed at little cost and by deputy. The vestry, the buttery, the kitchen, the almonry, the sartry, the gate, and the liberty all had their perpetual serjeants, each of whom was entitled to a monk's corrody.[3]

The monks enjoyed certain advantages in negotiations for the purchase of land on their own fee. When alienation was by sub-infeudation, they would be asked, as chief lords, to confirm the enfeoffment; if by substitution, the purchaser owed them fealty, and, in the case of a fee simple on a demesne manor, the transaction required their licence. They were thus exceedingly well placed to learn of opportunities to purchase. A number of their thirteenth-century charters may have required tenants in fee to give them the first refusal in the event of sale.[4] Moreover, when, after 1279, the system of mortmain licences

---

[1] Above, pp. 64-7.

[2] For the extent of such tenures by the early fourteenth century, see above, pp. 121-2.

[3] For the serjeanties of the vestry, the gate, the buttery, the liberty (the sphere of duty of the forinsic bailiff) and the sartry, see *Customary* ii. 73. The serjeanty of the almonry was granted to Gilbert de Claygate, *temp.* Henry III, as part of the price at which he parted with his land in Claygate to the monks; see below, p. 415 (no. 7). For the serjeanty of the kitchen, see W.A.M. 5886*, W.D., 94-94ᵛ. The serjeanties of the vestry and buttery were redeemed by the monks in 1298, that of the kitchen in 1373 (W.A.M. 5906; below, pp. 393-4 (no. 39). The stewardship of the Abbey, a serjeanty granted to Hugh de Coleham and his heirs by Gilbert Crispin, was redeemed from Walter, son of Thurstan de Coleham, in 1198 (W.D., 91ᵛ).

[4] For an example see above, p. 118 and n.

was in force, purchases on the fee of another lord required his permission; acquisitions in chief required that of the king, which was not readily given.[1] For all these reasons, the properties which the monks purchased belonged with scarcely an exception to their own fee.

Among possibilities open to them here, the repurchase of their knights' fees was apparently the least attractive or the most difficult, and there are few transactions of this kind to be reported. Many of these properties had passed out of the demesne of the church when Domesday Book was made.[2] On the other hand, the monks were reminded at their every scrutiny of the Domesday record that all their fee-farmed estates had once belonged to their demesne. It was these that provided them with their greatest triumphs in the land market. Richard de Berking's most important purchase of this kind brought back into the demesne of the church a moiety of the manor of Longdon, which manor one of his twelfth-century predecessors had fee-farmed to a member of the Foliot family.[3] The vendors were Avice de Foliot and Philip de Coleville, each of whom held a fourth part of the fee in Longdon formerly of Reginald de Foliot, the last of the direct line of the Foliots. Avice was one of the four sisters of Robert de Foliot, Reginald's father, among whom Reginald's lands had been divided; Philip, the son of Agnes de Foliot, another of the sisters. Avice and Philip at first proposed to sell their inheritance to the abbot of Gloucester, but in 1235 Berking obtained royal letters close forbidding any sale of the lands to the abbot of Gloucester without his consent.[4] Soon afterwards, he bought Philip's share for £228; for Avice's he paid £73. 6s. 8d.[5] Berking's acquisition comprised part of three vills—Longdon itself, Chaceley and Castlemorton; for the time being, however, Margaret, Reginald de Foliot's widow, had her dower in Chaceley.[6] The fee-farm rent for the whole manor of Longdon at the time of Reginald de Foliot's

---

[1] Below, p. 182. For the effects of the Statute of Mortmain, see also S. Raban, 'Mortmain in Medieval England', *Past and Present* 62 (Feb. 1974), 3–26. Mrs. Raban's important essay appeared after this chapter was written.

[2] Above, pp. 71 ff.

[3] For the purchase of Longdon, see below, pp. 414–15 (no. 3).

[4] *Close Rolls, 1234–7*, p. 67. From these letters it appears that Amphyllis de Foliot, another of the heirs of Reginald de Foliot, also intended to sell her share of the manor to the abbot of Gloucester. See also *V.C.H. Worcs.* iv. 113.

[5] W.D., 299–299ᵛ.   [6] *Flete*, p. 104.

death was £28 per annum.[1] Berking's outlay of £301. 6s. 8d. represented, therefore, a little more than twenty years' purchase of the farm of the moiety.

The redemption of fee-farms was a persistent thread in estates policy at Westminster for as long as the monks remained active in the purchase of land. But even so, not all the mistakes of the twelfth century could be put right. One exceedingly valuable property that finally eluded their grasp was the manor of Chelsea, which Gervase de Blois had granted to Dameta, his mother, for a rent of £4 per annum. In 1367 Richard de Heyle, the tenant in demesne of this property, demised it to the monks for his life, in return for a rent of £20 per annum, a daily corrody of bread and ale, a yearly livery of a robe, and the promise of alternative accommodation in a house in the precincts of the Abbey.[2] But this arrangement was not, as might be expected, and as the monks themselves probably intended, a preliminary to the sale of the property to the Abbey; for reasons now obscure, the monks were never able to consolidate their new foothold in Chelsea, and, later, we find them, once again, without a demesne interest there.[3] The most valuable estate recovered at any point in the Middle Ages was undoubtedly the manor and half-hundred of Deerhurst, which Walter de Wenlok purchased from the Abbey's fee-farm tenant, William de Derneford, in 1299.[4] Probably the latest transaction of this kind was the bargain which brought Birlingham back into the demesne of the church in 1378; in this year, Nicholas de Litlington remitted the rent of £11. 12s. 5d. per annum to the tenant in demesne, John Sapy, for his lifetime and secured the reversion of the manor in return.[5]

---

[1] W.D., 299. Cf. *C.R.R.* ix. 268. The issue in this plea between the abbot of Westminster and Robert de Foliot about customs and services in Longdon was probably the right of hospice claimed by the former in this manor; see above, p. 83 and n.

[2] *Cal. Cl. R., 1364–8*, pp. 385–6. The house was to be that formerly occupied by Sir John de Molyns. See also W.A.M. 19863, the account of the conventual treasurers for 1368–9, where Richard de Heyle's 'pension' of £20 per annum is in fact the rent which the monks owed him for the manor in the current year. For the tenement which the monks provided for Heyle, said to be near St. Margaret's church, see also W.A.M. 19861.

[3] Hence, all that the Abbey was receiving from Chelsea in 1535 was the old fee-farm rent, and a small payment in respect of cert money (below, p. 350).

[4] Below, p. 416 (no. 8).

[5] Below, p. 421 (no. 29).

The repurchase of the fee simples on their manors would have been a task of Herculean dimensions, and the monks of Westminster never took it in hand in the sense in which they undertook the recovery of fee-farms. Yet they frequently bought such property. This may indeed be described as the characteristic purchase of both the thirteenth century and the fourteenth; the cartularies of this period are full of charters relating to transactions of this kind. Over the whole period, from the beginning of the thirteenth century to the end of the fourteenth, the manor of Great Amwell was their only large purchase of land held in chief of the Crown,[1] and they bought even less property on the fee of other lords after 1279 than their licences in mortmain would have permitted.

It goes almost without saying that the monks usually bought agricultural land; urban property accounted for only a small proportion of their purchases. However, in the course of the long period under consideration, the regional focus of their activity shifted from the Western Parts to the Home Counties. Richard de Berking's major acquisition, the moiety of Longdon, was situated in the west, and, similarly, Walter de Wenlok's greatest success, the recovery of Deerhurst, was achieved here; but their fourteenth-century successors bought mainly in Buckinghamshire, Essex, and Middlesex. Flete's pages reflect the change in the monks' policy: Berking bought property at Castlemorton, Chaceley, and Longdon, but Langham, at Finchley and Wandsworth, and Litlington, at Denham, Pyrford, and Staines.[2]

Moreover, in the fourteenth century, the monks often favoured land in or near semi-urbanized settlements like Chelmsford and Staines, which possessed built-up areas as well as fields. They were continually active in the property market in Westminster itself, and at Eye and Knightsbridge, and here their purchases included a number of houses and shops. Thus although the abbot and convent were mainly buyers of agricultural land throughout, their activities show a distinct shift of interest towards the urban and semi-urban forms of investment. In London itself, however, they were markedly uninterested, or at least unsuccessful. After the beginning of the fourteenth

[1] Below, p. 415 (no. 6).
[2] *Flete*, pp. 103–4, 133–4. (Allfarthing was in Wandsworth.)

century, their only acquisitions here probably came through gift and not by purchase; chief among them were rents worth *c.* £13 per annum, and probably much more, which Sir John de Shorditch gave for the endowment of his chantry in 1339.[1] For much of the period, mills were attractive investments. Thomas de Henle bought a mill at Birdbrook; and Litlington bought mills or the reversion of mills at Moulsham, Stratford and Wandsworth.[2]

(ii) *The Element of Usury*

So far in this account it has been assumed that purchases of property by the monks of Westminster were in reality what the sources make them appear—transactions intended from the beginning by both parties to effect such transfers. This, however, is an assumption that no one will happily make who is familiar with the ways and means of borrowing money in the Middle Ages and knows how often land was given as gage for a loan.

By the thirteenth century, the institutions of the money-market could help a landholder who was anxious to augment his estates in three principal ways.[3] First, since land was often given as the security for a loan, the purchase of a professional money-lender's bonds could be the means of acquiring a long-term interest in land on highly beneficial terms. One of the complaints voiced in the so-called Petition of the Barons in 1258 was that magnates of the realm who engaged in this practice refused to release the gage, even when the debtor was able to pay what he owed.[4] In the second place, landholders who had gaged their property for a loan but had no hope of discharging the debt themselves might be persuaded to sell their interest in the land, and a purchaser who bought in these circumstances had only to pay off the debt to establish a permanent right in

---

[1] For this chantry, see below, p. 395 (no. 44). The sum of *c.* £13 per annum is derived from the mortmain licence.

[2] Below, pp. 417, 423, 424 (nos. 13, 38, 40, and 43). Berking's acquisition of a fulling mill and two corn mills in Pershore was probably effected, as Flete implies, by litigation, not by repurchase; see *Flete*, pp. 104–5.

[3] The following remarks relate to ways and means of acquiring encumbered estates in fee or for a long term; for seisin of such estates for a limited term, see H. G. Richardson, *The English Jewry under Angevin Kings* (London, 1960), pp. 84 ff.

[4] *Documents of the Baronial Movement of Reform and Rebellion, 1258–67*, ed. Treharne and Sanders, p. 86, cap. 25. Cap. 25 seems to have related, in particular, to the plight of minors whose ancestors had not been allowed to release their estates from a burden of debt.

the property. Finally, some creditors, in particular Jews, preferred to sell encumbered property that came into their hands on the failure of debtors to meet their obligations; land was thus put into circulation that would not otherwise have come on to the market. *Mutatis mutandis*, such arrangements have always been a feature of the land market in England, but how much property was transferred by this means in any period of the Middle Ages, and into what social pattern, if into any, the transfers fall—these are among the discoveries still awaiting the historian.

In due course, many thirteenth-century bonds to Jewish money-lenders, and related documents, found their way into the monastic archives at Westminster, although the monks themselves were not the debtors whom they named; no doubt because of its proximity to the Exchequer of the Jews, the Abbey became the place of deposit of a substantial cache of the records of the Norwich Jewry.[1] But the monks themselves had dealings with the impecunious owners of encumbered estates. The name of one man who sold some of his property to them after he had fallen into the clutches of the money-lenders must have been known to the community at Westminster for as long as the *Customary* made under Abbot Ware continued in use. He was Laurence de Wendlesworth, a landholder in Worcestershire and Gloucestershire. In or about 1248, the monks took over Laurence's debt to Moses, son of Benedict Crespin, and it was almost certainly at that time that they began to acquire parts of Laurence's estate. More of it came into their hands in Abbot Ware's time, and it was probably an integral part of these transactions that Laurence was granted a corrody, of which the daily allowances were to be handed over at the monastic infirmary. Evidently such an arrangement was a novelty, for the *Customary* gives particular instructions about the handing over of Laurence's dole: it was to be delivered to the servant in charge of the north side of the Infirmary.[2]

Another transaction, of a different kind, provides a tenuous connection between the greed of the monks of Westminster for

---

[1] V. D. Lipman, *The Jews of Medieval Norwich* (Jewish Historical Soc. of England, London, 1967), pp. 187 ff.

[2] *Customary* ii. 244; *Close Rolls, 1247–51*, p. 24; and for grants of property by Laurence de Wendlesworth to the Abbey *temp.* Ware, see W.A.M. 8207, 22442.

land and the central crisis of Henry III's reign. In 1252, Richard Goscelin and his son, Ralph, demised land at Park, in Stanwell, to the abbot of Westminster for ten years, on condition that the abbot repaid his debt to the Jews. After six years, however, none of the debt had been discharged, and, in one of its early decisions, the Council set up in 1258 took this land into royal custody.[1] Since the abbot of Westminster was one of England's great landowners and Ralph's estate probably a very small one, the episode belongs in the social setting which nurtured Chapter 25 of the Petition of the Barons; the precise abuse, however, is different from that complained of there.

We do not know how often the abbot and convent of Westminster were attracted by any of these forms of speculation. Quite probably they were deeply involved in them in the first half of the thirteenth century, but from that time onwards evidence of such transactions grows sparser in the Abbey muniments, and there is no good reason to doubt that this reflects a real change in the monks' activities. Thereafter, although some of those who sold their land to the Abbey— perhaps many of these people—were financially embarrassed when they did so, we rarely uncover property that was actually gaged for a loan when the monks purchased it. From the beginning of the fourteenth century, if not earlier, it is more appropriate to think of debt as part of the general context of the land transactions in which the monks took part—some of the vendors from whom they purchased property were, as a matter of fact, hard up—than as determining the very mechanism by which the exchanges were effected. Even their thirteenth-century speculations in the money market brought the monks none but small gains—a few acres here, a small fee there. As far as we know, none of the acquisitions which Flete saw fit to record was gained in this way.

(iii) *Procedure*

Among all the Abbey's purchases of property in the thirteenth and fourteenth centuries, there is only one where a broker or middleman is explicitly mentioned in the surviving sources. This is the purchase of a messuage and 80 acres of land at

[1] *Close Rolls, 1256–9*, pp. 345–6. Subsequently, as this entry shows, Richard Goscelin was reseised of the land.

Knowle for Queen Eleanor's foundation, from John and Alice Hyntone, in 1359. The accounts of the wardens of the foundation record that the expenses of the deal—£46. 13*s*. 4*d*.—included 'brokerage'.[1]

It is safe to assume that the monks resorted to middlemen and dealers in land on more than a single occasion. Yet they may have done so rather infrequently, for, more often than not, they were acquainted with the vendors of the property which they purchased, and the transaction merely added one more strand to an existing relationship. This followed from the fact that so much of the property in question was situated on their own fee. Buyer and seller were lord and tenant, perhaps also neighbours with interests in the same fields; occasionally, since in the thirteenth century and even later some of the final concords to which the monks were party had a background in litigation, they were plaintiffs and defendant in an action begun in the king's court. The monks seem as a rule to have navigated the rocks and shoals of the land market on their own, providing all the services for the operation, except in its legal stages, from their own resources.

Large purchases of land were apt to be long in preparation and enmeshed in the web of obligations that is characteristic of an economy where men rarely come together in a simple relationship for a single purpose. The purchase of the property in Hendon known as 'Brauncestr' land' suggests what may have been the typical circumstances.[2] The monks bought this land in 1362–3, at the beginning of Nicholas de Litlington's abbacy, and the vendor received £63. 6*s*. 8*d*. on this occasion; but they did not buy it from the eponymous Brauncestr'. Gilbert de Brauncestr' had disposed of the land twenty years earlier to one Roger Gerard, who happened to be a corrodian of Westminster Abbey,[3] and it was probably Gerard who eventually sold the land to the monks. Even when the abbot and convent had the necessary money in hand for the purchase of property, as was presumably true in the case of Litlington's and Langham's benefactions in the fourteenth century, they were often slow

---

[1] Below, p. 419 (no. 21). [2] Below, p. 422 (no. 34).
[3] P.R.O., C.P. 25 (1) 150/59/170; *Cal. Fines, London and Middlesex*, p. 118, no. 170. The property is described in the fine as 100 acres of arable, 10 acres of meadow, and 10 acres of woodland. Gerard is said to have paid £20 on this occasion.

to spend it. Litlington began the endowment of a chantry for his parents in or about the year 1351, when he obtained the king's permission to amortize land to the value of £20 per annum for the purpose.[1] Yet he was still acquiring the necessary properties nearly thirty years later; Birlingham, purchased in 1378, was the last of them.[2] All the indications are that it was always difficult for the monks to buy the kind of interest in land that they wished to buy, in the places where they wished to buy it or were permitted by the king or the chief lord of the fee to do so.

Throughout the period under consideration, the central formalities in a sale of land were the final concord and the livery of seisin. In the thirteenth century, the abbot's proctor at the making of the fine was sometimes a monk of the house. However, even in the early years of the century, he often seems to have employed a professional attorney for this purpose, as he did almost invariably in litigation. His proctors at the ceremony of livery of seisin would very likely be a monk and one or two officials from the neighbourhood of the estate. The stages of the redemption of the fee-farm of the manor of Deerhurst show how such a transaction might be arranged at the end of the thirteenth century. In one respect, namely, the need to obtain a royal licence in mortmain, this exchange belongs essentially to the period after 1279, but its other features, including the vexatious aftermath of litigation, are characteristic of the land transactions of the whole period.

Abbot Wenlok and William de Derneford formally agreed to exchange Islip and Deerhurst, the one estate to be held by Derneford and Cecily, his wife, for their joint and several lives, the other by Wenlok and his successors in perpetuity, on 9 July 1299. William and Cecily were to receive, in addition to the manor of Islip, a pension of £10 per annum, payable at Todenham. Each party would give the other seisin within fifteen days of Wenlok's obtaining the necessary licence for an alienation in mortmain, and the Dernefords were to come into

[1] Below, pp. 418–19 (nos. 18–20); and for the chantry, see below, p. 395 (no. 48). In the event, Litlington founded an anniversary for himself; the more grandiose scheme of a chantry for his parents fell through, but this fact does not affect the argument in the text, except perhaps to underline the difficulty the monks were under in any search for property to purchase.
[2] Below, p. 421 (no. 29).

the king's court to make the fine on a date chosen by the abbot.[1]
The licence is dated 3 August 1299.[2] We do not know when the
fine was made. By 1 November, however, the monks had paid
Derneford the sum of £100, which was one of the cash elements
in the bargain, and £77 for stock;[3] and it was specified in the
agreement of 9 July that Derneford should be paid on the day
on which the abbot received seisin of Deerhurst. When William
de Derneford died in 1303, his widow quitclaimed her rights in
Deerhurst to the monks of Westminster, and the demise to her
of Islip for life was confirmed; so, too, the pension of £10 per
annum.[4] It appears, however, that Cecily had been William de
Derneford's second wife, and in 1318, probably the year of her
death, Derneford's son, another William, refused to warrant
Deerhurst to the abbot and convent of Westminster. His claim
was that the manor had been given by his father to Clementia
Bluet, his mother, and the heirs of her body. The dispute was
compromised in 1319, when the younger Derneford released
his right in the manor and was granted in return a pension of
£11 per annum and the yearly livery of a squire's robe.[5]

The monks of Westminster were rarely in a position to pay
over the full purchase price of their newly acquired properties
on the conclusion of the formalities of the sale, but they did not
make the fine unless they knew that they could complete the
payment within a matter of weeks or at least months. Equally,
the vendor of the property did not enter this crucial stage of the
deal unless he knew that he would get his money soon. A
recognizance or a bond minimized whatever risk existed for
the vendor in the short delay between the making of the final
concord and the completion of payment. Thus when Wenlok
bought land at Spoonhill from Hugh de Clun for his mother,

[1] W.A.M. 32691. For this transaction, see also below, p. 416 (no. 8).

[2] *Cal. Pat. R., 1292–1301*, pp. 429–30.

[3] W.A.M. 32694. Of the sum paid for stock, £27 was the price of 32 oxen at
Hardwicke, one of the members of the manor of Deerhurst, and £50 the price of
corn and hay at Deerhurst and Hardwicke. On 8 Aug. 1299, Wenlok appointed
Br. Adam de Warefeld and two lay officials, Nicholas de Stebbynge and Richard
de Blebure, as his proctors at the livery of seisin (W.A.M. 32692).

[4] W.A.M. 32696.

[5] W.D., 319ᵛ; *Cal. Cl. R., 1318–23*, pp. 503–4 ff.; cf. *V.C.H. Glos.* viii. 38 and n.,
where it is assumed that Cecily de Derneford and Clementia Bluet were one and the
same person. It was agreed in 1319 that William de Derneford the younger should
receive two robes yearly if the Abbot's squires should ever receive two yearly.

for the sum of £87, a chancery recognizance was executed and the debt was paid in instalments, within six months;[1] and when Nicholas de Litlington incurred a debt of £33. 6s. 8d. to Roger Belet for Belet's land in Laleham, in c. 1366, he bound himself in the sum of £133. 6d. 8d. to pay what he owed in four instalments, of which the last would fall due at the beginning of August 1367.[2]

Even in the periods when the records are most abundant at Westminster, it is impossible to estimate the cost of these formalities, for we do not know how many of their lay servants and retainers the monks could and would have dispensed with but for the need for their services on such occasions; the burden which land transactions placed on the overheads of what was in the thirteenth century, if not at all times, a large monastic establishment is unknown. However, the *ad hoc* expenses of conveyancing seem to have been small. The formalities of the purchase at Spoonhill, from the writing of the final concord onwards, cost the abbot £1. 12s. 8d., but his account makes no mention of the expense of the recognizance;[3] presumably, if a vendor of land wished for this safeguard, he paid for it himself. In 1364–5, when the conventual treasurers at Westminster disbursed a little more than £200 in the purchase of property, they reckoned an additional £12. 3s. 4d. as the expenses of the several transactions; the expenses included, however, a number of unspecified gifts.[4]

Litigation was a different matter. It did not in fact add much to the bill, but this only because the monks rarely pursued a major issue to its conclusion in the courts; they compromised, as in the case of Deerhurst in 1319, and we can perhaps read in the terms of such a compromise their own estimate of what it would have cost them to maintain the action in the courts. In 1316, they paid £133. 6s. 8d. to Sir Peter de Limesy for the

[1] *Cal. Cl. R.*, *1288–96*, p. 126. The sum of £33. 13s. 4d. had been paid to Clun before the making of this recognizance; see *Walter de Wenlok*, p. 176 and n.

[2] W.A.M. 4928; see also below, p. 422 (no. 35).

[3] *Walter de Wenlok*, pp. 176–7.

[4] W.A.M. 19859. For the transactions, see below, pp. 420, 422–3, 424 (nos. 25, 27, 36, and 40). A fifth, the purchase of a newly built grange in Finchley, in Hendon, for £20, is not listed in this Appendix. The treasurers disbursed £213. 6s. 8d. on these items, excluding the expenses referred to in the text; £40 of a debt of £60 incurred in respect of one purchase was still owing at the end of the year.

surrender of his rights in the manor of Great Amwell, which his ancestor, Ralph de Limesy, sold to the Abbey in 1270. This was a sizeable addition to the original purchase price of £566. 13s. 4d.; but the agreement of 1316 terminated a plea of warranty begun by Peter in the king's court in 1314, in respect of 80 acres of woodland and £13. 6s. 8d. per annum in rent in this manor.[1]

(iv) *The Rules of Mortmain*

Several of the features of land purchase at Westminster which have been described can be traced from beginning to end of the monks' period of activity. The Statute of Mortmain, however, cuts across the period, and fifty or sixty years after the enactment of this statute, but for reasons connected with it, the practice developed at the Abbey of buying land, not in the name of the abbot and convent themselves, but through nominees.

As early as 1245, the Crown had forbidden religious and other persons to enter the fee of Westminster Abbey in the counties where the Abbey's principal estates were situated.[2] Thus Henry III protected the monks against the possibility that their own mesne tenants would alienate their land in mortmain, but he also, it appears, allowed them the right, soon to be claimed for all chief lords by the Barons in 1258–9, of deciding for themselves whether or not they would permit such transactions. In this respect the monks may not have lost freedom of action as a result of the enactment of the statute of 1279, for, as is well known, this gave rise to a system of controlled alienation, in which the principle of 1258 was in fact honoured.[3]

In so far as they were purchasers of land, the monks were caught up in new formalities after 1279. It was indeed to the records thrown up by these that Flete owed some of his information about the purchases made from the last years of Richard de Ware's abbacy onwards, although he nowhere mentions the statute by name. Henceforth the monks' purchases were licensed by the Crown; and an inquisition *ad quod damnum*,

---

[1] W.A.M. 4250; *Cal. Cl. R., 1313–18*, p. 204; and see below, p. 415 (no. 6).
[2] *Close Rolls, 1242–7*, p. 377.
[3] Statute, 7 Edward I; T. F. T. Plucknett, *Legislation of Edward I* (Oxford, 1949), p. 94 ff.; Bean, *Decline of English Feudalism*, pp. 53 ff.

which laid bare the particulars of the land in question, preceded the grant of the licence. Since nearly all the land which the monks purchased was held of their own fee, the consent of anyone other than the king himself to the transaction was rarely needed, and it was only his loss that the inquest had regard to.

At first licences were issued *ad hoc* for each purchase as it was made, unless, indeed, the rules were evaded altogether. Subsequently, however, as general licences came into common use, the abbot and convent of Westminster were able to benefit from this more flexible system. Each general licence permitted the acquisition in mortmain of lands to a certain value. All that the licence defined was the value of the lands and their mode of tenure—whether they might be held in chief or not, and, if not in chief, whether only on the Abbey's fee or on the fee of other lords as well. Nothing more could be said, because the purchases and gifts that would result in their acquisition lay in the future. Once acquired, the lands were still the subject of an inquest, and it was still necessary to seek a particular licence to cover their acquisition.

Six general licences in mortmain were issued in favour of Westminster Abbey. One, however, the latest, related to Henry V's chantry in the Abbey.[1] It was not so much permission for the monks to buy lands to the value of £100 per annum as a promise that Henry VI's government would give them such an endowment when possible, and it falls outside the scope of the transactions which are of concern to us. The earliest of the five licences of the normal type was granted to Abbot William de Curtlington and his monks in 1316; it permitted them to acquire lands to the value of £10 per annum to augment Queen Eleanor's foundation, which now carried a greater burden of masses, pittances, and alms than the provision made by Edward I in 1292 could well bear.[2] Curtlington was still abbot when a licence for the acquisition of lands to the value of £20 per annum not held in chief was granted by Edward III in 1332.[3] Prior Litlington, in 1351, made his own application for the licence that would enable the monastery to buy the lands

---

[1] *Cal. Pat. R.*, *1429–36*, p. 213. This licence was granted in May 1432, with the assent of the lords spiritual and temporal in parliament.

[2] Ibid., *1313–17*, p. 521; the licence limited the monks' choice to property on their existing fee in the manors of Eleanor's foundation.

[3] Ibid., *1330–4*, p. 280.

for a chantry for his parents, and ten years later, shortly before his departure for Ely, Simon de Langham obtained another general licence.[1] Both these licences were for lands worth £20 per annum; the earlier specified that the property acquired should be on the Abbey's fee; the later, that it should not be held in chief. Finally, in 1372, the Abbey was permitted to acquire lands worth £40 per annum in compensation for the fact that the new tower of the Palace of Westminster and the adjacent close encroached on land within the monastic precinct.[2]

Between the purchase of property by the monks of Westminster and their decision to bring it before the escheator and apply for the final licence there was often a considerable lapse of time, and the intervals grew longer in the course of the fourteenth century. Thus the purchase of lands and tenements at Turweston for Queen Eleanor's foundation in February 1340 was licensed in December of that year,[3] and the licence to acquire a mill at Birdbrook, which the monks in fact purchased between September 1341 and September 1342, was granted in October 1343;[4] but property at Longdon, in Warwickshire, amortized in January 1369, was purchased ten years previously,[5] and some of the acquisitions which the Chancery finally swept into its net in 1392, in the largest single amortization of the century at Westminster, had been made some twenty years or more earlier.[6]

Moreover, the interval between the grant of a general licence and its surrender, on the completion of all the transactions which it could be made to cover, might be very long indeed. It was fifty years before Queen Eleanor's foundation exhausted the licence of 1316,[7] and, as we have seen, Nicholas de Litlington's licence for his chantry was finally satisfied in 1378, nearly thirty years after its issue.[8]

The general licences in mortmain which Westminster Abbey acquired in the course of the fourteenth century ostensibly permitted the monks to acquire lands worth, in sum, £110 per annum. At its face value, the figure may suggest a somewhat

---

[1] *Cal. Pat. R.*, *1350–4*, p. 102; ibid., *1361–4*, p. 34.
[2] Ibid., *1370–4*, p. 193 (a licence to acquire lands not held in chief).
[3] Below, p. 417 (no. 15).   [4] Ibid. (no. 13).
[5] Below, p. 419 (no. 21).
[6] Below, pp. 420, 422 (nos. 27, 33); and see also p. 419 (no. 22).
[7] See below, p. 420 (no. 24).   [8] Above, p. 173.

niggardly attitude on the part of the Crown to the monks' need for land. Mortmain licences, however, had regard to the extended value of the land, a notoriously inadequate form of valuation.[1] Moreover, since it was in the interests of both the vendor and the purchaser of land that the transaction should be licenced, it was also in both their interests to obtain as low a valuation as possible. This, no doubt, was one of the purposes served by the gratuities which the monks of Westminster customarily gave to the escheator and his underlings at the inquest. In 1392, when amortizing property in Westminster, Eye, and Knightsbridge, the conventual treasurers spent £5. 13s. 8d. on gifts to the escheator, his clerk, their own forinsic bailiff, and the jurors, and on food and drink for the occasion.[2] Many valuations were in fact ludicrously low. In 1361, a property at Westerham, comprising two messuages, 222 acres of land, 7 acres of meadow, 10 acres of woodland, and 3s. per annum in rent, was extended at 10s. per annum.[3]

Chancery officials seem to have been well aware of what was happening, and they frequently raised the valuation of the lands before finally granting the licence; where rounding off was desirable, they invariably chose a noticeably higher figure. Moreover, they sometimes declared a general licence in mortmain to have been satisfied long before this was so according to the escheator's figures. The lands bought for Queen Eleanor's foundation at Turweston in 1340 had been valued by the escheator at £1. 17s. per annum, but they were held to satisfy £3 per annum of the foundation's current licence,[4] and in 1377, Downe, in Wandsworth, which the escheator had valued at £4 per annum, was amortized at £5 per annum.[5] The licence of 1332 to acquire lands not held in chief to the value of £20 per annum was cancelled in 1344, after amortizations valued by the escheators at no more than £13. 15s. 8d. per annum;[6] and

---

[1] In cases where the property which the monks wished to amortize was already held of them at fee-farm, the inquest *ad quod damnum* returned a value that was exclusive of the fee-farm; for an example, see below, p. 416 (no. 8).

[2] W.A.M. 19876. The property in question consisted of eleven messuages, two tofts, twelve shops, 6 acres of land, and an acre of meadow in Westminster, three messuages, thirteen shops, and 10 acres of land in Eye, Knightsbridge, and Westminster (*Cal. Pat. R., 1391–6*, p. 133).

[3] Below, pp. 419–20 (no. 23).   [4] Below, p. 417 (no. 15).

[5] Below, p. 421 (no. 31).

[6] *Cal. Pat. R., 1343–5*, p. 353. For the two major properties acquired under this

as far as we know, the gains which satisfied the licence for the acquisition of property to the value of £20 per annum on the Abbey's fee for Litlington's chantry had been valued by the escheator at £17. 13s. 4d. per annum.[1]

The situation of the monks of Westminster was thus at once better and worse than the contents of their mortmain licences suggest: better, because acquisitions of property could be expected to yield considerably more than the sum at which they were valued for the purposes of mortmain; worse, because the promise in a general licence was not often honoured in full—rather, it provided the broad framework in which subsequent negotiations took place. In an age when monks were supposed to acquire new property only if they did not already possess enough to live on,[2] promises permitting the monks of Westminster to acquire additional properties worth £110 per annum in the course of half a century reflect a sympathetic attitude to their needs; in the fourteenth century many English baronies were not worth more than £110 per annum according to the extent. But in the event the monks had to work within a significantly smaller figure.

This, however, need not mean that the mortmain system was a serious hindrance to the monks of Westminster in their purchases of land—that they would have bought on a much larger scale but for this limitation on their activity. This wider problem must now be considered.

It must first be said that successive kings appear to have been more interested in controlling the monks' activity in the land market than in profiting by it. Unhappily, we do not know what if anything Westminster Abbey paid for its general licences, but the sums which it had to pay for the final legitimation of its acquisitions were moderate; and this, after all, was the moment

licence, see below, pp. 417, 418 (nos. 14, 16). In addition, the licence covered the acquisition of a messuage and 3 acres in Paddington and a messuage in Wandsworth (*Cal. Pat. R.*, *1334–8*, p. 508).

[1] The amortizations covered by this licence were probably those of 29 Jan. 1354, 23 Oct. 1366, and 12 Apr. 1378 (ibid., *1354–8*, p. 5; ibid., *1364–7*, p. 328; and ibid., *1377–81*, p. 182). For some of the properties in question, see below, pp. 418–19 (nos. 18–20), and for the abortive Litlington chantry, below, p. 395 (no. 48 and n.). On discrepancies between the face value of general licences and the escheator's valuation of the several alienations that they subsequently covered, see also *Past and Present* 62 (1974), 20–1.

[2] Bean, op. cit., p. 56.

when the king really had the monks at his mercy. A licence to amortize two messuages, 222 acres of land, 7 acres of meadow, 10 acres of woodland, and 3*s.* per annum in rent at Westerham, in 1361, cost £1. 3*s.* 4*d.*[1] In 1367 the licence for their acquisition of the manor of Chelsea for the life of Richard Heyle cost £1. 8*s.* 8*d.*[2] For the large-scale amortizations of 1392 the monks paid £20.[3]

On the other hand, it was difficult to evade the rules for any length of time. Over the fourteenth century as a whole, very few among the purchases mentioned in the accounts of the Abbey's treasurers seem never to have been brought before the royal officials for licencing, and, of these, only three had been expensive; these were purchases of mills. In 1363–4, the monks purchased the unexpired portion of the term of their own mill at Wandsworth;[4] in the second transaction, in 1364–5, they purchased a mill at Stratford, in Essex;[5] and in the third, in 1375–6, the reversion of a mill and some meadowland in the same place.[6] For the first of these transactions, no licence may have been needed; the third probably fell through at the time, for in 1392 the monks parted with a valuable corrody in order to secure what looks like the same property. Clearly, the Abbey had little hope of making large purchases of property unknown to the king. In the end even small ones came to light, as the monks found to their cost in 1319, when they had to pay £10 for a pardon to cover sundry small acquisitions during the abbacy of Walter de Wenlok, for which their predecessors had not obtained licences.[7] In 1472, Edward IV, evidently in a severer mood than Edward II on the earlier occasion, declared certain lands acquired by the monks to be forfeit to the Crown because no licence had been granted for the acquisition.[8]

---

[1] W.A.M. 23698; and for the property in question, see below, pp. 419–20 (no. 23).

[2] W.A.M. 19862. The monks in fact paid 6*s.* 8*d.* for the licence and £1. 2*s.* for the writing of the letters patent; for this transaction, see above, p. 167.

[3] *Cal. Pat. R., 1391–6*, p. 133; cf. W.A.M. 19876. On fines for mortmain licences, see *Past and Present* 62 (1974), 19–23, where it is suggested that the Crown became more exigent after the mid-fourteenth century.   [4] Below, p. 424 (no. 43).

[5] Ibid. (no. 40).   [6] Ibid.

[7] *Cal. Pat. R., 1317–21*, p. 356. For the one considerable acquisition of property by the *abbot* of Westminster after this time which was never amortized, see below, p. 424 (no. 41). See also below, p. 420 (no. 28).

[8] *Cal. Pat. R., 1467–77*, p. 308. The lands in question, however, had been acquired by gift, not by purchase.

Despite the constant vexation which it entailed, the mortmain system was not a source of great hardship to the Abbey, except perhaps at the end of the thirteenth century, when Edward I briefly restricted the issue of licences allowing alienations notwithstanding the statute. Since the monks took several decades to exhaust the general licences that they were granted in the early fourteenth century, it hardly seems possible that the explanation of the modest scale of their investment in new property in this period lies here. In one respect, however, the rules to which the monks had to conform after 1279 were influential on the pattern of their purchases. By the restrictions which the rules imposed on the purchase of other tenures, they fortified the monks in the practice, already in evidence by 1279, of buying mainly properties that were situated on their own fee. The relevant enactments begin at least fifty years before 1279, in the ordinance of 1228 forbidding tenants-in-chief to alienate any of their lands to the church without the king's consent.[1] Chapter 14 of the Provisions of Westminster, forbidding alienations in mortmain without the consent of the chief lord of the fee, may have continued to have the effect of law, despite its omission from the Statute of Marlborough.[2] Finally, after 1292, the Statute of Mortmain was interpreted in this sense: churches might acquire land on other men's fees only with the prior consent of the chief lord.[3] In practice, the monks of Westminster do not seem to have found it easy to obtain this, and they came nowhere near to buying other men's fees up to the limits which the king would have permitted. As to acquisitions of land held in chief, these were excluded by all the general licences in mortmain which the king granted to the abbot and convent of Westminster in the fourteenth century.[4] The whole tendency of the rules about mortmain was thus to

[1] Bean, op. cit., p. 58.

[2] Ibid., p. 51. On this and other clauses in the Provisions of Westminster, their antecedents and effects, see P. A. Brand, 'The Contribution of the Period of Baronial Reform (1258–67) to the Development of the Common Law in England' (Oxford University D.Phil. thesis, 1974).

[3] Bean, op. cit., pp. 56–7; cf. Plucknett, *Legislation of Edward I*, pp. 100–1. In the aftermath of the enactment of the Statute of Mortmain, the Church seems to have tried, though unavailingly, to obtain the exemption from its provisions of acquisitions of property on the fees of religious or prelates (*Councils and Synods*, ed. Powicke and Cheney, ii. 885–6).

[4] Above, pp. 177–8 and nn.

confine the Abbey's speculations in property to the narrow base of its own fee.

Not only the location of purchases was affected, but also the scale of the individual transaction, for, if the monks of Westminster were to be confined mainly to their own fee, it followed that they would normally be dealing in small properties, the possessions of their own free tenants. Even Langham's gift of 1,000 marks (= £666. 13*s*. 4*d*.) had to be frittered away on relatively small properties. Flete knew of two which had been purchased with this money—the manor of Beckswell, and Moulsham mill, worth together about £16 per annum.[1] In the thirteenth century, before the full restrictions on the amortization of land were formulated, the monks might have hoped to buy a single large property with such a bequest, as Richard de Ware and his monks bought Great Amwell. This manor, however, was not on the fee of the Abbey; a scoop of that kind was impossible in the fourteenth century.

(v) *Purchase through Nominees*

Westminster Abbey adopted the system of buying land through nominees about sixty years after the enactment of the Statute of Mortmain.[2] One or two examples will show how it worked. An early one concerns the land purchased for Queen Eleanor's foundation at Turweston in 1340.[3] The vendor of this property was Henry Terry, of Brackley, and he received £66. 13*s*. 4*d*. from the warden of Queen Eleanor's manors at the time. However, Terry's grant of this land, on 13 February 1340, was not to the abbot and convent of Westminster, but to Adam de Northwyk and Alan de Curtlyngton, and it was from these two men that the Abbey was permitted to acquire this property by the mortmain licence issued in the following December; Northwyk and Curtlyngton enfeoffed the abbot and convent, to hold of the chief lords,[4] in February 1341.

---

[1] *Flete*, p. 133; see also below, p. 423 (nos. 37–8). For Langham's benefaction, see below, p. 396 (no. 51). Flete believed that more than one mill in Moulsham had been purchased with it.

[2] For the practice, see J. L. Barton, 'The Medieval Use', *Law Quarterly Review* 81 (1965), 562 ff.; Bean, op. cit., pp. 104 ff.; Milsom, *Historical Foundations of the Common Law*, pp. 173–4.

[3] Below, p. 417 (no. 15).

[4] The abbot and convent of Westminster themselves.

Downe, in Wandsworth, was a more considerable property. The treasurers of the Abbey paid Robert and Alice Fynnesford £100 for the so-called reversion of it in 1370, but the final concord (which transferred the whole interest of the vendors in the property) named Robert and Alice, on the one hand, and John de Whitewell and Thomas Pernel, both described as chaplains, on the other.[1] Whitewell is subsequently lost to sight, and we can safely assume that he released his interest in the property to Pernel. Seven years later, in 1377, the monks obtained a royal licence to acquire Downe from Pernel.

Here was a system whereby the deeds effecting a sale did not name the true purchasers of the property, or licences in mortmain the true vendors; and it triumphed very thoroughly at Westminster for, over a period of some fifty or sixty years, between the 1330s and the 1390s, the monks bought scarcely any property except in this way. Who, then, were Adam de Northwyk, Alan de Curtlyngton, and their like? What was their relationship with the parties to the transactions in which they are named? And what was the purpose of this cumbersome system?

Some whose names appear in the fines and licences of this period were clerics. Adam de Northwyk was vicar of Feering, a church appropriated to Westminster Abbey, and we are told that Alan de Curtlyngton was a chaplain; so too were Whitewell and Pernel.[2] One, Geoffrey de Norton, was rector of Launton, in Oxfordshire, a church the advowson of which belonged to the Abbey.[3] Others belonged to the monastery's army of servants. Thomas de Aston, for example, who is named in a fine by which, in effect, the monks acquired lands in Battersea, Wandsworth, and Rydon, in 1390, was an official of the cellar.[4] Sayer Bunde was serjeant of the Abbey's manor of Ashwell and of the appropriated rectory there;[5] Thomas Durdent held at one time the office of janitor at the Abbey and later was probably one of the lay officials of the abbot's household; his family

---

[1] For references, see below, p. 421 (no. 31).

[2] W.A.M. 1548, 1774, 7620.

[3] W.A.M. 17677. Norton was used in transactions relating to lands in Westminster, Eye, Battersea, Knightsbridge, Great Amwell, and to Longdon in Warwickshire.   [4] W.A.M. 1895, 5994, 28117.

[5] W.A.M. 26276 ff. For Bunde see also W.A.M. 18519–24, 24263–5, and below, p. 185 n.

held land in fee of the abbot at Denham.¹ But the name that appears most frequently is that of Richard le Rook. There were in fact two brothers of this name, sometimes, though not invariably, distinguished as the elder and the younger. One was employed in 1361–2 to put a new roof on the abbey cloister.²

Nearly all the names in question were those of men whose connection was with the monks of Westminster, not with the vendors of the property. As the examples given above tend to show, their role was played out between the making of the deeds effecting the sale—pre-eminently the final concord—and the amortization of the property. During this period they were enfeoffed with the property, but as the nominees of the abbot and convent of Westminster. It is possible that some of them doubled the role of nominee with that of middleman and dealer in land. If so, however, we should expect their names to appear in mortmain licences involving other religious houses in addition to the Abbey; in fact they seem rather rarely to do so. As far as we know, these men received no specific reward from the monks for acting in the capacity of nominee. The service was an unremarkable extension of their normal activity; some, like Richard le Rook, performed it many times; others, only once or twice.

The interval between the two stages in the transaction that are represented by the final concord and the enfeoffment of the abbot and convent of Westminster was sometimes bridged by a lease of the property to the monks. Thus Roger Basset, their nominee in the purchase of the land known as 'Feliceland', at Wickford, in 1335, subsequently leased the property to the abbot and convent for eighteen years for the rent of a rose yearly.³ More often, the nominees acted as farmers or bailiffs of the land, administering it on behalf of the monks, to whom they rendered account and to whom they paid the surplus issues.⁴

¹ Durdent was janitor from 1369 to 1371 and is mentioned in the accounts of the steward of the abbot's household c. 1380 (W.A.M. 19865, 24527 ff.). For the manor of Denham Durdent's, see *V.C.H. Bucks.* iii. 259.

² W.A.M. 17681, 19857. For Bunde, Durdent, and Rook, see also *Cal. Pat. R., 1364–7*, pp. 298, 328; ibid., *1377–81*, pp. 182, 534.

³ W.A.M. 1240; and see below, p. 418 (no. 16).

⁴ For an example, see W.A.M. 18519–24, the accounts for property in Westminster which Thomas Aston, John Thurston, John Kinbell, Sayer Bunde, and others held as the monks' nominees from 1385 until 1391. W.A.M. 4818 is the roll of courts held in the name of Richard le Rook, senior, at Finchley, in Hendon,

The arrangement was thus a primitive form of the use, with the monks of Westminster in the role of *cestui que use*. They depended on the probity of their chosen nominees, and the latter's sense of a binding obligation to make over the land to them, for the eventual fulfilment of the intention behind the original conveyance.[1] At first the interval between the sale of the property to the Abbey's nominees and the final conveyance to the monks was short—a year, as in the case of Henry Terry's land, or less. Later, as the case of Downe suggests, it grew longer, and among the properties which the monks were forced to amortize when, in 1392, Richard II forbade the Church to use such means of evading the rules about mortmain, were some the fruits of which they had effectively enjoyed for twenty years or more.[2]

In adopting this system, towards the middle of the fourteenth century, the monks of Westminster fell in with an established fashion in conveyancing and at first, so short were the periods for which nominees held lands to their use, legal fashion seems to provide the only explanation of their actions: they were doing what their lawyers advised as the current practice. Later, they learnt to benefit from the arrangement, and it was when this happened that they became slower in bringing about the final conveyance. Their motive was hardly that of postponing the necessary payment for licences in mortmain—hardly, at least, can the Abbey's reason for delay have been financial, for a monastery with an income of *c.* £2,000 per annum could easily lay its hands on 20*s.* or 30*s.* for a Chancery fine.[3] The system in fact multiplied the costs of conveyancing. If we are to understand the advantages we must take into account the fact that the monks of Westminster were now restricted, not only in the acquisition of property, but also in the alienation of it. From 1256, the king's licence was needed for an alienation of land held in chief;[4] from 1285, the Abbey could hardly expect to

---

le Fryth, in Wandsworth, and at Thorne, in 1364–5, when he held properties here on behalf of the Abbey.

[1] Cf. Bean, op. cit., p. 115; Milsom, op. cit., pp. 174–6.   [2] Above, p. 178.

[3] Cf. *Law Quarterly Review* 81 (1965), 565; Milsom, op. cit., p. 173; see also *Past and Present* 62 (1974), 18 ff., and, on the fines paid by those *alienating* land in mortmain in the fifteenth century, K. B. McFarlane, *The Nobility of Later Medieval England* (Oxford, 1973), p. 54.

[4] *Close Rolls, 1254–6*, p. 429; Bean, op. cit., pp. 67 ff.

find purchasers for property donated by the king or his forebears, since the purchaser of such property was threatened
with the forfeiture of the land, without compensation;[1] nor,
without the king's licence, could the monks sell any of their
property to another religious house, for the Statute of Mortmain
applied to such transactions.[2] It was indeed unlikely that the
monks of Westminster would now wish to alienate any considerable part of their estate. The same restrictions, however, made
it more difficult than it would otherwise have been for the monks
to improve their properties by means of exchanges—a well-
attested feature of medieval landholding—or to find an outlet
in land purchase for their short-term investments. But a nominee,
during his tenure of the lands, was normally a sub-tenant of
the Abbey, since the land in question was normally on the
Abbey's fee and he necessarily entered by substitution; and
such tenants were free to alienate to laymen. Therefore, by
allowing some of their purchases to be held by nominees, the
monks won for themselves a liberty of action in the land
market that they would not otherwise have enjoyed. It was
particularly important to have this freedom to speculate in
Westminster itself and in the adjacent vills of Eye and Knightsbridge, where all the indications are that property was bought
and sold rapidly at this time. At least one example of alienation
by a nominee, however, occurs at Pyrford, in Surrey, where
John Pecche, one of the Abbey's nominees in the purchase of
the estate of the Toundesle family in that manor, in 1362,
exchanged some of the land two years later with one John
Thornle.[3]

In the second place, the monks may have found some little
advantage in the practice of bringing forward their properties
for mortmain licences, not one by one, but several at a time,
as they were enabled to do by this system. If Chancery officials
were in the habit of raising the escheator's valuation and depriv-
ing the monks of the full benefit of their general licences in
mortmain, there was much to be said for giving them as few
occasions as possible of doing so; better a single strike on a

---

[1] 13 Edward I, Westminster II, cap. 41.   [2] Above, p. 182 n.
[3] W.A.M. 1656. (This indenture is now extremely difficult to read; I have
relied in part on the summary of its contents in the index in the Muniment Room
at Westminster Abbey.) See also below, p. 423 (no. 39).

short front than the hazards of an extended line. We can see
the monks carrying out this policy in 1366, when the acquisitions of several years were licensed in two batches, in July and
October.[1] Thus the purchase of land through nominees directs
attention to the petty annoyances of the mortmain system—to
the apprehension with which even highly favoured churches
entered its toils.

(vi) *The Vendors*

Although, after 1279, the monks of Westminster were driven,
as a rule, to buy property that belonged to their own fee, if
they bought at all, their sub-tenants were not under the same
compulsion to prefer the monks, the chief lords of the fee, to all
other possible purchasers. By now such landholders had great
liberty in disposing of their property, for the long struggle over
freedom of alienation had gone their way, and *Quia Emptores*,
enacted in 1290, underlined their victory. The fact that so many
of the tenants holding of the Abbey in fee did sell to the monks
and to no one else suggests that their freedom at law to do
otherwise was only one factor, and that not the most important,
in the situation.

The vendors of the thirteenth and fourteenth centuries fall
into two distinct categories. On the one hand were those who
not only owned land but depended on it as their main or only
source of livelihood. Most of these are to be classified as small
landowners—men who numbered their acres in scores or
hundreds, but rarely in thousands. In terms of the social
distinctions that became ever more marked as the period wore
on, most of them were knights, squires, or yeomen. Several
were, like William de Derneford, employed on the king's business
in the shire or beyond it.[2] As a rule, vendors of this type had
inherited the property which they sold, and some could boast
of a long family connection with it. The Dernefords held
Deerhurst of the abbot and convent of Westminster from the
mid-twelfth century, and the family of Ralph de Limesy, who
sold Great Amwell to the monks in 1269, already held this
property in 1086.[3]

---

[1] *Cal. Pat. R., 1364–7*, pp. 261, 298, 328–9; below, pp. 418, 420–4 (nos. 17, 24–5, 30, 32, 34–5, 39, 42).
[2] For Derneford, see *Cal. Pat. R., 1281–92*, p. 399; ibid., *1292–1301*, p. 148.
[3] *B.I.H.R.* 40 (1967), 131–2, 139–40; *V.C.H. Herts.* iii. 415–16.

Distinct from this type of vendor were those whose livelihood did not depend on landholding and whose material fortunes had been only in small measure made or marred by the possession of it. Among these, Mr. Roger Belet is an unusually interesting figure, for he combined most successfully the assured position of a landowner with the plentiful rewards of royal office. Belet's family had held one of the serjeanties of the royal butlery from the early twelfth century, and Belet himself was butler to Philippa of Hainault.[1] He was styled *magister*, in recognition of his profession as a canonist or civilian. His principal estate was at Southcote, near Reading.[2] In 1337, however, Edward III granted him the manor of La Hyde, in Laleham, and Belet himself seems to have augmented this property with purchases in Staines and neighbouring places.[3] It was this relatively new estate in Middlesex that Westminster Abbey bought from him sometime before 1366, the year in which the acquisition was amortized.[4]

Most of the group, however, were citizens of London and members of the London guilds, but with property to sell in the Home Counties, and from this it follows that they were chiefly important in the later, fourteenth-century phase of land purchase at Westminster, when the monks' attention was focused as never before on this region. It was from Robert Aleyn, a London fishmonger, that the monks bought or attempted to buy one of the mills at Stratford in 1364–5;[5] from Richard de Weston, a goldsmith, they purchased the manor of Rosamund, in Westminster and Eye, on the very doorstep of the Abbey, in 1361–2.[6] John de Farnebergh, Roger Fynch, Guy de Hoddesdon, and John Southam, all members of the London guilds, also sold property to the monks in this decade.[7]

What these men sold they had, as a rule, not long possessed. For example, six years before Richard de Weston sold Rosamund to the Abbey, the property belonged to Thomas de

---

[1] W.A.M. 16781, 16783; J. H. Round, *The King's Serjeants and Officers of State, with their Coronation Services* (London, 1911), pp. 165 ff.

[2] W.A.M. 16777.

[3] W.A.M. 4969, 4887, 4896, 16779, 16783–4; *Cal. Pat. R., 1334–8*, p. 410; see also *V.C.H. Midd.* ii. 399.   [4] Below, p. 422 (no. 35).

[5] Below, p. 424 (no. 40).   [6] Below, p. 422 (no. 32).

[7] Below, pp. 420, 424 (nos. 25, 43). For the purchase of property in Hendon from Farnebergh and Hoddesdon, respectively cofferer and fishmonger, see *Cal. Fines, London and Middlesex*, p. 146, no. 463.

Baldeswell, himself a goldsmith, Baldeswell having acquired it from yet another member of the company, John de Chichestre.[1]

The appetite of citizens of London for land in the neighbouring counties was already an old feature of the landholding scene by the fourteenth century; it can be copiously illustrated from the earliest surviving feet of fines. Nevertheless, a century or so before Fynch, Southam, and the rest entered into their bargains with the monks of Westminster, some at least of their properties had a very different kind of owner: they belonged to small or middling landowners, not to the middle class. The middle-class phase of ownership was thus the intermediate stage in the passage of the property from the hands of a small landowner to those of an exceedingly large one. Downe, in Wandsworth, is a case in point. The monks paid Robert and Alice de Fynnesford £100 for this property in 1370.[2] We are never told explicitly that Robert de Fynnesford's primary source of livelihood was trade, but this seems very likely from the fact that, at the time of the deal, he undertook to indemnify the nominees of the abbot and convent against any proceedings under statute merchant bonds.[3] The property may have been that in Wandsworth which Fynnesford bought from John de Chestre and Agnes, his wife, in 1350.[4] Whether or not this was so, Downe had a long history as a separate estate, for it probably represents the Domesday holding of William, son of Ansculf the sheriff, in Wandsworth.[5] Robert de Fynnesford's willingness to sell enabled the monks, at last, to tidy up the feudal geography of this corner of their estate.

We know little about the circumstances of those who sold property to the monks of Westminster, but enough to realize the importance of dynastic misfortune—the failure of heirs—and debt.[6] The latter is to be thought of, in the present context, less as hopeless insolvency than as a degree of indebtedness that would impair the running of the estate for years to come and

---

[1] W.A.M. 17660.

[2] The accounts of the conventual treasurers seem to show that this was the sum received by the Fynnesfords, but the fine mentions the sum of 200 marks (= £133. 6s. 8d.) (W.A.M. 19864–5, 1774; and see below, p. 194, and p. 421 (no. 31).

[3] W.A.M. 1783.   [4] *Surrey Fines*, p. 122 (no. 65).

[5] *V.C.H. Surrey* iv. 110–11.

[6] See, on the importance of the failure of heirs in the dispersal of estates, K. B. McFarlane, *Nobility of Later Medieval England*, pp. 55–6.

absorb the lion's share of its surplus issues. Placed in these circumstances, a landowner who was childless or who had only daughters might well be tempted to sell the land and so capitalize his diminished assets. Accordingly, we find that the two factors were sometimes present in a single situation. In particular, they helped the monks of Westminster to the purchase of Great Amwell, their most notable success.

Ralph de Limesy, the owner of Great Amwell, had been an adherent of Simon de Montfort; he was one of those who found a refuge in Kenilworth Castle immediately after the Battle of Evesham, and the likelihood is that he subsequently incurred a heavy fine for the redemption of his lands.[1] However, by 1265 he already had financial problems, and the monks of Westminster were already caught up in them. This we know from the terms on which Limesy leased the manor of Great Amwell to Abbot Ware in 1263. Ware was granted the manor for his own lifetime, but the initial rent of £10 per annum would rise to £40 per annum after twelve years.[2] Clearly, the terms agreed for the first twelve years of this arrangement were highly beneficial to the abbot of Westminster, and we may safely assume that Ware and his monks had lent Limesy a substantial sum of money. Other loans followed; these, however, were small.[3] Then, in 1269, Limesy agreed to sell the manor to the monastery for 850 marks, 200 of which were to be paid by the end of January in the following year.[4]

Here, it seems, is a straightforward case of a sale of land necessitated by the poverty of its owner. But Ralph de Limesy was to die without issue and may already have known in 1269 that this would be so. His brother, Richard, was granted the manor of Arley, his other substantial property;[5] Great Amwell he perhaps felt free to sell. The death of Reginald de Foliot without issue explains how it was that Longdon came on the market in the 1230s;[6] and much later, in 1362, John de Toundesle's lack of issue no doubt explains his readiness to sell the

---

[1] *Cal. Pat. R., 1258–66*, p. 488.   [2] W.A.M. 4255.
[3] W.A.M. 4258, 4261–5.
[4] W.A.M. 4256, 4259. 850 marks = £566. 13s. 4d.; 200 marks = £133. 6s. 8d. The fine, however, which was made in Feb. 1270, names the sum of 700 marks (= £466. 13s. 4d.); see W.A.M. 4246, the counterpart. For the whole transaction, see also *V.C.H. Herts.* iii. 416.
[5] *Knights of Edward I* iii. 88.   [6] Above, p. 166.

Toundesle lands in Pyrford to Abbot Litlington.[1] Finally, there is the case of Richard de Heyle, from whom the monks obtained the demise of Chelsea in 1367.[2] We know that twenty years earlier Richard had a son and two daughters, Nicholas, Margaret, and Elizabeth.[3] It does not follow that he had any surviving issue in 1367, when he surrendered his own life-interest in the manor to the monks of Westminster. On the contrary, he was now probably childless, with no near relative to relieve him of the care of the property in his old age; better far than struggling on, a house in the shadow of St. Margaret's and the security of a pension.

In these cases, the acquisition of property by Westminster Abbey signalled failure of one kind or another on the part of the individuals who sold it, and it is possible that the fortunes of small landowners were, as a whole somewhat undermined by the encroachment of larger interests on their share of the wealth of the kingdom in these two centuries.[4] But how should we interpret the sales by men such as Robert Aleyn and Richard de Weston, which played a crucial part in enlarging the possessions of the Abbey in the fourteenth century? In what sense, if in any, are these an index of the fortunes of those who made them?

Many considerations prompted men like Robert Aleyn and Richard de Weston to buy land. Among them was the absolute necessity of possessing a landed estate for anyone who aspired to be accepted into the ranks of the gentry. But the purchases, the fruits of which eventually found their way into the hands of the monks of Westminster, seem to belong in a different category. Several had been acquired relatively early in the lifetime of the merchants who bought them, before social ambition can

---

[1] Below, p. 423 (no. 39). The arrangement recorded here suggests that John de Toundesle's heir was his brother, William.

[2] Above, p. 167.

[3] W.A.M. 16366*. In this document, dated 22 Feb. 1349, the feoffees to whom Richard de Heyle had granted the manor re-enfeoffed him, for life, with remainder to Nicholas, his son, and his issue, Margaret, sister of Nicholas, and her issue, Elizabeth, sister of Nicholas, and her issue, John de Bray of Chiswick, and Joan, wife of the latter, for their lives, William, son of William atte Watere, of Ware, and his issue, Robert, son of the last named, and the right heirs of Richard, in that order.

[4] For this suggestion in respect of the thirteenth century, see *Cambridge Economic History of Europe* i (2nd edn., 1966), 592–5.

have made many claims on capital; they were probably straightforward investments in real property from economic motives—the wise underpinning of trading profits with the steadier returns that could be expected from land. Such properties might, with advantage, be sold again, but it is unlikely that they were purchased with the intention that they should be quickly resold. If the average rate of turnover was high, it is still true to say that many of these properties lodged in the hands of their merchant owners far longer than we should expect in the case of mere speculations. Robert de Fynnesford began to build up his property in Wandsworth not later than 1350, twenty years before selling a major part of it to the monks of Westminster.[1] James Andrew, the London clothier whose property in Denham Abbot Litlington purchased in 1366, had owned land in Denham for at least nine years.[2]

In disposing of such investments, their owners looked for the advantage which had been the whole purpose of the original outlay—a secure, if unspectacular income. The bargains which middle-class vendors of land struck with the monks of Westminster, including, as they often did, the grant of a corrody or pension to the vendor, reflect something of this search for security. Robert Aleyn, for example, though he rose to be a knight, was not above ending his days as a corrodian of the Abbey, in receipt of 14 loaves and 14 gallons of ale a week and a pension of £6. 13s. 4d. per annum.[3]

In cases where the promise of a pension or corrody was not enough to tempt the vendor to sell, the monks offered a livery of robes as well. Robert de Fynnesford and his wife both received robes annually for the remainder of their lives after the conclusion of the bargain about Downe, and Richard Sandhill, from whom the monks purchased marshland in South Benfleet in 1364–5, was similarly rewarded.[4] A squire's robe—for this is what Sandhill received, and probably Fynnesford, too—was an expensive garment, and the promise of one may have been translated by those who received it into economic terms. More probably, however, they valued it for what it usually signified, the protection and goodwill of the monastery; livery is an aspect

---

[1] *Surrey Fines*, p. 122 (no. 65); and see below, p. 421 (no. 31).
[2] Liber Niger Quaternus, 40; and see below, p. 421 (no. 30).
[3] Below, p. 424 (no. 40).   [4] Below, pp. 420, 421 (nos. 27, 31).

of the purchase of land at Westminster that has a social rather than an economic reference.

(vii) *Price*

It will be clear that in the thirteenth and fourteenth centuries the monks of Westminster rarely bought land in a free market, where the vendor was under no constraint to prefer them to other purchasers and where, conversely, they were free to compete on equal terms with other prospective purchasers. It may indeed be doubted whether they brought off a single large purchase in such conditions before the early sixteenth century and the purchases which completed the endowment of Henry VII's chantry—if, indeed, any of the latter were made in that way. The price of their purchases was, then, the price of property purchased under conditions of greater or less constraint.

The accounts of the treasurers and obedientiaries on whose behalf the purchases were made appear to record the price in simple, straightforward terms. Often the figure named in the smaller transactions is £100 or 100 marks—'Item solut' pro terra adquisita apud Hendon' vocata Brauncestr' lond', lxiij li. vjs. viijd.'[1]; '. . . in reversione terrarum et tenementorum Roberti atte Doun' apud Wandlesworth' emptarum, in partem solucionis c li., lx li.,'[2] and so on; and if we had nothing more to go on than these bare entries in the section customarily set aside for land purchase in these accounts, we should be tempted to say that 'Brauncestr' land' in Hendon cost £63. 6s. 8d., and Downe, in Wandsworth, £100. In fact many of these entries, perhaps all of them, are misleading if taken at their face value.

Two of the reasons why this is so have been mentioned.[3] In the first place, the sum named in the obedientiary's account may include a payment to a middleman, the element of brokerage. Secondly, the purchase of property might well be followed by litigation on a scale sufficient to alter the order of magnitude of the cost of the original transaction. Abbot Ware and his monks paid £566. 13s. 4d. for the manor of Great Amwell in 1270; forty-six years later, their successors paid a further £133. 6s. 8d. to terminate a plea of warranty in respect of this land.[4] Twenty

---

[1] W.A.M. 19858; and see below, p. 422 (no. 34).
[2] W.A.M. 19864; and see below, p. 421 (no. 31).
[3] Above, pp. 171–2, 175–6. [4] Above, pp. 175–6.

years after the purchase of Deerhurst from William de Derneford, the monks were obliged to placate Derneford's son with a
pension of £11 per annum and livery of a squire's robe.[1]

Pensions and robes, however, belonged not only to the liti-
gious aftermath of land purchase: they were often part and
parcel of the original bargain. This is the third and most weighty
reason why the lump sum which changed hands in such a
transaction should not be accepted without question as the
'price' of the land. The sales involving pensions and robes are
often represented in the record of the transaction as leases. The
vendor leased the property in question to the monks of Westminster for his life, and at the same time sold them the reversion,
to take effect after his death. For the reversion the monks paid
a lump sum, and for the lease a pension, with or without a robe.
Since such a lease created a freehold interest in land, it was
accompanied by livery of seisin, and sometimes, indeed, the
fine transferring all the vendor's legal rights in the property was
made at this juncture.

An arrangement of this kind was often convenient for both
the monks and the vendor of the property: it enabled the
former to pay for their purchases of land in instalments and, on
the other hand, assured the latter of some little security for the
remainder of his life. The agreement made about Downe, in
Wandsworth, will show how the system worked.

The monks paid Robert and Alice de Fynnesford £100 for
the reversion of Downe in 1370, and evidently, at the same time,
they agreed to farm the property from the Fynnesfords at a
rent of £14 per annum.[2] This, however, was simply a way of
representing the fact that Robert and Alice were to receive part
of the purchase price of their land in the form of an annuity; a
final concord was executed in which Robert and Alice made
over all their rights in Downe to nominees acting on behalf of
the monastery. Robert lived until *c.* 1382; during this time both
he and his wife received annual liveries of robes in addition to
their pension, and Alice lived to enjoy her annuity and her
livery until 1386.[3]

---

[1] Above, p. 174.
[2] Below, p. 421 (no. 31). For the identity of the Robert atte Doune from whom
the monks purchased this property with Robert de Fynnesford, see W.A.M. 1774.
[3] W.A.M. 19864 ff.

A different terminology hides the basically similar arrangement that brought Henry Terry's land at Turweston into the
hands of the monks thirty years earlier. They bought, not the
so-called reversion of Terry's land, but his whole interest in
the property, and the treasurer of Queen Eleanor's foundation
entered a payment of £66. 13s. 4d. for it in his account for the
year 1339–40.[1] At the same time, however, the monks granted
Terry a pension of £10 per annum for life, and a squire's robe
annually into the bargain, and they agreed to pay his wife
£3. 6s. 8d. per annum as her dower after his death.

Unlike Terry and Fynnesford, John de Sapy, the Abbey's
fee-farm tenant at Birlingham, insisted on keeping the estate
for his lifetime, and consequently what the monks were able to
purchase of him was in fact as well as in name only the reversion
of the property.[2] Here also, however, payment was spread over
several years. In 1378 it was agreed between the parties that
Sapy should hold the manor rent-free for the rest of his life—
a concession that cost the monks £11. 12s. 5d. per annum—but
that it should revert to the Abbey on his death. Sapy died in
1388.

Even if all the costs of subsequent litigation are excluded, it
is clear that the monks often paid rather highly for their
purchases. About the time of the purchase of Great Amwell,
ten years' purchase was a common price to pay for land.[3] The
monks paid £566. 13s. 4d. for this manor, and it seems likely
that the rent of £40 per annum, that Abbot Ware had earlier
promised to pay when his beneficial lease ran out, represented
the true rental value of the property at this time.[4] If so, the
sum paid fell only a little short of fifteen years' purchase.

Deerhurst, acquired thirty years later, was certainly more
expensive. This manor had been fee-farmed to the Derneford
family in the twelfth century, before the goods of the Abbey
were divided between the abbot and convent, but after 1299
Walter de Wenlok kept it for the abbot's portion. His action
gave rise to bitter controversy with the prior and convent, and
to this circumstance we owe our knowledge that the monks

---

[1] W.A.M. 23680; and see below, p. 417 (no. 15).
[2] Below, p. 421 (no. 29).
[3] *Cal. Pat. R., 1266–72*, pp. 140–1.
[4] Above, p. 191.

valued the assets which Wenlok exchanged for Deerhurst at *c.*
£60 per annum, for when, in 1307, Wenlok finally promised to
assign Deerhurst to the convent, the monks promised to allow
the abbot £60 per annum during the lifetime of Derneford's
widow—that is, for as long as his portion should be the poorer
for the transaction.[1] These assets, together with a pension of
£10 per annum, William de Derneford and, later, his widow
held for nineteen years in all, and Derneford received an
additional payment of £100 on the conclusion of the exchange
in 1299. On the crudest calculation, which makes no allowance
for the possibility that any part of the money might have been
gainfully employed in the meantime, it cost the monks £1,430
to acquire Deerhurst. But when the exchange was effected, they
were already receiving £34 per annum from the manor, as the
fee-farm rent of their tenant; all that they gained by the transaction of 1299 was, therefore, the clear value of the manor over
and above this farm. The escheator put this no higher than £36
per annum, but his estimate was, no doubt, too low.[2] However,
even if this sum is doubled, an outlay of £1,430 will still represent nearly twenty years' purchase, and this is to take no
account of the expense which the monks incurred in settling
their dispute with the younger Derneford in 1319.

In the second half of the fourteenth century, Cardinal Langham assumed that the monks of Westminster would need a
capital sum of 1,000 marks to purchase a net income of 40
marks per annum from land;[3] unless his gift included a generous
allowance for litigation and other expenses, he in fact assumed
a purchase price of twenty-five years.

But would Langham and his former brethren at Westminster
have thought in these terms at all? As evidence for the existence
of a fairly uniform and predictable price, the testimony of
Henry III's chancery in 1267, that land commonly changed

---

[1] *Walter de Wenlok*, p. 239, n.; see also above, pp. 173–4 and below, p. 416 (no.
8). Deerhurst never in fact came into the possession of the prior and convent.
It was also agreed in 1307 that the prior and convent would meet the expenses of
Abbot Wenlok's anniversary from the issues of Deerhurst—i.e. the arrangement
made in 1288, whereby the sum of £13. 6s. 8d. per annum from the rents of the
fair at Westminster was assigned to this anniversary, was set aside. But this proposal
lapsed with the rest of the agreement of 1307, on Wenlok's death.

[2] *Inquisitiones Post Mortem for Gloucestershire* iv (Index Library, xxx, British
Record Soc., 1903), 218.

[3] *Flete*, p. 133; and see below, p. 396 (no. 51).

hands at ten years' purchase,[1] not only seems to stand alone in its own age but also to be without parallel for more than 150 years to come. It is not until the fifteenth century that a relatively uniform price, now twenty years' purchase, emerges from the mists enveloping these matters for most of the Middle Ages.[2] And the religious were perhaps among the last to experience the benefits of this phenomenon when it appeared. They were much more restricted than laymen in their choice of land for purchase. If, like the monks of Westminster, they were often restricted to purchases on their own fee, they probably found, as the monks did, that some under-tenants were less ready to sell than their chief lords to buy. Further, to dispense with the middleman, as the monks of Westminster may have done rather frequently, is not always to save money: it may actually multiply costs by substituting a long search on the part of the amateur for what a professional may be able to lay hands on at once. Despite the social factors that may seem on the face of it to have worked so much in favour of the monks, as they set about coaxing their tenants into selling them their interest in the land, the market where they were forced to operate was in reality a seller's market throughout the thirteenth and fourteenth centuries.

The Sixteenth Century

The purchases of land that were made for Henry VII's foundation at Westminster were remote in time and circumstances from those considered worthy of record by John Flete. Henry intended his foundation to have an income of c. £800 per annum, and about half this sum was obtained by deflecting into the Abbey's coffers the income of a number of other churches, of which by far the largest was that of the collegiate church of St. Martin-le-Grand, valued at £266. 13s. 4d. per annum in 1504.[3] However, despite this generous use of property already

---

[1] *Cal. Pat. R., 1266–72*, pp. 140–1.

[2] McFarlane, *Nobility of Later Medieval England*, pp. 56–7. See, however, Rogers, *History of Agriculture and Prices* i. 688; and idem, *Six Centuries of Work and Wages: The History of English Labour* (12th edn., London, 1917), pp. 287–8.

[3] *Cal. Cl. R., Henry VII* ii, pp. 148–9. For the value of St. Martin-le-Grand to the monks of Westminster in 1535, see above, p. 31 n. The greater part of the large

belonging to the Church, it was necessary to buy lands and rents on a large scale: property worth *c.* £230[1] per annum was purchased, and for this purpose, in or about 1503–4, the king provided capital sums amounting to £5,150.[2] When the letters close in which this sum is recorded were made, the transactions were complete; £5,150 represents, therefore, not a guess on the king's part at the sum that would be needed for the purchase of lands worth *c.* £230 per annum, but the actual cost of the completed operation.

One circumstance distinguishing these purchases from earlier ones by the monks of Westminster is the existence of the developed entail and, in consequence, the acceptance of collusive litigation between prospective sellers and buyers of property as a means of circumventing it; common recoveries are therefore in evidence, and something must be allowed under this head in estimating the expenses of the whole operation. But the most important change concerns the situation of the new acquisitions. It is clear that on this occasion the monks were restricted neither explicitly by the king, who still licensed alienations in mortmain, nor by any other circumstance to the purchase of land belonging to their own fee. Had they been so restricted the purchases could hardly have been completed so quickly. As it was, Henry VII's chantry and that of his mother were the only major royal foundations at Westminster the endowment of which was all but complete in the lifetime of the persons whom they chiefly commemorated. The king's intention that the endowment of his own chantry should not be delayed no doubt explains why some of the purchases were outside the geographical range of the monks' activity as landlords down to the sixteenth century. But the king was more than paymaster and dispenser of mortmain licences: although their part in some of the transactions is now hidden from view, he and his counsellors almost certainly guided the whole operation. It is then in this special sense that these transactions are to be deemed

income which the monks drew as appropriators of this church was in fact consumed by the collegiate establishment which continued in existence, but Henry's endowment of his chantry with as much as £800 per annum took this need into account. Cf. *The Will of Henry VII*, ed. T. Astle (London, 1775), pp. 14–15, where the annual endowment is said to be 1,000 marks (= £666. 13*s*. 4*d*.) 'and aboue'.

[1] £231. 6*s*. 8*d*.
[2] *Cal. Cl. R., Henry VII* ii, pp. 148–9.

purchases of property on the part of the monks of Westminster.

Two properties in Essex, the manors of Pinchpol and Bullington, together with Plumstead Boarstall, in Kent, were purchased
from John Cutte, a royal servant and citizen of London.[1] In the
letters close recording the foundation of Henry VII's chantry,
these lands were valued at £40 per annum—Pinchpol and
Bullington at £20 and Plumstead Boarstall at the same amount.[2]
Like all the valuations given on this occasion, these were
intended to be a more or less exact estimate of what the monks
would actually receive from their new acquisitions; they were
intended to be clear yields, not values according to the extent
and need not be regarded with the scepticism merited by
fourteenth-century valuations for the purpose of mortmain.[3] In
paying John Cutte £800, as they did, the abbot and convent
therefore paid about twenty years' purchase for these properties. William Esyngton, the vendor of Fenne and Skreyne, in
Lincolnshire, did less well. He received £578 for property of
the annual value of £34, a price representing seventeen years'
purchase.[4]

[1] Below, pp. 425, 426 (nos. 47, 50).

[2] *Cal. Cl. R., Henry VII* ii, p. 149. The several members of the manors of Pinchpol
and Bullington appear in *V.E.* (i. 411–12, 418–19) under the entries 'Pinchpol in
Clavering', 'Bullington in Clavering', 'Bullington in Ugley', and 'Elsenham', and
the total net value was then £18. 7s. ½d. per annum. Plumstead Boarstall and
lands in Wickham belonging to this manor were valued at only £5. 13s. 1d. on
this occasion, but the manor included lands in several vills which are not mentioned in *V.E.* by name; the low valuation may be explained by this omission.

[3] Above, pp. 178–9. In two cases, however, the values assigned to properties
acquired for Henry VII's foundation were considerably higher in 1503–4 than in
1535. Two of the properties in question were rectories: the rectory of St. Bride's,
Fleet Street, London, was valued at £26. 13s. 4d. per annum in 1503–4, but at
£18. 18s. 5d. per annum (exclusive of reprises) in 1535; the rectory of Swaffham
Market, at £40 per annum in 1503–4 and £22 per annum in 1535 (*Cal. Cl. R.,
Henry VII* ii, pp. 148–50; *V.E.* i. 411–12, 419). The value of St. Bride's to the
monks of Westminster was apparently much depleted by a dispute about tithes,
terminated by an arbitration in 1534. The less considerable fall in values that
occurred in the case of a few other properties is probably to be explained by the
fact that Henry VII and his officials took no account, in 1503–4, of some permanent
rent-charges of a kind that were later allowed as reprises at the making of *V.E.*

[4] Below, p. 426 (no. 49). The value of £34 per annum for Fenne and Skreyne
in *Cal. Cl. R., Henry VII* ii, p. 149, is corroborated by an autograph letter of Abbot
Islip, dated 14 Dec. 1503 (W.A.M. 14708*). A few years later, the monks estimated
the clear value of this property to be £40. 7s. 9½d. per annum, together with 1lb. 2oz.
pepper, and 1½lb. cumin per annum (W.A.M. 14758). By 1535, however, the manors
were on lease for £33. 6s. 8d. per annum, and this is the value recorded in *V.E.*

These properties, with a rent of £26. 13*s*. 4*d*. per annum in Stanway, in Gloucestershire, which the monks purchased from the abbot and convent of Tewkesbury,[1] made up rather less than half the sum of *c*. £230 per annum. Most of the short-fall was endowed by means of purchases from two vendors of a very different stamp: George Neville, lord Bergavenny, and Maurice, lord Berkeley. From the former, the monks acquired Oswald Beck Soke, in Nottinghamshire, and the manors of Alkborough, Burton Stather, and Halton, in Lincolnshire;[2] from the latter, the manor of Great Chesterford, in Essex.[3] These transactions betray the direct initiative of the king or his advisers. Numbered among the nominees who acted for the Abbey were some of the most favoured of the king's servants and confidants. In the case of Great Chesterford, for example, the nominees included Richard Fox, bishop of Winchester, Sir Thomas Lovell, and Sir Richard Empson.[4] Berkeley, moreover, was in no position to resist a suggestion that he sell one of his manors to a purchaser of the king's choice, for at this time he was only beginning to repair the damage he had suffered by his brother's settlement of the remainder in many of his estates on the king in tail male; Great Chesterford was in fact one of the manors that he recovered by act of parliament in 1503, but many of the family estates remained in the king's hands.[5]

However, it will not do to magnify the element of royal persuasion in these transactions, for Neville and Berkeley seem to have received a fair, perhaps even a generous price for their properties. Exclusive of *ad hoc* expenses, the purchase of Pinchpol, Bullington, Plumstead Boarstall, and Fenne and Skreyne consumed £1,378 of the total amount which Henry VII gave the monks for the endowment of his foundation; this, as we have seen, was £5,150. It is perhaps a fair guess that the monks

---

[1] Below, p. 427 (no. 51). For the plight of the abbot and convent of Tewkesbury at this time, see *V.C.H. Glos.* ii. 64.

[2] Below, p. 425 (no. 46).   [3] Below, p. 426 (no. 48).

[4] Ibid. Fox, Lovell, and Empson were named among the executors of Henry VII's will (*Will of Henry VII*, ed. Astle, pp. 42–3; cf. pp. 11–12).

[5] *Rot. Parl.* vi. 529–30; John Smyth of Nibley, *Lives of the Berkeleys*, ed. J. Mac-Lean (Glos., 1883–5), ii. 129–30. For George Neville's deep indebtedness to Henry VII towards the end of the reign, see J. R. Lander, 'Bonds, Coercion and Fear: Henry VII and the Peerage', in *Florilegium Historiale: Essays presented to Wallace K. Ferguson*, ed. J. G. Rowe and W. H. Stockdale (University of Toronto Press, 1971), pp. 344–5.

paid about twenty years' purchase ($= £533. 6s. 8d.$) for their rent at Stanway, since property in general tended to fetch this price in the fifteenth century, and, of all the forms of property coming on the market, rent-charges fetched the steadiest price.[1] If this was so, there remains of Henry's gift *c.* £3,239. But no account has been taken so far of the expenses of these and the other transactions in addition to the sum which the vendor received—conveyancing fees, the costs of litigation, and so on; Henry's outlay of £5,150 probably included these. Moreover, in 1503, Neville gave the abbot and convent of Westminster a conditional remainder in the manors of Beverington and Lancing, in Sussex, in case the transfer of the other manors should fall through, and this transaction, too, must have consumed the normal expenses of a conveyance.[2]

If this reasoning is correct, the sum of £3,239 covered the purchase price of the lands that were finally sold by Neville and Berkeley and the *ad hoc* expenses of these transactions and other consequential ones, together with those of the purchases from John Cutte and William Esyngton. Granted even a generous allowance on the score of expenses, it seems possible that Neville and Berkeley received at least twenty years' purchase. Between them they sold the monks of Westminster property worth £130. 13s. 4d. per annum.[3] At twenty years' purchase, they would have received £2,613. 6s. 8d., a figure leaving *c.* £626 for the *ad hoc* expenses of all the transactions that have been described; the sum represents *c.* 12 per cent of Henry VII's total outlay of £5,150. This is indeed a possible figure for the incidental costs of land purchase on this scale at the end of the Middle Ages— half a century earlier, Sir John Fastolf would certainly have considered himself lucky to have escaped so lightly[4]—but it is perhaps an ample one for transactions where the litigation was collusive—designed, that is, to break entails but probably reflecting no true challenge on anyone's part to the monks' wish to buy the property in question and the vendor's agreement to sell it to them.

---

[1] McFarlane, *Nobility of Later Medieval England*, p. 57.

[2] W.A.M. 14647, 14649, 4030, 4053, 4056; *Cal. Pat. R., 1494–1509*, p. 304.

[3] Great Chesterford, £66. 13s. 4d.; Oswald Beck Soke etc., £64.

[4] K. B. McFarlane, 'The investment of Sir John Fastolf's profits of war', *Trans. Royal Historical Soc.*, 5th ser., 7 (1957), 111 ff.

VII

Customary Land to 1348: the
Size of Holdings

(i) *Holdings on the Manors in Middlesex in 1086*

I T is only in Middlesex that Domesday Book consistently records the size of holdings, and only *c.* 16 per cent of the landed wealth of the monks of Westminster lay in this county at that date.[1] If, however, it cannot be assumed that the situation here was a microcosm of that on the estate considered as a whole, the number of the manors involved lends it intrinsic interest. As a rule, the Survey describes holdings as hides, half-hides, virgates, or half-virgates, but occasionally it refers to acres, and it frequently forbears to describe the holdings of cottagers at all; in such cases we should probably assume that these were very small indeed.[2] As in the case of the hidage of the manorial unit as a whole, these modes of reckoning have a fiscal significance: they refer to units on which the local assessment of geld, and of other dues and services as well, was based; but the hides and virgates in question would have been related much more closely than the manorial hidage was to the real area of the land in question. Thus Domesday Book probably gives a reasonably accurate account of the actual holdings on the Abbey's manors in Middlesex at the end of the eleventh century. About 43 per cent of the tenants in question held virgates and half-virgates; a very small percentage held more, and *c.* 52 per cent less.[3] If Westminster itself and Staines,

---

[1] £82: £515. These figures exclude sub-tenancies valued separately from the Abbey's demesne manors; for the latter figure, see also above, p. 56.

[2] Lennard, *Rural England*, pp. 340 ff.

[3] 277 landholders are enumerated in the nine demesne manors of the Abbey in Midd. in 1086; see above, Table VII, pp. 123–6. Of these, 143 held less than half a virgate of land, 55 held half-virgates or (in seven cases) a little more, 65 held virgates, and 13 held more than a virgate. The holding of one tenant cannot be categorized. Where entries are in the form 'vj bordarii de iij virgatis', it has been

where the number of small holdings was particularly high, are excluded from the reckoning, it is still the case that *c.* 36 per cent of the recorded landholders in these manors held less than half a virgate of land.

(ii) *Holdings on the Manors of the Prior and Convent in* c. *1225*

With only few exceptions, every inhabitant of the manors of Westminster Abbey who is mentioned in the Domesday Survey was of dependent status, but at this date the line separating these men from the rare *liberi homines* is not to be thought of as a clear-cut division, a gulf not easily traversed in the one direction or the other by those on either side. By the early thirteenth century, however, categories had hardened, and the custumal which the prior and convent made of their manors at this time relies on the sharp distinction between so-called free land and customary land which had become a premiss of manorial tenures generally in the intervening period.[1] The description 'customary land' need imply no more than the juridical principle that the freehold of the land belonged to the lord of the manor, who was competent to transact all litigation concerning it in his own courts. On the estates of Westminster Abbey, however, and on many others beside, very nearly all customary land was held in villeinage—now a much more sharply defined institution than had been the case when Domesday Book was made—until the mid-fourteenth century, if not indeed beyond that term. Free land, by contrast, was land held by one or other of the recognized forms of free tenure, which tenure itself warranted the free status of the tenant in question. The custumal is to be understood, therefore, as a record of free land in the hands of free men and customary land in the hands of villeins. Though at odds with some accounts of English rural society in this period, the marshalling of free

assumed that the tenants shared more or less equally in the land—i.e. in this case, that each bordar had half a virgate; see, on this point, Lennard, *Rural England, 1086–1135*, p. 342. Thus the figures comprise an element of guess-work. Ten bordars at Staines who held 5 acres each have been counted as half-virgaters, since later evidence shows that the virgate in this manor was of *c.* 10 acres; and it has been assumed that the four bordars holding 40 acres in this manor were, severally, virgaters; see below, p. 235 n. The burgesses at Staines, the knights and other *homines* at Westminster, and the *servi* mentioned in every manor with the exception of Cowley and Westminster, have been excluded from the reckoning.

[1] B.L. Add. Ch. 8139. For the date of this custumal, see above, p. 104.

tenants and tenants in villeinage as distinct groups, having no personnel, or scarcely any, in common, is appropriate in the case of the Abbey's estates at the beginning of the thirteenth century, for only a tiny proportion of the tenants known to us here at this date held both free land and customary land. The custumal records the names of the free tenants as well as those of the villeins in five manors—Battersea and Wandsworth, Greenford, Morden, Teddington, and Aldenham—and in each place mixed holdings, comprising both land held freely and land held in villeinage, seem to have been rare or non-existent. At Aldenham, for example, where sixty-seven tenants are named, there were no such holdings, and at Battersea and Wandsworth only two holdings among ninety-one were of this kind.[1]

On the Abbey's customary land a virgated structure of holdings was well preserved, and the fragmentation of the latter less in evidence than is perhaps to be expected, given the demographic history of the preceding century; these, almost certainly, had been years of rapid growth in population. In each of the seven manors for which we have evidence at this date,[2] the commonest size of holding was a virgate or half- or quarter-virgate. Thus at Aldenham, where the virgate was of *c.* 40 acres, a holding of 10 acres occurs more frequently than any other; at Teddington, where the virgate was of *c.* 16 acres, the mode was also 16 acres; and at Battersea and Wandsworth, a manor with a virgate of *c.* 15 acres, it was 7½ acres. Moreover, these facts are not statistical illusions: half-virgate holdings, and, in one or two manors, whole virgates were in practice common. Of the seven manors, it was only at Feering and Aldenham that holdings of less than half a virgate each preponderated; most tenants of customary land in the other manors where the detailed structure of holdings is recorded held half a virgate or more of land.[3] And few of the untidy holdings that cannot be classified as virgates or fractions of the virgate were in fact

[1] See below, p. 432.
[2] The custumal enumerates customary holdings at Knightsbridge and Feering, in addition to the five manors mentioned in the preceding paragraph of the text.
[3] The number of customary tenants holding half a virgate or more of land in each manor was as follows: at Aldenham, 21 of a total of 59; at Battersea and Wandsworth, 63: 73; at Feering, 22: 47; at Greenford, 36: 46; at Knightsbridge, 29: 30; at Morden, 17: 18; at Teddington, 14: 21. For the holdings of this period classified by acreage, see Appendix VII (below, pp. 434 ff.). Two of the customary tenants at Battersea and Wandsworth were also tenants of free land.

random agglomerations of acres; most comprised a half or whole virgate, together with a little extra land that the tenant had been fortunate enough to acquire in addition to his standard holding.

(iii) *Holdings on the Manors of the Abbot and Convent in the Early Fourteenth Century*

A century later, in the time of Abbot Kedyngton and Abbot Curtlington, free tenants and the tenants of customary land were still, as a rule, distinct groups on the Abbey's estates.[1] The significant exceptions to this rule occur in the Abbey's semi-urbanized manors, precisely in the setting where we should expect legal and social distinctions to be first obscured, and where many of the tenants in question were probably no ordinary tenants of agricultural land. At Battersea and Wandsworth, for example, *c.* 18 per cent of the Abbey's tenants[2]— themselves a large group—held both free and customary tenements. In several cases, however, the mixed holding comprised a house or garden in the town quarters of Battersea and Wandsworth, held freely, and a customary holding in the fields.[3] Evidently, some townsmen possessed of free messuages had found an outlet for their surplus capital in customary land; even in this manor, the number of tenants who held both free land and customary land in the fields was small.

The virgate had proved a less resilient feature of manorial life. At South Benfleet, Hampstead, and Hendon, the practice of reckoning by virgates was itself more or less a thing of the past; the overwhelming majority of the holdings listed in the custumals of these manors is described in terms of messuages and their appurtenant acres, and it is to be presumed that, to a large extent, if not entirely, the virgate itself had been dissolved in the process of much buying and selling and exchange.[4] At Aldenham, where the virgate was still in use as the unit of

---

[1] Below, pp. 432-3. [2] 24: 134. [3] C.U.L. MS. Kk 5. 29, fos. 46 ff.
[4] Ibid., fos. 31ᵛ ff., 116ᵛ ff.; *Trans. London and Middlesex Archaeological Soc.* N.S., 6 (1929–32), 580–630. Morden is a special case: holdings here were now reckoned in terms of the acre and not the virgate, but the 20-acre and 10-acre holdings, which were characteristic of the early fourteenth-century manor, were in fact virgate and half-virgate holdings; see C.U.L. MS. Kk 5. 29, fos. 41ᵛ–2. At Claygate, a sufficient number of the holdings enumerated in the custumal made of this manor in 1341 were of 20 acres or fractions thereof to suggest that a virgate of 20 acres and its fractions, though not the prevailing units of land-holding, still had a real existence (W.A.M. 27228).

assessment for rents and services, there was little correspondence between this unit or any fraction of it and the actual unit of landholding. Most virgates here were shared by parceners—as many as eleven are mentioned in one case[1]—and, conversely, the holding of the individual tenant was made up, in many cases, of parcels in more than one virgate, if not in several. Here, in fact, the virgate was little more than a fiscal tenement.

But in some other manors the impressive feature of the tenemental patterns of the early fourteenth century is the continued prominence of the virgate or of sizeable fractions of the virgate, the ancient unit of landholding—and this in the face of so many pressures tending towards fragmentation. In this respect Battersea and Wandsworth still conformed to the old ways: of seventy-one tenants holding in villeinage here in 1312, no fewer than sixty-five (= 92 per cent) held half a virgate or more of land, and in nearly every case the basic holding was in fact a standard half-virgate or virgate.[2] At Stevenage—like Battersea and Wandsworth a partly urbanized manor—the half-virgate was the standard unit of customary landholding; of thirty tenants holding in villeinage here in 1315, twenty-five (= *c.* 83 per cent) held half-virgates.[3] If the conventual manors where a virgated structure of holdings persisted at this date are considered as a single group, it can be said that *c.* 51 per cent of the tenants holding in villeinage possessed a standard virgate or half-virgate holding, although in many cases this was not their entire holding.[4] Yet the convent's manors were in those

---

[1] C.U.L. MS. Kk 5. 29, fos. 65–65ᵛ. See also below, p. 211 n. Early enclosure and consolidation of strips may explain the fate of the virgate at Aldenham.

[2] Ibid., fos. 48 ff.

[3] Ibid., fos. 81ᵛ ff. In fact the custumal from which the figures in the text are derived mentions only one customary half-virgate at Stevenage; all the other tenants described as half-virgaters in the text are entered in this source as, in each case, one of two tenants of a virgate. This usage, however, is explained by the fact that the virgate was the basic unit for the assessment of rents and services at Stevenage; it is to be understood that the real unit of land-holding was now the half-virgate.

[4] 175: 345. (The latter figure is only an approximate one, since the full number of villein tenants at Ashwell is not precisely recorded; on this point see below, p. 432 and n.) The manors in question were Ashford and Teddington (Midd.); Ashwell, Stevenage, and Wheathampstead and Kinsbourne (Herts.); and Battersea and Wandsworth, and Morden (Surr.). Without Ashwell, where the great majority of tenants held less than a quarter-virgate each, the proportion was *c.* 71 per cent. Tenants who severally held both freely and in villeinage have been included in these figures.

very parts of England where we might expect an active land market and a light attachment to traditional units of tenure. On the abbot's portion of lands, at Pyrford, *c.* 77 per cent of the tenants of customary land had holdings of which the core was a standard half-virgate or virgate of land.[1] At Islip two-thirds of the body of customary tenants held half-virgates.[2]

(iv) *The Significance of the Virgate and Half-Virgate*

What then was the virgate and how had it come about that the fragmentation of this customary unit of landholding had so often been halted in time to save the half-holding from erosion or extinction? It seems likely that for a time in the early Middle Ages the virgate was the ideal family holding of rural society, the *terra unius familie* of the period, as the hide had been in Bede's day. Later, the half-virgate filled this role, and the line was evidently still drawn at this point on many of the Abbey's manors in the early fourteenth century. But the acreage of the virgate varied quite remarkably. On the Westminster estates, it was, for example, *c.* 40 at Aldenham, 32 at Islip, 20 at Morden and Pyrford, and 16 at Teddington; an 80-acre virgate occurs at Wheathampstead, and one of only 10 acres at Staines.[3] Moreover, the acre itself was not yet a standard unit of land measurement. Not only were customary acres—acres 'sicut jacent', as the sources of the period put it—different from, and often[4] considerably smaller than, measured acres: the former differed among themselves in size from place to place, and, occasionally, within the confines of a single vill or manor; and peasant holdings were normally measured in terms of these acres.[5] Even where the size of the acre was constant, the real number of acres in a virgate or half-virgate holding might

---

[1] 56: 73 (W.A.M. 27469).

[2] Glos. Records Office, D. 1099/M37, mm. 1–1ᵛ. This rental, compiled not long after the Hundred Rolls of 1279, lists ninety-one tenants in the manor of Islip who were, almost certainly, tenants of customary land, holding in villeinage, but the Hundred Rolls themselves, only sixty-nine. It is, however, the information given about villein dues at Islip in the Hundred Rolls that enables us to infer from the extremely brief entries in the rental that sixty of the ninety-one held half-virgates.

[3] For a longer list, see below, p. 434.

[4] Not, however, invariably. See, on the large customary acre of Cumberland, R. S. Dilley, 'The Customary Acre: an Indeterminate Measure', *Agricultural History Rev.* 23 (1975), 173–6.

[5] See also below, pp. 236–7.

differ from the number nominally comprised in these standard units; it was possible to have a large virgate or a small one, even where all virgates were in theory of the same acreage.

These are some of the awkward facts laid bare in recent studies of the agrarian landscape of medieval England.[1] If they do not mean—and they surely do not mean this—that holdings of the same nominal size, such as virgates, were not, as a rule, more or less commensurate with each other in the same manor or vill, they do make it impossible to believe that virgates, or half-virgates, had the same economic potential from place to place. The diverse acreages of these holdings is alone enough to make this conclusion impossible. On the estates of Westminster Abbey, the half-virgater at Battersea and Wandsworth, possessed of some $7\frac{1}{2}$ acres, must be reckoned, by absolute standards, a small-holder; at Islip, however, with 16 acres, he was assured, as a rule, not only of his own subsistence crops, but also of a surplus to sell each year; and the half-virgater of Wheathampstead, who had as many as 40 acres, was an aristocrat among the peasants of this period.

Must we, after all, abandon the notion that this holding, or the virgate, was ever a common family holding—the fair share of a family in the local fields? It would probably be better to see in the heterogeneous acreages of virgates and half-virgates a reflection of very diverse views, not often the same from place to place, but tenaciously held over a long period of time, of family needs and fair shares. That virgates and half-virgates were not in fact commensurate from place to place compels us to find the rationale of these units of land-holding in the presuppositions and distinctive modes of life of the peasant communities that made use of them; only if they were natural,

[1] For a conspectus of the evidence, see *Studies of Field Systems in the British Isles*, ed. A. R. H. Baker and R. A. Butlin (Cambridge, 1973). A number of studies in this volume rely on the hypothesis that the actual bundle of selions and acres making up a particular virgate or half-virgate holding could be and sometimes was changed, by, for example, the fitting into it of bits of newly assarted land; indeed, they demonstrate the truth of this hypothesis. The text above is concerned, not with the actual selions and acres in a holding, but with the number of the real or notional acres in the latter. A somewhat cursory examination of the evidence suggests that the composition of holdings changed little on the manors of Westminster Abbey for which we have evidence between *c.* 1200 and the mid-fourteenth century. For the period after 1348, see below, p. 286. On the composition of virgates see also R. A. Dodgshon, 'The Landholding Foundations of the Open-Field System', *Past and Present* 67 (May 1975), 1 ff.

authentic features of the rural economy could such diverse views of family needs have endured for so long.

However large or small it was, the ideal family holding of each village community was for a long time threatened, if not entirely dissipated, by the deep-rooted custom of providing for more than one child out of the family patrimony. It was the adoption of one or other of the forms of impartible inheritance on the Abbey's estates that saved, not often, indeed, the virgate itself, but in many cases the half-virgate from destruction. When did this happen?

On most of the manors for which we have evidence, the division of customary holdings and, by implication, the practice of partible inheritance, seems to have continued after the assessment of villein rents and services had settled into something very like its final form. In nearly every case the basic unit used in this assessment was the virgate, but most of the virgates in question, though retaining their function as the unit of assessment, ceased to be actual units of tenure; this role passed to the half-virgate or some smaller holding. Thus at Stevenage, though villein dues were still assessed on the virgate in the early fourteenth century, the standard holding in the case of customary land was the half-virgate;[1] evidently, division of the family inheritance had continued among the villeins of Stevenage into the period when rents and services had assumed their final form, based on the virgate.

This helps very little towards establishing an exact chronology, for, of the assessment of villein dues on the Abbey's manors, we can say only that the definitive arrangements were probably already old by the thirteenth century and may have been made in some places before the Domesday period.[2] An early date for the change from partibility to impartibility on these manors would not be surprising. It would be consonant, in the first place, with what is known—with the little that is known—of the timing of the change in English rural society considered more generally,[3] and, secondly, with our information about

[1] Above, p. 207 and n. Cf. G. C. Homans, *English Villagers of the Thirteenth Century* (New York, 1960), p. 116 and n.

[2] Below, pp. 218–19.

[3] See Pollock and Maitland, *History of English Law* ii. 279, where it is suggested that primogeniture was a common rule of inheritance on villein land from a time that was 'remote' in the age of copyhold. Partibility, however, is now known to

villein holdings on the Westminster manors in the thirteenth century. Where the matter can be put to the test, the fragmentation of standard holdings does not seem to have been carried much beyond the limits already established on these manors at the beginning of the century. At Feering, for example, the proportion of the Abbey's customary tenants holding less than half a virgate of land was virtually the same in the 1280s as it had been in the 1220s—52 or 53 per cent at each date.[1] Quite probably, when the custumal of *c.* 1225 was made, peasant society on most of these manors had already adopted the feudal rule that a single heir took all, except when there were daughters but no son; among daughters the land was divided.[2]

Was the influence of the monks of Westminster in their capacity as landlords therefore of little account in determining the size of customary holdings in their manors? This by no means follows from the fact that virgates and half-virgates were, in the sense set out in the preceding paragraphs, natural features of peasant life. Circumstances often weakened a tenant's resolve or capacity to maintain the level of activity to which he was in principle committed by the tenancy of half a virgate

have survived more widely than Maitland's sources led him to suppose; see R. J. Faith, 'Peasant families and inheritance customs in medieval England', *Agricultural History Review* 14 (1966), 77 ff.

[1] 25: 47 in *c.* 1225; 23: 44 in 1289 (B.L. Add. Ch. 8139; W.A.M. 9287; C.U.L. MS. Kk 5. 29, fos. 103 ff.). The term *parcenarii*, which is used in the custumal of 1289, denotes, not those having shares of land in accordance with the principle of parage, but 'peers' or 'equals' in a tenurial sense—those possessed of like holdings who owed like services.

Aldenham is an exception to the remarks in the text, and a difficult case. To all appearances, standard holdings were not more fragmented here towards the end of the thirteenth century than near the beginning: *c.* 64 per cent (= 38: 59) of the tenants of customary land held less than half a virgate in *c.* 1225, and 62 per cent (=38: 61) in the second half of the century (B.L. Add. Ch. 8139; W.A.M. 9287; W.A.M. 4616). By 1315, however, *c.* 83 per cent (= 99: 120) did so (C.U.L. MS. Kk 5. 29, fos. 64ᵛ–68). The probable explanation of the doubling of the number of tenants in a relatively short space of time before 1315 is the insistence of the monks of Westminster of that period upon bringing to the surface all inter-tenant sales of land; thus the custumal of 1315 lays bare a tenurial pattern that may have been long in existence. On the other hand, it is possible that partibility persisted late at Aldenham, but that the full number of parceners was not recorded in the custumals until the early fourteenth century.

[2] A crude summary of feudal primogeniture, which in practice often found ways of making some provision for younger sons and daughters; see *Past and Present* 57 (Nov. 1972), 3 ff.; and for similar strategems on the part of the tenants of the Westminster manors, see below, pp. 295 ff., and, for peasants more generally, *Agricultural History Review* 14 (1966), 85-6.

of land: he might, for example, be sick or aged, or impoverished by the failure of his crops. A free tenant so placed could reduce his scale of activity and replenish his little store of capital by selling an acre or two of his land; though without a strip or two here and there, he would still be in business. In the case of customary land, however, the monks evinced in many of their manors a strong and enduring hostility to the piecemeal fragmentation of holdings.[1]

One reason for their attitude was the administrative convenience of neat tenemental patterns, made up of half or whole virgates, for long ago these, but particularly the latter, had been adopted as the basis for the assessment of villein rents and services. Yet, as the example of Aldenham shows,[2] assessments based on the virgate could be made to function even when the latter had been superseded as the real unit of landholding. A much more weighty consideration with the abbot and convent was the necessity of preserving from destruction the units of landholding that were the livelihood of their dependent villein families. In adopting this attitude, the monks were thinking, not of this or that component of villein dues and how it could be most easily collected, but of the villein himself as one who, in a quite general sense, existed for their service; the continuance of his family on its virgated holding was considered indispensable to their exercise of lordship in the broad sense of this word. For the tenant of customary land in the early Middle Ages, therefore, it was usually a case of all or nothing: in sickness or in health, young or old, he either continued as tenant of his entire holding or surrendered it in its entirety; even his freedom to lease unwanted acres was much circumscribed.[3]

How important seignorial influence was in the long term in halting the fragmentation of holdings can be seen in the contrast between the customary and the free holdings in one of the manors of the abbot of Westminster—Pyrford, in Surrey. A rule of impartible inheritance had been adopted here in time to preserve virgates and half-virgates of, respectively, 20 and 10 acres as very common units of landholding on customary land in the early fourteenth century.[4] But despite the fact that the

---

[1] Below, pp. 299 ff.   [2] Above, pp. 206–7.   [3] Below, pp. 307 ff.
[4] W.A.M. 27469. A few of the customary half-virgates and virgates recorded in this extent were now notional units of tenure, in the sense that part of the land

customary tenants of Pyrford were mainly tenants of this kind, the very numerous free tenants were, almost to a man, small-holders having less than a quarter-virgate—less, that is, than 5 acres—each.[1] The free tenants of this manor had retained the capacity to alienate their holdings piecemeal, even in the period when family sentiment favoured the preservation of the hold-ing in its entirety; on customary land, however, the monks of Westminster intervened to prevent such transactions.

(v) *The Acreage of Holdings*

Despite the long-continued family and seignorial hostility towards fragmentation, most holdings of customary land in the Abbey's manors *were* small. After all, one could be a half-virgater at Greenford with only 8 acres, at Battersea and Wands-worth, with only $7\frac{1}{2}$. In the early thirteenth century, as the figures in Appendix VII show,[2] *c.* 48 per cent of the customary tenants in the manors for which we have evidence held only 10 field-acres or fewer than 10. A century later, the proportion was rather higher—52 per cent—and on some manors considered individually much higher—at Ashwell, in Hertfordshire, perhaps as high as *c.* 73 per cent. Only 7·5 per cent[3] of the customaries of these manors certainly held more than 30 acres of arable land at the earlier date; at the later, only *c.* 6 per cent.[4]

(vi) *The Significance of Tenurial Patterns*

The holdings which have been the topic for study in this chapter were all held of the abbot and convent of Westminster; in each manor they formed the very top layer of customary tenures. Yet, as every student of manorial history knows, to lay bare these arrangements is not necessarily to discover the pattern of the occupation of land at the time. For one thing, the

---

belonging to them had in fact been alienated, but the acreage affected by the transactions in question was very small; see below, pp. 301–2. See also above, p. 208.

[1] W.A.M. 27469.

[2] Below, pp. 435–7. The figures in this appendix relate to all customary holdings, but they take no account of the free holdings of those—as a rule, few—tenants who held both freely and by custom. In most such cases the tenant's customary holding was considerably larger than his free holding. The figures given in the remainder of this paragraph are approximate figures only, because, both in the early thirteenth century and in the early fourteenth, the size of a few holdings is not known.

[3] 22: 294.   [4] 46: 764.

manor was not always, and in medieval England perhaps not often, co-terminous with the vill where its complex of rights was exercised; many tenants therefore had interests in land that extended to more than a single manor. And further, whatever the relationship between manor and vill, sub-tenancies were common on customary land;[1] it cannot be assumed that the tenant holding directly of the lord of the manor himself exploited the whole of his land year by year.

On both counts we must be wary of identifying the pattern of customary landholding on the manors of Westminster Abbey with the pattern of the occupation of land in the vills in question. The monks of Westminster were hostile, not only to the piecemeal fragmentation of customary land, but also to demises on the part of tenants, other than those made for a very short term.[2] The latter, however, they tolerated, and, although they were reluctant to allow even these to affect the major part of any holding, the cumulative effects on patterns of landholding of such subleasing as they did permit were probably large. Certainly the existence of subtenants was an open secret between the monks of Westminster and some of their customary tenants at the beginning of the thirteenth century. It is surely implied at Greenford, for example, in the rule that every household there—not every tenant, but every household—send a man to the work of fencing in Spring.[3] Later, towards the end of the century, a custumal of the manor of Aldenham concludes with the words 'memorandum quod quilibet subtenentium invenit j hominem ad levandum fenum'.[4] As for vills of divided lordship, many of the Abbey's manors were situated in such places; many of its tenants may have had interests that spilled over into another lordship. The holdings considered in this chapter were, then, tenurial units, but perhaps not in many cases the actual farms worked by the Abbey's villeins year in, year out; small though many of them were, they represent, not the basic ground-plan of customary landholding, but the superstructure.

---

[1] See, in general, Postan, *Essays on Medieval Agriculture and General Problems of the Medieval Economy*, pp. 121 ff.

[2] Below, pp. 307 ff.

[3] B.L. Add. Ch. 8139; W.A.M. 9287.

[4] W.A.M. 4616; and for the undersettles of Aldenham, see also above, p. 211 n.

Yet down to the fourteenth century, and, indeed, for a much longer period than this, the peasant economy as a whole in these manors was deeply affected by arrangements at this level of manorial tenures. This was so for two reasons, one already anticipated in this chapter, the other to form the subject matter of the next. On customary land few tenants, if any, other than those holding directly of the abbot and convent possessed long-term interests in the land; at the level of sub-tenancies, men had to make do with short-term arrangements that offered no solid base for family fortune, no real security even for the year after next. This was a consequence of the restrictions imposed by the abbot and convent on the land transactions of their villeins, but also of a natural preference on the part of many of the lessors and lessees of this period for short terms.[1] By contrast, villeins holding of the abbot and convent had a fully heritable interest in their land; but given the situation which has just been described, the heritable holdings were inevitably the dominant features of the tenurial scene, the landmarks that never moved, however frequently their outline might be for a time obscured.

Though possessed of heritable interests in their land, the Abbey's tenants in villeinage probably did not enjoy the lion's share of its issues, as did tenants in fee, their counterpart, in the matter of heritability, on free land. On the contrary, it is probable that down to the fourteenth century many of them carried a grievously heavy burden of rent.[2] This is the second reason why their situation is germane to an understanding of the peasant economy as a whole, for, of course, no one with an interest in customary land, whatever place he occupied in the hierarchy of tenures, escaped without paying a rent that was proportionate to the burden carried by those at the top; every rent paid by a subtenant reflected the maladjustment of arrangements higher up. Thus the following account of villein dues, though true in a literal sense only of the manorial super-structure, describes the common plight of villein society in general on these manors.

[1] Below, p. 321.   [2] Below, pp. 236 ff.

VIII

Customary Land to 1348: Rents and Services

(i) *Labour Services, Renders in Kind, and Rents of Assize*

UNTIL 1348, nearly all the Abbey's customary land was held in villeinage, and villein rents were made up of the three classic components, labour services, renders in kind, and cash payments. The custumal of *c.* 1225 records the proportions in which these were mixed on the manors of the prior and convent at that time.[1]

At two of the manors surveyed in this custumal, Stevenage and Wheathampstead, the burden of week-work was still relatively heavy. Virgaters at Stevenage owed three days' work a week outside the harvest season; in harvest, they owed the reaping of half an acre each day. Those at Wheathampstead owed four days' work a week, beside the service of carrying corn to Westminster on Saturday; and these villeins too owed daily reaping services during the harvest season. But in general the commutation of week-work was well advanced. At Greenford, outside the harvest season, the most heavily burdened virgater did not owe more than five such works a month. At Launton, between 29 September and 24 June, virgaters owed as little as one day's work a month; this, however, was to be a full day's work, lasting until evening.

Two features of the occasional services demanded by the Abbey of its villeins at this date are noteworthy. First, ploughing services were common. They are mentioned in ten of the eleven manors the customs of which are described, and at Wheathampstead they appear heavy, until the extraordinary size of the virgate here (80 acres) is recalled: the virgater at Wheathampstead, burdened as he was with four days' work a week,

---

For the following dues, see B.L. Add. Ch. 8139, and W.A.M. 9287.

could be required to plough and harrow 15 acres of the demesne each year. At Aldenham, even a customary tenant with only 5 acres owed ploughing service three times a year, if he owned a plough; at Stevenage, a quarter-virgater—one having, that is, 10 acres—owed the ploughing of half an acre every Thursday; and at Ashwell every plough owed two ploughings a year without food.

Secondly, some villeins owed heavy carrying services. The virgater at Stevenage could be asked to carry 20 quarters of oats or 15 quarters of any other grain to Westminster each year. His counterpart at Wheathampstead owed regular carrying services on Saturday; and at Launton, remote though it was from Westminster, the virgater owed the carriage, not only of a load of oats or half a load of wheat to the Abbey in the summer, but also of wood at Christmas.[1]

Renders in kind, if always in sum much lighter than money rents and labour services, occur in nearly every manor, although they were not in every manor the common lot of every villein. They were heaviest at Ashwell, where each virgate owed as much as 1 quarter and 2 bushels of corn per annum. At Wheathampstead, a much larger virgate owed 2 bushels of good corn and 1 quarter of malt per annum; the corn render was for the sowing of the demesne.

With very few exceptions, the assessment of labour services and renders in kind was uniform for the category of holding in question, but this was not always the case with the money rents recorded in the custumal. At Aldenham, Feering, and Green-ford, these rents, though not entirely lacking in consistency from holding to holding, are noticeably varied, and the same is true of money rents at Wandsworth, in the manor of Battersea and Wandsworth. Thus at Feering some virgates owed 6s. per annum, one 9s. 4d., and two, 8s.; at Wandsworth, rents for half-virgate holdings fell in the range of 1s. 10d. to 3s.; but at Ashwell, Battersea, Morden, Stevenage, Teddington, and Wheathampstead, money rents show a high degree of uniformity

---

[1] Cf. villein obligations in the neighbouring vill of Islip, an abbatial property; we learn from a late-fourteenth-century custumal of this vill that the obligations of a half-virgater here had once included one day's *averagium* per week, with horse and sack, the service being valued in the custumal at 1½d. ('Custumal (1391) and Bye-Laws (1386–1540) of the Manor of Islip', ed. B. F. Harvey, *Oxfordshire Record Soc.* 40 (1959), 84).

—2*s*. per annum for a virgate at Morden, 1*s*. 4*d*. at Stevenage, and so on.

This difference between the standard money rent, on the one hand, and the apparently arbitrary figure, on the other, must reflect differences in methods of assessment: it appears that on most of their manors the monks of Westminster had made a collective bargain with the whole body of their tenants, but on a few the bargain had been made with the individual tenant. Aldenham, Feering, and Greenford, three of the manors where individually negotiated bargains seem to have been common, were still colonizing manors in the thirteenth century;[1] it seems likely that here the monks and their villeins agreed on rents for newly asserted land piecemeal, as this came under cultivation. It is possible, moreover, that the heterogeneity of cash renders in these manors reflects some little diversity in the real acreage of virgates and half-virgates. At Teddington, in the other group of manors, money rents clearly originated in the commutation of labour services. Unusually for the Abbey's manors, the basic unit of assessment for labour services here seems to have been the half, not the whole virgate. In *c.* 1225, a half-virgater at Teddington owed 3 works a week during the harvest season and 3 works a fortnight for the greater part of the year, and the labour service obligation of all multiple holdings was exactly the same. But a virgater owed, in addition, 2*s*. in rent per annum, the tenant of a virgate and a half, 4*s*., and so on. In this way the feudal principle that a tenant having a multiple holding must make other provision for the bodily service due in respect of all except the basic unit was honoured. In the other conventual manors, it is not evident that rents of assize originated in commutation payments, although they may have done so.

Even in the manors where rents lacked uniformity in *c.* 1225, it is sometimes possible to distinguish a rent more common than others that was probably the proto-payment for a standard holding, dating from a much earlier period. At Greenford this sum was 9*d*. per half-virgate, and seven half-virgate holdings were still paying it in *c.* 1225. Since the custumal is the earliest source of its kind to survive at Westminster, it is impossible to

---

[1] The custumal of *c.* 1225 notes that there are 3¼ virgates and 20 acres of asserted land at Aldenham (= *c.* 150 acres *in toto*).

say how long ago the arrangements recorded had been agreed between the monks and their villeins. Yet it may perhaps be inferred from some details in the Domesday description of the Abbey's manors that the assessment of rents and services had already begun to harden into a form that was difficult to change by 1086. One puzzling feature of this description is its reference to hides and half-hides in multiple occupation. Four *villani* holding 1 hide, and thirty-six bordars holding 3 hides are mentioned at Staines; at Greenford, four *villani* holding 1 hide and seven bordars holding 1 hide; and at Hendon, twelve bordars holding half a hide.[1] It is hard to explain such entries except on the assumption that the hides and half-hides in question had already become traditional units for the assessment of rent and services by 1086; the monks of the Domesday period were in the habit of dealing with the tenants in occupation as a group, not as individuals, because the current assessment of services had been settled before the lands were split up.

By the early thirteenth century, and not surprisingly, if the process had begun so much earlier, the definition of the villein's obligations on this estate had been taken a long way—further, indeed, than the bare fixing of money rents, renders in kind, and quotas of service would seem to suggest. A customary virgater at Teddington was to have ale at the first harvest boon, but his men, only water; at Launton, his men were to have food at the fourth boon only; a tenant of 2 virgates at Greenford was to have no food when he did his harrowing and hoeing, and he was to work until noon—these details[2] belong to a regimented system in which little was left to chance.

Remarkably, in view of the inflationary character of the period, the annual dues for villein holdings on these manors changed little in the century that separated the making of the custumal of *c.* 1225 from the Black Death. How little they changed at Teddington is shown in Table X, where the dues of a customary virgater, as set out in the custumal of *c.* 1225, are compared with those prescribed in the extent of this manor

[1] *D.B.* i. 128–128b.

[2] For which see B.L. Add. Ch. 8139, and W.A.M. 9287. Presumably at Teddington the virgater's men were given some of the large allowance of ale that was the virgater's customary right at the first boon.

that was made in 1312. In the latter source, the virgater's services are defined with greater particularity, but, even so, it is clear that minimal changes had occurred during the intervening period. Those that had occurred favoured in some cases

TABLE X. *The Annual Dues Owed by a Tenant in Villeinage of a Virgate of Customary Land at Teddington in the Early Thirteenth and Early Fourteenth Centuries*

	Early 13th Cent.	*Early 14th Cent.*
Labour Services Week-Work	3 works per week during harvest, but not on feast days.*	3 works per week, each for the whole day, during the 6 weeks of harvest, but not on feast days; tenant and his peers receive 16 gallons of ale. Value of each work: 2*d*.
	3 works per fortnight during remainder of year; but one work is remitted for each ploughing service performed. If threshing is done, 3 works are allowed for each quarter of corn threshed; if compost is spread, 2 works for each ½ acre.	3 works per fortnight between 24 June and 29 Sept. except during the above 6 weeks, the work to be done on Monday in the first week of each fortnight, and on Wednesday and Friday in the second week. Tenant receives bread @ ¼*d*. on one day. Value of each work: 1*d*.
		3 works per fortnight, on the days specified above, between 29 Sept. and 24 June. Value of each work: ½*d*. For each work he does what he is told to do for a day. If threshing is done, 3 works are allowed for the threshing of 1 quarter of rye or barley, or of 2 quarters of oats, or of 1 quarter of beans and peas.
		No works are owing in the week following Xmas, Easter, or Whitsun, or at other times of the year, if the day for work is a feast day.
Other Work	If tenant owns a plough, he ploughs and harrows 3 acres for seed and ploughs 2 acres fallow; he shares in the ploughing of *Eilwoldescroft*, for which 1 work is remitted.	If tenant owns a plough, he ploughs and harrows 2 acres in winter and 2 acres in Lent; if he owns plough beasts but no plough, he works with them for 2 days at winter

	Early 13th Cent.	*Early 14th Cent.*

Labour Services

Early 14th Cent.

sowing and 2 days at Lent sowing. The work is not valued because only tenants owning ploughs or beasts owe it.

With other customaries, the tenant mows the demesne meadow; dinner is provided, and 6*d.* for ale.

He mows for 1 day in *North-mead*, receiving bread @ ½*d.* and 4 eggs; he and peers receive cheese @ 4*d.*, and 6*d.* in cash. One day's week-work is remitted for this work. Value of mowing work: 2*d.* He mows for ¼ day with 1 man in *Southmead*, mowing and spreading hay. Value of work: ¾*d.* He contributes ¼ scythe in the demesne meadow at West-minster. Value of work: 1½*d.*

He finds 2 men for each of 3 boons in the corn harvest, at which he also works him-self. He has 32 gallons of ale at the first boon, and his men bread, water, and 2 dishes; at the second, they all have bread, water, and 2 dishes; at the third, he has bread, cheese, and ale. At the great boon, he has ale at dinner and his men water and 2 dishes; at supper, all have food and ale. The second day after the great boon, all customaries have dinner provided; when harvest is over, they have a sextar of ale.

He finds 2 men for 2 boons in the corn harvest, at which boons he also works himself. Each man has bread @ ½*d.* and fish and cheese @ ½*d.* on each occasion. Value of each man's work: 1*d.* At one boon† he supervises the reapers, carrying a staff; food is provided. Value of work: *nil.*

Renders in Kind

Every 2 such tenants give 15 sheaves of rye, barley, and oats at Michaelmas, to acquit damage done to the lord's corn and grass in the course of the year. Every such tenant renders 1 bushel (= 1/8 quarter) of barley at Whitsun and 5 eggs at Easter. Every two render a hen at Xmas.

Tenant renders 1 bushel of barley (= *churchscot*). Value: 6*d.* Also 1 peck of rye and 1 peck of barley at Michael-mas (= *unthankenbotecorne*). Also ½ hen at Xmas; value: 1*d.* Also 5 eggs at Easter; value: ¼*d.*

TABLE X (*cont.*)

	Early 13th Cent.	Early 14th Cent.
Money Dues	2s. per annum.‡	2s. per annum.
	Pannage @ 1d. for every year-old pig belonging to a holding for which works are done, and ½d. for every younger pig.	Pannage @ ½d. for each year-old pig which he has, and ¼d. for each younger pig.§ Tenant contributes to fixed tallage of £1. 1s. 2d. per annum and to cert money of 4s. at Hoketide view of frankpledge.

Sources: For the early thirteenth century: B.L. Add. Ch. 8139; W.A.M. 9287; for the early fourteenth century: W.A.M. 27197; C.U.L. MS. Kk 5. 29, fos. 21ᵛ–25ᵛ.

* A provision showing that week-work was already owing on certain days of the week and not on others, as it was a century later; a lord able to summon his labourers on any day of the week would not, in any case, have chosen a feast day.

† i.e. the third.

‡ Despite the omission of reference to tallage at this date, this levy may already have been a part of villein dues at Teddington; the custumal of the Abbey's manors from which the above entries for the early thirteenth century are derived is haphazard in its record of this payment.

§ Each tenant of 1½ virgates owed 1d. for every third year-old pig, and ½d. for every third younger pig. Each tenant of 2 virgates owed 1d. for every fourth year-old pig, and ½d. for every fourth younger pig. Each half-virgater owed 1d. for every year-old pig and ¼d. for every younger pig.

the villein, in others, the monks; one or two were compromises. Thus instead of coming himself with two men to the third harvest boon, the villein virgater was now required to do nothing on that occasion except supervise reapers who were, it seems, recruited in other ways; but the other boons were now dry boons for himself as well as his men. His quota of ploughing services had been reduced, but that of his harrowing services increased. It may have been to his advantage that his work at the hay harvest at Teddington was now precisely defined in terms of a day's work. On the other hand, the innovation of work in the meadows at Westminster—if, indeed, this service was an innovation and not an ancient custom that the earlier source failed to particularize—can hardly have been welcome. But the overriding impression conveyed by a comparison of the virgater's dues at these two dates is how little was changed in the meantime. And the prior and convent had not marked time more resolutely at Teddington than in their other manors; the same conservatism could be illustrated several times over on their portion of lands.

None of the abbot's manors comes into view before the middle of the thirteenth century, and we do not begin to be well informed about conditions here before 1270 or 1280. By then, it seems clear, villein dues on these manors too had settled into a mould that was difficult to break—that was not in fact to be broken until the mid-fourteenth century. Moreover, some of the dues in question have an air of real antiquity about them. At Islip, for example, a half-virgater worked for two and a half days a week or paid 3*s*. rent of assize per annum instead[1]— an arrangement that must have been made at a time when the virgater here, the possessor of a full land, was liable for five days' work a week the year round. But this is a heavier quota of service than we ever glimpse on the Abbey's entire estate in the thirteenth or fourteenth century—everywhere else, except during the harvest season,[2] the work of one or two of the days that made up the full working week had already been permanently commuted when the villein's quota of services first comes into view. The half-virgater's obligation at Islip must already have been very old by the second half of the thirteenth century; indeed, the very nature of the arrangement—the proffer of rent of assize and service as stark alternatives—argues for their antiquity.[3]

(ii) *Tallage and Entry Fines*

By the thirteenth century, the ability of the abbot and convent of Westminster to keep villein rents moving depended, not on their capacity to change the basic assessment of rents and services, but on three other features of the tenure. The first

[1] For rents and services at Islip, see *Rot. Hund.* ii. 831–2; Glos. Records Office, D. 1099/M 37, m. 1; W.A.M. 14776 ff. The manor included the Westminster fee in three vills—Islip, Murcot, and Fencot. The remarks in the text apply only to Islip, week-work at Murcot and Fencot having been permanently commuted into a money rent before 1279.

[2] At Deerhurst and Hardwicke the half-virgater still owed five days' work per week between 1 Aug. and 29 Sept. (W.A.M. 8422 ff.); at Pershore and Wick, the virgater owed as much between 24 June and 29 Sept. (W.A.M. 22100 ff.). These were abbatial manors, but Deerhurst and Hardwicke were out of the demesne between the mid-twelfth century and the end of the thirteenth; see below, p. 344. For Staines, where the half virgater owed three days' work per week, and the virgater, six days' work per week, between 24 June and 29 Sept., see below, p. 227.

[3] Below, pp. 226 ff.

was the liability of the tenant in villeinage to tallage at the will
of the lord. This device the abbot used more effectively in his
manors than his monks in theirs, and the practice whereby he
took, in addition to a yearly tallage from all tenants holding in
villeinage, a special levy on his election and receipt of the
temporalities continued into the fifteenth century; Richard
Harwden took this tax from his villeins, or attempted to take it,
on his election in 1420.[1] But already, by the second half of the
thirteenth century, this levy had lost its arbitrary character on
the abbatial manors; fixed tallage was the rule. At Sutton-under-
Brailes and Todenham, for example, where rents of assize
amounted to *c.* £17 per annum, the amount due in respect of
tallage was now £10 per annum, and the liability of the individual tenant was probably limited as well.[2] On the manors of
the prior and convent, where also fixed tallages were now usual,
the payments were in general lower. In the early fourteenth
century, this tax represented *c.* 10 per cent of the extended
value of all villein dues on their five principal manors.[3] In the
case of some of the convent's manors, the amount due was so
low as to suggest that the assessment had become fixed in
the distant past; at Wheathampstead, the tax yielded £2 per
annum;[4] at Morden, 5*s.*[5]

Entry fines were another adaptable component of villein dues.
Inevitably, however, the level of these was influenced by the
monks' recognition that villein tenure was fully heritable.
Within modest limits, these payments could be used to increase
the profitability to them of customary land; used to introduce
an element of real competition into the succession to villein
tenancies, they would have defeated the purpose for which the
latter existed—the support of the Abbey's villeins, the better

[1] W.A.M. 27490, the court rolls for Pyrford for 1421–2, where it is said that
every abbot may tallage at his entry and that the homage of Pyrford holding by
tallage owes £10. 6*s.* 2*d.* on Harwden's entry.

[2] W.A.M. 25900 (the minister's account for Todenham and Sutton-under-
Brailes for 1252–3, and the earliest such account to survive for any Westminster
manor). Rents of assize at Todenham and Sutton, excluding tallage, amounted
this year to £16. 12*s.* 7*d.*, and Peter's Pence to 2*s.* 4*d.*

[3] £14: £144. The manors in question were Aldenham, Battersea and Wandsworth, Feering, Stevenage, and Wheathampstead. For the dues, see C.U.L. MS.
Kk 5. 29, fos. 48 ff., 64ᵛ ff., 75ᵛ ff., 81ᵛ ff., and 103 ff. Cert money and court
profits have been excluded from consideration.

[4] Ibid., fo. 77.   [5] Ibid., fo. 43ᵛ.

to serve the Abbey. Few absolutely high entry fines are recorded in the thirteenth or fourteenth century, and those that are recorded were in most cases not fines for agricultural land. Thus at Wheathampstead, in 1304, Adam atte Rothe paid a fine of 16*s*. for an acre of land that he was to build on, and Elias Wadelowe paid 5*s*. for 1½ roods, again for building;[1] but the fine for a quarter-virgate of land which a tenant entered, in this manor of 80-acre virgates, in 1309, was 13*s*. 4*d*.[2] In most parts of the estate for which we have evidence a villein inheriting a virgate of land at this time could probably expect to escape with a fine in the range of 13*s*. 4*d*. to £2. One who had no family claim on the lands probably paid more. At Launton, such a tenant may have been asked for double the sum for which the family heir was liable; it was probably in these circumstances that two tenants, each taking a virgate of land in this manor, were asked for, respectively, £2. 13*s*. 4*d*. and £4 in 1294—sums that were at least double the normal entry fine for a virgate at Launton at this date.[3] The frequent use of the mark and the pound and of fractions of these common units of account, whatever the size of the virgate or level of the annual dues, underlines the fact that in general neither the abbot nor the convent of Westminster attempted to adjust fines closely to the value of the holding in question or to the income which they were destined to receive from the new occupant.

(iii) *Commutation and the Sale of Works*

Finally, something could be gained from the manipulation of labour services and renders in kind, particularly from the former. Custumals and extents recorded the utmost in the way of service that villeins could be asked to render each year. Should these services be used, or should these also be commuted into money payments, and, if so, at what price were villeins to be

---

[1] W.A.M. 8938 (court of 11 June, 1304); Adam received his acre with the growing crops. See also below, p. 446 n.

[2] W.A.M. 8940 (court of 25 June 1309). For the annual dues of customary tenants at Wheathampstead at this date, see below, p. 441.

[3] W.A.M. 15420. At the court held on 2 June 1294, John, son of Alice, paid a fine of £2. 13*s*. 4*d*. for a messuage and virgate of land surrendered by Agnes de Schithenhech' at the previous court; at the court held on 3 Aug. 1294, Richard atte Breche paid a fine of £4 for a virgate of land formerly held by Robert Clerk. Annual dues at Launton in the 1290s were the same as those of the early fourteenth century, and for these, see below, p. 441.

allowed or required to redeem them? Here the monks of Westminster still had a little room for manoeuvre, and the evidence
suggests that, towards the end of the thirteenth century, they
began to consider these questions with new attention.

Two different methods were used in the commutation of
labour services on this estate at this time, one undoubtedly
much older than the other. The older system was that of the
rent option, well known to historians from its appearance in
twelfth-century surveys of some other estates, including those
of Burton Abbey, in Staffordshire.[1] In the manors where this
system obtained, each villein at a given time was either on a
works option or on a rent option. If on the former, he was
liable for regular week-work, in addition to whatever other,
occasional services he might owe. If on the latter, he might
still owe some occasional services, but a lump sum of rent
acquitted his burden of week-work for an agreed period, which
was often a year, but sometimes only three, six, or nine months.
During that period, it was all or nothing: either the villein
owed week-work, or he did not. Islip and Hardwicke, two of
the manors where this system was certainly in use at the end
of the thirteenth century, had spent a long time in the hands
of other landlords than the monks of Westminster—the monks
did not enter into final possession of Islip until the reign of
John and did not hold Hardwicke in demesne between the
mid-twelfth century and the very end of the thirteenth.[2] But
this was also the method in use at Staines, Yeoveney, and Laleham, none of which had ever been, to our knowledge, outside
the demesne of the church.[3] It belongs to a certain period in
estates administration, a period long past in most places by the
end of the thirteenth century, but it was probably never the
preserve of a particular class of landlords.

The newer system was evidently in use at Teddington when
the extent of 1312 was made, and its essential features can
be deduced from Table X.[4] Where this applied, week-work
ceased to be treated as an obligation that a villein either did or

---

[1] 'The Burton Abbey Twelfth Century Surveys', ed. C. G. O. Bridgeman, in
Historical Collections for Staffordshire, 1916 (William Salt Archaeological Soc.,
1918), pp. 212 ff.

[2] Below, pp. 344–5, 356. For commutation arrangements at Islip, see W.A.M.
14776 ff., and at Hardwicke, W.A.M. 8422 ff.

[3] W.A.M. 16907 ff., 16828 ff., 27106 ff.   [4] Above, pp. 220–2.

did not owe over a relatively long period of time. The work of each day or half-day was valued in the manner already usual in the case of occasional services, and the work itself either performed by the villein or commuted at this price, which was recorded in the extent. From the point of view of any landlord, this arrangement had two great advantages. First, it recognized that there were intermediate positions between having a villein's entire week-work and having none of it; thus it was the more flexible system. And secondly, it was the more profitable arrangement, since the value of the works reckoned item by item usually exceeded the lump sums which were payable in lieu of them under the system of the rent option. This was so for two reasons. Not only had the value of labour risen since the lump sums were fixed, perhaps in the distant past: even when they were relatively new, these sums probably did not reflect the full value of the villein's services, reckoned day by day; they were unlikely to do so because the system of labour services itself was not yet administered in the rigorous, business-like way that is implied in the assumption that the work of each day was either used or sold but never wasted, forgotten or waived.[1] This method of commutation it is convenient to call 'sale of works', from the heading, *vendicio operum*, of the section in the ministers' accounts where the transactions in question were normally recorded.

By the end of the thirteenth century, the abbot of Westminster was using both methods of commutation simultaneously at Staines and Laleham.[2] In these manors some tenants were still on a rent option of the old type for the whole year or part of it, but even those on a works option were allowed—or required—to buy some of the services that they owed piecemeal, a price being set on each day's work. The sums of money involved at Staines show the advantage to the abbot of the new arrangement. A half-virgater here who was on a works option owed two days' work a week from 29 September to 24 June, and three a week from 24 June to 29 September. According to the newer system, a day's work in the former period was valued

---

[1] Below, p. 239.
[2] At Staines from 1295–6; at Laleham from *c.* 1287–8 (W.A.M. 16917 ff., 27106 ff.). In both manors, the value of the works that were used exceeded that of the works that were sold in each year down to 1348 for which we have evidence.

at $\frac{1}{2}d.$, and in the latter, at $1d.$, making 6s. 8d. per annum *in toto*;[1] but a half-virgater on a rent option of the old type paid only 6d. per term—that is, 2s. per annum.[2] The same practice, combining old and new, had been introduced at Yeoveney by 1300,[3] and at Hardwicke by 1317.[4] The prior and convent followed it at Ashford from *c.* 1323,[5] but 'sale of works' was probably the system in force in most of their manors by the end of the thirteenth century; that is to say, this was the method used if any labour services were in fact commuted into money payments. At Islip, the abbot allowed the old system of the rent or works option to persist unchanged.[6]

If the piecemeal sale of labour services was to be efficient, detailed accounts were needed year by year of the works owing in each manor and the use made of those which the villeins were in fact required to perform; in the absence of accounts, the local bailiffs and reeves, who were mainly responsible for the deployment of services, had too much scope for malpractice. The abbot and convent of Westminster were surprisingly slow to appreciate this point; a section devoted to works was introduced into ministers' accounts haphazardly and, on the whole, late in the history of this attempt to exploit week-work obligations more effectively.[7] Abbot Wenlok made the innovation at

---

[1] But only 6s. 5d. per annum if the appropriate deduction is made for the weeks following, respectively, Christmas, Easter, and Whitsun, when villeins at Staines owed no services. Between 1320 and 1329, the value of the works done between 29 Sept. and 24 June each year was reduced to $\frac{1}{4}d.$ each. The total value of a half-virgater's works thereafter was 5s. 1d. per annum, or 4s. 11$\frac{1}{2}d.$ per annum, taking into account the festival weeks.

[2] W.A.M. 16907 ff. For rents and services here, see also below, p. 440. The value (2s. 3$\frac{1}{2}d.$ per annum) of the labour services of a half-virgater at Staines shown here comprises the sum of 2s. mentioned above in the text, and 3$\frac{1}{2}d.$ per annum in respect of occasional services, other than week-work.

[3] W.A.M. 16842.   [4] W.A.M. 8428.   [5] W.A.M. 26718 ff.
[6] W.A.M. 14776 ff.

[7] Though not late in comparison with the practice of some other landlords. Crowland Abbey, for example, did not introduce works accounts in its Cambridge-shire manors until the second or third decades of the fourteenth century (between 1314 and 1321) and had not done so at Wellingborough (Northants.) by 1322. See F. M. Page, *The Estates of Crowland Abbey* (Cambridge, 1934), pp. 226 ff.; *Wellingborough Manorial Accounts, A.D. 1258–1323*, ed. Page (Northants. Record Soc., 1965), pp. xlii, 122 ff. The fact that such accounts in the early fourteenth century tended to record week-work obligations more often than occasional services suggests that the attempt on the part of the monks of Westminster to exploit the former more intensively may have had many parallels. See also J. Z. Titow, *English Rural Society, 1200–1350* (London, 1969), p. 25 and n., and, on the

Yeoveney in 1285–6, and at Staines a little later,[1] but it was to be twenty or thirty years before the practice was introduced in the abbot's manors in Gloucestershire,[2] and the prior and convent were still more dilatory: on their manors, works' accounts were probably not introduced before the 1330s. Nevertheless, the practice of selling unused works, with or without the safeguard of a written account, implied a closer scrutiny of the way in which bailiffs and reeves managed the local labour force than had been the lot of those officials earlier, and a stricter scrutiny on their part of the works actually done and of the occasions of abstaining. It all made for friction in the relations of the monks with their villeins, and on at least two of the abbot's manors, Bourton-on-the-Hill and Todenham, a hard-fought struggle over labour services distinguished the opening decades of the fourteenth century.

In each of these manors, villeins still performed week-work at this date. At Bourton-on-the-Hill, each virgate owed four days' work a week for the greater part of the year.[3] At Todenham, the holdings burdened with this kind of service were those of the so-called *cotmanni*, most of whom owed two or three days' work a week throughout the year.[4] Wherever week-work was performed, the feast days which the Church prescribed as holidays, on which men must abstain from all unnecessary forms of servile, or worldly, work, were apt to be a problem. Arrangements at Bourton-on-the-Hill were such as to raise this issue in an acute form, for here the customary rule was that the villein performed his services on Mondays, Tuesdays, Wednesdays, and Thursdays, but not on Fridays or Saturdays, and not, of course, on Sundays. What was to be done, therefore, in a week when a feast day of the Church fell on a Monday, Tuesday,

late-thirteenth-century ideal, *Walter of Henley and other Treatises on Estate Management and Accounting*, ed. D. Oschinsky (Oxford, 1971), pp. 278–9.

[1] W.A.M. 16828, 16911–12. The innovation was made at Staines in 1291–2 or a little earlier.

[2] At Bourton-on-the-Hill, Sutton-under-Brailes (now in Warwicks., but then in Glos.), and Todenham in 1312–13 (W.A.M. 8259, 25943; Glos. Records Office, D. 1099/M31/29). At Deerhurst and Hardwicke, the change was made between 1314 and 1317 (W.A.M. 8427–8).

[3] W.A.M. 8259 ff. Although the half-virgate was now the common unit of tenure on the land in question, the whole virgate was still the unit of assessment for villein rents and services at Bourton-on-the-Hill.

[4] W.A.M. 25943 ff.

Wednesday, or Thursday, or in the week following the great
feasts of Christmas, Easter, and Whitsun, when the bishops
normally prescribed at least two days' abstention from work?[1]
Were the monks of Westminster to remit the work that was due
on such days or the money payment in lieu of it? Could they, on
the contrary, require the villein to make up the work later
on, when the feast was past, or, if the day's work would in any
event have been sold, to pay the money equivalent as though
the day had been an ordinary working day after all? At Todenham, where the burden of week-work was smaller, the occasions
of conflict were to that extent fewer—there were in fact fewer
days in the year which might prove to be both feast days of the
Church and days when by custom labour services were due.
But here, too, it seems, although we are never told so explicitly,
week-work was customarily performed on certain days of the
week and not on others; had this not been so, Abbot Curtlington's skirmishes with his villeins at Todenham early in the
fourteenth century would be inexplicable.

Both at Bourton-on-the-Hill and at Todenham, Curtlington,
who was abbot from 1315 until 1333, refused to remit any day's
work on account of a festival, except during the weeks after
Christmas, Easter, and Whitsun; for a time, moreover, even
this minimum allowance was denied to his villeins.[2] In effect,
Curtlington challenged the tradition that works in these manors
were due on certain days of the week and not on others. Almost
certainly, in adopting this attitude, he reversed a more tolerant
policy on the part of some of his predecessors, and there can be
little doubt that the occasion of his doing so was the introduction
of written accounts for labour services in these manors, with the
revelation these brought of the actual cost to him of *festa ferianda*
here. In the very first such account put together at Bourton-on-
the-Hill, his auditors made the marginal note: 'Inquiratur si
debet [sc. prepositus] habere allocationem pro diebus festivis

---

[1] C. R. Cheney, 'Rules for the observance of feast days in medieval England',
B.I.H.R. 34 (1961), 117 ff.; B. Harvey, 'Work and *festa ferianda* in medieval
England', *Journal of Ecclesiastical History* 23 (1972), 1 ff.

[2] W.A.M. 8260 ff., 25944 ff.; Glos. Records Office, D. 1099/M 30/3 ff. These
sources show that it was Curtlington's predecessor, Richard de Kedyngton, who
initiated the new policy in the early fourteenth century and, further, that for
several years the villeins of these manors were denied a remission of services even
during the weeks of the three major festivals. Todenham and Bourton-on-the-Hill
belonged to the same administrative bailiwick.

per extentam.'[1] The abbot carried the day, and in each manor
all that was subsequently allowed to the villeins in recognition
of their need to abstain from servile work on feast days was the
bare minimum: two days' remission of work at each of the
great festival seasons—Christmas, Easter, and Whitsun. But in
1321, as a peace-offering to his disappointed villeins, he offered
to wipe out the money payments that were then over-standing in
each manor in respect of the disputed days' work. At Bourton-
on-the-Hill, the offer was accepted, but when Henry Melksop,
the reeve of Todenham, appeared before the abbot to be told of
the offer, he refused to be grateful, and his surly behaviour led
to a change of mind on the abbot's part. This confrontation
was later described by Curtlington himself in the following
words: 'Mes Henri Melksop lour messager, homme de bele
viere e de gros greyn, ne se deyna mie la bouche overir de nous
mercier, e pur soun groundilement nostre dite bone volente
avoms retret a ceste feche.'[2]

(iv) *The Move away from Labour Services before 1348*

The ways and means of commuting labour services into
money rents have been described. To what extent were such
services used or commuted on this estate in the course of the
thirteenth and early fourteenth centuries? The possibility of
answering this question depends on the existence of ministers'
accounts, but none of these has survived on this estate before
the second half of the thirteenth century. It is therefore the
century before the Black Death, but no earlier period, that lies
open to inspection.

As the figures in Appendix VIII show, more than half the
rent of virgated villein holdings was assessed in the form of
labour services in more than half the number of abbatial
manors for which we have evidence in this period.[3] In the manors
administered by the conventual treasurers, the ingredients of
villein dues more often varied according to the size of the
holding. In more than half the manors of these officials for

---

[1] W.A.M. 8259.

[2] W.A.M. 8356, a writ addressed by Curtlington to the bailiff and the reeve of
Bourton-on-the-Hill. Mrs. E. A. Armstrong has kindly verified my reading of this text.

[3] Below, pp. 439–40. Labour rent preponderated in the assessment of villein
dues at Bourton-on-the-Hill, Islip, Laleham, Staines, Yeoveney, Chaceley,
Pershore and Wick, and Pinvin.

which we have evidence, the labour-service component pre-ponderated in the assessment of the dues of the holdings that occur most frequently, if not in all holdings.[1] In several manors, labour rent was much more onerous than this; in some cases these are manors where the number of villein holdings was itself small, but not in all. Moreover, the figures in this appendix tend to undervalue labour rent in a number of manors. Where the system of the 'rent or works' option was in force, the value of the week-work is assumed to have been the rent payable in lieu of it by a villein who was on a rent option—at Staines, for example, the value is reckoned as 2*s*. per annum per half-virgate; but such a villein might now be asked for more than this traditional sum as the price of escape from week-work.[2] And as a rule, ploughing and harrowing services were not valued in the Abbey's extents if the liability to perform them was conditional on the tenant's possession of draught animals—he might possess none, and in that case it was not the monks' practice to demand cash in lieu of service.

In this period, the monks of Westminster were apt to use a high proportion of the available labour services in the manors where these were in fact the major or at least a notable part of the villein's total burden of rent. At Battersea and Wandsworth, where half the virgater's dues and rather more than half the dues of the half-virgater were assessed in the form of labour services, no sales of work are recorded in the ministers' accounts surviving from the late thirteenth century, and for a consider-ably longer period than this none may have been made.[3] A high proportion of the services owing at Stevenage was perfor-med down to 1348, and in most years before *c.* 1320, all were.[4]

---

[1] i.e. at Kelvedon, Stevenage, Wheathampstead and Kinsbourne, Ashford, Teddington, Battersea and Wandsworth, and Morden; see below, p. 441.

[2] Above, pp. 227–8.

[3] W.A.M. 27495 ff. Between 1300 and 1354, the only ministers' accounts surviving for this manor are those for 1304–5 and 1315–16.

[4] St. Paul's Cathedral MSS., Press B, Boxes 81, 92, 111; P.R.O., S.C. 6/870/9 ff.; W.A.M. 26344–8. Works accounts do not begin at Stevenage until 1315–16, but before this the proportion of works used can be inferred from the number sold; in the decade before the Black Death of 1348–9, *c.* 75 per cent of the works nominally owing at Stevenage were in fact performed. The only years before 1320 when relatively heavy sales of work are recorded were 1295–6, when harvest works were sold for £4. 14*s*. 10*d*. (in 1295) and £6. 0*s*. 3¾*d*. (in 1296); these sums probably represented between one-quarter and one-third of the total value of villein labour services at Stevenage at this date.

Both on the abbot's portion of lands and on that of the convent, there were manors where not only the theoretical but the actual burden of labour dues was heavy.

In both parts of the estate, however, labour rent lost ground to money rent in this period. Initially, the abbot was perhaps readier than his monks to experiment; but he was also more prone than they to repent of changes once made. At Bourton-on-the-Hill, where, as we have seen,[1] a relatively heavy burden of week-work persisted, the abbot normally used the entire amount that was owing until the early fourteenth century. In 1287–8, however, he sold all these services over a nine-month period.[2] At Islip, only 5 virgates of customary land were *ad opus* in 1276–7, except during August and September, the harvest months, but in 1279–80, the corresponding figure was between 7 and 15, depending on the exact season,[3] and in the 1330s and 1340s, between 13 and 15.[4] On the other hand, labour services seem to have been little used at Pensham, Pinvin or Pershore and Wick in the two or three decades before the Black Death.[5] At Bourton-on-the-Hill, their use somewhat declined in the 1340s, just before the Black Death.[6] When Abbot Wenlok recovered the manors of Deerhurst and Hardwicke from the hands of his fee-farm tenant there in 1299, it was to find that the only labour services still owing from his villeins were those which fell in the period from 24 June to 29 September.[7] At Sutton-under-Brailes, the abbot himself seems permanently to have commuted all week-work and most other forms of service as well, in the course of the second half of the thirteenth century, if not in an even earlier period.[8]

The prior and convent proceeded more cautiously than this on most of their manors down to the end of the thirteenth

---

[1] Above, p. 229.   [2] W.A.M. 8239.   [3] W.A.M. 14776–7.

[4] W.A.M. 14789 ff. The remarks in the text apply to the vill of Islip but not to Murcot or Fencot, for which see above, p. 223 n., and below, p. 440 n. No works accounts were kept at Islip before *c.* 1390. Earlier, however, ministers' accounts show how many villeins were on a works option. These sources show also that the sale of other, occasional labour services was rare in the first half of the fourteenth century: it is mentioned only once in the surviving accounts, in 1330–1 (W.A.M. 14789).

[5] W.A.M. 22112 ff.   [6] W.A.M. 8276–81.   [7] W.A.M. 8422 ff.

[8] Glos. Records Office, D. 1099/M 48. This extent was made in 1327, but the ministers' accounts of this manor suggest that there had been no major reassessment of obligations since *c.* 1275, and perhaps none since an earlier date (ibid., D. 1099/M 31/2 ff.; W.A.M. 25900–2).

century and for some little time thereafter; they were perhaps more committee-minded than their abbot, less volatile than he in approach to these matters. But after *c.* 1320 they probably showed a clearer preference than he for money rent. 'Sale of works' now begins to be a frequent entry in the ministers' accounts at Stevenage; in the decade before the Black Death *c.* 25 per cent of the villein services due in this manor were affected, on average, each year.[1] From *c.* 1320, it was the usual practice of the prior and convent to sell *c.* 80 per cent or more of the services still due, according to the extent, at Aldenham;[2] in the 1330s and 1340s they sold the greater number of the works due at Launton each year.[3] In the years immediately before the Black Death *c.* 70 per cent of the works of the villeins of Wheathampstead were sold.[4] Over the estate considered as a whole, the move away from labour rent and towards money payments is unmistakable in the decade before 1348.

(v) *The Level of Villein Rents*

These comments on the composition of villein rents in the early Middle Ages are preliminaries to the most important question of all: how heavy was the total burden of rent carried at this time by the tenant who held customary land in villeinage? An attempt to answer this question must focus attention, not on the virgates and half-virgates, the units of landholding that were in fact commonly used for the assessment of dues, but on the acres in the fields that made up each such holding. The reason for this is not simply that virgates varied in size from manor to manor,[5] for, even so, conclusions relating to each manor considered severally could be based on them. Nearly all the contractual rents—the rents, that is, that were paid for land on lease or at farm—recorded in this period were assessed on the acre, and it is with these that customary rents must be compared if we are to form an impression of the real level of

---

[1] W.A.M. 26344–8; P.R.O., S.C. 6/871/7 ff.; St. Paul's Cathedral MSS., Press B, boxes 92, 111. Seven ministers' accounts survive from the decade 1338–48.
[2] W.A.M. 26068 ff. [3] W.A.M. 15339 ff.
[4] Average annual value of works sold, Sept. 1344 to Sept. 1347: *c.* £9. 10*s.*; total value of works due: *c.* £13. 15*s.* per annum (Herts. Record Office, D./Elw M 146, 148–9). Between Sept. 1340 and Sept. 1347, the average annual value of works sold was *c.* 60 per cent of the whole (ibid., D/Elw M 142, 144–9).
[5] Above, p. 208.

the latter. Yet the choice of rents per acre as the basis for comparisons is open to several objections, among which two must certainly be noted here.

In the first place, the acre was itself not a uniform measure from manor to manor. Although, by the early fourteenth century, the monks of Westminster were probably using measured acres on all their demesnes, and measuring these acres on some demesnes by the royal perch of 16½ feet,[1] it can be assumed that, on their tenant land, the use of customary acres persisted, and with it much variety in usage from manor to manor. Such acres were often smaller than acres measured by the perch of 16½ feet. That in use at Islip, for example, was equivalent to only five-sixths of the acre so measured.[2] But it cannot be assumed that the difference was normally of this order of magnitude, for customary acres differed in size from place to place, and this, indeed, is only what we should expect, given their traditional origin in the day's work of man and beasts in the fields[3]—the terrain was not uniform from place to place, nor, perhaps, human capacity, or that of the plough-beast.

Secondly, the customary arable acres comprised in virgates and half-virgates were components of units of landholding which included other assets as well, and the extent and quality of the latter no doubt affected the level of the rent considered appropriate for the unit as a whole. At Staines and Yeoveney, customary virgaters probably had, not only 10 acres of arable, but also the generous stint of 1½ to 2 acres of meadow;[4] Richard Hathemar, a virgater at Chaceley in the early fourteenth

---

[1] This perch is mentioned in the early-fourteenth-century extents of Ashford, Ashwell, Battersea and Wandsworth, Hampstead, Hendon, Knightsbridge, Morden, Teddington, and Wheathampstead and Kinsbourne (W.A.M. 26703, 27197; C.U.L. MS. Kk 5. 29, fos. 30ᵛ, 36ᵛ, 39ᵛ, 44, 53, 69ᵛ, 77, 83ᵛ; *Trans. London and Middlesex Archaeological Soc.*, N.S., 6 (1929–32), 582). It may be fortuitous that all these were conventual manors—in fact, nearly all the extents surviving from this period relate to conventual manors. On the perch, see P. Grierson, *English Linear Measures: An Essay in Origins* (Reading, 1972), pp. 20 ff. For light on the problems to which medieval measurement of land gives rise, I am also much indebted to an unpublished paper by Mr. Andrew Jones, entitled, 'Land Measurement in England, 1150–1350: An Introduction'. See also above, p. 208.

[2] *V.C.H. Oxon.* vi. 215.

[3] F. W. Maitland, *Domesday Book and Beyond* (Cambridge, 1921), p. 377.

[4] See e.g. Walter Takepenny's half-virgate in Staines, said in 1349–50 to consist of 5 acres of arable and 1 acre of meadow, and the messuage, 10 acres of arable and 1½ acres of meadow, in sum a virgate, of William le Man in Yeoveney, in 1391 (W.A.M. 16873, 16967, fo. 3ᵛ).

century, is known to have had at least 7 acres of meadow, all
of it perhaps appurtenant to his arable holding.[1] Everywhere,
the tenant of a virgated holding had a large messuage, with an
ample garden and perhaps several dwellings, in addition to his
own, that were themselves exploitable assets, beside a stint in
the common pastures of the vill. All these things his rent purchased for him, and in most of the manors of the monks of
Westminster it was indeed their practice to insist that field-
acres, meadow, and messuage must be held as a single unit of
tenure or not at all.

Appendix IX,[2] therefore, has been put together with a proper
sense of the liberties which it takes with its subject matter. Here
the rents for virgated villein holdings shown in Appendix VIII[3]
are expressed as rents per acre, in accordance with the number
of acres in the virgate, and compared with contractual rents for
piecemeal acres in arable land in the same manors. The latter
are unhappily few in number and of assorted character. Some
were paid for short-term tenancies at will; others, for demises for
years or—but these arrangements are rare—for life; some relate
to tenant-land, but most, in all probability, to demesne land and
are therefore to be regarded as rents for relatively well-kept
acres, and, in many cases, acres measured by the perch of $16\frac{1}{2}$
feet. In contrast to customary rents on the Abbey's estates at
this time, contractual rents were sensitive to differences in the
quality of land; even in the same place, therefore, their range
might be wide.

Despite its imperfections, the usefulness of Appendix IX as
a rough guide to the level of customary rents in the early
fourteenth century can be too much disparaged. If tenants in
villeinage enjoyed other assets beside arable acres, the latter
were, as a rule, by far and away the most important part of
their holdings. Few manors had the resources in meadow land

---

[1] W.A.M. 21072. The holding formerly in Hathemar's possession that is mentioned in this account is known, from previous references to it in the ministers'
accounts of this manor, to have been a virgate. The villeins of Bourton-on-the-Hill
had generous stints of meadow below the vill, in Moreton-in-Marsh. In 1326, the
abbot of Westminster sold the hay crops of the meadow appurtenant to the holdings
of two fugitive villeins of this manor for 16s. 2d. (W.A.M. 8271). The villeins in
question probably held a virgate *in toto*.

[2] Below, pp. 443–7.

[3] But with the addition of figures for South Benfleet and Fanton, Hampstead,
and Hendon, three manors which do not appear in Appendix VIII.

of Chaceley and Staines; in most, a villein had a meagre share of meadow and of pasture rights as an appurtenance of arable land. As for his messuage, it was indeed an asset, but at times a costly one, for he was responsible for the repair of all the buildings on it.[1]

The lesson of the appendix, where customary rents are often at a level comparable with, if not higher than, that of contractual rents, is surely that the monks of Westminster demanded much of their villeins at this time. For the acre purchased by the customary rent was almost certainly smaller, in the greater number of cases, than that purchased by the contractual rent— the disparity between the levels of the two types of rent was in general greater than these figures suggest. Moreover, the obligations of the Abbey's tenants in villeinage were by no means discharged when the dues taken into account here had been paid. They owed, for example, entry fines and heriots in addition to their annual dues, pannage for the agistment of their pigs or for the liberty of killing or selling them,[2] and the so-called cert fine at the Hoketide view of frankpledge.

The level of customary rents tended to be high in relation to that of contractual rents where a significant proportion of the former was assessed in the form of labour services.[3] At Islip, Staines, and Laleham the difference between the two is indeed marked; and if at Staines customary tenants were exceptionally well provided with meadow, at Islip the whole body of tenants probably made do with *c.* 30 acres. At Bourton-on-the-Hill, the difference is striking. At Ashford, where *c.* 67 per cent of the dues of virgaters and half-virgaters was still assessed in the form of labour rent, the former may have compared favourably with contractual rents at the beginning of the century; by the 1330s, however, this had probably ceased to be the case. But the correlation between heavy labour rent and high annual dues is by no means perfect. At Sutton-under-Brailes, villeins

[1] Below, pp. 273–4 ff., and for rents per acre at Ashwell, Aldenham, and Hendon with and without messuage, see below, pp. 445–6 and nn.

[2] For this variant of pannage at Battersea and Wandsworth, see C.U.L. MS. Kk 5. 29, fo. 63.

[3] For the breakdown of these customary rents into the three components of cash, labour services, and renders in kind, see below, pp. 439–41. The method of assessing the value of labour dues adopted here tends to undervalue them in some manors; see above, p. 232. In this respect, therefore, the level of customary rents is unduly minimized in Appendix IX.

may not have escaped lightly, despite the insignificant proportion of labour rent in the annual dues of standard holdings
here:[1] the holdings of the *cotmanni*, most of which comprised 14
acres of arable, bore a heavier burden of rent than the virgates
and half-virgates of this manor, the rents for which are those
shown in Appendix IX—the rent of 6s. $\frac{1}{2}d.$ per annum which
each of these tenants paid for his holding is equivalent to a rent of
5·18d. per annum per acre, and the latter is more than double
the amount of the only contractual rent per acre recorded at
Sutton-under-Brailles in this period.[2]

On the whole, it is true to say, the smaller the holding—
within the virgated structure of holdings—the heavier the
burden of rent. At Feering, the tenant of the twelfth part of
a virgate, a relatively common holding, paid more than twice
the rent per acre of his neighbour, the half-virgater;[3] at Aldenham, the quarter-virgater paid a little more than the half-
virgater, the half-virgater, a little more than the virgater;[4] in
many places half-virgaters paid more per acre for their holdings
than virgaters. The level of customary rents shown in Appendix
IX goes far to explain why contractual tenancies were rare on
the Abbey's estates in this period; on balance, the monks of
Westminster would have lost by resorting to such tenancies. But
some other landlords were making this very change in the late
thirteenth century and the early fourteenth.[5]

Yet the annual dues for villein holdings—the rents of assize,
the quotas of service, and the capons and bushels of corn—were
little different in these manors from what they had been a
century earlier; they may indeed have hardened into their
early-fourteenth-century shape at a much earlier period than
this.[6] How was it that they still favoured the landlord so much,

---

[1] *c.* 13 per cent in the case of the virgater, and *c.* 14 per cent in that of the half-
virgater.

[2] For the holdings of the *cotmanni*, see below, p. 440 n. It is noted in the Liber
Niger Quaternus (fo. 74ᵛ) that at Sutton-under-Brailes pasture is scarce, tillage
abundant, and the meadows of moderate size.

[3] 10·89d.: 5·35d.

[4] They paid, respectively, 5·13d., 4·66d., and 4·34d. per acre. The tenant of
a quarter-virgate of *mondayland* here paid 5·6od. per acre; the one molman,
4·ood. per acre.

[5] For examples, see Miller, *Abbey and Bishopric of Ely*, pp. 109 ff.; J. Hatcher,
Rural Economy and Society in the Duchy of Cornwall, 1300–1500 (Cambridge, 1970),
pp. 52 ff.; Hilton, *The English Peasantry in the Later Middle Ages*, pp. 145 ff.

[6] Above, p. 219.

despite the inflationary trends of the centuries in question? The answer to this puzzle lies in a period earlier than any that can be brought to life again now—in that remote time when the proto rents and services of a dependent peasantry began to take shape in these manors—a time that may already have been past when the manors came into the hands of the monks of Westminster; this happened for the most part in the tenth and eleventh centuries. These dues, it appears, bore little relation to the realities of the demand for land or the potential yield of land, and this is not surprising, since the relationship of dependence that they enshrined did not yet belong in an economic context; its point of reference was, not the scarcity or abundance of land, but the need that peasants living in an insecure society had of lords, and the right of lords to live by the labour of their men. Though money rents may have been part of the obligation of the dependent peasant of this early period, as we know they were on some other estates, this was without doubt pre-eminently a time of bodily service and renders in kind, and probably one in which a good deal of slack was tolerated in the system; nobody thought in terms of a full exaction of services or of a comprehensive definition of the obligations of dependent tenure, one by one.

On the Abbey's estates, as on all others, the subsequent commutation of bodily service into money rents was a liberating process—in the end, cash payments and villeinage were proved to be, quite simply, incompatibles. But the time-span which fits this conclusion was a long one, more aptly measured in centuries than in decades. On a shorter view, one may wish to place more emphasis on the startling disproportions between rent and the livelihood that it purchased for the tenant that were laid bare by translating the old, ill-defined services into nicely calculated cash equivalents. In some cases, of course, it was the monks of Westminster who suffered the rude awakening. Thus, in common with other landlords, they discovered that there was little or no profit to them in the harvest boons at which lavish refreshments were by custom provided for workers; some of these had no value at all according to the extent by the beginning of the fourteenth century.[1] Quite probably the cost to a landlord of such boons had always been excessive, but they originated in

[1] C.U.L. MS. Kk 5. 29, fos. 65 (Aldenham), and 104 (Feering).

a period when services did not in fact have a cash value put upon them. By and large, however, it seems to have been the monks' villeins who found themselves at a disadvantage, as obligations which had taken shape in a basically natural economy were defined, measured, and valued, so that they might be absorbed into the cash economy of the twelfth and thirteenth centuries. Around 1300, when the demand for land was, by all accounts, at its medieval peak, some of them carried a burden of rent that the monks of Westminster would almost certainly have found it impossible to negotiate in a free market. Many derived little or no benefit in respect of their obligations as tenants from the fully heritable nature of their tenure; the point at which their ancestors and forebears had entered the nexus of cash relationships and defined services had been so unreasonably high on the scale of rents that the effects still showed at this late date.

In the century before 1348, the rents that were owing from the Abbey's customary tenants were normally paid. What happened earlier is now lost to our sight, but there is little doubt but that after *c*. 1250 or *c*. 1270 villeins paid their money rents and their rents in kind, and, from the time when works accounts begin to survive, we know that they performed their services after a fashion, or paid cash in lieu. Arrears of rent are rarely mentioned in ministers' accounts; resistance, such as that offered by the villeins of Todenham to William de Curtlington,[1] seems to have been rare. The monks of Westminster proved themselves capable of netting rents that were uneconomically high both where villeinage prevailed more or less to the exclusion of other tenures, as it did at Islip and Launton, and where, as at Staines and Stevenage, their tenants in villeinage were a small, underprivileged group living in a predominantly free society. The abbot, however, seems to have been at once more old-fashioned in his ways and more oppressive in his demands than the prior and convent. The archaic system of the 'rent or works' option was used more frequently in his manors than in theirs, and it is in his manors that the disparity between customary and contractual rents seems to have been most marked. At the very time when the abbot was bringing to an end all but the bare minimum of allowances for feast days for his customary

---

[1] Above, pp. 230–1.

labourers, the prior and convent were actually writing far more generous rules about such days into some of their extents.[1] Yet both parties were in general demanding landlords, both capable here and there of great severity towards their tenants.

The rights of jurisdiction which the abbot and convent possessed over the customary land of their estate help to explain their success. Access to the royal courts was still normally denied to the tenants of all such land. Accordingly, the villeins of Bourton-on-the-Hill and Todenham had to defend their claim to their accustomed holidays before the abbot and his officials or not at all. The acknowledged legal status of the Abbey's tenants in villeinage, as opposed to that of the land they held, was not uniform over the estate as a whole; it varied from manor to manor. At Oakham, the monks now recognized that some of the tenants of their so-called bond-land here were of free status—the fact is recorded in a custumal made at Oakham in 1341.[2] In some other manors—and these were perhaps more typical than Oakham of the estate as a whole—tenants in villeinage were considered to be villeins in respect of their personal status also; moreover the strong word, *nativi*, meaning 'serfs' was often used of them. They are described as *nativi* at Pyrford, for example, in 1330,[3] and at Wick, by Pershore, in 1352;[4] and the customary land unoccupied at Launton after the Black Death was *terra nativa* to the monks.[5] This terminology did not mean that still, in the mid-fourteenth century, the monks of Westminster drew no distinction between this man who had been born unfree and would, unless manumitted, die in that condition, and that other, who was a serf by virtue of holding land in villeinage. It did, however, imply that the latter was more or less as the former for the duration of his tenure. If the customaries of Battersea and Wandsworth, of Ashford, Hendon, and Teddington, Aldenham, Wheathampstead, and Stevenage were in danger of forgetting this fact, they were perhaps reminded of it by the requirement, set out in the extents of those manors made at the beginning of the

---

[1] C.U.L. MS. Kk 5. 29, fos. 73ᵛ, 77ᵛ, 82.   [2] W.A.M. 20632.

[3] W.A.M. 27469. With one exception, those tenants of free land who also held customary land in the manor are severally identified in this extent as *nativi*.

[4] W.A.M. 32742, a rental which categorises as *nativi* all the tenants of Wick who did not hold freely.

[5] W.A.M. 15345.

century, that they obtain the licence of the monks of Westminster as a preliminary to the marriage of their sons and daughters.[1] Certainly, there was no general recognition on this estate of the distinction between tenure in villeinage and villein status for which Bracton had argued nearly a century earlier; to hold in villeinage was to be a villein, with all the impairment of opportunity, esteem, and capacity for independent action that this still implied.[2]

Other circumstances, too, told in favour of the monks. The society which submitted to this degree of seignorial exploitation was, without doubt, a relatively immobile one, in which men and women made do, as a rule, with the given circumstances of the place where it so happened they had been born. This may seem an improbable conclusion to reach in respect of an estate comprising so much land within one or two days' journey of London. But where movement was illicit, as it was in the case of most *nativi*, the price of it was the heavy one of a decisive break in family ties that few may have been ready to pay at this time. Perhaps even a manor such as Stevenage or Battersea and Wandsworth can be peopled with villeins who were, for sentimental and other reasons, *adscriptitii glebae*.

More important was the fact that the tenants of Westminster Abbey, in common with their landlords, the monks, were unaccustomed to thinking in the terms that we have used in weighing their situation. In most of the manors of the estate, most of the land was customary land. The monks themselves granted few or no contractual tenancies, and, although sub-tenancies may have existed in great numbers,[3] the rents asked for these no doubt reflected the burden on the tenant who granted them. In fact, until the leasing and farming of demesne

---

[1] C.U.L. MS. Kk 5. 29, fos. 48ᵛ, 65, 73ᵛ, 82; W.A.M. 26703, 27197; *Trans. London and Middlesex Archaeological Soc.*, N.S. 6 (1929–32), 600. On merchet, see, most recently, Scammell, 'Freedom and marriage in medieval England', *Economic History Rev.*, 2nd ser., 27 (1974), 523–35, where it is pointed out that this form of the marriage fine became a distinctive mark of unfree status only in the course of the twelfth and early thirteenth centuries.

[2] For Bracton's view of villeinage, see Pollock and Maitland, *History of English Law* i. 415 ff., and P. R. Hyams, 'Legal Aspects of Villeinage between Glanvill and Bracton' (Oxford D.Phil. thesis, 1968). I am also much indebted to Mr. Hyams for the opportunity of reading a relevant chapter of his forthcoming book, *King, Lords and Peasants in Medieval England*.

[3] Above, p. 214.

acres began, many of the Abbey's customary tenants must have been without first-hand experience of the economic rent for land in their locality; the inequalities of treatment that were so plain for all to see when, after 1348, contractual tenancies made headway on customary land, were not yet in evidence.

IX

Customary Land from 1348 to *c.* 1390

THOUGH uneven in its incidence from manor to manor, the mortality of 1348–9 was severe in every part of the Abbey's estate where the matter can be put to the test. Everywhere in England, one feature distinguished this from the typical demographic disasters of the earlier Middle Ages. As far as we know, these were occasioned by harvest failures and famines, and their main victims were probably the utterly poor, that is, in rural society, the landless or nearly landless. In the Black Death, however, the landholding peasantry suffered, if not as grievously as the utterly poor—this we have no means of discovering—then certainly to a remarkable extent. On the monastic estate it is clear that an exceptionally high proportion of the tenants who were in possession of holdings in the summer of 1348 died in the course of the following year. The speed with which most of the holdings found tenants again should not blind us to the real violence done at this time to the structure of the landholding group. The tenants who held of the lord of the manor were a distinctive group in every local society: on the Westminster estates, they were the people, theirs the families, who could afford to hold land on the conditions on which the monks made it available; their tenacious hold on the land, despite the grievous disabilities of the tenure by which most held, is attested by the central role of rights of inheritance in the transmission of holdings down to the mid-fourteenth century. The reduction of their numbers eroded the foundations of the monks' policy on customary land.

The response of the abbot and convent of Westminster to the new situation was, quite simply, a resolve to restore the *status quo* as soon as possible. This was the meaning of their oft-repeated desire that the lands which they found so unexpectedly on their hands should be taken on the customary terms. More particularly, they determined that all the tenant-land of their estate should eventually be held in villeinage again, whatever other arrangements might have to be tolerated here for the time being, and, secondly, that their tenants should hold in the accustomed way, for rent and services—not, as so many wished to do, for rent alone. The dates at the head of this chapter enclose the very long period when these backward-looking aims were the mainspring of the monks' policy. It is a period that takes us, in demographic matters, far beyond the proper context of the Black Death, though not beyond the range of the influence of that tremendous event and its sequels, the epidemics of the later fourteenth century. Never sensitive to economic trends, the monks of Westminster were never more heroically indifferent to them than they were in this period.

In fact the major part of the tenant-land of Westminster Abbey continued to be held in villeinage until the fifteenth century, but after the year of the Black Death this tenure no longer had the virtual monopoly of the land that it was accorded on most of the manors for which we have evidence down to 1348; it is in this respect that the catastrophe marks a turning-point in the tenurial history of the estate. The intruders were the contractual tenancies which the monks had in the past more or less confined to their demesnes. These tenancies were not regulated, as villein tenure was, by the custom of the manor, and the monks and their tenants would have been acutely aware of the two principal consequences of this fact: whereas villein tenure was normally fully heritable and villein rents often far from being a *verus valor*, contractual tenancies were granted for a limited term and in return for an economic rent. Both ideas proved infectious, and before long a novel form of villein tenure, which to some extent conformed to these principles, appeared; those who held by it enjoyed only a life-interest or a term of years, and some had the advantage of paying rents that were akin to, if not exactly identical with, a *verus valor*. Since this arrangement was very likely the origin on this estate of copyhold tenure without the right of renewal, it would be difficult to exaggerate its long-term importance. Until the last two decades of the fourteenth century, however, most of the villein tenures of the estate continued on the old lines: they were fully heritable, and their rents were often unreasonably high; infection had robbed the leopard of only a few of his spots. Thus gross inequalities characterized the monks' treatment of their tenants in this period; old and new were juxtaposed in a most inflammatory way, in the same street and the same fields.

The following account of these developments will be more clear-cut than is warranted by the surviving evidence, which is treacherous to a degree. Not only are the relevant sources now far from complete: those that survive are often exceedingly ambiguous. Court rolls, recording the admittance of tenants, often fail to specify the mode of tenure. Every kind of source betrays the lack of a vocabulary to describe the changes that were so rapidly in train. To our great confusion, one over-worked word, *firma*, is used to describe a tenancy at will, a lease, the tenure of a villein whose services had been commuted into a money rent, and, finally, the rent that was owing in each of these cases.

(i) *Contractual Tenancies after 1348*

The contractual tenancies of this period were of two kinds: some were tenancies at will, others, leases for a term of years or for a life or lives.

The first attribute of tenancy at will that calls for explanation is its name. Juridically, all forms of landholding on the customary land of the Abbey's estate were *ad voluntatem*, since all were justiciable in the Abbey's own courts and not elsewhere. One of these, villein tenure, was protected by the custom of the manor; the rest were not, and the description 'at will' is applicable more particularly to these. But tenancies that were 'at will' in this sense may themselves be divided into two main categories, and it is these that concern us at present. On the one hand were leases, tenancies unprotected by the custom of the manor which nevertheless conferred the security of a term on those who held by them; these will be referred to as 'contractual leases', to avoid the possibility of confusion with grants made for a limited term within the system of villeinage. On the other, were tenancies which lacked both the protection of custom and the security of a term, and it is in this sense that the description 'tenancy at will' is used in the following pages.

Some of these tenancies endured for an extremely short period of time and conferred on the tenant no more than the right to harvest the growing crops on arable acres that had unexpectedly fallen vacant since the beginning of the manorial year, or to use the agistment that pertained to the holding in question for a few months. In these cases the only record of the transaction is likely to be an entry in the *exitus manerii* section of the minister's account for the year. But from the beginning of the extensive use of this arrangement, most of the Abbey's tenancies at will seem to have endured for at least a year, and it was probably understood that they would do so. Yet the court rolls, where they were recorded, afforded the tenant no security in this matter; it is not until the fifteenth century that yearly tenancies are mentioned explicitly in Abbey sources.[1]

Beyond the twelve-month period, most fourteenth-century tenancies at will were utterly insecure: they were terminated if anyone else offered to hold the land for a higher rent at will, or to hold on the customary terms. The most that a tenant at will could hope for was the first refusal of holding himself for the higher rent or on the customary terms, if anyone else came forward with such an offer. In 1355, a proviso of this kind was written into a tenancy of the fishery in the waters above Pershore: Richard le Fisher and John Ballard were to hold the fishery for as long as they would pay what anyone else offered for it.[2] No exact parallel has come to light among tenancies at will on agricultural holdings, but in time it became not uncommon for such tenancies to include the proviso that they would endure until another tenant was willing to hold on the customary terms. At Islip, for example, Thomas Honte took a messuage and half-virgate of land on these terms in October 1380, and Richard Lake a similar holding on the same terms in March of the following year.[3]

If the tenant at will could not count on being in possession of the land next year or the year after, it cost him nothing to surrender his holding, since, unlike the customary tenant, he was not liable for a heriot when he did so. Moreover, every tenant at will probably entered on his holding without paying a fine. He owed nothing except his annual dues. The major

---

[1] For an early example, see W.A.M. 15716, a rental of the manor of Launton, made in 1416–17, which mentions 'firme per annum'. For fourteenth-century formulae relating to tenancies at will, see e.g. W.A.M. 21952 (Pershore, 1352).

[2] W.A.M. 21954. Initially, they were to pay a 'farm' of 13s. 4d. per annum.

[3] W.A.M. 14866.

part of these—the major part by far—was always a money rent, but in due course many of the Abbey's tenants at will were required to perform occasional labour services. Harvest boons and mowing services are mentioned at Islip in 1357–8, in connection with 'farms' that were almost certainly tenancies at will,[1] and the obligations undertaken by Richard Lake here in 1381 included mowing works, in addition to a rent of 6s. 8d. per annum and tallage.[2]

The monks of Westminster occasionally made contractual leases of customary land by indenture, but this method, which conferred an estate at common law on the lessee and thus removed the lease from the jurisdiction of the manorial court, was reserved, understandably, for exceptional arrangements made with exceptional people. A case occurred at Islip in 1377, when two men, Thomas Durdent and Godfrey atte Pyrie, were granted a lease of the customary land of the reeve of the manor, William Dolle, for Dolle's lifetime, by an indenture executed, not at Islip, but at Westminster.[3] Durdent, however, was no ordinary tenant: when the Islip arrangement was made, he was already a pensioner in receipt of an allowance of £1. 6s. 8d. per annum from the abbot.[4] From this circumstance we should probably conclude that he was or had been one of the abbot's household servants; we know that he was also janitor of the Abbey.[5] A lease of agricultural land at Islip was perhaps a way of employing some of the surplus capital that Durdent had accumulated over the years at Westminster. Better acquainted than others with the wider world that fell under the jurisdiction of the common law, such people desired the additional security conferred by an indenture. Further, a lease such as this one, granted for a life other than the life of the lessee himself, was highly exceptional on the Abbey's estate; the special form of

---

[1] W.A.M. 14799. Only isolated court rolls survive for this manor before 1376; our knowledge of earlier developments comes, as in this case, mainly from ministers' accounts.

[2] W.A.M. 14819, 14866 (court of 10 Mar. 1381).

[3] W.A.M. 14814; cf. *Oxfordshire Record Soc.* 40 (1959), 102, where the instrument is described as a charter. In 1394, the lease was extended to cover the lifetime of William Dolle's widow; it continued to be mentioned in the Islip accounts until 1431 (W.A.M. 14831 ff.). The holding consisted of two messuages and half-virgates and a piece of so-called common land.

[4] W.A.M. 27155; the pension was payable from the issues of Laleham.

[5] Above, pp. 184–5 and n.

the lease recognised this fact too. But as a rule leases of tenant-land were made by agreements recorded in the court rolls of the manors in question, and at first perhaps nowhere else. Very soon, however, the monks began to keep copies of their leases, in addition to the record on the court rolls; another copy may have been given to the tenant. Their own copy of a lease made at Great Amwell in 1352 or 1353 enabled the monks to prove some thirty years later that the term had expired.[1]

From their first introduction, contractual leases of customary land were made for terms that varied, not only from manor to manor, but also from holding to holding in the same manor. The tenants who took the first such leases at Staines were granted terms varying from five to nine years;[2] at Stevenage, terms of four, six, nine, ten, and twelve years are mentioned.[3] Very soon longer terms became usual. Thus at Stevenage, terms of, respectively, eighteen, twenty, twenty-four, and thirty years, and some life-terms, are mentioned in the 1360s;[4] at Staines, twenty-year terms were being granted on agricultural land by c. 1370.[5] In 1360, a lease of a messuage and virgate of land at Castlemorton for a term of ten years was converted into a joint tenancy for the lives of the lessee, his wife, and his son.[6] But in general the term of years was commoner than the life-term at this time.

It is implied in many fifteenth-century leases that the lessee had the right to assign the unexpired portion of his term. Fourteenth-century leases, by contrast, rarely suggest this in so many words; but the right to assign is implied in the very grant of terms as long as twenty or thirty years—the monks must have realized from the beginning that many of the tenants enjoying terms such as these would wish, in due course, to relinquish

---

[1] Below, p. 285 n.

[2] W.A.M. 16873–4. Some demesne land in this manor was concurrently on lease for a term of nineteen years.

[3] P.R.O., S.C. 6/871/18–20; St. Paul's Cathedral MSS. Press B, Boxes 81, 84. It is, however, difficult to distinguish leases of customary land from leases of demesne land in this manor.

[4] P.R.O., S.C. 6/871/21 ff.

[5] W.A.M. 16934 (the account for 1387–8, which mentions twenty-year leases, now in their eighteenth year). In 1382, the abbot leased a curtilage at Yeoveney, in the bailiwick of Staines, for sixty years (W.A.M. 16954).

[6] W.A.M. 21122. The original lease was granted in 1356. In 1360, the lessee, Richard Meleward, paid a fine of £1. 10s.; the rent (12s. per annum) was to continue unaltered.

their interest in the land, that many, indeed, would not live to see the end of their term. Some leases, however, were for years terminable on lives. A twenty-year lease of tenant-land at Eye to William and Matilda Chidyngefold in 1332 provided that, if William and Matilda died within the term, the abbot could re-enter.[1]

As in the case of tenancies at will, so with contractual leases, the major part of the rent was nearly always, if not invariably, a money payment, but some lessees owed labour services, and small renders in kind were another feature of many such rents. For example, six contractual leases of tenements with customary land appurtenant are recorded in the rental that was made at Teddington in 1379; in four cases the tenant was free of every form of praedial service, but in two, a very small number of harvest boons was owing.[2] Occasionally, labour services were imposed in the case of leases that were in fact interim arrangements, preparing the way for the restoration of the customary conditions of tenure. An arrangement of this kind was made with a tenant named William le Reve at Stevenage in 1353. William took a messuage and three-quarters of a virgate on lease for six years at a rent of 13s. 4d. per annum, and six harvest boons; but it was also agreed between William and the monks that when this lease ran out he would continue to hold the land on the customary terms—that is, in villeinage.[3] But provision for a return to villein tenure was included in some leases which carried no burden of labour services in the interim. At Laleham, for example, at the very end of 1353, Walter Sabine was granted a three-year lease of half a virgate of land for a money rent, with the proviso that when his term ran out he would hold *ad opera*;[4] and at Todenham, in 1360–1, Alice,

[1] W.A.M. 27001. If, however, William and Matilda, or the survivor, departed within the term, they were to have the growing crops during the last year for which rent had been paid. Exceptionally for the estate as a whole, several leases of tenant-land are recorded at Eye in the early fourteenth century.

[2] W.A.M. 27198. Four of the leases, including the two that carried the obligation to render harvest boons, were for terms of years; one was for the lives of two spouses holding jointly; in one case the term is not recorded. It does not, of course, follow from the imposition of services that they were in fact performed. For leases in villeinage at Teddington at this date, see below, p. 256 and n.

[3] P.R.O., S.C. 6/871/18; for the harvest boons, however, see ibid., S.C. 6/871/19.

[4] W.A.M. 27139.

daughter of William Bryan, was granted a four-year lease of a messuage and virgate of land with a similar proviso.[1]

The scarcity of court rolls for the years immediately after the Black Death makes it difficult to say whether or not the tenants who took the first contractual leases of customary land paid fines. By the 1370s and 1380s, the situation is clearer: then, leaseholders were liable to an entry fine—it was the fine that signified the security of their tenure compared to that of the tenant at will—but many exceptions were admitted. Moreover, the great majority of the fines for such leases that have come to light anywhere on the Abbey's estates, not only in the fourteenth century but at any date before the end of the Middle Ages, were small. Few exceeded a year's rent for the land in question; most did not approach that level. This is only what we should expect, given the fact that a leasehold rent was normally a *verus valor*, as this term was understood by the monks and their tenants at the time—an up-to-date assessment of the burden that could reasonably be imposed on the land; in these circumstances, there was little scope for substantial fines.

Logically, the same consideration precluded the taking of heriot from leaseholders on the expiry of their term, and the evidence suggests that contractual leases, whether for a life or for a term of years, were in fact exempt from this burden in the period with which we are concerned. At Launton the exemption is stated as a matter of principle: William Jones owed a heriot for the messuage and virgate of land which he held in villeinage, but not for another holding which he had on lease for his life, 'quia tenuit ad firmam et non pro serviciis et consuetudinibus'.[2] Since leaseholders sank little or no capital in fines at the beginning of their term and had not to contemplate

---

[1] W.A.M. 25968. Some contractual leases at Todenham included a provision that, after the expiry of the term, the tenant would hold for a larger rent and pay tallage; we should probably understand the projected tallage-paying tenancy as a lease in villeinage for life—the form of tenure that prevailed at Todenham in the fifteenth century. For such leases, see below, pp. 254–6.

[2] W.A.M. 15455 (court of 5 Dec. 1394). William's death was reported at this court. It is also noted here that he took the lease of the messuage and half-virgate in 1373. However, Roger, his son, who now took the holding, was to be liable to a heriot; but this probably means that it was in fact a villeinage lease; William is described as *nativus*, and so is his son. In 1421, the court rolls of Islip note the non-liability to heriot of a leasehold for a term of years, as though it were a matter of principle (W.A.M. 14899, court of 1 Apr. 1421).

paying a heriot on surrender, there was a risk that they would fail to see out their term, and occasionally the monks required safeguards against this eventuality. These cases, however, seem to have been very rare and were probably confined to manors where this type of tenure was itself a rarity. A case occurs at Great Amwell. Richard Rolf, on being granted a twelve-year lease of 2 acres of land here in 1381, was required to find pledges who would ensure, not only that he paid his fine (6*d.*) and his rent (1*s.* per annum), but also that he held the land until the end of the term.[1] But only small pieces of land were put on lease at Great Amwell; most of the holdings in this manor were still held in villeinage on the customary terms. Moreover, there had been violence here earlier in the year in which Rolf was admitted to his lease; the condition in the lease may have been an exceptional arrangement for exceptional times.

Finally, the responsibility of those holding contractual leases for the good repair of their property should be noted. The sources shed no light at all on the liability or non-liability of the tenant at will for repairs and are not much more communicative about this matter in the context of leases. A few incidents, however, point to the conclusion that these tenants were normally liable for repairs; some of these occur in the early fourteenth century, on manors which already made use of leases at that time. At Pinvin, for example, in 1336, John Vypel incurred a penalty for allowing the condition of the cottage which he held on lease to deteriorate.[2] In fact both the monks and their lessees took it for granted that the latter were responsible for ordinary repairs. The obligations that needed to be mentioned explicitly in the lease were major repairs, made necessary by a longer period of dilapidation; the tenant who undertook these probably enjoyed a beneficial assessment of rent. In 1363, Nicholas Godram explicitly undertook repairs to a messuage in Birdbrook which he was to have on lease for nine years, but the wording of the covenant in the lease suggests that the so-

[1] W.A.M. 26151 (court of 14 Dec. 1381).

[2] W.A.M. 21941. The penalty was a fine of 2*s.*, the amount of the alleged damage to the cottage. Moreover, the abbot took the cottage into his hands, but his decision to do so is probably explained by the fact that Vypel's predecessor as tenant had put in a claim to it once again; she was a serf named Alice Hobbes, who had herself earlier forfeited the cottage on the grounds of neglect.

called 'repairs' were of a fundamental kind, for Godram, having repaired the buildings on the messuage, was to maintain them in that condition throughout his term;[1] the initial repairs probably amounted to the restoration of seriously dilapidated buildings to a habitable condition.

It follows from the fragmentary nature of the surviving sources that we cannot measure at all precisely the extent to which the monks of Westminster used tenancies at will and contractual leases to fill their vacant holdings in this period; but where measurement is out of the question, guess-work is not to be despised. Both expedients can be traced to the year of the Black Death itself, though not in many places to an earlier period. At first, however, they were not often tried together in one and the same place. Leases were characteristic of the economically advanced manors, such as Staines and Stevenage, where a basically agrarian way of life was diversified by the existence of burgage plots and a market; in one or two such manors they had already begun to invade the tenant-land before 1348. Elsewhere, tenancies at will were at first much more common. The contrast probably owed more to the determination of prospective tenants in the Staines–Stevenage type of manor to have the greater security conferred by a lease than to a judgement on the part of the monks of Westminster that leasing was in fact the right practice to adopt there; and the custom of the region no doubt influenced both parties— the tenants in asking, and the monks in granting. Quite soon leases began to gain ground at the expense of tenancies at will in many different places, and they were almost certainly the commoner of the two arrangements over the estate as a whole by the end of our period.

If, overlooking the differences between these two forms of contractual tenancy, we ask in what circumstances the one or the other, or both together, made headway at the expense of villein tenure after 1348, the answer is not in doubt. The manors characterized by a relatively large number of contractual tenancies at this time were for the most part those where villein dues still included labour rent on a significant scale down to 1348: it was on labour services that the tenant at will and

---

[1] W.A.M. 25569. With the messuage, Godram took 8 acres of land; he was to manure half an acre each year.

the leaseholder turned their backs. Thus contractual tenancies were relatively common at Islip, where *c.* 84 per cent of villein dues was made up of labour rent down to 1348, but much less so at Launton, only a few miles away, where the corresponding figure is *c.* 34 per cent.[1] There is a similar contrast between Todenham and its near neighbour, Sutton-under-Brailes, the former having some customary tenants heavily burdened with labour services down to 1348 and many contractual tenancies thereafter, the latter, already free of all but very light services by 1348 and much less given to contractual tenancies on tenant-land by the end of our period.[2] At Stevenage, where villein dues were exceedingly heavy in the first half of the century, an appreciable extent of customary land was held contractually in the 1350s and 1360s, and the area of such land held on these terms was subsequently enlarged.[3] At Pyrford, where the villein's labour services were already light before 1348, contractual tenancies were virtually unknown after 1348.[4]

(ii) *Leases in Villeinage*

Although every leaseholder enjoyed the security of a term, none whose case we have so far considered was protected by the custom of the manor. But a further innovation of the years after 1348 was a different kind of lease, that held in villeinage 'according to custom'. Normally on the Abbey's estates at this time, the records of admittances to villeinage tenancies included the words 'sibi et suis', 'sibi et heredibus suis', or—and these words had a special taint of servility—'sibi et sequele sue'.

---

[1] W.A.M. 14798 ff., 15345 ff.; and for the relative importance of labour services at Islip and Launton before 1348, see below, pp. 440, 441. Many so-called 'farms' are mentioned in the Launton accounts after 1348, but most of these were in fact heritable tenancies in villeinage for a money rent; see also below, pp. 260–1.

[2] For Todenham, see W.A.M. 25964 ff., Glos. Records Office, D. 1099/M 30/10 ff.; and for Sutton-under-Brailes, ibid., M 31/44 ff. (There is, however, a gap in the Sutton accounts between 1331 and 1377. Very few of the contractual tenancies mentioned here in 1377 and subsequently related to holdings that had been held on customary terms before 1348.) The holdings referred to at Todenham, heavily burdened with labour dues before 1348, were those of the *cotmanni*, for which see below, p. 439 n.

[3] P.R.O., S.C. 6/871/17 ff.; St. Paul's Cathedral MSS., Press B, Boxes 81, 84; and see below, p. 441. In 1360, between 20 and 25 per cent of the area of customary land in this manor was held on contractual terms; by the mid 1370s, more than 40 per cent was so held. It is, however, difficult to distinguish contractual tenancies from other forms of 'farms' at Stevenage.

[4] W.A.M. 27416 ff.; and see below, p. 440.

These phrases ensured that the land in question would descend to the issue or to the heirs general of the tenant in question.[1] However, the lessee who held in villeinage held for a defined and limited term. By the end of the century he held more often for life than for a term of years, but it cannot be assumed that this had always been so; the term of years may have been in common use in the generation after the Black Death.

This type of lease had another feature, beside its limited duration, in common with the contractual leases granted by the monks of Westminster in this period: in some cases the tenants' annual dues consisted exclusively of a money rent. This is true, for example, of William Hanew and Richard Pygon, each of whom was granted a life-lease in villeinage of a messuage and half-virgate of land at Pensham in 1368.[2] Where the arrangement was of this kind, it is easy to understand why the abbot and convent should have preferred to make a grant of limited duration; because they hoped eventually to reimpose the old services, the rent-paying tenant, though he held in villeinage, was to be only a termor. But the advantage to the tenant of such an arrangement is harder to discern, for manors where leases in villeinage for a money rent are found are also manors where to our knowledge contractual leases for money rents were granted in this period. What consideration persuaded tenants to hold on the former terms? Who would hold for life in villeinage who could hold for life outside that unlikable system? We can only make sense of the situation if we assume that such a tenant, though nominally holding for a term, had an expectation of passing on his holding to his heir that other lessees for life did not enjoy. His heir could not claim the right to succeed; but custom may soon have allowed something akin to the first refusal of the lands on terms little changed, if indeed they were changed at all.

If this suggestion is correct, the more prodigal the grant of leases in villeinage, the remoter became the prospect of restoring the old, pre-plague conditions of villein tenure, for each such lease half committed the monks to another similar arrangement in the next generation. Yet throughout this period, a return to the past was the overriding ambition of the monks and the officials who supervised the running of their estates—not, of

---

[1] Below, p. 278.   [2] W.A.M. 21961 (court of 17 Feb. 1368).

course, to a past that was in all respects unchanged, but to a situation where labour services should be once again more prominent in manorial dues than they were in the dues of leaseholders in the second half of the fourteenth century. No doubt for this reason, customary leases were used sparingly in this period. Examples have come to light at Wick, by Pershore,[1] at Pensham,[2] and Todenham,[3] at Teddington,[4] and at Wheathampstead and Harpenden.[5] It can safely be assumed that such tenancies occurred more widely than these examples suggest, but the real importance of the institution was still in the future in 1390.

(iii) *Labour Services and Commutation*

In the pursuit of their aim that land held in villeinage should be held, in the accustomed way, for a money rent and labour services, and not for a money rent alone, the monks of Westminster met, once again, with chequered success. Without attributing to the pattern of events a neatness which it did not possess, it can be said that success and failure here bore a certain relationship to success and failure in the restoration of villein tenure where it had lapsed on customary land: the manors where villeins continued to hold for labour services as well as money rents were, on the whole, those where it proved exceedingly difficult to persuade tenants to hold in villeinage at all, and vice versa, for the existence or non-existence of a labour-service obligation was the paramount consideration at this time in determining whether tenants would or could accept lands in villeinage. And so, although labour services were often

---

[1] See Richard and Margery Bradestoke's life-estate in a messuage and half-virgate of land, a toft and croft in Wick in 1368; the report of Richard's death the next year shows that he held in villeinage (W.A.M. 21961–2, courts of 28 Oct. 1368 and 8 Nov. 1369).

[2] Above, p. 255.   [3] Above, pp. 250–1 and n.

[4] W.A.M. 27198. The lessees in villeinage mentioned in this rental of 1379 are John Beaumond, junior, and John Gooz, each of whom held a messuage and virgate on such terms. These arrangements are distinguishable from the contractual leases mentioned in the rental by the nature of the annual dues, and specifically by the tenant's liablity to pay tallage.

[5] See, e.g., the holding of 5 acres which Vincent Martyn (d. 1388) held in villeinage for life (W.A.M. 8943). Many other, very small, holdings in this manor were held for life in villeinage at this time; in the court rolls they seem normally to be distinguished from contractual leases by the words 'ad voluntatem' in the formula of admittance.

a relatively small component of the dues owing from tenants in villeinage after 1348, as they had been earlier, and an even smaller component of the dues that were actually rendered, in this period they nevertheless eclipsed the other obligations of the tenure in importance; the very existence of the institution, the mere threat that the obligation would be enforced, largely determined the pace and direction of change in the sphere of peasant landholding considered as a whole.

In the two or three years following the catastrophe of 1348–9, the abbot and convent of Westminster did not follow identical policies on labour services. On the abbot's manors, a higher proportion than previously of the available services was sold to the villeins who owed them. The total number of works at his disposal was now, of course, much smaller than before 1348, because the number of tenants holding in villeinage was much smaller; for those who did still hold in villeinage, the balance between rent and work was tilted further in the direction of rent. At Islip, for example, where half-virgaters owed, and, down to 1348, usually performed two and a half days' work a week throughout the year, the whole of this obligation was commuted into a money rent for a time after 1349.[1] At Deerhurst and Hardwicke, the entire labour-service obligation of the customary tenants, with the exception of three days' mowing per half-virgate, was at once commuted.[2] At Bourton-on-the-Hill, half the week-work owed by the surviving villeins during the harvest season was commuted in 1350.[3]

How exactly these concessions were put into effect depended on existing arrangements. Thus where the system of the 'rent or works' option was in force, the services of the villeins were commuted by placing them on a rent option; where 'sale of works' was the favoured method of commutation before 1348, it continued to be used subsequently.[4] That existing methods of commutation should have been used in this period may seem

[1] W.A.M. 14798 (the minister's account for 1351–2). From the summer of 1352, however, some week-work was reimposed; see below, p. 259 and n.

[2] W.A.M. 8438A–40 (the ministers' accounts for 1349–52). For the labour-service obligation on this manor, see above, p. 223 n.

[3] W.A.M. 8282. This arrangement became permanent in the sense that customary tenants at Bourton-on-the-Hill were never again, to our knowledge, asked to perform more than half their harvest works; in some years, they performed precisely half.

[4] For these methods of commutation, see above, pp. 226 ff.

so obviously what was to be expected as to be hardly worth stating at all. But to the villeins whose lot we are considering, it mattered greatly that the abbot continued to use the method we have called 'sale of works' on some of his manors, even for large-scale acts of commutation, for in these cases he continued also, as a rule, to sell works at their pre-plague valuations, notwithstanding the dramatic rise since 1348 in their real value. But where the rent option was in force, he seized the opportunity of making substantial increases in the rents of assize payable by the villeins to whom it applied. At Islip, the rents of assize for a half-virgater on a rent option rose from 3s. to 5s. 5d. per annum in the aftermath of the Black Death;[1] at Deerhurst and Hardwicke, a half-virgater now paid 5s. instead of 3s. 4d. per annum to be quit of his summer and autumn works.[2] Here was the first of many anomalies in the treatment which the abbot meted out to his villeins in this period.

On the lands of the prior and convent of Westminster, who had probably advanced further than the abbot on the road of commutation before 1348 yet who were, in general, more cautious when confronted with new situations, we find a greater variety of practice, but, on the whole, stouter resistance to change than the example of the abbot could have inspired. At Launton, the prior and convent sold all the available week-works in 1350–1 and again in 1351–2, yet heroically used nearly all the ploughing services of their surviving villeins, though few types of service can have been more difficult to enforce than this, notoriously contentious as it was at the best of times;[3] in both these decisions they followed the practice of the years before the plague. At Feering, the acreage reaped by customary labour in 1350–1 (209½ acres) was not much less than the acreage so reaped in 1347–8 (237 acres).[4] In some manors the effective burden of labour services on the tenements that continued to be occupied on customary terms increased by a

---

[1] W.A.M. 14798. Cf. R. H. Hilton, *The Decline of Serfdom in Medieval England* (Economic History Soc., 1969), pp. 41–2.

[2] W.A.M. 8438A–40.

[3] W.A.M. 15345–6. The account for 1351–2 runs from 28 Sept. 1351 to 1 Aug. 1352. The number of available week-works was in fact very small in both the years mentioned in the text.

[4] W.A.M. 25668; P.R.O., S.C.6/841/9. The figure for 1347–8 represents *c.* 65 per cent of the whole demesne acreage reaped (367 acres); that for 1350–1, *c.* 59 per cent of the whole (353½ acres).

significant margin in the immediate aftermath of the Black Death. This happened at Stevenage. Here, in 1347–8, works valued at *c.* £14. 19*s.* according to the extent were provided by 12½ virgates of customary land, and in 1349–50, 8 virgates provided works valued at *c.* £9. 13*s.*[1] The burden per virgate according to the extent was £1. 3*s.* 11*d.* in 1347–8, and £1. 4*s.* 1½*d.* in 1349–50. But values according to the extent are, of course, a quite inadequate assessment of the value of the works performed in the latter year; the real burden of works per virgate had much increased.

In the longer term, the abbot's policy ceased to be as liberal as it was in the immediate aftermath of the Black Death. At Islip, half the week-work owed by his villeins in the summer and harvest months had been reimposed by 1358,[2] and at Hardwicke, by 1366, customary half-virgaters were deemed to owe six days' work a week during the three weeks of the harvest season; yet each continued to pay the additional money rent imposed immediately after the Black Death as the price of quittance from all works due throughout this season and during the summer.[3] On the convent's portion, the variety of practice of the years 1349–52 persisted throughout the next two or three decades. Even within the confines of a single manor, the prior and convent must sometimes have appeared changeful landlords—selling, for example, the ploughing services at Launton between 1359 and 1364 but later using these works again, as they now used harvest works in this manor.[4] Of the Abbey's

---

[1] P.R.O., S.C.6/871/16–17. In fact 14½ virgates of customary land at Stevenage were normally held in villeinage in the early fourteenth century, but by 1347–8, two of these were no longer held on these terms; and in 1349–50, 6½ virgates were untenanted for the whole year or for part of it (in most cases, for the whole year). In both years, some of the services of the customary half-virgate of the bedel of the manor were remitted. In the text above, his holding has been included among those providing works, but only the works that he actually performed have been counted. In 1350–1, 7⅝ virgates of customary land provided works valued at £6. 1*s.* 8*d.* according to the extent (= 15*s.* 11½*d.* per virgate); see St. Paul's Cathedral MSS., Press B, Box 84.

[2] W.A.M. 14799. An entry in the minister's account for Islip in 1351–2 suggests that, initially, in 1352, a more severe quota of works was reimposed, after the large measure of commutation which was found necessary here between 1349 and 1351; see W.A.M. 14798, and above, p. 257 and n.

[3] W.A.M. 8442, where the works are said to be owing 'de nova convencione'. (This account relates only to Hardwicke, not to Deerhurst and Hardwicke.)

[4] W.A.M. 15356 ff.; *V.C.H. Oxon.* vi. 239. The sale of ploughing works in 1363–4 appears as a 'vendicio super compotum' entry in the minister's account.

estates as a whole, it is true to say that even in the 1370s, tenants holding in villeinage by customary services might well be required to perform some week-work and a considerable number of other services.

Yet the inefficiency of labour services can hardly have been greater in any earlier period than it was in this, when they were so clearly to the disadvantage of the villein performing them. It is the antiquated level of the valuations of services in use in the Abbey's manors, the impossibility that the abbot and convent evidently felt themselves to be under of persuading their villeins to buy their works at anything like the high market price of the labour in question, that explains the extent to which such labour continued in use on their manors after 1348. At the time when harvest services were reimposed at Launton, it cost 9*d.* or 10*d.* to reap an acre by hired labour; if, however, the monks sold the three works that traditionally sufficed to reap an acre, they would gain only 7½*d.*[1] Only where the demesne was small or on lease could villeins hope to be safe from demands for labour services, and in practice not even the leasing of the demesne necessarily saved them, for, down to the end of the fourteenth century, lessees were offered, as a rule, some at least of the labour services of the villeins of the manors in question.

It was in these circumstances, with the monks of Westminster still hopeful of actualizing labour-service obligations and their tenants no less anxious to avoid these, that some wholly rent-paying villein tenancies were introduced after 1348. Villeins who held on these terms owed suit to the manorial court but, as a rule, no other form of bodily service. Their situation was thus different from that of villeins holding on a rent-paying option of the classic type, for these, although free of week-work, still owed in many cases a wide variety of occasional services.

One form of such a tenancy, the life-grant, has already been described.[2] By the 1370s, however, rent-paying tenancies in villeinage were being granted on heritable terms, in the familiar words 'sibi et suis', 'sibi et heredibus suis', 'sibi et sequele sue'.

---

[1] *V.C.H. Oxon.* vi. 239. Although an allowance of three reaping works per acre was traditional when customary labour was used for this purpose, the monks' practice in this period was in fact to allow only two.

[2] Above, pp. 254–6.

The first admittances on these terms at Launton probably occurred in *c.* 1370, and in this manor such tenancies soon became fairly common.¹ At Wheathampstead and Harpenden, a little under half the admittances in villeinage of which a record survives in the decade 1380–9 were probably of this kind.² In this manor, most of the admittances in question were to small tenancies which can never have owed a standard assessment of labour services. As late as *c.* 1390, heritable grants in villeinage for a money rent may have made little progress on larger holdings anywhere on the estate; but by that date three half-virgates at Islip were held on these terms,³ and in that year or the following, Abbot Colchester substituted money rents of 10*s.* and 5*s.* per annum for the old dues (which included labour services) of, respectively, villein virgates and half-virgates at Todenham, and proportionate money rents for the cotlands—the holdings of the so-called *cotmanni*—there.⁴

(iv) *The Level of the Annual Dues for Customary Land in c. 1390*

If, therefore, the abbot and convent of Westminster had taken stock of arrangements on the customary land of their estate towards the end of this period, they would have noticed

---

¹ W.A.M. 15369 ff. Both 'sibi et suis' and 'sibi et heredibus suis' occur at Launton in this context.

² Of forty admittances to tenements and tenant-land of which record survives at Wheathampstead and Harpenden in this decade, thirty were probably in villeinage, and, of these, fourteen related to tenants who were admitted to hold heritably for a money rent, and seven were admittances for life or for a term of years. 'Sibi et heredibus suis' is the usual, though not invariable, formula in heritable grants. The evidence is, however, difficult to interpret, because the court rolls describe villein tenancies in several different ways: those who had them held 'at will', 'at will by the rolls', and 'at will in bondage'. It is possible, moreover, that the figure of forty includes some admittances to tenancies of demesne acres. Recent court rolls were destroyed at Wheathampstead and Harpenden in 1381, and the first roll to survive after the Revolt of that year is that for the court held on 2 Dec. 1382. Some of the forty admittances to which this note relates were in fact confirmations of arrangements dating from the period before 1381. See W.A.M. 8941–3.

³ *Oxfordshire Record Soc.* 40(1959), 90. The half-virgates in question were those held, respectively, by Richard Webbe and John Englys, by William Bryd, and by John Taylor.

⁴ The change is referred to in the rental of Todenham that was made in 1406, but the ministers' accounts for this manor show that it was made between 1 Dec. 1390 and 29 Sept. 1391 (Glos. Records Office, D 1099/M 38; W.A.M. 25981). The tenants of some of the holdings in question continued to owe poultry rents; see below, p. 270 n.

some attesting marvellous success for the conservative policy on tenures of the last thirty or forty years, and others, its dismal failure. On the one hand were scores of holdings still occupied by villeins on customary terms—and in most cases these words are to be understood quite literally as denoting the survival, unchanged, of quotas of rents and services dating from the early fourteenth century. On the other, were the holdings which they had managed to fill only by recourse to the expedients described in this chapter, that is, by contractual tenancies or by a much modified form of villein tenure. Worse still, for some of their land, though not a great deal, they had been unable to find tenants on any terms at all that they would countenance. At Launton, for example, four virgates, representing about one-ninth of the total area of customary land, were untenanted,[1] and a number of the so-called cotlands at Todenham were without tenants for many years.[2] Vacancies seem to have been less of a problem near London than in the remoter parts of the estate; they therefore troubled the abbot more than the prior and convent, whose portion consisted, with few exceptions, of manors in the Home Counties.

To all departures from customary conditions of tenure, whether the result was a contractual tenancy, a villein lease, or a tenancy in villeinage for a money rent, the monks of Westminster applied one elastic term: land held in any of these ways was 'at farm', and as late as the 1380s they still hoped that eventually the need for 'farms' would disappear. To some extent their attitude is explained by the fact that even now not a few of the manorial demesnes were still in hand,[3] and still, therefore, in need of the labour that only customary tenure could provide cheaply. Moreover, whether or not demesnes were on lease, the institution of villeinage, articulated as nowhere else in the classic system of rents and services, stood in a more general sense for the right of the aristocracy to the support

---

[1] *V.C.H. Oxon.* vi. 237.

[2] W.A.M. 25971 ff., Glos. Records Office, D 1099/M 30/10 ff. The cotlands were situated in Homestall End, in Todenham, near the church and manor house. The minister's account for this manor in 1368–9 refers to a new ditch enclosing a croft 'in quo v cotmanni solebant inhabitare'—an interesting reference, if it may be taken to mean that these very dependent tenants not only lived in a particular quarter of Todenham, but cheek by jowl there; see W.A.M. 25971. Five cotlands were still untenanted in 1370–1.

[3] Above, pp. 150–1.

of a dependent class of labourers that was so essential and—by its beneficiaries—so little questioned a part of the feudal ethos of the fourteenth century.

But perhaps the level attained by customary rents was a more weighty consideration with the monks of Westminster than either of these, for in most places these were probably still higher than those yielded by any type of 'farm'. The following annual dues for holdings of standard size are recorded at Pinvin, for example, in 1382–3:[1]

Customary Holdings		'Farms'	
Virgate	18s. 5¼d.	Virgate	——
(1)		(0)	
Half-Virgate	8s. 10½d.	Half-Virgate	6s. 8½d.
(5)		(13)	

and at Islip, in 1391, the following:[2]

Customary Holdings		'Farms'	
Virgate	——	Virgate	16s. 6d.
(0)		(1)	
Half-Virgate	11s. 3½d.	Half-Virgate	10s. 2¾d.
(18)		(14)	

In 1372–3, four half-virgate holdings were 'at farm' at Wheathampstead and Harpenden, and the rents owing for these were, on average, 21 per cent lower than the current

[1] W.A.M. 22514. The figures in this paragraph and the next relate to the extended cash value of the annual dues, in whatever form they were assessed and paid. The 'farms' at Pinvin were in fact leases in villeinage. More than half the dues of customary half-virgaters here were still assessed in the form of labour rent.

[2] *Oxfordshire Record Soc.* 40 (1959), 82–102. The figures relate to the vill of Islip, but not to Murcot and Fencot, the other members of the manor. Two customary half-virgates which owed a smaller rent of assize than the rest (respectively, 3s. 8d. and 3s. 6d. per annum, compared to the standard 6s. per annum) have been omitted from the reckoning; one was certainly, and the other probably, a service-holding, the tenant of which owed special duty on the demesne. Three half-virgates held exclusively for money rents have been counted among the 'farms', despite the fact that the custumal from which these figures are derived enumerated them with the villein holdings; they were in fact held heritably in villeinage, but on terms that were exceptional at Islip in this period. If the practice of the custumal is followed, the average dues for customary half-virgates fall to 11s. 3½d. per annum and those of the 'farms' to 9s. 11d. per annum; thus the disparity between these two kinds of rents is enhanced. For these holdings, see also above, p. 261 and n. Tallage was assessed on villeinage holdings and on those at 'farm' at 1s. 8d. per annum per half-virgate, and the rents recorded in the custumal have been adjusted upwards in the text accordingly.

rents for customary holdings of this size;[1] the corresponding figure in respect of the half-virgates 'at farm' at Stevenage, on the one hand, and those still held on customary terms there, on the other, is *c*. 54 per cent.[2] Over the estate as a whole, few, perhaps, of the tenants who were in a position to bargain with the abbot and convent and their officials for holdings would offer as much as their luckless neighbours holding in villeinage on customary terms had to pay. Yet even in Stevenage, two or three virgates of land were still held on the latter terms.

(v) *Resistance to the Fragmentation of Holdings, and its Consequences*

After 1348, in situations where the customary conditions of tenure were in any case to be breached, the monks of Westminster sometimes disposed of the arable land of a holding, and the meadow and pasture appurtenant to it, without insisting that the new tenant take the messuage as well. But it is unlikely that they were ever very willing to take upon themselves in this way responsibility for the repair of so many unwanted buildings, and quite soon 'farmers', no less than customary tenants, were probably willy-nilly in possession of a messuage. In the case of villein tenancies, the monks had a second reason for insisting that messuage and virgate were not parted, for in some manors liability to the heriot payment was associated with occupation of the messuage.[3]

Similarly, the abbot and convent were reluctant to dispose of the arable land of their customary holdings piecemeal, despite the fact that it was now often easier to find tenants for the part than for the whole. Real fragmentation, the demising of selions and acres one by one or in small numbers, was rare, even in the aftermath of the Black Death, but for many years to come some

---

[1] 16*s*. 7½*d*.: £1. 1*s*. ¼*d*. For the farms, see W.A.M. 8926, and for the customary dues for a half-virgate, unchanged since the early fourteenth century, see below, p. 441. About half the customary land at Wheathampstead and Harpenden was now 'at farm'; about half was held for the customary rents and services.

[2] Eleven half-virgate holdings were at farm at Stevenage at this date; the average annual dues were 8*s*. 2¼*d*.; the customary dues of a standard half-virgate holding in this manor were still at their pre-plague level of 17*s*. 10¼*d*. (= half the annual dues of £1. 15*s*. 8½*d*. owing from a virgate, the unit of landholding on which customary rents and services here were traditionally assessed). See P.R.O., S.C. 6/872/5; above, p. 207 and n., and below, p. 441. *c*. 17 per cent of the entire extent of the customary land at Stevenage was now held on customary terms.

[3] Below, p. 308 and n.

holdings 'at farm', which had been in the hands of sole tenants before 1348, were divided among two or three. Thus of twelve holdings, each consisting of a virgate or half-virgate of land, said to be 'at farm' in the custumal of Islip made in 1391, only four were certainly in the hands of sole tenants; in eight cases, two tenants, or even three, are named.[1] At Wheathampstead and Harpenden, in 1372–3, the half-virgate held at one time by a tenant named William Kyng was now divided between two tenants, Stephen Kyng and John Top.[2] Such arrangements were less readily tolerated in respect of holdings occupied on customary terms; most of these tenancies probably went in this period, as earlier, to sole tenants who assumed entire responsibility for the rents and services. Towards the end of the century, therefore, virgates and half- and quarter-virgates were still a common unit of tenure on the customary land of this estate.

Yet in most of the Abbey's manors the virgate had no topographical cohesion: it was made up of scattered strips in different parts of the village arable, and, after 1348, the family sense of identification with the holding, which in the past helped to keep these strips together as a single unit of tenure, was much weakened.[3] Even in the period when the link between a holding and the family in occupation was very strong, the bundle of strips making up the virgate or half-virgate had probably not been unalterable.[4] Further, the labour resources of the peasants who survived the mortalities of the mid-fourteenth century were often better suited to a small holding than to a virgate or half-virgate. On all these counts, the survival of so many of the old units of landholding in this period must be deemed yet one more proof that lordship was strong on this estate. The main reason underlying the resistance of the monks to the fragmentation of holdings after 1348 was their conception of the holding in its entirety as the necessary portion of a dependent household, but they were also, no doubt, unwilling to undertake the fuss and bother of collecting the rents and administering the services of fragmented holdings.

---

[1] *Oxfordshire Record Soc.* 40 (1959), 100–2. It seems likely, however, that William Gorge held the entire half-virgate belonging to the toft and half-virgate of land of which he and William Cowpere were tenants. We do not know how Godfrey atte Pyrie and Thomas Durdent divided the two messuages and half-virgates of which they were tenants.

[2] W.A.M. 8926.   [3] Below, pp. 318–19.   [4] Above, p. 209 n.

It has become a commonplace of manorial studies that the landless families of rural England in the Middle Ages may appropriately be imagined as standing in a queue—a queue made up of men and women whose prospects of attaining the universal desideratum, land, were marvellously improved in the fourteenth century by the decline in population; and there is, of course, a very rough sense in which the analogy is just. In a period when land was the basic source of wealth, everyone may be assumed to have coveted it and to have been in a sense in position, ready to seize any chance of its acquisition. But where, as on this estate, the lord made land available in relatively large units or not at all, and at rents that could perhaps scarcely be paid except by those who put the entire holding to productive use, the hopes of many in the queue after 1348 must have been directed to tailor-made subtenancies; the utterly poor, as we must imagine most of the landless to have been, had little chance of staying the course in a tenancy held of such a lord.

It is therefore likely that most of the candidates coming forward for the surplus holdings on the Abbey's manors in the second half of the fourteenth century were either members of the existing land-holding group there or recruits from sectors of society, whether inside or outside the manor, where opportunities existed for amassing the capital so badly needed before Lackland could seriously set about improving his position. Nor can those who relied on subtenancies have escaped the consequences of oppressive lordship, for villeins holding on customary terms must have asked their subtenants to pay rents that were proportionate to the total burden on the holding. Moreover, subtenancies, though numerous and of cardinal importance in the peasant economy, were of necessity insecure, since the abbot and convent would rarely permit tenants of customary land to demise land for any term other than a very short one.[1]

(vi) *The Rarity of Large Holdings*

Although the abbot and convent of Westminster are known to have made many new custumals of their manors towards the end of the fourteenth century, few of these productions now

---

[1] Below, p. 321, where another reason for the short terms of inter-tenant leases is also considered.

survive. It is difficult, therefore, and in most parts of the estate impossible, to piece together the pattern of land-holding in this period. Where this is possible, the tenemental patterns which it reveals are, as we should expect, less neat than those of the early fourteenth century: the integrity of the standard holdings was not so well preserved at the later date; more piecemeal acres were on the market. Here and there a few holdings that may be deemed large by any standard that it is sensible to apply to peasant holdings had been created out of customary land—as a rule, by the putting together of customary holdings and 'farms'. At Pinvin, for example, in c. 1380, one Richard Selk held half a virgate in villeinage and two other half-virgates 'at farm', in addition to a couple of small free holdings; he had c. 75 acres of arable in all.[1] At Sutton-under-Brailes, by 1406, there were four customary holdings, each comprising a virgate and a half of land; and the virgate in this manor was of c. 48 acres.[2] Yet even at this date, such holdings are in general conspicuous by their absence; the large holdings of this period were not much larger or more numerous than those of the early fourteenth century. In the vill of Islip in 1391, probably only one of the holdings made up in part or in whole of customary land exceeded a virgate in size.[3] At Teddington, perhaps only five holdings made up of such land exceeded 20 acres at this time—two more than at the beginning of the century.[4] On the whole, the times had proved discouraging for the acquisitive peasant.

[1] W.A.M. 22514. The virgate at Pinvin was probably of c. 48 acres.

[2] W.A.M. 25983. John Handes, the tenant of one of these holdings, was also the free tenant of 2 virgates, and he held an additional odd acre of customary land. Thus he had c. 170 acres in all. The Sutton rental of 1327 shows that no tenant then held more than a single virgate of customary land; one, however, held 16 acres of demesne land on customary terms in addition to a customary virgate (Glos. Records Office, D 1099/M 48).

[3] This was the holding of Thomas Hunt, comprising two half-virgates, a cottage, and a plot of land, all of customary land—and a number of demesne acres. See *Oxfordshire Record Soc.* 40 (1959), 88 ff. The virgate at Islip was of c. 32 acres.

[4] W.A.M. 27198. Twenty-two tenants of customary land, whether in villeinage or 'at farm', are listed in this rental; the number at the beginning of the fourteenth century was the same. It is, however, possible that one or two such holdings are omitted from the later rental. Moreover, all the free holdings are omitted. Spouses holding jointly have been counted as single tenants.

X

From Villeinage to Customary Tenure, *c.* 1390 to *c.* 1490

MANY of the tenurial arrangements described in the previous chapter defied the economic realities of their time. Rents did not fall equally with the demand for land on this estate after 1348, if indeed they fell at all; villeins continued to be asked for, and to pay, rents that the monks of Westminster had no hope of exacting from tenants holding on contractual terms. Towards the end of the century, however, even tenants holding of the Abbey in villeinage began to enjoy some of the advantages that normally belong to tenants—to many of them, at least—when land is in plentiful supply; holding 'by custom' began to shed its heavily pejorative associations.

Very tentatively, the turn of the tide may be placed around the year 1390, soon after the election of William Colchester to the abbacy, in succession to Nicholas de Litlington, and it is tempting to see a connection between these two events. In the long line of abbots of Westminster, there is none whom one can more readily envisage at the helm of the monastery's affairs in a period of seignorial resurgence than the aristocratic Litlington; none less likely than his humane and compassionate successor to be in sympathy with the stern mood of that time. But the changes, if in train from the beginning of Colchester's abbacy, were too piecemeal, too slow to penetrate all parts of the estate, for the hypothesis of a prime mover to be plausible. It is simply the case that, about this time, the conflict between the traditional landlordism of the monks of Westminster and the aspirations of the peasants who were its main subjects began to go more often in favour of the latter than had ever been the case previously.

Underlying this change were other changes in the structure and ways of thought of rural society. The keystone of the monks' policy on customary land in the decades after 1348 had been the villein status of most of their tenants: in this period the abbot and convent dealt with the latter as with serfs, not free men. By the end of Edward III's reign, however, landlords could no longer count on the passive acceptance by peasant society of the disabilities of villeinage. Goodwill these can never have evoked; now even acceptance was in question. The riots of 1381 made the point explicit, and we know that these extended to some of the manors of Westminster Abbey.[1]

When William Colchester became abbot of Westminster, in 1386, it was thus already inevitable that conditions of tenure on the Abbey's estates should be ameliorated. In the event, the changes took much longer to work themselves out than might have been expected in the circumstances; not even by the middle years of the fifteenth century were the monks' demands on their tenants always such as the land would readily bear. Eventually, however, the pendulum swung beyond that point, and the monks of Westminster, who had once been landlords of the most exigent kind, taking as much as they could get, became easy-going, if not indeed ineffective, in their dealings with tenants, about some of whom they were now remarkably ill informed. It is this transformation of monastic practice that carries us forward to *c.* 1490, the term of the present chapter.

(i) *The Tenant's Obligations*

Labour Services and Money Rents

By the end of the fourteenth century, few labour services were still used, either on the abbot's estate or on that of the convent; indeed, in both cases, many of the manorial demesnes were now on lease.[2] But many tenants of customary land still owed a rent

---

[1] viz. Great Amwell, Moulsham, Pyrford, and Wheathampstead and Harpenden. Other manors may also have been affected; destruction of court rolls by rioters in 1381 may be one of the reasons why these records, in contrast to ministers' accounts, are in short supply for this estate down to the end of the fourteenth century. For destruction of court rolls at Great Amwell, see W.A.M. 26151; and at Moulsham, Essex Record Office, D/DM/M30, m 5ᵛ. For Pyrford, W.A.M. 27484; and Wheathampstead and Harpenden, W.A.M. 8941. In the case of Pyrford, however, and that of Wheathampstead and Harpenden, the evidence is circumstantial and a little later in date than 1381. On the decline of villeinage see, more generally, Hilton, *Decline of Serfdom in Medieval England*, pp. 32 ff.

[2] Above, pp. 150–1.

that was assessed partly in this form, and this mode of assessment, dependent as it was on the value of labour which no
longer operated under the conditions envisaged when the
arrangements were first made, was a serious hindrance to the
discovery of the economic rent for land. In some manors, though
not perhaps in many, labour-service obligations were terminated by agreements made for this purpose between the abbot and
convent and the whole body of tenants holding on these terms.
Such agreements seem to have been more often resorted to by the
abbot than by the prior and convent, but the higher survival-
rate of records relating to the abbot's manors in this period
makes it difficult to know the truth of the matter. At Todenham
it soon became clear that the new rent was too high. In 1390 or
1391, William Colchester commuted all the labour services of
his customary virgaters and half-virgaters here, conceding that
instead they should hold their lands for, respectively, 10s. and
5s. per annum.[1] By 1406, however, six virgates in this manor
were held for rents of 8s. or 9s. per annum.[2] When labour
services were finally commuted at Islip in 1433, Richard Harwden imposed a rent of 10s. 6d. per annum per half-virgate.[3]
This, if not too heavy a burden at the time, may quite soon have
become so; at all events, vacant holdings and the flitting of
tenants from the manor are features of the scene at Islip in the
1450s and 1460s.[4]

More satisfactory, for, after all, holdings that were nominally
of the same size often differed in the quality, if not in the
number, of their acres, was the *ad hoc* agreement, substituting
a money rent for labour services, made by the abbot or the
prior and convent with the individual customary tenant when
the latter took up his holding. Down to c. 1390, the monks of

---

[1] Above, p. 261 and n. Some virgaters and half-virgaters owed two hens
per annum each, in addition to their money rents. The labour services of the
holdings of the *cotmanni* (for which see below, p. 439 n.) were commuted on the
same occasion. The average rent for these in 1406, apart from the hens which
were owed by some, but not by all, and excluding from consideration one such
holding, part of which remained in the abbot's hands, was 5s. 10¾d. per annum.

[2] Glos. Records Office, D 1099/M 38; and for the situation in 1442, the date of
the next surviving rental, see ibid., D 1099/M 41. Not a single virgate was then
rendering as much as 10s. per annum.

[3] W.A.M. 15207; and, for the date of the change, see W.A.M. 14912. The
remarks in the text apply to the vill of Islip. The standard rent for a half-virgate
at Murcot and Fencot was now 8s. 6d. per annum.

[4] W.A.M. 14923 ff.

Westminster hesitated to make such agreements, except in the case of small holdings,[1] but now more tenants of standard holdings were permitted to hold on these terms. In 1401, for example, it was agreed that six of the Abbey's tenants at Wheathampstead and Harpenden should, for the future, owe a money rent, mowing works and suit of court, instead of the customary dues and services, which were, to a large extent, still assessed in the form of labour services.[2]

Best of all, from the point of view of the tenant, was it when labour services lapsed without an effective demand for a *quid pro quo*. This happened at Deerhurst, where, in the mid-fourteenth century, some customary tenants began to withhold payments due for works 'sold' to them and were allowed to do so with impunity.[3] Many of the lessees of the Abbey's demesnes, who were often entitled in principle to call upon customary tenants for services, may have preferred to let the latter fall into disuse, rather than expose their crops to the mercy of impressed labourers. It was probably in this fossilized sense that demesne leases continued into the sixteenth century to convey to lessees the right to use customary labour services. Such a clause is found in leases at Knowle and at Steventon in 1502,[4] at Parham in 1519,[5] and at Hardwicke in 1520.[6]

Entry Fines and Heriots

In the second half of the fourteenth century, entry fines for land held in villeinage, where their level is known, were normally, though not invariably, equivalent to less than one year's dues in cash, service and kind, and they did not rise higher than this in the first half of the fifteenth century. On some manors, indeed, they fell in this period, and it now seems to have been accepted by the monks that a tenant paying an economic rent could not reasonably be asked for an entry fine, except perhaps a small fee for the registration of his tenure. At Islip, in 1434,

---

[1] Above, pp. 260–1.

[2] W.A.M. 8945 (court of 3 Dec. 1401). Numbered among the six tenants were two pairs of spouses; thus only four holdings are in question. Three of these were quarter-virgates; the fourth, a holding of 15 acres.

[3] W.A.M. 8462. It is noted in this account (for the year 1493–4) that the sum of 8s. 10d. per annum had been withheld for thirty-four years. The works in question were due in the harvest season.

[4] W.A.M. Reg. Bk. i. 137, 138ᵛ.   [5] Ibid. ii. 136ᵛ.   [6] Ibid. 162.

this principle was stated as though it were a matter of course: Gerard Braban' did not owe a fine for the cottage and two acres of land that he was in fact to hold for the customary rents and services 'quia cepit ad verum valorem'.[1]

The fall in the level of entry fines left the heriot as the most considerable down-payment for which a tenant in villeinage, or his family, was liable, and, as long as the abbot and convent claimed the best beast in the flesh, little, other than a timely removal of beasts from the holding on the occasion of the vacancy, could be done to mitigate this due. By the end of the fourteenth century, however, the monks were commonly accepting a money payment in lieu of the beast, and from this arrangement it was a short step to the levy of a cash heriot that bore no relation to the value of any beast, best or otherwise, on the holding. By the mid-fifteenth century, the amount of the heriot payment that would eventually fall due was often agreed between the monks and their tenant at the outset of the tenancy. Such agreements were being made at Bourton-on-the-Hill and Sutton-under-Brailes in the 1430s and 1440s;[2] the first cases noticed at Islip occurred in 1416,[3] but at Launton, not until 1439.[4] In 1427, however, a widow at Launton promised to pay the monks 4s. or her best beast when her jointure was up,[5] and a case of this kind occurs at Wheathampstead and Harpenden in 1395.[6] By such arrangements the monks and their officials were saved the trouble of identifying a tenant's best beast when the time came, and perhaps that of circumventing attempts to spirit it away. The tenant was advantaged by knowing in advance how much he or his family would have to pay; and it seems likely that often, in practice, less was paid under the new

---

[1] P.R.O., S.C. 2/197/48 (court of 11 Oct. 1434). Gerard and his wife were admitted as joint tenants.

[2] Glos. Records Office, D 1099/M 1 (court rolls of these manors for the 1470s, when some of the heriots agreed in the 1430s and 1440s were paid).

[3] W.A.M. 14894 (court of 6 Apr. 1416). Each of these agreements, however, related to a cottage that was to be held on customary terms for life. For another case of the kind noted in the text, see W.A.M. 14898 (court of 28 Oct. 1420).

[4] W.A.M. 15500 (court of 18 Mar. 1439).

[5] W.A.M. 15488 (court of 11 Sept. 1427); and for jointure in the case of customary holdings, see below, pp. 298–9.

[6] W.A.M. 8944 (court of 26 Mar. 1395). Elena, widow of John Eston, was admitted to her jointure in a messuage and virgate of land and gave pledges in respect of the heriot owing for their joint tenancy, which was payable at her death; it was to be at least 10s. in value.

system than would have been the case under the old. Further-more, on manors where copyhold for lives or arrangements akin to this developed in the fifteenth century, the monks sometimes agreed to waive every heriot except that owing in respect of the last life.[1]

Repairs

In this period, the abbot and convent evidently considered ways and means of effecting a general improvement in the state of repair of customary holdings, and they had reason to be concerned about this problem. During the interlude after the Black Death, when tenancies at will were fairly common in a number of their manors, repairs, even to buildings still in occupation, were neglected; not a few messuages were in fact unoccupied for some time; and the weakening of the family hold on property, which is a feature of the rural scene after 1348, made for a feckless attitude on the part of many tenants to the upkeep of their buildings—why bother with repairs, when the holding might well pass outside the family at the next taking? All these developments are reflected in the dilapidated condi-tion of many villein tenements towards the end of the fourteenth century, a period when amercements for the offence of having a *tenementum ruinosum* were a common feature of proceedings in manorial courts. And the fact that tenements had become dilapidated in the course of the last few decades hindered a return to the customary conditions of tenure in villeinage, the great *desideratum* of monastic policy, for anyone taking such property on these terms could be held responsible for its repair. Probably no period has ever demonstrated more perfectly the necessity of compensating tenants for repairs, if a system of farming in which tenancies are at will or for a short term is to operate efficiently.

By the end of the fourteenth century, the prior and convent were promising compensation for repairs and improvements to certain tenants at Wheathampstead and Harpenden. These were tenants with leases for lives which were, however, termin-able if anyone else offered to hold the land in question on the customary terms. Thus in 1393, Andrew and Matilda Leyghton were granted a messuage and quarter-virgate of land in this

[1] For examples, see below, pp. 281-2 nn.

manor for their joint and several lives, for a money rent, suit
of court, and heriot, with that proviso, but with the promise of
compensation for their expenditure on the tenement in the
meantime, if the proviso were ever to take effect,[1] and a similar
arrangement was made in the case of Adam and Margery
Plomer and their son, Geoffrey, who took a messuage and
quarter-virgate here for the lives of the last two named.[2]
The tenant in villeinage who surrendered his holding rarely
received compensation for the unexhausted part of repairs or
improvements executed in the course of his tenancy; after all,
he had done no more than was his duty, and, in any case,
surrenders were not to be encouraged. But assistance for work
in progress was a different matter, and this the tenant in villeinage could now occasionally hope for. He might perhaps be
provided with the large timbers that were necessary for major
repairs; his entry fine might be waived on account of the
dilapidated condition of the holding, or the first year's rent
remitted to help pay for the repairs.[3]

More obtrusive in the records than the monks' readiness to
help with repairs is their insistence that these should in fact
be executed. New tenants were sometimes asked to name
pledges who would underwrite the obligation, and tenants
surrendering holdings to execute repairs. Details of the work
are rarely specified in the court rolls; they must have been
agreed orally between the monks and their tenants. Chattels of
deceased tenants might be, and sometimes were, seized to meet
the cost of necessary repairs to their holdings. If the case was a
really bad one, the offending tenant might actually forfeit his
holding, as Stacey Bechamp forfeited his messuage and lands at
Great Amwell in or about 1439, on the grounds that he had
failed to keep them in a proper state of repair.[4] As a rule, however, the monks' bark proved worse than their bite, and many
were the tenants in villeinage who, for years on end, disregarded
injunctions to repair, without incurring any more serious
penalty than a trifling amercement, now and again, of a few
pence.

[1] W.A.M. 8943 (court of 11 June 1393).
[2] W.A.M. 8944 (court of 11 June 1395).
[3] For examples of these practices at Islip, see W.A.M. 14901, 14909, 14916.
[4] W.A.M. 26200.

(ii) *Nomenclature*

In sum, by the mid-fifteenth century, the typical tenant in villeinage on the Abbey's estates no longer performed any form of bodily service, except suit of court, although he may still in theory have owed such service. His obligations, which, with the exception of suit of court, were probably all of the cash kind, were more nearly adjusted to the quality and condition of the holding they purchased for him than had been the case in the fourteenth century, and he was much more likely than his predecessors of that time to be paying an economic rent, no more, for his land. Perhaps no less important than these changes in bringing about a renewal of popularity for his tenure was the fact that the monks of Westminster now rarely referred to him, and probably rarely thought of him, as a villein; only the luckless *nativi de sanguine*, those who had been born unfree, were still bondmen in their eyes; tenants who would formerly have been described as tenants in villeinage now held 'according to custom' or 'by the rolls'. This change in nomenclature, however, was not made at the same time in every part of the estate. At Castlemorton, Chaceley, and Longdon, the words 'in villenagio', 'in bondagio', and 'native' were already dropping out of the conveyancing vocabulary used in respect of customary land by 1400.[1] At Launton, however, tenants are often described as holding 'in bondagio' down to c. 1420,[2] and at Sutton-under-Brailes the land of tenants holding by custom was still 'terra nativa' when a new rental was made of this manor, in 1443.[3] In most places where the matter can be put to the test, words with a servile meaning or implication fell out of use in the context of the tenure of land between c. 1430 and c. 1470.

(iii) *Residence Requirements*

Notwithstanding these changes, the abbot and convent of Westminster continued to associate landownership with lordship over the occupants of the land. Customary tenants, therefore, were still required to live in the manor where they held their lands, or at least in the liberty to which it belonged. It was no longer possible to insist, as so often in the fourteenth century,

---

[1] W.A.M. 21116 ff. But in these manors much land was held by one or other of the free tenures.
[2] W.A.M. 15460 ff.   [3] Glos. Records Office, D 1099/M 40.

that each messuage be occupied by the tenant of the lands to which it was appurtenant, for such a rule would have prevented even a bona fide inhabitant of the manor from taking on more than a single holding, but residence within the jurisdiction of the Abbey was probably the invariable rule. Occasionally, the point is made explicit in the court rolls. It was noted at Islip, in 1410, that Richard Bannebury's lease of a messuage and half-virgate of land would be terminated if he left the manor.[1]

There were, of course, other reasons beside the jurisdictional one why tenants should be required to live on their messuage or not far away from it. A non-resident would probably allow the buildings on the messuage to deteriorate and would very likely wish to sublet part of the holding, if not the whole; the monks of Westminster encouraged neither of these practices. The residence rule came to be of particular importance in the wool-producing manors of the Western Parts, of which Todenham and Sutton-under-Brailes are two examples. In the course of the fifteenth century, outsiders, some of whom were probably men of considerable means, began to cast covetous eyes on the pastures of these manors and the tenancies having the right of access to them, but the monks clung to their preference for home-spun tenants, though to do so meant, in the end, a sacrifice of income.

(iv) *The Triumph of Customary Tenure*

Before these changes in the obligations of customary tenure were complete, contractual tenancies had become, once again, of small importance on the agricultural land of the estate. The latest use of the term of years on tenant-land which has been noticed in the court rolls of Great Amwell occurred in 1393.[2] At Wheathampstead and Harpenden, contractual leases on tenant-land were less common in *c.* 1420 than they had been

---

[1] W.A.M. 14888 (court of 22 Oct. 1410). The lease was for four years. Banne-bury was a smith. A puzzling entry is that relating to the admittance of Richard Harries to a messuage and virgate of land at Todenham, in 1470: 'Et preceptum est quod morabitur super dictum messuagium cum uxore et sua familia continue per festum Natalis Domini proxime futurum, sub pena forisfacture et omissionis tenementi sui' (Glos. Records Office, D 1099/M 1, court of 10 May 1470).

[2] W.A.M. 26164. Later leases for terms of years at Great Amwell were probably of demesne land; contractual leases for life were rare here from 1381, the date at which the surviving court rolls begin.

in *c.* 1400,¹ and at Islip, few have been noticed after that date.² At Launton, although such tenancies still occur in the second half of the fifteenth century, customary tenancies were gaining ground from the second decade of that century.³ It must be said, however, that there are many manors where we do not know the state of affairs at this time. In the end, although contractual tenancies, particularly those for a term of years, had been much used at the beginning of the century in the case of urban and semi-urban properties, these, too, were swept along by the same movement. By *c.* 1435 the great majority of demises at Staines, whether of arable land, meadow, shops, or built-up tenements, were made according to custom, with the 'sibi et suis' formula;⁴ if, however, the term of years was used here, it was now unlikely to be of less than twenty years, and terms of forty and sixty years are mentioned.⁵

(v) *Estates in Customary Land*

The triumph of customary tenure over contractual arrangements recalls the situation on the Abbey's estates before 1348, when, indeed, contractual tenancies on customary land seem to have been virtually unknown; if, however, we consider, not the tenures, but the estate which each tenant enjoyed in his land—did he hold heritably, or for life, and so on—the period after 1348 will more often appear to be the time of origins.

Perhaps because the rebels of 1381 did their work so well, few court rolls dating from the first half of the fourteenth century survive for the Abbey's manors, and very few indeed from any earlier period than this. Moreover, on manors where some

---

¹ W.A.M. 8945 ff. ² W.A.M. 14898 ff.

³ W.A.M. 15470 ff. A custumal made at Launton in 1416–17 shows that, of the 31½ virgates of customary land then tenanted, 25½ were held by the customary rents and services, or heritably for a money rent, with or without certain services, and the remainder by demises for life or a term of years or on yearly tenancies (W.A.M. 15716).

⁴ W.A.M. 16958 ff., 16967, fos. 11ᵛ ff. However, the extent of customary land at Staines was small; see below, p. 428.

⁵ For forty-year terms in 1437 and 1460 (but in the latter year, in a lease of demesne land), see W.A.M. 16967, fos. *m*[= 13] and 17; for a sixty-year term in 1454, see W.A.M. 16959. W.A.M. 16967, however, is a court book, made for the purpose of recording the tenurial business of the court at Staines; it may omit some demises for short terms—arrangements that would soon have lost their interest for the abbot. (The folios of this manuscript are numbered alphabetically to fo. *m*; the numbering thereafter is my own.)

relatively early court rolls do survive, it was not yet the practice
to record anything other than the bare details of an admittance;
in some cases we are told only the tenant's name, that of his
predecessor, and the amount of his fine. Piecing together the
conventions of this period is therefore a singularly difficult task.
Nevertheless, outlines of a system emerge from the mists.[1]

Although life-interests and terms of years are mentioned in
the case of the Abbey's urban property at this time, the villein
tenancies, which all but monopolized agricultural land, were
heritable. The monks recognized that villeins, in common with
free men, had heirs, and they did their best to ensure that the
latter took over the lands when the time came; they might
indeed constrain the son of a deceased tenant to take up his
holding. In some manors, if not in all, the heritability of
villein holdings was made explicit in the words used on the
occasion of an admittance: land was granted to the incoming
tenant in the formula 'sibi et suis', 'sibi et heredibus suis', or
'sibi et sequele sue'. A villein, it is true, did not enter on his
inheritance without paying a fine at the will of the abbot and
convent, and the fine, though not absolutely large, probably
made a big hole in his pocket. In levying it, however, the monks
challenged the heritability of his tenure in much the same degree
as their early twelfth-century predecessors challenged the
heritability of tenure in fee when they levied arbitrary reliefs—
that is, hardly at all.

In other respects local custom was paramount: granted the
heritability of villein holdings, the identity of the heir or heirs
was discovered by applying the custom of the manor or vill.
Although impartibility and primogeniture prevailed by the
fourteenth century, practice in this matter was still not uniform;
nor, of course, should we expect it to have been so. At Launton,
Borough English, giving the inheritance to the youngest son,
was the rule.[2]

---

[1] The following account of practice before 1348 is based mainly on court rolls
for Wheathampstead and Harpenden (W.A.M. 8937–40; Herts. Record Office,
D/Elw M 128, 134, 136), Staines (W.A.M. 16952–3), Pyrford (W.A.M. 1685,
27468–70), Islip (W.A.M. 14861–2), Launton (W.A.M. 15420 ff.), Pershore
(W.A.M. 21935 ff.), Eye (W.A.M. 27000–2), Birdbrook (W.A.M. 25567–8), and
Morden (W.A.M. 27384–90).

[2] The rule is implied in, for example, the undertaking of Hugh, son of William
Agate, in 1290, to relinquish his father's land, to which he was then admitted, if John,
his younger brother, were ever to claim it (W.A.M. 15420, court of 30 Sept. 1290).

Later in the century, some of the Abbey's tenants in villeinage began to be admitted for a limited term—occasionally for
a term of years, but more usually for life. This happened in the
decades immediately following the Black Death, when tenants
were reluctant to take holdings in villeinage on customary
terms, if these included labour services, and the monks of
Westminster reluctant, for their part, to demise holdings on
terms other than these.[1] Since these attitudes were long-lasting,
life-tenancies in villeinage continued in certain manors into the
fifteenth century. By the mid-fifteenth century, when villeinage
had given way in most places to tenure by custom or by the
rolls, three basic arrangements can be distinguished.

Probably the most common form of admittance to customary
holdings was that using the words 'sibi et heredibus suis'. The
form, 'sibi et suis', though still in use, is less often encountered
and may now have been understood as applying only to the
tenant's issue, not to his heirs. In the manor of Islip, the words
'sibi et suis' were occasionally used in the conveyance of
tenancies for life.[2] The use of 'sibi et sequele sue' naturally
declined with the decline of villeinage. But many admittances
of this period in the form 'sibi et heredibus suis', and, indeed,
many using the 'sibi et suis' formula, differed in one important
respect from the examples which have survived from the early
fourteenth century. The frequent addition of the words 'et
assignatis suis' reflects the more liberal attitude of the late
medieval monks of Westminster towards the land transactions
of their customary tenants, who were now in a position to buy
and sell interests in villeinage holdings with a freedom unknown
before.[3] The purchaser of such a holding would probably be
asked to pay no more than a small, though still arbitrable, fine.
Given the alienability of his holding, and its heritability, the
customary tenant of this period admitted with the words 'sibi
et heredibus suis' may be deemed to have possessed a fee-
simple interest in his land.

---

[1] Above, pp. 245 ff.

[2] W.A.M. 14889 (court of 3 Aug. 1412), 14895 (court of 10 Mar. 1418). On
'sibi et suis' and the customary law relating to tenures, see E. Kerridge, *Agrarian
Problems in the Sixteenth century and After* (London, 1969), p. 36 and *passim*.

[3] Below, pp. 299 ff., and for court rolls which reflect this change, see
W.A.M. 15452 ff. (Launton), and W.A.M. 8943 ff. (Wheathampstead and
Harpenden).

Also possessed of a freehold interest in his land was the tenant who held according to custom for life, the successor of the fourteenth-century tenant in villeinage for life. At Bourton-on-the-Hill, Sutton-under-Brailes, and Todenham, admittances to hold for life seem to have become the norm by *c.* 1470; in the 1470s, the life is much the commonest form of estate recorded in the court rolls of these manors.[1] In a number of cases, reversioners are mentioned, some of whom were relatives of the tenant in possession. The fine that a reversioner would pay was agreed when his interest in the land was first recognized, and it was then entered in his copy. In at least one case, he undertook to pay a higher rent than the tenant in occupation. In 1478, Thomas Eddon claimed the reversion of 2 virgates of land which Alice Yate had surrendered in Sutton-under-Brailes, in accordance with a copy made ten years previously.[2] He was to pay an increment of rent of 7s. 4d. per annum, but not, it appears, an entry fine.

In some other places, life-interests occur concurrently with heritable tenancies of the traditional kind. They had become quite common in the manor of Islip by the 1420s.[3] Reversions, though more rarely mentioned here, do occur from time to time. In 1401, for example, William Webbe surrendered a messuage and the moiety of a half-virgate of land, together with the reversion of the other moiety, to the use of Thomas Nelme.[4]

---

[1] Glos. Records Office, D 1099/M 1.

[2] Ibid. (court of 6 July 1478). At the same court, Thomas Eddon surrendered a messuage and virgate and a messuage and 14½ acres of land, the latter holding being one of the so-called cotlands of Sutton-under-Brailes, for which see below, p. 440 n. In 1469, John Stevens was granted the reversion of the messuage and virgate of Richard Stevens in Bourton-on-the-Hill, for his own life and the lives of his wife and John, their son (ibid., court of 30 Oct. 1469). But nearly all the reversions recorded in these manors at this time conferred life-interests.

It is sometimes hard, in the sources of this period, to distinguish reversions from remainders. For examples of the use of *remanere* in a tenurial context, at Launton, see W.A.M. 15480 (court of 10 July 1419) and W.A.M. 15517 (court of 14 Mar. 1468); and for 'reversion' and 'remainder' as terms of art, see below, p. 450. Throughout this study, I have tried to follow the usage of the sources, if the latter use one or other of these words or a cognate.

[3] W.A.M. 14898 ff.

[4] W.A.M. 14878 (court of 23 July 1401). The lands in question were in Murcot and Fencot. It is said of the quarter-virgate of which Webbe had the reversion that Alice Trute and Joan Caldecote hold it 'per copiam'. This phrase rarely occurs in records relating to the estates of Westminster Abbey before the end of the fifteenth century. (Thomas Nelme = Thomas atten Elme.)

Somewhere between these two kinds of interest in customary land—the tenancies for life and heritable tenancies—comes the joint tenancy of husband and wife and one or more—but, as a rule, one, and he a son—of their children. Estates of this kind were common on some of the Abbey's manors in the early fifteenth century. Although in the case of such a tenancy, the son was admitted as tenant during his parents' lifetime, this step was sometimes, and perhaps as a rule, taken before he was of an age to be a real partner in the working of the holding. At Launton, for example, Richard Bygge married Katherine, daughter of Richard Hebbe, in 1409 and so became joint tenant with her of the messuage, virgate, and quarter-virgate of land which she had inherited four years earlier, on the death of Thomas Hebbe, her brother.[1] In 1411, Richard and Katherine were readmitted to their lands with an explicit mention of heirs and assigns, but in 1421, having once again surrendered the lands, they were admitted with their sons, Walter and Richard—both of whom are likely to have been under twelve years of age—as joint tenants with them.[2] It may have been understood by the parties most intimately concerned in such arrangements that the son, though now an admitted tenant, would not be entitled to a full share of the issues of the holding during the lifetime of his parents. If so, the joint tenancy of parents and child resembled in practice the later copy for lives with a jointure for the wife added in, for, under the system of copies for lives, each life took successively.

Such tenancies can be traced in the Western Parts in the second half of the fourteenth century.[3] At Castlemorton, for example, Richard and Agnes Meleward and Henry, their son,

[1] For the following case, see W.A.M. 15456 (court of 28 Feb. 1396), 15469 (court of 27 Feb. 1409), 15472 (court of 4 Dec. 1411), and 15482 (court of 9 July 1421); see also W.A.M. 15716. At the time of her marriage to Richard Bygge, Katherine Hebbe was the widow of William Baldwin, d. 1407. Agnes, the child of this earlier marriage, probably died soon after her father. See W.A.M. 15468 (court of 5 Dec. 1407).

[2] In 1445, Richard and Katherine Bygge surrendered the lands and were readmitted as joint tenants with William and Margery Freeman (W.A.M. 15506, court of 14 July 1445). Walter and Richard were now probably dead. When Richard himself died in 1449, the monks did not take a heriot (W.A.M. 15510, court of 8 July 1449).

[3] However, the earliest example so far noticed on the Abbey's estates occurs at Stevenage in 1345–6, when 8 acres of land were 'farmed' to John le Smyth, Joan, his wife, and John, their son, for their lives. See P.R.O., S.C. 6/871/15.

were admitted as joint tenants of a messuage and virgate of land in 1360,[1] and similar entries occur in the court rolls of Chaceley and Longdon before the end of the century.[2] In common with the life-interest, tenancies of this kind had become popular at Islip by the 1420s.[3] Only a few miles away, however, at Launton, neither this nor any other form of the limited estate in customary land was ever in frequent use;[4] in resorting to it, the Bygges were untypical of the whole body of tenants in this manor.

How exactly should we think of the joint tenancy of parents and child? Was it derived from the heritable tenancy or from the tenancy for life? In the case of the Bygge holding at Launton the parents in effect surrendered a heritable tenancy in order to settle the lands on their two sons, and perhaps their motive was the desire that both sons, not only the younger of the two, should share the inheritance; the custom of the manor would have given the whole of it to the younger. It is also possible to argue, though perhaps not with great conviction in a period of land surplus, that the abbot and convent of Westminster became somewhat hostile about this time to the idea that customary holdings should be fully heritable and, in granting joint tenancies for parents and child, were saying in effect that only the issue was entitled to inherit.

Though at times ambiguous, the evidence suggests that, on the contrary, most joint tenancies of this kind developed in association with the tenancies for life that appear on customary land after 1348. The prior existence of life tenancies was, in a general sense, conducive to the development of this other form of limited estate; and some life-tenancies were specifically extended to include the tenant's issue. Joint tenancies of parents and children are in fact least in evidence where the customary conditions of tenure were little disturbed, and tenancies of a limited duration therefore little in evidence, in the second half of the fourteenth century. The manor of Pyrford is a case in point. The abbot filled his villein holdings here rapidly and,

---

[1] W.A.M. 21122 (court of 24 Mar. 1360). Richard Meleward surrendered the unexpired part of the term of ten years which he had been granted in this holding four years previously.   [2] W.A.M. 21125 ff.

[3] W.A.M. 14898 ff. It was stipulated in the case of many of these tenancies that a heriot would be paid at the death of the last survivor.

[4] W.A.M. 15460 ff.

as a rule, on customary terms, after 1348; heritable tenancies remained the norm on customary land.¹ Where, on the other hand, joint tenancies of parents and child became common, life tenancies are also mentioned and seem in fact to occur more frequently than heritable grants. Thus the former arrangement is in evidence in the Western Parts, at Castlemorton, Chaceley, and Longdon, but so are tenancies for life.² Moreover, such joint tenancies were sometimes created on the surrender, by one of the parents, of a tenancy for life.

Yet the transition from tenancies for life to the joint tenancy of parents and child was not a matter of course; nor was the development everywhere sustained for long. The latter seems to have been virtually unknown at Bourton-on-the-Hill, Sutton-under-Brailes, and Todenham in the 1470s, although life-interests were well established here.³ At Islip, moreover, the practice of bringing sons into the tenancy during the lifetime of the parents did not retain the popularity it acquired early in the century; by *c.* 1470 the life-interest, with or without jointure for the wife, was more common.⁴ And, irrespective of all these considerations, it may be the case that the abbot of Westminster was more apt to make trial of new kinds of estates in customary land than the prior and convent. So, for example, grants in the form 'sibi et suis' and 'sibi et heredibus suis' have serious rivals at Islip and in his manors in Gloucestershire and Worcestershire, but at Launton, Great Amwell, and Wheathampstead and Harpenden, all conventual manors, they more than held their own in this period.

In the sixteenth century, it mattered greatly what estate a customary tenant enjoyed in his lands. Was the copyhold for life, for several lives or of inheritance? By then such distinctions determined in no small degree the fortunes of individual land-holders and their families. It must be conceded that, in this

---

¹ W.A.M. 27480 ff., 1685; and for the situation at Pyrford after 1348, see also W.A.M. 27416 ff. However, some admittances to customary land in this manor were now for terms of years. In the case of heritable tenancies, 'sibi et sequele sue' occurs as an alternative to 'sibi et suis' in this manor.

² W.A.M. 21128 ff. In 1470, however, a joint tenancy of Walter Hill's messuages and cotland in Bourton-on-the-Hill was granted to Isabel, Walter's widow, and William, her son; heriot was payable on the death of each (Glos. Records Office, D 1099/M 1, court of 10 May 1470).

³ Glos. Records Office, D 1099/M 1; and see above, pp. 279–80.

⁴ W.A.M. 14938 ff.; P.R.O., S.C. 2/197/48.

earlier period, they were in large measure distinctions without a difference, and it is probably this very fact that explains why diverse practices were tolerated, not merely in the monastic estate considered as a whole, but in the setting of the individual manor. But here another distinction is needed; it is that between the family and the seignorial aspects of conveyancing practice. Within the family, the arrival of the widow's jointure, of reversions and something akin to if not exactly identical with a copy for lives was profoundly important. These innovations meant, in sum or individually, a more honorable estate for widows, greater freedom for parents in devising land away from the customary heir, and perhaps a more equitable distribution of property than had previously been possible between the children of a twice-married parent.

As between lord and tenant, however, all the arrangements that have been considered probably worked out much the same in the end for the greater part of this period; a family claimant, if one existed, would almost certainly be admitted to a vacant holding in preference to others, if the last tenant had held by custom. He might be a reversioner, able to support his claim with a copy; on the other hand, he might have no formal claim on the land, only the first refusal that manorial custom probably allowed even to the issue of a tenant for life. Given the slackness of the demand for land, lasting on some manors into the second half of the fifteenth century, it probably did not matter much whichever was the case, for when fines are low and rents falling, the first refusal is all that a man needs.

(vi) *The Copy*

These developments gave rise to a diplomatic innovation, the copy. At first, this was quite literally a copy of the entry in the court rolls relating to the holding in question. That the rolls themselves now recorded in detail the tenure, estate, rent, and services of each newly admitted tenant is explained by the fact that manorial arrangements had lost their earlier uniformity; the individualized record was needed. But the practice of giving tenants a copy of the rolls also denotes a growing regard in peasant society for written evidence, and perhaps a desire on the part of customary tenants to emulate the freeholder's possession of a charter.

For the abbot and convent, too, the innovation was convenient. At Great Amwell, and presumably in other manors as well, they made copies for their own use. After the Peasants' Revolt, when the court rolls of Great Amwell were destroyed, the monks were able to verify the details of some earlier conveyances by reference to their copies.[1] When these special circumstances no longer existed, the monks and the officials assisting at their courts must nevertheless have found copies still useful. In some manors, if not in all, they insisted that one who claimed by copy produce it for their inspection.[2] The copy was the claimant's proof of title, but the monks had perhaps another reason for calling for it: this document, which bore the date of the court where it was made, saved them a tedious hunt through the manorial archives in search of the entry in question. Eventually, the so-called 'copy' may have become more informative than the court roll itself. It is possible, for example, that permission to sublet was sometimes spelt out in the copy but not in the roll.[3] Useful though copies were to the monks and their tenants, even at the end of this period, little or nothing in the records relating to the Abbey's estates suggests that customary tenure would come to be called after them, much less that, as Littleton's *Tenures* show,[4] this had already happened in some influential circles. The Abbey's tenants were said as a rule to hold 'by custom' or 'by the rolls'.

(vii) *The Size and Composition of Holdings*

Although in the semi-urbanized possessions of the Abbey, many mixed holdings, comprising free land and customary

---

[1] See W.A.M. 26155, the roll of the court held at Great Amwell on 5 May 1386, where, however, the reference is to the copy of a lease for a term of years. It is said here that the lease of a plot of land for a term of twenty years, in 1352–3, is recorded in a copy 'in ista bagga contenta'; finding that the term is over, the monks order that the tenement be taken in hand again. Presumably the copies of customary admittances etc. were kept at Westminster in bags, or files, thus escaping the fate of destruction that overtook some court rolls kept locally in 1381. In 1315, the court at Wheathampstead ordered that a charter taken from a villein who had acquired an acre of free land be kept 'in bagga domini' (Herts. Record Office, D/Elw M 128, court of 14 Mar. 1315).

[2] For examples, see Glos. Records Office, D 1099/M 1.

[3] Below, p. 311.

[4] *Littleton's Tenures*, ed. E. Wambaugh (Washington, D.C., 1903), pp. 33 f. For a rare example of the holding 'per copiam' so called, in this period, see above, p. 280 n.

land, had come into existence by the mid-fifteenth century, in the countryside proper, this arrangement may still have been uncommon. Early in the fifteenth century, at Aldenham, for example, c. 91 per cent[1] of the Abbey's tenants held either free land by free tenure or customary land by customary tenure; a mixture of lands or of tenures was rare. At Sutton-under-Brailes, in the 1440s, only c. 19 per cent of the tenants held both freely and by custom,[2] and at Todenham only one tenant among twenty-nine did so.[3] That the separation of free tenure and customary tenure was so marked even now, when the latter was fast losing its servile associations, suggests perhaps that we are dealing with different layers of society—that the Abbey's free tenants were still not often peasants.[4]

The semi-urbanized manors differed from the rest in another respect that is important in the present context. Although much land was still used in the former for husbandry, only vestiges of the system of measuring by virgates survived here. At Denham, for example, the riverside, countrified town that Edward I had restored to the monks' possession, a tenant was admitted to a messuage and half-virgate of land as late as 1489, but such holdings seem to have been rather rare here at this time and had been so, very likely, for more than a century.[5] By contrast, in parts of the countryside—the real countryside—the virgate was still much in evidence, not only into the second half of the fifteenth century, but until the surrender of the Abbey's estates to Henry VIII and, no doubt, later. We should envisage the virgate of this period as being often a little different in its detailed composition of acres and strips from the virgate of the thirteenth and early fourteenth centuries, for late-medieval changes in land-use would have been impracticable without concomitant changes of this kind, but nevertheless identical with that earlier unit of landholding in its main features. It is, therefore, a very conservative state of affairs that is revealed at

---

[1] c. 72: c. 79; but some entries in the rental from which these figures are derived have been lost and the figures are inexact. See W.A.M. 4599.

[2] 5: 27. See Glos. Records Office, D 1099/ M 40 (a rental of 1443).

[3] Ibid., D 1099/M 41–2 (a rental of 1442). William Bennet held a messuage and virgate of land by free tenure and two plots of common land at will (i.e. by custom).

[4] See also above, pp. 115 ff.

[5] W.A.M. 3404; and for admittances at Denham in the late fourteenth century and in the fifteenth century, see W.A.M. 3400–7.

Pensham, Pinvin, and Wick, where about half the copyholdings listed in the record of attornment of tenants to the king in 1540 were made up of virgates or fractions of virgates.[1] Although the holding of the individual tenant was now sometimes larger than a virgate in these places, the traditional virgates and half-virgates were its components: it had grown, where it had grown at all, by the putting together of these ancient units of landholding. A rental made in 1525 records a similar state of affairs on customary land at Turweston, one of the manors of Queen Eleanor's foundation.[2] Earlier, in the two decades 1450–69, *c.* 64 per cent of the admittances to customary holdings recorded in the manor of Islip related to virgates or to half- or quarter-virgates,[3] and nearly all those recorded at Launton in the decade 1460–9 were of this kind.[4]

Perhaps it is only because the Abbey's manors in the West and South Midlands are better documented than its other manors in this period that the survival of the virgate as a unit of landholding seems particularly strong in these parts. As in the late fourteenth century, so now, the situation owed much to the preference of the abbot and convent of Westminster for this kind of holding. They were not, of course, unusual among late-medieval landlords in this respect—a point driven home by the tenemental pattern on one of their own manors. This is Brickle-hampton, where most of the customary holdings in the mid-fifteenth century were made up of virgates; yet this property had only recently been acquired in demesne by the monks of Westminster.[5]

[1] W.A.M. 21827 B.

[2] W.A.M. 7695. However, although the virgate was a common component of holdings at Turweston, engrossment had taken place on a considerable scale. $18\frac{1}{2}$ virgates of customary land were now divided among only eight tenants, one of whom held 6 virgates freely, in addition to his customary holding. (These figures take no account of the demesne, reckoned to be 7 virgates in extent, which was in the hands of a lessee.)

[3] 35: 55 (W.A.M. 14923 ff., P.R.O., S.C. 2/197/48). The jointures of widows, which took effect without a formal admittance, have been excluded from consideration. It should be noted, however, that the court rolls of Islip are not complete for this period. The decades mentioned in the text run from Jan. 1450 to Dec. 1469.

[4] Eighteen admittances are recorded in this decade; in each case, the main holding was a virgate or the fraction of a virgate, but five holdings comprised a cottage, curtilage, or piecemeal acres as well; see W.A.M. 15511–19. The decade mentioned in the text runs from Jan. 1460 to Dec. 1469. The court rolls for Launton in this period are not complete.

[5] W.A.M. 22131; and see below, p. 361.

It goes almost without saying that, where agriculture was not the sole or the main means of livelihood for the tenant, the typical holding continued small in this period. Thus, of more than seventy tenants holding property of any kind of the monks at Staines in 1490, probably only sixteen held as much as 10 acres in the fields, although the great majority held some land there—very few were content with merely a house or two, or with a shop.[1] Even where most people did live by husbandry, many farmers continued to work on a small scale. At Aldenham, *c.* 43 per cent of the recorded tenants of customary land had fewer than ten acres each in the early fifteenth century.[2] In the vill of Islip, which, despite its position in the neighbourhood of Shotover and Stowood, had never been the habitat of small-holders, as Aldenham was, *c.* 35 per cent[3] of the tenants of customary land almost certainly held less than a quarter-virgate—less, that is, than 8 acres, or thereabouts—as late as 1435.

Yet in general the mean size of holdings grew larger in the course of the fifteenth century, and more holdings were large, in an absolute sense, than had been the case in the fourteenth century. The virgate, the *terra unius familie* of a now remote past,[4] will serve as a rough and ready standard in this context. At Pinvin, five tenants of customary land held more than a virgate each in 1442; in 1382–3, only one had done so.[5] At Todenham, there were at least nine tenants of customary land

---

[1] W.A.M. 16807. The figures in the text relate to every kind of property and every kind of tenure. The virgate at Staines was of 10 field-acres.

[2] *c.* 30: *c.* 70; see W.A.M. 4599. But on the imperfections of this rental, see above, p. 286 n. The figures in this paragraph and the next take into account the free holdings possessed by some of the Abbey's customary tenants at this time—i.e. although all the tenants taken into account were tenants of customary land, their holdings comprised, in some cases, free land in addition to customary land. The figures exclude free holdings not held in conjunction with customary holdings; of nine such holdings at Aldenham at this date, four were of less than 10 acres.

[3] 15:43; see W.A.M. 15207. Of the forty-six tenants named in this rental, three—Margery Clerk, John Swyft, and Alice Wynbush—were freeholders. The fifteen tenants who make up the 35 per cent mentioned in the text were classified as cottagers in the rental; but two other 'cottagers' are enumerated there, each of whom certainly held more than a quarter-virgate.

[4] See above, pp. 208 ff.

[5] W.A.M. 32821, 22514. One of the holdings that exceeded a virgate in extent in 1442 did so by only a small margin. The virgate at Pinvin was probably of *c.* 48 acres.

holding more than a virgate each in 1442, compared to five in
1406.¹ Further, in a number of manors, one holding of customary land outstripped by a considerable margin even the
largest of the rest. At Aldenham, early in the century, this was
John Wykebourne's holding of *c.* 100 acres;² at Todenham, in
the 1440s, Robert Heth's holding, of *c.* 94 acres;³ at Sutton-
under-Brailes, Nicholas atte Welle's, of 216 acres.⁴ But, of
course, the manorial demesnes, which were now often on lease
to a customary tenant of the manor, have to be taken into
account at this point. With these included, there were now
quite probably two farms considerably larger than any of the
others that were occupied by peasants. Equally, the leasing of
the demesnes could act as a brake on the accumulation of
customary holdings, and this, perhaps, was the case at Launton.
There was no customary holding here larger than *c.* 45 acres
in the mid-fifteenth century.⁵ The demesne, however, was on
lease to a tenant named John Cottesford, whom we should
classify as a cottager if we had only the rental of the time to go
by, for it is as a cottager that he is listed there.⁶

The tenants of these large farms were local residents—the
monks saw to that. Some, moreover, were people with deep
roots in the manor. Wykebournes are mentioned among the
tenants at Aldenham in the early fourteenth century,⁷ and a
family called 'atte Welle' had been established as long as this

¹ Glos. Records Office, D 1099/M 38, M 41. The figure for 1442 excludes
a virgater who also held a toft and a garden.
² W.A.M. 4599. In 1419–20, the prior and convent of Westminster manumitted
a son of one John Wykebourne of Aldenham, in return for the payment of £10
(W.A.M. 19915).
³ Glos. Records Office, D 1099/M 41–2. Heth held three messuages and virgates, together with a messuage and half-virgate. On the likelihood that the virgate
at Todenham was of *c.* 27 acres, see below, p. 434 n.
⁴ Glos. Records Office, D 1099/M 40. This holding comprised 2 virgates of free
land demised by indenture, 2 virgates of customary land, and half a virgate of
customary land demised by indenture. The virgate at Sutton-under-Brailes was
of *c.* 48 acres.
⁵ W.A.M. 15717. The reckoning in this rental is by the virgate and its fractions,
but the virgate is known to have been of *c.* 20 acres at Launton.
⁶ Ibid.; and see W.A.M. 15410. This John Cottesford was probably the son of
the man of the same name who took a farm of the demesne at Launton in 1423;
see below, p. 311 n. The arable demesne here was of *c.* 330 acres at the beginning
of the fourteenth century. Though the extent of tillage had been reduced since
then, the demesne was still not much eroded by piecemeal leasing when Cottesford
took it.
⁷ C.U.L. MS. Kk 5. 29, fos. 66–7.

at Sutton-under-Brailes.[1] If more ambitious than their neigh-bours, such tenants were not always more successful in the long run. In many cases their farms fell apart after a remarkably short space of time, into their component virgates and fractions of virgates. Their fate is a reminder how extraordinarily difficult it was even now for peasant families to amass the capital for relatively large-scale enterprise. As though to drive home the point, many of the families in possession of the demesne farms, whom the monks provided initially with basic livestock and equipment, held their ground for generation upon generation. Among the dynasties that took root in this easier soil was that of the Cottesfords of Launton, who emerge as armigerous gentry in the seventeenth century.[2]

(viii) *Standards of Administration*

In carrying through all these changes, in acquiescing where they acquiesced, and in opposing, where they opposed, the abbot and convent of Westminster enjoyed the minimum of professional advice, and that perhaps not often of the highest quality. Gone were the days that we glimpse in the records of Walter de Wenlok's abbacy, when the abbot of Westminster's employment was attractive to administrators who had done well in the royal service or that of the secular aristocracy.[3] More commonly found on the abbot's pay-roll from the end of the fourteenth century onwards than the true professional are small landowners like Alexander Besford, for whom office-holding can never have been more than bye employment, a make-weight to his fortunes. Besford, who was steward of the Western Parts in Abbot Colchester's early years, was a free tenant of the abbot's in Pinvin—a servant who was, no doubt, glad of the fee of £4 per annum which he received from the abbot, but un-

---

[1] Glos. Records Office, D 1099/M 48. The Welle virgate of customary land mentioned here was still in the hands of a family of that name in 1406 (W.A.M. 25983). By 1443, however, it was held by Richard Eddon, and the Welle of this date—the Nicholas mentioned in the text—was in possession of customary holdings which had formerly been in the hands of tenants named Fawkes, Handes, Undirwode, and Pepyn (Glos. Records Office, D 1099/M 40).

[2] *V.C.H. Oxon.* vi. 238.

[3] See in particular the case of William Merre, the steward of Wenlok's lands in that abbot's very last years, and one-time steward of the earl of Cornwall at Berkhampstead (*Walter de Wenlok*, p. 25 and n.).

likely to move elsewhere for more.[1] In wealth and standing, he is probably to be compared, *mutatis mutandis*, with the enfeoffed knights who so often witnessed the Abbey's charters in the twelfth and early thirteenth centuries. The Abbey's administration as a whole now depended principally on men of this stamp, and the later Middle Ages also witnessed the abandonment of another of Wenlok's practices, that of retaining at fee many lawyers and royal clerks;[2] such advisers were now, as a rule, employed *ad hoc*, as each situation where advice of this kind was deemed necessary arose. Thus the abbot's council, to which the knottier problems relating to tenures and rents were referred, is to be imagined in the fifteenth century as a rather amateur body, and one that had, moreover, not a few members who were personally interested, as tenants of the Abbey, in the outcome of the debate.

The scarcity of professional skills may explain the rather poor standard of record-keeping on the late medieval estate. The lay-out of the accounts of some of their local officials became archaic to a degree that is notable even by medieval standards of accounting. At Launton, for example, the rent-collectors' accounts name the sum of £18. 19s. 4d. per annum as the gross value of the rents of assize owing to the monks from 1374 until the sixteenth century.[3] As time passed, this sum bore less and less relation to the actual yield of rents, most of which was recorded later in the account, under the heading of 'Farms'; but, notwithstanding every change in the actual state of affairs, the accounts continued to enshrine the old sum.

It would not have mattered much, for ministers' accounts were extraordinarily conservative compilations throughout the Middle Ages, had these quaint practices not been the outward

---

[1] For Besford's fee, see W.A.M. 24537, 24410–11. Besford held the site of the old manor house at Pinvin as a free tenant (W.A.M. 22514). He relinquished office as steward in 1400. See also *V.C.H. Worcs.* iv. 21. The principal sources for the personnel of the monastic administration in the period covered by this chapter are the accounts of, respectively, the steward of the abbot's household, the receiver in the Western Parts, and the conventual treasurers (W.A.M. 24541 ff., 24410 ff., 19876 ff.).

[2] See *Walter de Wenlok*, pp. 30–2 and nn.

[3] W.A.M. 15370 ff. A new custumal of this manor was made in 1416–17, and a new rental in 1449–50 (W.A.M. 15716–17). Thus from 1450 it would certainly have been possible to bring the entries about rent in the ministers' accounts up to date.

sign of an inward reluctance on the part of the monks of Westminster to admit that what was done was done. Although, after the beginning of William Colchester's abbacy, they travelled a long way on the path of realism in the exploitation of their tenant-land, still they could not quite bring themselves to think of the world as it was and not as it had once been. By the mid-fifteenth century, this attitude no longer showed itself in a desire to return to bodily service as a component of customary rents, but it did mean that the monks continued to think of each of the adjustments that brought rents in general down from their high fourteenth-century level as, quite probably, a temporary measure. A search through the records to discover what the rent for land had been in the remote past became one of the employments of antiquarian-minded monks at this time. In the reign of Henry VI, one such monk nostalgically traced the changes that had occurred in rents for customary holdings at Laleham since the mid-fourteenth century and carefully recorded his findings in a rental which spanned this long period.[1]

Moreover, where there was any uncertainty as to the economic rent for land, as was frequently the case in this period of rapid social and economic change, the monks preferred to settle with their tenant on a rent that was, if anything, too high, and to adjust it subsequently by means of *ad hoc* rebates. In consequence, by c. 1450, the customary land of the Abbey's estate was studded with tenants who were not expected actually to pay the rent that they in theory owed. In the early fifteenth century, the abbot of Westminster was nominally entitled to rents amounting to c. £18 per annum from the tenant-land at Todenham, but each year he conceded that his rent-collector here could not collect the whole of this sum. By c. 1430, it had become normal practice to allow a 'respite' of £1. 6s. 8d. per annum to the collector.[2] What began, quite probably, as the practice of agreeing upon rebates of rent individually with deserving tenants developed insidiously into tolerance for unilateral

---

[1] W.A.M. 27171.

[2] Glos. Records Office, D 1099/M 30, M 42 ff. On the subject matter of this paragraph see also C. Dyer, 'A Redistribution of Incomes in Fifteenth-Century England', *Past and Present* 39 (Apr. 1968), 11–33; cf. R. R. Davies, 'Baronial Accounts, Incomes and Arrears in the Later Middle Ages', *Economic History Rev.*, 2nd ser., 21 (1968), 211–29.

decisions on the part of many tenants to withhold some of their rents. Hence the distinction which appears in the Abbey's rentals towards the end of this period, between rent that was *levabilis* and that which was *non levabilis*. The Abbey's rents at Westerham in 1487 amounted to £46. 14*s*. 7½*d*. per annum, of which sum £43. 1*s*. 8½*d*. per annum was *levabilis*.[1] At Staines, in 1490, the abbot's rents amounted to £33. 6*s*. 5½*d*. per annum, but £1. 7*s*. 9¾*d*. per annum of this sum is described as *redditus retractus*—rent withheld by the tenants.[2] In 1463, the abbot's free and customary tenants at Murcot and Fencot were permitted to compound for their rents at a farm of £12 per annum, despite the fact that the abbot would in theory lose £2. 3*s*. 6*d*. per annum by this arrangement, for the rents due from his tenants in the two vills amounted to £14. 3*s*. 6*d*.[3] The mood was indeed different from that of the monks of Westminster a century earlier, as Nicholas de Litlington succeeded to the place of Simon de Langham—rent had been *levabilis* then, and in the teeth, one would suppose, of much greater odds.

[1] W.A.M. 5132.   [2] W.A.M. 16807, fo. 15.
[3] W.A.M. 14847. The farm was agreed in Oct. 1463. The rental enumerating rents amounting to £14. 3*s*. 6*d*. per annum was not made until Dec. 1464, but the rental itself probably recorded quotas of rent that were already in existence by that date. The farm was continued after the making of the new rental.

XI

The Land Transactions of the Abbey's Tenants

OF all the problems posed by the village land market in the Middle Ages, none has proved more intractable than that of its origins. Did the sale and purchase of land, and inter-tenant leasing, have a regular place in village life in the twelfth century or at an even earlier date,[1] and, if so, in what type of village? Were there natural buyers and sellers of land, whose needs and capacities began to break through the restraints imposed on a free system of exchanges by inheritance customs and feudal law almost as soon as these took shape? Or was the village land market essentially a concomitant of the decline of feudalism and the wrenching apart of customary patterns of inheritance that characterized the later Middle Ages? Though the answers to these questions may one day become clearer to the historian than they are at present, the villages where the monks of Westminster helped, as landlords, to shape developments can never contribute much to their elucidation, for here the surviving evidence hardly extends to this early period; the market that comes into view on this estate is that of the period after *c.* 1280, and it must be confessed that even in this relatively late period the view that we have of it is a highly imperfect one.

In this period, there were principally three sets of factors that interacted, the one with the other, to foster certain kinds of land transactions among the Abbey's tenants and to inhibit others.

---

[1] As suggested in Postan, *Essays on Medieval Agriculture and General Problems of the Medieval Economy*, pp. 115 ff. Professor Postan's essay was first published in *Carte Nativorum: A Peterborough Abbey Cartulary of the Fourteenth Century*, ed. C. N. L. Brooke and M. M. Postan (Northants. Record Soc. XX, 1960), pp. xxviii ff. See also, on the Peterborough evidence, E. King, *Peterborough Abbey, 1086–1310: A Study in the Land Market* (Cambridge, 1973), pp. 99 ff.; and, more generally, P. R. Hyams, 'The origins of a peasant land market in England', *Economic History Rev.*, 2nd ser., 23 (1970), 18 ff.

These were, in the first place, family attitudes to the inheritance and alienation of land; secondly, the attitude of the monks of Westminster to such transactions; and, finally, the broadly economic factors of supply and demand.

(i) *The Rules of Inheritance*

Family attitudes to the inheritance and alienation of land were never the same in differently constituted communities and cannot be assumed to have remained unaltered over a long period of time. In nearly all the Abbey's manors where practice is known to us, impartible inheritance was the rule by the beginning of the fourteenth century, and very likely this had long been the case.[1] The better-documented conventions of aristocratic landholding at this time, which so ingeniously softened the rigours of impartibility for the children whom this practice excluded from the inheritance, prepare us to find, as we do, that some of the peasant communities which adopted that rule found ways and means of giving children other than the heir at least a small provision of land. This could be done, as it had often been done, *mutatis mutandis*, in aristocratic society since the mid-twelfth century, by the parent's making over of land during his own lifetime to a child who was not the heir and who would therefore take nothing at his death. A dispute about a heriot brings such a case to our notice at Pyrford in 1347.[2] When Walter atte Moor died, in that year, his cottage and virgate of land passed to Henry, his son and heir, who duly surrendered an ox valued at 10*s.* as heriot. But Walter held at one time other tenements as well as this one, and for these also the abbot claimed and took a heriot—a cow valued at 7*s.* Henry atte Moor, however, pleaded that Walter had made over these tenements to another son before he died—in effect, that, since Walter was not the tenant at death, no heriot was due for them.[3] Much earlier, in 1275, Simon atte Lane, of Wheathampstead, was presumably doing the same kind of thing when he surrendered 1½ roods of land to the use of Christina, his daughter; Simon did not lack an heir—he had a son

---

[1] Above, pp. 210–11, 278.   [2] W.A.M. 27478 (court of 23 Jan. 1347).

[3] Henry appealed to the record of the transaction in the court rolls, and, pending a decision based on this evidence, the cow was released to him, Henry having named two pledges for its return and for payment in lieu, should his claim fail. The outcome of this case is not known.

named Nicholas—but his daughter, if she was to have anything, must receive it during his lifetime.[1]

Where provision of this kind was made for any of the brothers
or sisters of the heir, it was understood that they had, even so,
not the smallest claim on the main family holding—their hopes
were pinned on what was sometimes called the land of acquisition—that is, on the assarts or the purchases of land made in
the lifetime of their parents.[2] Thus Walter atte Moor's virgate
of land at Pyrford, which was, no doubt, the main holding of
his family, descended entire to his heir. A little earlier, in 1335,
Henry atte Mulle, another of the customary tenants of this
manor, made over to his daughter, Juliana, his acquired lands,
that is, an acre taken from the manorial waste and two-thirds of
an acre of free land which he had been able to purchase; his
customary messuage and quarter-virgate, the family holding,
was destined for his heir.[3]

If, however, this was now the accepted convention, the
practice of providing land for younger (or elder) sons or for
daughters can have been a common one only in those vills
where there was a considerable area of land which no longer,
and perhaps had never, belonged to the standard holdings,
the virgates and half- and quarter-virgates. Such vills were not
rare on the Abbey's estates by the fourteenth century, but most
of the available bits and pieces of land were probably free land,
as they were, for example, at Pyrford; customary land was still
often tightly parcelled in virgates or fractions of virgates.[4] But
free land was forbidden fruit to a villein—family custom and the
manorial rule were at odds with each other.

The claims of a widow on the family holding were much
harder to contain and more or less impossible to eliminate. On
free land in the fourteenth century, a landholder's widow could

---

[1] W.A.M. 8937 (court of 18 Feb. 1275). Simon had at least three children—
Nicholas, Christina, and another son, Elias. The last-named died in or about
1275, and Nicholas, described as his heir, took his tiny holding of 1½ roods. This
seems to have been deemed to release one and a half roods of Simon's holding for
Christina.

[2] The description 'terra de adquisitione' is applied to such land in the extent
of Pyrford made in 1330 (W.A.M. 27469).

[3] W.A.M. 27470. In the extent of 1330, Henry's lands, other than the messuage
and quarter-virgate, are described as 'diverse parcelle terre et prati de adquisitione' (W.A.M. 27469).

[4] See above, pp. 207–8.

probably expect no more than dower in a third of the holding, and in some vills this was all that she normally had in the case of customary land. If, however, the heir was not yet of age, custom sometimes conferred on her, not the mere wardship of the heir and his lands, but a tenancy with remainder to the heir on attainment of his majority. When Robert Sterling, a tenant in villeinage of 4 acres, died at Eye in 1329, his widow was admitted as tenant until their three daughters and only son, the heir, should be of age.[1] In certain places, moreover, the widow of a customary tenant had rights akin to those of a jointure and, indeed, more ample rights than these, before that arrangement can truly be said to have existed at this level of landholding on the estate. She enjoyed such rights at Islip, in Oxfordshire.[2] Here, after enjoying her spouse's tenement for a year and a day, the widow of a customary tenant chose between two options: dower in a part of the land or of its issues —this is never described as a fixed proportion of the whole and seems to have been assessed *ad hoc*—and a continued tenancy of the entire holding for life. Provided a heriot had been paid in respect of her husband's tenancy at the time of his death, she could have the holding—if she chose the latter option—without paying a fine. If, however, she ever married again, a fine was owing, and this admitted her new spouse as joint tenant with her in the lands.

A few miles away, at Launton, the custom was similar, but, when we first see it in operation, in the late thirteenth and early fourteenth centuries, less considerate of the widow's feelings about remarriage.[3] Here, too, the widow had her spouse's tenement for a year and a day and then chose between dower— which included a third of the curtilage—or a tenancy of the entire holding. But it was expected that, if she chose the second

---

[1] W.A.M. 27000 (court of 14 July 1329). It is to be understood that the daughters were the older children of the marriage; they would in fact be of age before the son and heir.

[2] The following reconstruction of the rules at Islip is based on cases recorded in the court rolls from the late fourteenth century onwards; see W.A.M. 14863 ff. There is little or no information about the widow's rights at Islip until the late fourteenth century.

[3] See W.A.M. 15420 ff. Custom relating to widows is stated more explicitly at Launton than at Islip; see in particular W.A.M. 15428 (court of 30 Sept. 1324), 15430 (court of 4 Oct. 1330), 15446 (court of 5 Mar. 1384), 15452 (court of 20 Feb. 1391).

of these options, she would marry again without delay, and from her would-be husband the monks took a substantial fine— perhaps 20*s.* in the case of a half-virgate holding.[1] Marriage could be deferred by the widow on payment of a much smaller sum, but such fines purchased only temporary respite: in the end, the widow had to marry or surrender the holding. For a widow anxious to keep her holding but able to find no willing partner herself, a spouse was chosen in the manorial court.[2] The remainder in the holding at Launton was to the children, if any, of the second marriage. Later in the fourteenth century, as the demand for land fell, and, with it, the supply of men willing to accept a holding encumbered with a widow, a small fine purchased for a widow here the right to remain in that condition for life without forfeiting her lands; perhaps also society was becoming, quite simply, more considerate of human feelings in these matters.

The widow's jointure in the strict sense of the word, that is, her remainder in lands of which she and her husband had been joint tenants, made its appearance on the Abbey's customary land in the second half of the fourteenth century. It did so at first in association with another innovation of the period, life-tenancies in villeinage, and it is easy to see why these should have been the tenancies that precipitated the arrangement.[3] In the case of heritable tenancies in villeinage of the traditional type, the widow's rights were enshrined in custom and well known to everyone in the vill; there was no need to be explicit about them when customary land changed hands. But life-tenancies in villeinage were themselves a departure from custom; here, if the tenant's wife were not to be mentioned explicitly when he was admitted, she might be allowed nothing in her widowhood. The practice of admitting man and wife jointly became common, it being understood that remainder was to the survivor.

---

[1] For the level of fines for heirs here in this period, see above, p. 225.

[2] The conscript might escape with a fine. Thus in 1326, two husbands-elect refused, in turn, to marry the widow Agnes le Kyng and escaped with fines of, respectively, 3*s.* 4*d.* and 1*s.* 6*d.* Agnes herself refused a third candidate and was obliged, in the end, to surrender her holding, with the exception of her dower (W.A.M. 15429, courts of 19 Nov. 1326 and 10 Feb. 1327). A widow who, like Agnes, kept possession of the holding for more than a year and a day but then surrendered it, owed a second heriot; the first had been paid at her husband's death.   [3] For such tenancies, see above, pp. 254 ff.

Where the joint tenancy was of this kind, the widow's position was unambiguous. But what exactly could she claim in cases where the joint tenancy had embraced, not only herself and her spouse, but a child of the marriage, an arrangement in frequent use on some of the Abbey's manors in the fifteenth century?[1] It is likely, though incapable of proof, that the widow had in practice a larger claim on the land than her son, whose hopes were deferred until she chose to make it over to him. In general, the widow's jointure does mark an erosion of the rights of the heir in respect of the family holding. However, in a period such as the fifteenth century, when the monks of Westminster had, in many manors, more holdings than tenants to occupy them, the heir did not necessarily have a long wait before becoming a tenant himself. Tired of waiting, some in this position took other holdings as these became vacant; some who did this never entered into effectual occupation of the patrimonial holding. Jointures thus helped to bring into existence one notable feature of peasant landholding on the monastic estate in the late Middle Ages, the fading importance of inheritance as the mode of transmission of land.[2]

(ii) *The Attitude of the Monks of Westminster*

To Sales of Customary Land

To the abbot and convent of Westminster, about the year 1300, each customary holding on their estate was the necessary provision of land for a dependent household; hence their stout opposition to any transaction that would result in the permanent fragmentation of a holding—that is, to the sale and purchase of anything less than the whole.

How was it, then, that holdings had been fragmented even to the limited extent that is true of this period—that hides and half-hides had given way to virgates, and virgates to half- or quarter-lands, if indeed these basic units of landholding had not completely vanished? Very likely this process is to be explained mainly by a widespread practice of partible inheritance among the Abbey's tenants in an early period that lies beyond our range of vision now. It was the tenemental pattern

---

[1] Above, pp. 280 ff.   [2] See also below, pp. 318–19.

thrown up by this phase in the history of their manors that the
monks of the thirteenth and fourteenth centuries tried to
preserve intact; as we have seen, the dominant feature in this
pattern was often a half-virgate holding.[1]

For a long time after the triumph of impartible inheritance,
the monks' hostility to the fragmentation of holdings may have
been easy to reconcile with the usual desires of their tenants;
after all, the latter had adopted impartibility with the very
purpose of preventing the further break-up of the family
holding. The rub came towards the end of the fourteenth
century, when, despite the weakening of the peasant's own sense
of the need to preserve the integrity of holdings on account
of their place in long-established patterns of inheritance, the
monks of Westminster continued firmly opposed to fragmentation. To the end of the Middle Ages, it was only in manors of
a certain type that either the abbot or the convent readily
permitted their customary tenants to sell their holdings piecemeal.

These were manors such as Aldenham, belonging to the
portion of the prior and convent, or the abbot's manor of
Pyrford, where assarting in the early Middle Ages brought
under cultivation a considerable extent of arable land that
never became part of the virgated structure of holdings that it
was the monks' great desire to preserve. In the context of the
peasant land market such land was apt to prove the thin end
of a sizeable wedge, for, if traffic was permitted in this—and
why not?—it was in practice hard to treat the rest of the
tenant-land differently. Moreover, since the physical geography
of most of the assarting manors, in particular the proximity of
woodland and waste, made sense of small-holding as a way of
life, the peasant family's own zeal for keeping its holding intact
was at its weakest here. And finally, as in the case of Aldenham
and Pyrford, the assarting manors tended also to be manors with
a significant proportion of freeholders among the tenantry;[2]
but by the end of the thirteenth century, freeholders were prac-

---

[1] Above, pp. 207–8.
[2] The free tenants of Aldenham represented only *c.* 16 per cent of the whole
body of tenants there in the early fourteenth century, but they held *c.* 30 per cent
of the tenant-land. At Pyrford, *c.* 59 per cent of the Abbey's tenants in that period
were free, and they held *c.* 30 per cent of the tenant-land. See above, p. 114, and
below, p. 432.

tised buyers and sellers of land—it was natural that their way
of doing things should spread beyond the confines of the free
land of the manors in question.

In the early fourteenth century, whenever the monks permitted one of their customary tenants to sell an acre or two
of his holding piecemeal, they seem to have insisted that
the purchaser and his heirs owed them an annual rent for the
future, in addition to the rent already owing in respect of the
land, and, notwithstanding any premium that had been paid
to the vendor of the land. This rent, though always very small,
was sometimes, and, down to the late fourteenth century,
perhaps invariably, larger than the rent remitted to the vendor
in recognition of the sale. Thus William de Preston, who was
permitted to purchase certain meadowland and woodland
belonging to William Serych's customary holding at Pyrford
in 1329, was charged with a so-called new rent of $\frac{1}{2}d.$ per annum,
but only $\frac{1}{4}d.$ per annum of Serych's rent was remitted for the
future.[1] Moreover, the holding in its entirety continued to
appear against the name of the vendor or that of his heirs in
custumals and extents of the manor, and, as though to drive
home the lesson that customary holdings could not in fact be
fragmented, the purchaser of the fragment appeared in these
records as a free tenant—this despite the fact that he had
entered by surrender and admittance, the mode of entry that
was distinctive of customary land. All the anomalies of the
system are displayed in the extent of Pyrford that was made in
1330.[2]

This large manor, situated on the edge of Windsor Forest,
comprised three vills beside Pyrford itself: Woodham, Horsehill,
and Sidewood. In each there was a considerable area of free
land in addition to the customary land, and the total tenant
population of *c.* 160 included between ninety and a hundred
who held freely.[3] Among the latter were eight beside William

---

[1] W.A.M. 1685 (court of 16 Nov. 1329). Preston acquired this land, not from
Serych himself, but from one Thomas Lowys, to whom, evidently, Serych had
first made it over. It is to be understood that Preston would from now on owe, not
only the rent of $\frac{1}{2}d.$ per annum mentioned in the text, and payable to the monks of
Westminster, but also a contribution to the rent payable by Serych for his customary lands, the proportion being, very likely, that already agreed between Lowys
and Serych.

[2] W.A.M. 27469.

[3] Of whom six also held land in villeinage. For the figures, see below, p. 432.

Preston whose holdings included land taken from the customary holdings of the manor. In Horsehill, for example, the free cottage holding of William atte Lane junior had been taken from the customary land of William Golie, but Golie is later listed as the tenant of a messuage and 12 acres of customary land, with no hint that part of the holding had in fact been alienated. In addition to the meadowland and woodland taken from William Serych's holding, William Preston held by free tenure 2 acres of the customary land of William de þecthere, two pieces of arable land and meadow of the customary land of Walter atte Style, and 1 acre of the land of William Quinchald. But later in the extent, William de þecthere, Walter atte Style, and William Quinchald are credited with customary holdings that are, to all appearances, still intact.[1]

The increment of rent imposed on the fragment of land that was sold and the continued liability to the monks of Westminster of the vendor for virtually the whole of the rent originally assessed on the undivided holding—but particularly, perhaps, the latter—proved, in combination, an effective antidote to the fragmentation of customary holdings. Even in manors where the monks were not hostile in principle to sales of this kind, few were made. At Pyrford, not much more than 15 acres of arable and a little meadow had been affected by 1330.

Later, the practice of the abbot and convent changed, yet only in certain parts of the estate, and those probably a small proportion of the whole. The purchaser of a fragment of a customary holding was still sometimes required to pay an increment of rent in respect of his purchase. When, for example, John Berd sold half an acre of arable land to Walter Chertesey at Horsehill, in Pyrford, in 1440, Walter undertook to pay a rent of $\frac{1}{4}d.$ per annum to the principal tenement of the holding, which was to continue in Berd's hands; Berd, in effect, undertook to collect this increment of rent on behalf of the abbot.[2] But towards the end of the fourteenth century, the abbot and convent began to show more interest than hitherto in the way in which the main rent and services, as distinct from tiny

---

[1] William de Preston's holding was in the vill of Woodham. The other free tenants of the manor of Pyrford whose holdings included land that had once been part of a customary holding were: Alice Prentout, William Goym, Emma Serych, Gilbert Sabyne, Robert Hamond, Richard Cosyn and Peter *faber*.

[2] W.A.M. 27492 (court of 28 June 1440).

increments of rent, were apportioned between the vendor and
the purchaser of the fragment of a customary holding. The
portions were sometimes entered in the court roll, with other
details of the transaction agreed between vendor and purchaser,
and, in these cases, the monks dealt in future directly with
both parties. When Thomas Cook sold the messuage appurtenant to his 6-acre holding at Staines in 1395, the purchaser,
Robert Lodelowe, undertook to pay the abbot 1s. 3d. per
annum, and Thomas's rent and services were reduced proportionately.[1]

It may seem that the monks of Westminster were actually
strengthening their hold on the customary land of their estates
by such a measure, and so, in a sense, they were, for tenants like
William Serych, who answered to them for a holding that was,
though undivided in theory, in practice somewhat fragmented,
may have been inefficient collectors of the portions of rents
owed by their co-tenants. But when we consider how, over
a very long period of time, the monks had been able to insist
that the tenant of a customary holding accept entire responsibility—if a responsibility that was at times imperfectly
discharged—for all the rents and services owing from it, and
how manorial administration had been in this way simplified,[2]
the main significance of the change, where it occurred, appears
quite different: it marks a decline in the demands which could
be placed upon customary tenants. The practice of so appor-
tioning rents and services between the parties to a transaction
in customary land was probably not a common one on the
Abbey's estates, even in the fifteenth century. At Staines seignorial control had been weak for many years, and it is not surprising to find such a development there. Even where the
tenants of customary land were now allowed to dispose permanently of fragments of their holdings, the monks still taxed
the transactions in question by levying entry fines, or, if not

---

[1] W.A.M. 16967, fo. *d*ᵛ (court of Hil. Term, 1395). In fact, Lodelowe undertook
to pay 1s. per annum in rent, and to render three reaping works per annum, or
3d. per annum in lieu thereof.

[2] Above, p. 265. The apportionment of rents and services in the case of
transactions in free land has a different significance. This was a necessary concomitant of procedure by substitution instead of subinfeudation, and substitution
itself the means of saving for the chief lord of the fee incidents that he would
otherwise have lost. For such apportionment on the Abbey's lands, see below,
p. 314.

entry fines, then fines for the apportionment of rents and services. These payments, however, were not large—Cook and Berd paid 1s. for the apportionment of their rent in 1395—and would probably not have been in themselves a deterrent to many buyers and sellers of land in this period.

The attitude of the abbot and convent of Westminster to the sale of a holding of customary land in its entirety appears at first sight very different. Since the holding was not only the means of livelihood for a dependent household, but also a direct source of their own income, it had never to be without a tenant. From this it followed that it might be to their advantage to permit a customary tenant to sell his interest in his land—if for any reason the tenant could not continue to work the land himself, the alternative to sale was an untenanted holding and a gap in their rent-roll. Their concern in these cases was not to prevent the transfer of holdings outside the family at present in occupation, but to see that the proper formalities of surrender and admittance in the manorial court were observed. Accordingly, transactions apparently involving the passage of land outside the family are recorded in some of the earliest court rolls to survive for this estate. But what interest did a customary tenant possess in his land? It is when we probe this question that the ambivalence of the monks' attitude becomes apparent.

In fact down to the closing decades of the fourteenth century, the monks of Westminster allowed their customary tenants very little freedom of manœuvre in the sale of holdings. It is true that they tolerated traffic in such holdings, but their tolerance often proves, on dissection, to have been little more than a readiness to allow tenants wishing to relinquish their holdings the privilege of finding their own successors. The conditions of tenure on their estate ensured that the vendors in these transactions would derive little profit from the deal. For, if the purchaser was not asked for a higher entry fine than the tenant who took customary land by inheritance, there is certainly nothing to suggest that he paid less.[1] Yet the annual rent that he would have to pay as one of the Abbey's tenants was likely to be a high one—higher perhaps in many cases than the land would readily bear.[2] It was a rash purchaser who offered a

---

[1] He may in fact have paid considerably more; see above, p. 225.

[2] Above, pp. 234 ff.

premium of any size to the vendor of the land in these circumstances. Further, the stigma still attaching to villein tenure
must have limited the potential market for customary land by
scaring off many free men, the very people who could best
afford the capital outlay entailed in the purchase of land.

Over the estate as a whole, the fifteenth century may have
been well advanced before customary rents were adjusted to
an economic level.[1] In a sense, therefore, it is true to say that
the general conditions of customary tenure continued to inhibit
inter-tenant sales and purchases until that date. But the fall in
rents was heralded on some manors by the reduction of entry
fines to a low or nominal level; this, indeed, was the first and
most important instalment of the change. By reducing to
a minimum the premium which passed between the incoming
tenant and the monks of Westminster at the outset of a customary tenancy, this change freed more of the former's capital
for his deal with the vendor of the holding.

On some of their manors, the monks of Westminster now
acknowledged at the very moment when the customary tenant
was admitted the likelihood that he would want to sell his
interest in the land instead of transmitting it to his heir. 'Sibi
et suis', 'sibi et heredibus suis' in the words of the conveyance
became, very frequently, 'sibi et suis et assignatis suis', 'sibi et
heredibus suis et assignatis suis'. At Great Amwell, for example,
assigns begin to be mentioned in *c.* 1386, and such an entry soon
becomes a standard item in admittances to customary holdings;[2]
at Launton, they begin to be mentioned explicitly early in the
1390s.[3] The change at Great Amwell is of particular interest,
since we know that there had been violence here on the part of
the Abbey's tenants, and some burning of court rolls in 1381.[4]

Yet it would be a mistake to attach too much significance to
the presence or absence of an explicit reference to assigns in the
formulae of admittances, now or later. At Staines, for example,
such references remain rare far into the period in which there
is every other sign of a lively traffic in customary holdings.[5]
At Pyrford, where the traffic in holdings was certainly as lively
as it was at Launton, assigns may not have begun to be mentioned regularly until two or three decades after their intrusion

---

[1] Above, p. 269. [2] W.A.M. 26155 ff. [3] W.A.M. 15452 ff.
[4] Above, p. 269 n. [5] W.A.M. 16952–67.

into the words of conveyance in the latter place.[1] Although it can be assumed that inter-tenant sales of customary holdings were a familiar feature of village life in places where the tenant was given explicit liberty to assign his interest in the land to another, it does not follow that the monks were less favourably disposed to such transactions in manors where 'sibi et suis', 'sibi et heredibus suis' never, or rarely, became 'sibi et suis et assignatis suis', 'sibi et heredibus suis et assignatis suis'. The real importance of this difference in wording falls in a later period.

The Abbey's check on the enforcement of all these rules was the procedure of surrender and admittance used in all lawful transactions in customary land, whether within the family or outside it. This procedure made it easy for the abbot and convent to tax the transactions, and their taxation was often heavy, but they probably valued it mainly for other reasons than the financial. The procedure gave them, quite simply, an opportunity of seeing that the arrangements were as they should be—above all, that the purchaser was capable of meeting the obligations that he was about to undertake as a tenant of customary land on their fee. If tolerated in the case of customary land, procedure by the execution of charters, which miscreant vendors and purchasers sometimes attempted, could have reduced the monks' role, as happened eventually in the case of sales of free land, to that of receiving a fealty that could not be refused. Moreover, one who transferred his tenement by charter and not by surrender and admittance *ipso facto* called in question its villein status, since the power to transfer a tenement belonged to the owner of the freehold.[2]

A sale of customary land by charter had little chance of going undetected if accompanied by the ceremony of livery of seisin, for this act had to take place in public. But, down to the end of the thirteenth century, the status of some holdings—were they free or villein?—may have been in doubt, and, if so, it was possible in this period for the parties to a transaction to adopt the wrong procedure without an intention to deceive. This arose from the brevity of many of the

[1] W.A.M. 27484 ff., 1685.

[2] See Bracton, *De Legibus et Consuetudinibus Angliae*, ed. G. E. Woodbine, trans. and revised S. E. Thorne (Harvard University Press, Cambridge, Mass., 1968–), ii. 90.

manorial records of this time, and the similarity between some free and villein services; very often there was no authoritative record that could settle a genuine doubt. The more ample records of the fourteenth century helped to remedy this situation. Even so, some uncertainty persisted, as a case occurring at Pyrford in 1347 suggests. In that year, John le Shepherde of Woking surrendered a curtilage and cottage to the use of Thomas de Horsehull', who is described as a clerk, Matilda, wife of Thomas, and Walter, their son; and Thomas, Matilda, and Walter were duly admitted to hold of the abbot of Westminster. Thomas had first acquired the curtilage by charter and now he surrendered his charter, to be admitted, as was appropriate in the case of a customary tenant, by surrender and admittance. Yet the abbot evidently did not regard the previous transaction as wholly blameworthy, for, in return for Thomas's surrender of the charter, he remitted his entry fine.[1] This was probably a case where the legal status of the land had been truly in doubt.

To Leases of Customary Land

The interest of the monks of Westminster in the leases made by their customary tenants began on the messuage of the holding. Although the exact measurements of the messuage are rarely recorded in our sources, in the case of virgate and half-virgate holdings this was no doubt an ample plot of land, part curtilage or garden, part set aside for the principal dwelling and necessary outbuildings and for a number of minor dwellings and hovels. The last-mentioned, though needed from time to time by dependent relatives of the tenant of the holding, were an asset that could occasionally be leased outside the family, and the evidence suggests that these leases did not need a licence from the abbot or convent; only in this way can the rarity of references to such leases in the court rolls be explained.

The chief dwelling, however, had normally to be occupied by the tenant himself. A tenant who leased this part of the

---

[1] W.A.M. 27478 (court of 10 Nov. 1347). The curtilage had been taken by John le Shepherde from the waste. In 1475, the status of a toft and its appurtenances at Sutton-under-Brailes was in dispute between the abbot of Westminster and the tenant, John Lennard (Glos. Records Office, D 1099/M 1, court of 20 Sept. 1475).

messuage was probably on the point of quitting the manor altogether—the monks were in danger of losing one of their villeins. Then again, tenants of customary land were responsible for all necessary repairs to their holdings; but one who leased the main dwelling on his holding disburdened himself of the very item that was likely to need the most costly repairs. And finally, at Stevenage—and perhaps in other parts of the estate—the tenant of a customary holding escaped liability for a heriot at death or surrender if he was not resident on the capital messuage.[1] Where this was the rule, the abbot and convent had a strong financial incentive to restrict the sub-leasing of the main dwelling on the messuage, or even that of the messuage in its entirety. Perhaps only in the towns on the Abbey's fee—and Stevenage was itself partly urbanized—was it easy to obtain a licence for a lease of this kind.

Before the second half of the fourteenth century, few people may have felt this as a hardship. Then, as rather more tenants than previously began to have plural holdings, each furnished with a messuage, it became impossible to enforce the rule. In the fifteenth century, tenants of customary land had still to reside in the manor or within the liberty to which it belonged, but the monks were no longer able to insist that each messuage be occupied by the tenant who had taken it of them.[2]

In the case of the field-acres appurtenant to the messuage, the abbot and convent were for a long time hostile to piecemeal leases, as they were to sales of this kind. Until the fifteenth

---

[1] An inquest summoned at Stevenage in 1349, to decide whether a villein named John atte Dane, who held a free messuage and acre of land in addition to his villein tenement, which had no messuage, owed a heriot at his decease for the latter, returned the verdict: 'quod non est consuetudo manerii predicti quod aliquis nativus perques' liberi tenementi in quo mansit dare heriettum nisi manserit in messuagio quod tenet de domino in bondagio' (P.R.O., S.C. 2/178/48, court of 14 Feb. 1349). The principle may have been expressed in this manor in a form apparently limiting its application to mixed holdings, comprising both free and villein tenements, because the relevant cases were all in fact of this type—i.e. tenants at Stevenage were not yet permitted to hold two *bond* tenements concurrently. John atte Dane was a *nativus de sanguine*, and he had acquired his free tenement unknown to his lord, the abbot of Westminster. These facts made the court hesitate to allow his relatives the benefit of the above custom, and the matter was adjourned for decision by the abbot.

For a late-fifteenth-century entry at Islip, associating heriot with, in particular, the messuage of a customary holding, see W.A.M. 14943 (court of 16 Oct. 1475).

[2] Above, pp. 275–6.

century, therefore, the leases that they licensed were of odd-
ments of land—the additional acres and roods that the family
in possession of the main holding might well need in one
generation but not in another. In this way, the monks ensured
that their tenants continued in a position to answer for the
entire burden of rent and services—they did not intend that
their customary holdings should dissolve in a cloud of sub-
tenancies.

However small the acreage involved, all except short-term
leases of customary land required the monks' consent. The
court rolls, it is true, are not explicit about the exemption of
short-term arrangements from the need for a licence; that
these transactions were normally exempt can be inferred from
the fact that such short-term leases as were licensed at the
manorial court—and some for periods as short as a year are
mentioned—seem to have been exceptional in another respect:
they involved, not a mere acre or two, but a large proportion
of the holding, if not the whole. It is hard to discover where the
line was drawn, but quite possibly anything more durable than
an annual tenancy needed its licence.

Needless to say, every such licence was bought with a fine.
The fines, though not prohibitively large, were certainly
obligations that a poor man would gladly avoid. Six pence
from Nicholas le Clerk at Eye, in 1328, to sublet 1 acre of
arable and ¼ acre of meadow for five years;[1] 1s. the following
year from William by Southe, a serf of Eye, to sublet 2½ acres
of arable for five years[2]—these fines were not absolutely high
in relation to the rental value of land in a manor in the environs
of London, but, if paid by the lessor, they were the means of
deflecting part of his profit on the transaction into the abbot's
coffers during the first year of the term; if the lessor passed on
the burden to the lessee, the latter had an expensive first year.

On the other hand, fines did not rise proportionately in the
case of long terms, and deserving lessors and lessees were well
treated. The fine of 6d. taken from Juliana le Wyse when she
assumed the subtenancy of a cottage at Launton in 1314 was
equivalent to only half the annual rent which she was to pay
the lessor;[3] perhaps it was as an elderly spinster or a widow that

[1] W.A.M. 27000 (court of 5 July 1328).   [2] Ibid. (court of 2 Oct. 1329).
[3] W.A.M. 15424 (court of 14 Mar. 1314). The lessor's name was John le Wyse.

Juliana was considered a deserving case. A more unusual case was that of John atte Hulle, who was allowed to demise 5 acres of customary land, together with some free land, at Pyrford, for a term of ten years, on setting out for the Holy Land in 1361. When the abbot of Westminster heard what had been done, John had already departed, but, for a fine of 4*s*., his tenant, Cecily Hamond, secured recognition of her term, attested by other tenants of the manor, and exemption from suit of court while it lasted.[1] At Wheathampstead, in 1383, Margery Lyne was permitted, in her widowhood, to sublet 10 acres of customary land for a year at a rent of 6*d*. per acre, and she paid only 4*d*. for the fine.[2] But fines for licences to sublet customary land were now in general low.

Those who were most severely hindered by the restrictions on subleasing were, almost certainly, the small-scale capitalist farmers who appeared on the Abbey's customary land in the fifteenth century—men such as John Wykebourne, the tenant of *c*. 100 acres at Aldenham, and Nicholas atte Welle, who had more than 200 acres at Sutton-under-Brailes.[3] But, not much later than the appearance of such tenants, the court rolls begin to hint at a more liberal attitude on the part of the abbot and convent towards subleasing. For example, Abbot Colchester and his successor, Richard Harwden, occasionally gave tenants in the manor of Islip *carte blanche* to have subtenants at the beginning of their tenancies and without restriction as to the acreage to be leased or, so it appears, the term. In 1400, a tenant at Longdon was allowed to sublet two so-called 'day-works' of land for his life for a fine of only 6*d*., notwithstanding his prior offence in leasing what was probably a greater extent of customary land without a licence.[4] In 1420, John Cottesford

---

[1] W.A.M. 27481 (court of 28 June 1361). The lease stipulated that John atte Hulle should have the right of re-entry should he return within the term, and that his heir might enter, should his death within the term be properly attested. See also below, p. 320.

[2] W.A.M. 8941 (court of 14 Sept. 1383). In the following year, Margery was permitted to demise her messuage and all her land to Nicholas Carter for her life; the fine on this occasion was of 6*d*. She survived until 1395, when the holding was granted to Nicholas Carter, his wife, and his son, for their joint and several lives (W.A.M. 8944, court of 26 Mar. 1395).

[3] Above, p. 289.

[4] W.A.M. 21132 (court of 6 Oct. 1400). A 'day-work' of land was probably an acre.

was allowed to demise his villein holding at Launton for three years, with, so it seems, no inquiry being made as to the identity of the lessee; Cottesford was to find a man of 'good condition'.[1]

Yet few licences to sublet the major part of a holding or any part of it for a long term are recorded in the court rolls which survive from the second half of the fifteenth century. This may signify only a decline in punctilio on the part of the officials responsible for these records—they were perhaps less careful than formerly to enter such items; or perhaps it was now considered more important to enter the tenant's capacity to sublet in his copy than in the court roll itself. More probably, there were, even now, relatively few tenants anxious to make such arrangements; it was not in this way that the subsistence farmers who made up the great majority of the Abbey's tenants, normally exploited their holdings.[2]

To Transactions in Free Land

Until the abbacy of Richard de Ware, the monks of Westminster continued to limit the freedom of their tenants in fee to alienate, and their insistence that alienations required their formal licence long survived the retreat on the issue of principle that becomes noticeable in the time of this abbot.[3] The monks had two reasons for interest in such transactions. On the one hand were all those considerations relating to the bond between lord and tenant and to the incidents of feudal tenure that made the alienability of lands held in fee a burning issue in feudal society in the thirteenth century; on the other, the Abbey's need to increase its estate and so its rental income from land—an end that might be conveniently achieved by absorbing into the demesne of the estate a proportion of the lands too generously subinfeudated in earlier periods. Often, in fact, the monks wished themselves to buy the land that their tenants in fee put on the market. In the thirteenth century,

---

[1] W.A.M. 15481 (court of 10 Jul. 1420). Cottesford is described as a tailor; the holding in question was presumably the messuage and half-virgate of land to which he and his wife were admitted in 1419 (W.A.M. 15480, court of 4 Dec. 1419). This is probably the John Cottesford who became farmer of the demesne at Launton in 1423; see W.A.M. 15408, and above, p. 289 and n.

[2] See also below, p. 321.　　　　　　　　　　　　　　[3] Above, pp. 118–19.

they can be found claiming the first refusal of land on their fee, should the feoffee ever wish to alienate it;[1] even when the monks' scrutiny of alienations became formalized, as it did towards the end of the century, the knowledge of the parties that this stage in the transactions existed at all still gave the monks a certain advantage if they coveted the land for themselves. Overtly, however, they now imposed only two conditions before licensing an alienation on their fee and, after 1290, receiving the fealty of the purchaser of the land, in accordance with the principle of *Quia Emptores*: the new tenant might not be a religious body; nor might he be one of their own villeins, for a villein who possessed himself of a freehold interest in land was well on the way to throwing off the condition of villeinage altogether; he must surrender his charter and accept the status of a tenant at will on the purchased land, or give up the land itself.

If they so wished, the monks were in a position to enforce the latter rule strictly, for the identity of the purchaser in a sale of land was always made public in the act of livery of seisin; they needed only the co-operation of their local officials to discover which of their villeins had received such livery. The fact that free and unfree were, to such a large extent, separate tenurial groups on the Abbey's estates in the thirteenth and fourteenth centuries suggests that the monks were then usually of this mind. But exceptions are recorded at this time. At Birdbrook, in 1294, a villein who had earlier acquired a messuage and $1\frac{1}{2}$ acres of free land surrendered her charter but was allowed to sell or assign the holding;[2] in 1276, Thomas atte Hulle, a villein of Wheathampstead, was explicitly allowed to keep the free land which his brother, Richard, also presumably a villein, had held before him.[3] At Stevenage, it was stated as the custom of the manor in 1349 that a villein who acquired a free tenement and lived on it thereby escaped liability for heriot in respect of his customary holding.[4] Later

---

[1] Above, p. 118 and n.

[2] W.A.M. 25568 (court of 20 July 1294). The monks stipulated that the new feoffees should hold of them by substitution. The delinquent in this case, Elena daughter of Ralph *ad pontem*, is described as a *nativa*, and the word *nativus* is applied severally to the villeins mentioned in the cases cited in the remainder of this paragraph.

[3] W.A.M. 8937 (court of 25 June 1276).   [4] Above, p. 308 n.

in the century, however, practice seems to have become stricter. So, for example, in 1379, William Sabyn, a villein of Pyrford, was deprived of his status as a free tenant of one-third of an acre of free land, which he had acquired from another tenant, and required to hold the land on customary terms;[1] in 1384, a selion of land acquired by Henry Ody, a villein, was taken in hand at Castlemorton;[2] and in 1389, an acre acquired in fee by Geoffrey Hulok, a villein, was taken in hand at Wheathampstead.[3]

The insistence of the monks of Westminster that tenants who possessed a fee simple interest in their lands nevertheless required their licence before alienating made the transition to the world of *Quia Emptores* easy, ensuring as it did that a procedure for the scrutiny of charters was already in existence in 1290. As substitution replaced subinfeudation in this period, the abbot and convent reaped the benefit of innumerable reliefs that had previously eluded them; every tenant holding of the Abbey in fee owed relief if he came into his lands by inheritance. The tenant who entered by purchase might or might not be required to pay a small fine. At Pershore in 1402, the exaction of such a payment is described as the custom of the fee of Westminster Abbey, as though it was not paralleled on the fees of other lords holding lands in Pershore.[4] Whether or not he owed a fine, the purchaser of a free tenement on the Abbey's estate now required the monks' licence before entering their fee; this licence had replaced that required in the thirteenth century by the vendor of the property. The rule was

[1] W.A.M. 1685 (court of Hil. Term, 1379). In 1423, a plot called *Whapshoteshawe* was taken into the abbot's hands at Pyrford because it had been acquired by William Smyth', who is described as a *nativus de sanguine* (ibid., court of St. John the Baptist term, 1423).

[2] W.A.M. 21124 (court of 21 Apr. 1384).

[3] W.A.M. 8943 (court of 10 Sept. 1389); for Hulok's status, see also ibid. (court of 2 Sept. 1388). In Dec. 1389, the bailiff of the manor answered for 5 bushels of wheat as the issue of the land; this grain was presumably the harvest of the previous autumn (ibid., court of 2 Dec. 1389).

[4] W.A.M. 21988 (court of 17 Jan. 1402). For some examples of such fines at Castlemorton in 1400–1, see W.A.M. 21131–2. Some entries in the late-fourteenth-century court rolls of this manor imply that the fines were penalties for entering the Abbey's fee without the monks' licence. In the majority of cases, the payments are entered without a gloss of this kind; it is probable, however, that a purchaser of property who neglected this due formality paid, in the end, a larger fine than he would otherwise have been asked for. See W.A.M. 21124, and, more generally, Sutherland, *Assize of Novel Disseisin*, p. 96.

important to the monks, providing as it did a safeguard against the intrusion of other religious into their fee.

After the enactment of *Quia Emptores* and the end of sub-infeudation in the case of fee simple, a sale relating to a part but not the whole of a free tenement necessitated the apportionment between vendor and purchaser of the rent owed to the monks of Westminster as chief lords. This task was the responsibility of the parties to the transaction. Thus, to take a late example, at Wheathampstead and Harpenden in 1409, the eight persons among whom the free holding known as 'Longes' was now divided were ordered to agree before the next meeting of the court on the proportions in which the rent owing from that holding to the monks of Westminster was to be shared by them.[1] The result of such an apportionment, though scrutinized at a meeting of the court of the manor in question, was apparently not, as a rule, recorded in the court roll; until such time as the shares could be incorporated in a new rental, they were presumably entered on separate schedules or loose membranes.

(iii) *Economic Factors*

Demand

From the beginning of the thirteenth century, the keenest demand for land on the fee of Westminster Abbey was generated by the monks of Westminster themselves. It was largely by repurchasing the freehold of the property too readily alienated in the eleventh and twelfth centuries that the monks of this later period achieved the augmentation of their estate that was made necessary by an ever-rising cost of living.[2] Naturally, many of their purchases were on a scale that would take us, were we to pursue them, outside the range of the village land market that is the main topic of the present chapter. Some, however, belong in this humble context. At the end of the twelfth century, or very early in the thirteenth, the monks purchased the freehold of a virgate of land in Morden, where the virgate was of 20 acres,[3] and Richard de Berking's acquisitions

---

[1] W.A.M. 8945 (court of 13 Mar. 1409).
[2] Above, pp. 165 ff.
[3] W.D., 170ᵛ. The monks paid the grantor £5. 13s. 4d. and undertook to pay him a rent of 4s. 2d. per annum; he was to pay 4s. per annum to his chief lord.

included free tenements comprising, respectively, a messuage and 5 acres at Aldenham, and 2 acres at Parham.[1]

Other members of the landowning class seem rarely to have fished these waters; or, if they did so, it was with small rewards, for their holdings, large or small, on the fee of Westminster Abbey, did not significantly increase after the beginning of the thirteenth century; indeed, they diminished. Yet in many of the vills where the Abbey had its manors, other lords had manors too. The monks' practice of buying up the freeholds of which they were chief lords, which Berking's successors continued vigorously for some 150 years, must have been well known to all their neighbours and perhaps discouraged bids from members of this class. Religious, moreover, were specifically discouraged from attempts to buy land anywhere on the Abbey's fee; even before the enactment of the Statute of Mortmain in 1279, the monks of Westminster are found invoking the help of their royal patron to keep such unwelcome intruders out.[2]

The situation of the Abbey's manors, and the semi-urban characteristics that not a few of them developed in the early Middle Ages, ensured the existence of a middle-class demand for land on this estate. At Staines, for example, the abbot was the lord, not only of a demesne and dependent peasantry, but also, as early as 1086, of a town peopled by a relatively large community of burgesses.[3] His manor of Eye, though, even in the fourteenth century, still rich in meadowland and abundantly endowed with rough grazing, was less than an hour's walk from the City of London, and a mere stone's throw from the Palace of Westminster, the administrative heart of the kingdom. Feering, on the convent's estate, was only a few miles distant from the town of Colchester.

In all these places, and in others like them, the appetite of townsmen nearby for arable land, pasture, and meadow is well attested. At Battersea and Wandsworth, some of the customary holdings were probably occupied by local townsmen at the beginning of the fourteenth century, but as a rule such people were still shy of these tenancies, and the Abbey, for its own

[1] Ibid., 188–188ᵛ, 573.
[2] *Close Rolls, 1234–7*, p. 67; and see above, p. 166.
[3] See Table VII, p. 124 above.

part, reluctant to see shopkeepers and artisans in possession of holdings that were intended for the support of its villeins and their households.[1] In general, and understandably, the middle-class demand was for free land. Very often, moreover, it was a small-scale demand, representing the overflow of capital resources that were only a little too large to be wholly contained in a strictly urban range of investments. Those among whom it originated were probably shopkeepers and craftsmen, who did not trust wholly to their trade or their craft for a livelihood. John *mercator* and Roger *mercator*, who are mentioned among the free tenants of Feering towards the end of the thirteenth century, held only a very little land there; and, despite their high-sounding name, it is likely that they were quite ordinary tradesmen, or of a family that had once belonged to this class.[2] True merchant capitalists rarely, it seems, bought land in the Abbey's manors. Predictably, however, the possessions in the environs of London are an exception to this rule. Some substantial citizens of London were buying land of the Abbey's free tenants here in the fourteenth century; and in or about 1392, John Sandhill, a London chandler, acquired a carucate of free land in the manor of Wheathampstead and Harpenden.[3]

In common with shopkeepers and artisans, most peasants wanted to buy or lease land in small amounts or not at all. Here, if anywhere, the difference between vague desire and effective demand needs emphasis. In a general sense, nearly all the inhabitants of the medieval countryside wanted to possess land, and many, no doubt, dreamt of possessing a considerable extent of it; but, for the greater part of the Middle Ages, the omnipresent poverty of rural society reduced effective market demand to a small thing relating to acres and roods, even to odd bits and pieces of land. As a rule, the destination of substantial holdings in the manors of Westminster Abbey was

---

[1] Above, pp. 206 ff.

[2] C.U.L. MS. Kk 5. 29, fos. 101–101ᵛ. John *mercator* held two cottages, 1½ acres of arable, and ½ acre of meadow. Roger *mercator* held, in Pattiswick, a messuage and 4 acres of free land, and, in Feering, a messuage and 2½ acres of land formerly belonging to a customary holding; but he held this land freely. For similar cases of free holdings that had been carved out of customary land, at Pyrford, see above, pp. 301–2.

[3] W.A.M. 8943 (court of 11 June 1392); and see above, pp. 189–90.

decided outside the nexus of market transactions—by inheritance, by marriage, or by escheat into the hands of the abbot
and convent and the subsequent grant of the lands in question
to a new tenant.[1] Transactions *inter vivos* were the net that
saved the casualties of this system, and especially those who
could expect no share in the family inheritance, from too hard
a fall; they were, in the second place, an outlet for the aspirations of the acquisitive peasantry, whose energies and resources
transcended the limits of a standard holding; and, finally, they
were a means of improving upon an awkward distribution of
strips in the common fields. Whatever the circumstances of the
transaction, more often than not, the demand was on a small
scale; this followed inescapably from society's lack of capital
resources. Essentially, in the countryside, the demand was for
acres and roods that could be bought and sold or leased without
detriment to the virgated structure of holdings that, down to
the fourteenth century, family and feudal sentiment both
cherished in many places; and, since it cost less in capital
outlay to take land on lease than to buy it, the demand was, on
the whole, for a demise of land.

Supply

The circumstances of the tenants who were willing to demise
their land or any part of it, or who were driven by force of
circumstance to do so, are a matter of guess-work throughout
the Middle Ages on this estate; it is, for example, only a guess
that in the fifteenth century the tenants of large customary
holdings chose to exploit some of their land in this way. The
licences noted in court rolls do not help us at this juncture, for
they relate, not to typical arrangements, but to the exceptional
—to the long lease and the large-scale lease that can provide
no basis for generalization about the situation as a whole. It is
likely—but this again is incapable of proof—that the first object
of many lessors was, not to dispose for the time being of some
of their land, but to borrow money on the security that the
land would provide if so demised; the lease was the concomitant
of the borrowing and lending of money.[2]

---

[1] For the truth of this statement on two manors of the estate, see below,
pp. 322 ff.

[2] See the important conclusions, for an earlier period, of Hyams, in *Economic
History Rev.*, 2nd ser., 23 (1970), 28–31.

Perversely, since these transactions were almost certainly much less common than leases, the sources are more informative about the supply of land for inter-tenant sales and purchases. It can safely be assumed that in the early Middle Ages most of the land that changed hands in this way *inter vivos* was free land or newly assarted land (itself often free). Here a virgated structure of holdings was apt to be not much in evidence; the difficulties of detaching acres from their parent holdings were minimized. By contrast, much of the older customary land was still held in virgates and half-virgates, even around the year 1300.[1] It follows from this dependence on the availability of free land and assarts that the late thirteenth century was a crucial period in the history of the village land market, for by then the pace of assarting was probably slow on all parts of the estate. If the intending purchaser of this period could not lay his hands on free land long since colonized, he probably went unsatisfied. Not surprisingly, therefore, it is at this time that evidence of an extreme degree of fragmentation in the case of free holdings begins to accumulate. A free holding comprising $32\frac{1}{2}$ acres of arable land at Ashford, for example, was now divided among twenty-six tenants.[2] For the same reason, this was also a time of particular frustration for would-be purchasers of land who were of villein status. If newly colonized land was now hard to come by, so, too, in their case, was free land, for a villein could not, or at least should not, acquire a free tenement.

To the end of the Middle Ages, the abbot and convent of Westminster did their best to ensure that, if customary land changed hands *inter vivos*, the transaction embraced the entire holding; the difficulties which they now experienced in finding tenants did not shake their hostility to permanent fragmentation over the greater part of the estate.[3] To the end, therefore, it was still normally the case that customary land must be bought and sold in what were, according to the scale of measurement appropriate to a self-sufficient economy, relatively large units, or not at all.

In another respect, the conditions of supply in the village land market were significantly different in the late Middle Ages from what they had been earlier. The family sense of

[1] Above, pp. 206–7.   [2] W.A.M. 26703.   [3] Above, pp. 300–1.

inseparable association with a particular holding, which had been so marked a feature of rural society in the early Middle Ages, weakened; indeed, in some places it more or less disappeared. That sense belonged to a period when holdings commonly remained in the hands of the same family over several generations; but this seems to have happened much less frequently after *c.* 1350 than previously. The change reflects the unwonted abundance of land in this period, and the declining importance of inheritance as the mode of acquiring it. Many heirs now probably found that there was no need to wait long years for the succession to the family holding; other land became available in the meantime and proved attractive—the inheritance they might or might not take up when the time came.

A bizarre result of this development, as well attested on the Abbey's manors as it is elsewhere, was the fifteenth-century habit of naming holdings after families who had been in possession of them in a now remote past; currently, family connections were not long-lasting enough to affect nomenclature. As late as the 1430s, Islip, the abbot's manor in Oxfordshire, possessed a half-virgate of customary land known as 'Geytis', despite the fact that the last member of the Geyt family, which gave its name to this holding, died in the Black Death of 1348–9, or just after that event.[1] Was the loosening of the family hold on customary land associated with a quickening of the rate of transactions *inter vivos*? Was the destiny of a holding now more often settled by agreement among tenants and would-be tenants and less frequently by the direct resort of the interested parties to the monks of Westminster, or on the initiative of the latter? These are questions that it is hoped to illumine in the last section of this chapter.

(iv) *The Transactions*

Despite the paucity of explicit references to inter-tenant leases, these arrangements were, almost certainly, the commonest form

---

[1] W.A.M. 14798, 15207. For the transmission of this holding after the mid-fourteenth century, see W.A.M. 14799, 14878 (court of 10 Mar. 1401), 14904 (court of 1 Apr. 1426), 14909 (court of 30 Nov. 1430); *Oxfordshire Record Soc.* 40 (1959), 86. For the declining importance of inheritance in the transmission of peasant holdings after *c.* 1350, see R. Faith, 'Peasant families and inheritance customs in medieval England', *Agricultural History Rev.* 14(1966), 86 ff.

of the transaction *inter vivos* in every part of the Abbey's estate throughout the Middle Ages. At one time or another, all the main factors that we have considered—the interest of the family and that of the abbot and convent, and the ineradicable poverty of rural society—told against sales and in favour of leases. It seems to have been assumed by the monks in the thirteenth century that some of the tenants of their customary land had under-tenants, and such arrangements may well have existed at a much earlier date than this.[1]

Indentures were probably the preferred form of lease when the tenement in question was a free one. It is likely, for example, that the free tenants at Pershore, who demised their messuages for life-terms, as we know some of them did in the fourteenth century,[2] made use of indentures. For customary land, the oral *conventio*, recited in the presence of witnesses, seems to have been considered appropriate. John atte Hulle's lease to Cecily Hamond at Pyrford in 1361 was evidently made in this way.[3] The unusual circumstances made it desirable to record the conditions of this lease in the court rolls. This, however, happened after John's departure for Syria; he had made the demise in the presence of other tenants of the manor, and it was their witness to it that was recorded in the rolls.

It follows from the fact that leases of customary land were made orally that we know next to nothing about their terms. Champarty leases are mentioned at Launton in 1301–2,[4] at Pinvin in 1343,[5] and at Longdon in 1400,[6] and this form of arrangement was probably very common. But money rents are also mentioned, and occasionally it becomes clear that the lessor was asking of his lessee a rent that was proportionately higher than that which he himself owed to the monks of Westminster for his land. Presumably, the rent paid by Margery

---

[1] Above, p. 214.

[2] W.A.M. 21964 (court of 21 Apr. 1372), 21971 (court of 10 June 1376), 21978 (court of 30 May 1381). The demises recorded were for life, and this fact explains why they were of interest to the abbot of Westminster: as tenants for life, the lessees were possessed of a freehold interest in their land and therefore owed him a fine for entering his fee.

[3] Above, p. 310.

[4] W.A.M. 15421 (court of 15 June 1301); cf. W.A.M. 15422 (court of 24 Mar. 1302).

[5] W.A.M. 21948 (court of 2 Oct. 1343).

[6] W.A.M. 21132 (court of 6 Oct. 1400).

Lyne's tenant at Wheathampstead left her something for herself after the discharge of her own obligations to the monks of Westminster each year, for it is likely that her entire holding in the fields was comprised in the ten acres which she had demised to him.[1]

Down to the fifteenth century, as we have seen, the monks of Westminster rarely allowed tenants of customary land to make leases for other than very short terms, and there is no reason to suppose that their prohibition of longer terms was often flouted. A tenant who demised his land for an illicit term *ipso facto* forfeited all hope of legal redress should the conditions of the lease be broken—he would never be able to air the matter in public at all. Moreover, land could not be worked year after year by someone other than the tenant holding of the abbot and convent of Westminster without the circumstance becoming a matter of common knowledge; not even a demise within the family, by brother to brother or parent to child, could be concealed for long.

Although, in the fifteenth century, the abbot and convent were probably much readier to license demises for a relatively long term than had been the case earlier, it does not follow that such terms then became common. On the contrary, most of their tenants may well have continued to prefer the old arrangements when demising land, for implied in a readiness to admit a subtenant for a long term was an assurance about the future that few or no lessors can have possessed in a period such as this, when the term of life itself was so unpredictable. Short terms were of a piece with the precarious character of peasant existence as a whole and probably remained the typical arrangement until the end of the Middle Ages and beyond.[2] Occasionally, however, the situation of a lessor made a demise for the remainder of his own lifetime—a demise, that is, *pur auter vie*—appropriate. Margery Lyne's demise at Wheathampstead in 1384 was of this kind. Such arrangements need not endure for a long time, but they could do so; Margery Lyne lived for eleven years after making this demise.[3]

---

[1] Above, p. 310.

[2] In the case of leases associated with loan agreements, for which see above, p. 317, the propriety of short terms presumably affected the scale on which money was loaned and borrowed.

[3] Above, p. 310 n.

Sales of customary land are not identified as such in manorial court rolls. Fortunately, however, for the historian, they included one necessary formality which helps in their identification. This was the vendor's surrender of the holding in question into the hands of the abbot and convent of Westminster— a surrender made on the understanding that the abbot and convent would immediately admit the purchaser as tenant. In some cases the vendor is said explicitly to make his surrender to the use (*ad opus*) of or in favour (*in favorem*) of the purchaser, but it cannot be assumed that either of these forms will be used—sometimes only the bare notice of a surrender betrays the fact that a sale has taken place. Transfers of property within the family were also made in this way; thus a parent who wished to make over his holding to his son had first to surrender it into the monks' hands before the latter could be admitted; one who wished to create a jointure for his wife or his heir, as many tenants did on this estate in the fifteenth century,[1] had to surrender the holding as a preliminary to his readmittance as tenant jointly with the other person. Procedurally, therefore, sales are merely one species of a genus, the transfer of land *inter vivos*. When we have isolated the latter from other changes of tenancy recorded in the rolls, such, for example, as the admittance of an heir to the holding of a deceased parent, we have still to decide which among the transfers *inter vivos* were family transactions and which were sales.[2]

How frequent was either of these forms of the transfer *inter vivos* on the estates of Westminster Abbey? We shall never know the answer to this question, even in respect of the later Middle Ages, when the Abbey's court rolls probably included the information that is needed to answer it, for relatively few of these records have survived. The following remarks are based on two of the best series among the rolls that do survive—those for, respectively, the manor of Islip and the manor of Launton.

Both these manors were in Oxfordshire, and, although the vill of Islip itself was only six or seven miles distant from the

---

[1] Above, pp. 280 ff.

[2] It will be plain that matters have been simplified in this paragraph. Not all surrenders set in train a transaction *inter vivos* of either kind described here; but on this point, see Table XI, note (p. 325 below).

town of Oxford, both manors comprised essentially rural settlements, where the strength of the demand for land depended on the local inhabitants; outside investment was of negligible importance, as, indeed, the insistence of the monks of Westminster on the duty of the tenants of customary land to reside within their jurisdiction helped to ensure.[1] In each case, but particularly at Launton and at Murcot and Fencot, the two vills which, with that of Islip itself, made up the manor of Islip, the way of life of the inhabitants was coloured by the proximity of Otmoor, then a daunting expanse of waste land, which nevertheless afforded some grazing for beasts, beside fowl and rabbits for those who could trap them. Arable cultivation can never have been easy on the heavy soils of this region, and we know that this part of Oxfordshire was touched by the late-medieval shift from corn to grass.[2] Both at Islip and its dependent vills and at Launton, a predominantly virgated structure of holdings survived into the fourteenth century and beyond.[3]

There were also important differences between the two manors. Though Islip was one of the Confessor's gifts to the monastery, the monks of Westminster did not enter into possession of it until John's reign;[4] subsequently, this manor was assigned to the abbot's portion. Launton, which the prior and convent took at the division of goods, was in the unbroken possession of the Abbey from the late eleventh century. At Islip, the virgate was of *c.* 32 acres and the rule of inheritance primogeniture. Here the abbot was obliged to fill not a few of his holdings in the late fourteenth century by means of contractual tenancies, and for part of the fifteenth century life-tenancies in villeinage were in vogue.[5] At Launton, the position of villeinage as the prevailing mode of tenure was not shaken in the fourteenth century, and heritable tenancies, conveyed in the formula 'sibi et suis' or 'sibi et heredibus suis'

---

[1] Above, pp. 275–6.
[2] *V.C.H. Oxon.* vi. 27–8, 337. Cf. K. J. Allison, M. W. Beresford, and J. G. Hurst, *The Deserted Villages of Oxfordshire* (Leicester, 1965), p. 22, where the immunity of Islip from the decay of settlement in the Middle Ages and later is noted. The remark is true only in respect of the total desertion of vills; changes in land-use and a retreat of arable almost certainly occurred here in the late Middle Ages.
[3] *V.C.H. Oxon.* vi. 214, 237–8.   [4] Below, p. 356.
[5] For late-medieval tenurial conditions at Islip and Launton, see above, pp. 247 ff., 276 ff.

TABLE XI. *The Number of Admittances to Customary Land and of Transfers inter vivos recorded in the Manors of Islip and Launton in the Later Middle Ages*

Date	ISLIP			LAUNTON		
	Admittances	Transfers *inter vivos*		Admittances	Transfers *inter vivos*	
		in the family	outside the family		in the family	outside the family
1280–99				32	16	1
1300–19				31	11	2
1320–39				49	12	5
1340–59				11	0	0
1360–79				11	0	4
1380–99	45	6	6	53	10	15
1400–19	73	8	8	57	8	7
1420–39	82	1	13	68	15	19
1440–59	62	7	12	18	5	5
1460–79	48	2	9	35	11	9
1480–99	37	2	5			
1500–19	11	0	0			
1520–39	26	2	4			
Total	384	28	57	365	88	67
Percentage	100	*c.* 7	*c.* 15	100	*c.* 24	*c.* 18

remained the norm. The virgate here was of *c.* 20 acres, and the customary rule of inheritance Borough English.

Some of these points are germane to a consideration of land transactions and help to explain why, as Table XI shows, the pattern of these may have been somewhat different in the two manors. In this table, the number of recorded transactions which were made *inter vivos* at Islip and Launton is compared with the total number of recorded admittances to customary land; and transactions *inter vivos* are subdivided into those, on

---

Sources For Islip: W.A.M. 14865 ff., 15203; P.R.O., S.C. 2/197/48–9. For Launton: W.A.M. 15420 ff.

Note to Table XI

All transfers *inter vivos* were effected by means of a surrender of the holding in question on the part of the existing tenant; a person designated by the latter was thereupon admitted by the abbot and convent of Westminster. But not all surrenders recorded in the court rolls have this significance: some mark the end of a tenancy but have no bearing on the monks' subsequent admittance of a new tenant. Surrenders of this kind are easily identified when, as often happened in the late Middle Ages, they were followed by a vacancy of short or long duration. If, however, a new tenant was at once admitted, it may be impossible to distinguish the transaction from a transfer *inter vivos*. For this reason, the figures given in the Table under this head, but particularly those relating to transfers *inter vivos* outside the family, are to be understood as maxima; they probably take into account some surrenders which do not have that significance.

The admittance of a widow to her spouse's holding for a year and a day has been counted among the total number of admittances, but not her subsequent admittance as tenant for life, if she chose this option at the end of the year; there may in any case be no reference in the court roll to this second admittance. The admittance of her second husband to a tenancy of her holding, in the case of her remarriage, has been counted as a transfer *inter vivos* within the family. So, too, have two other types of admittance: that of a husband to the holding of an heiress who became his wife, and that of a wife to a joint tenancy with her husband, or of wife and son to such a tenancy.

It must be emphasized that the figures in the table relate to *recorded* admittances and transfers *inter vivos* in the period indicated. Fluctuations from one twenty-year period to another have no intrinsic significance, since the number of court rolls surviving from each such period is not constant. In the case of Islip, however, the few court rolls extant for the period down to 1380 have been excluded from consideration; these relate to the years 1275, 1325, and 1376–9. It perhaps goes without saying that, in the case of both manors, only those admittances are deemed to be 'recorded' that are still legible in the rolls.

For the pioneer analysis of court-roll evidence along the lines attempted, with some degree of simplification, above, see A. Jones, 'Land and people at Leighton Buzzard in the later fifteenth century', *Economic History Review*, 2nd ser., 25 (1972), 18 ff.; and for widows' rights and other family aspects of customary landholding in these manors, see above, pp. 296 ff.

the one hand, which kept the land in question in the same family group, and, on the other, those which gave possession to a new family. It has been suggested above that the latter, but not the former, are to be deemed 'sales'.[1] The distinction is, of course, too clear cut to be entirely safe in the present instance, for members of the same family sometimes entered into mercenary transactions in respect of their land—some transfers of land within the family were in fact sales. Moreover, it was very possible for the parties to a transaction to be related without the betrayal of this relationship in the court rolls; we must allow for a wide margin of error on this score. But, as a very rough indication of the order of magnitude of the two kinds of transactions *inter vivos*, the figures will probably serve. The errors, which probably arise mainly from a failure to identify parties to a transaction as relatives, will, if that is so, tend to inflate the number of apparent sales.

At Islip, inter-tenant sales of land were infrequent in the fifteenth century and perhaps remained so after 1500—the number of court rolls surviving from the latter period is too small for the truth to be discovered from them. It is likely that a mere 15 per cent of all the admittances recorded in this manor between 1380 and 1539 were made in this context. At Launton, the comparable figure was very little higher—*c.* 18 per cent for a period beginning and ending earlier, in, respectively, 1280 and 1479. But in the second of these two centuries, between 1380 and 1479, the village land market was, it seems, more active at Launton than at Islip: in this period, when, again, *c.* 15 per cent of all recorded admittances at Islip were associated with sales of land,[2] the comparable figure at Launton is *c.* 24 per cent.[3]

Statistically, this difference, thrown up as it is by relatively small samples of imperfect data, is without significance. Yet these figures may in fact reflect some small difference in the activity of the land market in Launton, compared to Islip. Greater use was made at Islip in this period of life-tenancies on customary land. A life-tenant had much less to sell than a tenant enjoying a fully heritable interest in his land, as most of the customary tenants of Launton continued to do at this time. He had nothing at all to devise, and this fact suggests that the

---

'family' type of transfer *inter vivos* may indeed have been less common at Islip than at Launton, as Table XI implies; *c.* 8 per cent of the admittances recorded at Islip between 1380 and 1479 related to this type of transaction; the comparable figure at Launton for this period is *c.* 21 per cent.[1] Some of the transfers of this kind recorded at Launton were probably of a testamentary kind, representing a distribution of property made at the point of death or with this eventuality in mind.

Even if the percentages in Table XI faithfully reflect real differences between Islip and Launton, they point, in each place, to an economy where the sale of a holding of customary land was unusual—the last resort, it may be, of the elderly and infirm or the widowed, unable to persevere longer, and a necessary course of action for the tenant who was about to move away from the manor altogether, but hardly a regular occurrence. What, then, was the usual mechanism for transferring holdings when the appropriate time came, in these manors?

Inheritance and marriage were important, though less important in the fifteenth century as a means of acquiring land than in the fourteenth. Where an existing family association with the holding was not prolonged in one or other of these ways, other aspirants to the tenancy, if any there were, applied directly to the monks of Westminster or to their officials. In both manors, but particularly at Islip, it was difficult to fill holdings in the fifteenth century, and many were untenanted at one time or another. At Launton, some tenants were conscripts, even in the early fourteenth century. In 1325, for example, one John Baldwin was compelled to take up the half-virgate holding of the late Agnes Pipat here, her son being incapable of doing so.[2]

It cannot be assumed that the village land market was as inactive in all parts of the Abbey's estate as it was at Islip and Launton. But even in some places that were economically much more advanced than north Oxfordshire, its part in the transmission of holdings was, it seems, relatively small. At

[1] Islip, 24: 310; Launton, 49: 231.

[2] W.A.M. 15428 (court of 12 Feb. 1325). Consideration of the amount of John's entry fine was deferred, since he was unwillingly a tenant, but later the sum was fixed at 2*s*. (ibid., court of 8 July 1325). For the conscription of men to marry landholding widows in this manor, see above, p. 298.

Wheathampstead and Harpenden, for example, not more than *c*. 30 per cent of the transfers of customary holdings recorded between 1380 and 1419, four decades for which the evidence is relatively abundant, are to be categorized as sales, and the exact figure may in fact be smaller.[1] Yet this manor, situated as it was well within the range of influence of the metropolitan market, was almost certainly more prosperous, more attractive to would-be tenants in the late Middle Ages than Islip or Launton. More than half the number of customary holdings bought and sold at Wheathampstead and Harpenden between 1380 and 1419 comprised 5 acres or less in the fields; some were mere cottages and gardens, or building plots. It was no doubt the availability of holdings of this kind that helped to stimulate a rather more active market than is found either at Islip or at Launton. What is known of land transactions *inter vivos* on free land in the Abbey's manors supports the conclusion that even in the late Middle Ages the effective demand was still, as a rule, for something small. Thus at Castlemorton, Chaceley, and Longdon, in Worcestershire, most of the free tenements that were bought and sold in this period comprised only a few acres of land, if as much.[2]

Nothing need surprise us in these case histories, nor is it unlikely that they are in fact typical of the Abbey's estate as a whole, or at least of the rural part of the estate. To the end of the Middle Ages, most of the Abbey's tenants were subsistence farmers who had nothing to sell except the holding that was their livelihood in the literal sense of the word, the direct source of their bread and ale, of their bacon, cheese, and pottage; and the monks seem rarely to have made any concessions to the parties to a transaction *inter vivos*—heriot and entry fine were as much owing in these circumstances as in any

---

[1] Number of recorded admittances, 1380–1419: 132, of which 5 (= *c*. 4 per cent) related to transactions *inter vivos* within the family, and perhaps 39 (= *c*. 30 per cent) to transactions *inter vivos* taking land outside the family. See W.A.M. 8941–6. The figures take no account of twenty-three admittances which probably or certainly related to demesne land. Thirty-nine is the maximum figure for transactions *inter vivos* taking land outside the family; it includes several admittances made after surrenders which are not described explicitly as surrenders *inter vivos* and may not have been such. At Islip, as Table XI shows, *c*. 12 per cent (14: 118) of recorded admittances may have related to sales in the period 1380–1419; at Launton, *c*. 20 per cent (22: 110).

[2] W.A.M. 21116 ff.

other. Moreover, in the small village societies of this period, everyone knew when this or that holding was likely to fall vacant and could make a direct approach to the monks and their officials at the appropriate time. In a sense, it is remarkable that inter-tenant sales of land attained even the proportions that we have been able to claim for them at Islip and Launton and at Wheathampstead and Harpenden.

Perhaps it is as much the circumstances of the vendors as the appetite for land of the purchasers that accounts for the volume of the transactions. It follows from the mode of life of country-dwellers, which was only to a limited extent integrated in a system of exchanges, that many needing to disburden themselves of their holdings were nevertheless unwilling to do so unless assured of at least a small share of the issues for the future. How these matters were arranged within the family is not in doubt: many heirs received the family holding encumbered with the obligation of paying a pension to an aged or ailing parent, whose surrender of the lands had been conditional on this very undertaking.[1] But what was to be done if the holding had to pass outside the family of the present tenant on surrender? A similar arrangement was needed, this time between unrelated parties. It was hardly to be expected that the monks of Westminster would negotiate it; the situation called for preliminary treaty before the matter reached their ears. Hence the sale of land that was made in exchange, not for cash—at least, not only for cash—but on terms that included a promise of housing and food for the vendor. When, for example, Alice Fulkes surrendered her messuage and half-virgate of land in Murcot in 1416 to the use of William, son of John Palmer, it was part of the agreement that William would allow Alice 4 bushels of wheat and a quarter of barley each year;[2] eight years later, John Wylcockes promised to allow William Smyth, whose cottage holding he then took over, easement in a room in the cottage;[3] and the following year, William Bryd's messuage and half-virgate passed into the hands of John Adam and Margaret, his wife, encumbered with

---

[1] For these arrangements in an earlier period, see Homans, *English Villagers of the Thirteenth Century*, pp. 144 ff.

[2] W.A.M. 14894 (court of 21 July 1416).

[3] W.A.M. 14902 (court of 5 May 1424).

the obligation of feeding and clothing Bryd and allowing him easement in a room for the rest of his life.[1] All these transactions were probably sales; concessions such as these were unlikely to be obtained except by means of a privately negotiated transaction *inter vivos*.

[1] W.A.M. 14903 (court of 9 Apr. 1425). This holding and William Smyth's were in one or other of the vills of Murcot and Fencot.

Conclusion

I F the evidence has been rightly interpreted, the abbot and convent of Westminster were remarkably insensitive, as landlords, to market forces. In the long run, of course, their policies always responded to major changes in the demand for land, but in the later Middle Ages, if not in earlier periods, their response was so slow that the situation which evoked it was apt to change profoundly before the monks showed a willingness to come to terms. This conservatism in the estate-office at Westminster means that the rents which the monks asked of their tenants are treacherous data for the economic historian; the demand for land which these express is perhaps not often that of the period from which they come.

Two qualitative changes in landlordism at Westminster have been described—one beginning in *c.* 1220; the other in *c.* 1390. The latter change took almost a century to complete, and the attitudes which it fostered were those which the monks brought to bear on the problems, economic and political, facing them in the first half of the sixteenth century. There is a passing resemblance between these attitudes and the easy-going outlook sometimes imputed, after the Dissolution, to the monastic landowner in general.[1] The monks of Westminster were, as landlords, not benevolent, but ineffectual. Without becoming the friends of their tenants, they had ceased to be adversaries whom the latter respected; that is the lesson of the phenomenon of *redditus retractus*.[2] On demesne land, indeed, they were no longer in day-to-day or even year-by-year control: the initiative in exploitation here had passed to their lessees, and the monks of Westminster were no more eager than other religious of the period, similarly placed, to retrieve it.[3] On most of the

---

[1] *A Discourse of the Common Weal of this Realm of England*, ed. E. Lamond (Cambridge, 1929), p. 39, where lands are mentioned, formerly in monastic ownership, which 'were neuer surueyhed to the vttermost'. But on the realities of monastic practice in the early sixteenth century, see *Agrarian History of England and Wales*, vol. iv, *1500–1640*, ed. Thirsk, pp. 311 ff.   [2] On which see above, pp. 292–3.
[3] Above, pp. 160 ff.

tenant-land of the estate, they were still the key figures in the transmission of holdings; more often than not, the tenants in occupation had obtained their copies or their leases by direct application to the monks of Westminster and to no one else— that is the conclusion to be drawn from the small scale of the development of the local land market.[1]

With the advantage of hindsight, we can see that, had a monastic foundation survived at Westminster into the second half of the sixteenth century, the economic trends of the period would have forced upon the monks changes in policy on estates administration analogous to those which, long ago, had enabled their predecessors to survive the thirteenth-century rise in prices. These changes, however, would not have been easy to carry through, for the situation of the monks of Westminster as landowners at the beginning of the sixteenth century was much less propitious than that of their predecessors in *c.* 1220 or *c.* 1250. The latter-day monks were, for example, more isolated than their predecessors; the positive content of their status as an exempt house, subject, *nullo mediante*, to Rome, had evaporated, leaving only its negative concomitant, exemption from the authority of the ordinary. For the protection of their possessions, they were more dependent on their royal patron and on the actions of his courts than their predecessors had been. In the exploitation of their estates, they could no longer rely on the specific ties of dependence between lord and man that had done so much to swell the rents collected by thirteenth- and fourteenth-century monks of Westminster. Moreover, they were more dependent than the monks of Westminster of earlier periods on income derived from properties in the City of London and its environs. In 1535, *c.* 12 per cent of the Abbey's net income was derived from properties in Westminster,[2] and *c.* 36 per cent from properties in the county of Middlesex;[3] in 1086, Westminster provided *c.* 2 per cent of the Abbey's net income,[4] and Middlesex *c.* 16 per cent.[5] In and around Tudor London, however, the layman's jealous view of the Abbey's privileges made it wise for the monks to make friends of their tenants, if they could.

[1] Above, pp. 319 ff.
[2] £341: £2,827. The figures in this and the following note take appropriated churches into account.
[3] £1,016: £2,827.　　　　[4] £10: £515.　　　　[5] £84: £515.

These and other circumstances would have obliged the monks of Westminster to proceed carefully when a revision of the comfortable mode of exploiting their estates, which had been inherited from the fifteenth century, should become inescapable. But the additions made by Henry VII and Margaret Beaufort to the Abbey's income had the effect of postponing this day,[1] and, in the event, it was not the ancient monastic foundation at Westminster but the collegiate bodies established there by Henry VIII and Elizabeth and the transient monastic foundation of Mary which experienced the full rigours of the Tudor inflation and, with these, the difficulty and the inevitability of change.

[1] Above, pp. 67–8.

APPENDIX I

The Demesne Manors of Westminster Abbey, to 1540

THE attempt has been made in this appendix to list all the manors of which the abbot and convent of Westminster were the tenants in demesne in 1086 or at a later date, to record how each was acquired, for how long it was in demesne, to which obedience it was assigned, and, finally, its value *T.R.E.* and in 1086, if in the monks' possession then, and in 1535.

The later the period, the more difficult does it become to identify the places that were and those that were not 'manors'. Down to the fourteenth century, the touchstone is a juridical one. In their so-called manors, the abbot and convent of this period were not only the principal landholders: they were the lords of a court for the whole of the estate in question; elsewhere, though they might hold land, they owed suit to the courts of other men. Moreover, down to the fourteenth century, a list of manors in this sense of the word comprises all the important possessions of the Abbey. From the fourteenth century, however, the term was used by the monks of Westminster, not only in this sense, but also to denote any large agrarian property, whether or not this comprised tenant-land as well as demesne, and in cases where the abbot and convent were not the lords of the local court. The monks now described as 'manors' properties which a Cistercian might have described as 'granges'; and their new acquisitions were increasingly of this kind. By the early sixteenth century, the shrunken meaning of *manerium* was so well established that the term is used consistently in the *Valor Ecclesiasticus* to denote the manor house and demesne, or home farm, of the Abbey's several properties. Reflecting this change in usage, the following list includes some estates which gave the monks of Westminster little or no scope for the exercise of jurisdiction. Though not by any means a complete record of all the places where the monks of Westminster held land or other forms of property, it does in fact include all their principal holdings. It provides a conspectus of the growth of one of medieval England's great estates.

Not less difficult than the task of identifying 'manors' has been that of discovering when each such property was in demesne, and this for two reasons. First, even at Westminster, where the records of the medieval foundation have survived in such abundance, the period down to *c.* 1300, which saw both many alienations of property and the beginning of the attempt to reverse this trend, is not in all respects well documented; some manors moved in and out of the demesne with scarcely a trace in writing of the transactions to guide the historian. Secondly, even when a transaction is recorded, the record may be difficult to interpret. Was this the farm that took the manor outside the demesne of the church, into the hands of a tenant holding heritably, in fee? It is often hard to be sure one way or the other, and, indeed, the very distinction between a freehold and other interests in land, on which this question turns, was slow to be hammered out at the time. The limiting dates given below for the period in demesne are those which seem, on balance, probable; but many are open to question. Moreover, the statement that a manor was in demesne 'at all times' should be understood with the same proviso: it means that, on balance, this is probably the case. By the sixteenth century many of the Abbey's manors were on lease again, but this does not mean that the Abbey's monks were no longer the tenants in demesne: in nearly every case the lease was for a term of years, an arrangement which did not confer on the lessee a freehold interest in his land.

All values given in this appendix are annual values. As a rule, Domesday values are entered only if the Abbey possessed the manor in question at the time. In a few cases, however, where the monks acquired a manor after 1066 but before 1086, the value *T.R.E.* has been included; in these circumstances it is clearly of interest. The figures for 1535 are the valuations recorded in the *Valor Ecclesiasticus*, after deduction of reprises. Since the veracity or otherwise of the *Valor* is of intrinsic interest, the leasehold rents which the Abbey was in fact drawing from its demesnes and manors in 1535 have been noted wherever possible, for the sake of comparison; it will be clear that, in recording these, Henry VIII's commissioners achieved a high degree of accuracy. However, the *Valor* omits certain fee-farm rents due in respect of manors that had passed out of the demesne, and a few corn rents, and it almost certainly undervalues the sources of income that the monks customarily described as 'things pertaining to the regality'—feudal incidents and court dues. Its estimate of the Abbey's income must be regarded as in general an undervaluation.

Although a useful comparison can be made between the values of a manor *T.R.E.* and in 1086, it must be emphasized that a comparison between these values on the one hand and that for 1535 on the other is in many cases misleading, for the manorial unit itself was subject to change in the meantime: it was perhaps diminished by the hiving off of once subordinate estates as independent manors, or augmented by the purchase of neighbouring fees.

BEDS.

Holme with Langford Given by Richard II in 1399; in demesne at all times; assigned to the anniversary of Richard II and Anne of Bohemia. Value in 1535: £7. 17s. 4d.[1]

    Cal. Ch. R. v. 376–7; *V.E.* i. 417.

Holwell See under HERTS.

BERKS.

Bagnor (in Speen) Acquired by exchange in 1531; in demesne thereafter.[2]

Betterton (in Lockinge) Acquired with Bagnor. q.v.

Curridge (in Chieveley) Acquired with Bagnor, q.v.

Easthampstead Given by Edward the Confessor; demised to Hurley Priory @ £5 per annum by 1225; granted to the priory in fee between 1231 and 1236; recovered, with the site and possessions of the priory, in 1536; the fee-farm rent was assigned in the meantime to the convent for the upkeep of its buildings. Value *T.R.E.*: £5; in 1086: £3.

    W.D., 446ᵛ; W.A.M. 2251; *Sawyer*, 1039; *D.B.* i. 59ᵇ; *Walter de Wenlok*, p. 218; *Letters and Papers of Henry VIII* xi, p. 84; Dugdale, *Mon. Ang.* iii. 436–9.

Hurley The site and possessions of the dissolved priory of St. Mary at Hurley, including the manors of Hurley and Easthampstead, were given by Henry VIII in 1536, in exchange for Chelsea, Eye, and Teddington (Midd.), q.v., and other possessions of the Abbey in or

---

[1] Farm of the manor: £7. 15s. 4d.; profits of the court: 2s. The manor was in fact on lease @ £8 per annum (W.A.M. Reg. Bk. ii. 182ᵛ–183).

[2] The manors of Bagnor, Betterton, Curridge, and Peasemore, together with other possessions of the dissolved priory of Poughley (Berks.), were granted to Westminster Abbey by Henry VIII in 1531, in exchange for certain properties belonging to the Abbey in Westminster, some of which Henry wished to include in Hyde Park. The income accruing from these lands was shared among the abbot's portion and the other monastic offices which lost by the surrender of the lands in Westminster, that is, the offices of the sacrist, cellarer, intern treasurer, warden of St. Mary's chapel, and precentor. In 1535, the income from the whole estate amounted to £66. 18s. 4d. per annum. See *Letters and Papers of Henry VIII* v, no. 627 (23).

near Westminster and for a rent of £14 per annum. The whole was valued @ £111. 1s. 9½d. per annum in 1544.[1]

Dugdale, *Mon. Ang.* iii. 436–9; *Letters and Papers of Henry VIII* xi, p. 84.

Letcombe Regis   Given with Offord Cluny (Hunts.) by Henry VI in 1445, in fulfilment of the will of Henry V; in demesne at all times; assigned to Henry V's chantry. Value in 1535: £55. 6s. 8d.[2]

 Foedera xi. 89–93; cf. *Cal. Ch. R.* vi. 196–7; *V.E.* i. 417, 423; and see below, p. 398 (no. 58).

Peasemore   Acquired with Bagnor, q.v.

Poughley (in Chaddleworth)   The site of the dissolved priory of Poughley, together with the manor of Bagnor, q.v., and other possessions of the priory, was acquired by exchange in 1531; in demesne thereafter; assigned to the abbot's portion and the cellar. Value of the whole estate in 1535: £66. 18s. 4d.

 V.E. i. 411–18.

Steventon   Given by Richard II in 1399; in demesne at all times; assigned to the anniversary of Richard II and Anne of Bohemia. Value in 1535: £68. 3s. 3¼d.[3]

 Cal. Ch. R. v. 376–7; *V.E.* i. 417, 423–4.

Windsor   Given by Edward the Confessor; surrendered to William I in exchange for Battersea and Wandsworth (Surr.), Feering, and Ockendon (Essex), q.v.[4] Value *T.R.E.* and in 1086: £15.

 Harmer, no. 97; *D.B.* i. 32, 56[b]; *Regesta* i. 45, 86–7.

BUCKS.

Burnham, East. See below, under *Cippenham.*

Cippenham (in East Burnham)   Given by William I; in demesne until farmed to William de Buckland, 1115–17; assigned to the chamber. Value *T.R.E.*: £6; in 1086: £5. 2s. 4d.; in 1535: £2. 10s.

 Regesta i. 370; *D.B.* i. 145[b]; *V.E.* i. 414; *Gilbert Crispin*, p. 154; and see above, p. 79.

Denham   Given by Ulstan, a thegn, *T.R.E.*; out of the demesne by 1171;[5] given, secondly, by Edward I in 1292; assigned thereafter

---

[1] The properties were by then in the possession of Charles Howard.

[2] £60, less reprises of £4. 13s. 4d. £60 per annum was in fact the current leasehold rent of the manor (W.A.M. Reg. Bk. ii. 220).

[3] Of which sum, £27 gross is derived from the demesne. The demesne, together with the tithes owing from it, was in fact on lease @ £32 per annum (W.A.M. Reg. Bk. ii. 239–239ᵛ).

[4] In addition, Benfleet (Essex) and Pyrford (Surr.) may have come to the monks as part of this exchange, which facilitated the making of Windsor Forest.

[5] Abbot Walter of Winchester (1175–90) fee-farmed the main manor in Denham to Martin de Capella @ £15 and one hospice per annum, but the manor was

to the anniversary of Eleanor of Castile and to the abbot's portion.[1]
Value *T.R.E.*: £10; in 1086: £7; in 1535: £52. 3s. 11d.[2]
   Sawyer, 1040, 1043; *D.B.* i. 145ᵇ; *V.C.H. Bucks.* iii. 257; *Cal. Ch.
   R.* ii. 411; *V.E.* i. 411, 418.

Luffield Priory, site and possessions of   See under NORTHANTS.

Stokenchurch (Malletts Court)   Given by Richard II in 1399; in
demesne at all times; assigned, first, to the anniversary of Richard
II and Anne of Bohemia, but later to the abbot's portion. Value in
1535: £3. 6s. 8d.[3]
   Cal. Ch. R. v. 375–6; *V.C.H. Bucks.* iii. 98; *V.E.* i. 411.

Thornborough   Given by Henry VII in 1503, with other possessions
of Luffield Priory (Northants.), q.v.; in demesne thereafter; assigned
to Henry VII's chantry. For the value in 1535, see below, under
Luffield.
   Cal. Pat. R., 1494–1509, p. 304; *V.C.H. Bucks.* iv. 238–9.

Turweston   Given by Edward I in 1292; in demesne at all times;
assigned to the anniversary of Eleanor of Castile. Value in 1535:
£13. 12s. 4½d.[4]
   Cal. Ch. R. ii. 424–6; *V.C.H. Bucks.* iv. 252; *V.E.* i. 417, 423.

CANTAB.

Duxford   Acquired from Hugh of Envirmeu in exchange for Doddington and Thorpe (Lincs.), q.v., *temp.* William II; surrendered
to the king between 1102 and 1107.[5]
   Regesta ii. 818.

already in the hands of the Capella family by 1171 (W.D., 178ᵛ–179; *Pipe Roll,
17 Henry II* (P.R.S. xvi), p. 60. For the farm, see also above, p. 81. The hospice
was later commuted into a payment of £3 per annum. Half a knight's fee, comprising the manor later known as Denham Durdent's, was alienated before 1166
(*V.C.H. Bucks.* iii. 259).

   [1] For most of the ensuing period, the abbot took the surplus issues left after
payment of alms of £30. 6s. 8d. per annum on Queen Eleanor's anniversary and
the old fee-farm rent of £15 per annum, which was assigned to the prior and convent. The payment of £3 per annum in lieu of hospice rights lapsed. £1. 10s.
per annum from the issues of Denham had been assigned to the high altar *temp.*
Abbot Herbert (1121–36) (W.A.M. 3435).
   [2] Of which sum, £15. 13s. 4d. gross is derived from the demesne. The latter was
in fact on lease @ £15. 6s. 8d., one boar, or 6s. 8d. in lieu thereof, 6½ quarters
of wheat and half a quarter of peas per annum (W.A.M. Reg. Bk. ii. 100ᵛ–101).
   [3] The current leasehold rent of the manor (ibid. ii. 227ᵛ–228).
   [4] Rents of assize: £8. 13s. 11½d.; farm of the demesne: £4. 13s. 4d.; profits of
the court: 19s. 11d.; reprises: 14s. 10d. The manor of Turweston, excluding the
profits of the court, was in fact on lease @ £5. 6s. 8d. per annum, to Richard
Noterell, yeoman, of Westminster (ibid. ii. 194ᵛ–195).
   [5] The king restored the manor to Count Eustace III of Boulogne.

ESSEX

Beckswell (in Moulsham)   Purchased in 1374; in demesne at all times; assigned to the conventual treasury. Value in 1535: £4. 6s. 8d.
   V.E. i. 416; below, p. 423 (no. 37).

Benfleet (in South Benfleet)   Given by William I, possibly in part exchange for Windsor (Berks.), q.v.; at farm to William de Eynesford III for his life in the late twelfth century;[1] assigned in the early twelfth century to alms and pittances; the residue of the issues was later assigned to the conventual treasury.[2] Value *T.R.E.*: £4; in 1086: £6; in 1535 (with the rectory of South Benfleet): £59. 9s. 2d.[3]
   W.D., 602ᵛ; *D.B.* ii. 14; *V.E.* i. 416, 422; *Gilbert Crispin*, p. 41.

Birdbrook   Given by Edward I in 1292; in demesne at all times; assigned to the anniversary of Eleanor of Castile. Value in 1535: £31. 14s. 1½d.[4]
   Cal. Ch. R. ii. 424–6; *V.E.* i. 417, 423.

Bonvilles (in North Benfleet)   Probably acquired in c. 1504 with other possessions of the collegiate church of St. Martin-le-Grand and possibly identical with the manor in North Benfleet later known as 'Berdfelds', 'Bradfields', or 'Boadvills'; in demesne thereafter; assigned to Henry VII's chantry. Value in 1535: £5. 6s. 8d.[5]
   V.E. i. 411; for 'Berdfelds' see P. Morant, *History and Antiquities of the County of Essex* (London, 1768), i. 261.

Bullington (in Clavering and Ugley)   Purchased in 1504 with funds provided by Henry VII; in demesne thereafter; assigned to Henry VII's chantry. Value in 1535: £9. 13s. 2d.[6]
   V.E. i. 411; below, p. 425 (no. 47).

---

[1] Above, pp. 78–9 and n.

[2] In the early thirteenth century, the prior and convent granted this manor for a term to Abbot Ralph de Arundel (W.D., 602ᵛ).

[3] Of which sum, £20 gross is derived from the demesne; but this was the current leasehold rent of demesne and rectory together (W.A.M. Reg. Bk. ii. 205–205ᵛ). The net value of the rectory, after deduction of reprises, was c. £4. 3s. 4d.; see below, p. 405 and n.

[4] Of which sum, £12 gross is derived from the farm of the demesne, and this was the current leasehold rent (W.A.M. Reg. Bk. ii. 251ᵛ).

[5] The current leasehold rent for the manor (ibid. ii. 115ᵛ). For an eighteenth-century survey of Bonvilles, see W.A.M. 55898; at that time, the estate comprised 187 acres of arable.

[6] £10. 2s. 2d., including reprises, of which sum, £6. 2s. 2d. is derived from Bullington in Clavering and £4 from Bullington in Ugley. The latter part of the manor was in fact on lease @ £4 per annum (W.A.M. Reg. Bk. ii. 236ᵛ). Bullington, together with Pinchpol, q.v., and lands in Elsenham valued at £3. 6s. 8d. in *V.E.*, made up the so-called manors of Pinchpol and Bullington purchased for Henry VII's chantry in 1504 and then valued at £20 per annum; see above, p. 200.

Chesterford, Great   Purchased in 1504 with funds provided by Henry VII; in demesne thereafter; assigned to Henry VII's chantry. Value in 1535: £67. 6s. 8d.[1]
> *V.E.* i. 411; below, p. 426 (no. 48).

Coggeshall (in Feering)   Acquired with Feering, q.v.   In demesne until fee-farmed to Leovegar @ £2 per annum, *temp.* Abbot Herbert (1121–36)[2]
> W.D., 266ᵛ.

Coggeshall, Little (in Feering) Acquired with Feering, q.v.   In demesne until granted in fee to Aubrey de Vere in 1201, in return for de Vere's quitclaim of Feering.
> *Essex Fines* i. 24 (no. 53); *C.R.R.* i. 464–5.

Fanton[3] (i)   A manor here was confirmed to the Abbey by Edgar, and probably in demesne at all times. It was assigned in the early twelfth century for alms and pittances; later, the residue of the issues was assigned to the conventual treasury. Value *T.R.E.*: £3; in 1086: £6; in 1535: £25. 6s. 11d.[4]
> *Sawyer*, 774; *D.B.* ii. 14; *Gilbert Crispin*, p. 41; *V.E.* i. 416.

(ii)   Another estate in Fanton, allegedly confirmed to the Abbey by Edward the Confessor, was the subject of a dispute with William I in 1086. Value *T.R.E.*: £1; in 1086: 10s.
> *Sawyer*, 1039; *D.B.* ii. 14.

Feering[5]   Given by William I in part exchange for Windsor (Berks.), q.v.; Aubrey de Vere quitclaimed this manor to the abbot of Westminster in 1201;[6] it was subsequently in demesne and assigned to the conventual treasury. Value *T.R.E.*: £22. 10s.; in 1086: £34. 10s.;[7] in 1535: £62. 12s. 2d.[8]

[1] The current leasehold rent (W.A.M. Reg. Bk. ii. 287). An estate called 'Bawdland' in the vill of Great Chesterford, not mentioned in *V.E.*, was on demise to the same lessee @ £6 per annum (ibid.).

[2] Leovegar quitclaimed this rent to the monks, for alms, for his lifetime (W.D., 266ᵛ).   [3] Now Fanton Hall.

[4] Of which sum, 3d. is derived from the profits of the court. The manor of Fanton, with 'Brownes land', was in fact on lease @ £25 and 12 quarters of oats per annum (W.A.M. Reg. Bk. ii. 127ᵛ–128ᵛ).

[5] A discrete manor, comprising lands in the vills of Bradwell, Coggeshall, Feering, Fordham, Inworth, Little Teye, Messing, Pattiswick, Sisted, and Tolleshunt. Except in Feering, and possibly in Pattiswick, all holdings were held by free tenure.

[6] De Vere traced his claim to hold in fee for a farm of £40 per annum to the time of Gervase de Blois (1138–57) (*C.R.R.* i. 464–5).

[7] The Domesday manor included houses in Colchester.

[8] Of which sum, £25 gross is derived from the demesne. But demesne and rectory were on lease together @ £25 per annum (W.A.M. Reg. Bk. ii. 186ᵛ). The net value of the rectory, after deduction of reprises, was c. £9. 9s.; see below, p. 406.

Regesta i. 86–7, 163; *D.B.* ii. 14; *Essex Fines* i. 24 (no. 53); *V.E.* i. 416, 422–3; and see also above, under *Windsor* (Berks.) and *Little Coggeshall* (Essex).

Good Easter Given by Henry VII, with other possessions of the collegiate church of St. Martin-le-Grand, in 1503; in demesne thereafter; assigned to Henry VII's chantry.[1] Value in 1535: £16. 10s.[2]

Cal. Pat. R., 1494–1509, p. 304; *V.E.* i. 411.

Ham (in East Ham) Confirmed to the Abbey by Edgar; in demesne until fee-farmed to Alger, a clerk, *temp.* Gervase de Blois (1138–57); also in demesne in the later Middle Ages. Value *T.R.E.*: £1; in 1086: £3; in 1535: £4.[3]

Sawyer, 774; *D.B.* ii. 14; *V.E.* i. 414; *B.I.H.R.* 40 (1967), 135; and see above, p. 79.

Ingatestone Given by Leofric *T.R.E.*; in demesne in 1086. Value *T.R.E.* and in 1086: £1.

Sawyer, 1039; *D.B.* ii. 15.

Kelvedon Confirmed to the Abbey by Edward the Confessor as the gift of Guthmund; probably in demesne at all times; in the early thirteenth century part of the issues was assigned to the kitchen; *temp.* Gervase de Blois (1138–57) the manor was assigned to the Corpus Christi lamp and the other needs of the high altar; the conventual treasury was charged with the administration of the manor. Value *T.R.E.*: £5; in 1086: £8;[4] in 1535 (with Kelvedon Hatch, q.v.): £28. 11½d.[5]

Sawyer, 1040, 1043; *D.B.* ii. 14; *W.D.*, 377ᵛ; *V.E.* i. 416, 422; *Walter de Wenlok*, p. 215.

---

[1] This manor, when in the hands of the canons of St. Martin's, had been shared between six prebends—Imber, Paslowes, Fawkeners, Burghs, Newarks, and Newlands—and is sometimes described as six separate manors of these names. The share of the prebend of Newlands in Good Easter was excepted from Henry's gift. For the spiritualities annexed to these prebends, see below, pp. 403 ff. For the possessions of St. Martin's, see also *V.C.H. London* i. 562–3.

[2] A seriously inadequate figure, since it relates only to Good Easter Newarks, which was in fact on lease (without the profits of the court) @ £16 per annum; see W.A.M. Reg. Bk. ii. 269–269ᵛ. The manor of Good Easter Imber was on lease @ £12 per annum (ibid. ii. 140–140ᵛ).

[3] The land 'by Barking', where *V.E.* records an income of £4 per annum for the monks, was in fact the manor of Ham. The sum represents the current leasehold rent of the manor (W.A.M. Reg. Bk. ii. 213ᵛ).

[4] The Domesday value; it is also said, however, in *D.B.* that the abbot has £12 [per annum] from the manor.

[5] Of which sum, £13. 6s. 8d. is derived from the demesne. But demesne and rectory were on lease together @ £13. 6s. 8d. per annum (W.A.M. Reg. Bk. ii. 263–263ᵛ). The net value of the rectory was c. £11. 6s. 8d.; see below, p. 407.

Kelvedon Hatch   Given by Ailric, chamberlain, in *c.* 1066; probably in demesne at all times; assigned to the conventual treasury. Value *T.R.E.*: £2; in 1086: £3. For the value in 1535, see above, under *Kelvedon*.

Harmer, no. 74; *D.B.* ii. 14.

Moulsham   Bequeathed to the monks by Leofcild, *T.R.E.*; in demesne until fee-farmed @ £9 per annum, *temp.* Gervase de Blois (1138–57); recovered in demesne *c.* 1337; in the early thirteenth century, the farm was assigned to the kitchen; later, the residue was assigned to the conventual treasury, which was charged with the administration of the manor. Value *T.R.E.*: £9; in 1086: £12; in 1535: £48. 12*s.* 7¾*d.*[1]

Harmer, no. 84; *D.B.* ii. 15; *V.E.* i. 416, 422; *Walter de Wenlok*, p. 215; *B.I.H.R.* 40 (1967), 130–1; and see below, p. 417 (no. 14).

Newarks Norton (in High Ongar, Norton Mandeville, and Shelley) Given by Henry VII, with other possessions of the collegiate church of St. Martin-le-Grand, in 1503; in demesne thereafter; assigned to Henry VII's chantry. Value in 1535: £6. 13*s.* 4*d.*[2]

Cal. Pat. R., 1494–1509, p. 304; *V.E.* i. 412; *V.C.H. London* i. 562–3; and see above, p. 342 nn.

Ockendon (in North Ockendon)   Given by William I in part exchange for Windsor (Berks.), q.v.; in demesne in 1086; demised *temp.* Herbert (1121–36) to Henry fitz Wlured and thereafter outside the demesne. In the early thirteenth century the farm was assigned temporarily to the kitchen; subsequently it went to the cellar. Value *T.R.E.*: £4; in 1086: £10; in 1535: £10. 4*s.*[3]

Regesta i. 86–7; *D.B.* ii. 15; *V.E.* i. 413; *Walter de Wenlok*, p. 215; and see above, p. 81 and n.

Paglesham   Given by Ingulf, a thegn, *temp.* Harold; not in demesne after 1189–90, when a final concord was made confirming a heritable tenancy in the manor to Nicholas de Paglesham @ £9 per annum; assigned in the early twelfth century to alms and pittances. Value *T.R.E.*: £4; in 1086: £6.

W.D., 613ᵛ; cf. *Sawyer*, 1040, 1043; *D.B.* ii. 15; *Gilbert Crispin*, p. 41.

---

[1] Of which sum, £15 gross is derived from the demesne, and this was in fact the current leasehold rent (W.A.M. Reg. Bk. ii. 280).

[2] The value assigned to the so-called prebend of Norton Newarks in *V.E.* was in fact the leasehold rent of the manor of Newarks Norton at this date (W.A.M. Reg. Bk. ii. 310).

[3] A sum comprising the twelfth-century farm of £10 per annum and cert money of 4*s.* per annum from the view of frankpledge. In 1086 William *camerarius* held one hide of the Abbey in Ockendon, but this property does not appear later among the demesne possessions of the Abbey.

Pinchpol (in Manewden)   Purchased in 1504 with funds provided by Henry VII; in demesne thereafter; assigned to Henry VII's chantry. Value in 1535: £5. 7s. 2½d.[1]

V.E. i. 411, 419; below, p. 425 (no. 47).

Wennington   Given by Aetsere Swearte and Aelfgyth, his wife, 1042–4; in demesne in 1086; assigned in the early twelfth century to alms and pittances; in the early thirteenth century, however, the farm of this manor was assigned to the kitchen, and, in the fifteenth century, to the monk-bailiff; it was administered by the conventual treasury. Value *T.R.E.*: £2; in 1086: £3. Not mentioned in 1535. *D.B.* ii. 15; *Harmer*, no. 73; *Gilbert Crispin*, p. 41; *Walter de Wenlok*, p. 215.

GLOS.

Bourton-on-the-Hill[2]   Acquired with Deerhurst, q.v.; probably in demesne at all times; assigned to the abbot's portion. Value in 1535: £28. 17s. ¾d.[3]

V.E. i. 410, 418.

Deerhurst, alias *Plaistow*[4]   Given by Edward the Confessor; in demesne until fee-farmed *temp.* Gervase de Blois (1138–57) to William de Derneford; purchased by the Abbey from the fee-farmer in 1299 and thereafter in demesne; assigned to the abbot's portion. Value *T.R.E.*: £10;[5] in 1086: £10;[6] in 1535 (with Hardwicke): £64. 7s. 11¾d.[7]

---

[1] The value including reprises was £6. 13s. 4d., and this was the current leasehold rent of the manor (W.A.M. Reg. Bk. ii. 236ᵛ). Lands in Elsenham, valued in *V.E.* at £3. 6s. 8d., were included in the manor of Pinchpol at the time of purchase; for the value in 1504, see above, under *Bullington*.

[2] For some administrative purposes the manor included Moreton-in-Marsh, q.v.

[3] The sum includes rents and profits of the court from the abbot's tenants at Moreton-in-Marsh. It also includes £8. 6s. 8d. in respect of the demesne, and this was the current leasehold rent for the demesne at Bourton, together with the abbot's sheepfold, and three meadows in Moreton-in-Marsh (W.A.M. Reg. Bk. ii. 143).

[4] This manor was administered with Hardwicke (Glos.), q.v., until the second half of the fourteenth century. Parts of it were in the hands of tenants before 1066 and subsequently; Bourton-on-the-Hill, Hardwicke, Sutton-under-Brailes, and Todenham are described as berewicks of Deerhurst in 1086.

[5] The farm *T.R.E.* for the whole manor, including the subinfeudated portions, was £41 and 8 sextars of honey.

[6] Two other figures are given for 1086: £26 for Deerhurst, together with its four berewicks; and £40 for the whole manor, including the subinfeudated portions.

[7] Of which sum, £16 gross is derived from the demesne. The demesne of Deerhurst (exclusive of the lands already in the hands of tenants) was on lease @ £6 per annum, and that of Hardwicke, with two water mills, @ £10 per annum (W.A.M. Reg. Bk. ii. 162, 262).

Harmer, no. 99; *D.B.* i. 166; *V.E.* i. 410, 418; *V.C.H. Glos.* viii. 37–8; *B.I.H.R.* 40 (1967), 132–3; and see below, p. 416 (no. 8).

Hardwicke (in Elmstone Hardwicke) Acquired with Deerhurst, q.v., and administered with it as a single manor until the later fourteenth century. For the value in 1535, see above, under *Deerhurst*.

Moreton-in-Marsh A town plantation of the early thirteenth century; in demesne at all times; the rents were assigned to the anniversary of Richard de Berking; the residue of the issues, to the abbot's portion. Valued in 1535 with Bourton-on-the-Hill, q.v.
   Flete, p. 104.

Sutton-under-Brailes See below, under WARWICKS.

Todenham Acquired with Deerhurst, q.v.; probably in demesne at all times; assigned to the abbot's portion. Value in 1535: £28. 11*d.*[1]
   V.E. i. 410, 418.

HANTS

Eversley Given by Edward the Confessor, 1053–66; in demesne in 1086. Value *T.R.E.*: £5; in 1086: £4.
   Harmer, no. 85; *Sawyer*, 1039; *D.B.* i. 43ᵇ; *V.C.H. Hants.* iv. 33.

HERTS.

Aldenham Reputedly given by Offa the Great; confirmed to the Abbey by Edgar; in demesne at all times except between 1315 and 1321, when demised in part exchange for Hendon, q.v.; assigned to the conventual treasury. Value *T.R.E.*: £8; in 1086: £3; in 1535 (with the rectory of Aldenham): £44. 11*s.* 10*d.*[2]
   Sawyer, 124, 774; *D.B.* i. 135; *V.E.* i. 415, 422; *V.C.H. Herts.* ii. 150; and see below, p. 416 (no. 11).

Amwell, Great Purchased in 1270; in demesne at all times until the sixteenth century; assigned to the conventual treasury. Value in 1535: £20. 6*s.* 6*d.*[3]
   V.E. i. 415, 416; below, p. 415 (no. 6); *V.C.H. Herts.* iii. 416.

---

[1] Of which sum, £10 gross is derived from the demesne; this was in fact the current leasehold rent (ibid. ii. 104).

[2] Of this sum, £8. 6*s.* 2*d.* should be allowed for the rectory; see below, p. 403.

[3] Farm of the manor: £18; sale of wood: £1. 10*s.*; profits of the court: 16*s.* 6*d.* The manor was in fact on lease @ £18 per annum. The lessees, Gilbert and Jocosa Rokes, had a life-interest; thus, legally, the manor had passed out of the demesne of the Abbey (W.A.M. Reg. Bk. ii. 184ᵛ–185).

Ashwell   Given by Edward the Confessor; in demesne at all times; the main issues were assigned in the early thirteenth century to the kitchen; later, the residue went to the conventual treasury, which was charged with the administration of the manor. Value *T.R.E.*: £22; in 1086: £20; in 1535: £40. 19s. 4d.

> *Sawyer*, 1040, 1043; *D.B.* i. 135–135ᵇ; *V.E.* i. 415–16, 422; *Walter de Wenlok*, p. 215.

Datchworth with Watton   Given by Edgar and confirmed to the Abbey by Edward the Confessor and William I. By 1192 Hugh de Buckland was tenant in demesne, and William de Buckland had been so before him. Value *T.R.E.*: £4; in 1086: £2. 10s.[1]

> *Harmer*, no. 79; *D.B.* i. 135; *Regesta* i. 16; *Feet of Fines, Henry II and Richard I* (P.R.S. xvii), pp. 13–14; *V.C.H. Herts.* iii. 78, 159.

Harpenden   See below, under *Kinsbourne*, and *Wheathampstead and Harpenden*

Holwell[2]   Given by Edgar; in demesne until the twelfth century; the fee-farm rent thereafter was assigned to the conventual treasury. Value *T.R.E.* and in 1086: £5.

> *Sawyer*, 774; *D.B.* i. 211; *V.C.H. Beds.* ii. 286.

Kinsbourne   (in Harpenden) Acquired with Wheathampstead, q.v., and administered with it as a single manor until the thirteenth century; in demesne at all times; assigned to the conventual treasury. Value of the demesne in 1535: £14.[3]

> *V.E.* i. 415.

Stevenage   Given, with Tewin, by Edward the Confessor; in demesne at all times; assigned to the conventual treasury. Value *T.R.E.*: £13; in 1086: £12; in 1535: £42. 9½d.[4]

> *Sawyer*, 1040, 1043; *D.B.* i. 135; *V.E.* i. 415–16, 422.

Tewin   Acquired with Stevenage, q.v.

Titeburst   Acquired with Aldenham, q.v. Not in demesne after the twelfth century; in the late thirteenth century, the fee-farm tenant, Alexander de Cheny, owed £1 per annum. Value *T.R.E.*: 13s. 4d.; in 1086: 10s.

> *Cal. Inq. post mortem* iii. 335; *D.B.* i. 135.

Watton   See above, under *Datchworth with Watton*.

---

[1] Datchworth: £3, *T.R.E.*; £2 in 1086. Watton: £1, *T.R.E.*; 10s. in 1086.
[2] Formerly in Beds.
[3] The current leasehold rent (W.A.M. Reg. Bk. ii. 269ᵛ).
[4] Of which sum, £5. 12s. is derived from the demesne. The latter was in fact on lease @ 24 quarters of good barley per annum (ibid. ii. 280ᵛ).

Wheathampstead and Harpenden[1]   Given by Edward the Confessor; in demesne at all times; assigned to the conventual treasury. Value *T.R.E.*: £30; in 1086: £16; in 1535 (with a portion of the tithes): £82. 19*s.* 6¼*d.*[2]

Sawyer, 1031, 1040, 1043; *D.B.* i. 135; *V.E.* i. 415–16, 422; *V.C.H. Herts.* ii. 297–8; see also *B.I.H.R.* 40 (1967), 133.

HUNTS.

Offord Cluny   Given by Henry VI in 1445, with Letcombe Regis (Berks.); in demesne at all times; assigned to Henry V's chantry. Value in 1535: £20.

V.E. i. 417. For other references, see under *Letcombe Regis* (Berks.).

KENT

Combe (in Greenwich)   Acquired between 1245 and 1257, perhaps by purchase. Assigned, *temp.* Richard Ware (1258–83), to the sacrist and, subsequently, to Ware's anniversary, when this should be observed, but, in 1283–4, to the kitchener. Later, the manor was administered by the conventual treasurers. It was surrendered to Henry VIII in 1536.[3] Value in 1535: £2.[4]

V.E. i. 416; *Cal. of Kent Feet of Fines, to the end of Henry III's reign*, ed. I. J. Churchill, R. Griffin, and F. W. Hardman, pp. 188, 288; *Flete*, p. 116; *Walter de Wenlok*, pp. 232 and n., 237; *Letters and Papers of Henry VIII* xi, p. 85; *Hasted's History of Kent*, ed. H. H. Drake, pt. i, *The Hundred of Blackheath* (London, 1886), p. 51 and n.; below, p. 392 (no. 31).

Edenbridge   See below, under *Stangraves*, and *Westerham.*

Plumstead Boarstall (in Plumstead, Boarstall, Crayford, Erith, Lessness, and East Wickham)   Purchased in 1504 with funds

---

[1] The manor comprised lands in Wheathampstead, Harpenden, and Kinsbourne (itself in Harpenden). In *D.B.* and in twelfth-century sources, the name 'Wheathampstead' is used; later, 'Wheathampstead and Harpenden' is the usual form. Kinsbourne, q.v., acquired a separate manorial identity in the course of the thirteenth century. The values of the late eleventh century and that of 1535 are, therefore, not exactly comparable; on this point, however, see also the following note.

[2] Of which sum, £26. 6*s.* 8*d.* gross is derived from the demesne. The monks were in fact receiving a leasehold rent of only £7 per annum from the demesne at Wheathampstead; however, the tithes of Wheathampstead were demised to the same lessee @ £6 and 40 quarters of good wheat per annum. It appears, therefore, that a cash value of £13. 6*s.* 8*d.* per annum was set on this corn rent. See W.A.M. Reg. Bk. ii. 88ᵛ.   [3] When the property was described as three closes.

[4] The current leasehold rent (ibid. i.133–133ᵛ). In 1271, an income of at least £8 per annum could be anticipated from this property (below, p. 392, no. 31).

provided by Henry VII; in demesne thereafter; assigned to Henry VII's chantry. Value in 1535: £5. 13s. 1d.[1]

V.E. i. 412, 419; below, p. 426 (no. 50).

Stangraves (in Edenbridge) Acquired in *c.* 1351, probably by purchase; in demesne at all times; assigned to the anniversary of Eleanor of Castile. For the value in 1535, see below, under *Westerham*, and n.

Below, p. 419 (no. 22).

Westerham Given by Edward I in 1292;[2] in demesne at all times; assigned to the anniversary of Eleanor of Castile. Value in 1535: £68. 15s. 8¾d.[3]

Cal. Ch. R. ii. 425; *V.E.* i. 417, 423.

LINCS.

Alkborough Purchased in *c.* 1504, together with Belchford, q.v., with funds provided by Henry VII.[4]

Belchford Purchased in *c.* 1504, together with Alkborough, Burton Stather, and Halton (Lincs.), and Oswald Beck Soke (Notts.), with funds provided by Henry VII; thereafter in demesne; assigned to Henry VII's chantry. For the value in 1535, see below, under *Burton Stather*.

Below, p. 425 (no. 46).

Burton Stather Purchased with Belchford, q.v. Value in 1535 (with Belchford and Halton): £30.[5]

V.E. i. 412.

Doddington and Thorpe Given by Ailric son of Mariete *T.R.E.*; exchanged for Duxford (Cantab.), q.v., *temp.* William II, but recovered between 1102 and 1107; not in demesne after 1191–1200, when the manor was fee-farmed to William Picot @ £12 per annum. Rents from this manor were assigned in the early twelfth century to the chamber. Value in 1086: £4; in 1535: £12.

W.D., 501, 505ᵛ; *Regesta* i. 212; ibid. ii. 818; cf. *D.B.* i. 346; *Gilbert Crispin*, p. 41; *V.E.* i. 414.

---

[1] The value includes that of lands in East Wickham, which is recorded separately in *V.E.* Even so, it is an undervaluation of the manor as a whole; see above, p. 200 n.

[2] Edward I's grant carried manorial rights in Edenbridge.

[3] The sum includes £5. 2s. 8d. from the farm of land called *Chermans*, and £10 from the demesne. The two properties were in fact on lease @ £15. 2s. 8d. per annum (W.A.M. Reg. Bk. ii. 257–257ᵛ). It is to be understood that the figures for Westerham in *V.E.* include the monks' income from Stangraves manor, q.v.

[4] The manor is mentioned neither in *V.E.* nor in the sixteenth-century leasebooks of the Abbey.

[5] This was the current leasehold rent of Burton Stather, Halton, and Belchford (W.A.M. Reg. Bk. ii. 277).

Fenne (in Fishtoft) and *Skreyne*[1] (in Frieston)   Purchased in 1504 with funds provided by Henry VII; thereafter in demesne; assigned to Henry VII's chantry. Value in 1535: £33. 6s. 8d.[2]

V.E. i. 412; below, p. 426 (no. 49).

Halton   Purchased with Belchford, q.v. For the value in 1535, see above, under *Burton Stather*.

Below, p. 425 (no. 46).

Skreyne   See above, under *Fenne and Skreyne*.

Thorpe   See above, under *Doddington and Thorpe*.

MIDD.

Ashford   Acquired with Staines, q.v.; in demesne at all times; assigned to the conventual treasury. Value in 1535 (with the rectory of Staines): £38. 15s. 6d.[3]

V.E. i. 415, 422; V.C.H. Midd. ii. 306.

Billetts (in Laleham)   Purchased in c. 1366; in demesne at all times; assigned to the abbot's portion.[4] Value in 1535: £6. 11s. 10½d.[5]

V.E. i. 410, 418; below, p. 422 (no. 35); V.C.H. Midd. ii. 399.

Chalkhill (in Kingsbury)   Given by William, the king's chamberlain, in the late eleventh century.[6] Value T.R.E.: £3; in 1086: £1. 10s.

Gilbert Crispin, p. 130; cf. D.B. i. 128[b], and above, p. 39 and n.

---

[1] Now Crane End.

[2] This was the current leasehold rent of Fenne and Skreyne (ibid. ii. 279[v]).

[3] £40, less reprises of £1. 4s. 6d. The sum of £40, which V.E. derives from the manor of Ashford, represents the current leasehold rent for the manor and the church of Staines, with the dependencies of the latter at Ashford, Laleham, and Yeoveney; it was made up of a cash rent of £20 per annum and 60 quarters of wheat, valued at £20, per annum (W.A.M. Reg. Bk. ii. 195[v]–196). The net value of the rectory of Staines was c. £29 per annum; see below, p. 409 and n.

[4] This acquisition compensated the abbot and his successors for the loss of £6. 13s. 4d. per annum from their portion, in consequence of Abbot Litlington's surrender to the prior and convent of a yearly hospice at Oakham valued at this amount; the prior and convent were to have this income for the upkeep of the plate which Litlington gave to the refectory in 1378 (Liber Niger Quaternus, 102; and see above, p. 42).

[5] £6. 13s. 4d., less reprises of 1s. 5½d. The current leasehold rent of the manor is said to be £6. 13s. 8d. per annum, and this sum is probably a scribal error for £6. 13s. 4d. per annum (W.A.M. Reg. Bk. ii. 310[v]).

[6] This is probably the land at 'Cealchithe' which the Abbey had been claiming since before the Conquest as the gift of Thurstan, a housecarl of Edward the Confessor (*Regesta* i. 89). For the identification as Chalkhill, see ibid. ii, p. 392. Its subsequent history is obscure, and there is indeed no firm evidence that the Abbey ever held this land in demesne. In 1086 William the chamberlain held it 'sub abbate'.

Chelsea   Mode of acquisition uncertain; the manor, which included land in Westbourne and Kensal, was possibly comprised in the estate of 13½ hides attributed to the monks of Westminster in Westminster itself in 1086. It was at farm to William de Buckland *temp.* Gilbert Crispin (1085–1117/18) and fee-farmed *temp.* Gervase de Blois (1138–57) to the abbot's mother. The farm of £4 per annum was assigned in the early thirteenth century to the kitchen but subsequently to the office of the monk-bailiff; it was surrendered to Henry VIII in 1536. In 1367, the monks obtained a lease of Chelsea from the tenant in demesne for his lifetime. Value in 1535: £4. 3s.[1]

   Gilbert Crispin, p. 154; *V.E.* i. 417; *B.I.H.R.* 40 (1967), 131; *Letters and Papers of Henry VIII* xi, p. 85. See also *Cal. Cl. R., 1364–8*, pp. 385–6, and above, pp. 78–9, 167.

Cowhouse (in Hampstead)   See below, under *Hodford*.

Cowley Peachey   Given by St. Dunstan. Farmed to Hugh de Coleham @ £1. 10s. per annum, *temp.* Herbert (1121–36), and not in demesne thereafter; the farm was assigned to the cellar. Value *T.R.E.*: £2; in 1086: £1. 10s.; in 1535: £1.

   W.D., 129, 629; *Sawyer*, 894, 1293; *D.B.* i. 128b; *V.E.* i. 413; *V.C.H. Midd.* iii. 172.

Down (in Northolt)   Given by Richard II in 1399; in demesne at all times; assigned to the anniversary of Richard II and Anne of Bohemia. Value in 1535: £16. 2s.[2]

   Cal. Ch. R. v. 376; *V.E.* i. 417, 424; *V.C.H. Midd.* iv. 114–15.

Drayton (in West Drayton)   Given by Margaret, countess of Richmond, in 1506; thereafter in demesne; assigned to the anniversary of the donor. Value in 1535: £9. 6s. 8d.[3]

   V.E. i. 411; *V.C.H. Midd.* iii. 194.

Eye[4]   Given by Geoffrey de Mandeville I and Lecelina, his second wife (i.e. probably before 1100); in the king's hands 1316–27; with that exception, in demesne until surrendered to Henry VIII in 1536, in exchange for the site and possessions of Hurley Priory, q.v.; assigned to the abbot's portion. Value in 1535: £31.[5]

---

   [1] Of which sum, 3s. was cert money from the view of frankpledge.

   [2] Of which sum, £13. 6s. 8d. gross is said to derive from the farm of the manor. The manor was in fact on lease @ £6. 13s. 4d. and 20 quarters of wheat per annum (W.A.M. Reg. Bk. ii. 281ᵛ).

   [3] The manor was in fact on lease @ £10. 6s. 8d. per annum (ibid. ii. 206ᵛ).

   [4] The manor house and adjacent lands in this manor were usually known as 'La Neyte', and in the thirteenth century the name 'Ebury' began to be used of Eye excluding 'La Neyte'. For the site of the whole manor, see *Archaeologia* 62 (1910), i. 31–53. Eye is not mentioned in Domesday Book.

   [5] The sum takes no account of the house at La Neyte, which, as the abbot's

Regesta ii. 769; *Gilbert Crispin*, p. 139; *Cal. Cl. R., 1327–30*, p. 4; *V.E.* i. 410, 415; *Letters and Papers of Henry VIII* xi, p. 84.

Finchley Bidek's manor here was purchased between 1349 and 1362; in demesne at all times; assigned to the conventual treasury. Probably valued with Hampstead, q.v., in 1535.
Below, p. 418 (no. 17).

Frith (in Hendon) Purchased *temp.* Richard de Berking (1222–46); in the course of the same abbacy a heritable grant of this property @ a rent of £1. 6s. 8d. per annum was made to Walter de Frith, son of Walter de Frith, who had sold it to the monks. Part of the manor was recovered by the monks before 1246; the date when the rest was recovered in demesne is uncertain. The issues were assigned, first, to Berking's anniversary; later, the residue went to the conventual treasury. Value in 1535: £13. 17s. 5d.[1]
W.D., 374ᵛ–375ᵛ; *V.E.* i. 415; below, p. 414 (no. 2).

Fulham[2] Given, with other possessions of the collegiate church of St. Martin-le-Grand, by Henry VII in 1503; thereafter in demesne; assigned to Henry's chantry. Value in 1535: £3. 12s. 2d.
Cal. Pat. R., 1494–1509, p. 304; *V.E.* i. 411, 419; *V.C.H. London* i. 562–3.

Greenford Given by Ailric, 1051–66; probably in demesne at all times; assigned to the conventual treasury. Value *T.R.E.*: £10; in 1086: £7; in 1535 (with Hanwell): £30. 6s. 6¼d.[3]
Harmer, no. 89; *V.C.H. Midd.* iii. 209; *D.B.* i. 128ᵇ; *V.E.* i. 415, 422.

Halliford Acquired with Staines, q.v.; in demesne until farmed to Robert Crevequer, probably *temp.* Herbert (1121–36); given, secondly, by Geoffrey de Aspale in 1285, as the endowment of his

own residence, was regarded by the commissioners of 1535 as being without value; but it includes the value of meadows in La Neyte, Market Mead, Longmore, and Le Burgoyne, all of which were in fact in Eye, though mentioned separately in *V.E.* The current leasehold rent for the demesne and meadows, with certain lands excepted, was £21 and 12 cartloads of hay and a boar per annum; six of the cartloads of hay were valued @ 3s. 4d. per annum in the lease, and six @ 4s. per annum. See W.A.M. Reg. Bk. ii. 135.

[1] The estate known as Newhall, in Hendon, was administered as part of this manor, and the value of 1535 includes the income from both.

[2] The manor lay in the parishes of Fulham and Chelsea (D. Lysons, *Environs of London* (4 vols., London, 1792–6), ii. 359–60).

[3] Of which sum, £18 gross is derived from the demesne. The current leasehold rent was in fact £8 and 30 quarters of good wheat per annum (W.A.M. Reg. Bk. ii. 254ᵛ).

chantry;[1] assigned to the conventual treasury. Value in 1535: £18. 13*s.*[2]

W.D., 129; *V.E.* i. 415; *V.C.H. Midd.* iii. 6; and see below, p. 393 (no. 36).

Hampstead Given by Aethelred II. A fee was created here *temp.* Stephen, and later in the twelfth century the whole manor was fee-farmed. It was redeemed from the farmer *temp.* Richard de Crokesley (1246–58). The main issues were assigned to the conventual treasury, but the sum of £6. 13*s.* 4*d.* per annum was assigned to Crokesley's anniversary. Value *T.R.E.*: £5; in 1086: £2. 10*s.*; in 1535: £31. 2*s.* 5*d.*[3]

  Sawyer, 894; *Regesta* iii. 925; *D.B.* i. 128; *V.E.* i. 415, 422.

Hanwell Given by St. Dunstan; in demesne at all times; assigned to the conventual treasury and administered with Greenford. Value *T.R.E.*: £7; in 1086: £5. 10*s.* Valued with Greenford, q.v., in 1535.

  Sawyer, 894, 1293; *D.B.* i. 128[b]; *V.C.H. Midd.* iii. 224.

Hendon Given by St. Dunstan; at farm *temp.* Gilbert Crispin (1085–1117/18), but possibly not on fully heritable terms until *temp.* Gervase de Blois (1138–57), when the manor was in the hands of Gilbert fitz Gunter; in demesne from 1315. In the early thirteenth century, the farm was assigned to the kitchen; after the recovery of the manor, the main part of the residue was assigned to the conventual treasury, which was also charged with the administration of the manor. Value *T.R.E.*: £12; in 1086: £8; in 1535: £73. 14*s.* 10¼*d.*[4]

  Sawyer, 1293, 1295; *D.B.* i. 128[b]; *V.E.* i. 415, 422; *Walter de Wenlok*, p. 215; *B.I.H.R.* 40 (1967), 135–6; *Flete*, p. 89; above, p. 80; and below, p. 416 (no. 11).

Hodford (in Hendon) Given by Edward I in 1295 for the anniversary of Eleanor of Castile; alienated to Richard le Rous in 1312. Given, secondly, by Richard II in 1399, with lands in Cowhouse (in Hampstead); the manor was thereafter in demesne and assigned to the anniversary of Richard II and Anne of Bohemia, but later to the abbot's portion. Value in 1535 (with Cowhouse): £19. 15*s.*

---

  [1] Geoffrey de Aspale retained a life-interest in the manor. For Halliford, see also above, p. 40.

  [2] From the manor: £18; from the court: 13*s.* The manor was in fact on lease @ £11. 6*s.* 8*d.* and 21 quarters of good corn per annum (W.A.M. Reg. Bk. ii. 182).

  [3] Of which sum, £15 gross is derived from the demesne, and this was the current leasehold rent (ibid. ii. 287). The value probably includes that of Finchley, q.v.

  [4] Of which sum, £24 gross is derived from the demesne, and this was the current leasehold rent (ibid. ii. 178[v]–179).

Cal. Ch. R. ii. 461; ibid. v. 375; *Cal. Pat. R.*, *1307–13*, p. 438; cf. Lysons, *Environs of London* iii. 4–5; *V.E.* i. 410; below, p. 416 (no. 11).

Hyde[1] Purchased in 1350; in demesne until 1536, when surrendered to Henry VIII; assigned, first, to the cellar, but later to the new work. Value in 1535:[2] £13. 13*s.*
    V.E. i. 413, 421; *Letters and Papers of Henry VIII* xi, p. 84; below, p. 418 (no. 19).

Knightsbridge[3] Confirmed to the Abbey by Edward the Confessor; in demesne at all times; assigned to the conventual treasury. In 1535, probably valued with Hyde, q.v.
    Sawyer, 1039.

Laleham Acquired with Staines, q.v.; in demesne at all times; assigned to the abbot's portion. Value in 1535: £27. 14*s.* 1*d.*[4]
    V.E. i. 410, 418.

Northolt Given by Richard II in 1399; in demesne at all times; assigned to the anniversary of Richard II and Anne of Bohemia. Value in 1535: £16. 19*s.* 8*d.*[5]
    Cal. Ch. R. v. 376; *V.E.* i. 417, 424; *V.C.H. Midd.* iv. 113.

Paddington[6] Confirmed to the Abbey by Edgar and Aethelred II; in demesne at all times; assigned, first, to the almonry; later, the issues were divided between the new work, the almonry, and St. Mary's chapel. Value in 1535: £21.[7]
    Sawyer, 1293; cf. ibid. 894; *V.E.* i. 413–14.

---

[1] Hyde was probably at one time part of the manor of Eye, q.v., as given by Geoffrey de Mandeville I to the Abbey; if so, an alienation of land by the monks in the twelfth century is indicated.

[2] Probably with Knightsbridge.

[3] This manor is not mentioned by name in *D.B.* but may be included in the Domesday estate of the Abbey in Westminster; it extended into the vills of Littleton, Paddington, and Westbourne. See below, under *Paddington*.

[4] Of which sum, £8 gross is derived from the demesne and £4 from New Place, alias Clement's messuage; these were the current leasehold rents for the properties in question (W.A.M. Reg. Bk. ii. 266ᵛ).

[5] Of which sum, £15. 8*s.* gross is derived from the farm of the manor. The current leasehold rent was in fact £15. 8*s.* and 10 quarters of oats per annum (ibid. ii. 257ᵛ).

[6] The manor, which included land in Westbourne, is not mentioned among the Abbey's possessions in *D.B.*; it may have been included in the estate in Westminster. In 1506, Margaret, Countess of Richmond, augmented the Abbey's estate in Paddington and Westbourne with lands that were valued at £10 per annum in 1535; these were assigned to her anniversary (*Cal. Pat. R.*, *1494–1509*, pp. 517–18; *V.E.* i. 411).

[7] The main item was the sum of £19 entered with the income of the warden of the new work. This was in fact the current leasehold rent of the manor of Paddington (W.A.M. Reg. Bk. ii. 62ᵛ–63).

Shepperton Given by St. Dunstan and confirmed to the Abbey by Edward the Confessor; in the possession of Ranulf Flambard for a time in the early twelfth century; not in demesne after *temp.* Herbert (1121–36), when the manor was farmed to Robert Crevequer. Value *T.R.E.*: £7; in 1086: £6. 16s. 6d. The fee-farm rent was later assigned to the office of the monk-bailiff.

  Harmer, no. 86; *Sawyer*, 1293; cf. ibid. 894; *D.B.* i. 128ᵇ; *Regesta* ii. 1881; *V.C.H. Midd.* iii. 5.

Staines Given by Edward the Confessor; in demesne at all times; assigned to the abbot's portion. Value *T.R.E.*[1]: £40; in 1086: £35; in 1535: £35. 2s.

  Harmer, nos. 97–8; *D.B.* i. 128–128ᵇ; *V.E.* i. 410, 418; *V.C.H. Midd.* iii. 18–19.

Sunbury Given by St. Dunstan; in demesne until 1222,[2] when surrendered to the bishop of London as part of the settlement of the monks' dispute with him concerning the parish of St. Margaret's, Westminster. Value *T.R.E.*: £7; in 1086: £6.

  Sawyer, 894, 1293; cf. ibid., 1447; *D.B.* i. 128ᵇ; *V.C.H. Midd.* iii. 54.

Teddington Acquired with Staines, q.v.; in demesne at all times until 1536[3] when surrendered, with other properties, to Henry VIII in exchange for the site and possessions of Hurley Priory (Berks.), q.v.; assigned to the conventual treasury. Value in 1535: £22. 4s. 6d.[4]

  Letters and Papers of Henry VIII xi, p. 84; *V.E.* i. 415, 422; *V.C.H. Midd.* iii. 69.

Westminster Given or restored to the Abbey by Edgar; in demesne at all times, with the exception of three hides in Tothill that were subinfeudated before 1086; the issues were divided between the prior's office, the cellar, sacristy, chamber, infirmary, refectory,

---

  [1] The value now and in 1086 includes that of four berewicks; these were probably Ashford, Halliford, Laleham, and Teddington, q.v. Moreover, Yeoveney, q.v., had not yet acquired an administrative identity of its own and was probably valued with Staines in the Survey. But on the berewicks, see also *V.C.H. Midd.* iii. 109.

  [2] See, however, n. 3 below.

  [3] However, between 1159 and 1175, Hugh fitz Warner surrendered his claim to 3 hides in Teddington and Sunbury and was granted 3 virgates there in fee (W.D., 155ᵛ–156).

  [4] Of which sum, £14. 6s. 8d. gross is derived from the farm of the demesne. The demesne was in fact on lease with the rectory and the great and small tithes @ £7. 6s. 8d. and 21 quarters of good wheat per annum (W.A.M. Reg. Bk. ii. 97). The glebe seems to have been excluded from this arrangement; see below, p. 410 n.

almonry, and new work. Value *T.R.E.*[1]: £12; in 1086: £10; in 1535: *c.* £312.[2]

Sawyer, 670, 1293; *D.B.* i. 128; *V.E.* i. 412 ff.

Yeoveney Acquired with Staines, q.v.; in demesne at all times; assigned to the abbot's portion. Value in 1535: £17. 6s. 8d.[3]

V.E. i. 410; *V.C.H. Midd.* iii. 18–19.

NORTHANTS.

Deene Given by Edward the Confessor;[4] not in demesne after the twelfth century; the fee-farm rent was later assigned to the office of the monk-bailiff. Value *T.R.E.* and in 1086: £6; in 1535 (with Sudborough): £25.

Sawyer, 1040, 1043; *D.B.* i. 222; *V.E.* i. 417; F. M. Stenton, *The First Century of English Feudalism, 1066–1166* (2nd edn., Oxford, 1961), pp. 267–9.

Luffield Priory, site and possessions of[5] The estate of the dissolved priory of St. Mary the Virgin at Luffield, in Luffield and elsewhere, was given by Henry VII in 1503, together with the site of the priory, and held thereafter in demesne; assigned to Henry VII's chantry. Value of the whole in 1535: £45.[6]

Cal. Pat. R., 1494–1509, p. 304; *V.E.* i. 412.

Sudborough Given by Edward the Confessor; not in demesne after the twelfth century;[7] the fee-farm rent was later assigned to the

[1] The value now and in 1086 may include that of the Abbey's lands in the manors of Chelsea, Knightsbridge, and Paddington, q.v.

[2] The value of 1535, though large, reflects the fact that many properties in Westminster had been surrendered to Henry VIII in 1531 (*Letters and Papers of Henry VIII* v, pp. 286–7).

[3] The manor was on lease @ £17 and one boar, or 10s. in lieu thereof, per annum (W.A.M. Reg. Bk. ii. 161ᵛ).

[4] According to *Sawyer*, 1039, however, Deene was the gift of Edward's chamberlain, Hugelinus.

[5] The main estates, outside Luffield, lay in Silverstone and Whittlebury (Northants.), and Evershaw, Shalstone, and Thornborough (Bucks.); see G. R. Elvey, *Luffield Priory Charters*, i (Bucks. and Northants. Record Societies, 1968), pp. vii ff. The priory site itself extended into Bucks. and Northants. It may have been only in Thornborough, q.v., that the Abbey now acquired manorial rights.

[6] The possessions of Luffield Priory, excluding its advowsons but including income from spiritualities, were currently on lease @ £45 per annum (W.A.M. Reg. Bk. ii. 305ᵛ). If the proportions of 1291 were still maintained, *c.* £25. 4s. of this sum (= 56 per cent) was derived from spiritualities.

[7] The fee-farm of Sudborough, the terms of which were modified in the king's court in 1224, was certainly an old one then (*C.R.R.* xi. 2575). The fee-farm tenant in 1224 was Bartholomew de Sudborough.

office of the monk-bailiff. Value *T.R.E.* and in 1086: £5. Valued in 1535 with Deene, q.v.

    Sawyer, 1040; cf. ibid., 1039; *D.B.* i. 222; *V.C.H. Northants.* iii. 245.

Sulby Mode of acquisition uncertain; probably outside the demesne by 1196;[1] the fee-farmers were the abbot and convent of Sulby; the farm was assigned to the chamber. Value in 1535: £5. 2*s.*

    Chancellor's Roll, 8 Richard I (P.R.S., N.S., vii), p. 190; *Gilbert Crispin*, pp. 48–9; *V.E.* i. 414.

NOTTS.

Oswald Beck Soke (in South Wheatley) Purchased in *c.* 1503–4 with funds provided by Henry VII; in demesne thereafter; assigned to Henry VII's chantry. Value in 1535: £34.[2]

    V.E. i. 412; below, p. 425 (no. 46).

OXON.

Islip[3] Given by Edward the Confessor, but not in the Abbey's possession until 1203;[4] in demesne thereafter, except between 1299 and 1318, when the manor was alienated in part exchange for Deerhurst, q.v. (Glos.); assigned to the abbot's portion. Value in 1535: £49. 10*s.* 1*d.*

    Harmer, nos. 103–4; *V.E.* i. 411, 418; *V.C.H. Oxon.* vi. 208–9.

Launton Given by Edward the Confessor; in demesne at all times; the main issues were assigned in the early thirteenth century to the kitchen; later, the residue was assigned to the conventual treasury, which was charged with the administration of the manor. Value in 1535: £23. 4*s.* 7½*d.*[5]

    Harmer, no. 95; *V.E.* i. 416, 423; *V.C.H. Oxon.* vi. 234.

RUTL.

Oakham with Barleythorpe[6] Claimed by the Abbey in virtue of the

---

[1] The Abbey's farm of £5 per annum in respect of Sulby is mentioned in the Chancellor's Roll of 8 Richard I (1196–7); W.D., 129, however, attributes this fee-farm to Abbot Ralph de Arundel (1200–14).

[2] The current leasehold rent (W.A.M. Reg. Bk. ii. 169ᵛ).

[3] The manor included land in the vills of Islip, Murcot, and Fencot.

[4] Edward's gift included land in Marston, but the Abbey never gained possession of this.

[5] Of which sum, £4 gross is derived from the farm of the demesne, and this was in fact the current leasehold rent (ibid. ii. 225ᵛ). Launton is not valued in *D.B.*

[6] After the appropriation of Oakham rectory in 1231 (for which see below, p. 404), the manor of Oakham with Barleythorpe and the appropriated church were known together as 'Oakham Church'.

Confessor's grant of the reversion of Martinsley wapentake, but not in its possession until the appropriation of the church of Oakham in 1231;[1] in demesne at all times; assigned to the office of the warden of the churches; the first call on the issues was an allowance of 6*s.* a day to the prior and convent for pittances. Value in 1535: £25. 3*s.* 9½*d.*[2]

W.D., 596; *Harmer,* no. 94; *V.E.* i. 416, 423; *V.C.H. Rutland,* ii. 14.

STAFFS.

Perton   Given by Edward the Confessor; the period when this manor was in demesne is uncertain.[3] The fee-farm rent was assigned to the monk-bailiff. Value *T.R.E.* and in 1086: £2; in 1535: £5.

Harmer, no. 96; *D.B.* i. 247[b]; *V.E.* i. 417.

SURR.

Allfarthing (in Wandsworth)   A manor here known as 'le Frithe' was purchased *temp.* Simon de Langham (1349–62); it was in demesne at all times; assigned, first, to the conventual treasury but, later, to the abbot's portion.[4] Value in 1535: £26. 13*s.* 4*d.*[5]

V.E. i. 411; below, p. 418 (no. 17 and n.).

Battersea and Wandsworth[6]   Given by William I, in part exchange for Windsor (Berks.), q.v.; in demesne at all times;[7] assigned to the

---

[1] Earlier, however, the Abbey may have possessed a soke in Oakham; see *V.C.H. Rutland* i. 133.

[2] The figure arrived at if half the reprises of £3. 16*s.* allowed to the warden of the churches in Rutland is deducted from the gross value of the manor; it seems appropriate to allocate half to the rectory of Oakham, for which see below, p. 404 and n.

[3] The monks lost possession of Perton after 1086 but were restored to it by Richard I in 1189–90; immediately, however, they farmed the manor to Hugh de Nonant, bishop of Coventry, for his life @ £2 per annum, and this arrangement was probably part of the bargain whereby they recovered the manor (W.D., 648). There is no later evidence of a demesne manor here.

[4] In 1499, however, the manor was demised to Prior John Islip for his life, with the proviso that after his death it was to go to his successors (W.A.M. Reg. Bk. i. 110[v]). This arrangement is probably relevant to the note in *V.E.* that the manor was then in dispute between the abbot and the prior.

[5] The current leasehold rent (W.A.M. Reg. Bk. ii. 292[v]).

[6] This manor comprised land in six vills: Battersea, Bridges, Hese, Penge, Wassingham, and Wandsworth, and, for a time, perhaps land in Tooting also. In *D.B.* the name 'Battersea' is used; later, 'Battersea and Wandsworth' became usual, but in 1535, Wandsworth, q.v., was valued separately.

[7] Ranulf Flambard was briefly in possession of this manor in the early twelfth century (*Regesta* ii. 1881).

conventual treasury.[1] Value *T.R.E.*: £80; in 1086: £75. 9s. 8d.; in 1535 (excluding Wandsworth, q.v.): £65. 19s. 8½d.[2]

D.B. i. 32; *V.E.* i. 416; *V.C.H. Surrey* iv. 11, 110.

Claygate   Given by Tostig and Leofrun, his wife, and confirmed to the Abbey by Edward the Confessor, 1058–66. The monks were disseised of part of their estate here in the mid-twelfth century but probably reseised of it by Henry II. The manor was on demise for his lifetime to Geoffrey fitz Peter, earl of Essex, *temp.* Ralph de Arundel (1200–14); the issues were assigned to the almonry. Value *T.R.E.*: £2; in 1086: £2. 10s.; in 1535: £7. 5s. 4d.[3]

Harmer, no. 93; T. A. M. Bishop, *Scriptores Regis* (Oxford, 1961), plate xxv(b); W.D., 465ᵛ, 471; W.A.M.1842; *D.B.* i. 32; *V.E.* i. 413.

Downe (in Wandsworth)   Purchased in 1370; in demesne at all times; assigned to the conventual treasury. Value in 1535: £6. 6s. 8d.[4]

V.E. i. 416; *V.C.H. Surrey* iv. 111; below, p. 421 (no. 31).

Finches (in Wandsworth)   At an unknown date, but probably *temp.* Simon de Langham (1349–62) and by purchase, the Abbey acquired the estate in Wandsworth known as 'Finches', which Roger Finch, a vintner of London, sold to Sir Robert de Congham and others in 1354.[5] The property was not valued separately in 1535.

Cal. Cl. R., 1354–60, pp. 99, 108; *V.C.H. Surrey* iv. 111–12.

Morden   Confirmed to the Abbey by Edgar; in demesne at all times; the main issues were assigned in the early thirteenth century to the kitchen; later, the residue was assigned to the conventual treasury, which was charged with the administration of the manor. Value *T.R.E.*: £6; in 1086: £10;[6] in 1535 (with the rectory of Morden): £10.[7]

---

[1] In 1535, however, the sacrist had a rent of 5s. 4d. per annum in this manor (*V.E.* i. 413).

[2] Of which sum, £29. 17s. 1d. gross is derived from rents of assize, £22. 13s. 4d. from the demesne, £10. 18s. from mills, and £2. 5s. 11½d. from the court. The manor, with exceptions which included the profits of the court and 10 acres of meadow, was in fact on lease @ £24. 13s. 4d., 8 quarters of oats and 2 quarters of barley per annum (W.A.M. Reg. Bk. ii. 284ᵛ).

[3] Of which sum, £6 is derived from rents of assize, rents and farms, and 12s. from sale of wood. The manor was in fact on lease @ £6 per annum (ibid. ii. 254). It should be noted that the Abbey's demesne holding in Claygate now included the estate purchased from Gilbert de Claygate in the thirteenth century, for which see below, p. 415 (no. 7).

[4] The current leasehold rent for the Abbey's estate in Downe (W.A.M. Reg. Bk. ii. 232).

[5] W.A.M. 1793 is a fourteenth-century rental of this estate and of land in All-farthing (in Wandsworth).

[6] However, the annual render in 1086, as distinct from the value, is said to be £15.

[7] The current leasehold rent for both properties (W.A.M. Reg. Bk. ii. 212). The

Sawyer, 774; *D.B.* i. 32; *V.E.* i. 416; *Walter de Wenlok*, p. 215.

Pyrford[1] Given by William I, possibly in part exchange for Windsor (Berks.), q.v.; in demesne at all times;[2] assigned to the abbot's portion. Value *T.R.E.*: £12; in 1086: £18; in 1535: £42. 7s. 11½d.
Regesta i. 45, 162; *D.B.* i. 32; *V.E.* i. 411, 418; *V.C.H. Surrey* iii. 431–2.

Tooting Given by Alnod of London, *temp.* Harold;[3] perhaps comprised later in the manor of Battersea and Wandsworth, q.v. Value *T.R.E.* and in 1086: £2.
D.B. i. 32; *V.C.H. Surrey* iv. 98.

Wandsworth A member of the manor of Battersea and Wandsworth, q.v., until the fourteenth century; assigned, first, to the conventual treasury, but, later, to the abbot's portion.[4] Value in 1535: £26. 14s.
V.E. i. 411, 413, 420.

SUSS.

Chollington (in Eastbourne)[5] Given by Edgar; outside the demesne by 1086.
Sawyer, 774; *V.C.H. Sussex* i. 408[b] and n.

Parham The reversion was given by St. Dunstan. The Abbey's title in this manor was disputed by Herbert fitz Herbert, *c.* 1130–3, and in 1211–12 by Peter fitz Herbert, whose claim the Abbey pacified with a payment of £100. From the latter date the manor was probably in demesne. In the early twelfth century the rents of Parham were assigned to the chamber; William Postard (1191–1200) assigned the whole manor to the prior and convent, who were to pay £8 per annum from its issues to the kitchen;[6] later, the residue of the issues went to the infirmary. Value in 1086: £4; in 1535: £11. 6s.[7]

net value of the rectory was *c.* £7. 12s.; see below, p. 412. The lessee, who may have enjoyed beneficial terms, was William Porter, a Chancery clerk.

[1] The manor included land in four vills: Horsehill, Pyrford, Sidewood, and Woodham.

[2] Ranulf Flambard was briefly in possession of this manor in the early twelfth century (*Regesta* ii. 1881).

[3] So *D.B.* i. 32; cf. *Harmer*, no. 92, which names Swein, Edward the Confessor's kinsman, as the donor.

[4] By 1535, however, the sacrist had rents amounting to £1. 8s. 8d. per annum from shops in Wandsworth and £4. 6s. 8d. per annum from the farm of a mill there.

[5] For the identity of the 'Sillinctune' of Edgar's charter with Chollington in Eastbourne, see W. Bugden, 'The manor of Chollington in Eastbourne', *Sussex Archaeological Collections* 62 (1921), 128 ff.; see also *Gilbert Crispin*, p. 41.

[6] Ralph de Arundel (1200–14) confirmed this grant (W.D., 572–572ᵛ).

[7] Of which sum, £10. 6s. gross is derived from the farm of the manor, and this was in fact the current leasehold rent (W.A.M. Reg. Bk. ii. 136ᵛ).

Sawyer, 1293; cf. ibid., 1040; W.D., 571ᵛ–572; *Regesta* ii. 1879; *C.R.R.* vi. 176–7, 287, 296, 393; *Gilbert Crispin*, p. 41; *V.E.* i. 414.

WARWICKS.

Grafton Minor   See next entry.

Knowle, with Grafton Minor   Given by Edward I in 1292 for the anniversary of Eleanor of Castile; in demesne at all times, except when demised to Ralph de Perham for his lifetime, in the early fourteenth century.[1] Value in 1535: £58. 16s. 8d.[2]
  Cal. Ch. R. ii. 425; *Cal. Pat. R., 1313–17*, p. 435; *V.E.* i. 416, 423; *V.C.H. Warwicks.* iv. 94; above, pp. 31–2.

Sutton-under-Brailes[3]   Acquired with Deerhurst (Glos.), q.v.; probably in demesne at all times; assigned to the abbot's portion. Value in 1535: £21. 10s. 11½d.[4]
  V.E. i. 410, 418.

WILTS.

Westbury Priory (in Westbury)   Given by Richard II in 1399; in demesne at all times; assigned to the anniversary of Richard II and Anne of Bohemia. Value in 1535: £10. 10s.
  Cal. Ch. R. v. 376; *V.E.* i. 417; *V.C.H. Wilts.* viii. 154.

WORCS.

Besford   Acquired with Pershore, q.v.; not mentioned in demesne after 1086. Value in 1086: £1.
  D.B. i. 174ᵇ; *V.C.H. Worcs.* iv. 20.

Binholme   See below, under *Pershore*.

Birlingham   Acquired with Pershore, q.v.; in demesne until the twelfth century; the first fee-farm tenant was a D'Abitot. The reversion was purchased from John de Sapy in 1378 and took effect in 1388; in demesne thereafter; assigned to the abbot's portion. Value in 1086: £2. 10s.; in 1535 (probably with Defford, q.v.): £19. 14s. 3d.
  D.B. i. 174ᵇ; *V.E.* i. 410, 418; *V.C.H. Worcs.* iv. 24–5; below, p. 421 (no. 29).

---

[1] The rent agreed when the demise was made, in 1316, was £46. 13s. 4d. per annum for the first ten years and £52 per annum thereafter (*Cal. Pat. R., 1313–17*, p. 435).
[2] Of which sum, £12 gross is derived from the demesne, and this was the current leasehold rent (W.A.M. Reg. Bk. ii. 197).   [3] Formerly in Glos.
[4] Of which sum, £4 gross is entered separately from the main issues of the manor. This was in fact the current leasehold rent of the demesne (ibid. ii. 289).

Bricklehampton (i)   A manor here was acquired with Pershore, q.v., and in demesne until the late twelfth century, when it was farmed to Peter de Wick and subsequently to Robert, his son. Value in 1086: £1.[1]

> D.B. i. 174ᵇ; *V.C.H. Worcs.* iv. 166.

(ii)   A manor here was in demesne from *c.* 1445; it was assigned to the abbot's portion. Value in 1535 (with Comberton, q.v. and rents in Elmley, Worcs.): £16. 11s. 8¾d.

> W.A.M. 24445 ff.; *V.E.* i. 410, 418.

Castlemorton[2]   Acquired in 1235 with a moiety of Longdon (Worcs.), q.v.; in demesne at all times; assigned to the abbot's portion. For the value in 1086, see below, under *Longdon*. Value in 1535 (with Castlemorton Greyndour, q.v.): £25. 11s. 1½d.

> *V.E.* i. 410, 418.

Castlemorton Greyndour   Acquired in 1397 with Longdon Greyndour, q.v.; in demesne at all times; assigned to the abbot's portion. Valued in 1535 with Castlemorton, q.v.

Chaceley[3]   The reversion was acquired in 1235 with a moiety of Longdon (Worcs.), q.v. The manor was in demesne at all times thereafter and assigned to the abbot's portion. For the value in 1086, see below, under *Longdon*. Value in 1535 (with Chaceley Greyndour, q.v.): £14. 4s. 2½d.[4]

> *V.E.* i. 410, 418; *V.C.H. Worcs.* iv. 54.

Chaceley Greyndour   Acquired in 1397 with Longdon Greyndour, q.v.; thereafter in demesne; assigned to the abbot's portion. For the value in 1086, see below, under *Longdon*, and in 1535, above, under *Chaceley*.

Comberton (in Great and Little Comberton)[5]   Acquired with Pershore, q.v., but in the hands of Gilbert fitz Turold in 1086. Restored to the church by Robert Dispenser, *temp.* Henry I; in demesne until the early thirteenth century and from the mid-fifteenth; assigned to the abbot's portion and administered with Bricklehampton. Value T.R.E.: £16; in 1086: £8. 10s.[6] For the value in 1535, see above, under *Bricklehampton*.

> D.B. i. 175; *Gilbert Crispin*, p. 146; *Regesta* ii. 903; *V.C.H. Worcs.* iv. 57.

---

[1] A striking assessment, since there were 10 hides at Bricklehampton.
[2] Formerly Morton Foliot.   [3] Now in Glos.
[4] Of which sum, £4. 6s. 8d. gross is derived from the demesne; this was the current leasehold rent (ibid. ii. 243ᵛ).
[5] Another estate in Comberton had already been subinfeudated by 1086.
[6] *T.R.E.*, Comberton, £6; its berewick, £10. In 1086, Comberton, £5; its berewick, £3. 10s.

Cradley, and *Hagley*   Two parts of the manors of Cradley and Hagley, together with the reversion of the third part, were given by Elizabeth Woodville in 1479, as the endowment of a chantry. The Abbey lost possession of Hagley, and, almost certainly, of Cradley, soon after this grant.

Below, p. 398 (no. 61); *V.C.H. Worcs.* iii. 133.

Defford   Acquired with Pershore, q.v.; in demesne until the twelfth century and from the early fifteenth, from which date it was administered with Birlingham;[1] assigned to the abbot's portion. Value in 1086: £2. 10s. For the value in 1535, see above, under *Birlingham*.

D.B. i. 174^b; *Feudal Aids* v. 327.

Eckington (i)   One manor here, acquired with Pershore, q.v., was in demesne in 1086 but in the hands of William de Leigh by 1193–5. Value in 1086: £5.

(ii)   Another manor, part of that held of the Abbey by Urse the sheriff in 1086, was given by Richard II in 1397; it was in demesne thereafter and assigned to the abbot's portion. For the value in 1086, see below, under *Pershore*. Value in 1535: £15. 13s.

D.B. i. 174^b; *V.E.* i. 410, 418; *Cal. Pat. R., 1396–9*, pp. 206, 261; *V.C.H. Worcs.* iv. 69, 71.

Hagley   See above, under *Cradley*, and *Hagley*.

Hussingtree (in Martin Hussingtree)   Acquired with Pershore, q.v.; in demesne in 1086. Value in 1086: £1. 10s.

D.B. i. 174^b; *V.C.H. Worcs.* iv. 135–6.

Longdon   Acquired with Pershore, q.v.; out of the demesne by 1166, when William Foliot was the tenant in fee. A moiety was repurchased in 1235 from the tenants in fee and held thereafter in demesne; a fourth part (Longdon Greyndour) was given by Richard II in 1397 and held thereafter in demesne. All issues of the manor were assigned to the abbot's portion. Value in 1086: £9;[2] in 1535: £18. 2s. 7d.[3]

D.B. i. 174^b; *V.E.* i. 410, 418; below, pp. 414–15 (no. 3); *Cal. Pat. R., 1396–9*, pp. 206, 261; *V.C.H. Worcs.* iv. 113.

---

[1] There is, however, no trace of a demesne manor at Defford in the late fourteenth century, and this makes it seem improbable that Defford was recovered *with* Birlingham (i.e. in 1388), as suggested in *V.C.H. Worcs.* iv. 167.

[2] This sum includes the value of the lands later comprised in the manors of Chaceley, Chaceley Greyndour, Castlemorton, and Castlemorton Greyndour, q.v.

[3] Of which sum, £3. 6s. 8d. gross is derived from the demesne, and this was in fact the current leasehold rent (W.A.M. Reg. Bk. ii. 47^v).

Longdon Greyndour   See above, under *Longdon*.

Morton Foliot   See above, under *Castlemorton*.

Morton Foliot Greyndour   See above, under *Castlemorton Greyndour*.

Pensham   Acquired with Pershore, q.v.; probably in demesne at all times; assigned to the abbot's portion. Value in 1086: £3; in 1535: £16. 5s.[1]
    D.B. i. 174^b; *V.E.* i. 410, 418; *V.C.H. Worcs.* iv. 167.

Peopleton   Acquired with Pershore, q.v.; in demesne in 1086. For the value in 1086, see below, under *Pershore*.
    D.B. i. 175; *V.C.H. Worcs.* iv. 148.

Pershore, alias *Binholme*[2]   Given by Edward the Confessor; in demesne at all times; assigned to the abbot's portion. Value in 1086: £14;[3] in 1535: £28. 13s. 9d.[4]
    Harmer, no. 99; *D.B.* i. 174^b; *V.E.* i. 410, 418; *V.C.H. Worcs.* iv. 166.

Pinvin   Acquired with Pershore, q.v.; in the hands of Urse the sheriff in 1086; recovered in demesne by the late thirteenth century; assigned to the abbot's portion. Value *T.R.E.*: £4;[5] in 1086: £6;[6] in 1535: £11. 19s. 6d.
    D.B. i. 175; *V.E.* i. 410, 418; *V.C.H. Worcs.* iv. 168.

Powick   Acquired with Pershore, q.v.; in demesne until farmed to Great Malvern Priory @ £24 per annum, *temp.* Herbert (1121–36). Value in 1086: £20; in 1535: £24. 13s. 4d.
    W.D., 293–293^v; *D.B.* i. 174^b; *V.E.* i. 410; *V.C.H. Worcs.* iv. 186.

---

[1] Of which sum, £8 gross is derived from the demesne, and this was in fact the current leasehold rent (ibid. ii. 217–217^v).

[2] In the fifteenth century, the name 'Binholme' began to be used frequently as the name of the manor house and agricultural demesne of the manor of Pershore and of the whole complex of lands belonging to the Abbey in this part of Worcs., of which Pershore was the administrative centre; 'Pershore' now more often denoted the town of that name. Westminster Abbey held little property in the town of Pershore by the fifteenth century; see Hilton, *English Peasantry in the Later Middle Ages*, p. 81 and n.

[3] The value given for the chief manor of Pershore. It is said, however, of Besford, Birlingham, Bricklehampton, Comberton, Defford, Eckington, Hussingtree, Longdon, Pensham, Peopleton, Powick, Snodsbury, and Wick, and of some vills where the Abbey had no land in demesne in 1086, 'omnes hae supradictae terrae jacuerunt et jacent ad Persore', and it is recorded that this whole complex, itself described as a manor, rendered £83 and 50 sextars of honey *T.R.E.* (*D.B.* i. 175).

[4] From 'Pershore', £11. 2s. 1d. gross; from 'Binholme', £18. 6s. 8d.

[5] The combined value of the two manors in Pinvin which Urse held at this date; the several values were: £1. 10s.; £2. 10s.

[6] Each of Urse's manors is valued at £3 at this date.

Snodsbury (in Upton Snodsbury)[1]   Acquired with Pershore, q.v.; in demesne until granted to Peter de Wick *temp.* Laurence (1158–73). Value in 1086: £7. 10*s.*

   D.B. i. 174ᵇ; *V.C.H. Worcs.* iv. 209.

Wick   Acquired with Pershore, q.v.; in demesne at all times;[2] assigned to the abbot's portion. Value in 1086: £3; in 1535: £13. 5*s.* 5½*d.*

   D.B. i. 174ᵇ; *V.E.* i. 410, 418; *V.C.H. Worcs.* iv. 168.

---

[1] Another manor here was held by Urse the sheriff in 1086.

[2] With the exception of 1½ hides in the hands of Urse the sheriff and Gilbert fitz Turold by 1086, and of 3 virgates granted by Abbot Laurence (1158–73) to Peter de Wick.

APPENDIX II

Burials, Confraternity, Perpetual Anniversaries and Chantries, and Other Forms of Spiritual Benefit

LISTING the tombs in Westminster Abbey was already a task that excited the antiquary before the monastery was dissolved, in 1540, and it continued to interest him in the seventeenth century, when the publication of Camden's guide to burials in the Abbey might have been expected to bring the work to an end.[1] The list now surviving in All Souls College, Oxford, MS. 126 was made early in the seventeenth century, apparently without reference to and certainly without much reliance upon Camden's work, by a compiler whose Puritan sympathies are betrayed by the description of the high altar of the church as 'the communion table'. Camden's guide, however, is the authoritative work on burials in the Abbey down to the end of the sixteenth century, and an indispensable source for the location of tombs and monuments at that date—an important consideration where, as in this church, some remains have been moved from their original place of burial. But this mutability of arrangements in the Abbey is one reason why, even so, the tomb-lists compiled before Camden's retain their value and importance. Camden, moreover, naturally recorded the funeral monuments of the Abbey as the latter existed in his own day, with Henry VII's chapel, at the east end. The earlier lists record burials in the old Lady Chapel, which Henry's chapel, itself a lady chapel, replaced. Then, again, the sixteenth century was a period in the history of the Abbey when legend grew fast; the early tomb-lists usefully enshrine the traditions that were in existence before the upheavals of the mid-century. On the other hand, if memories sometimes luxuriated under the influence of the events of this period, they could also fade into oblivion, and some relating to burials in the Abbey did so. Some lists compiled before Camden's include nearly a dozen burials at the north door of the church which are very likely authentic but of which Camden was, it seems, ignorant. For all these reasons, historians still need to consult the early lists.

[1] *Reges, Reginae, Nobiles et Alii in Ecclesia Collegiata B. Petri Westmonasterii Sepulti usque ad Annum Reparatae Salutis 1600* (London, 1600). This work, which is without pagination, is cited henceforward as *Camden*. See also the guide to burials in the Abbey compiled *c.* 1645 by Jack Mostyn; this is now W.A.M. Mostyn Hall MS. The essential later work is J. Dart, *Westmonasterium* (2 vols., London, n.d.).

Six such lists are known to survive. Each derives from a list, or from lists, now lost, which were made between the building of the chapel of St. Erasmus, completed in 1486–7, and the destruction, in 1502, of the old Lady Chapel, to make way for Henry VII's chapel; the Lady Chapel that appears in each is, therefore, the old chapel, not the new. Though having these and some other features[1] in common, the six lists fall into two distinct categories. In the first category are those recording, not only the burials, nearly all of which were attested by tombs and monuments, in the Confessor's chapel, alias the chapel of kings, the presbytery, the sequence of chapels extending from the east aisle of the north transept, through the old Lady Chapel, to the chapel of St. Benedict at the south entrance to the ambulatory, and the ambulatory itself, but also burials at the north door of the church and in the cloister and chapter-house; even in the sixteenth century, there was probably no monumental evidence of burials at the north door, and most of the burials assigned to the cloister and chapter-house were, indeed, mythical. It seems clear from the surviving texts, which record burials in other churches in London beside the Abbey, or survive in association with such lists, that these lists were the fruit of a wide-ranging antiquarian or genealogical interest in their subject. Lists belonging to the second category omit burials at the north door of the Abbey and those claimed for the cloister and chapter-house; these lists are more strictly concerned than the others with monumental evidence, and there is no sign that the interest of their compilers extended beyond the Abbey.

Four of the surviving lists belong to the first category. The earliest of these is, almost certainly, that surviving in College of Arms MS. A. 17.[2] This manuscript, which belonged to Thomas Benolt,

---

[1] Among which may be noted here the practice of referring to the chapel of St. Edmund and St. Thomas the martyr as the chapel of St. Thomas; Camden, however, refers to this as the chapel of St. Edmund. The primary dedication was in fact to St. Edmund; but the chapel also contained an altar dedicated to St. Thomas the martyr. The popularity of the cult of St. Thomas among those who knew the Abbey is attested, not only by the neglect of St. Edmund in references to the chapel where both were commemorated, but also by the number of the burials taking place there: it was, in this respect, the most popular of the Abbey's chapels in the late Middle Ages.

[2] The collection of coats of arms and standards forming the main part of the manuscript is concluded on fo. 62. The lists of burials forming the second part of the book, and extending over 18 folios, begins on fo. 62ᵛ, but its folios are numbered separately (down to fo. 16), and the earlier numbering discontinued after fo. 62. The list of burials in the Abbey occupies fos. 1–3 of the new sequence. The manuscript is described in the *Catalogue of the Burlington Fine Arts Club Exhibition*, 1916, p. 64 (a reference which I owe to Mr. Michael Maclagan).

Clarenceux King of Arms, is to be dated *c.* 1520, but the list of burials in the Abbey included in it was probably put together between 1499 and 1508, for it records the burials of John, viscount Welles, d. 1499, in the Lady Chapel, but omits all reference to Giles, baron Daubeney, d. 1508; Daubeney, however, was buried in the chapel of St. Paul in the Abbey.[1] This is the only list to say explicitly that the door where burials took place was the north door. The other lists in the first category are now, respectively, College of Arms MS. F 9, fos. 1–2ᵛ, B.L. Add. MS. 38133, fos. 98ᵛ–100, and ibid., Harleian MS. 544, fos. 65–65ᵛ, 67. These, however, are all redactions, with only minor variants, of a single list, itself little different from that in College of Arms MS. A 17, fos. 1–3, made between 1508, the year of the burial of Daubeney, which is recorded, and 1523, the year of the burial of Thomas Ruthall, bishop of Durham, which is omitted in the first two of these texts and appears only as an addition to the third.[2] College of Arms MS. F 9, fos. 1–2ᵛ may be the source from which the other two lists were copied. The exemplar, whatever its identity, from which these three copies derive recorded the burial of Sir Thomas Vaughan, d. 1483, twice—once in the chapel of St. Michael, and once in the chapel of St. Mary Pew; the double entry is repeated in each copy, though rectified, by cancellation of the former entry, in B.L. Harleian MS. 544, fo. 65. Vaughan's namesake, Sir Hugh Vaughan, d. 1500, was buried in the chapel of St. Michael. Sir Thomas Vaughan was buried in the chapel of St. John the Baptist, but on the side adjacent to St. Mary Pew; to place him in the latter chapel was thus to achieve a near miss. It appears, moreover, that the common source of these three lists committed the egregious blunder of making Anne Neville the wife of Henry III. This error is in College of Arms MS. F 9 and in B.L. Harleian MS. 544; the copyist of B.L. Add. MS. 38133, evidently realizing that something was amiss in his text, leaves a blank space at this point.

College of Arms MS. F 9 was probably written in the second quarter of the sixteenth century, or a little later; the contents of B.L. Add. MS. 38133 were bound together as a book not later than about the mid-sixteenth century. B.L. Harleian MS. 544

---

[1] The omission of the burial of Elizabeth, wife of Giles Daubeney, d. 1500, is less significant, since the lists in B.L. Harleian MS. 544, fos. 65–65ᵛ, 67, B.L. Add. MS. 38133, fos. 98ᵛ–100, and College of Arms, MS. F 9, fos. 1–2ᵛ also omit this burial.

[2] Ruthall was buried in the chapel of St. John the Baptist. In B.L. Harleian MS. 544, fo. 65ᵛ, his name is added at the end of the section on the chapel of St. Paul, which follows that on the chapel of St. John the Evangelist. The chapel of St. John the Baptist, with St. Mary Pew adjacent, lay between the chapel of St. John the Evangelist and the chapel of St. Paul.

belonged to John Stow, and fos. 65–65^v and 67, like most of the book, are written in his hand; these folios are the principal source of the list of burials in Westminster Abbey which Stow included in the *Survey of London*.[1] Stow, however, made some corrections and additions of his own.

Of the surviving lists, B.L. Egerton MS. 2642, fos. 322–323^v and —most probably—W.A.M. 53318 belong in the second category. These lists differ from those in the first category in more respects than the one noticed above. They are in Latin, the others, in English; and each makes some attempt to record the tombs and monuments of the abbots of Westminster—a subject of no interest, it seems, to the compilers of the lists in the first category. Both lists adopt a stance facing west in the Confessor's chapel, but east in the presbytery.[2] But there are also differences between the two lists. That in B.L. Egerton MS. 2642, fos. 322–323^v includes the names of one or two of the monks of Westminster other than the abbots, who were buried in the church and not in the monastic cemetery; its latest abbot is George Fascet, d. 1500; its latest burial, that of John Stanley, d. *c.* 1528; in it, the comment, unique in all extant tomblists, that Richard, duke of York and his brother, Edward V, were suffocated in the Tower of London by their uncle, Richard III, follows the entry relating to the burial of Anne Mowbray, Richard's wife, in the chapel of St. Erasmus.[3] This list was probably put into its final shape in *c.* 1530. The surviving text of it, however, was written in the late sixteenth century, by a copyist who found some of his exemplar baffling; hence, in his version, *capella regum* becomes *capella regis*, and Abbot Milling, Abbot *Azoling*. B.L. Egerton MS. 2642, for which it was made, is a common-place book, chiefly of heraldic interest.

The list in W.A.M. 53318 includes the tomb of John Islip, d. 1532, but excludes the tombs of monks of Westminster who were not abbots. In the case of secular burials in the Abbey, however, this list is more thorough than B.L. Egerton MS. 2642, fos. 322–323^v, over the ground that they have in common. The surviving copy is written in a scholarly hand, probably of the first half of the seventeenth century; it includes corrections and annotations in a different hand and has the general appearance of being a working copy.

---

[1] John Stow, *A Survey of London*, ed. C. L. Kingsford (2 vols., Oxford, 1971), ii. 108–11. The list here includes burials in the post-Dissolution church.

[2] The lists in the first category awkwardly change their stance in the course of enumerating the burials in the Confessor's chapel: the burials of Matilda, Henry I's wife, and Edith, Edward the Confessor's, are located from the viewpoint of one facing west; other burials in the chapel, from that of one facing east.

[3] fo. 323.

Unfortunately, the manuscript is torn, and no entries survive for the south ambulatory west of the chapel of St. Nicholas; the entries relating to the chapel of St. Nicholas itself are incomplete. The conclusion that this list belongs in the second category has been inferred from its resemblance, in the respects noted above, to B.L. Egerton MS. 2642, fos. 322–323ᵛ.

Even when the earliest of the extant tomb-lists was made, traditions relating to monuments in the Abbey were not in every case reliable. Moreover, it was not only at the north door that burials could leave no trace above ground. By no means everyone buried elsewhere in the Abbey was buried in a tomb: some were placed in coffins under the floor, or in the vaults, and, if this was done, an inscription recording the burial might or might not be provided; if provided, it might or might not be long-lasting. It can safely be assumed that the number of burials in the old Lady Chapel far exceeded the small number that is all that even the most informative of the tomb-lists record there. Where neither tomb nor inscription has survived, and where tomb-lists are silent, we are dependent on literary or documentary evidence. In the late Middle Ages, the rolls of the sacrist, the official who arranged funeral rites and received the payments made for them by the relatives and executors of the deceased, are the most precious form of this now extant, but these records are often ambiguous; we do not always know whether or not burial in the monastic church or its precincts followed the obsequies to which they refer. Some other forms of literary evidence were used by Camden and earlier compilers of tomb-lists. The belief of the latter that Fulk de Novo Castro, Henry III's cousin, had been buried in the cloister or chapter-house derived, no doubt, from references in chronicles of the time to the burial of Fulk in the Abbey and from the lack of evidence of burial elsewhere in the church.[1] Camden's belief that Geoffrey de Aspale, Roger le Brabazun and John Halengrett had all been buried in the Abbey is, almost certainly, explained by his discovery in the Abbey's cartularies that each founded a chantry or anniversary there. Burial, however, was not invariably associated with liturgical commemoration in medieval practice at Westminster. In each of these cases Camden may have been mistaken; in one, he was certainly mistaken.[2] Yet when all possible sources of error have been taken into account, it remains true that the list of burials in this appendix is far from complete. This can be inferred, for example, from an entry in

---

[1] For references see below, p. 374 and n.
[2] i.e. in Brabazun's case, for which see below, p. 376 and n. For Aspale and Halengrett, see below, p. 374 and nn.

the sacrist's roll for the year 1443–4.[1] The sacrist here records the receipt of £2 'de sepultura diversorum generosorum infra ecclesiam hoc anno'; yet not one of the burials known to us belongs unquestionably to that year. It is not too much to say that, by 1540, thousands of people had been buried in the Abbey church or its precincts whose names are now lost beyond recall.

In this appendix, the following categories of burials are distinguished:

*** Burials attested by a tomb or brass surviving to this day.

** Burials not so attested but mentioned in one or more of the tomb-lists, down to and including Camden's, and confirmed by documentary or literary evidence.

* Burials unattested by tomb or brass, or by any of the tomb-lists, down to and including Camden's, but for which literary or documentary evidence exists.

†† Burials mentioned in one or more of the tomb-lists, down to and including Camden's, but otherwise not confirmed.

† Burials mentioned in one or more of the tomb-lists, down to and including Camden's, but doubtful.

In fact these categories represent a simplification of the problems involved in making the list. Some tombs and brasses surviving to this day can be identified only because John Flete, in the fifteenth century, or Camden, at the end of the sixteenth, made a note of the inscription. Some of the monuments, though marking a burial that is attested by other medieval evidence, are themselves modern. And, finally, in medieval practice, tomb and effigy were sometimes in position in advance of the death that they were intended to commemorate, and the tomb was not always, in the event, the repository of the remains that it had been made to accommodate. It has seemed better, however, that such difficult cases should be noticed as they arise, than that categories should be multiplied.

Burials of monks of Westminster have been ignored, unless they took place elsewhere but in the monastic cemetery, north of the church. Abbots were buried, either in the cloister (their eleventh- and twelfth-century place of sepulture) or in the church, and in the late Middle Ages some other monks attained this privilege; one or two of those who did so were university graduates.

The list of *confratres*, the second item in this appendix, is also incomplete, and inevitably so, given the loss of the martyrology in which the names of *confratres* were written. Confraternity is best recorded at the end of the fifteenth century and early in the sixteenth, when some grants, though not all, were entered in the current lease-book of the Abbey. These grants show that the formal content of confraternity had not altered since the mid-thirteenth century, when the institution is described in the Abbey's *Customary*.[1]

The practice of endowing anniversaries and chantries with real property ensured that the Abbey's cartularies would provide a more or less complete record of these institutions. But the date of foundation of anniversary or chantry is often difficult to discover, since protracted negotiations, themselves punctuated by written deeds, might precede the final agreement. In most cases, the date given below as the date of foundation is that of the final ordination of the institution; at this relatively late stage in the negotiations, the exact scale of the endowment was known and the liturgical observations, the pittances, and the alms were prescribed accordingly. No attempt has been made to describe the first two of these three essential components of every anniversary, but the elemosinary provisions are briefly summarized.[2]

The forms of association with the monastery described in the final section of the appendix are heterogeneous. In the early Middle Ages, a grant of spiritual benefits, without further elaboration, need mean no more than the grant of a regular share in the intercessions of the monks. As some entries in the list show, in the thirteenth century such grants helped to settle legal disputes and clinch transactions in real property. Some of the other privileges mentioned in the grants recorded in this section were part and parcel of confraternity, as that institution is described in the time of Abbot Ware. Thus the privileges of the *confrater* of this period included the enrolment of his name in the Abbey's martyrology and the announcement of his decease in the next brief going out for a monk. Specific grants of privileges such as these, which are recorded from the end of the thirteenth century, might seem to indicate a narrowing of the scope of confraternity from this time onwards, but, as we have seen, this is not the case. The opposite is in fact true. The content of 'spiritual benefits' was becoming at once enlarged and more precisely defined, until, by the end of the fifteenth century, a grant in

---

[1] *Customary* ii. 232 ff.; and for references to the late-fifteenth- and the sixteenth-century grants, see below, pp. 386–7, nn. See also above, p. 39.

[2] One chantry to which reference survives has nevertheless been omitted from the list. B.L. Harleian Charter 45.c.50 appears to be a deed relating to the foundation of a chantry in the Abbey in 1397 by Sir William de Arundel, son of Sir John de Arundel; the endowment was to be the manor of Brandon (Warwicks.). There is, however, no evidence that the Abbey was ever seised of this manor, and Arundel's foundation probably never took effect. The charter is now exceedingly difficult, and in large part impossible, to read.

which these words were specifically used was in fact a grant of confraternity, as this institution had been understood at Westminster
since the early Middle Ages; accordingly, in the grants recorded in
the late fifteenth and early sixteenth centuries, 'spiritual benefits'
and 'confraternity' are interchangeable terms.

(i) *Burials*

Seventh Century

    † [Saebert, king of the East Saxons, d. 616/17][1]
    † [——, Ethelgoda, wife of, d. *c.* 615][2]

Eleventh Century

    *** Edward the Confessor, d. 1066[3]
    ** ——, Edith, wife of, d. 1075[4]
    * Edwin, abbot of Westminster, d. *c.* 1071[5]
    * Harold Harefoot, d. 1040[6]
    * Hugh, chamberlain of Edward the Confessor[7]
    ** Mandeville, Athelaise de[8]
    † [Sulcard][9]
    * Vitalis, abbot of Westminster, d. *c.* 1085[10]

[1] Richard of Cirencester records Saebert's burial and that of his wife near the high altar, and a translation, 700 years later, to a nobler site (*Speculum Historiale* i. 95). The tomb reputedly Saebert's was, by the sixteenth century, in the presbytery, on the south side. However, the tradition that Saebert and his wife were buried at Westminster is worthless.

[2] In the sixteenth-century tomb-lists, among those buried in the cloister or chapter-house; but see previous note.

[3] For the thirteenth-century shrine, of which the base remains, in its position behind the high altar, see *History of the King's Works*, ed. Colvin, i. 147–50. In the church built by the Confessor himself, his place of burial was before the altar (*Traditio* 20 (1964), 91).

[4] Edith's tomb in the Confessor's church was on the north side of the altar (*Customary* ii. 45). Sixteenth-century tomb-lists place her on the left of the shrine— left, to one facing west—i.e. they place her on the south side in Henry III's church. Camden, perhaps in ignorance of the west-facing stance of the compilers of the lists at this point, places her north of the shrine. See also *Joannis Abbatis Epistolae*, in Migne, *Patrologia Latina* cxlvii. 463.

[5] Buried in the cloister; translated to the chapter-house *temp.* Henry III (*Flete*, p. 83).

[6] According to the E version of the Anglo-Saxon Chronicle, s.a. 1039. Harold's body was later disinterred and reburied elsewhere (*Florentii Wigorniensis monachi Chronicon ex Chronicis*, ed. B. Thorpe (2 vols., English Historical Soc., London, 1848–9), i. 194.

[7] See above, n. 5.

[8] First wife of Geoffrey de Mandeville I, d. 1100, q.v.

[9] Monk of Westminster; for his account of the foundation of the Abbey, see above, pp. 20 ff. He is listed in *Camden*, among those buried in an unknown spot

[*see opposite for note 9 cont. and note 10*

Early Twelfth Century

*** Crispin, Gilbert, abbot of Westminster, d. 1117/18[1]

* Deorman, the three daughters of[2]

* Herbert, abbot of Westminster, d. *c.* 1136[3]

** Mandeville, Geoffrey de, I, d. 1100[4]

† [———, II, earl of Essex, d. 1144][5]

** Matilda, first wife of Henry I, d. 1118[6]

Late Twelfth Century

* Blois, Gervase de, formerly abbot of Westminster, d. 1160[7]

* Haverhill, Deonise[8]

† [———, William de][9]

*** Laurence, abbot of Westminster, d. 1173[10]

* Winchester, Walter of, abbot of Westminster, d. 1190[11]

there. He was presumably buried in the monks' cemetery and therefore has no proper place in this list.

[10] The burials of Vitalis, Gilbert Crispin, Herbert, Gervase de Blois, Laurence, Walter of Winchester, William Postard, and William de Humez in the south cloister are recorded in *Flete*, pp. 85 ff.; effigies of Gilbert Crispin, Laurence, and William de Humez are still *in situ* there, though much defaced.

[1] See previous note; and for the inscription on Crispin's tomb, *Flete*, p. 87.

[2] They obtained the right of burial and confraternity, 1107–15, with a gift of land in London (*Regesta* ii. 1123). For Deorman, see J. H. Round, *The Commune of London and Other Studies* (Westminster, 1899), p. 106. Theoderic, son of Deorman, was justiciar of London and Midd., 1143–52 (*History* 57 (1972), 354).

[3] See above, n. 10; and for the inscription, *Flete*, p. 91.

[4] Athelaise, the first wife of Geoffrey de Mandeville I, was buried in the cloister, and Geoffrey expressed a wish to be buried beside her (*Gilbert Crispin*, p. 139). Geoffrey's own burial in the Abbey, in an unknown spot, is recorded in *Camden*. Other tomb-lists confuse him with Geoffrey de Mandeville II, first earl of Essex, d. 1144, who is next in the above list. There is no evidence, other than de Mandeville's expressed wish, that he was in fact buried at Westminster. For the probable date of the death of Geoffrey de Mandeville I, see *Regesta* ii. 769 n.

[5] Included in sixteenth-century tomb-lists among burials in the chapter-house or cloister, but probably in error for Geoffrey de Mandeville I, d. 1100, q.v. However, in *Camden* both men appear.

[6] By the high altar, on the south side (*Customary*, ii. 45); see also below, p. 388 (no. 3). According to the early tomb-lists, Matilda's place in Henry III's church was on the right of the shrine, to one facing west—i.e. on the north side. Camden, however, places her on the south side.

[7] See above, n. 10; and for the inscription, *Flete*, p. 91.

[8] W.D., 367ᵛ. Deonise was the wife of Brictmar de Haverhill, who was twice sheriff of London and Midd.; for him, see *History* 57 (1972), 355, and below, p. 386.

[9] Son of Brictmar de Haverhill, for whom see previous note. William founded an anniversary in the Abbey and had confraternity there; see below, p. 386, and below, p. 388 (no. 6). His burial in the Abbey, in an unknown spot, is recorded in *Camden* but there is no earlier mention of this tradition.

[10] See above, n. 10; and for the inscription, *Flete*, p. 94.

[11] See above, n. 10; and for the inscription, *Flete*, p. 96.

Early Thirteenth Century

    * Arundel, Ralph de, formerly abbot of Westminster, d. 1223[1]
    * Berking, Richard de, abbot of Westminster, d. 1246[2]
    † [Halengrett, John, d. in or before 1246][3]
 *** Humez, William de, abbot of Westminster, d. 1222[4]
  ** Novo Castro, Fulk de, d. 1247[5]
    † [Oliver, natural son of King John, d. 1219][6]
    * Postard, William, abbot of Westminster, d. 1200[7]

Late Thirteenth Century

    * Almain, Henry, d. 1271[8]
    * Alphonso, son of Edward I, d. 1284[9]
    † [Aspale, Geoffrey de, d. 1287][10]
  †† Calhan, Peter, d. 1258[11]
    * Crokesley, Richard de, abbot of Westminster, d. 1258[12]

---

[1] In the nave (*Flete*, p. 100).

[2] In the Lady Chapel (*Flete*, p. 106).

[3] Alias John Alyngreth, whose burial in the Abbey, in an unknown spot, is recorded in *Camden*. For Halengrett, see below, p. 391 (no. 23).

[4] See above, p. 372, n. 10; and for the inscription, *Flete*, p. 102.

[5] A knight, and a cousin of Henry III; for his burial in the Abbey, see M. Paris, *Chronica Majora* iv. 604; *Rolls of Arms, Henry III*, ed. T. D. Tremlett and H. S. London (Harleian Soc., 1967, for 1961–2), pp. 30, 71, *s.n.* Châteauneuf.

[6] In *Camden*, among those buried in the church, in an unknown spot. For Oliver, who died at Damietta, see *D.N.B.* xiv. 1035.

[7] See above, p. 372, n. 10; and for the inscription, *Flete*, p. 98.

[8] Henry's body was buried at Hailes Abbey, but his heart in Westminster Abbey, by the shrine of the Confessor (*Flores Historiarum* iii. 22).

[9] Alphonso's body was buried in the Abbey, but his heart in the Dominican friary in London; for his burial in the Confessor's chapel, and the burials there of the other children of, respectively, Henry III and Edward I included in this list, see J. D. Tanner, 'Tombs of Royal Babies in Westminster Abbey', *Jnl. of the British Archaeological Assoc.*, 3rd ser., 16 (1953), 25 ff., and references given there. Eventually, the remains of a number of these children—according to sixteenth-century tomb-lists, nine—were placed in the mosaic tomb made by Edward I for his son, John, and now placed between the chapel of St. Edmund and St. Thomas the martyr and that of St. Benedict. It is not known which children, other than John, were so buried.

[10] In *Camden*, among those buried in the Abbey, in an unknown spot. Aspale was the founder of a chantry in the Abbey, and this very fact makes the lack of an earlier tradition of burial there seem conclusive; see below, p. 393 (no. 36); and for the date of Aspale's death, see *Cal. Inq. post mortem* ii. 635.

[11] In the chapel of St. Paul. This burial is mentioned only in W.A.M. 53318 and in *Camden*; Calhan is described in the former as a citizen of London, and the precise date, 26 May 1258, is given.

[12] In the chapel of St. Edmund, built by Crokesley himself, at the north door (*Flete*, pp. 109–10).

*** Edmund, earl of Lancaster, d. 1296[1]
*** ——, Aveline, first wife of, d. 1274[2]
*** Eleanor of Castile, wife of Edward I, d. 1290[3]
†† Eleanor, countess of Bar, daughter of Edward I, d. 1298[4]
*** Henry III, d. 1272[5]
* ——, Henry, son of, d. 1260[6]
* —— John, son of, d. 1252[6]
* —— Katherine, daughter of, d. 1257[7]
* —— Richard, son of, d. 1250[8]
* Henry, son of Edward I, d. 1274[9]
*** John, son of Edward I, d. 1271[10]
*** Valence, William de, d. 1296[11]
*** ——, John, son of, d. 1277[12]
*** ——, Margaret, daughter of, d. 1276[13]
* Ware, Richard de, abbot of Westminster, d. 1283[14]
* Wendene, Richard de, d. 1250[15]
* Wroxhille, Hamo de[16]

Early Fourteenth Century
* Beauflour, Joan, d. 1326–7[17]

---

[1] Edmund and Aveline, his first wife, who is next in the above list, were buried in the presbytery, on the north side.   [2] See previous note.

[3] In the Confessor's chapel. For her tomb, see *History of the King's Works*, ed. Colvin, i. 481–2.

[4] According to sixteenth-century tomb-lists, in the cloister or chapter-house—an unlikely location. See also *Jnl. of the British Archaeological Assoc.*, 3rd ser., 16 (1953), 31.

[5] Before the high altar; later, in the Confessor's chapel (*History of the King's Works*, ed. Colvin, i. 479). Later still, in 1292, Henry's heart was reinterred at Fontevrault.   [6] See above, p. 374, n. 9.

[7] See *History of the King's Works*, ed. Colvin, i. 478–9; see also above, p. 374, n. 9.

[8] See above, p. 374, n. 9.

[9] See ibid. Henry's heart was buried in the Dominican friary at Guildford.

[10] *Jnl. of the British Archaeological Assoc.*, 3rd ser., 16 (1953), 28–9; and see above, p. 374, n. 9. The tomb reputedly John's is without an inscription.

[11] In the chapel of St. Edmund and St. Thomas the martyr.

[12] John and his sister, who is next in the above list, were buried in the Confessor's chapel (*Jnl. of the British Archaeological Assoc.*, 3rd ser., 16 (1953), 31). Two grave slabs and fragmentary inscriptions survive.

[13] See previous note.

[14] In the presbytery, on the north side (*Flete*, p. 115).

[15] *Flores Historiarum* ii. 369. Wendene was bishop of Rochester. He is the holy but unnamed bishop of Rochester listed in *Camden*, among those buried in the Abbey in an unknown spot.

[16] The burial is noted in W.D., 482ᵛ, where Wroxhille is described as a clerk; see also below, p. 392 (no. 29).

[17] Widow of Thomas Beauflour; for her request for burial in the Abbey see below, p. 394 (no. 42). Camden's belief that a Thomas Bounflower and his wife

    * Bircheston, Simon de, abbot of Westminster, d. 1349[1]
 *** Blanche, daughter of Edward III, d. 1342[2]
 *** Bohun, Humphrey de, d. 1304[3]
 *** ———, Mary de, d. 1305[4]
    † [Brabazun, Roger le, d. 1317][5]
    * Bykenore, Sir Thomas de, d. 1316[6]
    * Curtlington, William de, abbot of Westminster, d. 1333[7]
 *** Edward I, d. 1307[8]
 *** Eltham, John of, earl of Cornwall, d. 1336[9]
    * Henle, Thomas de, abbot of Westminster, d. 1344[10]
    * Kedyngton, Richard de, abbot of Westminster, d. 1315[11]
    † [Romayne, Thomas, d. 1313][12]
   †† Rous, Richard le[13]

were buried in the Abbey no doubt derived from this burial and the foundation of a chantry in the Abbey for Joan and Thomas. However, the wife's name, according to Camden, was Philippa.

[1] In the east cloister (*Flete*, pp. 129–30).

[2] Blanche of the Tower. She and her brother, William of Windsor, d. 1348, q.v., were probably buried in the Confessor's chapel; later, their tomb, for which see *Jnl. of the British Archaeological Assoc.*, 3rd ser., 16 (1953), 34, was moved to the chapel of St. Edmund and St. Thomas the martyr. See also *History of the King's Works*, ed. Colvin, i. 486 and n.

[3] Humphrey and Mary de Bohun, who is next in the above list, were children of Humphrey de Bohun, earl of Hereford and Essex. For their tomb, originally in the chapel of St. Nicholas, but subsequently in the chapel of St. John the Baptist, see C. Peers and L. E. Tanner, 'On Some Recent Discoveries in Westminster Abbey', *Archaeologia* 2nd. ser., 43 (1949), 151–5.

[4] See previous note.

[5] Listed, as Roger Braharsen, in *Camden*, among those buried in the Abbey, in an unknown spot. Brabazun was in fact buried in St. Paul's Cathedral (*Chronicles of the Reigns of Edward I and Edward II*, ed. W. Stubbs (2 vols., Rolls Ser., 1882–3), i. 280). See also below, p. 394 (no. 40 and n.).

[6] Died in the Palace of Westminster; buried in the Abbey (Liber Niger Quaternus, 139). For Bykenore, see *Knights of Edward I* i. 94.

[7] Before the altar of St. Benedict (*Flete*, p. 123).

[8] In the Confessor's chapel. For his tomb, see *History of the King's Works*, ed. Colvin, i. 486.

[9] In the chapel of St. Edmund and St. Thomas the martyr.

[10] In the presbytery, before the high altar, on the north side (*Flete*, p. 126). The expenses of Henle's funeral amounted to £26. 3s. 3¼d., and his tomb cost an additional £8. 16s. 10d. (W.A.M. 5467A).

[11] In the presbytery, before the high altar, on the south side (*Flete*, p. 122).

[12] A pepperer of London, for whom see *Walter de Wenlok*, p. 246 and n. Camden's belief that Romayne was buried in the Abbey may have derived from the fact that he bequeathed a substantial legacy (£66. 13s. 4d.) to the abbot and convent of Westminster; the Abbey, however, was not the only church that he so benefited. See *Cal. of Wills proved and enrolled in the Court of Husting, London*, ed. Sharpe, i. 238.

[13] A burial located by sixteenth-century tomb-lists in the cloister or chapter-house and included by Camden among those that he cannot locate. Burial in

† [Shorditch, Sir John de, d. 1345][1]
† [——, Elena, his wife][2]
†† Trussell, Sir William, d. *c.* 1346–7[3]
*** Valence, Aymer de, earl of Pembroke, d. 1324[4]
  * Wenlok, Walter de, d. 1307[5]
*** Windsor, William of, son of Edward III, d. 1348[6]
  * Woodstock, Edmund of, earl of Kent, d. 1330[7]

Late Fourteenth Century

*** Anne of Bohemia, first wife of Richard II, d. 1394[8]
 ** Berners, Sir James, d. 1388[9]
 ** Beverley, John de, d. 1380[10]

the Abbey may have been one of the inducements that persuaded Richard le Rous to surrender his interest in the manor of Hendon to the monks, as he did between 1312 and 1315 (below, p. 416, no. 11).

[1] Camden's belief that Shorditch and his wife were buried in the Abbey probably derived from the fact that they founded a chantry and had spiritual benefits there (below, p. 395, no. 44). But these very facts make the lack of an earlier tradition of burial in the Abbey seem conclusive.

[2] See previous note.

[3] In the east aisle of the north transept, later the chapel of St. Michael. Trussell was parliamentary spokesman at the deposition of Edward II; for his career, see *D.N.B.* xix. 1197–8. The date of his death is indicated by the sacrist's receipt of a legacy from him in 1346–7; the exact sum is not given, but this legacy and one other amounted to £13. 6s. 8d. (W.A.M. 19622).

[4] In the presbytery, on the north side.

[5] In the presbytery, on the south side of the high altar (*Flete*, p. 119). The expenditure on Wenlok's burial and tomb—the items are conflated in the account— amounted to £70. 13s. 7¼d. (*Walter de Wenlok*, p. 214).

[6] See under Blanche, daughter of Edward III, d. 1342.

[7] In his will, Edmund of Woodstock left the choice of his place of sepulture to his widow. He was buried, first, in the church of the friars minor at Winchester, but reinterred, in 1331, in the Abbey; the site of the burial in the Abbey is not known. See *Cal. Papal Letters*, ii. 349; *G.E.C.* vii. 147 and n.

[8] In the Confessor's chapel. For the tomb, see *History of the King's Works*, ed. Colvin, i. 487–8.

[9] Berners and Sir John Salisbury, d. 1388, q.v., were included in sixteenth-century tomb-lists among those buried in the cloister or chapter-house. In fact these knights of Richard II's chamber, condemned in the Merciless Parliament and subsequently executed, were buried in the chapel of St. John the Baptist (*Polychronicon Ranulphi Higden monachi Cestrensis*, ed. C. Babington and J. R. Lumby (9 vols., Rolls Ser., 1865–86), ix. 178).

[10] In the south ambulatory. Beverley was one of Edward III's squires; for his will, in which he requested burial near the tomb of Edward III and left £5 to the monks of Westminster, see A. H. Cooke, *The Early History of Mapledurham* (Oxfordshire Record Soc. vii), p. 34.

    * [Blokkele, John de][1]
*** Brocas, Sir Bernard, d. 1395[2]
*** Edward III, d. 1377[3]
    * Elmham, Robert de, d. 1364–5[4]
*** Golafre, Sir John de, d. 1396[5]
  ** Hawley, Robert, d. 1378[6]
    * Hemenhale, Sir Robert de, d. 1391[7]
    * Holland, Maud, countess of Ligny and St. Pol, d. 1392[8]
*** Langham, Simon de, formerly abbot of Westminster, d. 1376[9]
    * ——, Thomas, father of,[10]
    * Leycestre, Walter[11]

[1] In 1382, Blokkele was granted the right of burial in the Abbey, should he die in or near London (below, p. 397, no. 53). It is not known where or when he died.

[2] In the chapel of St. Edmund and St. Thomas the martyr. Brocas was chamberlain to Anne of Bohemia (*D.N.B.* ii. 1273). The sacrist received £16 for the hearse and candles used at his funeral (W.A.M. 19655).

[3] In the Confessor's chapel. For his tomb, see *History of the King's Works*, ed. Colvin, i. 487.

[4] A king's clerk (*Cal. Pat. R., 1361–4*, p. 107). The sacrist's account for 1364–5 records the receipt of 2s. 6½d. on the day of his funeral (W.A.M. 19630).

[5] In the south ambulatory. Golafre was a knight of the king's chamber (*Cal. Pat. R., 1391–6*, pp. 536, 658, etc.).

[6] In the south transept, near the door of the chapel of St. Benedict; the indent is still visible, but the inscription is modern. For a drawing of the brass see Bodleian Library, Oxford, MS. Wood D 4, fo. 126ᵃ, and for the original inscription, *Camden*. For Hawley's murder before the high altar, and his burial in the Abbey, see *Anonimalle Chronicle, 1333 to 1381*, ed. V. H. Galbraith (Manchester, 1927), pp. 121–2; and for the circumstances and aftermath, in so far as these concerned the ransom of the count of Denia, A. Rogers, 'Hoton versus Shakell: a Ransom Case in the Court of Chivalry, 1390–5', *Nottingham Mediaeval Studies* 6 (1962), 74–108; and ibid. 7 (1963), 53–78. See also below, under Shakell, John, d. 1396.

[7] First of the five husbands of Joan de la Pole, baroness Cobham. According to Holinshed, Sir John Harpeden, the fifth husband, d. 1437, q.v., was buried beside Hemenhale. The tradition, if correct, establishes Hemenhale's place of burial as the chapel of St. John the Evangelist in Westminster Abbey. See *G.E.C.* iii. 345; and *Holinshed's Chronicles of England, Scotland and Ireland* (6 vols., London, 1807–8), iv. 788–90.

[8] Wife of Waleran de Luxemburg, count of Ligny and St. Pol, and a half-sister of Richard II (*G.E.C.* iv. 325). She is styled 'the countess of St. Paul's' in the sacrist's account. On the occasion of her funeral, on 23 April—an event attended by the king—the sacrist spent 14s. 8d. on meat and 15s. 5d. on wine; subsequently, he received £1. 13s. 4d. for the black cloth used for the hearse (W.A.M. 19650). See also *Polychronicon Ranulphi Higden* ix. 265.

[9] Langham died at Avignon and was first buried in the Charterhouse there; he was later reinterred in the Abbey, by the altar of St. Benedict (*Flete*, p. 132).

[10] In the nave (ibid.).

[11] A royal serjeant at arms. In his will, made in 1389, Leycestre asked for burial in the church of St. Margaret's, Westminster; but in a codicil made in 1391, he asked that he should be buried in the Abbey, north of the Holy Cross altar (in the

 * Litlington, Nicholas de, abbot of Westminster, d. 1386[1]
 * Lucas, Robert, d. 1382[2]
 * 'Palacio', William de[3]
 * Palmer, James[4]
*** Philippa of Hainault, wife of Edward III, d. 1369[5]
 ** Salisbury, Sir John, d. 1388[6]
 * [Shakell, John, d. 1396][7]
 * Shirforde, William[8]
 * ——, Alice, wife of[9]
*** Waldby, Robert de, d. 1397[10]

nave). He left £2 to the fabric and £1 for pittances for the monks. See W.A.M. 23462, 25355, and Liber Niger Quaternus, 87ᵛ.

 [1] In the south transept, before the altar of St. Blaise (*Flete*, p. 137).

 [2] A citizen and goldsmith of London. In his will, Lucas asked for burial in Westminster Abbey and left £40 to the abbot and convent (Guildhall Library, London, Commissary Court of London (London Division), Register 1, fos. 93ᵛ–94; see also *Cal. of Wills proved and enrolled in the Court of Husting, London*, ed. Sharpe, ii. 230–1).

 [3] Said in Liber Niger Quaternus, 80ᵛ to be keeper of the Palace of Westminster and described as 'vir bonus et simplex et semper ecclesie Westm' multum amabilis'. He requested burial in the Abbey, by the holy water stoup, next to the cloister door, on condition that a *socius*, named John, should be buried beside him and that the said John should make a gift to the monks for these concessions. William, it is noted, was buried in the above spot, but, once this was done, John 'non est visus' (ibid.). William was, almost certainly, William de Sleford, dean of St. Stephen's chapel in the Palace of Westminster, d. 1396. Sleford acquired a share, with five others, in the keepership of the Palace, in 1380 (*Cal. Pat. R., 1377–81*, p. 524; ibid., *1391–6*, p. 685).

 [4] A king's clerk. Palmer was buried at the altar of St. Andrew. He was the donor of the enclosure making this altar into a chapel; he furnished the altar and gave the monks a picture of St. Andrew. See Liber Niger Quaternus, 92ᵛ. In *Camden*, both Palmer and Joan, his sister, are included among those buried in the Abbey, in an unknown spot.

 [5] In the Confessor's chapel. For the tomb, see *History of the King's Works*, ed. Colvin, i. 486–7.

 [6] See above, under Berners, Sir James, d. 1388.

 [7] Joint claimant, with Robert Hawley, d. 1378, q.v., to the ransom of the count of Denia; Shakell, moreover, narrowly escaped death with Hawley. In his will, he requested burial in the Abbey, next to Hawley and left £6. 13s. 4d. to the monks for pittances on the day of his burial, and £100 to the new work, conditionally upon recovery of the ransom (Guildhall Library, London, Commissary Court of London (London Division), Register 1, fos. 390–390ᵛ). (I am indebted to Mr. N. H. MacMichael for this reference.) However, there is no reference to Shakell's burial in the sacrist's rolls for 1395–6 and 1396–7 (W.A.M. 19655–6).

 [8] In 1363, Shirforde and his wife were granted the right of burial in the Abbey, where they also founded an anniversary; see below, p. 396 (no. 49).

 [9] See previous note.

 [10] In the chapel of St. Edmund and St. Thomas the martyr. For Waldby, who was archbishop of York at his death, see Emden, *Biographical Register of the University of Oxford to A.D. 1500* iii. 1958.

*** Waltham, John de, d. 1395[1]
*** Woodstock, Thomas of, duke of Gloucester, d. 1397[2]
*** ——, Eleanor, wife of, d. 1399[3]

Early Fifteenth Century

*** Amundesham, William, d. 1420[4]
** Buxhill, Amice, d. 1416[5]
* Ca'brige, ——, wife of John de, d. 1448–9[6]
* Chaucer, Geoffrey, d. 1400[7]
* [Chesterfield, Richard de, d. *c.* 1405][8]
† [Cockayne, Joan][9]

[1] In the Confessor's chapel. For Waltham, bishop of Salisbury and treasurer of England, see *D.N.B.* xx. 720–2. The sacrist received £40 for the hearse and candles used at the funeral (W.A.M. 19655); see also below, p. 397 (no. 57).

[2] In the chapel of St. Edmund and St. Thomas the martyr; but the remains were moved, *temp.* Henry IV, to the Confessor's chapel (Westlake, *Westminster Abbey*, ii. 305). The sacrist spent 10*s.* 8*d.* on hospitality for the duchess of Gloucester, when she visited the church after her husband's death, 9*s.* on the occasion of a later visit, and 18*s.* 10*d.* at the reception of the duke's body (W.A.M. 19657).

[3] In the chapel of St. Edmund and St. Thomas the martyr. The hearse and black cloth used on this occasion had been used in 1397 at the burial of Eleanor's husband; subsequently, the sacrist received £2 for them (W.A.M. 19658). For her will, requesting burial in the Abbey, see N. H. Nicolas, *Testamenta Vetusta* (2 vols., London, 1826), i. 146–9.

[4] In the north ambulatory; so *Camden*. The monument is no longer identifiable. The words 'receptor nostri canonici', in Camden's notice, should, no doubt, read 'inceptor juris canonici'. For Amundesham, who was a monk of Westminster, see *Monks*, p. 122, and Emden, *Biographical Register of the University of Oxford to A.D. 1500* i. 31–2.

[5] Formerly wife of John de Beverley, d. 1380, q.v., beside whom she was buried, in the south ambulatory. Amice was the daughter of Alan Buxhill, constable of the Tower and one of the slayers of Robert Hawley, d. 1378, q.v. She married, secondly, Sir Robert Bardolf. In her will, she left £3. 6*s.* 8*d.* to the monks of Westminster, and a further sum of £6. 13*s.* 4*d.* to find a priest who should celebrate masses for her, her benefactors, and all faithful departed, for the year following her death (*Some Oxfordshire Wills proved in the Prerogative Court of Canterbury, 1393–1510*, ed. J. R. H. Weaver and A. Beardwood (Oxfordshire Record Soc. xxxix), p. 8).

[6] The burial is noted in the sacrist's roll (W.A.M. 19698). A tenant named John de Caubrege held land in Eye of the warden of the new work (W.A.M. 23510 ff.).

[7] In the south transept, before the chapel of St. Benedict; see W. R. Lethaby, *Westminster Abbey and the Kings' Craftsmen. A Study of Mediaeval Building* (London, 1906), p. 344. Chaucer was the tenant of a house in the precincts of the Abbey (W.A.M. Charter LVII).

[8] A king's clerk, for whom see Emden, *Biographical Register of the University of Oxford to A.D. 1500* i. 408–9. In 1366, Chesterfield was granted the right of burial in the Abbey, before the Holy Trinity altar, should he die in or near London (below, p. 396, no. 50). It is not known where he died.

[9] According to sixteenth-century tomb-lists, at the north door. She was the wife of Sir John Cockayne and daughter of Sir John Dabridgecourt. Her burial has also been claimed for Ashbourne church, in Derbyshire; see A. E. Cockayne,

*** Colchester, William, abbot of Westminster, d. 1420[1]
 * Courtenay, Richard, d. 1415[2]
 * Girdeler, John, d. 1402[3]
*** Harpeden, Sir John, d. 1437[4]
*** Harwden, Richard, formerly abbot of Westminster, d. 1441[5]
*** Henry V, d. 1422[6]
 ** ——, Katherine, wife of, d. 1437[7]
 * [Lewis III, count palatine, d. 1436][8]
*** Mohun, Philippa, duchess of York, d. 1431[9]

Cockayne Memoranda (Congleton, 1873), pp. 195–6; cited in Stow, *Survey of London*, ed. Kingsford, ii. 376–7. Her husband died in 1447.

[1] In the chapel of St. John the Baptist.

[2] Died at Harfleur; buried in the Confessor's chapel; see *Gesta Henrici Quinti*, trans. and ed. F. Taylor and J. S. Roskell (Oxford, 1975), p. 45; John Leland, *De Rebus Britannicis Collectanea*, ed. T. Hearne (2nd edn., 6 vols., London, 1774), ii. 353; H. Wharton, *Anglia Sacra* (2 vols., London, 1691), i. 416; L. E. Tanner, *Recollections of a Westminster Antiquary* (London, 1969), pp. 179–81. For Courtenay, who was bishop of Norwich and a servant of Henry IV and Henry V, see *D.N.B.* iv. 1265–7; and Emden, *Biographical Register of the University of Oxford to A.D. 1500* i. 500–2.

[3] In his will, Girdeler requested burial in the Abbey, in a place to be chosen by the abbot, and left £6. 13s. 4d. to the monks, and £2 to buy six candles for the high altar 'in the worship of God'. He was of Harefield (Midd.). See *The Fifty Earliest English Wills*, ed. F. J. Furnivall (Early English Text Soc. lxxviii), pp. 10–11.

[4] According to the tomb-lists, in the chapel of St. John the Evangelist; subsequently, Harpeden's tomb was moved to the north ambulatory. For the date of his death see P.R.O., C.139/86/28; *Cal. Fine R.*, *1437–45*, pp. 2, 3, 51. (For these references and for that dating the death of Lewis Robsart, lord Bourchier, q.v., to 1430, I am indebted to Mr. N. H. MacMichael, who has thus generously made available to me material collected for a forthcoming paper on the deaths of these two men.)

[5] In the ambulatory, by the south door of the Lady Chapel. The monument is now defaced, but B.L. Egerton MS. 2642, fo. 323, and W.A.M. 53318 locate Harwden's burial here.

[6] In the Confessor's chapel; for the sacrist's perquisites on the occasion, see Westlake, *Westminster Abbey* ii. 307. For the making of Henry's chantry, subsequently, over the ambulatory, see *History of the King's Works*, ed. Colvin, i. 488–9.

[7] Katherine of Valois. She was buried in the Lady Chapel; for the subsequent removal of the coffin, which, after several vicissitudes, was placed in Henry V's chantry, see Westlake, *Westminster Abbey* ii. 361.

[8] See the sacrist's roll for 1436–7, which includes the following entry: *Et pro hercia in eadem ecclesia in exequiis domini ducis Bavar', c. marcas, nil adhuc quia nondum receptas* (W.A.M. 19678). For Lewis III, who used the style 'count palatine and duke of Bavaria', see H. J. Cohn, *The Government of the Rhine Palatinate in the Fifteenth Century* (Oxford, 1965), pp. 26–7, and J. Ferguson, *English Diplomacy, 1422–1461* (Oxford, 1972), pp. 70–3. He married Blanche, daughter of Henry IV, d. 1409. (I owe this identification to Mrs. J. G. Russell.)

[9] In the chapel of St. Nicholas. For her will, see Nicolas, *Testamenta Vetusta* i. 218.

†† Peverell, Thomas, d. 1419–20[1]
*** Richard II, d. 1400[2]
*** Robsart, Lewis, Lord Bourchier, d. 1430[3]
*** ——, Elizabeth, wife of, d. 1433[4]
 * Russell, John, d. 1445–6[5]
*** Selby, Ralph, d. 1420[6]
*** Windsor, Sir John, d. 1414[7]

Late Fifteenth Century

 ** Anne, wife of Richard III, d. 1485[8]
 * Bonefaunt, Thomas de, d. 1470[9]
 ** Bourchier, Humphrey, lord Cromwell, d. 1471[10]
*** ——, —— son of John Bourchier, lord Berners, d. 1471[11]
 † [Bridgewater, Edward, d. 1471–2][12]

[1] At the entrance to the chapel of St. Edmund and St. Thomas the martyr (B.L. Egerton MS. 2642, fo. 323ᵛ). For Peverell, who was a monk of Westminster, see *Monks*, pp. 111–12.

[2] Buried, first, at Langley, but reinterred in the Abbey, in the Confessor's chapel, in 1413 (Thomas of Walsingham, *Ypodigma Neustriae*, ed. H. T. Riley (Rolls Ser., 1876), p. 446). For the tomb, see *History of the King's Works*, ed. Colvin, i. 487–8.

[3] The sacrist received £10 for hearse and candles (W.A.M. 19671). Robsart and his wife were buried in the chapel of St. Paul. For the date of Robsart's death, see *John Benet's Chronicle for the years 1400 to 1462*, ed. G. L. Harriss and M. A. Harriss, *Camden Miscellany* xxiv (Camden, 4th ser. ix), 183 and n.

[4] See previous note.

[5] In 1445–6, the sacrist received 13s. 4d. from one Richard Walth' for permission (*licencia*) to bury Mr. John Russell in the church (W.A.M. 19695).

[6] In the south ambulatory. The indent of the tomb-slab is now worn away, but see L. E. Tanner and N. H. MacMichael, 'An Indent in Westminster Abbey', *Trans. Monumental Brass Soc.* 10. 2 (Dec. 1964), 95–6. For Selby, who was a monk of Westminster, see *Monks*, pp. 128–9, and A. B. Emden, *Biographical Register of the University of Cambridge to 1500* (Cambridge, 1963), p. 517.

[7] In the north ambulatory.

[8] According to the tomb-lists, 'under the presbytery', on the south side; the burial is now commemorated by a modern brass in the south ambulatory. The sacrist received £42. 12s. on the occasion of this burial, of which sum, £9. 5s. 4d. was received in offerings at the mass (W.A.M. 19730).

[9] For whom see Emden, *Biographical Register of the University of Oxford to A.D. 1500* i. 217–18. In his will, Bonefaunt asked for burial in the Abbey. The sacrist received 5s. for candles on the occasion of his obsequies (W.A.M. 19717).

[10] In the chapel of St. Edmund and St. Thomas the martyr. The sacrist received £6 on the occasion of his obsequies and those of his namesake, Humphrey, son of John Bourchier, who is next in the above list and who, in common with the lord Cromwell, was killed at Barnet (W.A.M. 19717).

[11] In the chapel of St. Edmund and St. Thomas the martyr; and see previous note.

[12] A doubtful case. For Bridgewater, who was a monk of Westminster, see *Monks*, p. 161; he may be identical with the Edward Tudor, whose burial in the chapel of St. Blaise is recorded in *Camden*.

*** Carew, Nicholas, d. 1470[1]
  ** ——, Margaret, wife of, d. 1470[2]
*** Dudley, William, d. 1483[3]
  ** Edmund, son of Henry VII, d. 1499[4]
*** Elizabeth, daughter of Henry VII, d. 1495[5]
*** Estney, John, abbot of Westminster, d. 1498[6]
  ** Hatclyff, William, d. 1480[7]
  †† Hungerford, Sir Thomas, d. *c.* 1494[8]
  †† ——, Sir Walter, d. 1464[9]
*** Kyrton, Edmund, formerly abbot of Westminster, d. 1466[10]
*** Margaret, daughter of Edward IV, d. 1472[11]
  †† Milling, Thomas, formerly abbot of Westminster, d. 1492[12]
  †† Mowbray, Anne, wife of Richard, duke of York, d. 1481[13]

[1] In the chapel of St. Nicholas. The tomb is now defaced, but the site of the burial is recorded in the tomb-lists. For Carew, see *Cal. Pat. R.*, *1467–77*, p. 189. The sacrist received £2 on the occasion of the burial of Carew and his wife; the sum included a payment for candles (W.A.M. 19717). However, no tomb-list earlier than Camden's mentions Carew's wife.

[2] See previous note. Margaret, who died within a week of her husband, was the daughter of John, lord Dinham; the inscription on the tomb, recording these facts, is in *Camden*.

[3] In the chapel of St. Nicholas. For Dudley, who was bishop of Durham, see Emden, *Biographical Register of the University of Oxford to A.D. 1500* i. 599–600.

[4] Edmund and his sister, who is next in the above list, were buried in the Confessor's chapel. His burial there is recorded in W.A.M. 53318; hers, in B.L. Add. MS. 38133, fo. 98ᵛ in ibid., Harleian MS. 544, fo. 65, in College of Arms, MS. F 9, fo. 1, in ibid. A 17, fo. 1, and in All Souls College, Oxford, MS. 126, beside. See also *Jnl. of the British Archaeological Assoc.*, 3rd ser., 16 (1953) 36–7.

[5] See previous note.

[6] In the chapel of St. John the Evangelist (B.L. Egerton MS. 2642, fo. 322ᵛ; W.A.M. 53318). Estney's monument was subsequently moved and is now in the north ambulatory.

[7] In the Lady Chapel. For Hatclyff, who was secretary and counsellor to Edward IV, see Emden, *Biographical Register of the University of Cambridge to 1500*, p. 292.

[8] In the chapel of St. Erasmus. Hungerford is identified in B.L. Harleian MS. 544, fo. 65ᵛ, as the father of Sir John Hungerford, of Down Ampney (Glos.). See also *Cal. Pat. R.*, *1494–1509*, p. 6.

[9] Outside the chapel of St. Nicholas. Walter, son of Edmund Hungerford, married Margaret, lady Clinton, widow of John, lord Clinton, and daughter of John St. Leger (*G.E.C.* iii. 316).

[10] In the chapel of St. Andrew.

[11] In the Confessor's chapel; see *Jnl. of the British Archaeological Assoc.*, 3rd ser. 16 (1953), 35–6.

[12] In the chapel of St. John the Baptist. A tomb which is possibly that of Milling is now in the north ambulatory.

[13] In the chapel of St. Erasmus. On the destruction of this chapel, the remains were taken to the London house of the Minoresses; they were later placed in Henry VII's chapel in the Abbey.

* Neville, Thomas, d. 1471[1]
* Southcot, John, d. 1453–4[2]
†† Stonor, Sir William, d. 1494[3]
** Vaughan, Sir Thomas, d. 1483[4]
†† Welles, John, viscount Welles, d. 1499[5]

Early Sixteenth Century

*** Beaufort, Margaret, countess of Richmond, d. 1509[6]
†† Bedel, William, d. 1518[7]
†† ——, Cecily, wife of[8]
*** Brown, Thomas, d. 1513–14[9]
*** Daubeney, Giles, baron Daubeney, d. 1508[10]
*** ——, Elizabeth, wife of, d. 1500[11]
*** Elizabeth, wife of Henry VII, d. 1503[12]
*** Fascet, George, abbot of Westminster, d. 1500[13]
*** Henry VII, d. 1509[14]
** Henry, son of Henry VIII, d. 1511[15]

[1] The so-called Bastard of Fauconberg, a natural son of William Neville, lord Fauconberg. For his death, see *Chronicles of London*, ed. C. L. Kingsford (Oxford, 1905), p. 185. His burial at Westminster is recorded in the sacrist's roll for 1471–2 (W.A.M. 19718).

[2] A squire. The sacrist received £1 for his burial in the Abbey (W.A.M. 19704).

[3] In the Lady Chapel. For Stonor's career and marriages, the third to Anne Neville, daughter of John, marquis of Montagu, see *Stonor Letters and Papers, 1290–1483*, ed. C. L. Kingsford (2 vols., Camden, 3rd ser., xxix–xxx, 1919), i. xxvi ff.

[4] In the chapel of St. John the Baptist. Vaughan was treasurer of the chamber to Edward IV (*The Household of Edward IV. The Black Book and the Ordinance of 1478*, ed. A. R. Myers (Manchester, 1959), p. 291).

[5] In the Lady Chapel. John Welles was the husband of Cecily, daughter of Edward IV, d. 1507.

[6] In the chapel which became known as the Lady Margaret Chapel, in the south aisle of the Lady Chapel. The sacrist received £20 on the occasion of the burial (W.A.M. 19765); see also below, p. 399 (nos. 62–3). For the tomb see R. F. Scott, in *Archaeologia*, 2nd ser., 16 (1914–15), 365–76.

[7] Bedel, who was treasurer to Thomas Wolsey, and his wife were buried in the south transept (*Camden*).

[8] See previous note.

[9] In the north ambulatory. For Brown, who was a monk of Westminster, see *Monks*, pp. 171–2.

[10] Daubeney and his wife were buried in the chapel of St. Paul. He was one-time lieutenant of Calais (*D.N.B.*, v. 540–2); see also below, p. 399 (no. 64).

[11] See previous note.

[12] The original site of burial is unknown; subsequently, the body was moved to the Lady Chapel (Westlake, *Westminster Abbey* ii. 361).

[13] In the chapel of St. John the Baptist.

[14] In the Lady Chapel. The sacrist received £158. 18s. on the occasion (W.A.M. 19765).

[15] At the door of the Confessor's chapel, on the north side (W.A.M. Mostyn Hall MS., fo. 37). The tomb-list in All Souls College, Oxford, MS. 126, which was

*** Humphrey, Robert, d. 1509[1]
*** Islip, John, abbot of Westminster, d. 1532[2]
* Kendale, ――, wife of John Kendale, d. 1501–2[3]
*** Ruthall, Thomas, d. 1523[4]
*** Stanley, Sir Humphrey, d. 1505[5]
† [――, Sir John, d. *c.* 1528][6]
* Turcas, J., d. 1501–2[7]
†† Vaughan, Sir Hugh, d. 1500[8]
†† ――, Anne, wife of, d. 1522[9]

Uncertain Period[10]

†† Aylmer, Katherine[11]
†† Browne, Robert, esq.

evidently put together before the discovery of the exact site, in 1645, locates the burial on the south side of the chapel. See also *Jnl. of the British Archaeological Assoc.*, 3rd ser., 16 (1953), 37.

[1] In the north ambulatory. For Humphrey, who was a monk of Westminster, see *Monks*, p. 172. Camden misread his name as 'Humphrey Roberts'.

[2] In the Jesus chapel, which was built by Islip and became known as the Islip chantry.

[3] The sacrist received 6*s.* 8*d.* from John Kendale (about whom nothing else is known) for this burial (W.A.M. 19757).

[4] In the chapel of St. John the Baptist. For Ruthall, who was bishop of Durham, see *D.N.B.* xvii. 492–3.　　　　　　　　　　[5] In the chapel of St. Nicholas.

[6] In the chapel of St. John the Baptist (B.L. Egerton MS., 2642, fo. 322ᵛ; the compiler of this list, however, did not know Stanley's first name). For Stanley, who was probably a monk of Westminster at his death, see below, p. 387, n.; that he was buried in a special place in the Abbey is, however, in doubt. The date of his decease is uncertain; for the suggestion that it was soon after the dissolution of his marriage, in June 1528, as a preliminary to his entering religion, see G. Ormerod, *The History of the County Palatine and City of Chester*, 2nd edn., rev. T. Helsby (3 vols., London, 1882), iii. 641.

[7] The sacrist received 6*s.* 8*d.* from one John Petwyn for this burial (W.A.M. 19757).

[8] Vaughan and his wife were buried in St. Michael's chapel.

[9] See previous note. Anne was the daughter of Henry Percy, 3rd earl of Northumberland; she married: (i) Sir Thomas Hungerford, of Rowden, in Chippenham, d. 1469; (ii) Sir Laurence Raynesford, d. 1490; and (iii) Sir Hugh Vaughan (*G.E.C.* ix. 717 n.; ibid. vi. 621–2; *Cal. Cl. R., Henry VII* i. 731).

[10] Most probably, all these burials took place in the late fifteenth or early sixteenth century. All except those of Katherine Aylmer and Ralph the chaplain are located by the tomb-lists which mention them at the (north) door of the church (B.L. Harleian MS. 544, fos. 65ᵛ, 67; ibid. Add. MS. 38133, fos. 99ᵛ–100; College of Arms MS. A 17, fo. 2ᵛ; and ibid. F. 9, fos. 2–2ᵛ).

[11] In the Lady Chapel. Katherine is described as the wife of Edward Aylmer and daughter of the duchess of Norfolk. This is likely to be a reference to a daughter of Margaret, dowager duchess of Norfolk, 1485–94, for whom see *G.E.C.* ix. 612. Margaret's first husband was Nicholas Wyfold, one-time mayor of London, d. 1456.

†† Browne, William, esq.
†† Constantyne, Ralph, gent.
†† Felby, John, esq.
†† Mortimer, George[1]
†† Ralph, chaplain[2]
†† Southcocke, William, esq.
†† Southwicke, William, esq.
†† Troffote, Arthur, esq.
†† Watkynnes, Anne[3]

(ii) *Confraternity*

Late Eleventh Century

William, chamberlain to William I[4]

Early Twelfth Century

Deorman, the three daughters of[5]

Late Twelfth Century

Haverhill, Brictmar de; William, his son; William's wife and their sons; and the ancestors and descendants of Brictmar[6]

Late Thirteenth Century

Giffard, John, 1298[7]
Wenden, William de, 1298[8]

Late Fifteenth Century

Fitzlewis, Elizabeth, 1497[9]
Horneby, Henry, 1497[10]

---

[1] Described as a bastard.
[2] In the chapel of St. Paul. W.A.M. 53318, the only source to mention this burial, describes Ralph as chaplain 'cuiusdam archiepiscopi Garlensis'.
[3] Wife of John Watkynnes.
[4] *Gilbert Crispin*, p. 130; and see above, p. 39 and n.
[5] For whom see above, p. 373 and n.
[6] W.D., 367ᵛ. For Brictmar de Haverhill see above, p. 373 n. ; and for his son, below, p. 388 (no. 6). For this grant and for spiritual benefits for the persons named above, Brictmar gave 6s. per annum in rents in London *temp.* Walter of Winchester (1175–90).
[7] See below, pp. 393–4 (no. 39).   [8] Ibid.
[9] W.A.M. Reg. Bk. i. 93. Elizabeth Fitzlewis was abbess of the minoresses of London.
[10] Ibid. For Horneby, who was secretary, chancellor, and dean of the chapel to Margaret, countess of Richmond, see Emden, *Biographical Register of the University of Cambridge to 1500*, pp. 313–14.

Morton, John 1496[1]
Shirwood, John, 1486[2]
Sholdham, Elizabeth, 1497[3]
Stratton, Thomas, 1477[4]
Thwaytes, Sir Thomas, and Alice, his wife, 1490[5]

Early Sixteenth Century

Brooke, Richard, 1500–32[6]
Stanley, Sir John; Margaret, his wife; John, their son; and Anne, sister of the first named, 1528[7]
——, Thomas, earl of Derby, 1500–4[8]
Underwood, Philip, 1500–32[9]

(iii) *Perpetual Anniversaries and Chantries*

1. An anniversary for Abbot Vitalis (d. *c.* 1085) was observed on 19 June. *Endowment*: None recorded.
   Flete, p. 85.

2. An anniversary for Abbot Gilbert Crispin (d. 6 Dec. 1117/18) was observed on 7 Dec. *Endowment*: No special assignment; the expenses were borne by the chamber, the office which owed its enjoyment of separate revenues to Crispin.
   Customary ii. 149; *Flete*, p. 87.

---

[1] W.A.M. Reg. Bk. i. 103–103ᵛ. Morton, who was archbishop of Canterbury and chancellor of England, was also granted a daily mass in the Lady Chapel for his good estate during life and his soul after death.

[2] Ibid. 7ᵛ. For Shirwood, who was bishop of Durham, see Emden, *Biographical Register of the University of Oxford to A.D. 1500* iii. 1692–3.

[3] W.A.M. Reg. Bk. i. 93. Elizabeth Sholdham was abbess of Barking.

[4] W.A.M. 12747. Stratton is described as a squire. See also below, p. 398 (no. 60). [5] W.A.M. Reg. Bk. i. 46ᵛ.

[6] Ibid. ii. 75ᵛ. Brooke is described as a serjeant at law.

[7] Ormerod, *History of the County Palatine and City of Chester* iii. 641. (I am indebted for this reference to Mr. N. H. MacMichael.) In his will, dated 20 June 1527, Sir John Stanley committed the custody of his son, then aged three, to the abbess and convent of Barking, until he should reach the age of twelve, and to the abbot of Westminster for the rest of his minority; he left the former £15 per annum for the duration of the minority, and to the abbot and convent of Westminster, £10 per annum for the same period; and he stipulated that the boy was not to marry before the age of twenty and that, if he then did so, he should be advised by the abbot of Westminster and Edmund Trafford. In June 1528, Stanley and his wife executed a deed of separation, as the preliminary to entering religion ('Will of Sir John Stanley, of Honford, Cheshire, dated June 20, A.D. 1527', *Archaeological Journal* 25 (1868), 72–84). He died soon after, and within a short time the tradition was already current that he was then a monk of Westminster (*Letters and Papers of Henry VIII* iv (3). 6075 (38). See also above, p. 385 and n.

[8] W.A.M. Reg. Bk. ii. 33.

[9] Ibid. 75–75ᵛ. Underwood was a monk of the London Charterhouse.

3. Between 1118 and 1124, an anniversary for Matilda, first wife of Henry I (d. 1118), and her parents was founded by David, her brother; Malcolm IV (1153–65) confirmed this and added David and his own parents to the commemoration. *Endowment*: Rents of £1. 10s. per annum in Tottenham.

W.D., 157–157ᵛ; *Papsturkunden in England* i, p. 322; see also William of Malmesbury, *Gesta Regum*, ed. W. Stubbs (Rolls Series, 1887–9), p. 494.

4. An anniversary was kept for the parents of Abbot Laurence (1158–73) on 28 Jan. *Endowment*: An assignment on the Abbey's pension (£5 per annum) from the church of Sawbridgeworth.

W.A.M. 8579; *Monks*, p. 44.

5. Abbot Laurence (d. 1173) founded an anniversary for himself; the observances included the distribution of 4s. 8d. in alms to the poor. *Endowment*: Rents of 18s. per annum in Battersea.[1]

Customary ii. 247; *Flete*, pp. 94–5.

6. Between 1189 and 1212, William de Haverhill, son of Brictmar de Haverhill (for whom see above, p. 373, n.), founded an anniversary for himself and his wife. *Endowment*: Rents of 14s. per annum in London.

W.D., 368–368ᵛ.

7. An anniversary was kept for Abbot Walter of Winchester (d. 1190) on 27 Sept.[2] The observances, as finally authorized, included the distribution of bread made from 2 quarters of wheat to the poor. *Endowment*: An assignment on the revenues of the almonry; at first, this consisted of the issues of the manor of Paddington, but later, of the sum of £6. 13s. 4d. per annum.[3]

W.A.M. 19840 ff.; *Customary* ii. 177; *Flete*, pp. 96–8.

8. An anniversary was kept for Prior Robert de Molesham (*c.* 1189–97) on the morrow of the feast of the Conception of the B.V.M. (9 Dec.). On the vigil, the sum of £1 was distributed in

---

[1] When, subsequently, the expenses rose to £4 per annum, they were borne by the infirmary, which owed its possession of the appropriated revenues of the churches of Battersea and Wandsworth to Laurence; see *Flete*, p. 94, and below, p. 411 n.

[2] The feast of SS. Cosmas and Damianus, and this was the name by which the anniversary was known in the Abbey.

[3] In an act that was probably made to ensure the better keeping of his anniversary, Walter of Winchester assigned the church of South Benfleet and the manor of Benfleet, with Fanton and Paglesham, to the convent for pittances (W.D., 603). In respect of the manor of Benfleet, and Fanton and Paglesham, however, this was merely a confirmation of an existing arrangement.

bread to the poor. *Endowment*: An assignment of £5 per annum on the revenues of the Lady Chapel.¹
Customary ii. 92.

9. *Temp.* King John (1199–1216), Edward, reeve of Westminster, founded an anniversary for himself. *Endowment*: £1. 10s. per annum in rents.
W.D., 552; cf. *Customary* ii. 101.

10. Abbot William Postard (d. 1200) founded an anniversary for himself. *Endowment*: £14 per annum from the issues of Oakham and Hambledon churches.²
Flete, pp. 98–9.

11. *Temp.* Abbot Ralph de Arundel (1200–14), an anniversary was founded for the mother of Geoffrey fitz Peter, earl of Essex.³ *Endowment*: £1 per annum in rents in London.
W.D., 492ᵛ.

12. An anniversary was kept for William de Ste-Mère-Église, bishop of London (d. 1224).⁴ *Endowment*: None; the expenses were met from the abbot's portion.
Walter de Wenlok, pp. 220–1.

13. Abbot William Humez (d. 1222) founded an anniversary for himself; the observances included a refection for 100 poor persons. *Endowment*: A rent of £2 per annum from the manor of Deene and the Abbey's portion of the tithes of Pershore (£8. 13s. 4d. per annum) were assigned to the infirmary for the purpose.
Flete, p. 102.

14. Between 1222 and 1231, Br. Richard le Gras, a monk of Westminster, founded an anniversary for himself, his father, William le Gras,⁵ and his kin. *Endowment*: A messuage and 46 acres and a rent of 3s. per annum in Stevenage.⁶
W.A.M. 5399*.

¹ Molesham was instrumental in securing separate revenues for the Lady Chapel.
² Postard assigned the above income from these churches to the infirmary and directed that the residue be used for sick brethren.
³ She was Matilda, wife of Peter de Lutegareshale.
⁴ The bishop who permitted the final appropriation of the rectory of Staines, for which see below, p. 409.
⁵ Perhaps the William Crassus alias le Gras mentioned in *Pat. R.*, *1216–25*, pp. 292, 454, 574. That his son retained his family name in religion suggests a relatively distinguished origin.
⁶ Provided, however, that, if the endowment were later to be augmented, the residue should go to the poor.

15. *Temp.* Richard de Berking (1222–46), Andrew Bucherel, one-time mayor of London, founded an anniversary for himself and his ancestors. *Endowment*: £1. 3s. per annum in rents.[1]

W.D., 493–493ᵛ; cf. *Customary* ii. 101.

16. *Temp.* Richard de Berking (1222–46), Robert de Wudegar, son of William de Wudegar, founded an anniversary for himself and his father, to be kept on 9 Feb. until Robert should die and there-after on the day of his death. *Endowment*: 30 acres of land in Ben-fleet, together with the tenement of Robert le Dragger', a rent of 4d. per annum, and all Robert's *sequela*.[2]

W.D., 604–604ᵛ.

17. *Temp.* Richard de Berking (1222–46), an anniversary was founded for Br. Gregory Tayleboys, monk of Westminster. *Endowment*: 1s. 1d. per annum in rents in Westminster.[3]

W.D. 460ᵛ–461.

18. In *c.* 1230, William Chenduit, rector of the church of St. Laurence on the Bank, London,[4] founded a commemoration[5] for himself and his father, to be observed on the day of his father's death. *Endowment*: Land and houses in London.[6]

W.D., 488ᵛ.

19. In 1231, on the occasion of the appropriation of Oakham church, the abbot and convent of Westminster granted a perpetual anni-versary to Hugh de Welles, bishop of Lincoln. The observances were to include a distribution of bread, *companagium*, and drink to 100 poor persons.

W.A.M. Bk. iii. 66; *Registrum Antiquissimum of the Cathedral Church of Lincoln* ii, ed. C. W. Foster (Lincoln Record Soc., xxviii), 75–6.

20. In 1240, Stephen de Chelmereford, a London vintner, founded prayers for himself and all faithful departed on the anniversary of his death. *Endowment*: 8s. per annum in rents in the parish of St. Leonard, Eastcheap.

W.D., 489; and for Stephen de Chelmereford, see *Cal. Pat. R.*, *1258–66*, pp. 145, 162, 238.

---

[1] The initial endowment was 8s. per annum, but the founder, who was about to set out for Jerusalem, stipulated that, when he should die, the monks were to receive the sum of £10 to purchase an additional 15s. per annum in rents.

[2] Robert de Wudegar also confirmed his father's gift of 15 acres in Benfleet to the monks.

[3] But this was perhaps not the complete endowment.

[4] St. Laurence, Candlewick Street.   [5] *memoria*.

[6] The property had been purchased from Augustine, son of Eustace, a mercer, and Bela, his wife.

21. In 1245, Henry III founded a chantry of one chaplain for Raymond-Berengar IV, count of Provence, his father-in-law. *Endowment*: £5 per annum.

    Cal. Ch. R. i. 289 (where, for 'Richard' read 'Raymond-Berengar'); M. Paris, *Chronica Majora* iv. 485.

22. In 1246, Henry III founded a chantry of one chaplain for Isabella of Angoulême, his mother. *Endowment*: £5 per annum.

    Cal. Ch. R. i. 304.

23. In 1246, Henry III founded a chantry, to be served by a secular priest, for John Halengrett and all faithful departed. *Endowment*: £2 per annum in rents from the lands of the Normans in Hadleigh; a further endowment was promised by Halengrett's father.[1]

    W.D., 497; cf. *Close R., 1242–7*, p. 532.

24. Abbot Richard de Berking (d. 1246) founded an anniversary for himself and his parents. The observances included a refection of bread, ale, pottage, and a dish of meat or fish for 100 poor persons. *Endowment*: The rents of Moreton-in-Marsh (for which see above, p. 345) and a rent of £1. 6s. 8d. per annum in Hendon.[2]

    W.D., 374ᵛ–375; *Flete*, p. 107.

25. In 1249, Henry III founded an anniversary for himself and Eleanor of Provence. *Endowment*: The issues of the rectory of Feering, for which see below, p. 406.[3]

26. In 1256, Abbot Richard de Crokesley (d. 1258) founded an anniversary for himself, and four daily masses, to be said by four monks.[4] The observance of the anniversary was to include a distribution of alms to 1,000 poor persons on the day and to 500 on each of the six following days, at the rate of 1d. per person. *Endowment*: An assignment of £47. 13s. 4d. per annum to the infirmary, which was charged with the anniversary, derived in part from the manors of Hampstead and Stoke[5] and the soke of Mohun.

    In 1267 this foundation was modified by a judgement of papal judges-delegate, and the endowment was reduced to an assignment of £6. 13s. 4d. per annum from the issues of Hampstead.

    W.A.M. 5400, 5405; *Flete*, pp. 111–12.

---

[1] The elder Halengrett was perhaps the royal serjeant and cross-bowman of this name who is mentioned *temp.* Henry III (*Cal. Ch. R.* i. 304; *Cal. Liberate R., 1245–51*, pp. 7, 75, 143–5, etc.).

[2] Until Berking's death the whole was to be assigned to his parents' anniversary; after that event, their share was to be £1 per annum.

[3] The further grant in 1265 of rebels' lands to the value of £100 per annum never took effect; see W.A.M. 1692; W.D., 61ᵛ.

[4] Crokesley envisaged the recruitment of four additional monks for the purpose and assigned £20 per annum to the cellar for their keep.   [5] Unidentified.

27. *Temp.* Richard de Ware (1258–83), Thomas de Stretford, a brewer of Stratford (Essex), founded an anniversary for himself and Br. John le Fundur, a monk of Westminster.[1] *Endowment*: A croft in Feering, and £10 for the purchase of rents.

    W.D., 252.

28. *Temp.* Richard de Ware (1258–83), an anniversary was endowed for Br. Robert Tayleboys, monk of Westminster.[2] *Endowment*: A tenement in Aldenham and rents in Aldenham and Westminster.

    W.A.M. 4506; W.D., 460–460ᵛ.

29. *Temp.* Richard de Ware (1258–83), a commemoration[3] at the altar of St. Nicholas was founded for Hamo de Wroxhille by his executors.[4] *Endowment*: £2. 2s. per annum in rents.

    W.D., 482ᵛ.

30. In 1261, Henry III founded an anniversary for Sanchia, queen of Almain. *Endowment*: £3. 6s. 8d. per annum.

    Cal. Pat. R., 1258–66, p. 195.

31. In 1271, Abbot Richard de Ware (d. 1283) founded an anniversary for himself. *Endowment*: Land in Kelvedon and £8 per annum from the issues of Combe.[5]

    Flete, pp. 115–16.

32. *Temp.* Edward I (1272–1307), an anniversary was founded for Br. Gregory de Stanes, a monk of Westminster. *Endowment*: 15 acres of arable, 1 acre of meadow, 15s. 8d. per annum in rents, and six tenements, all in Aldenham, together with the homage of six free tenants there and that of their heirs, and 6d. per annum in rents in Westminster.

    W.D., 195ᵛ–198, 460.

33. In 1275, Philip, clerk of the church of St. Maxentius, London, bequeathed the proceeds of the sale of houses in the parish of St. Peter the Less, London, to endow a chantry in Westminster Abbey for Henry III and the testator's parents, Odo and Alesia Russel.

    Cal. of Wills proved and enrolled in the Court of Husting, London, ed. Sharpe, i. 23.

---

[1] Thomas de Stretford is described as 'specialis amicus' of Br. John. In this and similar cases, where an anniversary was endowed for a monk by a layman, the former may have contributed to the outlay; if so, the layman's role was perhaps more complex than that of co-founder: he was the third party through whom one who legally owned nothing could in fact apply funds to a particular purpose.

[2] Br. Robert was already deceased.   [3] *memoria.*

[4] For Hamo see also above, p. 375 and n.

[5] In the vacancy after Ware's death, the prior and convent revoked the assignment of Combe to this anniversary without providing in any other way for the residue of the endowment (*Walter de Wenlok*, p. 232); see also above, p. 347.

34. *Temp.* Walter de Wenlok (1283–1307), an anniversary was endowed for Prior John de Coleworth. *Endowment*: A messuage in Eye.[1]

W.D., 331ᵛ–332.

35. *Temp.* Walter de Wenlok (1283–1307), Richard son of Geoffrey Baker[2] founded an anniversary for himself and Br. Nicholas de Ware, a monk of Westminster.[3] *Endowment*: 5s. per annum, to be paid at one of Richard's houses in Westminster.

W.D. 455ᵛ–456.

36. In 1285, Geoffrey de Aspale, a royal clerk,[4] founded a chantry of two monk-chaplains for himself, his kin, and all faithful departed. *Endowment*: The manor of Halliford, for which see above, pp. 351–2.

W.A.M. 5029; W.D., 149ᵛ.

37. In 1288, Abbot Walter de Wenlok (d. 1307) founded an anniversary for himself. *Endowment*: £13. 6s. 8d. per annum from the rents of the fair at Westminster.

Flete, p. 120; above, p. 197 n.

38. In 1292, Edward I founded a weekly and yearly anniversary for Eleanor of Castile; the observances included a weekly distribution of 1d. for food to each of 140 poor persons, the same on the eve of the yearly anniversary (kept on 29 Nov.), and, on the day itself, 1d. in food to every poor person who should present himself before the third hour.[5] *Endowment*: Lands worth £200 per annum.[6]

Cal. Ch. R. ii. 411, 424–6; and see above, pp. 31 ff.

39. In 1298, William de Wenden was granted a chantry of one chaplain (who was to receive £3. 6s. 8d. per annum from the monks of Westminster) for himself, John Giffard, Robert de Wenden, and Lucy, Robert's wife, and all faithful departed, the chantry to be at the altar of the Holy Cross, in the nave, together with confraternity for himself and Giffard, the enrolment of their names in

---

[1] The abbot and convent paid a *gersuma* of £3 for this messuage.

[2] 'Galfridus pistor'.

[3] The foundation also provided for the maintenance of a light in St. Dunstan's chapel in the subhostelry.

[4] For Aspale, see Tout, *Chapters in the Administrative History of Medieval England*, v. 236–8. Aspale was treasurer to Eleanor of Castile and therefore involved in the early stages of the endowment of Eleanor's anniversary, for which see below, no. 38 and n. See also *Mediaeval and Renaissance Studies*, v. 94–134.

[5] Perhaps anxiety about the coinage is reflected in the provision that the poor should always receive the equivalent of 1d. at the time of the foundation.

[6] The acquisition of these lands began before Eleanor's death and under her supervision.

all the missals of the Abbey, in the margin of the canon, and the enrolment of William's name in the martyrology of the Abbey, in exchange for the surrender of the serjeanties of the vestry and buttery at the Abbey, of which he was the tenant in fee.[1]

In 1300, the monks were released from the obligation to maintain the chantry; the grant of confraternity to Wenden and Giffard and of the enrolment of their names in the missals and that of Wenden in the martyrology was confirmed, and Wenden and Giffard were admitted to all other spiritual benefits.

W.A.M. 5903; W.D., 88ᵛ–89; *Flete*, p. 117.

40. In 1317, Roger le Brabazun[2] founded a daily mass at the altar of St. John the Evangelist and yearly anniversaries for himself, Edmund, earl of Lancaster, and Blanche, Edmund's wife, and all faithful departed. *Endowment*: A messuage and 57 acres of land in Hampstead.

W.A.M. 5401; *Cal. Pat. R.*, *1313–17*, p. 663; ibid., *1317–21*, p. 220.

41. In 1324, Abbot William de Curtlington founded an anniversary for himself and all faithful departed. The observances included the distribution of £1. 5s. in alms to 300 poor persons (i.e. 1d. per person), or of the equivalent in bread. *Endowment*: The sum of £6. 13s. 4d. per annum, which the abbot was entitled to receive from the prior and convent in lieu of a night's hospice at Hendon.

Flete, pp. 123–5.

42. In 1326–7, Joan, widow of Thomas Beauflour, bequeathed houses in the parish of St. Bride's, London, to found a chantry for herself, her husband, and Richard de Langeford, and others. She requested burial in the Abbey.

Cal. of Wills proved and enrolled in the Court of Husting, London, ed. Sharpe, i. 321.

43. In 1333, Abbot Thomas de Henle (d. 1344) founded an anniversary for himself. *Endowment*: The quitclaim to the prior and convent of nine dishes, six conventual loaves and three flagons of ale, which the abbot was entitled to receive daily from them when in Westminster or La Neyte, and of thirty rafters of oak which he was entitled to receive yearly from the wood of the prior and convent in Hendon.

Flete, p. 127.

---

[1] William de Wenden was also granted a pension of £16 per annum for life; and Margaret, daughter of John le Seler, of Westminster, was to receive £2 per annum for life.

[2] Judge of the King's Bench and one of the persons appointed by the king in 1308 to inquire into the condition of Westminster Abbey and the dilapidation of its goods (W.A.M. 12777; *Walter de Wenlok*, p. 126 and n.). See also above, p. 376 and n.

44. In 1339, Sir John de Shorditch[1] and Elena, his wife, founded a chantry of two monk-chaplains, who should celebrate daily at the altar of St. Benedict for the founders, their ancestors and successors, during the lifetime of the founders. After the death of the latter, anniversaries were to be kept by the monks of Westminster; the names of the founders were to be enrolled in the Abbey's martyrology, and their decease to be announced in the next brief going out for a monk; they were also granted spiritual benefits. *Endowment*: Houses and tenements in Wood Street and Gutter Lane, London.[2]

Liber Niger Quaternus, 109^v–110^v; *Cal. Pat. R., 1338–40*, p. 83, where, however, the chantry is said to be of three chaplains.

45. In 1347, Abbot Simon de Bircheston (d. 1349) founded an anniversary for himself. The observances included a distribution of 1*d.*, or of food to the value of 1*d.*, to each of 300 poor persons. *Endowment*: The abbot's portion of the issues of the fair at Westminster was made over to the convent and assigned to the new work.[3]

Flete, pp. 128–9.

46. Abbot Simon de Langham (1349–62) founded an anniversary for himself. *Endowment*: Bidek's manor, in Finchley, and the manor of Le Frithe, in Allfarthing.

Flete, p. 133; below, p. 418 (no. 17).

47. In *c.* 1350, Thomas Walden, an apothecary of London, founded a chantry, presumably for himself. *Endowment*: A lump sum of £100.

W.A.M. 19846.[4]

48. In 1360, Prior Nicholas de Litlington founded an anniversary for himself. The observances included the distribution of alms of 6*s.* 8*d.* per annum to the poor. *Endowment*: Lands and rents in Hyde, Knightsbridge, and South Benfleet.[5]

W.A.M. 5406–7.

---

[1] A royal clerk, who abandoned the clerical estate on assuming knighthood and was murdered in 1345 (*Cal. Pat. R., 1343–5*, pp. 458, 576). See also above, p. 377 and n.

[2] The mortmain licence permitted acquisitions to the value of £13. 6*s.* 8*d.* per annum.

[3] Since 1308 the profits of the fair had been divided equally between the abbot and the prior and convent. A half share was worth between £40 and £50 per annum at the beginning of the fourteenth century, but perhaps considerably less by the 1340s. See *Walter de Wenlok*, p. 239 and n.

[4] The account of the conventual treasurers for 1350–1, where the receipt of £80 of this sum is recorded.

[5] These lands were among those acquired in virtue of the licence granted in 1351, permitting the Abbey to acquire property to the value of £20 per annum, on its own fee, for the endowment of a chantry for Litlington's parents; see above,

49. In 1363, an anniversary was founded for William Shirforde and Alice, his wife,[1] their parents, benefactors, and all faithful departed, presumably by William and Alice, who were also granted the right of burial in the Abbey. *Endowment*: The reversion of some land and houses in Westminster of which the abbot and convent of Westminster were chief lords.

Liber Niger Quaternus, 113–113^v.

50. In 1366, Richard de Chesterfield, a canon of Lincoln,[2] founded a commemoration[3] for himself in the Abbey during his lifetime and an anniversary for himself after death, and obtained the right of burial in the Abbey, before the Holy Trinity altar, should he die in or near London. The observances on the anniversary included the distribution of 6s. 8d. in alms to the poor. *Endowment*: £40 for the purchase of lands.

Liber Niger Quaternus, 77.

51. Between 1368 and 1376, Cardinal Langham (d. 1376) founded a chantry of four monk-chaplains for himself and his parents. *Endowment*: 1,000 marks (= £666. 13s. 4d.) for the purchase of 40 marks (= £26. 13s. 4d.) per annum in rents.[4]

Flete, p. 133.

52. In 1377, in her will, Mary of St. Pol, dowager countess of Pembroke,[5] founded a chantry of one priest in the chapel of St. Mary Pew, near the tomb of Aymer de Valence, earl of Pembroke, her husband. *Endowment*: A lump sum of money.

Cal. of Wills proved and enrolled in the Court of Husting, London ii. 194–5; Westlake, *Westminster Abbey* ii. 351–2; L. E. Tanner, 'The Countess of Pembroke and Westminster Abbey', *Pembroke College, Cambridge, Society, Annual Gazette* 33 (Dec. 1959), 9–13; see also above, p. 377.

pp. 177–8, and below, pp. 418–19 (nos. 18–20). This chantry seems never to have been founded. In 1374, however, Litlington, then abbot of Westminster, endowed an anniversary for himself, at which his parents' names were also to be recited, at Hurley Priory (Liber Niger Quaternus, 77^v). He also founded an anniversary for himself, with the same proviso, at Great Malvern Priory (ibid. 100^v).

[1] Alice Warde.

[2] Also a canon of St. Stephen's, Westminster; for this and Chesterfield's other benefices, see Emden, *Biographical Register of the University of Oxford to A.D. 1500* i. 408. See also above, p. 380, n.

[3] 'specialis memoria inter vivos'.

[4] With this money the monks purchased Bekswell manor, in Moulsham, and one or more mills there (below, p. 423, nos. 37–8).

[5] For whom see H. Jenkinson, 'Mary de Sancto Paulo, Foundress of Pembroke College, Cambridge,' *Archaeologia*, 2nd ser., 16 (1914–15), 401–46.

53. In 1382, John de Blokkele[1] founded an anniversary for himself. He was also granted a special commemoration in the masses, psalms, vigils, and prayers of the monks during his lifetime, and the right of burial in the Abbey, should he die in or near London. *Endowment*: A lump sum of £40.

W.A.M. 5403.

54. In 1387, Thomas of Woodstock, duke of Gloucester, and Eleanor, his wife, were granted an anniversary for themselves in return for a gift of vestments, plate, and jewels. Later, however, Thomas and Eleanor released the abbot and convent from the obligation of keeping this anniversary.

Liber Niger Quaternus, 85ᵛ, 100; and see above, p. 380.

55. In 1394, Richard II founded a weekly and yearly anniversary for himself, when he should die, and Anne of Bohemia. The observances included the distribution of alms of 1*d.* for food to each of 140 poor persons weekly and, on the anniversary, 1*d.* to every poor person who should come to the Abbey before the third hour.[2] *Endowment*: £200 per annum from the Exchequer, or lands or churches to that value.

Cal. Ch. R. v. 347–8, 375–80; and see Table I (above, p. 34).

56. In 1397, Abbot William Colchester (d. 1420) founded a chantry of one monk-chaplain and an anniversary for himself. The observances on the anniversary (which was to be kept on 29 June) included the distribution of £1 in alms to the poor of Westminster and £2 (later reduced to £1) to the poor of Aldenham. *Endowment*: The issues of the church of Aldenham, for which see below, p. 403.

W.A.M. 4515, 5260A.

57. In 1412, the executors of the will of John Waltham, bishop of Salisbury (d. 1395), founded an anniversary for him, to be kept on 18 Sept. or in the course of the previous week.[3] The observances included the distribution of 1*d.* to each of eighty poor persons. *Endowment*: A vestment worth £40 and the sum of £333. 6*s.* 8*d.*[4]

W.A.M. 5262A.

---

[1] Described as a clerk and probably the John de Blokle who was a prebendary of St. Stephen's, Westminster (*Cal. Pat. R.*, *1381–5*, p. 193).

[2] This foundation superseded the anniversary mass for Richard II and Anne of Bohemia that the monks observed yearly on 16 July, Richard's coronation day, in accordance with an agreement made in 1391, when he licensed the appropriation of Aldenham church (ibid., *1388–92*, p. 470).

[3] In fact the monks were keeping an anniversary for Waltham by 1399–1400 (W.A.M. 19659; see also above, p. 380).

[4] Later, tenements were built in London to endow this anniversary. It is

58. In 1432, the executors of Henry V's will founded a chantry, where three masses were to be said daily, and an anniversary for Henry. The observances of the anniversary, on 31 Aug., as defined in 1445, included the distribution of £20 to the poor for his soul and the souls of his parents and progenitors and of all faithful departed; further, twenty-four poor persons were each to receive 10*d.* at the anniversary. *Endowment*: £100 per annum from the Exchequer, until the chantry should be endowed with lands or churches to this value.[1]

    Cal. Pat. R., 1429–36, p. 213; *Foedera* xi. 89–91.

In 1463, Edward IV burdened this foundation with the further obligation of saying prayers for himself and Cecily Neville, his mother, and keeping anniversaries (on 29–30 Dec.) for Richard, duke of York, his father, Edmund, earl of Rutland, his brother, and for Richard Neville, earl of Salisbury.

    Cal. Ch. R. vi. 196–7.

59. In 1476, Lettice, widow of Sir Richard Lee, citizen and alderman of London, founded an anniversary for her late husband and for herself, and for Richard their son, when they should die. *Endowment*: A lump sum, amount unspecified.

    W.A.M. 5261A.

60. In 1477, Thomas Stratton was granted an anniversary and confraternity.

    W.A.M. 12747; and see above, p. 387 and n.

61. In 1479, Elizabeth Woodville, Edward IV's queen, founded a chantry of two monk-chaplains in the chapel of St. Erasmus (which she had built), where daily masses were to be said for herself and her husband, in life and after death, and for the souls of their children; a yearly anniversary for Elizabeth and Edward was to be kept by the monks of Westminster, and the observances on this occasion were to include the distribution of 1*d.* to each of 240 poor persons. *Endowment*: Two parts of the manors of Cradley and Hagley (Worcs.), and the reversion of the third part.

    Cal. Pat. R., 1476–85, pp. 133–4.

recorded in the foundation deed of the latter that Richard II gave the monks of Westminster a vestment 'de historia Jesse' worth £666. 13*s.* 4*d.* when he viewed Waltham's body, on the latter's decease. See W.A.M. 5262A, 24622–49.

    [1] This was done in 1445; see above, p. 33. Although the monks' income from Offord Cluny and Letcombe Regis, the manors given for this endowment, declined to *c.* £80 later in the century, they at first received between £90 and £100 per annum from these properties (W.A.M. 24132 ff.).

62. In 1504, Henry VII founded a chantry of three monk-chaplains, who should celebrate daily and keep weekly and yearly anniversaries—the latter to be kept on 11 Feb. during his lifetime—for himself, and for Elizabeth, his wife, Edmund, earl of Richmond, his father, Margaret, countess of Richmond, his mother, and all his progenitors, and all faithful departed. The elaborate observances included, on the anniversary, a distribution of £20 in alms to needy persons coming to the monastery, the inmates (thirteen men and three women) of the almshouse founded at Westminster by the king and other needy persons in London and Westminster, none to receive more than 2*d.*, and, at the weekly obit, a distribution of 1*d.* to each inmate of the almshouse and to 124 other poor persons. *Endowment*: Lands and churches worth £804. 12*s.* 8*d.* per annum.[1]

Cal. Cl. R., Henry VII ii. 389.

63. In 1506, Margaret Beaufort, countess of Richmond, founded a chantry of two monk-chaplains, and an anniversary, to be kept on 31 May during her lifetime, for herself, Edmund, earl of Richmond, her late husband, her parents and other progenitors, Thomas earl of Derby, and Henry, lord Stafford, her late husbands, Elizabeth, Henry VII's wife, and their deceased issue, and all faithful departed.[2] The observances on the anniversary included a distribution of £10 to the poor who should come between 8 a.m. and noon, each receiving 1*d.*, the residue, if any, to be given to the poor of London and Westminster. *Endowment*: Lands and churches worth £87 per annum.

Cal. Cl. R., Henry VII ii. 770; *Collection of all the Wills now known to be Extant of the Kings and Queens of England*, etc., ed. J. Nichols (London, 1780), pp. 367 ff.; see also Table I (above, p. 34).

64. In his will, Giles Daubeney, baron Daubeney, d. 1508, bequeathed £13. 6*s.* 8*d.* per annum to found a chantry of two priests in the church where he should be buried; this was in fact Westminster Abbey.

D.N.B. v. 542; and see above, p. 384.

[1] The value which Henry VII put upon his gifts in 1504. The royal letters fail to show, however, that, from this sum, the monks of Westminster were to find, not only the expenses of Henry's chantry, but also c. £170 per annum to augment the income of c. £90 per annum still annexed to the church of St. Martin-le-Grand. This collegiate foundation, though appropriated to Westminster Abbey in 1503, was not dissolved until 1542. This sum was equivalent to the gross income of the properties in London and Midd. which the monks of Westminster acquired as appropriators of St. Martin's. See W.A.M. 13313 ff.; and for the income of Henry VII's foundation in 1535, see Table I (above, p. 34).

[2] The monks of Westminster had been saying a daily mass for Margaret since 1496 (*Cal. Cl. R., Henry VII* ii. 770).

(iv) *Other Spiritual Benefits*

Early Thirteenth Century

Coleville, Philip de, and his heirs, 1238[1]
Contributors to the new work in the Lady Chapel, 1214–22[2]
Dene, Simon de, and his heirs, 1210[3]
Thecheham, Gilbert de; Alice, his wife; and the heirs of Alice, 1244[4]

Late Thirteenth Century

Giffard, John, 1298[5]
Langedon, William de; Joan, his wife; and the heirs of Joan, 1254[6]
Ros, Geoffrey de, and his heirs, 1254[7]
Wenden, William de, 1298[8]

Early Fourteenth Century

Shorditch, Sir John de, and Elena, his wife, 1339[9]

Late Fourteenth Century

Litlington, Nicholas de, abbot of Westminster, 1378[10]

---

[1] Below, pp. 414–15 (no. 3 and n.).

[2] They were granted spiritual benefits in the Abbey, and at Fécamp, Malmesbury, [Great] Malvern, Hurley, and Sudbury, and in the cells of these houses, *temp.* William de Humez (W.D., 507ᵛ).

[3] Received into all the benefits and prayers of the monastery on recognizing the abbot of Wesminster's claim to the advowson of the church of Uppingham (P.R.O., C.P. 25 (i) 192/2/21).

[4] Granted all the benefits and the prayers of the monastery on recognizing the claim of the abbot and convent to a rent of 3*s.* per annum (W.D., 137ᵛ).

[5] Giffard and William de Wenden, q.v., were granted, in addition to confraternity, the enrolment of their names in all the missals of the Abbey, in the margin of the canon, and also, in Wenden's case, in the martyrology. In 1300, they were granted all other spiritual benefits. See above, pp. 393–4 (no. 39).

[6] Granted all the benefits and the prayers of the monastery on making a fine with the abbot and convent relating to a messuage, two virgates, and two acres of land in Hanwell (W.D., 132). Joan de Langedon was Abbot Berking's niece (ibid. 131).

[7] Granted all the benefits and the prayers of the monastery in settlement of a plea of warranty relating to 36 acres of land in Benfleet (*Essex Fines* i, p. 201, no. 1161).

[8] Above, n. 5.

[9] Above, p. 395 (no. 44).

[10] Granted the daily prayers of the monks in choir, on making a gift of plate to the refectory and misericord, for which see above, p. 42 and n.

Late Fifteenth Century

Beaufort, Margaret, countess of Richmond, 1493 and 1496[1]
Henry VII, 1493[2]
Morton, John, 1496[3]

[1] In 1493, Margaret and Henry VII were granted a daily mass of the Virgin in the Abbey and its federate houses, and, after death, an office of the dead; and Henry was granted, additionally, the right to the announcement of his death in the first brief going out for a monk, and the enrolment of his name in the martyrology (*Cal. Cl. R., Henry VII* ii. 197 (vii)). In 1496, Margaret was granted a daily mass in St. Edward's chapel (ibid. 770 (i)).

[2] See previous note.   [3] Above, p. 387 n.

APPENDIX III

Appropriated Churches

WITH few exceptions, the churches listed in this appendix were parish churches of which the rectories, and, in one or two cases, the vicarages also, were appropriated to Westminster Abbey. However, Wheathampstead (diocese of Lincoln) has been included, although here the monks possessed only half the rectorial tithes. The other exceptions, if few in number, were important in the history of the latter-day monastery, for they were the heterogeneous assortment of churches—free chapels, prebendal and collegiate churches—given by Henry VII for the endowment of his chantry. Outstanding among these was the collegiate church of St. Martin-le-Grand in London. Not all, and, indeed, not even the greater part of the revenues of these non-parochial churches came from spiritualities. St. Martin's, however, possessed a number of rectories and other churches at the time of the appropriation, and these have been entered separately in the following list; so, too, the churches once belonging to Luffield Priory, which Henry VII gave to the Abbey after the Dissolution of the priory in 1494.

The values given for 1535, which are derived from the *Valor Ecclesiasticus*, are net annual values after deduction of reprises. However, at Feering, Kelvedon, South Benfleet, and Staines (diocese of London), and at Morden (Winchester), *V.E.* gives a consolidated value for the rectory and the demesne of the manor, or for rectory and the manor itself. Here a tentative estimate of the value of the rectory on its own is made, based on the relative values of spiritualities and temporalities in each of the places in question in 1291.[1] Since the relative importance of spiritualities in the monks' income here almost certainly declined between 1291 and 1535, these estimates are probably a little too high—a consideration to be borne in mind in using the figures relating to parish churches in Table III above.[2] The values given for 1291, which are derived from the *Taxation of Pope Nicholas IV*, are also to be understood as net annual values.

[1] A guess along similar lines has been made in the case of Thornborough (Lincoln); *V.E.* gives a single value for this and all the other former possessions of Luffield Priory which the Abbey acquired in 1503.

[2] Above, p. 53.

DIOCESE OF CHICHESTER

Playdon (Suss.) Playdon Hospital was given by Henry VII in 1503 for the purpose of appropriation but not formally appropriated until 1521; it was assigned to Henry VII's chantry. Value in 1504[1] and in 1535: £10.

Cal. Pat. R., 1494–1509, p. 303; *Cal. Cl. R., Henry VII* ii, pp. 148–9; *V.E.* i. 412; *V.C.H. Sussex* ii. 104–5.

DIOCESE OF ELY

Bassingbourn (Cantab.) The rectory was given by Henry VII in 1503, with the rectories of St. Botulph's, Aldersgate, St. Andrew's, Good Easter, Newport Pound, and Whitham, the chapel of Cressing, the prebendal churches of Crishall, Cowpes, and Keton (diocese of London), and other possessions of the collegiate church of St. Martin-le-Grand; all were assigned to Henry VII's chantry. Value in 1535: £42. 16s. 8d.[2]

V.E. i. 412, 419; *V.C.H. London* i. 561–3.

DIOCESE OF LINCOLN

Aldenham (Herts.)[3] The rectory was appropriated in 1391 by a mandate of John Buckingham, confirmed by Boniface IX in 1392, the appropriation to take effect on the death of the present incumbent; the vicar's portion, already in existence, was to continue. The vicarage, ordained in 1399, comprised a hall, chambers, and other domestic buildings in the rectory, a garden, the offerings, chattel mortuaries and small tithes, an arable close 7 acres in extent, and 1 rood of meadow. The church was assigned to the anniversary mass for Richard II and Anne of Bohemia on the king's coronation day (16 July) and, from 1397, to the anniversary of William Colchester, who paid the costs of the appropriation. Value in 1291: £12. 13s. 4d.; in 1392:[4] £38. 13s. 4d.; in 1535: £8. 6s. 2d.[5]

W.A.M. 4515, 5260A; W.A.M. Bk. iii. 8–10; *Cal. Pat. R., 1388–92*, p. 470; *Cal. Papal Letters, 1362–1404*, pp. 430–1; *T.P.N.*, 36ᵇ; *V.E.* i. 415, 422; *V.C.H. Herts.* ii. 160.

---

[1] In Henry VII's recital, in that year, of his gifts to the Abbey.

[2] £50, less reprises of £7. 3s. 4d.

[3] The monks possessed a pension of 13s. 4d. per annum in this church before the appropriation (*T.P.N.* 36ᵇ).

[4] In Boniface IX's mandate.

[5] The rectory of Aldenham was on lease @ £10 per annum and the demesne @ £8 per annum (W.A.M. Reg. Bk. ii. 279). Conflating these two items, *V.E.* gives the value of the 'manor' as £18 per annum. From the sum of £10, the reprises of £1. 13s. 10d. noted in *V.E.* have been deducted.

Ashwell (Herts.)[1] The appropriation of the rectory, in accordance with a mandate of Honorius III in 1225, was upheld by Gregory IX in 1239, in the face of opposition from Robert Grosseteste; a vicarage, valued at £10 in 1291, was ordained in or about 1244; it comprised the buildings in the demesne court, with the exception of certain granges, altar dues, and one-third of the great tithes.[2] The church was assigned in the fourteenth century to the warden of the churches, but previously and subsequently to the conventual treasury. Value in 1291: £26. 13s. 4d.; in 1535: £36. 13s. 4d.

W.D. 450ᵛ ff.; W.A.M. Bk. iii. 13–14; *Les Régistres de Grégoire IX*, ed. Auvray *et al.*, 4822; *T.P.N.*, 37; *V.E.* i. 416; *V.C.H. Herts.* iii. 207.

Dodford (Northants.) The rectory was given by Henry VII in 1503, with other possessions of Luffield Priory, and assigned to Henry's chantry; it was not valued separately in 1535.

Cal. Pat. R., 1494–1509, p. 304; cf. *V.C.H. Northants.* ii. 95.

Oakham (Rutl.)[3] The main fruits were appropriated in 1231, before which date the monks possessed a pension of £20 per annum in this church; they were assigned, first, to the pittancer but, from the fourteenth century, to the warden of the churches. After 1231, the rector (as the incumbent continued to be called) had a house on the south side of the church, tithes of sheaves to the value of £2 per annum, altar dues, small tithes, half the tithes of hay, and one carucate of land, together with a pension of 13s. 4d. per annum owing to the church of Oakham. It is this portion which is described as the 'vicarage' of Oakham and valued at £20 in 1291. Value of the rectory in 1291 (with the manor of Oakham): £70; in 1535: £47. 8s. 8d.[4]

W.A.M. Bk. iii. 65–6; *T.P.N.*, 65ᵇ; *V.E.* i. 416, 423; *V.C.H. Rutland* i. 132–3; ibid. ii. 14.

[1] The monks possessed pensions amounting to £1. 11s. 8d. per annum in this church before the appropriation (Liber Niger Quaternus, 141, 143; *T.P.N.*, 37).

[2] In 1215, a dispute about the tithes of the demesne at Ashwell between the monks of Westminster and the rector of Ashwell was settled on the following terms: the rector was to have £1. 18s. per annum in rents but find a chaplain to celebrate a daily mass of the Virgin in Ashwell church (W.D. 451ᵛ–453; W.A.M. Bk. iii. 14–15).

[3] The rectory included dependent chapels at Brooke, Egleton, Gunthorpe, and Langham, and probably a chapel at Barleythorpe. The monks had a larger claim, dating from the late eleventh century, to all the tithes of Rutland (*Regesta* i. 381–2; and see above, p. 47).

[4] £49. 6s. 8d. gross, made up as follows: £14 from Oakham, £6 from Barleythorpe, £5. 6s. 8d. from Brooke, £6 from Egleton, and £18 from Langham. But it seems appropriate to assume that at least half the reprises of £3. 16s. per annum allowed by *V.E.* to the warden of the churches in Rutland were expenses incurred in respect of the rectory of Oakham.

Swineshead (Lincs.)   The rectory was given by Margaret Beaufort, countess of Richmond, in *c.* 1499 and assigned to her chantry. Value at the time of the appropriation: £26. 13*s.* 4*d.*; in 1535: £33.
  V.E. i. 411; *Cal. Cl. R., Henry VII* ii. 594, 770.

Thornborough (Bucks.)   The rectory was given by Henry VII in 1503, with other possessions of Luffield Priory, and assigned to Henry's chantry. Value in 1535: [£7. 5*s.*].
  Cal. Pat. R., 1494–1509, p. 304; cf. *V.C.H. Bucks.* iv. 238, 242.

Wheathampstead (Herts.)   In *c.* 1221, the monks succeeded in appropriating half the tithes of this rectory. Value in 1291: £20; in 1535: £19. 6*s.* 8*d.*[1]
  T.P.N., 36ᵇ; *Cal. Papal Letters* i. 82; *V.C.H. Herts.* ii. 312–13.

DIOCESE OF LONDON

Benfleet, South (Essex)   The rectory was appropriated between 1189 and 1198, in accordance with a mandate of Richard fitz Neal, which, however, assigned £2. 13*s.* 4*d.* per annum and all oblations, offerings, and small tithes to the vicar, together with a share of the rectorial tithes. The church was assigned to the pittancer but administered by the conventual treasury. Value in 1291: £6. 13*s.* 4*d.*; in 1535: [£4. 3*s.* 4*d.*].[2]
  W.D., 617ᵛ; W.A.M. Bk. iii. 23; *T.P.N.*, 22; *V.E.* i. 416, 422.

Cheshunt (Herts.)   The advowson of this church was given by Margaret Beaufort, countess of Richmond, in *c.* 1499, with the king's licence to appropriate; the appropriation was complete by 1503, when the rectory was leased to Nicholas Hill, gentleman of the king's household, for fifteen years @ £34 per annum. The church was assigned to the Countess of Richmond's chantry. Value at the time of the appropriation and in 1535: £26. 13*s.* 4*d.*
  W.A.M. Reg. Bk. i. 139–139ᵛ; *Cal. Cl. R., Henry VII* ii. 594, 770; *V.E.* i. 411; *V.C.H. Herts.* iii. 456.

Chesterford, Great (Essex)   The rectory was appropriated in accordance with a royal licence, granted in 1504, which required the ordination of a perpetual vicarage and a yearly distribution of alms from the issues of the rectory; it was assigned to Henry VII's chantry. Value in 1504: £22 per annum; in 1535: £21. 6*s.* 8*d.*[3]

---

  [1] See above, p. 347 and n.
  [2] After deduction of a vicar's stipend of £2. 18*s.* 4*d.* per annum; but the resulting figure is conjectural in the sense noted above, p. 402.
  [3] £26. 13*s.* 4*d.*, less £2. 13*s.* 4*d.* to the vicar in augmentation of his stipend and £2. 13*s.* 4*d.* to the bishop of London as indemnity for the appropriation. In 1532 this rectory was demised to John and Agnes Shether for forty years @ £26. 13*s.* 4*d.* per annum (W.A.M. Reg. Bk. ii. 287).

Cal. Cl. R., *Henry VII* ii, p. 149; *Cal. Pat. R.*, *1494–1509*, p. 364; *V.E.* i. 412, 419.

Cowpes and Keton (Essex) For the acquisition and assignment of the prebendal churches here, see above, under *Bassingbourn* (diocese of Ely). Value in 1535: £24. 1s. 8d.
V.E. i. 412.

Cressing (Essex) For the acquisition and assignment of the free chapel here, see above, under *Bassingbourn* (diocese of Ely). Value in 1535: £6.[1]
V.E. i. 412, 419.

Crishall (Essex) For the acquisition and assignment of the prebendal churches here, see above, under *Bassingbourn* (diocese of Ely). Value in 1535: £14. 2s.[2]
V.E. i. 412, 419.

Feering (Essex)[3] The rectory was appropriated in 1249, in accordance with a mandate of Innocent IV, as the endowment of the anniversary of Henry III and Eleanor of Provence; the papal mandate required the ordination of a vicarage.[4] Value in 1291: £16. 13s. 4d.;[5] in 1535: [£9. 9s.].[6]
T.P.N., 23; *Les Régistres d'Innocent IV*, ed. E. Berger (4 vols., Bibliothèque des Écoles françaises d'Athènes et de Rome, 1884–1919), 4570; *V.E.* i. 423.

Good Easter (Essex) For the acquisition and assignment of the rectory of St. Andrew's here, see above, under *Bassingbourn* (diocese of Ely). Value in 1535: £6. 5s. 10d.[7]
V.E. i. 412, 419.

Great Chesterford (Essex) See above, under *Chesterford, Great*.

Hendon (Midd.) An early claim to the rectory was compromised in 1258, when the monks of Westminster resigned the church into the hands of the bishop of London, reserving the advowson and the pension of £1. 6s. 8d. per annum which had been confirmed to them

---

[1] £8, less £2 in augmentation of the vicarage.   [2] £16, less reprises of £1. 18s.

[3] A pension of £1 per annum in this church was confirmed to the monks by Gilbert Foliot (1163–87) (*Letters and Charters of Gilbert Foliot*, ed. Morey and Brooke, p. 490).

[4] The vicarage was valued @ £2 in 1291, but by the early fourteenth century the vicar had, in addition, a portion of £3. 6s. 8d. per annum from the rectorial income (*T.P.N.*, 24; Liber Niger Quaternus, 140ᵛ).

[5] A vicar's portion of £3. 6s. 8d. per annum came out of this sum (Liber Niger Quaternus, 140ᵛ; C.U.L. MS. Kk 5. 29, fo. 95ᵛ).

[6] After deduction of a vicar's pension of £3. 6s. 8d. per annum. For the conjectural nature of the resulting figure, see above, p. 402.

[7] The reprises include a pension of £2 per annum for the vicar.

by Gilbert Foliot (1163–87). The rectory was appropriated in 1477, in accordance with a papal mandate requiring the ordination of a vicarage, and assigned thereafter to the abbot's portion; it included the chapel of St. Mary's, Hampstead.[1] The pretext for the appropriation was the Abbey's poverty and the decay of its buildings. Value in 1258 and 1291: £20; in 1535: £33. 6s. 8d.

W.D., 627; *Cal. Pat. R., 1467–77*, p. 601; *Cal. Papal Letters, 1471–84* ii, p. 579; *T.P.N.*, 17; *V.E.* i. 411; Lysons, *Environs of London* iii. 13.

Kelvedon (Essex)[2] The rectory was finally appropriated in 1356, in accordance with mandates of John XXII in 1330 and Clement VI in 1351, which required the ordination of a vicarage.[3] The vicarage, ordained in 1356, comprised personal tithes, tithes of hay, and all small tithes, altar dues and mortuaries, 62 acres of arable, a hall, chamber, solar, pantry, and buttery in the manor court, other buildings, and a curtilage and garden. Value of the rectory in 1291: £26. 13s. 4d.; in 1535: [£11. 6s. 8d.].

W.A.M. Bk. iii. 51–4; *Cal. Pat. R., 1330–4*, p. 180; *Cal. Papal Letters, 1305–42*, p. 350; ibid., *1342–62*, p. 386; *Chronica Johannis de Reading et Anonymi Cantuariensis, 1346–1367*, pp. 116, 252–3; *T.P.N.*, 22[b].

London and Westminster

St. Botulph's, Aldersgate For the acquisition and assignment of this rectory, see above, under *Bassingbourn* (diocese of Ely). It was not valued separately in 1535.

St. Bride's, Fleet Street[4] The rectory was appropriated in c. 1504, in accordance with a royal licence, to augment the endowment of Henry VII's chantry; a vicarage, worth £16 per annum, was in existence by 1535. Value in 1504: £26. 13s. 4d.; in 1535: £18. 18s. 5d.[5]

Cal. Cl. R., Henry VII ii, pp. 149–50; *V.E.* i. 411, 419.

St. Margaret's, Westminster (i) The monks possessed the *rectory* from an early date, as that of the church of the precinct. A portion of the issues was assigned by Herbert (1121–36) to the high altar and the needs of the church; the issues in the fourteenth century were

---

[1] The monks paid £24. 17s. 8d. for the mortmain licence needed on the occasion of the appropriation (*Cal. Pat. R., 1467–77*, p. 601).

[2] A pension of £5 per annum in this church was confirmed to the monks by Gilbert Foliot (1163–87) (*Letters and Charters of Gilbert Foliot*, ed. Morey and Brooke, p. 490). [3] For the costs of the appropriation, see above, p. 52.

[4] A pension of 13s. 4d. per annum in this church was confirmed to the monks by Gilbert Foliot (1163–87) (*Letters and Charters of Gilbert Foliot*, ed. Morey and Brooke, p. 490).

[5] £50, less reprises of £30. 19s. 7d. which included a vicar's pension of £16 per annum.

assigned to the almonry, but later the greater part went to the sacrist's office. Until the fourteenth century, the rectory included the chapel of St. Katherine's, Paddington, q.v. Value in 1291 (with Paddington): £20; in 1535 (with the vicarage): £24.[1]

W.A.M. 3435; *T.P.N.*, 17[b]; *V.E.* i. 413; and see above, pp. 45–6.

(ii) The *vicarage* was appropriated between 1291 and *c.* 1335.[2] Value in 1291: £8; in the early fourteenth century: £8. 13*s.* 4*d.*;[3] in 1535 (with the rectory): £24.[4]

T.P.N., 17[b]; *V.E.* i. 413.

St. Martin-in-the-Fields[5] The rectory was appropriated in 1275. The vicarage, ordained the same year, comprised a cell (*arca*) near the church, on the north side, small tithes, offerings, altar dues, and one-third of the great tithes. The rectory was assigned to the prior. Value in 1291: £10;[6] in 1535: £5. 6*s.* 8*d.*

W.A.M. Bk. iii. 59–60; *T.P.N.*, 17; *V.E.* i. 412.

St. Martin-le-Grand This collegiate church, together with most of its possessions, was given by Henry VII in 1503. The possessions, which were assigned to Henry's chantry, included the rectories of Bassingbourn (diocese of Ely), St. Botulph's, Aldersgate, St. Andrew's, Good Easter, Newport Pound, and Whitham, the chapel of Cressing and the prebendal churches of Crishall, and Cowpes and Keton (diocese of London), q.v. Value in 1535: *c.* £320.[7]

V.E. i. 411–12, 418–19; *V.C.H. London* i. 561–3.

Newport Pound (Essex) For the acquisition and assignment of this rectory, see above, under *Bassingbourn* (diocese of Ely). Value in 1535: £17. 6*s.* 8*d.*[8]

V.E. i. 412, 419.

Paddington (Midd.) This benefice, not called a rectory until the

---

[1] In the decade Sept. 1520–Sept. 1530, the monks' average annual income from the church, above the curate's stipend, was in fact *c.* £24 (W.A.M. 19782–804).

[2] i.e. between the making of, respectively, *T.P.N.* and the summary of the Abbey's goods according to *T.P.N.*, which is in Liber Niger Quaternus, 140[v] ff.; the *terminus ante quem* for the latter is *c.* 1335.

[3] The monks' own valuation, made between 1301, and 1335, for which see Liber Niger Quaternus, 141.   [4] See note 1 above.

[5] A pension of £1 per annum in this church was confirmed to the monks by Gilbert Foliot (1163–87) (*Letters and Charters of Gilbert Foliot*, ed. Morey and Brooke, p. 490).

[6] From this sum, however, the vicar was entitled to receive a pension or portion of £3. 6*s.* 8*d.* per annum (Liber Niger Quaternus, 142).

[7] *c.* £343, less reprises of *c.* £23. The figure is misleading, however, since *V.E.* takes no account of the cost to the monks of Westminster (*c.* £170 per annum) of maintaining a collegiate establishment at St. Martin's; see above, p. 399 and n.

[8] £18, less reprises of 13*s.* 4*d.*

late Middle Ages, was acquired with St. Margaret's, Westminster,
q.v. In the fourteenth century, the issues were divided between the
sacrist and the almoner; later, the sacrist took all. Valued in 1291
with St. Margaret's; value in 1535: £2. 6s. 8d.[1]
V.E. i. 413.

Pleshey (Essex) The free chapel in Pleshey Castle was given by
Henry VII in 1503 and assigned to his anniversary. Value in 1504:[2]
£6; in 1535: £3. 12s. 6d.[3]
Cal. Pat. R., 1494–1509, p. 304; *Cal. Cl. R., Henry VII* ii, p. 148;
V.E. i. 411–12.

Sawbridgeworth (Herts.)[4] The rectory was finally appropriated in
1356, in accordance with a mandate of John XXII in 1330 and
another of Clement VI in 1351, which required the ordination of
a vicarage; the rectory was assigned to the warden of the churches.
The vicarage, ordained in 1356, comprised a hall, two chambers,
and other domestic buildings, on a messuage, a garden, personal
tithes and small tithes, altar dues, mortuaries, and offerings at the
image of St. Mary. Value of the rectory in 1291: £46. 13s. 4d.; in
1535: £22. 13s. 4d.
W.A.M. Bk. iii. 51–4; *T.P.N.*, 18; *V.E.* i. 416; *Chronica Johannis
de Reading et Anonymi Cantuariensis, 1346–1367*, ed. Tait, pp. 116,
252–3; *V.C.H. Herts.* iii. 346; and see above, p. 52.

South Benfleet (Essex) See above, under *Benfleet, South*.

Staines (Midd.) The appropriation of the rectory, made probably
in the late twelfth century, was confirmed by papal judges-delegate
in *c.* 1217–18, when a vicarage was ordained; the vicar took the
small tithes, the offerings, and the glebe. The rectory included
dependent chapels at Ashford, Laleham, Yeoveney, and, until
c. 1217–18, Teddington, q.v. It was assigned, first, to the hostelry
and infirmary, but, later, to the conventual treasury. Value in 1291:
£46. 13s. 4d.;[5] in 1535: [*c.* £29].[6]
T.P.N., 17; *V.E.* i. 415, 422; *V.C.H. Midd.* iii. 28.

[1] This was in fact the current leasehold rent for the rectory (W.A.M. Reg. Bk.
ii. 63). [2] In Henry's VII's recital, in that year, of his gifts to the Abbey.
[3] Made up of £2. 12s. 6d. from rents, etc., and £1 from tithe.
[4] A pension from this church was confirmed to the monks by Gilbert Foliot
(1163–87). Though said in Foliot's confirmation to be of £15 per annum, it was
in fact of £5 per annum. See *Letters and Charters of Gilbert Foliot*, ed. Morey and
Brooke, p. 490, and above, p. 47, n.
[5] In *T.P.N.*, only Laleham is mentioned as a dependency of Staines, but Teddington was valued separately. The sum of £46. 13s. 4d. is probably an undervaluation; see above, p. 50 and n.
[6] After deduction of £1 per annum for the vicar of Ashford. On the conjectural
nature of the resulting figure, see above, p. 402.

Teddington (Midd.) This church, which was not a separate bene-fice until the thirteenth century, was acquired with that of Staines, q.v.; it was assigned to the sacrist's office. Value in 1291: £6; in the early fourteenth century: £8;[1] in 1535: [c. £9. 10s.].[2]

T.P.N., 17; V.E. i. 413; V.C.H. Midd. iii. 76.

Westminster See above, under *London and Westminster*.

Whitham (Essex) For the acquisition and assignment of the rectory, see above, under *Bassingbourn* (diocese of Ely). Value in 1535: £7.[3]

V.E. i. 412, 419.

DIOCESE OF NORWICH

Swaffham Market (Norf.) The rectory was given by Henry VII in or before 1504 and assigned to his chantry. Value in 1504:[4] £40; in 1535: £22.

Cal. Pat. R., 1494–1509, p. 378; Cal. Cl. R., Henry VII ii, p. 148; V.E. i. 412.

DIOCESE OF SALISBURY

Hurley (Berks.) The rectory was given, with the rectories of Streatley and Waltham St. Lawrence (Berks.), and with the site and other possessions of the dissolved priory of St. Mary's, Hurley, by Henry VIII, in 1536.

Letters and Papers of Henry VIII xi. 202(4); above, pp. 337–8.

Stanford-in-the-Vale (Berks.) The advowson of the church was given by Henry VII in 1500, with licence to appropriate, provided that a vicarage was ordained; the church was assigned to Henry's chantry. Value of the rectory in 1504:[5] £28; in 1535: £26. 13s. 4d.

Cal. Pat. R., 1494–1509, pp. 201, 245; Cal. Cl. R., Henry VII ii, p. 148; V.E. i. 412.

Steventon (Berks.) The rectory was given by Richard II in 1398 and assigned to his anniversary and that of Anne of Bohemia. Value in 1291: £10; in 1535: £19. 17s. 3½d.[6]

Cal. Ch. R. v. 375–8; T.P.N., 195b; V.E. i. 417, 424; V.C.H. Berks. iv. 369.

[1] The monks' own valuation, for which see Liber Niger Quaternus, 141.

[2] The value of £5 given in V.E. for this church is the value of the glebe; the rectory buildings and the tithes were on lease with the demesne, and the value of these was probably c. £4. 10s. See also above, p. 354 and n.

[3] £12, less reprises of £5; the latter included 6s. 8d. for an annual distribution of corn to parishioners of the church.

[4] In Henry's VII's recital, in that year, of his gifts to the Abbey.

[5] See note 4 above.

[6] £21, less £1. 2s. 8½d. in reprises, which included a pension of 13s. 4d. per annum to the vicar.

Streatley (Berks.) For the acquisition of this rectory, see above, under *Hurley*. Value in 1544:[1] £10.

Letters and Papers of Henry VIII xi. 202(4); Dugdale, *Mon. Ang.* iii. 439.

Uplambourn (Berks.) The free chapel here was given by Henry VII in *c.* 1501 and assigned to his chantry. Value in 1504[2] and in 1535: £6. 13*s.* 4*d.*

Cal. Pat. R., 1494–1509, pp. 245, 304; *Cal. Cl. R., Henry VII* ii, p. 148; *V.E.* i. 412.

Waltham St. Lawrence (Berks.) For the acquisition of this rectory, see above, under *Hurley*. Value in 1544:[3] £10. 15*s.* 8*d.*

Letters and Papers of Henry VIII xi. 202 (4); Dugdale, *Mon. Ang.* iii. 439.

DIOCESE OF WINCHESTER

Battersea (Surr.) The rectory was appropriated, with that of Wandsworth, q.v., in *c.* 1185, in accordance with a mandate of Richard of Ilchester that required the assignment of a vicar's portion;[4] in the fourteenth century, the vicarage was valued @ £4. 3*s.* 4*d.* per annum. Value of the rectory in 1291: £17. 13*s.* 4*d.*; in 1535: £6.

W.D., 570ᵛ–571, 583; Liber Niger Quaternus, 143ᵛ; *T.P.N.*, 207; *V.E.* i. 415.

Morden (Surr.)[5] The rectory was appropriated in 1301, in accordance with a mandate of John de Pontissara;[6] a vicarage was ordained in 1331; it comprised the house, curtilage, and garden customarily occupied by the parish priest, the tithes of hay and of the mill, the small tithes, offerings, legacies to the vicar, 13 acres of arable, half an acre of meadow, and 1 quarter of wheat and 1 quarter of beans per annum; a further ordination in 1442 gave the

[1] In the particulars of the post-Dissolution grant to Leonard Chamberlayne.

[2] In Henry VII's recital, in that year, of his gifts to the Abbey.

[3] See note 1 above.

[4] In 1161, Alexander III confirmed Abbot Laurence's assignment of the churches of Battersea and Wandsworth to the infirmary, in a decree which has often been cited as a mandate for appropriation; in fact both assignment and papal confirmation related only to a pension of £4 per annum which the monks already enjoyed in these two churches (*Papsturkunden in England* i. 85; *Flete*, p. 94).

[5] The monks possessed a pension of 6*s.* 8*d.* per annum in this church before the appropriation. In *V.E.* (i. 415) this is erroneously entered as a pension from the church of 'Morton' in Glos.; cf. *T.P.N.*, 207ᵇ.

[6] In 1319, Edward II fined the monks in the sum of £40, on the grounds that they had appropriated this church without obtaining a licence in mortmain (*Cal. Pat. R., 1317–21,* p. 344).

vicar the great and small tithes and 4 yards of coloured cloth per annum. The rectory was assigned to the conventual treasury. Value in 1291: £12; in 1535: [£7. 12s.].[1]

W.A.M. Bk. iii. 62–3; *Registrum Johannis de Pontissara*, ed. C. Deedes (2 vols., Canterbury and York Soc. xix, xxx), i. 117–18; *T.P.N.*, 207[b].

Wandsworth (Surr.) For the appropriation of this rectory in *c.* 1185, see above, under *Battersea*. The vicarage, ordained in 1249 and valued at £6. 13s. 4d. in 1291, comprised altar dues, offerings, the rents of the church's tenants, and a share in the great tithes and tithes of hay. Value of the rectory in 1291: £20; in 1535: £6. 13s. 4d.

W.A.M. Bk. iii. 21; *T.P.N.*, 207, 209; *V.E.* i. 415; *V.C.H. Surrey* iv. 117.

DIOCESE OF WORCESTER

Longdon (Worcs.) The rectory was finally appropriated in 1335, by Simon Montacute's confirmation of Adam Orleton's appropriation, executing a mandate of John XXII, issued in 1331. As finally ordained in 1335, the vicarage included 6 quarters of tithe-wheat and 6 quarters of tithe-barley per annum. The rectory was assigned to the new work. Value in 1291: £29;[2] in 1535: £26.[3]

T.P.N., 216[b]; *V.E.* i. 413; J. Nash, *Collections for the History of Worcestershire* (2 vols., London, 1781–2), ii. 115; R. M. Haines, 'The appropriation of Longdon Church to Westminster Abbey', *Trans. Worcestershire Archaeological Soc.*, N.S. 38 (1962), 39–52.

DIOCESE OF YORK

Tickhill (Yorks.) The free chapel in Tickhill Castle was given by Henry VII in *c.* 1503 and assigned to Henry's chantry. Value in 1504:[4] £40; in 1535: £45.

Cal. Pat. R., 1494–1509, p. 304; *Cal. Cl. R., Henry VII* ii, p. 148; *V.E.* i. 412.

---

[1] But the values given for Morden in *V.E.* may be uneconomically low; see above, p. 358 n.

[2] This figure may be compared with some of the mid-fourteenth century: in 1341 and 1342 the rectory was at farm @ £40 per annum, and in 1343 at £34. 14s. per annum (*Trans. Worcestershire Archaeological Soc.*, N.S. 38 (1962), 50).

[3] In 1524, Longdon rectory, excluding the profits of the court and feudal incidents, was leased for 35 years @ £26 per annum (W.A.M. Reg. Bk. ii. 206).

[4] In Henry VII's recital, in that year, of his gifts to the Abbey.

APPENDIX IV

Major Purchases of Property

THE task attempted in this appendix is not the impossible one of recording all the purchases of property made by the abbot and convent of Westminster from the thirteenth century onwards—for it was in this century that the monks first began to buy on a notable scale—but that of listing their major purchases and recording, wherever possible, the barebones of the arrangements by which these were effected. No doubt the list is, even so, incomplete.

In the fourteenth century, the sequence of formal moves in such a property deal included, as a rule, the vendor's enfeoffment of the Abbey's nominees with the property, to be held of the chief lords (who were often the abbot and convent of Westminster), the final concord between vendor and nominees, the royal licence permitting the nominees to alienate the property in mortmain, and, finally, their surrender of it to the abbot and convent of Westminster.[1]

By the sixteenth century, when, after the fifteenth-century suspension of activity, the monks of Westminster were once again buying property in the grand manner, the sequence usually, if not invariably, included a covenant in which the vendor and the Abbey's nominees agreed on the terms of a sale, or the former agreed to make an estate for the latter in the property within a stipulated period of time; and, indeed, since the monks were now buying at the behest of the king and need anticipate no difficulty over amortization, the covenant might be made between the vendor and the abbot and convent themselves. The moves in the sequence, however, no longer occurred in a regular and predictable order: the fine might precede the grant of the royal licence or be made later.[2] When, in the earlier period, the use of nominees was habitual, the Abbey's purchases often passed through several hands before they were finally amortized, and the nominees named in the mortmain licence may well not be those through whom the purchase was made. For this reason, the names of the latter have been included in the following list only if they can be discovered,

---

[1] Above, pp. 183 ff.

[2] See, more generally, *Abstracts of Surrey Feet of Fines, 1509–1558*, ed. C. A. F. Meekings (Surrey Record Soc. xix), pp. ix ff.

with reasonable certainty, from the enfeoffment, fine, or covenant made at an early stage in the proceedings.

From 1279, all acquisitions of property by the monastery needed a royal licence. In the fourteenth century, it was the monks' practice to obtain general licences permitting acquisitions up to a certain value, and five such licences were obtained before 1400.[1] Still, however, individual licences were required for each acquisition, when the time came to amortize it. The date when the purchases in the following list were amortized is not certain in every case. The uncertainty arises, not, as far as we know, from a failure on the part of Chancery to enrol every licence that was granted, but from the difficulty of matching the descriptions of property given in the enrolled licences with those given at other points in the sequence of events. The uncertain cases are nos. 17, 25, 32, 34, and 45. Here the date given is the probable one; but there is an element of uncertainty.

The price of the properties listed below is problematic in a different way. As a rule, the payment made by the monks included a lump sum of money, the details of which were recorded in the accounts of the obedientiary against whose funds it was charged. But, for reasons set out above, in Chapter VI, we should hesitate to regard such a lump sum as the whole price of the property in question; often it may not even have been the major part of this. Therefore, at the cost of some tedious circumlocutions, the use of the word 'price' has been avoided in this context. What *in toto* the monks paid for their acquisitions is considered above.[2]

Temp. Richard de Berking (1222–46)

1. The so-called 'island' in *Eye* (Midd.)—that is, the portion of the manor later known as 'La Neyte'—and a mill here were purchased in 1235 or 1236 from Laurence, son of William le Petit. The vendor was granted £10 per annum for life.

Fine, Mich. 1235/6: P.R.O., C.P. 25 (1) 146/10/144.
See also W.A.M. 4772.

2. The manor in *Hendon* (Midd.) known as 'Frith' was purchased.
W.D., 374^v–375^v; above, p. 351.

3. A portion of the Domesday manor of *Longdon* (Worcs.), said to be a moiety, was purchased in 1238 from Philip de Coleville and Avice de Foliot, two of the four heirs among whom the manor had been divided on the death of Reginald de Foliot; the vendors

---

[1] For details see above, pp. 177–8.   [2] pp. 194 ff.

received, respectively, £228 and £73. 6s. 8d.[1] The moiety included lands in Castlemorton and the reversion of lands in Chaceley which were subsequently administered as separate manors.

Fine between the abbot of Westminster and Philip de Coleville, Mich. 1238: P.R.O., C.P. 25 (1) 258/5/13.

See also W.A.M. 32674–5; *Flete*, p. 104; *Close Rolls, 1234–7*, p. 67; *V.C.H. Worcs.* iv. 113 f.; and above, pp. 166–7.

Temp. Richard de Crokesley (1246–58)

4. In 1252, the soke of Mohun in *London* and *Midd.* was purchased from Robert de Beauchamp and Alice, his wife, who received £56. 13s. 4d.

Fine, Hil. 1252: P.R.O., C.P. 25 (1) 147/17/318.

See also W.D., 87–87ᵛ.

5. Two carucates of land in *Yeoveney* (Midd.)[2] were purchased from William son of Walter de la Poylle in 1258. According to the fine, the vendor received £40.

Fine, Trin. 1258: P.R.O., C.P. 25(1) 147/20/390.

Temp. Richard de Ware (1258–83)

6. Ralph de Limesey's manor in *Great Amwell* (Herts.) was purchased in 1270. The vendor received £566. 13s. 4d.; but in 1316, the monks paid a further £133. 6s. 8d. to settle a plea of warranty in respect of 80 acres of woodland and £13. 6s. 8d. per annum in rent in this manor. The current leasehold value of the manor in 1270 was probably £40 per annum.

Fine, Hil. 1270: P.R.O., C.P. 25(1) 86/32/625.

See also W.A.M. 4246; and above, p. 191.

Temp. Berking, Crokesley, or Ware (1222–83)

7. An estate in *Claygate* and *Kingston* (Surr.) was acquired from Gilbert de Claygate in return for the grant in fee of a monk's corrody, a serjeant's corrody, 1 quarter of wheat, 1 quarter of rye, 2 quarters of oats, and 2 quarters of barley per annum, two houses, and the office of serjeant in the monastic almonry.

W.D., 465ᵛ; Liber Niger Quaternus, 78.

---

[1] The fine between the abbot and Philip de Coleville records the grant of spiritual benefits at the Abbey to the latter and his heirs; almost certainly, a similar grant was made to Avice de Foliot.

[2] Thus the fine; however, the vendor's quitclaim, dated 9 May 1258, describes the property as a messuage, 2 carucates of land, and two mills, in Staines and Yeoveney (W.A.M. 16746).

Temp. Walter de Wenlok (1283–1307)

8. The manor of *Deerhurst*, with *Hardwicke* (Glos.), was purchased by the abbot from William de Derneford in 1299, together with the half-hundred of Deerhurst, and amortized the same year. The vendor received the manor of Islip (Oxon.) and a pension of £10 per annum for his own and his wife's joint and several lives, together with the sum of £100, and £77 for manorial stock. The extended value of the manor, over and above the fee-farm rent of £34 per annum already owing to the monks, was £36 per annum. In 1319, a plea of warranty between the abbot and convent of Westminster, of the one part, and William de Derneford's son, of the other, was compromised by the grant of a pension of £11 per annum and an annual livery of a squire's robe to the latter.

Amortization, 3 Aug. 1299: *Cal. Pat. R., 1292–1301*, pp. 429–30. See also above, pp. 173–4 and references given there.

9. Simon de Ellesworth's manor in *Turweston* (Bucks.) was purchased by the wardens of Queen Eleanor's foundation, on Eleanor's orders and with funds provided by her, in *c.* 1286. The vendor received £133. 6s. 8d. However, the abbot and convent were not in possession of the manor until 1292, when Edward I formally granted it to them.

W.A.M. 23628; *Cal. Ch. R.* ii. 425; *V.C.H. Bucks.* iv. 252.

10. Some houses and messuages in *Westminster* (Midd.) were purchased from Stephen de Cornhill. An acquittance from Cornhill in 1289 shows that for one of the houses the monks paid £35. 6s. 8d.[1]

W.A.M. 28842; W.D. 86ᵛ–87; *Flete*, pp. 116; *Walter de Wenlok*, p. 239.

Temp. Richard de Kedyngton and William de Curtlington (1308–33)

11. The chief manor of *Hendon* (Midd.), which had been alienated in the twelfth century, was recovered from the fee-farm tenant, Richard le Rous, in 1312–15. The probable terms of the transaction were as follows. In 1312, Richard le Rous surrendered all but a life-interest in the manor, in return for the grant of Hodford manor in fee and £100; in 1315, he surrendered his life-interest and received in return a demise of the manor of Aldenham (Herts.), with the exception of the woods there, and two serfs, and their families, together with £40 per annum from the issues of Wheathampstead, each of these grants being for his life.

Fine, Trin. 1312:[2] P.R.O., C.P. 25(1) 149/42/88.

---

[1] This seems to have been one of Wenlok's unlicensed acquisitions, for which the monks were obliged to pay a fine, retrospectively, in 1319; see above, p. 181.

[2] It is noted in the fine that it was made by order of the king.

See also W.D., 124ᵛ–126ᵛ; *Cal. Pat. R., 1307–13*, p. 438; and for Richard le Rous, above, p. 376.

Temp. William de Curtlington (1315–33)

12. The reversion of five shops, two messuages, and other tenements in *Westminster* (Midd.), and of land in *Eye* (Midd.) was acquired from William son of John de Tyteburst in 1325, to take effect after the death of Alice, widow of Geoffrey, son of John de Tyteburst.

Amortization, 3 Aug. 1392: *Cal. Pat. R., 1391–6*, p. 133.

See also W.A.M. 17591A, 17616.

Temp. Thomas de Henle (1333–44)

13. A mill was purchased in *Birdbrook* (Essex) by the wardens of Queen Eleanor's foundation, from William Lengleys and Michael de Birdbrook, in 1341–2. The vendors received £20, but this sum may have been only part of the purchase price.

Amortization, 24 Oct. 1343: *Cal. Pat. R., 1343–5*, p. 136.

See also W.A.M. 23686.

14. An extensive property in *Chelmsford* (Essex) was amortized in 1344. This, almost certainly, was the manor of Moulsham, known from other sources to have been recovered in demesne in *c.* 1337. This property, which belonged to the Abbey's fee, was amortized in satisfaction of £8. 12s. 8d. per annum of the licence of 1332 to acquire lands not held in chief to the value of £20 per annum.

Amortization, 28 Sept. 1344: *Cal. Pat. R., 1343–5*, p. 353.

See also W.A.M. 19845 ff.; Essex Record Office, D/DM/M68 ff.

15. Land in *Turweston* (Bucks.), known subsequently as 'Terry's land', was purchased for Queen Eleanor's foundation from Henry Terry, of Brackley, in 1340, through nominees, Adam de Northwyk and Alan de Curtlyngton. In addition to the sum of £66. 13s. 4d., the vendor was granted a pension of £10 per annum and the annual livery of a squire's robe, in each case for life, and dower of £3. 6s. 8d. per annum for Alice, his wife, if she were to survive him. This land was amortized at the extended value of £1. 17s. per annum but in satisfaction of £3 per annum of the general licence of 1316 to acquire lands to the value of £10 per annum for Eleanor's foundation.

Enfeoffment of nominees by vendor, 13 Feb. 1340: W.A.M. 7639.

Amortization, 23 Dec. 1340: *Cal. Pat. R., 1340–3*, pp. 76–7.

Surrender by nominees to abbot and convent, 7 Feb. 1341: W.A.M. 7633. See also W.A.M. 7620, 7627, 7638, 23680.

16. Eighty acres of land and two of meadow in *Wickford* (Essex), known as 'Feliceland' were purchased from Peter fitz William, of Roxwell, Joan, his wife, and James de Burstalle, and Joan, his wife, in 1335, through a nominee, Roger Basset. According to the fine, the vendors received £26. 13*s*. 4*d*. Once enfeoffed, Basset demised the manor to the abbot and convent for a term of 18 years at a nominal rent. This property was amortized, with other lands on the Abbey's fee, in satisfaction of £5 of the licence of 1332 to acquire lands not held in chief to the value of £20.

Enfeoffment of nominee by vendors, 3 Aug. 1335: W.A.M. 1169.

Demise by nominee to abbot and convent, 1 Mar. 1336: W.A.M. 1240.

Fine, East. 1337: *Essex Fines* iii, p. 43 (no. 405); cf. W.A.M. 1177.

Amortization, 28 Aug. 1337: *Cal. Pat. R., 1334–8*, p. 508.

Temp. Simon de Langham (1349–62)

17. Langham purchased a manor in *Allfarthing*, in Wandsworth (Surr.), known as 'le Frithe',[1] together with a manor in *Finchley* (Midd.) known as 'Bidek's manor', for the endowment of his anniversary.

Amortization, 16 July, 1366: *Cal. Pat. R., 1364–7*, p. 298.

See also *Flete*, p. 133.

18. The remainder in a messuage, 60 acres of land, and 100 acres of marsh in *South Benfleet* (Essex) was purchased from John Handlo, through nominees, Thomas Byestetoun and John Pecche, in 1350. According to the fine, the vendors received £6. 13*s*. 4*d*. This purchase and nos. 19 and 20 below were financed by Prior Nicholas de Litlington for the endowment of his anniversary.

Fine, Hil. 1352: *Essex Fines* iii, p. 102 (no. 969).

Amortization, 29 Jan. 1354: *Cal. Pat. R., 1354–8*, p. 5.

See also W.A.M. 5406.

19. A messuage and 100 acres of land in *Eye* (Midd.) were purchased from Peter Alnemouth, of Newcastle-upon-Tyne, and Cristina, his wife, in 1350, through nominees, Thomas Byeston' and John Pecche. According to the fine, the vendors received £66. 13*s*. 4*d*. The property was known subsequently as the manor of Hyde.

Fine, Trin. 1350: *Cal. Fines, London and Midd.*, p. 128 (no. 274); cf. W.A.M. 4765.

---

[1] The manor was probably the agglomeration of lands belonging to the Abbey's fee in Wandsworth described in *V.C.H. Surrey* iv. 111. Another estate in Wandsworth, known as 'Finches', was probably purchased *temp.* Simon de Langham; see above, p. 358.

Amortization, 29 Jan. 1354: *Cal. Pat. R., 1354–8*, p. 5.
See also W.A.M. 5406; and no. 18 above.

20. Three messuages, 91 acres of land, and a rent of 10s. 2d. per annum in *Knightsbridge, Kensington, Chelsea,* and *Eye* (Midd.), all said to have belonged formerly to John Convers, were purchased from Peter Alnemouth (for whom see no. 19 above) and Cristina, his wife, in 1350–2, through nominees, William Lound, Thomas Byesteton, William atte Watre, and John Pecche. The vendors received £66. 13s. 4d.

Enfeoffment of nominees by vendors, 16 June 1350: W.A.M. 16209.

Fine, Easter, 1352: P.R.O., C.P. 25 (1) 150/64/288: cf. W.A.M. 16270.

Partial amortization, 29 Jan. 1354: *Cal. Pat. R., 1354–8*, p. 5.

Surrender of amortized portion by nominee, 23 Feb. 1354: W.A.M. 16180.

See also W.A.M. 5406; and no. 18 above.

21. A messuage and 80 acres of land, known as 'Ceppe', in *Longdon* (Warwicks.), a member of the manor of Knowle, were purchased by the wardens of Queen Eleanor's foundation from John Hyntone and Alice, his wife, in 1359, through nominees, Richard Hugyn, Richard Rook, senior, and John Pecche. The outlay of £46. 13s. 4d. recorded in the account of the wardens of the foundation included a payment, of unspecified amount, for brokerage (*brocagium*).[1]

Fine, Mich. 1359: *Warwickshire Feet of Fines*, ed. L. Drucker, E. Stokes, and F. C. Wellstood (3 vols., Dugdale Soc. xi, xv, xviii), iii. 2083; cf. W.A.M. 597, 32749.

Amortization, 18 Jan. 1369: *Cal. Pat. R., 1367–70*, p. 188.

See also W.A.M. 23696.

22. The manor of *Stangraves* (Kent), which was in the Abbey's possession from *c.* 1351, was, almost certainly, acquired by purchase.

Amortization, 3 Aug. 1392: *Cal. Pat. R., 1391–6*, p. 133.

See also W.A.M. 26437 ff.

23. Land in *Westerham* (Kent) was purchased before Mar. 1360, with funds provided by Prior Litlington to augment the possessions

---

[1] According to the fine, the 'consideration' was £13. 6s. 8d. In the same year, the reversion of a rent of 6s. 6½d. per annum in Longdon was purchased from William Coppethorn and Ella, his wife, together with the interest of the Coppethorns in half the messuage. The fine for this transaction also names the sum of £13. 6s. 8d.; but the wardens of Queen Eleanor's foundation accounted for an outlay of only £4. To Henry Middelmor', who was seised of the rent at the time, they paid an additional £5. 6s. 8d. See W.A.M. 23696; *Warwickshire Feet of Fines* iii. 2082.

of Queen Eleanor's foundation there. This was probably the estate of two messuages, 222 acres of land, 7 acres of meadow, 10 acres of wood, and 3*s.* per annum in rents, in Westerham, amortized in 1361 at the extended value of 10*s.* per annum, and in satisfaction of £1 per annum of a general licence. The account of the wardens of the foundation shows that the vendor was John de Cobham; William de Cothull, of Westerham, who is named in the licence, was, therefore, a nominee.

Amortization, 4 May 1361: *Cal. Pat. R., 1361–4*, p. 15.
See also W.A.M. 5406, 23698.

24. Other purchases of land in *Westerham* are indicated by the amortization of three messuages, a carucate and 5 acres of land, 13½ acres of meadow, 40 acres of pasture, 15 acres of wood, and rents of, respectively, £1. 6*s.* 8*d.*, 2 lb. wax, and 3 lb. pepper per annum, at the extended value of £4. 1*s.* 8¼*d.* per annum in 1366, in part satisfaction of the general licence of 1316, to acquire lands to the value of £10 per annum for Queen Eleanor's foundation.

Amortization, 16 July 1366: *Cal. Pat. R., 1364–7*, pp. 261–2.

Temp. Nicholas de Litlington (1362–86)

25. Land in *Battersea* (Surr.) was purchased by the conventual treasurers from John Southam, a stockfishmonger of London, in 1364–5. The vendor received £40.

Amortization, 16 July 1366: *Cal. Pat. R., 1364–7*, p. 298.
See also W.A.M. 19859.

26. The estate known as 'Bridges', or 'Bridgecourt', in *Battersea* (Surr.), was purchased by the conventual treasurers in 1369–70. The vendor received £68. 13*s.* 4*d.*

Amortization, 2 Aug. 1380: *Cal. Pat. R., 1377–81*, pp. 534–5.
See also W.A.M. 19864.

27. A marsh of 40 acres in *South Benfleet* (Essex), called 'Bartlescote', was purchased by the conventual treasurers from Richard Sandhill, in 1364–5. Sandhill received £66. 13*s.* 4*d.*; he also received a squire's robe annually until 1376, when, presumably, he died.

Amortization, 3 Aug. 1392: *Cal. Pat. R., 1391–6*, p. 133.
See also W.A.M. 5703, 19859.

28. The account of the wardens of Queen Eleanor's foundation records the purchase of lands and tenements of William Englissh in *Birdbrook* (Essex), in 1372, the vendor receiving £66. 13*s.* 4*d.* There is, however, no evidence that this property was ever amortized, and the transaction may not have been brought to a conclusion.

W.A.M. 23700.

29. The abbot obtained the reversion of John de Sapy's manor in *Birlingham* (Worcs.) in 1378, to take effect on the death of Sapy, who was the Abbey's fee-farm tenant. The farm of £11. 12*s*. 5*d*. per annum, which Sapy owed to the abbot and convent, was remitted for the remainder of his life; he died in 1388. Writing two or three generations later, John Flete valued this acquisition at £5 per annum beyond the reprises. The property was amortized at the extended value of £3. 13*s*. 4*d*. per annum and in satisfaction of £4. 13*s*. 4*d*. per annum of the general licence of 1351 to acquire lands to the value of £20 per annum for Prior Litlington's chantry.[1] The Abbey's nominees in this transaction were Sir Richard Scrope, Walter Parham, of Bourton, Richard Rook, of Westminster, and Thomas Durdent, of Denham.

Amortization, 12 Apr. 1378: *Cal. Pat. R., 1377–81*, p. 182.

See also Liber Niger Quaternus, 61–61ᵛ; *Flete*, pp. 134–5; and above, p. 196.

30. Two messuages, 126½ acres of land, 20 acres of meadow, and 10 acres of wood in *Denham* (Bucks.) were purchased from James Andrew, a clothier of London, and Matilda, his wife, in 1366, through nominees, Richard Rook, senior, Thomas Durdent, and John Pecche. According to the fine, the vendors received £66. 13*s*. 4*d*.[2]

Fine, Trin. 1366: P.R.O., C.P. 25 (1) 20/97/232; cf. Liber Niger Quaternus, 42ᵛ–43.

Amortization, 23 Oct. 1366: *Cal. Pat. R., 1364–7*, p. 328.

Surrender by nominees to the abbot and convent, 4 Dec. 1366: Liber Niger Quaternus, 43.

31. The manor of Robert de Fynnesford in *Downe*, in Wandsworth (Surr.), was purchased by the conventual treasurers from Fynnesford and Alice, his wife, in 1370, through nominees, John de Whitewell and Thomas Pernel. The vendors received the sum of £100, together with a pension of £14 per annum, and, severally, the annual livery of a robe, for their joint and several lives. The sum of £14 per annum may represent the current leasehold value of the manor. The property was amortized at the extended value of £4 per annum, but in satisfaction of £5 per annum of a general licence.

Fine, Mich. 1370: *Surrey Fines*, p. 139 (no. 60); cf. W.A.M. 1774.

Amortization, 7 June 1377: *Cal. Pat. R., 1374–7*, p. 478.

See also W.A.M. 1780, 19864 ff.; and above, p. 195.

---

[1] In fact Litlington founded an anniversary but not a chantry in the Abbey (above, p. 395, no. 48 and n.).

[2] Two other, smaller, properties were purchased in Denham at this time— a croft and meadow, from John Cooke, and *Balhammesgrove*, from Edward Durdent (Liber Niger Quaternus, 43).

32. Lands in *Eye* and *Westminster* (Midd.) known as the manor of *Rosamund* were purchased from Richard de Weston, a goldsmith of London, in 1361–2, through nominees, Richard Rook, senior, Geoffrey de Norton, chaplain, and John Pecche. Once in the monks' hands, they lost their identity as a manor.

Enfeoffment of nominees by vendor, 1361–2:[1] W.A.M. 17666.

Amortization, 16 July 1366: *Cal. Pat. R., 1364–7*, p. 298.

Surrender by nominees to abbot and convent, 9 Aug. 1366: W.A.M. 17681.

33. A messuage, 40 acres of land, 4 acres of meadow and 10*d.* per annum in rent were purchased in *Feering* and *Kelvedon* (Essex) from William atte Wode, of Feering, and Margery, his wife, in 1373, through nominees, Richard Stoke, William Norton, and Richard Rook. According to the fine, the vendors received £66. 13*s.* 4*d.*

Fine, East. 1373: *Essex Fines* iii, p. 168 (no. 1726).

Amortization, 3 Aug. 1392: *Cal. Pat. R., 1391–6*, p. 133.

34. Land in *Hendon* (Midd.) known as 'Brauncestr' land' was purchased by the conventual treasurers in 1362–3. The vendor received £63. 6*s.* 8*d.* He was probably a corrodian of the Abbey named Roger Gerard.

Amortization, 16 July 1366: *Cal. Pat. R., 1364–7*, p. 298.

See also W.A.M. 19858; and above, p. 172.

35. The manor in *Laleham* (Midd.) known as 'Billetts', or 'Belets', which Roger Belet held in chief, together with the reversion of the lands which he held of the abbot and convent of Westminster in *Laleham, Litlington*, and *Staines* (Midd.), was purchased in or before 1366; presumably the reversion was to take effect when Belet and his wife died. In fact Belet seems to have made over nearly all the property to the abbot's nominees, Richard Rook, John Pecche, and Thomas Durdent, in 1366, but Agnes Belet, the survivor, retained the chief messuage of the reversionary lands in Laleham until 1382. In 1378, the abbot and convent valued the acquisitions to date at £6. 13*s.* 4*d.* per annum.

Amortizations, 20 Mar. and 23 Oct. 1366: *Cal. Pat. R., 1364–7*, p. 230 (where for Robert Belet, read Roger Belet); ibid., p. 328.

See also W.A.M. 4920, 4970, 5255, 5256A; *V.C.H. Midd.* ii. 399; and above, p. 189.

36. A messuage, 70 acres of land, 5 acres of meadow, and 5 acres of woodland in *Longdon* (Warwicks.) were amortized in 1369. This may have been the property for which the conventual treasurers paid the widow of Robert Langeton £66. 13*s.* 4*d.* in 1364–5.

---

[1] 35 Edward III—i.e. between 25 Jan. 1361 and 24 Jan. 1362.

Amortization, 18 Jan. 1369: *Cal. Pat. R., 1367–70*, p. 188.
See also W.A.M. 19859.

37. *Beckswell* manor, in Moulsham (Essex), and a rent of £1. 16s. 5d.
per annum in *Moulsham* and *Chelmsford* (Essex) were purchased from
Sir Thomas Tirell and Alice, his wife, with moneys given by Cardinal
Langham to enable the monastery to recruit four additional monks
for the service of his own and his parents' chantry. The Abbey's
nominees were Richard de Stoke, John Scaldewell, and John Wroth,
junior.

Fine, Hil. 1374: *Essex Fines* iii, p. 169 (no. 1732).
Amortization, 3 Aug. 1392: *Cal. Pat. R., 1391–6*, p. 133.
See also *Flete*, p. 133; and above, p. 396 (no. 51).

38. According to Flete, mills in *Moulsham* (Essex) were also purchased with Cardinal Langham's benefaction (for which see above,
no. 37). In fact only one such acquisition has come to light: a mill
here, purchased through nominees, was amortized at the extended
value of £2 per annum and in satisfaction of £3. 6s. 8d. per annum
of a general licence.

Amortization, 1 Aug. 1380: *Cal. Pat. R., 1377–81*, p. 540.
See also *Flete*, p. 133.

39. The Toundesle lands in *Pyrford* (Surr.) were purchased by the
abbot from John, son of Robert de Toundesle, in 1362, through
nominees, Richard Rook and John Pecche. The vendor received
£66. 13s. 4d. Katherine, widow of Robert de Toundesle, who surrendered her dower in half the lands, received a pension of £2 per
annum, and William, Robert's son, received 5 quarters of wheat, or
£1 per annum, as he should choose. The payment of Katherine's
pension ceased, presumably on her death, before 1370; the last
recorded payment to William is that for the year 1377–8. The
estate included the messuage and carucate of land held by Agnes
de Toundesle of the abbot of Westminster at Pyrford earlier in the
century, for which see W.A.M. 27469. In 1364, part of it was
exchanged for other lands in Pyrford. The lands remaining in the
hands of the nominees after this exchange were amortized as a
messuage, 50 acres of arable, 7 acres of meadow, 60 acres of pasture,
6 acres of woodland and 13s. 4d. per annum in rent.

Enfeoffment of nominees by vendor, 4 Dec. 1362: W.A.M. 1662.
Amortization, 23 Oct. 1366: *Cal. Pat. R., 1364–7*, p. 328.
Surrender by nominees to abbot and convent, 6 Dec. 1366:
W.A.M. 1655.
See also W.A.M. 1648, 1659, 27420 ff.

40. The accounts of the conventual treasurers record the purchase of a mill in *Stratford* (Essex) from Robert Aleyn, a fishmonger of London, in 1364–5 and of the reversion of a mill and 12 acres of meadow here from the same person in 1375–6. The sums paid to Aleyn were, respectively, £60 and £66. 13s. 4d. Neither purchase seems ever to have been amortized, and it is possible that neither transaction was completed. However, in 1392, Robert Aleyn and Matilda, his wife, were granted a corrody of 14 loaves and 14 gallons of ale per week and £6. 13s. 4d. per annum in return for the grant of a mill at Stratford.

W.A.M. 19859, 19867; Liber Niger Quaternus, 88; above, p. 181.

41. In 1369, and almost certainly by purchase, the abbot acquired the manor of *Stourton*, in *Whichford* (Warwicks.), from Thomas West, through nominees, Walter de Parham, of Bourton, Richard Rook, and John Pecche. The manor was still in the abbot's possession in 1373–5, but it was never amortized and did not become a permanent part of the Abbey's estates.[1]

W.A.M. 636–7, 645, 653, 24513; cf. *V.C.H. Warwicks*. v. 205–6; W. Dugdale, *The Antiquities of Warwickshire* (London, 1730), p. 588.

42. A mill, two messuages, and 192 acres of land in *Sutton-under-Brailes* (Warwicks.) were purchased by Litlington and amortized in 1366. The property included a messuage and virgate of land and a messuage and 6 acres once held in fee here of the abbot and convent of Westminster by Mr. Laurence de Walker.

Amortization, 23 Oct. 1366: *Cal. Pat. R., 1364–7*, p. 328.
See also Glos. Records Office, D1099/M 31/44; W.A.M. 25983; *Flete*, p. 134.

43. The unexpired term of the lease of a mill in *Wandsworth* (Surr.) called 'Adekyns mill' was purchased from Roger Fynch, a vintner of London, in 1363–4. The vendor received £66. 13s. 4d.

W.A.M. 19858*; see also above, p. 181.

Temp. William Colchester (1386–1420)

44. A toft, 62 acres of arable, and 2½ acres of meadow, 25 acres of pasture, and a rent of 9s. 8d. per annum in *Battersea, Wandsworth,* and *Rydon* (Surr.) were purchased from John Norton, in 1390, through nominees, Simon Barton, John Thurston, and Thomas Aston. The vendor received £66. 13s. 4d.

[1] In 1375, however, 2 acres of land in Stourton were amortized on behalf of the Abbey. These were probably appurtenances of the so-called messuage purchased from Geoffrey de Chyriton for £4 in 1371–2 (W.A.M. 641–2, 24515; *Cal. Pat. R., 1374–7*, p. 101; see also W.A.M. 640).

Fine, Mich. 1390: *Surrey Fines*, p.156 (no. 17); cf. W.A.M. 1895.
Amortization, 3 Aug. 1392: *Cal. Pat. R., 1391–6*, p. 133.

45. Land in *South Benfleet* and *Moulsham*, in Chelmsford (Essex), was purchased by the conventual treasurers from John Godynow, in 1386–7. The vendor received £64. 1*s*. 10*d*.
Amortization, 3 Aug. 1392: *Cal. Pat. R., 1391–6*, p. 133.
See also W.A.M. 19874.

Temp. John Islip (1500–32)

46. The manors of *Alkborough*, *Burton Stather*, and *Halton*, with a third part of *Belchford* (Lincs.), and the manor of *Oswald Beck Soke* (Notts.) were purchased from George Neville, lord Bergavenny, in 1503–4,[1] with funds provided by Henry VII to endow his chantry. The property was valued @ £64 per annum.
Fine, Hil. 1504: W.A.M. 14624.[2]
Amortization, 2 Mar. 1504: *Cal. Pat. R., 1494–1509*, pp. 350–1.
See also *Cal. Cl. R., Henry VII* ii. 149; and above, pp. 201 f.

47. The manors of *Bullington*, in Clavering and Ugley, and *Pinchpol*, in Manewden (Essex), with lands in Langley, Berdon, Wicken Bonant, Manewden, Farnham, and Elsenham, were purchased for the sum of £400[3] from Sir John Cutte and Elizabeth, his wife, in 1504, with funds provided by Henry VII to endow his chantry, and amortized the same year. The property was valued at £20 per annum.
Covenant between vendors and abbot and convent, 1 Feb. 1504: W.A.M. 5242.
Amortization, 20 Feb. 1504: *Cal. Pat. R., 1494–1509*, p. 342.
Fine, Trin. 1504: *Essex Fines* iv, p. 110 (no. 123); cf. W.A.M. 5211.
See also *Cal. Cl. R., Henry VII* ii. 148–9, and above, p. 200 and n.

---

[1] Although the fine was not made until Hilary Term 1504, on 1 Mar. 1503 Neville surrendered the issues of Alkborough etc. to the abbot and convent of Westminster for the ensuing three years, and on 7 Dec. 1503 he undertook to make 'a sufficient and sure estate' in these properties for the abbot and convent before 25 Mar. next to come, and had already (in Hilary Term 1503) submitted to a common recovery in respect of them. The plaintiffs in the common recovery were Reginald Bray, Edward Poynings, Thomas Fenys, John Pecche, John Mordaunt, James Hoberd, Richard Empson, Thomas Lucas, and others. See W.A.M. 14646–7, 14650; P.R.O., C.P. 40/963, m. 459.
[2] Counterpart.
[3] However, the fine relating to this transaction and to no. 50 below names the sum of £100.

48. The manor and advowson of *Great Chesterford* (Essex) were purchased from Maurice, lord Berkeley, in 1504, with funds provided by Henry VII to endow his chantry, and amortized the same year.[1] The property was valued @ £66. 13s. 4d. per annum, exclusive of sales of wood, and, according to the fine, this was also the sum that Berkeley received.[2]

Common recovery against the vendors, East. 1504: C.P. 40/968, m. 316.

Amortization, 11 May 1504: *Cal. Pat. R.*, *1494–1509*, p. 365.

Fine, Trin. 1504: *Essex Fines* iv, p. 110 (no. 183); cf. W.A.M. 3168.

See also *Cal. Cl. R.*, *Henry VII* ii, p. 149.

49. The manors of *Fenne* and *Skreyne* (Lincs.), with lands and rents in Fishtoft, Boston, Skirbeck, Frieston, Bennington, Butterwick, and Sibsey, and the advowson of the chapel of Fenne, were purchased in 1502–3 for the sum of £578[3] from William Esyngton and his wife, with funds provided by Henry VII to endow his chantry, and amortized in 1504. The property was valued @ £34 per annum.

Fine, Hil. 1502: P.R.O., C.P. 25(1) 145/165/43.

Common recovery against the vendors, Hil. 1502: P.R.O., C.P. 40/959, m. 310; cf. W.A.M. 14722.

Amortization, 20 Feb. 1504: *Cal. Pat. R.*, *1494–1509*, p. 342.

See also *Cal. Cl. R.*, *Henry VII* ii, p. 149; and above, p. 200 and n.

50. The manor of *Plumstead Boarstall* (Kent), with lands in Plumstead, Boarstall, Erith, Lessness, Crayford, Wickham, and East Wickham, was purchased for the sum of £400 from Sir John Cutte and Elizabeth, his wife, in 1504, with funds provided by Henry VII to endow his chantry. The property was valued @ £20 per annum.

Covenant between vendors and abbot and convent, 1 Feb. 1504: W.A.M. 5242.

Amortization, 20 Feb. 1504: *Cal. Pat. R.*, *1494–1509*, p. 342; cf. ibid., p. 305.

---

[1] On 16 Feb. 1504, Berkeley and his sons agreed to give the abbot and convent of Westminster an estate in the manor and advowson before 13 July next; the plaintiffs in the common recovery of Easter Term 1504 demised the property to the abbot and convent on 13 May 1504. The plaintiffs on this occasion and in the common recovery relating to no. 49 below included Richard Fox, bishop of Winchester, Giles Daubeney, Thomas Lovell, Richard Empson, and other royal counsellors and confidants. See W.A.M. 3161, 3167.

[2] See, however, above, pp. 201 f.

[3] The price agreed between the vendors and the abbot and convent in Oct. 1503 (W.A.M. 14708; see also W.A.M. 14708*). This figure is to be preferred to that of £1,000 named in the fine.

Fine, Trin. 1504: *Essex Fines* iv, p. 110 (no. 123); cf. W.A.M. 5211.
See also W.A.M. 5172, 5172*; *Cal. Cl. R., Henry VII* ii, p. 149; and above, p. 200 and n.

51. A rent of £26. 13s. 4d. per annum in *Stanway* (Glos.) was purchased from the abbot and convent of Tewkesbury in 1504, with funds provided by Henry VII to endow his chantry.

Amortization, 15 Mar. 1504: *Cal. Pat. R., 1494–1509*, p. 353.
See also *Cal. Cl. R., Henry VII* ii, p. 149.

APPENDIX V

The Acreage of Demesne Land and of Customary Land in the Demesne Manors, *c.* 1300 to *c.* 1330[1]

I *The Abbot's Portion*

County and Manor	Demesne				Customary Land
	Arable	*Meadow*	*Pasture*	*Woodland*	
Bucks.					
Denham	450				
Glos.					
Bourton-on-the-Hill	350				245
Deerhurst	240				
Hardwicke	760	80	35		
Todenham	370				655+
Midd.					
Eye	295	100			
Laleham	205				100
Staines	145				110[2]
Yeoveney	230				40

[1] The figures are approximate and, in some instances, the minimum that is likely; all have been corrected to the nearest five. The absence of an entry indicates that the figure in question is not known. The acres shown are not identical units in every column. Demesne acres are probably in every case measured acres, but the perch used in their measurement may not have been in each case the same. On most of the manors of the prior and convent, the royal perch of $16\frac{1}{2}$ feet was in use; at Launton, however, the demesne may have been measured by the perch of 18 feet that was still in use on other land here in the sixteenth century (*V.C.H. Oxon.* vi. 235). We do not know what perch was in use on abbatial demesnes. Customary land was measured in customary acres, and such acres were in general smaller than measured acres.

At Ashwell, Battersea and Wandsworth, South Benfleet, Feering, Morden, Paddington, Staines, and Teddington, the figures for the demesne include the acreage of the demesne of the rectory.

Westminster itself presents special problems. The monks possessed extensive meadows in this vill in the early fourteenth century. Most of this land fell within the confines of the manor of Eye and is included in this appendix in the figure given for the meadows in Eye. A little, however, was administered with the manor of Paddington and is included in the corresponding figure for Paddington. A little may have escaped notice altogether.

[2] Including *c.* 65 acres of gavel-land.

I   *The Abbot's Portion* (cont.)

County and Manor	Demesne				Customary Land
	Arable	Meadow	Pasture	Woodland	
Oxon.					
Islip	485				1,175
Surr.					
Pyrford	120				1,060
Warwicks.					
Sutton-under-Brailes	200				755[1]
Worcs.					
Chaceley	220	35			130
Castlemorton	85				
Longdon	105				
Pensham	190	30			
Pinvin	145				560
Pershore and Wick	240	60			

II   *The Portion of the Prior and Convent*

County and Manor	Demesne				Customary Land
	Arable	Meadow	Pasture	Woodland	
Bucks.					
Turweston	265				
Essex					
Birdbrook	560				
Benfleet, South	280	25	5	55	} 175[2]
Fanton	400	10	55		
Feering	725[3]	35	70	100	680
Kelvedon	525	10		60	
Herts.					
Aldenham	430	20	10	35	1,105
Amwell, Great	175				
Ashwell	625	15	15		1,045
Kinsbourne	360	10	30		210
Stevenage	540	5	35	110	665
Wheathampstead	640	15	10		810

[1] Including *c.* 50 acres of one-time demesne land now in the hands of tenants holding by custom.

[2] See below, p. 432 n. 1.

[3] The demesne of this manor lay in the vills of Feering and Pattiswick and in a third vill, described as 'the berewick', but never identified more precisely than this.

II   *The Portion of the Prior and Convent* (cont.)

County and Manor	Demesne				Customary Land
	Arable	Meadow	Pasture	Woodland	
Kent					
Combe			95[1]		
Westerham	500[2]				
Midd.					
Ashford	200	20	25		390[3]
Greenford	425				
Halliford	130				
Hampstead	205	30	50		330
Hendon	470	35			1,050
Knightsbridge	230	5	100		
Paddington	155	10			
Teddington	160	10	80[4]		260
Westminster		15			
Oxon.					
Launton	330				725
Rutl.					
Oakham	130[5]				
Surr.					
Battersea and Wandsworth	425	55	120		800
Claygate	80				130
Morden	310	5	35		275
Suss.					
Parham	125[6]				
Warwicks.					
Knowle	280				

[1] A figure derived from the terrier (undated) in C.U.L. MS. Kk. 5. 29, fo. 125.

[2] The approximate acreage of the cleared area in *c.* 1300; the greater part of this, however, was only sporadically cultivated; see T.A.M. Bishop, 'The rotation of crops at Westerham, 1297–1350', *Economic History Rev.* 9 (1938–9), 39–40.

[3] Including 30 acres of gavel-land.   [4] Commonable heath-land.

[5] Excluding the rectory glebe at Oakham; no evidence relating to the area of this survives before *c.* 1330. In a custumal of 1341, however, it is described as 7 virgates of arable and 7 acres of meadow, in Oakham, Barleythorpe, and Langham, all of which were demised to tenants; but the acreage of the virgate at Oakham is not known. See W.A.M. 20632.

[6] A guess, based on the fact that in 1356–7, the first year in which we have evidence of demesne tillage in this manor, 71½ acres were reaped; one so-called *campum* was at farm at 4s. 6d. per annum. See W.A.M, 4069.

APPENDIX VI

Holdings in the Demesne Manors of Westminster Abbey, to 1348, Classified by Tenure

AN attempt to enumerate holdings must be confined to the manors for which custumals, extents, or rentals survive from this period. The result in the present instance is a set of figures relating, on the one hand, to a number of manors in the West Midlands belonging to the abbot of Westminster's portion of lands, and, on the other, to a number in Essex, Hertfordshire, Middlesex, and Surrey, most of which were assigned to the prior and convent.

Three categories of holding have been distinguished. The first comprises those held by any of the free tenures; the few contractual tenancies that existed on tenant-land in the Abbey's manors in this period have been included in this category. Secondly, villein holdings are enumerated; and, finally, the hybrids—the holdings that comprised land held freely and land held in villeinage.

Each of the holdings enumerated in this appendix[1] was the possession of a tenant who held directly of the abbot and convent of Westminster. At one end of the spectrum of landholding, that represented by the large free holdings, an investigation that stops at this level of the tenurial structure may leave us with very little knowledge of how the land was in fact occupied, for many of these holdings were not farms in single occupation: they were estates with their own structure of demesne and tenant-land. The smaller the holding, the more dependent its form of tenure, the greater is the likelihood that we are dealing with a single unit of husbandry, or at least with one eroded by no permanent alienations. But here, too, there is a sense in which the figures relate to a superstructure—this time, the superstructure of the peasant economy.[2] Since the topic for study is the tenurial unit, all holdings of land in the manor have been included, whether or not their tenants resided there. Numbered among the free holdings, therefore, are some belonging to tenants whose scale of operations as a whole far exceeded that suggested by the evidence of a single manor. Occasionally, extra-manorial holdings are mentioned in the surveys of this period, because the

---

[1] The following remarks apply no less to Appendix VII (below, pp. 434–7).
[2] Above, pp. 213 f.

rent of these was paid to the manor in question; these have been excluded from consideration.

County and Manor	Early 13th Cent.			Late 13th Cent.			Early 14th Cent.		
	Free	Villein	Both	Free	Villein	Both	Free	Villein	Both
Essex									
Benfleet, South } [1]							43	24	7
Fanton									
Feering[2]		47	0	100	40	4			
Kelvedon				c. 35	7	0			
Glos.									
Bourton-on-the-Hill				35	23	0			
Todenham				16	27+[3]	0			
Herts.									
Aldenham	8	59	0	21	61	0	15	113	7
Ashwell							12+[4]	128+[4]	3
Stevenage							90+[5]	17	13
Wheathampstead and Kinsbourne							98	35	4
Midd.									
Ashford							30	16	3
Greenford	3	46	0						
Hampstead							5[6]	45[6]	0
Hendon							49	69	2
Knightsbridge and Paddington[7]		29	1				38		
Teddington	5	21	0				13	13	9
Oxon.									
Islip				4	91	0			
Surr.									
Battersea and Wandsworth	18	71	2	50	65	0	63	47	24
Claygate							6	15	5
Morden	3	18	0				5	28	5
Pyrford							89	67	6
Warwicks.									
Sutton-under-Brailes				9	38		6	36	0

[1] Holdings in South Benfleet are not distinguished clearly from those in Fanton in the custumal of 1315.

[2] The early-thirteenth-century custumal of Feering omits free tenants.

[3] The rental from which this figure is derived omits the *cotmanni* of Todenham, of whom there were sixteen in the early fourteenth century; see below, p. 439 n.

[4] A few holdings at Ashwell were in the hands of parceners, whose numbers are not precisely recorded.

[5] A fee known as the Stonhall fee was divided between several tenants, but the number of the latter is not recorded.

[6] The figures take no account of a tenement and a pasture that were at farm to unnamed tenants.

[7] The early thirteenth-century custumal omits free tenants; the early-fourteenth-century extent, tenants of customary land. It is, however, possible that some of the twenty-nine tenants of customary land in the early thirteenth century held small amounts of free land in addition to their villein holdings; see above, p. 115 n.

County and Manor	Number of Holdings								
	Early 13th Cent.			Late 13th Cent.			Early 14th Cent.		
	Free	Villein	Both	Free	Villein	Both	Free	Villein	Both
Worcs.									
Castlemorton	57	22	0						
Chaceley	7	12	0						
Longdon	17	9	0						
Pensham							4	18	0
Pershore and Wick							53[1]	24	0
Pinvin							3	22	1

Sources.

Aldenham, c. 1225: B.L. Add. Ch. 8139; late 13th cent.: W.A.M. 4616; 1315: C.U.L. MS. Kk 5. 29, fos. 63ᵛ–69. *Ashford,* 1312: W.A.M. 26703. *Ashwell,* 1315: C.U.L. MS. Kk 5. 29, fos. 83ᵛ–89. *Battersea and Wandsworth, c.* 1225: B.L. Add. Ch. 8139; 1268: W.A.M. 27494; 1312: C.U.L. MS. Kk 5. 29, fos. 44–52ᵛ. *Benfleet, South,* and *Fanton,* 1315: C.U.L. MS. Kk 5. 29, fos. 116ᵛ–120. *Bourton-on-the-Hill, c.* 1280: Glos. Records Office, D 1099/ M37, mm. 4–4ᵛ, used in conjunction with W.A.M. 8230 ff. *Castlemorton, c.* 1280: Glos. Records Office, D1099/M37, m. 6. *Chaceley, c.* 1280: Glos. Records Office, D 1099/M37, m. 5; cf. W.A.M. 21066 ff. *Claygate,* 1341: W.A.M. 27228. *Feering, c.* 1225: B.L. Add. Ch. 8139; 1289: C.U.L. MS. Kk 5. 29, fos. 95ᵛ–111ᵛ. *Greenford, c.* 1225: B.L. Add. Ch. 8139. *Hampstead,* 1312: C.U.L. MS. Kk 5. 29, fos. 31ᵛ–36. *Hendon,* 1321: *Trans. London and Middlesex Archaeological Soc.,* N.s. 6 (1929–32), 580–630. *Islip, c.* 1280. Glos. Records Office, D 1099/M 37, mm. 1–1ᵛ; cf. *Rotuli Hundredorum* ii. 831–2, and W.A.M. 14776 ff. *Kelvedon,* 1294: C.U.L. MS. Kk 5. 29, fos. 112–16. *Knightsbridge, c.* 1225: B.L. Add. Ch. 8139; 1312: C.U.L. MS. Kk 5. 29, fos. 36–9. *Longdon, c.* 1280: Glos. Records Office, D1099/M37, m. 6ᵛ. *Morden, c.* 1225: B.L. Add. Ch. 8139; 1312: C.U.L. MS. Kk 5. 29, fos. 39ᵛ–43ᵛ. *Pensham, Pershore and Wick,* and *Pinvin,* 1338–49: W.A.M. 22515. *Pyrford,* 1330: W.A.M. 27469. *Stevenage,* 1315: C.U.L. MS. Kk 5. 29, fos. 78ᵛ–83. *Sutton-under-Brailes, c.* 1280: Glos. Records Office, D 1099/M37, m. 2; 1327: Glos. Records Office, D 1099/ M48. *Teddington, c.* 1225: B.L. Add. Ch. 8139; 1312: W.A.M. 27197. *Todenham, c.* 1280: Glos. Records Office, D 1099/M37, m. 3; cf. ibid. M 30/1 ff., and W.A.M. 25901 ff. *Wheathampstead and Kinsbourne,* 1315: C.U.L. MS. Kk 5. 29, fos. 69ᵛ–78ᵛ.

[1] The figure includes twenty-one contractual tenancies; eleven of these were probably of demesne land.

APPENDIX VII

Holdings of Customary Land in the Demesne Manors of Westminster Abbey, to 1348, Classified by Arable Acreage

THE purpose of this appendix is to record the distribution by acres of holdings of *customary* land in the manors of Westminster Abbey in the thirteenth and early fourteenth centuries. The holdings enumerated are, therefore, on the one hand, those classified as villein holdings in Appendix VI,[1] and, on the other, the villein part of the composite free-and-villein holdings enumerated there. Thus not all comprise the entire acreage which the tenant in question held of the abbot and convent of Westminster—the free part of the composite holdings is omitted—but the great majority do so.

In compiling these figures, it has often been necessary to convert virgates and fractions of the virgate into acres. The probable acreage of the virgate in manors where this has been done was as follows:[2]

In *Essex*, at Feering, 40 acres; in *Glos.*, at Bourton-on-the-Hill, 24, at Todenham, 27;[3] in *Herts.*, at Aldenham, Ashwell, and Stevenage, 40, at Wheathampstead and Kinsbourne, 80;[4] in *Midd.*, at Ashford, 20, at Greenford, 16, at Knightsbridge, 14, at Teddington, 16; in *Oxon.*, at Islip, 32; in *Surr.*, at Battersea and Wandsworth, 15, at Morden, and at Pyrford, 20; in *Warwicks.*, at Sutton-under-Brailes, 48;[5] in *Worcs.*, at Chaceley, 24, at Pinvin, 48.

---

[1] Above, pp. 431–3.

[2] On some of the pitfalls in thus assuming a uniform acreage, even for the virgates in a single manor, see above, pp. 208–9; see also above, pp. 234–5.

[3] See n. 5 below.

[4] For this extraordinarily large virgate see W.D., 207ᵛ–208. The existence of some even larger virgates in the later Middle Ages is indicated by references to, e.g., a 30-acre holding 'called a farthingland', and to half a farthingland of 15 acres (W.A.M. 8944, courts of 3 Dec. 1398 and 3 Dec. 1401).

[5] This acreage is explicitly recorded in Liber Niger Quaternus, 74ᵛ—a fifteenth-century source. The figure is consistent with other evidence from the late-medieval period; for example, the virgate of free land belonging to Mr. Laurence Walker, which the abbot of Westminster acquired in the mid-fourteenth century, and which he 'farmed' to three tenants, is represented in a rental of 1443 by three separate holdings, each of 16 acres (Glos. Records Office, D 1099/ M31/44; ibid. M 40). However, a survey of this manor, made in 1559, notes that, both at Sutton-under-Brailes and at Todenham, a yardland (i.e. a virgate) commonly comprises 80 lands or leys, and that every three such lands and leys contain, at an estimate,

Finally, it must be emphasized that the appendix as a whole relies to some extent on guess-work; some of the possible occasions of error are noted as they arise. The figures for, respectively, the early thirteenth century and the early fourteenth have been summed, but it should be noted that the totals relate only to the holdings in the manors where the size of holdings is *recorded* in each of these periods.

Early 13th Century

County and Manor	Number of Holdings						
	Up to 10 a.	10·25– 20 a.	20·25– 30 a.	30·25– 40 a.	Over 40 a.	Acreage not known	Total
Essex							
Feering	20	19	0	5	0	3	47
Herts.							
Aldenham	24	22	4	4	5	0	59
Midd.							
Greenford	25	12	4	5	0	0	46
Knightsbridge and Paddington	13	17	0	0	0	0	30
Teddington	10	5	4	2	0	0	21
Surr.							
Battersea and Wandsworth	44	22	5	0	1	1	73
Morden	5	11	2	0	0	0	18
Total	141	108	19	16	6	4	294
Percentage	*c.* 48	*c.* 37	*c.* 7	*c.* 5	*c.* 2	*c.* 1	100

Late 13th Century[1]

Essex.[2]							
Feering	20	17	1	6	0	0	44
Glos.							
Bourton-on-the-Hill	8	11	2			2	23
Todenham		7	20				27+[3]

1 acre (ibid. M 51). Very likely, the estimate that 3 lands, or selions, make an acre was made by someone thinking in terms of a statutory acre. If so, here is another example of the small size of some customary acres.

It may well be true that the yardland or virgate at Todenham was of *c.* 27 acres; it is recorded, not only in 1559, but also in 1391, that this was so. However, the actual number of acres in yardlands here described in sixteenth- and seventeenth-century deeds was sometimes considerably less than this, and sometimes a little more. See *V.C.H. Glos.* vi. 254–5.

[1] Since the entries for Todenham are incomplete, and the number of the holdings at Islip of which the acreage is not known is large, in this period, no totals or percentages, other than the totals for each manor severally, are given. Moreover, the rentals and custumals analysed in this section span a period of some thirty years.

[2] Excluding, of the manors for which custumals survive, Kelvedon. There were seven customary holdings here in 1294, made up as follows: 1½ virgates, 1; virgate, 2; half-virgate, 3; quarter-virgate, 1; but the acreage of the virgate at Kelvedon is not recorded. [3] See above, p. 432 n. 3.

Late 13th Century (cont.)

County and Manor	Number of Holdings						
	Up to 10 a.	10·25– 20 a.	20·25– 30 a.	30·25– 40 a.	Over 40 a.	Acreage not known	Total
Herts.							
Aldenham	27	21	6	7	0	0	61
Oxon.							
Islip		60				31[1]	91
Surr.							
Battersea and Wandsworth	35	26	4	0	0	0	65
Worcs.[2]							
Chaceley	8	2	1			1	12

Early 14th Century

	Up to 10 a.	10·25– 20 a.	20·25– 30 a.	30·25– 40 a.	Over 40 a.	Acreage not known	Total
Essex							
Benfleet, South } [3] Fanton	29	2	0	0	0	0	31
Herts.							
Aldenham[4]	83	20	9	4	3	1	120
Ashwell[5]	96	21	5	3	2	4+[6]	131+
Stevenage	3	20	5	2	0	0	30
Wheathampstead and Kinsbourne	7	15	2	12	3	0	39
Midd.							
Ashford	4	10	3	2	0	0	19
Hampstead	29	12	3	0	0	1	45
Hendon	27	32	9	3	0	0	71
Teddington	11	8	1	2	0	0	22
Surr.							
Battersea and Wandsworth	40	25	6	0	0	0	71
Claygate	16	4	0	0	0	0	20
Morden	23	7	3	0	0	0	33
Pyrford[7]	26	26	7	2	0	12	73

[1] The rents payable for these holdings show that at least twenty were each of less than half a virgate (= *c.* 16 acres).

[2] Excluding Castlemorton and Longdon. Although rentals are extant for these manors, and have been used in Appendix VI, it has not been possible to infer the acreage of holdings from the available evidence.

[3] See above, p. 432 n. 1.

[4] Some holdings at Aldenham were in the hands of parceners; the share of the individual parcener has been inferred from the apportionment of rent; thus the entries for this manor include an element of guess-work.

[5] It has been assumed that the holdings of the numerous so-called *bordelli* at Ashwell were small, each comprising not more than 5 acres.

[6] See above, p. 432 n. 4.

[7] Many of the tenants at Pyrford held small so-called purprestures in addition to standard holdings of a virgate or half-virgate. In cases where the rent for the purpresture was very small, the latter has been ignored in the classification of holdings; but, where it seems likely that the purpresture represented a sizeable addition—an acre in extent, or more—to the tenant's holding, the latter has been classified among those of which the acreage is unknown.

Early 14th Century (cont.)

County and Manor	Number of Holdings						
	Up to 10 a.	10·25– 20 a.	20·25– 30 a.	30·25– 40 a.	Over 40 a.	Acreage not known	Total
Warwicks.							
Sutton-under-Brailes	5	19	5	0	7	0	36
Worcs.[1]							
Pinvin	0	0	22	0	1	0	23
Total	399	221	80	30	16	18+	764
Percentage	*c.* 52	*c.* 29	*c.* 10·5	*c.* 4	*c.* 2	*c.* 2·5	100

Sources As for Appendix VI; see above, p. 433.

[1] Excluding, of the manors for which custumals or rentals survive, Pensham, and Pershore and Wick. The names of the customary tenants at Pensham in this period are recorded, but not the extent of their holdings. The customary holdings at Pershore and Wick enumerated above in Appendix VI were probably made up as follows: half-virgate, 17; virgate, 5; acreage not known, 2. But the acreage of the virgate in this manor is not recorded. Further, the rental in which these holdings are recorded (W.A.M. 22515) contains some demonstrable inaccuracies. It should be noted, therefore, that the figures for Pinvin shown above are derived from this source.

P 2

The Extended Value of the Annual Dues for Virgated Holdings of Customary Land in the Demesne Manors of Westminster Abbey in the Early Fourteenth Century[1]

(1) DUES shown in roman type are averages, based on a custumal or extent of the manor in question; the number of cases to which each average relates is shown in brackets beside the description of the holding in Column (ii). Dues shown in italics have been pieced together from the evidence of ministers' accounts, in the absence of custumal or extent; they are the standard dues of the basic holdings used in the assessment of rents and services—the virgate and/or half-virgate. In these instances, the figures in brackets in Column (ii) show the number of these basic holdings in existence in the early fourteenth century in the place in question; they are not necessarily a guide to the number of tenants, since allowance must be made for plural holdings.

The restriction of the data to virgated holdings has entailed the exclusion of the so-called cottages, though not of all holdings as small as some cottage holdings are known to have been. The dues for cottages lacked the homogeneity of those owing for standard holdings, as, indeed, cottages differed widely in size and amenity.

(2) The extended value of dues was, of course, the cash value set upon them in the current extent of the manor. As noted in the text,[2] the actual burden of villein dues in this period was in some manors heavier than the extended value may suggest.

(3) In manors where labour services were remitted on feast days of the Church, it has been necessary to guess the number of days affected by this practice. It has been assumed that, if a customary tenant owed four days' work per week throughout the year, twenty days per annum were lost, in addition to two days' holiday—the

---

[1] Not, however, all the demesne manors. The manors treated in this appendix were, with exceptions noted below: (i) those assigned to the abbot's portion; (ii) those assigned to the conventual treasurers; and (iii) those administered by the latter officials on behalf of other obedientiaries.

[2] Above, p. 237.

universal minimum—at Christmas, Easter, and Whitsun respectively; further, that fifteen of these days fell between 29 Sept. and 24 June, and five between 24 June and 29 Sept. Where the quota of works was larger or smaller than four days per week per annum, proportionate allowances have been made.

(4) Where tallage is recorded as a communal levy, but with no record of the liability of the individual tenant, it has been assumed that the payment was shared among all holdings comprising agricultural land, with or without messuage, in proportion to the size of the holding. If the whole burden of tallage was in fact borne by the holdings with messuage—i.e. by the type of holding with which this appendix is concerned—the rents shown here are unduly low. In several instances, however, ministers' accounts record the tallage quotas of the individual holding.

(5) The following manors, each of which belonged to one of the categories dealt with in this appendix, are, nevertheless, omitted: Denham (Bucks.); South Benfleet, Fanton, and Moulsham (Essex); Great Amwell (Herts.); Eye, Greenford, Halliford, Hampstead, Hanwell, Hendon, and Knightsbridge (Midd.), Castlemorton, Longdon, and Pensham (Worcs.). At South Benfleet, Fanton, Hampstead, and Hendon, the virgate-structure of holdings had virtually disappeared by the beginning of the fourteenth century; in these manors, therefore, customary rents cannot be expressed in figures that relate to the virgate, as do those set out in this appendix.[1] In the other manors, information about customary rents is exceedingly fragmentary or non-existent in the period *c.* 1300 to 1348.

I   *The Abbot's Manors*

(i) County and Manor	(ii) Holding	(iii) Annual Dues			
		Money	Labour	Kind	Total
		s. d.	*£ s. d.*	*s. d.*	*£ s. d.*
Glos.					
Bourton-on-the-Hill	Virgate (7½)	*2 1½*	*17 9*	*4*	*1 0 2¼*
Deerhurst and Hardwicke	¼ Virgate (38)	*10 1*	*3 4*	*Nil*	*13 5*
Todenham[2]	Virgate (20)	*6 0*	*2 4½*	*8*	*9 0¼*
	¼ Virgate (6)	*3 0*	*1 7*	*6*	*5 1*

[1] For customary rents expressed as rents per acre in these manors, see below, pp. 445–6.

[2] In addition to the rents shown here, those of the sixteen *cotmanni* of Todenham should be noted. Most of these tenants owed the following dues per annum: money rent, 1*s.* 3*d.*; labour services valued at 11*s.* 1½*d.*; renders in kind valued at 2*d.*; total, 12*s.* 6½*d.* One of these holdings comprised 22 or 23 acres of arable; the acreage of the others is not known.

I *The Abbot's Manors* (cont.)

(i) *County and Manor*	(ii) *Holding*	(iii) *Annual Dues*			
		Money	*Labour*	*Kind*	*Total*
		s. d.	*£ s. d.*	*s. d.*	*£ s. d.*
Midd.					
Laleham	½ Virgate (19½)	*1 9*	*2 10½*	*2¾*	*4 10¼*
Staines	½ Virgate (8½)	*1 6*	*2 3½*	*2½*	*4 0*
Yeoveney	½ Virgate (7½)	*1 4*	*2 0*	*2½*	*3 6½*
Oxon.					
Islip[1]	½ Virgate (*c.* 32)	*1 8*	*9 10½*	*2*	*11 8½*
Surr.					
Pyrford	2 Virgates (2)	15 11½	2 5½	Nil	18 5
	1½ Virgates (1)	13 2	3 7¾	Nil	16 9¾
	1¼ Virgates (2)	13 6	3 8¾	Nil	17 2¾
	Virgate (23)	8 11¾	2 5½	6¾	12 0
	¾ Virgate (2)	6 11½	1 3½	1 0	9 3
	⅔ Virgate (2)	6 5½	7½	Nil	7 1
	½ Virgate (26)	5 2	1 0½	Nil	6 2½
	⅓ Virgate (1)	3 8½	1½	Nil	3 10
	¼ Virgate (5)	2 10½	1 0½	2½	4 1½
Warwicks.					
Sutton-under-Brailes[2]	Virgate (7)	12 1	1 10½	Nil	13 11½
	½ Virgate (4)	6 1	1 0	Nil	7 1
Worcs.					
Chaceley	Virgate (1)	*3 11¼*	*1 15 0¾*	*Nil*	*1 19 0*
	½ Virgate (2)	*2 8¼*	*17 6½*	*Nil*	*1 0 2¾*
Pershore and Wick	Virgate (5)	*8 5½*	*10 11½*	*1*	*19 6*
	½ Virgate (17)	*4 3¼*	*5 5¾*	*1*	*9 10*
Pinvin	Virgate (1)	*8 0½*	*9 4*	*Nil*	*17 4½*
	½ Virgate (21)	*4 0¼*	*4 8*	*Nil*	*8 8¼*

II *Manors Assigned to or Administered by the Conventual Treasurers*

Essex[3]					
Feering	Virgate (7)	8 6	10 5	5¾	19 4¾
	½ Virgate (12)	5 3½	3 5	2½	8 11
	⅓ Virgate (3)	3 1	4 3	2¾	7 6¾
	¼ Virgate (4)	1 7¾	3 2¼	Nil	4 10
	$\frac{1}{12}$ Virgate (11)	11¾	2 0¼	¼	3 0¼

[1] The rents shown are the minimum that is likely; the extended value of labour rent per half-virgate may in fact have been as high as 12*s.* 3½*d.* per annum. They relate only to the vill of Islip; for rents at Murcot and Fencot, the other vills comprised in this manor, the evidence is tenuous at this time. According to the Hundred Rolls, a half-virgater at Islip owed 3*s.* rent per annum, 'et opera et consuetudines ad voluntatem domini' (*Rot. Hund.* ii. 831). The rent of 3*s.* per annum was in fact paid by a tenant not performing week-work; it is therefore subsumed in the value of the labour services shown above. The cash render of 1*s.* 8*d.* per annum shown above was a payment for tallage.

[2] In addition to the rents shown here, those of the twenty-five *cotmanni* of Sutton should be noted. The greater number of these (eighteen) held a messuage and 14 acres of arable and owed the following annual dues: money rent, 3*s.*; labour services valued at 1*s.* 0½*d.*; renders in kind valued at 2*s.*; total 6*s.* 0½*d.*

[3] The figures for Feering and Kelvedon are derived from extents made, respectively, in 1289 and 1294; they are, however, true of the early fourteenth century as well.

II *Manors Assigned to or Administered by the Conventual Treasurers* (cont.)

(i) *County and Manor*	(ii) *Holding*	(iii) *Annual Dues*									
		Money		*Labour*			*Kind*		*Total*		
		s.	*d.*	*£*	*s.*	*d.*	*s.*	*d.*	*£*	*s.*	*d.*
Kelvedon	1½ Virgates (1)	6	1	1	6	0¼		9	1	12	10¼
	Virgate (2)	2	4	1	6	0½		3	1	8	7½
	½ Virgate (2)	2	3¼		13	0½		1½		15	5¼
	¼ Virgate (2)	2	0		5	6	Nil			7	6
Herts.											
Aldenham[1]	Virgate (7)	9	4¾		4	6½		6¼		14	5½
	½ Virgate (13)	4	10		2	9½		1¾		7	9¼
	½ Virgate (*molman*) (1)	6	8		Nil		Nil			6	8
	¼ Virgate (29)	2	6½		1	8		¾		4	3¼
	¼ Virgate (*mondayland*) (8)		5		4	2		1		4	8
	⅛ Virgate (1)	2	1		1	8		1		3	10
	⅛ Virgate (*mondayland*) (1)		2		4	2		1		4	5
Ashwell[2]	Virgate (2)	12	6			6½	4	6		17	6½
	½ Virgate (23)	6	4			5½	2	3		9	0½
	⅓ Virgate (1)	4	2			3½	1	6		5	11½
	¼ Virgate (18)	3	1½			2	1	1½		4	5
Stevenage	Virgate (14)	4	1½	1	10	9¼		9¾	1	15	8½
	½ Virgate (1)	11	4¾		Nil		Nil			11	4¾
Wheathampstead	Virgate (1)	13	4	1	4	8½	3	4½	2	1	5
	⅔ Virgate (1)	12	3		16	6	2	1	1	10	10
	½ Virgate (8)	6	11½		12	4¼	1	8½	1	1	0¼
	⅓ Virgate (1)	15	10¾		Nil		Nil			15	10¾
	¼ Virgate (13)	4	2		6	1¾		10		11	1¾
—— Kinsbourne	½ Virgate (4)	3	2¾		19	4	1	2¼	1	3	9
	¼ Virgate (2)	2	7½		8	8¾	1	10		13	2¼
Midd.											
Ashford	2 Virgates (1)	5	11		19	0	3	5	1	8	4
	1 Virgate (13)	2	11½		9	6	1	8½		14	2
	½ Virgate (6)	1	5¾		4	9		10¼		7	1
	½ Virgate (*gavel-land*) (3)	3	9¼			4¼		11		5	0½
Teddington	2 Virgates (2)	8	7		7	7		10¼		17	0¼
	1½ Virgates (3)	5	9		7	4¼		10¼		13	11½
	Virgate (7)	3	1½		7	1½		10¼		11	1¼
	½ Virgate (3)		8		6	11¾		10¼		8	6
Oxon.											
Launton	Virgate (35¾)	*8*	*9½*		*4*	*6½*	*Nil*			*13*	*4*
Surr.											
Battersea and Wandsworth	2 Virgates (3)	6	7		6	6¾		3¼		13	5
	1½ Virgates (2)	5	5¾		3	6	Nil			8	11¾
	Virgate (23)	4	2¾		4	7¾		3		9	1½
	½ Virgate (37)	2	3		3	8½		2		6	1½
	¼ Virgate (4)	4	6¾			½	Nil			4	7¼
Morden	1½ Virgates (1)	3	8¼		4	9¼		½		8	6
	Virgate (9)	2	4½		3	5¼		½		5	10¼
	½ Virgate (3)	1	2¼		3	0		¼		4	2½

[1] The so-called molmen at Aldenham held 145½ arable acres outside the virgated pattern of holdings, in addition to the half-virgate shown in the text.

[2] A half-virgate, for which the sole recorded due was a money-rent of 8*d.* per annum, has been excluded from the reckoning; this was probably a service-holding, the tenant of which owed special duties on the demesne. Further, 98½ acres of land at Ashwell were held by customary tenants outside the virgated pattern of holdings and exclusively for money-rents. On these acres, see also below, p. 445 n. 4.

Sources

Aldenham: C.U.L. MS. Kk 5. 29, fos. 63ᵛ–69 (extent of 1315). Ashford: W.A.M.
26703 (extent of 1312). Ashwell: C.U.L. MS. Kk 5. 29, fos. 83ᵛ–89 (extent of
1315). Battersea and Wandsworth: ibid., fos. 44–52ᵛ (extent of 1312). Bourton-on-
the-Hill: W.A.M. 8237, 8250 ff. Chaceley: W.A.M. 21066 ff. Deerhurst and
Hardwicke: W.A.M. 8422 ff. Feering: C.U.L. MS. Kk 5. 29, fos. 95ᵛ–111ᵛ
(extent of 1289). Islip: W.A.M. 14787 ff.; cf. *Oxfordshire Record Soc.* 40 (1959), 84.
Kelvedon: C.U.L. MS. Kk 5. 29, fos. 112–16 (extent of 1294). Laleham: W.A.M.
27112 ff. Launton: W.A.M. 15312 ff. Morden: C.U.L. MS. Kk 5. 29, fos. 39ᵛ–43ᵛ
(extent of 1312). Pershore and Wick: W.A.M. 22092 ff., 22515. Pinvin: W.A.M.
22121 ff., 22515; cf. W.A.M. 22514, 22531. Pyrford: W.A.M. 27469. Staines:
W.A.M. 16857 ff., 16923 ff.; cf. W.A.M. 16786. Stevenage: C.U.L. MS. Kk 5.
29, fos. 78ᵛ–83 (extent of 1315). Sutton-under-Brailes: Glos. Records Office,
D 1099/M48 (extent of 1327). Teddington: W.A.M. 27197 (extent of 1312).
Todenham: W.A.M. 25929 ff., Glos. Records Office, D 1099/M 30/3 ff. Wheathampstead and Kinsbourne: C.U.L. MS. Kk 5. 29, fos. 69ᵛ–78ᵛ (extent of 1315).
Yeoveney: W.A.M. 16849 ff.

APPENDIX IX

Customary and Contractual Rents per Arable Acre in the Demesne Manors of Westminster Abbey in the Early Fourteenth Century

THE figures in Column (iii) of this table express the extended value of the annual dues for customary holdings recorded in Appendix VIII.[1] In Column (iv) these dues are expressed, in pence, as averages per arable acre for the holding in question, except in the cases of Deerhurst and Hardwicke, Kelvedon, and Pershore and Wick, where the acreage of the virgate is not known. Also included in Column (iv) are dues for South Benfleet and Fanton, Hampstead, and Hendon—manors where a virgated structure of holdings had all but disappeared by the early fourteenth century and which are omitted, therefore, from Appendix VIII. Holdings in these manors were reckoned by the acre and not by the virgate. The figures for South Benfleet and Fanton, Hampstead, and Hendon are, in each case, averages per acre of the extended value of the dues paid for holdings appurtenant to messuages. At South Benfleet and Fanton, considered together, such holdings comprised 141½ arable acres, at Hampstead, 307¼ acres, and at Hendon, 909 acres.

The contractual rents entered in Column (v) are those recorded for specified acreages of demesne land and tenant-land in the surviving ministers' accounts for the manors in question between 1300 and 1348. Rents relating to parcels of land of which the acreage is not given are omitted; these, however, are not numerous. Although the land to which these rents relate is described as demesne land in only a minority of cases, very likely it was so in nearly all. The figures in this column, therefore, relate mainly to measured acres. Each contractual rent is entered under the year in which the lease which gave rise to it was made or that of the first surviving reference to it. In the case of eleven manors, Column (v) is blank. Only two accounts for Fanton survive from this period, and none for South Benfleet. But accounts do survive, in some instances in good numbers, for Battersea and Wandsworth, Feering, Hampstead, Hendon, Pinvin, Pyrford, Teddington, Todenham,

---

[1] See above, p. 438 and n.

and Yeoveney. Here, the absence of references to contractual rents may well mean that few such arrangements, or none, were in use at this time.

The validity of the comparison between customary and contractual rents which this appendix is intended to facilitate is considered above.[1]

I *The Abbot's Manors*

(i) *County and Manor*	(ii) *Holding*	(iii) *Annual Dues for (ii)*	(iv) *Annual Dues expressed as dues per arable acre*	(v) *Contractual Rents per arable acre*
		£ s. d.		
Glos.				
Bourton-on-the-Hill	Virgate (7½)	1 0 2½	10·10*d.*	*1337–8* 11a. 3ro. @ 3·83*d.*; 10a. @ 3·00*d.*; 2a. @ 4·00*d.*
Deerhurst and Hardwicke	½ Virgate (38)	13 5		*1321–2* 2a. 3ro. @ 4·36*d.*; *1325–6* 1a. 2ro. @ 20·00*d.*; 1a. @ 18·00*d.*; 1a. @ 12·00*d.* *1328–9* 2a. @ 18·00*d.* *1329–30* 1a. @ 12·00*d.* *1333–4* 1a. 2ro. @ 16·00*d.* *1342–3* 1a. @ 13·50*d.*; 12a. 2ro. @ 6·00*d.*; 3a. @ 8·00*d.*
Todenham	Virgate (20)	9 0½	4·02*d.*	
	½ Virgate (6)	5 1	4·52*d.*	
Midd.				
Laleham	½ Virgate (19½)	4 10½	11·65*d.*	*1302–3* 123a. ½ro. demesne @ 6·00*d.*
Staines	½ Virgate (8½)	4 0	9·60*d.*	*1346–7* 23a. demesne @ 6·00*d.*
Yeoveney	½ Virgate (7½)	3 6½	8·50*d.*	
Oxon.				
Islip	½ Virgate (*c.* 32)	11 8½	8·78*d.*	*1331–2* 15a. 3ro. demesne @ 3·00*d.*, rising to 6·00*d.* in *1332–3.*
Surr.				
Pyrford	2 Virgates (2)	18 5	5·53*d.*	
	1½ Virgates (1)	16 9¾	6·73*d.*	
	1¼ Virgates (2)	17 2¾	8·27*d.*	
	Virgate (23)	12 0	7·20*d.*	
	¾ Virgate (2)	9 3	7·40*d.*	
	⅔ Virgate (2)	7 1	6·38*d.*	
	½ Virgate (26)	6 2½	7·45*d.*	
	⅓ Virgate (1)	3 10	6·91*d.*	
	¼ Virgate (5)	4 1½	9·90*d.*	
Warwicks.				
Sutton-under-Brailes	Virgate (7)	13 11½	3·49*d.*[2]	*1330–1* 32a. demesne @ 2·25*d.*
	½ Virgate (4)	7 1	3·54*d.*[2]	

[1] pp. 234–7.

[2] The corresponding figure in the case of the holdings of the *cotmanni* of Sutton-under-Brailes is 5·18*d.*; for these holdings, see above, p. 440 n. 2.

I *The Abbot's Manors* (cont.)

(i) *County and Manor*	(ii) *Holding*	(iii) *Annual Dues for (ii)*	(iv) *Annual Dues expressed as dues per arable acre*	(v) *Contractual Rents per arable acre*
		£ *s.* *d.*		
Worcs.				
Chaceley	Virgate (1)	1 19 0	19·50*d.*	*1313–14* 18a. 3ro. @ 4·00*d.* *1320–1* 4a. 2ro. @ 8·00*d.* *1343–4* 10a. @ 12·00*d.*
	½ Virgate (2)	1 0 2¾	20·23*d.*	
Pershore and Wick	Virgate (5)	19 6		*1321–2* 18a. @ 6·00*d.* *1343–4* 24a. @ 3·00*d.*; 15a. @ 6·00*d.*
	½ Virgate (17)	9 10		
Pinvin	Virgate (1)	17 4½	4·34*d.*	
	½ Virgate (21)	8 8¼	4·34*d.*	

II *Manors Assigned to or Administered by the Conventual Treasurers*

Essex				
Benfleet, South, and Fanton[1]			4·96*d.*	
Feering[2]	Virgate (7)	19 4¾	5·82*d.*	
	½ Virgate (12)	8 11	5·35*d.*	
	⅓ Virgate (3)	7 6¾	6·81*d.*	
	¼ Virgate (4)	4 10	5·80*d.*	
	1/12 Virgate (11)	3 0¼	10·89*d.*	
Kelvedon[2]	1½ Virgates (1)	1 12 10¼		*1327–8* 35a. @ 6·00*d.* *1336–7* 26a. @ 6·00*d.* *1337–8* 35a. @ 6·00*d.* *1338–9* 7a. 2ro. @ 8·00*d.*
	Virgate (2)	1 8 7½		
	½ Virgate (2)	15 5¼		
	¼ Virgate (2)	7 6		
Herts.				
Aldenham	Virgate (7)	14 5½	4·34*d.*	*1301–2* 8a. demesne @ 6·00*d.* *1303–4* 5a. @ 6·00*d.*
	½ Virgate (13)	7 9¼	4·66*d.*	
	½ Virgate (*molman*) (1)	6 8	4·00*d.*[3]	
	¼ Virgate (29)	4 3¼	5·13*d.*	
	¼ Virgate (*mondayland*) (8)	4 8	5·60*d.*	
	⅛ Virgate (1)	3 10	9·20*d.*	
	⅛ Virgate (*mondayland*) (1)	4 5	10·60*d.*	
Ashwell[4]	Virgate (2)	17 6½	5·26*d.*	*1305–6* 16a. @ 17·81*d.*; 1a. @ 5·00*d.* *1311–12* 25a. @ 18·80*d.* *1332–3* 100a. demesne @ 4·00*d.*; 161a. demesne @ 6·00*d.* *1341–2* 1a. @ 5·00*d.*; 1a. @ 6·00*d.*; 120a. [demesne] @ 6·00*d.*
	½ Virgate (23)	9 0½	5·43*d.*	
	⅓ Virgate (1)	5 11½	5·36*d.*	
	¼ Virgate (18)	4 5	5·30*d.*	

[1] See above, p. 432 n. 1. [2] See above, p. 440 n. 3.

[3] The rent per acre of the arable land held by molmen at Aldenham outside the virgated structure of holdings, and probably without messuage, was 5·20*d.* For this land, see above, p. 441 n. 1.

[4] Customary tenants at Ashwell held 98½ acres outside the virgated structure of holdings and probably without messuage; 75½ acres of this land was 'outland'. The average rent per acre in the case of the 98½ acres was 8·35*d.*, in that of the 75½ acres, 9·42*d.*

II *Manors Assigned to or Administered by the Conventual Treasurers* (cont.)

(i) *County and Manor*	(ii) *Holding*	(iii) *Annual Dues for (ii)*	(iv) *Annual Dues expressed as dues per arable acre*	(v) *Contractual Rents per arable acre*
		£ s. d.		
Herts. (*cont.*)				
Stevenage	Virgate (14)	1 15 8½	10·71*d.*	*1344–5* 8a. @ 8·00*d.*[1]
	½ Virgate (1)	11 4¾	6·84*d.*	
Wheathampstead[2]	Virgate (1)	2 1 5	6·21*d.*	*1326–7* 10a. @ 6·00*d.* *1339–40* 4a. @ 8·00*d.*; 11a. 2ro. @ 6·00*d.*
	⅔ Virgate (1)	1 10 10	6·94*d.*	
	½ Virgate (8)	1 1 0¼	6·31*d.*	
	⅓ Virgate (1)	15 10¾	7·15*d.*	
	¼ Virgate (13)	11 1¾	6·69*d.*	
—— Kinsbourne	½ Virgate (4)	1 3 9	7·13*d.*	*1345–6* 10a. @ 6·00*d.*; 10a. @ 8·00*d.*
	¼ Virgate (2)	13 2¼	7·91*d.*	
Midd.				
Ashford	2 Virgates (1)	1 8 4	8·50*d.*	*1299–1300* 1a. @ 12·00*d.* *1307–8* 1a. @ 10·00*d.* *1331–2* 20a. @ 6·00*d.* *1335–6* 3a. @ 6·00*d.* *1336–7* 156a. 3ro. @ 6·00*d.*; 8a. @ 6·00*d.*
	1 Virgate (13)	14 2	8·50*d.*	
	½ Virgate (6)	7 1	8·50*d.*	
	½ Virgate (*gavel-land*) (3)	5 0½	6·05*d.*	
Hampstead			5·41*d.*	
Hendon			7·62*d.*[3]	
Teddington	2 Virgates (2)	17 0¼	6·38*d.*	
	1½ Virgates (3)	13 11½	6·98*d.*	
	Virgate (7)	11 1¼	8·33*d.*	
	½ Virgate (3)	8 6	12·75*d.*	
Oxon.				
Launton	Virgate (35¾)	13 4	8·00*d.*	*1335–6* 3a. demesne @ 6·00*d.*[4]
Surr.				
Battersea and Wandsworth	2 Virgates (3)	13 5	5·37*d.*	
	1½ Virgates (2)	8 11¾	4·79*d.*	
	Virgate (23)	9 1½	7·30*d.*	
	½ Virgate (37)	6 1½	9·80*d.*	
	¼ Virgate (4)	4 7¼	14·73*d.*	
Morden	1½ Virgates (1)	8 6	3·40*d.*	*1311–12* 7a. @ 4·00*d.*
	Virgate (9)	5 10¼	3·51*d.*	
	½ Virgate (3)	4 2½	5·05*d.*	

[1] Note also the following 'new rents' recorded among rents of assize at Stevenage: *1327–8* 1a. @ 6·00*d.*; *1330–1* 1a. @ 8·00*d.*

[2] In 1303–4, 4a. 1ro. of land at Wheathampstead, of which at least 2a. 2ro. were demesne land, were granted heritably in seven lots, for rents equivalent to 2*s.* per acre per annum, and for relatively heavy fines (e.g. 16*s.* in the case of an acre lot). These were customary tenancies, and in five cases it is said explicitly that the land was to be built on. An eighth lot consisted of 1 rood of land @ 2*d.* per annum and for a fine of 6*d.* See W.A.M. 8938; Herts. Record Office, D/Elw M 122.

[3] The average rent per acre of 142 arable acres held by customary tenants without messuage was 7·15*d.*

[4] Some customary tenancies of demesne arable acres were granted at Launton at this time. The usual rent seems to have been 6*d.* per acre per annum. These acres, however, had pasture rights appurtenant to them; the tenants paid small entry fines. See W.A.M. 15340, 15431.

Sources

(i) *Customary Rents*: As for Appendix VIII (above, p. 442), but add: South Benfleet and Fanton, C.U.L. MS. Kk 5. 29, fos. 116ᵛ–120 (extent of 1315); Hampstead, ibid., fos. 31ᵛ–36 (extent of 1312); Hendon, *Trans. London and Middlesex Archaeological Soc.*, N.S. 6 (1929–32), 580–630 (extent of 1321).

(ii) *Contractual Rents*: Aldenham, W.A.M. 26048 ff.; Ashford, W.A.M. 26688 ff.; Ashwell, W.A.M. 26256 ff., P.R.O., S.C. 6/862/5; Bourton-on-the-Hill, W.A.M. 8250 ff.; Chaceley, W.A.M. 21066 ff.; Deerhurst and Hardwicke, W.A.M. 8422 ff.; Islip, W.A.M. 14787 ff.; Kelvedon, W.A.M. 25184 ff., P.R.O., S.C. 6/844/38; Laleham, W.A.M. 27112 ff., P.R.O., S.C. 6/916/26; Launton, W.A.M. 15312 ff.; Morden, W.A.M. 27297 ff.; Pershore and Wick, W.A.M. 22092 ff.; Staines, W.A.M. 16857 ff., 16923 ff.; Stevenage, P.R.O., S.C. 6/870/15 ff., W.A.M. 26344–8, St. Paul's Cathedral MSS., Press B, Boxes 81, 92, 111; Sutton-under-Brailes, Glos. Records Office, D 1099/M31/ 19 ff.; Wheathampstead and Kinsbourne, W.A.M. 8790 ff., 8918–22, Herts. Record Office, D/Elw M 119 ff.

Glossary[1]

Anniversary	An annual commemoration, usually of a deceased person on the day of his death; the central, but in some cases by no means the only, observance was a mass.
Appropriation	The take-over by a religious house or other party of the tithes and endowments of a parish or other church or of part of these; in its commonest form, the take-over by a religious house of the great tithes and glebe of a parish church, i.e. of the rector's benefice.
Assign, to	To transfer to another; to alienate.
Cestui que use	The beneficiary of an enfeoffment to uses. (Cf. the modern beneficiary of a trust: he enjoys the revenue for the time being but cannot consume the capital.)
Champarty lease	A lease giving the landlord a fixed share of the produce of the land so leased.
Chantry	An endowed, daily mass, usually in commemoration of a deceased person.
Chirograph	An indenture, q.v.
Contractual lease	A lease, the terms of which were agreed *ad hoc* between the parties; usually contrasted with an arrangement regulated by customary conditions of landholding.
Copy	A transcript of an entry in a manorial court roll, most characteristically recording the admittance of a tenant to hold according to the custom of the manor.
—— *hold*	The tenure of one so admitted.
Corrody	A regular allowance for maintenance, usually in kind, made from the revenues of a great estate, especially that of a religious house.
Customary land	Land on which conditions of landholding etc. were normally regulated within the manor and by recourse to custom; not free land, q.v.
Demesne	(i) That part of an estate or manor not alienated in fee and thus held by tenants for rent or services. (ii) The home-farm of the lord of the manor and its appurtenances.
——, *tenant in*	One seised of an estate of inheritance.

[1] I am greatly indebted to Dr. P. R. Hyams for help with this glossary.

Entry, right of	The right to enter on land without incurring the guilt of disseisin.
Estate	(Latin, *status*) A continuing free interest in land, classifiable by its duration (e.g., an estate in fee simple, q.v., or a life estate) and of a type recognized by the royal courts; several different people may have estates in the same piece of land at the same time.
Exemption	The freedom from all spiritual jurisdiction except that of the pope enjoyed by some ecclesiastical corporations, usually after a specific grant of privilege.
Farm	(i) The interest in a manor or manorial demesne of the official in charge of it; he would normally be expected to remit a fixed rent to the lord, whatever the level of revenue in a particular year. (ii) A lease, q.v. (iii) Any unaccustomed tenurial arrangement.
Fee	(i) A holding, usually of land, but occasionally of money or of an office. The original connotations were of reward for service; the later ones, of a permanent arrangement.
—— *farm*	A fee held by the service of paying a rent in money or in kind.
—— *simple*	A heritable and alienable fee; i.e., one that is permanent except at the option of the tenant.
—— *tail*	A conditional, inalienable fee, descending to a limited class of heir and reverting to the donor on failure of that class. Most characteristically, a conveyancing device to retain a landed patrimony within the control of the grantor's direct heirs.
Final concord, fine	(i) The bringing of a dispute etc. to an end (Latin, *finis*) often sealed by a payment as offering. (ii) A conveyance of property in the form of a compromise of a legal action; in the later Middle Ages, most such litigation was collusive. (iii) The tripartite indenture (q.v.) recording (i) and (ii).
Freehold	An estate (q.v.) in land of uncertain duration; i.e., not a fixed term.
Free land	Land which was held on terms which permitted the tenants (or their rivals) to sue about it in royal courts or the county court. Not customary land (q.v.) or other servile land.
Gavel-land	Customary land held for a money rent (O.E. *gafol*) and not for customary services.
—— *-man*	A tenant of gavel-land.
Grout	(i) An inferior kind of malt. (ii) The ale made from this.

Hoketide	The second Monday and Tuesday after Easter.
Indenture	A deed written with one counterpart, or with two, on a single piece of parchment, the two or three parts being severed by a zig-zag cut, or cut through the lettering of a word such as 'cirographum'. Each of those interested received one part.
Jointure	Co-tenancy in which the survivor takes the whole; especially used of married couples (e.g. widow's jointure).
Lease	A grant of land that is distinguished from a freehold (q.v.) or grant in fee (q.v.) by its limited duration, usually for a term of years or for a life or lives. Cf. champarty lease, contractual lease.
Livery of seisin	The public transfer of seisin between feoffor and feoffee, on the land or property in question, or within view of it.
Martyrology	Register of persons commemorated in the liturgy in a religious house.
Molman	A gavel-man, q.v.
Nativus	A serf.
—— *de sanguine*	A serf by reason of descent.
Parceners	Co-heirs of land which, nevertheless, was not partitioned but remained a single unit of tenure; often female, e.g. sisters.
Pittance	An additional allowance of food or drink on a special occasion, such as an anniversary, q.v.
Real actions	Actions in the royal or county courts for the recovery of the seisin (q.v.) of land; e.g. novel disseisin, writ of right.
Remainder	The interest of the person who was to succeed to property on the expiry of a previous estate.
Reprises	Regular charges on a manor or other property which are part of the gross but not the net income of the estate.
Reversion	The coming back of property to a donor on the expiry of a life-tenancy or failure of heirs in tail; a special case of remainder, q.v.
Seisin	Possession; used later only of possession of a free tenement recoverable by the real actions, q.v.
Selion	A unit of cultivation in an open field; i.e. a ridge.
Serjeanty	(i) A free tenure, for services other than knight service; in the present context, a tenure for services in and about the monastic household. The tenants (serjeants; Latin, *servientes*) might be called *ministeriales* on the Continent.

Tithes, great	Tithes of the major crops; the Church's tenth.
——, *personal*	Tithes other than those paid in respect of agrarian produce.
——, *small*	Tithes of agrarian produce other than the major crops; e.g. of lambs.
Waste	(i) Property not yielding its accustomed dues or profits, e.g. on account of neglect or damage. (ii) Land not appropriated for productive use in severalty. (iii) The diminution of the heritable assets of an estate; actionable by holders of remainder (q.v.) or reversion (q.v.).

Bibliography

I MANUSCRIPT SOURCES

Muniment Room, Westminster Abbey

(i) *Accounts of abbatial officials*

W.A.M. 9251–3, 24489–548 — Accounts of the steward, alias clerk, of the abbot's household 1275–1463

W.A.M. 33320, 33324 — Day-books of household expenses, 1500–2, 1509–10

W.A.M. 24404–88 — Accounts of the steward, alias receiver, in the Western Parts, 1352–1523

(ii) *Accounts of conventual officials*

W.A.M. 18962–19154 — Almoner, 1283–1539
W.A.M. 18717–827 — Chamberlain, 1291–1536
W.A.M. 19155–315 — Granger, 1349–1537
W.A.M. 19318–502 — Infirmarer, 1297–1537
W.A.M. 13313, 13315–19 — Receiver of the revenues of the church of St. Martin-le-Grand, 1503–27

W.A.M. 19618–837* — Sacrist, 1317–1540
W.A.M. 19838–20000 — Treasurers, 1297–1503
W.A.M. 23318–451 — Warden of the churches, 1349–1522
W.A.M. 23452–626 — Warden of the new work, 1341–1534
Wardens of the royal foundations
W.A.M. 23627–969 — Eleanor of Castile, 1286–1534
W.A.M. 23970–24121 — Richard II and Anne of Bohemia, 1394–1534
W.A.M. 24122–235 — Henry V, 1437–1535
W.A.M. 24236–50, 28043 — Henry VII, 1502–33
W.A.M. 23179–317 — Warden of St. Mary's chapel, 1298–1537

(iii) *Ministers' Accounts*

Bucks.

W.A.M. 3408–19 — Denham, 1369–1502
W.A.M. 7754–917 — Turweston, 1293–1517

Essex

W.A.M. 25395–566 — Birdbrook, 1292–1516

| W.A.M. 25572–775 | Feering (manor and rectory), 1271–1507 |
| W.A.M. 25776–894 | Kelvedon, 1292–1500 |

Glos.

W.A.M. 8230–350	Bourton-on-the-Hill, 1279–1497
W.A.M. 8422–66	Deerhurst and Hardwicke, 1306–1447
W.A.M. 25903–92	Todenham, 1281–1461
W.A.M. 25900–2	Todenham and Sutton-under-Brailes (Warwicks.), 1252–3, 1276–7[1]
W.A.M. 25993–26015	Todenham and Sutton-under-Brailes, 1461–97[2]

Herts.

W.A.M. 26016–144	Aldenham, 1278–1515
W.A.M. 26145–9	Amwell, Great, 1290–1517
W.A.M. 26248–300	Ashwell (manor and rectory), 1274–1502
W.A.M. 8914–16	Harpenden, 1280–2
W.A.M. 8761–883	Kinsbourne, 1273–1530
W.A.M. 26339–43	Stevenage, 1270–81
W.A.M. 26344–83	——, 1320–1502
W.A.M. 8913, 8918, 8920–36	Wheathampstead, 1271–2, 1305–6, 1339–1515

Kent

W.A.M. 26437*	Stangraves, 1351–2
W.A.M. 26386–437	Westerham, 1293–1350
W.A.M. 26438–519	——, 1357–97

Midd.

W.A.M. 26655–846	Ashford (manor and rectory), 1277–1500
W.A.M. 26848–998	Eye, 1275–1490
W.A.M. 27010–64	Halliford, 1289–1512
W.A.M. 32367–76, 32393–406, 32493–531	Hampstead, 1272–1412
W.A.M. 32532–622	Hendon, 1316–1502
W.A.M. 27067–104	Hyde, 1363–98
W.A.M. 16367–445	Knightsbridge, 1257–1404
W.A.M. 27105–68	Laleham, 1276–1476
W.A.M. 16907–30	Staines, 1281–1340
W.A.M. 16932	——, 1352–3
W.A.M. 16933–51	——, 1363–1498

[1] Joint accounts for the two manors.
[2] The accounts for this period are individual to the one manor or the other but they now form a single series.

W.A.M. 16857–64   Staines and Yeoveney, 1328–36[1]

W.A.M. 16870–4, 16931   ——, 1341–51[1]

W.A.M. 16822–56   Yeoveney, 1274–1328

W.A.M. 16865–9   ——, 1335–41

W.A.M. 16875–906, 16932*   ——, 1352–1497

W.A.M. 27173–83   Teddington, *c.* 1290–1357

W.A.M. 27186–94   ——, 1357–1517

Oxon.

W.A.M. 14776–860   Islip, 1276–1487

W.A.M. 15286–419   Launton, 1267–1517

Rutl.

W.A.M. 20218–336   Oakham with Barleythorpe, 1275–1517

Surr.

W.A.M. 27495–611   Battersea and Wandsworth and members (manors and rectories), 1277–1500

W.A.M. 27199–227   Claygate, 1310–75

W.A.M. 27282–382   Morden (manor and rectory), 1280–1502

W.A.M. 27391–467   Pyrford, 1276–1492

Suss.

W.A.M. 4069   Parham, 1356–7

Warwicks.

W.A.M. 27692–739   Knowle, 1293–1504

W.A.M. 27925   Sutton-under-Brailes, 1443–4

   ——, see also under Todenham (Glos.)

Worcs.

W.A.M. 22133, dorse, 24445–88   Bricklehampton, 1445–1523

W.A.M. 21046, 21050–65   Castlemorton, 1331–1492

W.A.M. 21047–9   —— and Longdon, 1314–30

W.A.M. 21066–115   Chaceley, 1313–1491

W.A.M. 22133, dorse   Comberton, 1445–6

W.A.M. 21015–33   Longdon, 1335–1497

W.A.M. 21034–46   —— rectory, 1340–51

W.A.M. 22213–82   Pensham, 1351–1497

W.A.M. 22118–19, 22121–5   Pensham, Pershore and Wick, and Pinvin, 1329–51

W.A.M. 22093–104, 22107–10, 22112–17, 22120, 22127–51, 22343–90   Pershore and Wick, 1306–1497

W.A.M. 22284–342   Pinvin, 1344–1502

[1] Joint accounts for the two manors.

(iv) *Court Rolls*

	Bucks.
W.A.M. 3400–7	Denham, 1374–1504
	Essex
W.A.M. 25567–71	Birdbrook, 1293–1536
	Glos.
W.A.M. 8358–68	Bourton-on-the-Hill and Moreton-in-Marsh, 1376–1539
W.A.M. 32737	Deerhurst, 1348
	Herts.
W.A.M. 26151–247	Amwell, Great, 1381–1508
W.A.M. 8937–50	Harpenden, Kinsbourne, and Wheathampstead, 1272–1509
W.A.M. 26385	Stevenage, 1293–4
	Midd.
W.A.M. 27000–2	Eye, 1327–47
W.A.M. 16952–66	Staines and Yeoveney, 1275–1504
W.A.M. 16967	——, book of extracts from court rolls, 1380–1470
	Oxon.
W.A.M. 14861–958	Islip, 1275–1540
W.A.M. 15420–525	Launton, 1287–1476
	Surr.
W.A.M. 27384–90	Morden, 1296–1328
W.A.M. 27468, 27470–4, 27476–93	Pyrford, 1283–1504
W.A.M. 1685	——, book of extracts from court rolls, 1283–1469
	Worcs.
W.A.M. 21116–38, 21140–66, 21169, 21175–9	Castlemorton, Chaceley, and Longdon, 1373–1540
W.A.M. 21935–22054	Pershore, 1320–1540

(v) *Custumals, extents, rentals, and surveys*

	Bucks.
W.A.M. 7695	Turweston, rental, 1525
	Essex
W.A.M. 55357	Benfleet, South, copy of rental, 1437
	Glos.
W.A.M. 27798	Bourton-on-the-Hill, custumal, 1380–1
W.A.M. 22211	Deerhurst and Hardwicke, extent, 1362–6

Herts.

W.A.M. 4616 — Aldenham, custumal, late 13th century

W.A.M. 4597–8 — ——, rental, late 14th century, and copy

W.A.M. 4599 — ——, rental, early 15th century

W.A.M. 4601 — ——, rental, early 16th century

Kent

W.A.M. 5133 — Westerham, rental, *temp.* Henry VI

W.A.M. 5132 — ——, abstract of rental, 1487

Lincs.

W.A.M. 14758 — Fenne and Skreyne, valor, early 16th century

W.A.M. 14744 — ——, rental, 1508

Midd.

W.A.M. 26703 — Ashford, extent, 1312

W.A.M. 26999 — Ebury, rental, 1372

W.A.M. 4977 — Halliford, rental, late 14th century

W.A.M. 5016 — ——, rental, 1425–6

W.A.M. 32361 — Hampstead, rental, 1280–1

W.A.M. 32363 — ——, rental, 1371

W.A.M. 4750 — Hendon, rental, 1371–2

W.A.M. 16334 — Hyde, rental, 1417

W.A.M. 27171 — Laleham, extracts from rentals, *temp.* Edward III–Henry VI

W.A.M. 16786 — Staines, rental, 1353

W.A.M. 16795 — ——, rental, late 14th century

W.A.M. 16804 — ——, rental, mid-15th century

W.A.M. 16807 — ——, rental, 1490

W.A.M. 27197 — Teddington, extent, 1312

W.A.M. 27198 — ——, rental, 1378

Oxon.

W.A.M. 15207 — Islip, rental, 1435

W.A.M. 15716 — Launton, custumal, 1416–17

W.A.M. 15717 — ——, rental, 1449–50

Rutl.

W.A.M. 20640 — Oakham with Barleythorpe, rental, 1513–14

W.A.M. 20632 — Oakham rectory, extent, 1341

Surr.

W.A.M. 1793 — Allfarthing and Finches (in Wandsworth), rental, 1390–1

W.A.M. 27494 — Battersea and Wandsworth, custumal, 1268

W.A.M. 1876 ————, rental, early 15th century

W.A.M. 27228 Claygate, extent, 1341

W.A.M. 27229A ————, rental, 1353

W.A.M. 27469 Pyrford, extent, 1330

W.A.M. 1644 ————, rental, 1390

Warwicks.

W.A.M. 25983 Sutton-under-Brailes, rental, 1406

Worcs.

W.A.M. 22131 Bricklehampton, Comberton, Elmley, and Wick, rental, 1453

W.A.M. 21170* Castlemorton, Chaceley, and Longdon, record of attornment of tenants, 1540

W.A.M. 22211 Castlemorton, Chaceley, Longdon, Pensham, Pershore, and Pinvin, extent, 1362–6

W.A.M. 32763 Chaceley and Eckington, rental, late 15th century

W.A.M. 22515 Pensham, Pershore and Wick, and Pinvin, rental, 1338–49

W.A.M. 21827B ————, record of attornment of tenants, 1540

W.A.M. 32742 Pershore and Wick, rental, 1352

W.A.M. 22531 Pinvin, rental, 1364

W.A.M. 22514 ————, rental, 1382–3

W.A.M. 32821 ————, rental, 1442

Essex, Herts., Midd., Oxon., and Surr.

W.A.M. 9287 Aldenham, Ashwell, Battersea and Wandsworth, Feering, Greenford, Knightsbridge and Paddington, Launton, Morden, Stevenage, Teddington, and Wheathampstead, custumal, *c.* 1225

(vi) *Charters and other deeds* See index and calendar in the Muniment Room

(vii) *Cartularies and other registers*

W.A.M. Book 11 'Westminster Domesday', early 14th century

W.A.M. Book 1 'Liber Niger Quaternus', late 15th century, renewal of an earlier cartulary

W.A.M. Book 3 Cartulary devoted to appropriations of churches, early 16th century

W.A.M. Register Books I–II Lease-books, 1485–1536

(viii) *Miscellanea*

W.A.M. 9243–5   Accounts of proctors to and from Rome, 1298

W.A.M. 53318   Tomb-list, early 17th century

Mostyn Hall MS   Guide to burials in the Abbey, *c.* 1645

Other Repositories

Cambridge, University Library

C.U.L. MS. Kk 5. 29, fos. 21ᵛ–128   A copy (late 14th or early 15th century) of extents of the manors of South Benfleet and Fanton (1315), Feering (1289), and Kelvedon (1294), in *Essex*; Aldenham (1315), Ashwell (1315), Stevenage (1315), and Wheathampstead and Kinsbourne (1315), in *Herts.*; Ashford (1312), Hampstead (1312), Hendon (1321), Knightsbridge (1312), and Teddington (1312), in *Midd.*; Battersea and Wandsworth (1312), and Morden (1312), in *Surr.*; together with terriers of the demesnes at Ashwell (*Herts.*), Combe (*Kent*), Greenford (*Midd.*), and Downe (*Surr.*)

Chelmsford, Essex Record Office

(i) Ministers' Accounts

Essex

D/DM/M 85, 98, 114   Beckswell, 1378–1424

D/DM/M 84, 87–8, 90–7 99–113, 115–17, 119–30, 132, 134–9, 141–50, 152; D/DGe/M 87   Beckswell and Moulsham, 1377–1513

D/DM/M 68–83, 118, 131, 133, 140, 151   Moulsham, 1337–1516

(ii) Court Rolls

Essex

D/DM/M 30   Moulsham, 1381

(iii) Rental

Essex

D/DM/M 57   Moulsham, 1413

(iv) Miscellanea

D/DM/M 153–9 — Dockets made at the audit of ministers' accounts of conventual manors, 1359, 1384, 1386, 1392–4

Gloucester, County Records Office, Shire Hall

(i) Ministers' Accounts

Glos.

D 1099/M30/1–64 — Todenham, 1311–1496

Warwicks.

D 1099/M31/1–80 — Sutton-under-Brailes, 1273–1496

(ii) Court Rolls

Glos. and Warwicks.

D 1099/M1 — Bourton-on-the-Hill, Moreton-in-Marsh, Sutton-under-Brailes, and Todenham, 1469–78

(iii) Extents, rentals, and surveys

Glos.

D 1099/M 37, mm. 4–4ᵛ — Bourton-on-the-Hill, rental, *c.* 1280

D 1099/M 37, m. 3, D 1099/M 38, 41, 44 — Todenham, rentals, *c.* 1280, 1406, 1442, 1545

Glos. and Warwicks.

D 1099/M 51 — Todenham, and Sutton-under-Brailes, surveys, 1559

Oxon.

D 1099/M 37, mm. 1–1ᵛ — Islip, *c.* 1280

Warwicks.

D 1099/M 48–9 — Sutton-under-Brailes, extent, 1327, and copy

D 1099/M 37, m. 2, D 1099/M 39–40 — ——, rentals, *c.* 1280, 1406, 1443

Worcs.

D 1099/M 37, mm. 5, 6–6ᵛ — Castlemorton, Chaceley, and Longdon, rentals, *c.* 1280

Hertford, County Record Office, County Hall

(i) Ministers' Accounts

Herts.

D/Elw M 79–91, 93–127, 130–3, 135, 137–50 — Wheathampstead, 1273–1360

Midd.

D/Elw M 118 — Yeoveney, 1299–1300

(ii) Court Rolls

	Herts.
D/Elw M 128, 134, 136	Wheathampstead, 1312–15, 1323–4, 1324–7

(iii) Extent

	Herts.
D/Elw M 129	Wheathampstead and Kinsbourne, 1315

London, British Library (formerly British Museum)

(i) Ministers' Accounts

	Herts.
Additional Rolls 26827, 26829, 66717–72	Amwell, Great, 1280–1410

(ii) Custumal

	Essex, Herts., Midd., Oxon., and Surr.
Additional Charter 8139	Aldenham, Ashwell, Battersea and Wandsworth, Feering, Greenford, Launton, Knightsbridge and Paddington, Morden, Stevenage, Teddington, and Wheathampstead, *c.* 1225

(iii) Charter

	Warwicks.
Harleian Charter 45. c. 50	

(iv) Cartulary

Cotton Faustina A III	*Temp.* Edward I

(v) Miscellanea

Additional MS. 38133, fos. 98^v–100; Harleian MS. 544, fos. 65–65^v, 67; Egerton MS. 2642, fos. 322–323^v	Tomb-lists, sixteenth century

——, *College of Arms*

MS. A. 17, fos. 62^v ff. MS. F 9, fos. 1–2^v	Tomb-lists, sixteenth century

——, *Public Record Office*

(i) Ministers' Accounts

	Essex
S.C. 6/841/3	Fanton, 1301–2
S.C. 6/841/6–9	Feering, 1332–48
S.C. 6/844/37–8	Kelvedon, 1318–19, 1337–8

S.C. 6/862/4–5
S.C. 6/870/9–20, S.C. 6/871/1–21, S.C. 6/872/1–8

S.C. 6/916/26
S.C. 6/919/12–23
S.C. 6/918/1–22

(ii) Court Rolls

S.C. 2/176/130–6
S.C. 2/178/47–52

S.C. 2/197/48–9

(iii) Feet of Fines
C.P. 25 (1) 20/97/232
C.P. 25 (1) 86/32/625
C.P. 25 (1) 145/165/43
C.P. 25 (1) 146/10/144
C.P. 25 (1) 147/17/318
C.P. 25 (1) 147/20/390
C.P. 25 (1) 149/42/88
C.P. 25 (1) 150/59/170
C.P. 25 (1) 150/64/288
C.P. 25 (1) 192/2/21
C.P. 25 (1) 258/5/13
C.P. 25 (1) 284/21/90

(iv) Plea Rolls
C.P. 40/959
C.P. 40/963
C.P. 40/968

(v) Miscellanea
S.C. 6/1109/4
S.C. 6/1261/6

S.C. 6, Henry VIII/2414

C. 139/86/28

——, *St. Paul's Cathedral Library*

Ministers' Accounts[1]
Press B, Box 92

Herts.
Ashwell, 1340–1
Stevenage, 1284–1405

Midd.
Laleham, 1327–8
La Neyte, 1315–27
Teddington, 1300–50

Herts.
Ashwell, 1329–74
Stevenage, 1298–1371

Oxon.
Islip, 1434–1523

Common Pleas, Hilary Term, 1502
——, Hilary Term, 1503
——, Easter Term, 1504

Vacancy account, 1307–10
Day-book of the abbot's household, 1371–3
View of the ministers' accounts for the possessions of the former monastery, 1542–3
Inquisition *post mortem*, 1438

Essex
Fanton, 1304–5

[1] The individual items in the boxes have no numbers.

Herts.

Press B, Boxes 81, 84, 86, 92, 111   Stevenage, 1273–1409

Oxford, Bodleian Library

Dodsworth MS. 76
Wood MS. D 4

    All Souls College Library

    MS. 126   Tomb-list, early 17th century

II PRINTED SOURCES

Anonimalle Chronicle, 1333 to 1381, The, ed. V. H. Galbraith (Manchester University Press, Manchester, 1927).

ASTLE, T., ed., *The Will of Henry VII* (London, 1775).

BISHOP, T. A. M., *Scriptores Regis: Facsimiles to identify and illustrate the hands of royal scribes in original charters of Henry I, Stephen, and Henry II* (Clarendon Press, Oxford, 1961).

Book of Fees, The (3 vols., H.M.S.O., London, 1920–31).

BRACTON, *De Legibus et Consuetudinibus Angliae*, ed. G. E. Woodbine, translated, with revisions and notes, by S. E. Thorne (2 vols., Harvard University Press, Cambridge, Mass., 1968).

BRETT-JAMES, N. G., 'Some extents and surveys of Hendon', *Transactions of the London and Middlesex Archaeological Society*, N.S. 6 (1929–32), 547–632.

BUTLER, C., ed., *Sancti Benedicti Regula Monasteriorum* (2nd edn., B. Herder, Freiburg-im-Breisgau, 1927).

Calendar of Charter Rolls (H.M.S.O., London, 1903–).

Calendar of Close Rolls (H.M.S.O., London, 1892–).

Calendar of Fine Rolls (H.M.S.O., London, 1911–).

Calendar of Inquisitions Miscellaneous (Chancery) (H.M.S.O., London, 1916–).

Calendar of Inquisitions post mortem (H.M.S.O., London, 1904–).

Calendar of Letters and Papers, Foreign and Domestic, Henry VIII, ed. J. S. Brewer, J. Gairdner, and R. H. Brodie (H.M.S.O., London, 1864–1932).

Calendar of Liberate Rolls (H.M.S.O., London, 1916–).

Calendar of Patent Rolls (H.M.S.O., London, 1901–).

Carte Nativorum: A Peterborough Abbey Cartulary of the Fourteenth Century, ed. C. N. L. Brooke and M. M. Postan (Northants, Record Society xx, 1960).

Chancellor's Roll for the Eighth Year of the Reign of King Richard the First, Michaelmas, 1196, The, ed. D. M. Stenton (Pipe Roll Society, N.S. vii, 1930).

Chronicles of London, ed. C. L. Kingsford (Clarendon Press, Oxford, 1905).

Chronicles of the Reigns of Edward I and Edward II, ed. W. Stubbs (2 vols., Rolls Series, 1882–3).

Chronicles of the Reigns of Stephen, Henry II, and Richard I, ed. R. Howlett (4 vols., Rolls Series, 1884–9).

CIRENCESTER, RICHARD OF, *Speculum Historiale de Gestis Regum Angliae*, ed. J. E. B. Mayor (2 vols., Rolls Series, 1863–9).

CLARE, OSBERT OF, *Letters of Osbert of Clare, prior of Westminster*, ed. E. W. Williamson (O.U.P., Oxford, 1929).

Councils and Synods, with other Documents relating to the English Church. II. A.D. 1205–1313, ed. F. M. Powicke and C. R. Cheney (2 vols., Clarendon Press, Oxford, 1964).

Curia Regis Rolls (H.M.S.O., London, 1922–).

Customary of the Benedictine Monasteries of Saint Augustine, Canterbury, and Saint Peter, Westminster, ed. E. Maunde Thompson (2 vols., Henry Bradshaw Society xxiii, xxviii, London, 1902, 1904).

DICETO, RALPH OF, *The Historical Works of Master Ralph de Diceto, dean of London*, ed. W. Stubbs (2 vols., Rolls Series, 1876).

Discourse of the Common Weal of this Realm of England, A, ed. E. Lamond (C.U.P., Cambridge, 1929).

Documents Illustrating the Activities of the General and Provincial Chapters of the English Black Monks, 1215–1540, ed. W. A. Pantin (Camden, 3rd. ser., xlv, xlvii, liv, 1931–7).

Documents of the Baronial Movement of Reform and Rebellion, 1258–1267, selected by R. E. [*sic*] Treharne and ed. I. J. Sanders (Clarendon Press, Oxford, 1973).

Domesday Book (2 vols., 1783).

DUGDALE, W., *Monasticon Anglicanum*, ed. J. Caley, H. Ellis, and B. Bandinel (6 vols., London, 1817–30).

DUNSTAN, ST., *Memorials of Saint Dunstan, archbishop of Canterbury*, ed. W. Stubbs (Rolls Series, 1874).

EDWARD THE CONFESSOR. *The Life of King Edward who rests at Westminster*, ed. and trans. F. Barlow (Nelson, London, 1962).

Entries in the Papal Registers relating to Great Britain and Ireland, ed. W. H. Bliss, C. Johnson, and J. A. Twemlow: *Calendar of Papal Letters* (H.M.S.O., London, 1893–).

Feet of Fines. *Feet of Fines of the Reign of Henry II and of the first seven years of the reign of Richard I. A.D. 1182 to A.D. 1196* (Pipe Roll Society xvii, 1894).

——, Essex. *Feet of Fines for Essex*, ed. R. E. G. Kirk, E. F. Kirk, P. H. Reaney, M. Fitch, *et al.* (4 vols., Essex Archaeological Society, 1899–1964).

——, Kent. *Calendar of Kent Feet of Fines to the end of Henry III's Reign*, ed. I. J. Churchill, R. Griffin, and F. W. Hardman, with an Introduction by F. W. Jessup (*Kent Records* xv, 1956).

——, London and Middlesex. *A Calendar to the Feet of Fines for London and Middlesex*, vol. i, *Richard I to Richard III*, ed. W. J. Hardy and W. Page (Hardy & Page, London, 1892–3).

——, Surrey. *Pedes Finium; or Fines relating to the County of Surrey levied in the King's Court from the seventh year of Richard I to the end of the Reign of Henry VII* (Surrey Archaeological Society, extra vol. i, 1894).

—— ——. *Abstracts of Surrey Feet of Fines, 1509–1558*, ed. C. A. F. Meekings (Surrey Record Society xix, 1946).

——, Warwickshire. *Warwickshire Feet of Fines*, ed. L. Drucker, E. Stokes, and F. C. Wellstood (Dugdale Society xi, xv, xviii, 1932, 1939, 1943).

Feudal Aids (6 vols., H.M.S.O., London, 1899–1920).

FLETE, JOHN. *The History of Westminster Abbey by John Flete*, ed. J. Armitage Robinson (C.U.P., Cambridge, 1909).

Flores Historiarum, ed. H. R. Luard (3 vols., Rolls Series, 1890).

FOLIOT, GILBERT. *The Letters and Charters of Gilbert Foliot, abbot of Gloucester (1139–48), bishop of Hereford (1148–63) and London (1163–87)*, ed. A. Morey and C. N. L. Brooke (C.U.P., Cambridge, 1967).

FURNIVALL, F. J., ed. *The Fifty Earliest English Wills in the Court of Probate, London, A.D. 1387–1439, with a Priest's of 1454* (Early English Text Society lxxviii, 1882).

Gesta Henrici Quinti, trans. and ed. F. Taylor and J. S. Roskell (Oxford, Clarendon Press, 1975).

GREGORY IX. *Les Régistres de Grégoire IX*, ed. L. Auvray, Mme. Vitte-Clémencet, et L. Carolus-Barré (4 vols., Bibliothèque des Écoles françaises d'Athènes et de Rome, 1896–1955).

HARMER, F. E., *Anglo-Saxon Writs* (Manchester University Press, Manchester, 1952).

HIGDEN, RALPH. *Polychronicon Ranulphi Higden monachi Cestrensis*, ed. C. Babington and J. R. Lumby (9 vols., Rolls Series, 1865–86).

Holinshed's Chronicles of England, Scotland and Ireland (6 vols., London, 1807–8).

INNOCENT III. *The Letters of Pope Innocent III (1198–1216) concerning England and Wales*, ed. C. R. and M. G. Cheney (Clarendon Press, Oxford, 1967).

INNOCENT IV. *Les Régistres d'Innocent IV*, ed. E. Berger (4 vols., Bibliothèque des Écoles françaises d'Athènes et de Rome, 1884–1919).

Inquisitions post mortem for Gloucestershire, ed. S. J. Madge, part iv, *20 Henry III to 29 Edward I (1236–1300)* (British Record Society xxx, 1903).

Islip, Custumal (1391) and Bye-Laws (1386–1540) of the Manor of, ed. B. F. Harvey (Oxfordshire Record Society xl (1959), 80–119).

Joannis abbatis Epistolae, in Migne, *Patrologia Latina* cxlvii. 463–76.

John Benet's Chronicle for the years 1400 to 1462, ed. G. L. Harriss and M. A. Harriss, in *Camden Miscellany* xxiv (Camden, 4th ser., ix), 151–233.

LELAND, J., *De Rebus Britannicis Collectanea*, ed. T. Hearne (2nd edn., 6 vols., London, 1774).

Lincoln, Registrum Antiquissimum of the Cathedral Church of, vol. ii, ed. C. W. Foster (Lincoln Record Society xxviii, 1933).

Lincolnshire Domesday and the Lindsey Survey, The, ed. C. W. Foster and T. Longley, with an introduction by F. M. Stenton (Lincolnshire Record Society, xix, 1924).

Littleton's Tenures, ed. E. Wambaugh (John Byrne and Co., Washington, D.C., 1903).

Luffield Priory Charters, part i, ed. G. R. Elvey (Buckinghamshire Record Society xv, 1968, and Northamptonshire Record Society xxii, 1968).

MALMESBURY, WILLIAM OF, *Gesta Pontificum Anglorum*, ed. N. E. S. A. Hamilton (Rolls Series, 1870).

——, *Gesta Regum Anglorum*, ed. W. Stubbs (2 vols., Rolls Series, 1887–9).

NICHOLS, J., ed., *A Collection of All the Wills now known to be extant of the Kings and Queens of England, etc.* (London, 1780).

NICOLAS, N. H., *Testamenta Vetusta* (2 vols., London, 1826).

Papsturkunden in England, ed. W. Holtzmann (3 vols., Abhandlungen der Gesellschaft der Wissenschaften zu Göttingen, Philologisch-historische Klasse, neue Folge, xxv; 3 Folge, 14–15, 33, Berlin and Göttingen, 1930–52).

PARIS, M., *Chronica Majora*, ed. H. R. Luard (7 vols., Rolls Series, 1872–83).

Pipe Roll, 17 Henry II. *The Great Roll of the Pipe for the Seventeenth Year of King Henry the Second, A.D. 1170–1* (Pipe Roll Society xvi, 1893).

——, 21 Henry II. *The Great Roll of the Pipe for the Twenty-First Year of the Reign of King Henry the Second, A.D. 1174–1175* (Pipe Roll Society xxii, 1897).

PONTISSARA, JOHN DE. *Registrum Johannis de Pontissara, episcopi Wyntoniensis, A.D. 1282–1304*, ed. C. Deedes (2 vols., Canterbury and York Society xix and xxx, 1915, 1924).

READING, JOHN OF. *Chronica Johannis de Reading et Anonymi Cantuariensis, 1346–67*, ed. J. Tait (Manchester University Press, Manchester, 1914).

Red Book of the Exchequer, ed. H. Hall (3 vols., Rolls Series, 1896).

Regesta Regum Anglo-Normannorum, 1066–1154 (4 vols., Clarendon Press, Oxford, 1913–69: vol. i, 1066–1100, ed. H. W. C. Davis and R. J. Whitwell; vol. ii, 1100–1135, ed. C. Johnson and H. A. Cronne; vols. iii–iv, 1135–54, ed. H. A. Cronne and R. H. C. Davis).

Rolls of Arms, Henry III, ed. T. D. Tremlett and H. S. London (Harleian Society ciii–civ, 1967, for 1961–2).

Rotuli Hundredorum, ed. W. Illingworth and J. Caley (2 vols., Record Commission, 1812–18).

Rotuli Parliamentorum (6 vols., Record Commission, 1783).

RYMER, T., ed., *Foedera, conventiones, literae et cujuscunque generis acta publica inter reges Angliae et alios quosvis imperatores, reges, pontifices, principes vel communitates* (20 vols., London, 1704–35).

SCHOLZ, B. W., 'Sulcard of Westminster: "Prologus de Construccione Westmonasterii" ', *Traditio* 20 (1964), 59–91.

SHARPE, R. R., ed., *Calendar of Wills proved and enrolled in the Court of Husting, London, A.D. 1258–A.D. 1668* (2 vols., London, 1889–90).

STANLEY, JOHN. 'Will of Sir John Stanley, of Honford, Cheshire, dated June 20, A.D. 1527', *Archaeological Journal* 25 (1868), 72–84.

Stonor Letters and Papers, 1290–1483, ed. C. L. Kingsford (2 vols., Camden, 3rd ser., xxix–xxx, 1919).

STOW, JOHN, *A Survey of London*, ed. C. L. Kingsford (2 vols., Clarendon Press, Oxford, repr. 1971, of 1st edn., 1908).

SULCARD, *Prologus de Construccione Westmonasterii*. See under Scholz.

Symeonis Monachi Opera Omnia, ed. T. Arnold (2 vols., Rolls Series, 1882–5).

Taxatio Ecclesiastica Angliae et Walliae, auctoritate P. Nicholai IV, circa A.D. 1291, ed. T. Astle, S. Ayscough and J. Caley (Record Commission, 1802).

THORPE, B., ed., *Diplomatarium Anglicum Aevi Saxonici. A Collection of English Charters, from the reign of King Aethelberht of Kent, A.D. DC.V to that of William the Conqueror* (Macmillan & Co., London, 1865).

Valor Ecclesiasticus, temp. Henrici VIII, auctoritate Regia Institutus, ed. J. Caley and J. Hunter (6 vols., Record Commission, 1810–34).

WALSINGHAM, THOMAS OF, *Ypodigma Neustriae*, ed. H. T. Riley (Rolls Series, 1876).

Walter of Henley and other Treatises on Estate Management and Accounting, ed. D. Oschinsky (Clarendon Press, Oxford, 1971).

WEAVER, J. R. H., and BEARDWOOD, A., ed., *Some Oxfordshire Wills proved in the Prerogative Court of Canterbury, 1393–1510* (Oxfordshire Record Society, xxxix, 1958).

WENLOK, WALTER DE. *Documents Illustrating the Rule of Walter de Wenlok, abbot of Westminster, 1283–1307*, ed. B. F. Harvey (Camden, 4th ser., ii, 1965).

WHARTON, H., *Anglia Sacra* (2 vols., London, 1691).

WHITELOCK, D., ed., *Anglo-Saxon Wills* (C.U.P., Cambridge, 1930).

WILKINS, D., *Concilia Magnae Britanniae et Hiberniae* (4 vols., London, 1737).

WORCESTER, FLORENCE OF. *Florentii Wigorniensis monachi Chronicon ex Chronicis*, ed. B. Thorpe (2 vols., English Historical Society, London, 1848–9).

III SECONDARY WORKS[1]

Agrarian History of England and Wales, The, vol. iv, *1500–1640*, ed. J. Thirsk (C.U.P., Cambridge, 1967).

BAKER, A. R. H., and BUTLIN, R. A., *Studies of Field Systems in the British Isles* (C.U.P., Cambridge, 1973).

BARLOW, F., *Edward the Confessor* (Eyre & Spottiswoode, London, 1970).

BARTON, J. L., 'The Medieval Use', *Law Quarterly Review* 81 (1965), 562–77.

BEAN, J. M. W., *The Decline of English Feudalism, 1215–1540* (Manchester University Press, Manchester, 1968).

BISHOP, T. A. M., 'The rotation of crops at Westerham, 1297–1350', *Economic History Review* 9 (1938–9), 38–44.

BUGDEN, W., 'The manor of Chollington in Eastbourne', *Sussex Archaeological Collections* 62 (1921), 111–32.

BUTTERWORTH, G., 'The Saxon Chapel at Deerhurst', *Transactions of the Bristol and Gloucestershire Archaeological Society* 11 (1886–7), 105–116.

CAMDEN, W., *Reges, Reginae, Nobiles et Alii in Ecclesia Collegiata B. Petri Westmonasterii Sepulti usque ad Annum Reparatae Salutis 1600* (London, 1600).

CHAPLAIS, P., 'The original charters of Herbert and Gervase, abbots of Westminster (1121–1157)', *A Medieval Miscellany for Doris Mary Stenton*, ed. P. M. Barnes and C. F. Slade (Pipe Roll Society, N.S. xxxvi, 1962 for 1960), 89–110.

CHENEY, C. R., *From Becket to Langton. English Church Government, 1170–1213* (Manchester University Press, Manchester, 1956).

——, 'Rules for the observance of feast-days in medieval England', *Bulletin of the Institute of Historical Research* 34 (1961), 117–47.

CHEW, H. M., *The English Ecclesiastical Tenants-in-Chief and Knight Service* (O.U.P., Oxford, 1932).

COKAYNE, G. E., *The Complete Peerage*, ed. V. Gibbs, H. A. Doubleday, *et al.* (St. Catherine's Press, London, 1910–).

---

[1] A select list, in which are included books and articles relating specifically to Westminster Abbey and its estates and the more important of the general works cited in the text.

Colvin, H. M., ed., *The History of the King's Works* (H.M.S.O., London, 1963–)

Darby, H. C., and Campbell, E. M. J., *The Domesday Geography of South-East England* (C.U.P., Cambridge, 1962).

——, and Terrett, I. B., *The Domesday Geography of Midland England* (2nd edn., C.U.P., Cambridge, 1971).

Dart, J. *Westmonasterium, or The History and Antiquities of the Abbey Church of St. Peter's Westminster* (2 vols., London, n.d.).

Dictionary of National Biography.

Du Boulay, F. R. H., *The Lordship of Canterbury. An Essay on Medieva Society* (Nelson, London, 1966).

Dugdale, W., *The Antiquities of Warwickshire* (2nd edn., rev. W. Thomas, 2 vols., London, 1730).

Dyer, C., 'A Redistribution of Incomes in Fifteenth-Century England', *Past and Present* 39 (Apr. 1968), 11–33.

Emden, A. B., *A Biographical Register of the University of Cambridge to 1500* (C.U.P., Cambridge, 1963).

——, *A Biographical Register of the University of Oxford to A.D. 1500* (3 vols., Clarendon Press, Oxford, 1957–9).

Faith, R. J., 'Peasant Families and Inheritance Customs in Medieval England', *Agricultural History Review* 14 (1966), 77–95.

Galbraith, V. H., 'A Visitation of Westminster in 1444', *English Historical Review* 37 (1922), 83–8.

Graham, R., *English Ecclesiastical Studies* (S.P.C.K., London, 1929).

Gransden, A., 'The Continuations of the *Flores Historiarum* from 1265 to 1327', *Mediaeval Studies* (Toronto), 36 (1974), 472–92.

Grierson, P., *English Linear Measures. An Essay in Origins* (University of Reading, Reading, 1972).

Haines, R. M., 'The appropriation of Longdon Church to Westminster Abbey', *Transactions of the Worcestershire Archaeological Society*, n.s. 38 (1962 for 1961), 39–52.

Harvey, B. F., 'Abbot Gervase de Blois and the Fee-Farms of Westminster Abbey', *Bulletin of the Institute of Historical Research* 40 (1967), 127–42.

——, 'The leasing of the abbot of Westminster's demesnes in the later Middle Ages', *Economic History Review*, 2nd. ser., 22 (1969), 17–27.

——, 'The Monks of Westminster and the University of Oxford', *The Reign of Richard II: Essays in Honour of May McKisack*, ed. F. R. H. Du Boulay and C. M. Barron (Athlone Press, London, 1971), pp. 108–30.

——, 'Work and *festa ferianda* in medieval England', *Journal of Ecclesiastical History* 23 (1972), 289–308.

Harvey, P. D. A., 'The Pipe Rolls and the adoption of demesne farming in England', *Economic History Review*, 2nd ser., 27 (1974), 345–59.

Harvey, S., 'The knight and the knight's fee in England', *Past and Present* 49 (Nov. 1970), 3–43.

Hasted's History of Kent, corrected, enlarged, and continued to the present time from the Manuscript Collections of the late Rev. Thomas Streatfield and the late Rev. Lambert Blackwell Larking, the Public Records, and other Sources, ed. H. H. Drake, pt. i. *The Hundred of Blackheath* (Mitchell & Hughes, London, 1886).

HILTON, R. H., *The English Peasantry in the Later Middle Ages* (Clarendon Press, Oxford, 1975).

——, *The Decline of Serfdom in Medieval England* (Economic History Soc., 1969).

HOLMES, G. A., *The Estates of the Higher Nobility in Fourteenth-Century England* (C.U.P., Cambridge, 1957).

HOLT, J. C., 'Politics and property in early medieval England', *Past and Present* 57 (Nov. 1972), 3–52.

HONEYBOURNE, M. B., 'The sanctuary boundaries and environs of Westminster Abbey and the college of St. Martin-le-Grand', *Journal of the British Archaeological Association*, N.S. 38 (1932), 316–32.

HYAMS, P. R., 'The origins of a peasant land market in England', *Economic History Review*, 2nd ser., 23 (1970), 18–31.

JONES, A., 'Land and people at Leighton Buzzard in the later fifteenth century', *Economic History Review*, 2nd ser., 25 (1972), 18–27.

KERRIDGE, E., *Agrarian Problems in the Sixteenth Century and After* (George Allen & Unwin, London, 1969).

KING, E., *Peterborough Abbey, 1086–1310: A Study in the Land Market* (C.U.P., Cambridge, 1973).

KNOWLES, D., 'The growth of exemption', *Downside Review* 50 (1932), 201–31, 396–436.

——, *The Monastic Order in England, 940–1216* (2nd edn., C.U.P., Cambridge, 1963).

——, *The Religious Orders in England* (3 vols., C.U.P., Cambridge, 1948–59).

——, BROOKE, C. N. L., and LONDON, V. C. M., eds., *The Heads of Religious Houses: England and Wales, 940–1216* (C.U.P., Cambridge, 1972).

KOSMINSKY, E. A., *Studies in the Agrarian History of England in the Thirteenth Century* (Basil Blackwell, Oxford, 1956).

LENNARD, R., 'The economic position of the bordars and cottars of Domesday Book', *Economic Journal* 61 (1951), 342–71.

——, *Rural England, 1086–1135. A Study of Social and Agrarian Conditions* (Clarendon Press, Oxford, 1959).

LETHABY, W. R., *Westminster Abbey and the Kings' Craftsmen. A Study of Mediaeval Building* (Duckworth & Co., London, 1906).

LUNT, W. E., *Financial Relations of the Papacy with England to 1327*; and *Financial Relations of the Papacy with England, 1327–1534* (Studies in Anglo-Papal Relations during the Middle Ages, i–ii: Mediaeval Academy of America xxxiii, lxxiv, Cambridge, Mass., 1939, 1962).

LYSONS, D., *The Environs of London* (4 vols., London, 1792–6).

——, *An Historical Account of those Parishes in the County of Middlesex which are not described in the Environs of London* (London, 1800).

McFARLANE, K. B., *The Nobility of Later Medieval England* (Clarendon Press, Oxford, 1973).

MAITLAND, F. W., *Domesday Book and Beyond* (C.U.P., Cambridge, repr. 1921, of 1st edn. 1897).

MILSOM, S. F. C., *Historical Foundations of the Common Law* (Butterworths, London, 1969).

MOOR, C., *Knights of Edward I* (5 vols., Harleian Society lxxx–lxxxiv, 1929–32).

MORANT, P., *History and Antiquities of the County of Essex* (2 vols., London, 1768).

NASH, J., *Collections for the History of Worcestershire* (2 vols., London, 1781–2).

PEARCE, E. H., *William de Colchester, abbot of Westminster* (S.P.C.K., London, 1915).

——, *The Monks of Westminster* (C.U.P., Cambridge, 1916).

——, *Walter de Wenlok, abbot of Westminster* (S.P.C.K., London, 1920).

PEERS, C., and TANNER, L. E., 'On Some Recent Discoveries in Westminster Abbey', *Archaeologia*, 2nd ser., 43 (1949), 151–63.

PLUCKNETT, T. F. T., *Legislation of Edward I* (Clarendon Press, Oxford, 1949).

POLLOCK, F., and MAITLAND, F. W., *The History of English Law before the Time of Edward I* (2nd. edn., with an introduction by S. F. C. Milsom, 2 vols., C.U.P., Cambridge, 1968).

POSTAN, M. M., *Essays on Medieval Agriculture and General Problems of the Medieval Economy* (C.U.P., Cambridge, 1973).

RABAN, S., 'Mortmain in medieval England', *Past and Present* 62 (Feb. 1974), 3–26.

RACKHAM, R. B., 'The nave of Westminster', *Proceedings of the British Academy*, 1909–10, pp. 33–96.

REYNOLDS, S., 'The rulers of London in the twelfth century', *History* 57 (1972), 337–57.

RICHARDSON, H. G., *The English Jewry under Angevin Kings* (Methuen & Co., London, 1960).

ROBINSON, J. ARMITAGE, *Gilbert Crispin, abbot of Westminster* (C.U.P., Cambridge, 1911).

——, *The Abbot's House at Westminster* (C.U.P., Cambridge, 1911).

——, *Somerset Historical Essays* (British Academy, London, 1921).

ROGERS, J. E. THOROLD, *A History of Agriculture and Prices in England from the year after the Oxford Parliament (1259) to the commencement of the Continental War (1793)* (7 vols., Clarendon Press, Oxford, 1866–1902).

Royal Commission on Historical Monuments (England.) An Inventory of the Historical Monuments in London. Vol. i, *Westminster Abbey* (London, 1924).

RUTTON, W. L., 'The Manor of Eia, or Eye next Westminster', *Archaeologia* 62 (1910), 31–58.

SAUNDERS, G., 'Results of an inquiry concerning the situation and extent of Westminster, at various periods', *Archaeologia* 26 (1836), 223–41.

SAWYER, P. H., *Anglo-Saxon Charters. An Annotated List and Bibliography* (Royal Historical Society, London, 1968).

SCAMMELL, J., 'Freedom and marriage in medieval England', *Economic History Review*, 2nd ser., 27 (1974), 523–37.

SCOTT, R., 'On the Contracts for the Tomb of the Lady Margaret Beaufort, Countess of Richmond and Derby, mother of Henry VII, and Foundress of the Colleges of Christ and St. John in Cambridge', *Archaeologia*, 2nd ser., 16 (1914–15), 365–76.

SIMPSON, A. W. B., *An Introduction to the History of the Land Law* (O.U.P., Oxford, 1961).

SOUTHERN, R. W., *Saint Anselm and His Biographer: A Study of Monastic Life and Thought, 1059–c. 1130* (C.U.P., Cambridge, 1963).

470   *Bibliography*

STANLEY, A. P., *Historical Memorials of Westminster Abbey* (1st edn., John Murray, London, 1868).

STENTON, F. M., *The First Century of English Feudalism, 1066–1166* (2nd edn., Clarendon Press, Oxford, 1961).

SUTHERLAND, D. W., *The Assize of Novel Disseisin* (Clarendon Press, Oxford, 1973).

SWEET, A. H., 'A papal visitation of Westminster in 1469', *Anglican Theological Review* 5 (1922), 29–34.

TANNER, J. D., 'Tombs of royal babies in Westminster Abbey', *Journal of the British Archaeological Association*, 3rd ser., 16 (1953), 25–40.

TANNER, L. E., 'Some representations of St. Edward the Confessor in Westminster Abbey and elsewhere', *Journal of the British Archaeological Association*, 3rd ser., 15 (1952), 1–12.

——, 'The Countess of Pembroke and Westminster Abbey', *Pembroke College, Cambridge, Society, Annual Gazette* 33 (Dec. 1959), 9–13.

——, *Recollections of a Westminster Antiquary* (John Baker, London, 1969).

——, and MACMICHAEL, N. H., 'An Indent in Westminster Abbey', *Transactions of the Monumental Brass Society*, 10. 2 (Dec. 1964), 95–6.

TAYLOR, C. S., 'Deerhurst, Pershore, and Westminster', *Transactions of the Bristol and Gloucestershire Archaeological Society* 25 (1902), 230–50.

THOMSON, J. A. F., 'Tithe disputes in later medieval London', *English Historical Review* 78 (1963), 1–17.

TOUT, T. F., *Chapters in the Administrative History of Mediaeval England* (6 vols., Manchester University Press, Manchester, 1920–33).

Victoria Histories of the Counties of England (in progress, London, 1900–).

WESTLAKE, H. F., *St. Margaret's, Westminster, the church of the House of Commons* (Smith, Elder & Co., London, 1914).

——, *Westminster Abbey. The last days of the monastery as shown by the life and times of Abbot John Islip, 1464–1532* (Philip Allan, London, 1921).

——, *Westminster Abbey. The Church, Convent, Cathedral and College of St. Peter, Westminster* (2 vols., Philip Allan, London, 1923).

WIDMORE, R., *An Enquiry into the Time of the First Foundation of Westminster Abbey* (London, 1743).

——, *An History of the Church of St. Peter, Westminster, commonly called Westminster Abbey* (London, 1751).

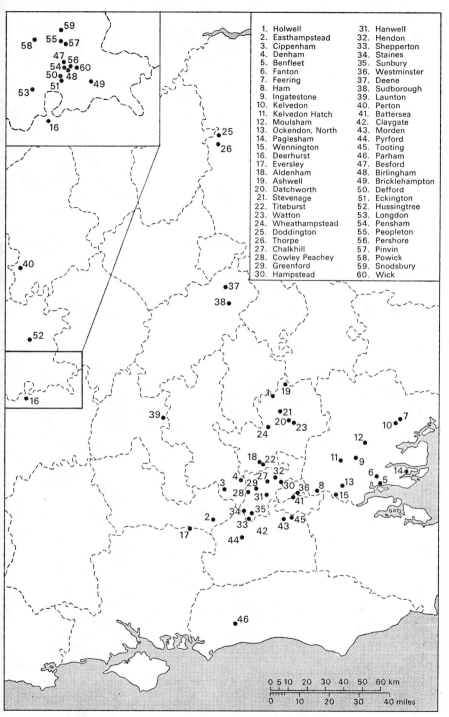

1. Holwell
2. Easthampstead
3. Cippenham
4. Denham
5. Benfleet
6. Fanton
7. Feering
8. Ham
9. Ingatestone
10. Kelvedon
11. Kelvedon Hatch
12. Moulsham
13. Ockendon, North
14. Paglesham
15. Wennington
16. Deerhurst
17. Eversley
18. Aldenham
19. Ashwell
20. Datchworth
21. Stevenage
22. Titeburst
23. Watton
24. Wheathampstead
25. Doddington
26. Thorpe
27. Chalkhill
28. Cowley Peachey
29. Greenford
30. Hampstead
31. Hanwell
32. Hendon
33. Shepperton
34. Staines
35. Sunbury
36. Westminster
37. Deene
38. Sudborough
39. Launton
40. Perton
41. Battersea
42. Claygate
43. Morden
44. Pyrford
45. Tooting
46. Parham
47. Besford
48. Birlingham
49. Bricklehampton
50. Defford
51. Eckington
52. Hussingtree
53. Longdon
54. Pensham
55. Peopleton
56. Pershore
57. Pinvin
58. Powick
59. Snodsbury
60. Wick

MAP I. THE DEMESNE MANORS OF WESTMINSTER ABBEY IN 1086

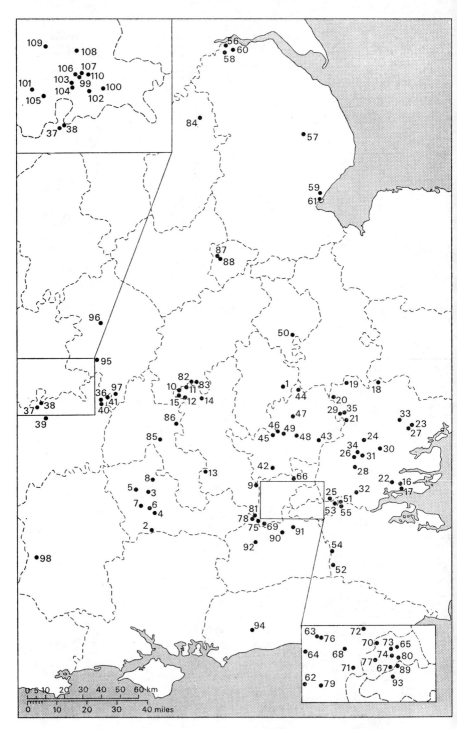

MAP II. THE PRINCIPAL ESTATES OF WESTMINSTER ABBEY IN 1535

MAP II. THE PRINCIPAL ESTATES OF WESTMINSTER
ABBEY IN 1535

Beds.
1. Holme with Langford

Berks.
2. Bagnor
3. Betterton
4. Curridge
5. Letcombe Regis
6. Peasemore
7. Poughley
8. Steventon

Bucks.
9. Denham
10. Evershaw
11. Luffield
12. Shalstone
13. Stokenchurch
14. Thornborough
15. Turweston

Essex
16. Benfleet, N.
17. Benfleet, S.
18. Birdbrook
19. Chesterford, Great
20. Clavering
21. Elsenham
22. Fanton
23. Feering
24. Good Easter
25. Ham
26. High Ongar
27. Kelvedon
28. Kelvedon Hatch
29. Manewden
30. Moulsham
31. Norton Mandeville
32. Ockendon, N.
33. Pattiswick
34. Shelley
35. Ugley

Glos.
36. Bourton-on-the-Hill
37. Chaceley
38. Deerhurst
39. Hardwicke

40. Moreton-in-Marsh
41. Todenham

Herts.
42. Aldenham
43. Amwell, Great
44. Ashwell
45. Harpenden
46. Kinsbourne
47. Stevenage
48. Tewin
49. Wheathampstead

Hunts.
50. Offord Cluny

Kent
51. Boarstall
52. Edenbridge
53. Plumstead
54. Westerham
55. Wickham, E.

Lincs.
56. Alkborough
57. Belchford
58. Burton Stather
59. Fenne
60. Halton
61. Skreyne

Midd.*
62. Ashford
63. Down
64. Drayton
65. Eye
66. Finchley
67. Fulham
68. Greenford
69. Halliford
70. Hampstead
71. Hanwell
72. Hendon
73. Hyde
74. Knightsbridge
75. Laleham
76. Northolt
77. Paddington
78. Staines
79. Teddington

80. Westminster
81. Yeoveney

Northants.
82. Silverstone
83. Whittlebury

Notts.
84. Oswald Beck Soke

Oxon.
85. Islip
86. Launton

Rutl.
87. Barleythorpe
88. Oakham

Surr.*
89. Battersea
90. Claygate
91. Morden
92. Pyrford
93. Wandsworth

Suss.
94. Parham

Warwicks.
95. Grafton Minor
96. Knowle
97. Sutton-under-Brailes

Wilts.
98. Westbury

Worcs.
99. Birlingham
100. Bricklehampton
101. Castlemorton
102. Comberton
103. Defford
104. Eckington
105. Longdon
106. Pensham
107. Pershore
108. Pinvin
109. Powick
110. Wick

* Including estates now in London.

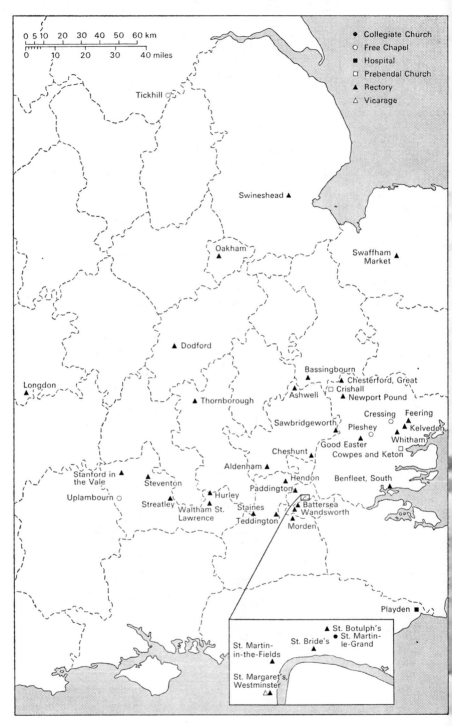

MAP III. CHURCHES APPROPRIATED TO WESTMINSTER ABBEY BY 1540

INDEX[1]

Acres, 128, 208, 235 ff., 310 n., 428 n., 443
Adam, John and Margaret, 329 f.
Adymer, abbot of Westminster, 17 n.
Aelfhelm Polga, 23, 37
Aelfhere, ancestor of Odda, 30
Aethelbert, king of Kent (560–616), 20, 22
Aethelred II (978/9–1016), 22, 352 f.
Aetsere Swearte and Aelfgyth, his wife, 344
Agate, Hugh, s. of William, and John, his brother, 278 n.
Ailric, 351
Ailric, chamberlain, 343
Ailric, s. of Mariete, 37, 348
Aldebury, Walter de, 150, 152
Aldenham (Herts.), 116, 119 n., 310, 315, 392, 397; assarts, 218; church and rectory, 51, 54, 62 n., 155 n., 345, 397, 403; demesne, 129, 155, 403 n., 429; holdings, 205 ff., 211 n., 288 f., 432, 435 f.; manor, 24 n., 86, 104, 113 n., 114, 124 (Table VII), 127 n., 150, 152, 155, 224 n., 300, 345, 416; meadow and pasture, 429; molmen, 238 n., 441 n., 445 n.; rents, 217 f., 234, 238, 392, 441, 445; sub-tenancies, 214; tenant-land, 114, 429; tenants, 115 n., 119 ff., 205, 241 f., 286, 300 n.; vicar, vicarage, 153 n., 403; virgate, 205 ff.; woodland, woods, 114, 120, 416, 429
Aleyn, Robert, fishmonger of London, 189, 192 f., 424; Matilda, wife of, 424
Alfgar, abbot of Westminster, 17 n.
Alfnod, abbot of Westminster, 17 n.
Alfric, abbot of Westminster, 17 n.
Alfwy, abbot of Westminster, 17 n.
Alger, clerk, 79, 82, 342
Alice, wife of Gilbert, 115 n.
Alienation: by abbot and convent, 83 f., 90, 186 f.; by customary tenants, 299 ff.; by free tenants, 83, 118 ff., 165, 176, 188, 311 ff.;

by nominees, 187; by religious, 154; see also assign, the right to
Alkborough (Lincs.), 201, 348, 425
Allfarthing, in Wandsworth (Surr.), 168 n., 358 n.; le Frithe, le Fryth, le Frythe, manor in, 185 n., 357, 395, 418
Almain, Henry (d. 1271), 374
Alms, 30, 33, 35, 99 n., 339 n., 388 ff., 393 ff., 405, 410 n.
Alnemouth, Peter, of Newcastle-upon-Tyne, and Cristina, his wife, 418 f.
Alnod of London, 359
Alphonso, s. of Edward I (d. 1284), 374
Alyngreth, John, see Halengrett, John
Ambrosius Aurelianus, 17
Amundesham, William, monk of Westminster (d. 1420), 380
Amwell, Great, 184 n., 249, 274; contractual tenancies, 252, 276; demesne, 276 n., 429; land transactions, 305; manor, 168, 176, 183, 184 n., 188, 191, 194, 196, 269 n., 283, 285, 345, 415, 439
Andrew, James, mercer of London, 193, 421; Matilda, wife of, 421
Anne of Bohemia, wife of Richard II (d. 1394), 377, 378 n.; see also Richard II and Anne of Bohemia
Anne, wife of Richard III, see Neville, Anne
Anniversaries, 28 ff., 39 f., 41, 53 n., 63, 371, 387 ff.
Anselm, St., 95
Apollo, 18 n.
Appropriation of churches, 48 ff., 65, 402 ff.; see also under individual parishes
Ardern, Amice de, wife of John le Lou, 31
Ardern, Sir William de, 31
Arley (Warwicks.), manor, 191
Artur, a sub-tenant, 71 n.
Arundel, Sir John de, 371 n.; Sir William, s. of, 371 n.

Arundel, Sir John de, and Sir William de, his son, 371 n.

Arundel, Ralph de, abbot of Westminster (1200–14, d. 1223), 83 f., 97, 99, 340 n., 356 n., 358, 359 n., 374, 389

Ashbourne (Derbys.), 380 n.

Ashby, Nicholas, prior of Westminster (d. 1458), 100 n.

Ashford (Midd.): chapel, 349 n., 409; customary land, 430; demesne, 149, 430; gavel-land, 430 n.; holdings, 207, 318, 432, 436; manor, 121, 127 n., 228, 349, 354 n.; meadow and pasture, 430; rents, 232 n., 237, 441, 446; tenants in villeinage, 241 f.; vicar, 409 n.; virgate, 434

Ashwell (Herts.): *bordelli*, 436 n.; burgesses, 101, 124 (Table VII); church and rectory, 49, 65, 184, 404; demesne, 150, 404 n., 428 n., 429; holdings, 6, 207, 213, 432, 436; manor, 27 n., 72 f., 104 f., 111, 113 n., 124 (Table VII), 127 n., 184, 346; meadow and pasture, 429; mill, 72; 'outland', 445 n.; rents, 217, 441, 445; serjeant of, 184; tenant-land, 106 n., 114, 429; tenants, 106, 207 n.; vicarage, 404; virgate, 434

Aspale, Geoffrey de (d. 1287), 40, 351 f., 369, 374, 393

Assarting, assarts, 113 f., 130, 218, 296, 300, 318

Assign, the right to, 156, 249 f.

Aston, Thomas, Thomas de, 184, 185 n., 424

Augustine, s. of Eustace, and Bela, his wife, 390 n.

Aula, Roger de, 110 n.

Avignon (France, Vaucluse), 378 n.

Aylmer, Edward, 385 n.; Katherine, wife of, d. of Margaret, dowager duchess of Norfolk, 385

Ayot (Herts.), 72, 74

Bagnor, in Speen (Berks.), manor, 337 f.

Baker, Geoffrey, 393 n.; Richard, s. of, 393

Baldeswell, Thomas de, goldsmith of London, 189 f.

Baldwin, a sub-tenant, 71 n.

Baldwin, Baldewine: Agnes, 281 n.; John, 327; Walter, 110 n., 115 n.; William, 281 n.

Ballard, John, 247

Bannebourn, Richard, 276

Bardolf, Sir Robert, and Amice, his wife (Amice Buxhill), 380 n.

Barking (Essex), 342 n.; abbess of, 387 n.; abbess and convent of, 387 n.

Barleythorpe (Rutl.), 404 n., 430 n.; rectory, *see* Oakham with Barleythorpe rectory

Barnet (Herts.), battle of (1471), 382 n.

Barton, Simon, 424

Basset, Roger, 185, 418

Bassingbourn (Cantab.), 403, 408

Battersea (Surr.), 75 f., 116, 119 n., 357 n., 388, 420; Bridgecourt, Bridges in, *see* Bridges; church and rectory, 54, 65 n., 164 n., 388 n., 411; demesne, 358 n.; free tenants, 71, 115 n., 116, 118 n.; knight in, 71, 76, 115 n.; manor, 73 f., 76 n., 125 (Table VII) (*see also* Battersea and Wandsworth manor); Penge in, *see* Penge; purchases of property in, 184, 420, 424; vicar, vicarage, 48, 411

Battersea and Wandsworth (Surr.): customary land, 430; demesne, 129, 150, 154, 157, 428 n., 430; holdings, 205 ff., 209, 213, 432, 435 f.; manor, 27, 86, 104, 121, 127 n., 224 n., 237 n., 242, 315, 338, 357 ff., 443; meadow and pasture, 430; mills, 358 n.; rents, 217, 231 f., 441, 446; tenants, 121, 205 ff., 241 f.; virgate, 434

Bavaria, duke of, *see* Lewis, count palatine and duke of Bavaria

Baynard, Ralph, 71 n.

Baynard, William, 71 n., 73 ff.

Beauchamp, Robert de, and Alice, his wife, 415

Beauchamp, William de, I, 76 n.

Beauchamp, William de, II, 76

Beauflour, Joan (d. 1326/7), 375, 394

Beauflour, Thomas, 375 n., 394

Beaufort, Margaret, countess of Richmond (d. 1509), m. (i) Edmund, earl of Richmond; (ii) Henry, lord Stafford; (iii) Thomas, lord Stanley, later earl of Derby, 29, 45 n., 67, 92, 199, 333, 350, 353 n., 384,

386 n., 399, 401, 405; foundation, 29, 34, 52; parents, 399

Beaumond, John, 256 n.

Bechamp, Stacey, 274

Beckswell manor, in Moulsham (Essex), 183, 340, 396 n., 423

Bedel, William (d. 1518), and Cecily, his wife, 384

Belchford manor (Lincs.), 348 f., 425

Belet, Mr. Roger, 175, 189, 422; Agnes, wife of, 422

Belets manor, in Laleham (Midd.), *see* Billetts

Benedict of Nursia, St., 95

Benfleet (Essex), *see* Benfleet, South

Benfleet, North (Essex), 340

Benfleet, South (Essex), 390, 395, 400 n.; demesne, 152, 154, 340 n., 428 n., 429; holdings, 206; manor, 28 n., 79, 81, 102 n., 123 (Table VII), 141, 338 n., 340, 402, 439, 443; marsh in, 193, 418, 420; meadow and pasture, 429; purchases of property in, 193, 425; rectory, 48, 58 n., 152, 340, 388 n., 402, 405; rents, 443, 445; tenant-land, 122 n., 429; vicar, vicarage, 48, 405; woodland, 429

Benfleet, South, and Fanton manor (Essex), 127 n., 236 n., 432, 436

Bennet, William, 286 n.

Bennington (Lincs.), 426

Benolt, Thomas, Clarenceux, King of Arms (d. 1534), 366 f.

Benson, William, abbot of Westminster (1533–40), 93 n., 94

Berd, John, 302, 304

Berdfelds manor (Essex), *see* Bonvilles

Berdon (Essex), 425

Bergavenny, George, lord, *see* Neville, George

Berkeley, Maurice, lord (d. 1506), 201 f., 426; William, brother of, 201

Berkhampstead (Herts.), 290 n.

Berking, Alice de, 121

Berking, Richard de, abbot of Westminster (1222–46), 52, 64 f., 86 f., 89, 92 ff., 96 f., 104, 115 f., 118 ff., 130, 143, 164, 166 ff., 169 n., 314 f., 351, 374, 390 f., 414 f.; anniversary, 345, 351; niece of, 400 n.; parents, 391; prior, 97

Berkinges, Geoffrey de, 115 n., 116 f.

Berners, Humphrey, lord, *see* Bourchier, Humphrey, lord Berners

Berners, Sir James (d. 1388), 377

Besford (Worcs.), 72, 76 n., 125 (Table VII), 360, 363 n.

Besford, Alexander, steward of the Western Parts, 290 f.

Betterton, in Lockinge (Berks.), 337

Beverington (Suss.), 202

Beverley, John (d. 1380), 377, 380 n.; Amice, wife of (Amice Buxhill), 380 n.

Bidek's manor, in Finchley (Midd.), *see* Finchley

Billetts manor, also known as Belets manor, in Laleham (Midd.), 175, 349, 422

Binholme manor, also known as Pershore (Worcs.), 363

Bircheston, Simon de, abbot of Westminster (1344–9), 66, 376, 395

Birchetts Green (Berks.), 133 n.

Birdbrook (Essex), 31, 169, 178, 252 f., 312, 340, 417, 420, 429

Birdbrook, Michael de, 417

Birlingham (Worcs.), manor, 102 n., 125 (Table VII), 133, 167, 173, 196, 360, 362, 363 n., 421

Black Death, the (1348–9), 42 n., 66, 112, 144, 157, 161, 219, 231, 233 f., 244 f., 253, 257 ff., 264, 273, 319

Blanche, d. of Edward III (d. 1342), 376

Blanche, d. of Henry IV (d. 1409), 381 n.

Blebure, Richard de, 174 n.

Blechenham, in Hendon (Midd.), 21

Blois, Gervase de, abbot of Westminster (1138–57), 79 ff., 84 f., 99 f., 118, 167, 341 n., 342 ff., 350, 352, 373; Dameta, mother of, 81, 167, 350

Blokkele, Blokle, John de, 378, 397

Bluet, Clementia, 174

Boadvills manor (Essex), *see* Bonvilles

Boarstall, in Plumstead (Kent), 347, 426; *see also* Plumstead Boarstall

Bohun, Humphrey de, earl of Hereford and Essex (d. 1322), 376 n.; Humphrey, s. of (d. 1304), and Mary, d. of (d. 1305), 376

Bohun, Joan and John de, 32

Bonefaunt, Thomas de (d. 1470), 382
Bonvilles manor, also known as Berd-felds, Boadvills, Bradfields, in N. Benfleet (Essex), 340
Bordars, 101 ff., 123–5 (Table VII), 203 n., 219
Boston (Lincs.), 426
'Bounflower', Thomas and Philippa, 375 n.
Bourchier, Humphrey, lord Berners (d. 1471), 382
Bourchier, Humphrey, lord Cromwell (d. 1471), 382
Bourchier, Lewis Robsart, lord, *see* Robsart, Lewis
Bourton-on-the-Hill (Glos.), 421, 424; cotland, 283 n.; customary land, 428; customary leases, 280; demesne, 128, 344 n., 428; heriots, 272, 283 n.; holdings, 432, 435; jointure, 280 n., 283 n.; labour services, 229 ff., 233, 257 n.; manor, 114 n., 128, 134 f., 150 f., 229 ff., 241, 283, 344 f.; rents, 237, 439, 444; sheep-fold, 344 n.; virgate, 236 n., 434
Braban', Gerard, 272
Brabazun, Roger le, *see* le Brabazun
Bracton, Henry (d. 1268), 82, 242
Bradestoke, Richard and Margery, 256 n.
Bradfields manor (Essex), *see* Bonvilles
Bradwell (Essex), 341 n.
'Braharsen', Roger, 376 n.
Brandon (Warwicks.), 371 n.
Brauncestr', Gilbert de, 172
Bray, John de, of Chiswick, and Joan, his wife, 192 n.
Bray, Sir Reginald (d. 1503), 425 n.
Breche, Richard atte, 225 n.
Brickendon (Herts.), 23, 37
Bricklehampton (Worcs.), 125 (Table VII), 287, 361, 363 n.
Brictric, 72
Bridgecourt, Bridges, also known as Bruges, in Battersea (Surr.), 108, 116, 121 n., 357 n., 420
Bridgewater, Edward, monk of West-minster (d. 1471/2), 382
Brocas, Sir Bernard (d. 1395), 378
Broghton, Ralph de, 32 n.
Brooke (Rutl.), 404 n.
Brooke, Richard, serjeant-at-law, 387
Brown, Browne, Robert, 385

Brown, Browne, Thomas, monk of Westminster (d. 1513/14), 384
Brown, Browne, William, 386
Bruges, in Battersea, *see* Bridgecourt
Bruges, Algar de, 108
Bruges, John and William de, 121 n.
Brun', Walter, 115 n.
Bryan, Alice, d. of William, 250 f.
Bryd, William, tenant at Islip, 261 n.
Bryd, William, tenant at Murcot or Fencot, 329 f.
Bucherel, Andrew, mayor of London, 390
Buckingham, John, bishop of Lincoln (1363–98), 403
Buckland, Hugh de, 346
Buckland, William de, sheriff of Berks., 79 f., 338, 346, 350
Bullington manor, in Clavering and Ugley (Essex), 200 f., 340, 425
Bunde, Sayer, 184, 185 n.
Bures (Essex), 102 n., 103 n., 113 n., 123 (Table VII)
Burghs prebend (church of St. Martin-le-Grand, London), 342 n.
Burials, 25, 28, 37 f., 365 ff., 372 ff.
Burnham, E. (Bucks.), 77, 79, 102 n., 123 (Table VII), 338
Burstalle, James and Joan de, 418
Burton (Staffs.), *see* Burton-upon-Trent
Burton Stather (Lincs.), 201, 348, 425
Burton-upon-Trent (Staffs.), abbey of St. Mary and St. Modwen at, 226
Butterwick (Lincs.), 426
Buxhill, Alan, constable of the Tower of London (d. 1381/2), 380 n.; Amice, d. of (d. 1416), m. (i) John Beverley; (ii) Sir Robert Bardolf, 380
Bybbesworth, Edmund, 158
Byesteton, Byestetoun, Byeston', Thomas, 418 f.
Bygge, Richard, snr., and Katherine, his wife, 281 f.
Bygge, Richard, jnr., 281
Bygge, Walter, 281
Bykenore, Sir Thomas de (d. 1316), 376
By Southe, William, 309

Caen (France, Calvados), 25
Calais (France, Pas-de-Calais), 384 n.
Caldecote, Joan, 280 n.
Calhan, Peter, citizen of London (d. 1258), 374

Cambridge, university, 30
Camden, William (d. 1623), 365, 369, 372 n., 373 n., 376 nn., 377 n., 380 n., 383 n., 385 n.
Camville, Sir Robert de, 32
Canterbury, archbishop of, 68, 387 n.; see of, 69
Canute, king of England (1016–35), 17 f.
Capella, Martin de, 338 n.
Cappere, Hugh, *see* le Kuver, Hugh
Carew, Nicholas (d. 1470), and Margaret (d. 1470), 383
Carter, Nicholas, 310 n.
Cassy, John, 162 f.
Castlemorton (Worcs.), formerly Morton Foliot, 166, 168, 275, 313, 415; assart, 130; contractual tenancies, 249; customary leases, 283; demesne, 429; holdings, 433, 436 n.; jointure, 249, 281 ff.; land transactions, 328; manor, 93, 275, 361, 362 n., 439; tenant-land, 122, 128 n., 275 n.
Castlemorton Greyndour manor (Worcs.), 361, 362 n.
Caubrege, Ca'brige, John de, 380
Cealchithe, 349 n.
Cecily, d. of Edward IV (d. 1507), 384 n.
Cecily, wife of Adam, 115 n.
Ceppe, in Longdon (Warwicks.), 419
cestui que use, 186
Chaceley (Glos., formerly Worcs.), 166, 168, 415; customary leases, 283; demesne, 152, 361 n., 429; holdings, 433, 436; jointure, 282 f.; land transactions, 328; manor, 275, 362 n.; meadow, 235 ff., 429; rents, 231 n., 440, 445; tenant-land, 275 n., 429; virgate, 235 f., 434
Chaceley Greyndour manor (Glos., formerly Worcs.), 361, 362 n.
Chaddleworth (Berks.), 338
Chalkhill, in Kingsbury (Midd.), 39 n., 349
Chamberlayne, Leonard, 411 n.
Chantries, 40, 371, 391 ff.
Charing (Midd.), 116
Charters, 11, 13, 22 f., 39, 117 ff., 165, 284, 285 n., 306 f., 312 f., 359 n.
Chaucer, Geoffrey (d. 1400), 380
Chelmereford, Stephen de, vintner of London, 390

Chelmsford (Essex), 168, 417, 423, 425; *see also* Moulsham
Chelsea (Midd.), manor, 77 ff., 167, 181, 337, 350, 351 n., 355 n., 419
Chenduit, William, 390
Cheny, Alexander de, 346
Chertesey, Chertseye, Benedict de, prior of Westminster, 97
Chertesey, Chertseye, Walter, 302
Cheshunt (Herts.), 405
Chesterfield, Richard de (d. *c.* 1405), 380, 396 n.
Chesterford, Great (Essex), 201 f., 341, 426; vicar, vicarage, 405
Chestre, John de, and Agnes, 190
Chichester (Suss.), diocese of, 403
Chichestre, John de, goldsmith of London, 190
Chidyngefold, William, and Matilda, his wife, 250
Chievely (Berks.), 337
Chollington (*Sillinctune*) manor, in Eastbourne (Suss.), 24 n., 85 n., 359
Chyriton, Geoffrey de, 424 n.
Cippenham manor, in E. Burnham (Bucks.), 77, 79, 338
Cirencester, Richard of, monk of Westminster, 15, 18, 372 n.
Clare, Osbert of, monk of Westminster, 18, 22, 85 n., 95
Clavering (Essex), 200 n., 340, 425
Claygate (Surr.), 78 f., 102 n., 125 (Table VII), 154 f., 165 n., 206 n., 358, 430, 432, 436
Claygate, Gilbert de, 165 n., 358 n., 415
Clerk, John, lessee of Kelvedon, 156
Clerk, John, rector of Launton, 153
Clerk, Margery, 288 n.
Clerk, Robert, 225 n.
Clifford, Walter de, 75
Clinton, John, lord (d. 1464), 383 n.
Clun, Hugh de, 174 f.
Cobham, Joan, baroness Cobham (Joan de la Pole), 378 n.
Cobham, John de, 420
Cockayne, Sir John, 380 n.; Joan, wife of, 380
Coggeshall (Essex), 341
Coggeshall, Little (Essex), 341
Colchester (Essex), 98, 315, 341 n.
Colchester, William, abbot of Westminster (1386–1420), 9 f., 14, 60, 90 n., 96, 98 f., 133, 261, 268 ff.,

Colchester, William (*cont.*):
290, 292, 310, 381, 424 f.; anniversary, 51 n., 397, 403; chantry, 397
Coleham, Hugh de, 165 n., 350
Coleham, Walter, s. of Thurstan de, 165 n.
Coleville, Philip de, 166, 400, 414 f.
Coleworth, John de, prior of Westminster (d. *c.* 1295), 393
Combe, in Greenwich (Kent), 347, 392, 430
Comberton manor, in Great and Little Comberton (Worcs.), 74, 141, 361, 363 n.
Commutation and sale of works, 4, 94, 112, 216, 218, 225 ff., 239 f., 256 ff.; *see also under individual manors*
Confraternity, 38 f., 370 ff., 373 n., 386 f., 393 f., 398, 400 n.
Congham, Sir Robert de, 358
Coningsby, Humphrey, serjeant-at-law, 155
Constantyne, Ralph, 386
Convers, John, 419
Cook, Cooke, John, 421 n.
Cook, Cooke, Thomas, 303 f.
Coppethorn, William, and Ella, his wife, 419 n.
Copy, copies, of court rolls, 249, 280, 284 f., 332
Cornhill, Stephen de, 416
Cornwall, earl of, 290 n., 376
Corrodians, corrodies, 120, 141 f., 165, 167, 170, 172, 181, 193, 415, 422, 424
Cosyn, Richard, 302 n.
Cothull, William de, of Westerham, 420
Cottars, 101 ff., 123–5 (Table VII)
Cottesford, John (i), 289 n., 310 f.
Cottesford, John (ii), 289
Courtenay, Richard, bishop of Norwich (1413–15), 381
Cowhouse manor, in Hampstead (Midd.), 35, 352
Cowley (Midd.), manor, 124 (Table VII), 203 n.; *see also* Cowley Peachey
Cowley Peachey (Midd.), manor, 350
Cowper, William, merchant of the Staple, 152, 154
Cowpes and Keton, in Maldon (Essex), prebendal churches of, 403, 406, 408

Cradley (Worcs.), 362, 398
Crane End (Lincs.), *see* Skreyne
Crassus, William, 389 n.
Crayford (Kent), 347, 426
Crespin, Moses, s. of Benedict, 170
Cressing (Essex), chapel, 403, 406, 408; vicarage, 406 n.
Crevequer, Robert, Robert de, 40, 351, 354
Cricklade (Wilts.), 101, 113 n., 125 (Table VII)
Crishall (Essex), prebendal church of, 403, 406, 408
Crispin, Gilbert, abbot of Westminster (1085–1117/18), 28, 64, 78, 80, 85, 87, 95, 117, 129, 132, 140 f., 143, 165 n., 350, 352, 373 nn., 387
Crokesley, Richard de, abbot of Westminster (1246–58), 97, 352, 374, 391, 415
Cromwell, Humphrey, lord, *see* Bourchier, Humphrey, lord Cromwell
Crowland (Lincs.), abbey of St. Mary the Virgin, St. Bartholomew and St. Guthlac in, 228 n.
Culworth, Richard de, 29
Curridge, in Chieveley (Berks.), 337
Curry family, the, of Chaceley, 152
Curtlington, Curtlyngton, Alan de, 183 f., 417
Curtlington, Curtlyngton, William de, abbot of Westminster (1315–33), 14 n., 129, 133, 177, 206, 230 f., 240, 376, 394, 416 f.
Cutte, Sir John, citizen of London, 200, 202, 425 f.; Elizabeth, wife of, 425 f.

D'Abitot family, the, 360
Dabridgecourt, Sir John (d. 1415), 380 n.
Dameta, mother of Gervase de Blois, 81, 167, 350
Damietta, 374 n.
Dane, John atte, 308 n.
Datchworth (Herts.), 124 (Table VII), 346 n.
Datchworth with Watton manor (Herts.), 24 n., 346
Daubeney, Giles, baron (d. 1508), 367, 384, 399, 426 n.; Elizabeth, wife of (d. 1500), 367 n., 384
David I, king of Scotland (1124–53), 388

Decanus, Clement, 56 n.
Deene (Northants.), 27 n., 102 n., 124 (Table VII), 355 f., 389
Deerhurst (Glos.): berewicks of, 71, 76 n., 114 n., 123 (Table VII), 174 n., 344 nn.; customary land, 128 n.; demesne, 71, 157 f., 162, 344 n., 428; fee-farm, 173, 196 f., 344, 416; half-hundred, 167, 416; Hasfield in, 72, 77 n.; hospice rights, 83 n.; labour services, 271; manor, also known as Plaistow, 27, 30, 71, 73, 78, 83, 88, 123 (Table VII), 139 n., 167 f., 173 ff., 188, 195 ff., 344, 356 (*see also* Deerhurst and Hardwicke manor); monastery, 30, 73; woodland, 114
Deerhurst and Hardwicke manor (Glos.), 121 n., 122, 229 n., 259 n., 416, 443; customary land, 122 n.; labour services, 223 n., 233, 257; rents, 258, 439, 444
Defford (Worcs.), 77, 125 (Table VII), 360, 362, 363 n.
Dene, Simon de, 400
Denham (Bucks.), 111, 168, 193, 421; abbot's house, 133; demesne, 128, 139 n., 150, 158, 339 n., 428; Durdent's manor in, 338 n.; fee-farm, 32, 60 n., 338 n., 339 n.; holdings, 286; hospice rights at, 83 n., 338 n., 339 n.; manor, 9, 32, 33 n., 35, 40, 59 f., 77, 81, 102 n., 113 n., 122, 123 (Table VII), 127 n., 133, 136, 138, 338, 439; tenant-land, 122 n., 128 n.; wood, 421
Denia, count of, 378 n., 379 n.
Deorhurste, Adam de, 110 n., 115 n.
Deorman, the daughters of, 38, 373, 386; Theoderic, s. of, 373 n.
Derby, John, 153 n.
Derby, Thomas, earl of, *see* Stanley, Thomas
Derneford, William de (mid-12th cent.), 344
Derneford, William de (late 13th cent.), 167, 173 f., 188, 195, 197, 416; Cecily, wife of, 173 f., 197; Clementia Bluet, wife of, 174; William, s. of, 174, 195, 197, 416
Dinham, John, lord (d. 1458), 383 n.
Diocletian, 17
Dispenser, Robert, 74, 78, 361

Doddington (Lincs.), 102 n., 124 (Table VII)
Doddington and Thorpe manor (Lincs.), 339, 348
Dodford (Northants.), rectory, 53, 404
Dolle, William, reeve of Islip (Oxon.), 248
Domesday Book, 55, 63, 71 ff., 77, 101, 123 ff. (Table VII), 203 f., 219
Doun', Doune, Robert atte, 194, 195 n.
Douraunt, John, 115 n.
Down, in Northolt (Midd.), 157, 161, 350
Downe, in Wandsworth (Surr.), 61 n., 150 n., 152, 179, 184, 186, 190, 193 ff., 358, 421
Drayton manor, in West Drayton (Midd.), 350
Droitwich (Worcs.), 71 n., 101, 113 n., 125 (Table VII)
Ducet, John, 110 n., 115 n., 117
Ducet, Nicholas, 117
Dudley, William, bishop of Durham (1476–83), 383
Dune, Robert de la, 76 n., 115 n., 117
Dunning, a tenant, 72
Dunstan, St., 17, 22 ff., 36, 46, 74, 141, 350, 352, 354, 359
Durdent, Edward, 421 n.
Durdent, Thomas, 184 f., 248, 421 f.
Duxford (Cantab.), 339, 348
Dytton, John, 150, 152

Easthampstead (Berks.), manor, 27 n., 113 n., 123 (Table VII), 337
Ebury, in Eye (Midd.), 350 n.
Eckington (Worcs.), 72, 77 n., 125 (Table VII), 362, 363 n.
Eddon, Richard, 290 n.
Eddon, Thomas, 280
Edenbridge (Kent), 348
Edgar, king of England (957–75), 22 ff., 37, 74, 341 f., 345 f., 353 f., 358 f.
Edith, wife of Edward the Confessor (d. 1075), 27, 47, 368 n., 372
Edmund, earl of Lancaster (d. 1296), 375, 394; Aveline, wife of (d. 1274), 375; Blanche, wife of (d. 1302), 394
Edmund, earl of Richmond (d. 1456), 399
Edmund, earl of Rutland (d. 1460), 398
Edmund, s. of Henry VII (d. 1499), 383

Edward I (1272–1307), 31 f., 58 n., 177, 182, 338 ff., 348, 352, 360, 374 n., 375 f., 392 f., 416; Eleanor, wife of, *see* Eleanor of Castile

Edward II (1307–27), 44, 154, 181, 377 n., 411 n., 416 n.

Edward III (1327–77), 15, 32, 44, 177, 189, 269, 376 ff.

Edward IV (1461–83), 181, 383, 384 n., 398

Edward V (1483), 368

Edward the Confessor, St., king of England (1042–66), 23 ff., 30, 36 f., 46 f., 55, 73, 78, 85, 132, 323, 337 f., 341 f., 344 ff., 349 n., 353 ff., 359 n., 363, 372; canonization, 28, 43; shrine, 25, 28, 43 ff., 372 nn., 373 n., 374 n.; thegn, thegns of, 32, 41, 55

Edward, reeve of Westminster, 389

Edwin, abbot of Westminster (1049–c. 1071), 16, 372

Egleton (Rutl.), 404 nn.

Eleanor, countess of Bar, d. of Edward I (d. 1298), 375

Eleanor of Castile, wife of Edward I (d. 1290), 31 f., 375, 393, 416; anniversary, 29 f., 148, 339 f., 348, 352, 360, 393; foundation, 10, 31 ff., 60 n., 61 n., 62, 91, 172, 177 ff., 183, 196, 287, 417, 419 f.

Eleanor of Provence, wife of Henry III (d. 1291), 391

Elena, d. of Ralph *ad pontem*, 312 n.

Elfgifu, the lady, 23

Elfrid, a sub-tenant, 71 n., 72

Elizabeth I (1558–1603), 333

Elizabeth, d. of Henry VII (d. 1495), 383

Elizabeth, wife of Henry VII (d. 1503), 384, 399

Ellesworth, Simon de, 31, 416

Elme, Thomas atten (Thomas Nelme), 280

Elmham, Robert de (d. 1364/5), 378

Elmley (Worcs.), 361

Elsenham (Essex), 200 n., 340 n., 344 n., 425

Eltham, John of, earl of Cornwall (d. 1336), 376

Elverding', John de, 115 n.

Ely (Cantab.), Benedictine abbey of St. Ethelreda at, 23, 37, 80 n.

Ely, bishop of, 1 n., 68 f.

Ely, diocese, see of, 178, 403, 408

Empson, Sir Richard (d. 1510), 201, 425 n., 426 n.

English, Englissh, Englys, John, 261 n.

English, Englissh, Englys, William, 420

Envirmeu, Hugh of, 339

Erith (Kent), 347, 426

Estney, John, abbot of Westminster (1474–98), 93, 97 n., 383

Eston, Elena, widow of John, 272 n.

Esyngton, William, 200, 202, 426

Ethelgoda, wife of Saebert, king of the E. Saxons (d. c. 615), 20, 372

Eustace III, count of Boulogne, 339 n.

Evershaw (Bucks.), 355 n.

Eversley (Hants), 27 n., 123 (Table VII), 345

Evesham (Worcs.), battle of (1265), 191

Ewell, James, haberdasher of London, 152, 161

Exchequer of the Jews, 170

Eye (Midd.), 43, 81 n., 87, 118, 168, 187, 189, 297, 350, 380 n., 393, 414, 417 ff., 422; contractual tenancies, 250; demesne, 158, 350 n., 428; land transactions, 309; le Burgoyne in, 350 n.; Longmore, 350 n.; manor, 38, 135, 139 f., 151, 315, 337, 353 n., 439; Market Mead in, 350 n.; meadows, 350 n., 428; purchases of property in, 179, 184 n., 414, 417 ff., 422; tenant-land, 122 n., 128 n.

Eynesford, William de, III, 79, 81, 340

Fanton (now Fanton Hall) (Essex): demesne, 429; free tenants, 118 n.; manors (i) 24 n., 78, 102 n., 103, 113 n., 123 (Table VII), 141, 341, 388 n., 439, 443 (*see also* Benfleet, South, and Fanton manor), (ii) 103, 123 (Table VII), 341; meadow and pasture, 429; rents, 443, 445; tenant-land, 122 n., 429

Farm, farms, 78, 80, 130, 141, 350; meaning of word, 246, 262; of manors, 77 ff., appendix I *passim*; of tenant-land, 263 f.; *see also* fee-farm; lease

Farnebergh, John de, cofferer of London, 189

Farnham (Essex), 425

Fascet, George, abbot of Westminster (1498–1500), 93, 97 n., 368, 384

Fastolf, Sir John (d. 1459), 202

Fauconberg, the Bastard of, *see* Neville, Thomas, s. of William

Fauconberg, William, lord, *see* Neville, William

Fawkeners (prebend of church of St. Martin-le-Grand, London), 342 n.

Fawkes, tenant at Sutton-under-Brailes, 290 n.

Fécamp, abbey at, 400 n.

Fee-farm, fee-farms, 77 f., 89, 120, 165 ff., 179 n., appendix I *passim*

Feering (Essex), 39, 72, 76, 84 n., 119, 392, 422; assarts, 218; berewick of, 429 n.; church and rectory, 29, 47 n., 49, 184, 341 n., 391, 402, 406; demesne, 129, 148, 150, 258, 341 n., 428 n., 429; free tenants, 105, 316, 432 n.; glebe, 129; holdings, 205, 211, 432, 435; labour services, 258; manor, 27 f., 86, 102 n., 103 ff., 122, 123 (Table VII), 127 n., 224 n., 338, 341, 402, 443 f.; meadows and pasture, 429; rents, 217 f., 238, 440, 445; tenant-land, 122 n., 429; vicar, vicarage, 50, 184, 406; virgate, 434; woodland, 429

Felby, John, 386

Feliceland, Felicelond', in Wickford (Essex), 185, 418

Fencot (Oxon.), 223 n., 233 n., 263 n., 270 n., 280 n., 293, 323, 330 n., 356 n., 440 n.

Fenne, in Fishtoft (Lincs.), 349, 426

Fenne and Skreyne manor (Lincs.), 200 f., 426

Fenys, Thomas, 425 n.

Fileby, John de, 32 n.

Fileby, Robert de, 32

Finch, Fynch, Roger, vintner of London, 189 f., 358, 424

Finches manor, in Wandsworth (Surr.), 358, 418 n.

Finchley, in Hendon (Midd.), 168, 175 n., 185 n.; Bidek's manor in, 351, 352 n., 395, 418

Fines: and tenancy-at-will, 247; for customary holdings, 224 f., 237, 271 f., 274, 278 ff., 284, 297 f., 303, 307, 327 n., 446 n.; for demesne leases, 158 f., 162; for entry on the Abbey's fee, 313, 320 n.; for leases of tenant-land, 249 n., 251; for marriage or refusal of marriage, 241 f., 298; for mortmain licences, 180 f.; for sub-tenancies, 309 f.

Fishtoft (Lincs.), 426

fitz Adam, Ralph, 115 n.

fitz Ailmar, Gilbert, 115 n.

fitz Baderon, William, 71 n.

fitz Corbuz, William, 71 n.

fitz Gunter, Gilbert, *see* Hendon, Gilbert de

fitz Herbert, Herbert, 359

fitz Herbert, Peter, 359

fitz Neal, Richard, bishop of London (1189–98), 48, 405

fitz Pentecost', Geoffrey, 110 n., 115 n.

fitz Peter, Geoffrey, earl of Essex (d. 1213), 79, 358, 389

fitz Ponz, Drogo, 71 n.

fitz Rou, Thurstin, 71 n., 72, 74, 76

fitz Turold, Gilbert, 71, 74, 361, 364 n.

fitz Walter, John, 115 n.

fitz Warner, Hugh, 354 n.

fitz William, Peter, of Roxwell, and Joan, 418

fitz Wlured, Henry, 80 n., 81 n., 343

Fitzlewis, Elizabeth, abbess of the minoresses of London, 386

Flambard, Ranulf, bishop of Durham (1099–1128), 354, 357 n., 359 n.

Flete, John, monk of Westminster, 12 ff., 21 f., 64 n., 65 n., 84, 89, 92, 94, 98 f., 164, 169 n., 171, 176, 183, 198, 370, 421, 423

Foliot, Agnes de, 166

Foliot, Amphyllis de, 166 n.

Foliot, Avice de, 166, 414 f.

Foliot, Gilbert, bishop of London (1163–87), 47 ff., 406 f., 408 n., 409 n.

Foliot, Reginald de, 166, 191, 414; Margaret, widow of, 166; Robert, father of, 166, 167 n.

Foliot, William, 362

Fontevrault (France, Maine-et-Loire), abbey at, 375 n.

Fordham (Essex), 341 n.

Fox, Richard, bishop of Winchester (1501–28), 201, 426 n.

Foxle, John de, 59 n.

Freeman, William and Margery, 281 n.

Freemen, 101, 103, 106, 123 ff. (Table VII)

Frieston (Lincs.), 426

Frith, Frithe manor, in Hendon (Midd.), 351, 414

Frith, Frithe manor, in Allfarthing (Surr.), also known as le Frithe, 185 n., 357, 395, 418

Frith, Frithe, Walter de, and Walter his son, 351

Fulham (Midd.), 351

Fulkes, Alice, 329

Fynnesford, Robert, Robert de, also known as Robert atte Doune, 184, 190, 193 ff., 421; Alice, wife of, 184, 190, 193, 195, 421

Galle, Thomas, haberdasher of London, 161 n.

Gerard, Roger, corrodian, 172, 422

Giffard, John, 386, 393 f., 400

Girard the chamberlain, 71 n.

Girdeler, John (d. 1402), 381

Glanvil, 82

Glastonbury (Som.), Benedictine abbey of St. Mary the Virgin at, 17 n., 26, 68

Gloucester, 25, 152; abbot of, 166

Gloucester, Thomas, duke of, *see* Woodstock, Thomas of

Godram, Nicholas, 252 f.

Godynow, John, 425

Golafre, Sir John de (d. 1396), 378

Golie, William, 302

Good Easter manor (Essex), 342, 403, 406, 408; vicar, 406 n.

Good Easter Imber manor (Essex), 342 n.

Good Easter Newarks manor (Essex), 342 n.

Gooz, John, 256 n.

Gorge, William, 265 n.

Goscelin, Richard, 171; Ralph, s. of, 171

Goym, William, 302 n.

Grafton Minor (Warwicks.), 360

Gratian, 84

Greenford (Midd.): assarts, 218; demesne, 351 n., 430; holdings, 205 n., 213, 219, 432, 435; manor, 104, 113 n., 116, 124 (Table VII), 351 f., 439; rents, 216 ff.; subtenancies, 214; tenants, 115 n., 205; virgate, 434

Grosseteste, Robert, bishop of Lincoln (1235–53), 49, 404

Guildford (Surr.), Dominican friary at, 375 n.

Gunter, farmer of Hendon, 80

Gunthorpe (Rutl.), 404 n.

Guthmund, 342

Hadham, Reginald de, monk of Westminster, 51, 100

Hadleigh (Essex), 391

Hagley (Worcs.), 362, 398

Hailes (Glos.), Cistercian abbey at, 374 n.

Haket, William, 75

Halengrett, John (John Alyngreth), 369, 374, 391

Halliford (Midd.), 40, 77, 157, 351 f., 354 n., 393, 430, 439

Halton (Lincs.), 201, 348 f., 425

Ham manor, in E. Ham (Essex), 24 n., 77, 79, 102 n., 123 (Table VII), 342

Hambledon (Rutl.), church, 389

Hamond, Cecily, 310, 320

Hamond, Robert, 302 n.

Hampstead (Midd.), 73, 118 n., 352, 394; chapel of St. Mary at, 407; customary land, 430; demesne, 352 n., 430; holdings, 206, 432, 436; manor, 24 n., 113 n., 124 (Table VII), 127 n., 236 n., 351 f., 391, 439; meadow and pasture, 430; rents, 443, 446

Handes, tenant at Sutton-under-Brailes, 290 n.

Handes, John, 267 n.

Handlo, John, 418

Hanew, William, 255

Hanwell (Midd.), 24 n., 124 (Table VII), 351 f., 439

Hardwicke, in Elmstone Hardwicke (Glos.), 114 n., 128, 140, 152, 154 f., 174 n., 226, 228, 259, 271, 344 f., 428

Harefield (Midd.), 381 n.

Harfleur (France, Seine-Inf.), 381 n.

Harold, earl of Wessex, 37; king of England (1066), 25, 343, 359

Harold Harefoot, king of England (d. 1040), 23, 372

Harpeden, Sir John (d. 1437), 378 n., 381

Harpenden (Herts.), 347 n.; manor, *see* Wheathampstead and Harpenden manor

Harries, Richard, 276 n.

Harwden, Richard, abbot of Westminster (1420–40, d. 1441), 12, 14, 96, 224, 270, 310, 381

Hasfield (Glos.), in Deerhurst, 72, 77 n.

Hatclyff, William (d. 1480), 383

Hathemar, Richard, 235 f.

Haverhill, Brictmar de, sheriff of London and Midd., 373 nn., 386; Deonise, wife of, 373; William, s. of, 373, 386, 388

Hawley, Robert (d. 1378), 15, 378, 379 n., 380 n.

Hebbe, Richard, 281; Thomas, s. of, 281; Katherine d. of, m. (i) William Baldwin; (ii) Richard Bygge, 281

Hemenhale, Sir Robert de (d. 1391), 378

Hendon (Midd.), 21 n., 111, 172, 175 n., 185 n., 189 n., 194, 351 n., 352, 416, 422; advowson, 406; church and rectory, 47 n., 51 f., 67, 406 f.; demesne, 129, 154, 352 n., 430; Frith manor in, 351, 414; holdings, 206, 219, 432, 436; hospice rights at, 83 n., 394; manor, 24 n., 77 f., 80, 113 n., 114 n., 122, 124 (Table VII), 127 n., 133, 236 n., 345, 352, 376 n., 416, 439; meadow, 430; rents, 391, 443, 446; tenant-land, 114 f., 122 n., 129, 430; tenants, 114 n., 118 n., 241 f.; tithes, 49; vicarage, 407; wood, 114, 394

Hendon, Gilbert de, also known as Gilbert fitz Gunter, 56 n., 80, 352

Henle, Thomas de, abbot of Westminster (1333–44), 96, 98, 169, 376, 394, 417 f.

Henry I (1100–35), 28, 94, 339, 361, 368 n., 373, 388

Henry II (1154–89), 95, 106, 115, 358

Henry III (1216–72), 25, 28 f., 40 n., 44, 64, 171, 176, 197, 367, 369, 374 nn., 375, 391 f.

Henry III and Eleanor of Provence: anniversary, 29, 49, 391, 406

Henry IV (1399–1413), 381 n.

Henry V (1413–22), 42 n., 45, 381; anniversary, 29 ff., 33, 398; chantry, 177, 338, 347, 398; foundation, 10, 29, 34

Henry VI (1422–61, 1470–1), 45, 177, 292, 338, 347

Henry VII (1485–1509), 33, 45, 53, 67 f., 333, 383 f., 401; anniversary, 29, 33, 53, 67, 92, 399, 409; chantry, 29 ff., 194, 199 f., 339 ff., 348 f., 351, 355 f., 399, 402 ff., 407 f., 410 ff., 425 ff.; foundation, 29 f., 33 ff., 52, 198 ff., 399

Henry VIII (1509–47), 63, 286, 333, 337, 347, 350, 353 f., 355 n., 384, 410

Henry, s. of Edward I (d. 1274), 374 n., 375

Henry, s. of Henry III (d. 1260), 374 n., 375

Henry, s. of Henry VIII (d. 1511), 384

Herbert, abbot of Westminster (1121–36), 80 f., 84, 94, 129, 132, 339 n., 341, 343, 350 f., 354, 363, 373, 407

Herevi, William, 115 n., 116

Heriot, heriots, 107 n., 108 f., 237, 247, 251 f., 264, 272 f., 281 n., 282 n., 283 n., 295, 297, 298 n., 308, 312

Herlane, William de, 118 n.

Hese (Surr.), 357 n.

Heth, Robert, 289

Heyford, Richard de, 115 n.

Heyle, Richard, Richard de, 167, 181, 192; Elizabeth, Margaret and Nicholas, children of, 192

High Ongar (Essex), 343

Hill, Isabel, 283 n.

Hill, Nicholas, 405

Hill, Walter, 283 n.

Hill, William, 283 n.

Hobbes, Alice, 252 n.

Hoberd, James, 425 n.

Hoddesdon, Guy de, fishmonger of London, 189

Hodford manor (Midd.), 35, 114 n., 352, 416

Holdy, John, 155

Holland, Maud, countess of Ligny and St. Pol, wife of Waleran de Luxemburg (d. 1392), 378

Holme with Langford manor (Beds.), 337

Holwell manor (Herts., formerly Beds.), 124 (Table VII)

Honte, Thomas, 247

Horneby, Henry, 386

Horsehill (Surr.), 301 f., 359 n.

Horsehull', Thomas de, clerk, Matilda, his wife, and Walter, their son, 307

Horsendune, William, William de, 110 n., 115 n.

Howard, Charles, 338 n.

Hubert, friend of William, chamberlain to William I, 39 n.

Hugelinus, Hugh, chamberlain to Edward the Confessor, 355 n., 372

Hugyn, Richard, 419

Hulle, John atte, 310, 320

Hulle, Richard atte, 312

Hulle, Thomas atte, 312

Hulok, Geoffrey, 313

Humez, William, William de, abbot of Westminster (1213–22), 64, 84, 86, 373 n., 374, 389, 400 n.

Humphrey, Robert, monk of Westminster (d. 1509), 385

Hungerford, Edmund, 383 n.; Sir Walter, s. of (d. 1464), 383

Hungerford, Sir Thomas (d. 1494), 383; Sir John, of Down Ampney (Glos.), s. of, 383 n.

Hungerford, Sir Thomas, of Rowden, in Chippenham (Wilts.), (d. 1469), 385 n.

Hunt, Hunte, Thomas, 267 n.

Hunt, Hunte, Walter, 107 n.

Hurley (Berks.), 133 n., 337; priory of St. Mary at (a cell of Westminster Abbey), 43, 337, 350, 354, 395 n., 400 n., 410; rectory, 410

Hussingtree, in Martin Hussingtree (Worcs.), 78, 102 n., 125 (Table VII), 362, 363 n.

Hut, Peter, 110 n., 115 n.

Hyde, in Eye (Midd.), 353, 395, 418

Hyntone, John and Alice, 172, 419

Idufestre, John de, 115 n.

Idufestre, William de, 115 n.

Ilchester, Richard of, bishop of Winchester (1174–88), 48, 411

Imber (prebend of church of St. Martin-le-Grand, London), 342 n.

Ingatestone (Essex), manor, 102 n., 103, 123 (Table VII), 342

Ingulf, a thegn, 343

Inheritance customs, 7, 210 ff., 278, 282, 295, 299 f., 323, 325

Inkman, Richard, gent., 161 n.

Inworth (Essex), 341 n.

Isabella of Angoulême (d. 1246), 29, 391

Islip (Oxon.): abbot's house, 133; assart, 130; chapel of St. Edward the Confessor, 153 n.; contractual tenancies, 251 n., 254, 276 f., 323; customary leases, 280, 283, 323, 326; demesne, 127 n., 128, 134, 153 n., 156, 263 n., 429; entry fines, 271 f., 297; heriots, 251 n., 272, 282 n., 297, 308 n.; holdings, 208 f., 261, 265, 267, 287 f., 432, 435 n., 436; jointure, 282 f., 287 n., 297; land transactions, 310, 322 ff.; manor, 27, 107, 127 n., 128, 133, 135, 139 n., 173 f., 223 n., 226, 240, 248, 274 n., 278 n., 279, 283, 322 f., 356, 416, 440 n.; meadow, 237; rents, 108 f., 217 n., 223, 226, 228, 231 n., 233, 237, 248, 254, 257 ff., 261, 263, 270, 440, 444; tallage, 248, 263 n., 440 n.; tenancy-at-will, 247; tenant-land, 319, 429; virgate, 434

Islip, John, abbot of Westminster (1500–32), 36, 93, 96, 97 n., 133, 200 n., 357 n., 368, 385, 425 ff.

Jerusalem, 390 n.

Jerusalem, patriarch of, 44

John, king of England (1199–1216), 226, 323, 374, 389

John, s. of Edward I (d. 1271), 374 n., 375

John, s. of Henry III (d. 1252), 374 n., 375

John, carpenter, 115 n.

John, *le marescal*, 121

John, *mercator*, 316

John, s. of Alice, 225 n.

Jones, William, 251; Roger, s. of, 251 n.

Jumièges, Geoffrey of, abbot of Westminster (c. 1071–c. 1075), 99, 100

Jumièges, Robert of, bishop of London (1050–1), 24 n.

Katherine, d. of Henry III (d. 1257), 375, 381

Katherine of Valois, wife of Henry V (d. 1437), 381

Kedyngton, Richard de, abbot of Westminster (1307–15), 206, 230 n., 376, 416

Kelvedon (Essex), 23, 392, 422; church and rectory, 47 n., 50 n., 51 f., 342 n., 402, 407; demesne, 342 n.;

holdings, 432, 435 n.; manor, 24 n., 78, 80, 123 (Table VII), 127 n., 156, 342, 402, 443; purchase of property in, 422; rents, 231 f., 440 n., 441, 445; tithes, 407; vicarage, 407

Kelvedon Hatch (Essex), 36 n., 123 (Table VII), 342 f.

Kempe, Thomas, 158

Kendale, John, 385

Kenilworth Castle (Warwicks.), 191

Kensal (Midd.), 350

Kensington (Midd.), 419

Keton, in Maldon (Essex), *see* Cowpes and Keton

Kinbell, John, 185 n.

Kingsbury (Midd.), 39, 349

Kingston (Surr.), 117, 415

Kinsbourne, in Harpenden (Herts.); demesne, 346, 429; manor, 114 n., 121 n., 346, 347 n. (*see also* Wheathampstead and Kinsbourne manor); meadow and pasture, 429; rents, 441, 446; tenant-land, 122 n., 429; virgate, 434

Knightsbridge (Midd.), 45, 168, 179, 184 n., 187, 395, 419, 430, 434; manor, 353, 355 n.; *see also* Knightsbridge and Paddington

Knightsbridge and Paddington manor (Midd.), 104 f., 115 n., 127 n., 205 n., 432, 435, 439

Knowle (Warwicks.), 31, 148, 154, 171 f., 271, 419, 430; *see also* Knowle with Grafton Minor

Knowle with Grafton Minor manor (Warwicks.), 360

Kyng, Stephen, 265

Kyng, William, 265

Kyrton, Edmund, abbot of Westminster (1440–62), 12, 14 n., 67, 90 f., 99 f., 133, 383

Labour services, 4, 6, 107 ff., 111 ff., 133, 163, chapters VIII and IX *passim*

Lacy, Roger de, 71

La Hyde manor, in Laleham (Midd.), 189

Lake, Richard, 247 f.

Laleham (Midd.), 175, 349, 422; chapel, 409; commutation and sale of works, 226 f.; contractual tenancy,

250; demesne, 134, 149, 353 n., 428; manor, 135, 248 n., 353, 354 n.; rents, 231 n., 237, 292, 440, 444; tenant-land, 122 n., 428

Lancing manor (Suss.), 202

Lane, Simon atte, 295 f.; Christina, d. of, 295 f.; Elias, s. of, 296 n.; Nicholas, s. of, 295 f.

Lane, William atte, 302

La Neyte, in Eye (Midd.), 81 n., 92 f., 118 n., 130, 133, 350 n., 394, 414; abbot's house at, 87

Langedon, William de, and Joan, his wife, 400

Langeford, Richard de, 394

Langeton, Robert, 422

Langham (Rutl.), 404 nn., 430 n.

Langham, Simon de, abbot of Westminster (1349–62), later bishop of Ely, archbishop of Canterbury and cardinal bishop of Praeneste (d. 1376), 16, 42, 66, 93, 95 ff., 140, 164 f., 168, 172, 178, 183, 197, 293, 357 f., 378, 418 ff.; anniversary, 395; chantry, 40, 42, 396, 423; Thomas, father of, 378

Langley (Essex), 425

Langley, King's (Herts.), 382 n.

Launton (Oxon.), 9, 240; contractual tenancies, 247 n., 251, 254, 277; customary tenancies, 254 n., 261, 277, 283; demesne, 153, 155, 157 f., 289, 356 n., 428 n., 430; entry fines, 225, 298; heriots, 251, 272, 281 n.; holdings, 287, 289; jointure, 272, 281 f., 297 f.; labour services, 216 f., 219, 234, 258 ff.; land transactions, 305, 309 ff., 320, 322 ff.; manor, 27 n., 56, 104 f., 126 n. 1, 155, 275, 278, 291, 356; mill, 157 n.; rector, 153, 184; rents, 254, 441, 446; tenant-land, 157 n., 241, 262, 430; virgate, 289 n., 325

Laurence, abbot of Westminster (1158–73), 56, 64, 94 n., 95, 129, 364, 373, 411 n.; anniversary, 388

Lease, leases: by indenture, 152 ff., 248, 320; by oral agreement, 320; champarty, 138 n., 153, 320; contractual, 246 ff.; for life or lives, 79 f., 118 n., 154, 173 f., 191, 236, 249, 250 n., 273 ff., 320 n., 340, 358, 360, 416; for term of years, 82, 154 ff.,

Lease, leases, (*cont.*):
162, 236, 249, 250 n., 276 f., 279,
282 n., 285 n., 309 f., 321, 418; for
years determinable on lives, 155, 250;
in villeinage, 245, 254 ff., 279, 298;
on part of the Abbey's tenants, 266,
276, 285, 307 ff., 320; *pur auter vie*,
167, 195, 248, 310 n., 321; stock and
land, 153 f., 290
Le Brabazun, Roger (d. 1317), 369,
376, 394
Le Clerk, Nicholas, 309
Le Dragger', Robert, 390
Lee, Sir Richard, citizen and alderman
of London, and Lettice, his wife,
398; Richard, s. of, 398
Le Fisher, Richard, 247
Le Frithe, le Fryth, manor in All-
farthing (Surr.), 185 n., 357, 395,
418
Le Fundur, John, monk of Westminster,
39, 392
Le Gras, Richard, monk of West-
minster, 39, 389; William, father of,
39, 389
Leigh, William de, 362
Le Kuver, Hugh, also known as Hugh
Cappere, 121 n.
Le Kyng, Agnes, 298 n.
Le Lou, John, 31
Le Man, William, 235 n.
Lengleys, William, 417
Lennard, John, 307 n.
Leofcild, possibly sheriff of Essex,
37, 343
Leofnoth, priest and sub-tenant, 71 n.
Leofric, 342
Leofwine, s. of Wulfstan, 23
Leovegar, 341
Le Petit, Laurence, s. of William, 118 n.,
414
Le Poher, Hugh, 76
Le Reve, William, 250
Le Rook, Richard, *see* Rook, Richard
Le Rous, Richard, 352, 376, 416
Le Seler, John, and Margaret, his d.,
394 n.
Le Shepherde, John, 307
Le Smyth, John, snr., Joan, his wife,
and John, their son, 281 n.
Lessness (Kent), 347, 426
Letcombe Regis (Berks.), 31, 338, 347,
398

Lewesham, Philip de, abbot-elect of
Westminster (1258), 89 n., 97
Lewis III, count palatine and duke of
Bavaria (d. 1436), 381
Le Wyse, John, 309 n.
Le Wyse, Juliana, 309 f.
Leycestre, Walter, 378
Leyghton, Andrew, and Matilda, his
wife, 273 f.
Limesy, Sir Peter de, 175 f.
Limesy, Ralph de, 176, 188, 191, 415
Limesy, Richard de, 191
Lincoln diocese, 403 ff.
Litlington (Midd.), 422
Litlington, Nicholas de, prior (1350–62)
and abbot of Westminster (1362–
86), 14, 42, 66, 92, 97, 167 ff., 173,
175, 268, 293, 349 n., 400, 419 f.,
424; anniversary, 173 n., 395, 418,
421 n.; burial, 379; chantry, 395 n.,
421; household and itinerary, 133,
135 ff., 147 f.; income, 60 n., 139 f.;
parents, 42 n., 173, 177 f., 180,
395 n.
Littleton (Midd.), 353 n.
Littleton, Sir Thomas (1422–81), 285
Lockinge (Berks.), 337
Lodelowe, Robert, 303
London, 28, 38, 41, 44, 54, 85, 116,
141, 160 f., 168 f., 242, 262, 309,
316, 332, 373 n., 378 n., 380 n.,
386 n., 388 ff., 395 ff.; bishop of, 24,
354, 405 n., 406 (*see also* fitz Neal,
Richard; Foliot, Gilbert; Jumièges,
Robert of; Mellitus; Ste.-Mère-
Église, William of); churches: St.
Botulph's, Aldersgate, 53, 407, St.
Bride's, Fleet Street, 47 n., 200 n.,
394, 407, St. Laurence, Candlewick
Street, also known as St. Laurence
near the Bridge, St. Laurence on the
Bank, 47 n., 50 n., 390, St. Leonard,
Eastcheap, 390, St. Martin-in-the-
Fields, 45, 47 n., 50, 408, St.
Maxentius, 392, St. Paul's Cathedral,
20, 376 n., St. Peter-the-Less, 392,
other churches, 47 n., 50 n.; citizens,
see under individual citizens; council
of (1268), 49; diocese, 405 ff.;
religious houses: Charterhouse,
387 n., Dominican friary, 374 n.,
Franciscan nunnery, 383 n., 386 n.,
St. Martin-le-Grand, 31, 53, 63,

198, 340, 342 f., 351, 399 n., 402 f., 408; Tower of, 16, 368

Longchamp, William, chancellor, and bishop of Ely (1189–97), 64 n.

Longdon (Worcs.), 72, 107, 166, 168, 363 n.; demesne, 155, 362 n., 429; holdings, 433, 436 n.; hospice rights, 83 n., 167 n.; jointure, 282 f.; land transactions, 310, 320, 328; manor, 125 (Table VII), 166, 168, 191, 275, 361 f., 414 f., 439; rectory, 51, 156 n., 412; tenant-land, 122 n., 128 n., 275 n.; woodland, 114

Longdon Greyndour manor (Worcs.), 361 f.

Longdon, in Solihull (Warwicks.), 178, 184 n., 419, 422

Lound, William, 419

Lovell, Sir Thomas (d. 1524), 201, 426 n.

Lowys, Thomas, 108, 301 n.

Lucas, Robert, goldsmith of London (d. 1382), 379

Lucas, Thomas, 425 n.

Lucius, king of the Britons, 17

Luffield, priory of St. Mary the Virgin at (Bucks. and Northants.), 339, 355, 402, 404 f.

Lutegareshale, Matilda, wife of Peter de, 389

Luxemburg, Waleran de, count of Ligny and St. Pol (d. 1415), 378 n.

Lyne, Margery, 310, 320 f.

Malcolm IV, king of Scotland (1153–65), 388

Malletts Court manor, in Stokenchurch (Bucks.), 339

Malmesbury (Wilts.), Benedictine abbey of St. Mary the Virgin at, 400 n.

Malvern, Great, Benedictine priory of St. Mary and St. Michael at, 81, 363, 395 n., 400 n.

Mandeville, Geoffrey de, I (d. *c.* 1100), 38, 43, 71 ff., 350, 353 n., 373; Athelaise, wife of, 38, 372 f.; Lecelina, wife of, 350

Mandeville, Geoffrey de, II, earl of Essex (d. 1144), 373

Manewden (Essex), 344, 425

Mannyng, John, yeoman of Westminster, 155

Margaret, d. of Edward IV (d. 1472), 383

Markham, Robert, gent., of London, 152, 154

Marston (Oxon.), 356 n.

Martin of Tours, St., 98

Martinsley wapentake (Rutl.), 27, 357

Martyn, Vincent, 256 n.

Mary, queen of England (1553–8), 333

Mary the Virgin, St.: cult, 39; girdle, 44; image of, in Sawbridgeworth church, 409; mass of, at Ashwell, 404 n.; mass of, in Westminster Abbey, 401 n.

Matham, Walkelin de, 116

Matilda, wife of Henry I (d. 1118), 28, 368 n., 373, 388

Mearcyncg Seollan, 23 n.

Meleward, Richard, 249 n., 281 f.; Agnes, his wife, 281 f.; Henry, their son, 281 f.

Melksop, Henry, reeve of Todenham, 231

Mellitus, bishop of London (601 × 604–17), 20 f., 25

Merleberg, Alured de, 72, 77

Merre, William, steward of the abbot's lands, 290 n.

Messing (Essex), 341 n.

Middelmor', Henry, 419 n.

Milling, Millyng, Thomas, abbot of Westminster (1469–74, d. 1492), 95, 97 n., 368, 383

Mohun, Philippa, duchess of York (d. 1431), 381

Mohun, soke of (London and Midd.), 391, 415

Molesham, Robert de, prior of Westminster, 39, 388 f.

Molyns, Sir John de, 167 n.

mondayland, 238 n., 441, 445

Monemouth, John, and Elizabeth, his wife, 152, 154, 155

Montacute, Simon, bishop of Worcester (1333–7), 412

Montagu, John, marquis of, *see* Neville, John

Montfort, Simon de, earl of Leicester (d. 1265), 191

Moor, Walter atte, 295 f.; Henry, s. of, 295

Mordaunt, John, 425 n.
Morden (Surr.), 314; church and rectory, 51, 155, 358, 402, 411 f.; demesne, 153, 428 n., 430; holdings, 206 n., 432, 435 f.; manor, 24 n., 78, 104, 125 (Table VII), 127 n., 155, 358; meadow and pasture, 430; mill, 411; rents, 217 f., 232 n., 441, 446; tallage, 224; tenant-land, 120, 430; tenants, 106, 115 n., 117, 205; virgate, 206 n., 434
Moreton-in-Marsh (Glos.), 72, 236 n., 344 nn., 345, 391
Mortimer, George, 386
Morton, John, archbishop of Canterbury (1486–1500), and chancellor, 387, 401
Morton Foliot, *see* Castlemorton (Worcs.)
Moulsham, in Chelmsford (Essex), 37, 77, 81, 103, 123 (Table VII), 169, 183, 269 n., 343, 396 n., 417, 423, 425, 439
Mowbray, Anne, wife of Richard, duke of York (d. 1481), 368, 383
Mulle, Henry atte, and Juliana, d. of 296
Murcot (Oxon.), 223 n., 270 n., 280 n., 293, 323, 329, 330 n., 356 n.

Nelme, Thomas, *see* Elme, Thomas atten
Neville, Anne, wife of Richard III (d. 1485), 367, 382
Neville, Cecily, duchess of York, mother of Edward IV (d. 1495), 398
Neville, George, lord Bergavenny (d. 1535), 201 f., 425
Neville, John, marquis of Montagu (d. 1471), 384 n.; Anne, d. of, m. Sir William Stonor, 384 n.
Neville, Richard, earl of Salisbury (d. 1460), 398
Neville, William, lord Fauconberg (d. 1463), 384 n.; Thomas, natural son of (d. 1471), 384
Newarks prebend (church of St. Martin-le-Grand, London), 342 n.
Newarks Norton manor (Essex), 343
Newlands prebend (church of St. Martin-le-Grand, London), 342 n.
Newmarket, Henry de, 76 f.
Newport Pound (Essex), 403, 408

Nicholas de Romanis, cardinal bishop of Tusculum (1205–19), 84
Nonant, Hugh de, bishop of Coventry (1188–98), 79, 82, 357 n.
Norfolk, Margaret, dowager duchess of (d. 1494), 385 n.
Northolt (Midd.), 157, 350, 353
Northwyk, Adam de, 183 f., 417
Norton, Geoffrey de, 184, 422
Norton, John, 424
Norton, William, 422
Norton Mandeville (Essex), 343
Norwich (Norf.): diocese, 410; Jewry, 170
Norwich, George, abbot of Westminster (1463–9), 67, 89 n., 90 f., 99
Noterell, Richard, yeoman of Westminster, 339 n.
Novo Castro, Fulk de (d. 1247), 369, 374

Oakham (Rutl.), 47, 49, 142, 241, 349 n., 357 n., 389, 404, 430; *see also* Oakham with Barleythorpe
Oakham with Barleythorpe (Rutl.): manor, also known as Oakham manor, 50, 356 f., 404; rector, rectory, 47 n., 49 f., 58 n., 65, 92 f., 356 n., 357, 390, 404
Ockendon manor, in N. Ockendon (Essex), 27 f., 80 f., 83 n., 103, 123 (Table VII), 338, 343
Ockendon, N. (Essex), church, 47 n., 50 n.
Odbert, a sub-tenant, 71 n., 72
Odda, earl, 30
Ody, Henry, 313
Offa, king of Essex (694 × 709), 21
Offa, king of Mercia (757–96), 21, 345
Offord Cluny manor (Hunts.), 31, 338, 347, 398 n.
Oliver, s. of King John (d. 1219), 374
Ordbriht, abbot of Westminster, 17 n.
Orleton, Adam, bishop of Worcester (1327–33), 412
Osbern, biographer of St. Dunstan, 23
Osbert, a palmer, 120
Osumull', Richard de, 118 n.
Oswald Beck Soke manor, in S. Wheatley (Notts.), 201, 348, 356, 425
Otmoor (Oxon.), 323
Ottobuono Fieschi, cardinal deacon of

St. Adrian (1252–76), later Pope Adrian V, 49, 90

Oxford, 23, 97; university, 30, 33 n., 96 n.

Paddington (Midd.), 24 n., 45, 78, 152, 158, 179 n., 353, 355 n., 388, 408 f., 428, 430; *see also* Knightsbridge and Paddington

Paglesham manor (Essex), 36 n., 77, 102 n., 123 (Table VII), 141, 343, 388 n.

Paglesham, Nicholas de, 343

Palacio, William de, *see* William *de palacio*

Palmer, James, 379; Joan, sister of, 379 n.

Palmer, William, s. of John, 329

Parceners, 206 f., 211 n., 432 n.

Parham (Suss.), 24 n., 85, 113 n., 125 (Table VII), 271, 315, 359

Parham, Thomas de, 153

Parham, Walter, Walter de, 421, 424

Park, in Stanwell (Midd.), 171

Paslowes prebend (church of St. Martin-le-Grand, London), 342 n.

Pattiswick (Essex), 149, 316 n., 341 n., 429 n.

Peasemore (Berks.), 337 n.

Pecche, Sir Gilbert, 31 f.

Pecche, John, 187, 418 f., 421 ff., 425 n.

Penge, in Battersea (Surr.), 115 n., 357 n.

Pensham (Worcs.), 125 (Table VII), 128 n., 154, 233, 255 f., 286 f., 363, 429, 433, 437 n., 439

Peopleton (Worcs.), 76 n., 101 n., 125 (Table VII), 363

Pepyn, tenant at Sutton-under-Brailes, 290 n.

Percy, Henry, 3rd earl of Northumberland (d. 1461), 385 n.

Perham, Ralph de, 154, 360

Pernel, Pernell, Thomas, butcher of London, 152

Pernel, Pernell, Thomas, chaplain, 184, 421

Pershore (Worcs.), 84 n., 102, 313, 320; Benedictine abbey of St. Mary the Virgin and SS. Peter and Paul at, 30, 73; burgesses, 101, 125 (Table VII); fishery, 247; manor, also known as Binholme, 27, 30, 47 n., 71 ff., 76 n., 78, 88, 102, 125 (Table VII), 134, 278 n., 360 ff. (*see also* Pershore and Wick manor); mills, 169 n.; tithes, 389; town, 111, 363 n.

Pershore and Wick manor (Worcs.), 128 n., 223 n., 231 n., 233, 429, 433, 437 n., 440, 443, 445; virgate, 437 n.

Pershore, Alexander de, monk of Westminster, 51

Perton (Staffs.), 27 n., 79, 82, 102 n., 125 (Table VII), 357

Peter, St., 20 f., 24 f., 44, 46 n.

Peter *faber*, tenant at Pyrford, 302 n.

Peter, sheriff, 71 n., 73

Peter, tenant at Battersea and Wandsworth, 110 n., 115 n.

Peterborough (Northants.), Benedictine abbey of St. Peter at, 94

Petwyn, John, 385 n.

Peverel, Peverell, Ralph, 71 n., 73, 126 n. 9.

Peverel, Peverell, Thomas, monk of Westminster (d. 1419/20), 382

Philippa of Hainault, wife of Edward III (d. 1369), 189, 379

Picot, Thomas, 110 n., 115 n., 116

Picot, William, 348

Pinchpol manor, in Manewden (Essex), 200 f., 340 n., 344, 425

Pinvin (Worcs.): customary land, 429; demesne, 149, 429; holdings, 267, 286 ff., 433, 437; land transactions, 320; manor, 252, 290, 291 n., 363, 444; rents, 231 n., 233, 263, 440, 445; virgate, 434

Pipat, Agnes, 327

Pirton (Worcs.), 76 n.

Plaistow manor (Glos.), *see* Deerhurst

Playdon Hospital (Suss.), 403

Pleshey (Essex), 409

Plomer, Adam, and Margery, his wife, and Geoffrey, their son, 274

Plumstead (Kent), 347, 426; *see also* Plumstead Boarstall manor

Plumstead Boarstall manor (Kent), 200 f., 347 f., 426

Pole, Joan de la, baroness Cobham (d. 1434), m. (i) Sir Robert de Hemenhale, and (v) Sir John Harpeden, 378 n.

Ponther, Walter, 71 n., 72, 76

Pontissara, John de, bishop of Winchester (1282–1304), 51, 411

Popes: Alexander III (1159–81), 43, 411 n.; Boniface IX (1389–1404), 403; Clement III (1187–91), 14 n., 48, 52; Clement VI (1342–52), 407, 409; Gregory IX (1227–41), 43, 404; Honorius III (1216–27), 49, 404; Innocent II (1130–43), 85; Innocent III (1198–1216), 13, 84; Innocent IV (1243–54), 29, 43 n., 49, 406; John XXII (1316–34), 51, 407, 409, 412; Nicholas IV (1288–92), Taxation of, 12, 46, 49 f., 52, 57 ff., 402; Paschal II (1099–1118), 24 n.; Sixtus IV (1471–84), 67

Porter, William, chancery clerk, 155, 358 n.

Postard, William, abbot of Westminster (1190–1200), 64 n., 84 f., 89, 94 n., 129, 359, 374, 389

Poughley, in Chaddleworth (Berks.), Augustinian priory of St. Margaret in, 337 n., 338

Powick (Worcs.), 72, 76 n., 81, 83 n., 125 (Table VII), 363

Poylle, William, s. of Walter de la, 415

Poynings, Edward, 425 n.

Prentout, Alice, 302 n.

Preston, William, William de, 301 f.

Puncelinus, grandfather of Alger, 79 n.

Pygon, Richard, 255

Pyrford (Surr.), 168, 359 n.; abbot's house, 133; contractual tenancies, 254, 283 n., 443 f.; demesne, 128 f., 429; fishery, 120 n.; holdings, 208, 432, 436; land transactions, 301 f., 305 f., 310, 313, 320; manor, 28 n., 125 (Table VII), 133 ff., 168, 187, 192, 269 n., 278 n., 282 f., 295 f., 300 ff., 307, 316 n., 338 n., 359, 423; *nativi*, 241, 313; rents, 440, 444; tallage, 108 n., 224 n.; tenant-land, 114, 128 f., 283 n., 296, 300 n., 301, 429; tenants, 108, 120, 208, 212 f., 241 n., 300 n., 301; virgate, 208, 434

Pyrie, Godfrey atte, 248

Quinchald, William, 302

Ralph, chaplain, 385 n., 386

Ramis, Roger de, 71 n., 72 f., 76

Ramsey (Hunts.), Benedictine abbey of St. Mary and St. Benedict at, 23, 37

Raymond-Berengar IV, count of Provence (d. 1245), 391

Raynesford, Sir Laurence (d. 1490), 385 n.

Reading (Berks.), 189

Reading, John of, monk of Westminster, 51, 66

Reimes, Richard de, 75 f.

Reinbald, a sub-tenant, 71 n.

Rheims, council of (1148), 95

Richard I (1189–99), 13, 357 n.

Richard II (1377–99), 45, 51, 92, 186, 337 ff., 350, 352 f., 360, 362, 378 n., 382, 397, 410

Richard II and Anne of Bohemia: anniversary and foundation, 10, 29 f., 33 ff., 62, 337 ff., 350, 352 f., 360, 397, 403, 410

Richard III (1483–5), 368; Anne, wife of, 367, 382

Richard, duke of York (d. 1460), 398

Richard, duke of York (d. 1483), 368; Anne, wife of, 368, 383

Richard, forester, 115 n.

Richard, s. of Henry III (d. 1250), 375

Robert *ad boscum*, 115 n.

Robert *de bosco*, 120; Walter, s. of, 120; William, s. of Walter, 120

Robert *dispensator, see* Dispenser, Robert

Robert, marshal (i) (mid-12th cent.), 118; (ii) (early 13th cent.), 110 n., 115 n.

Robsart, Lewis, lord Bourchier (d. 1430), 38, 382; Elizabeth, wife of (d. 1433), 382

Rodbert, chaplain, 132

Roger *de aula*, 115 n.

Roger *mercator*, 316

Rogers, Richard, fuller of London, 161 n.

Rokes, Gilbert, and Jocosa, his wife, 345 n.

Rolf, Richard, 252

Romayne, Thomas, pepperer of London (d. 1313), 376

Rook, Richard, also known as Richard le Rook, 422 ff.; snr., 185, 419, 421 f.; jnr., 185

Ros, Geoffrey de, 400

Rosamund manor (Midd.), 189, 422

Rothe, Adam atte, 225

Russel, Russell, Mr. John (d. 1445/6), 38, 382
Russel, Russell, Philip, and Odo and Alesia, his parents, 392
Ruthall, Thomas, bishop of Durham (1509–23), 367, 385
Rutland, tithes in, 47, 357 n., 404 n.
Rydon (Surr.), 184, 424

Sabin, Sabyn, Sabyne, Gilbert, 302 n.
Sabine, Sabyn, Sabyne, Walter, 250
Sabine, Sabyn, Sabyne, William, 313
Saebert, king of the E. Saxons (d. 616/17), 18, 20, 372; Ethelgoda, wife of, 20, 372
St. Leger, John, 383 n.; Margaret, d. of (d. 1496), m. (i) John, lord Clinton; (ii) Sir Walter Hungerford, 383 n.
Ste.-Mère-Église, William of, bishop of London (1199–1221), 389
St. Pol, Mary of, dowager countess of Pembroke (d. 1377), 396
Sakespeye, Geoffrey de, 121 n.
Sakespeye, Richard de, 117
Salisbury, diocese of, 410 f.
Salisbury, Sir John (d. 1388), 377 n., 379
Sanchia, queen of Almain (d. 1261), 392
Sandhill, John, chandler of London, 316
Sandhill, Richard, 193, 420
Sapy, John, John de, 167, 196, 360, 421
Sawbridgeworth (Herts.): church and rectory, 47 n., 51 f., 388, 409; vicarage, 409
Scaldewell, John, 423
Schithenhech', Agnes de, 225 n.
Scovill family, 31
Scrope, Sir Richard (d. 1403), 31, 421
Selby, Ralph, monk of Westminster (d. 1420), 382
Selk, Richard, 267
Serych, Emma, 302 n.
Serych, William, 301 ff.
Severn Stoke (Worcs.), 72, 77
Shakell, John (d. 1396), 379
Shalstone (Bucks.), 355 n.
Shelley (Essex), 343
Shepperton (Midd.), 24 n., 77, 124 (Table VII), 354

Shether, John, and Agnes, his wife, 405 n.
Shirforde, William, and Alice, his wife (Alice Warde), 379, 396
Shirwood, John, bishop of Durham (1484–94), 387
Sholdham, Elizabeth, abbess of Barking, 387
Shorditch, Sir John de (d. 1345), 40, 169, 377, 395, 400; Elena, wife of, 377, 395, 400
Shotover (Oxon.), 288
Sibsey (Lincs.), 426
Sidewood (Surr.), 301, 359 n.
Sillinctune, see Chollington
Silverstone (Northants.), 355 n.
Simon, chaplain, of Aldenham, 119 n.
Sisted (Essex), 341 n.
Siward, abbot of Westminster, 17 n.
Skirbeck (Lincs.), 426
Skreyne (Crane End), in Frieston (Lincs.), 349; *see also* Fenne and Skreyne
Sleford, William de, also known as William *de palacio*, 379 n.
Smyth, Smyth', William, villein of Pyrford, 313 n.
Smyth, Smyth', William, tenant at Murcot or Fencot, 329 f.
Snodsbury manor, in Upton Snodsbury (Worcs.), 125 (Table VII), 363 n., 364
Solas, John, Joan, his wife, and John and Thomas, their sons, 155
Southam, John, stockfishmonger of London, 189 f., 420
Southcocke, William, 386
Southcot, John (d. 1453/4), 384
Southcote (Berks.), 189
Southwicke, William, 386
Speen (Berks.), 337
Spoonhill (Salop), 174 f.
Stafford, Henry, lord (d. 1481), 399
Staines (Midd.), 111, 118, 168, 189, 303, 422; bailiwick, 249 n.; berewicks of, 126 n. 10, 354 n.; burgesses, 101, 124 (Table VII), 203 n., 315; contractual tenancies, 249, 253, 277; demesne, 102, 128, 149, 249 n., 428; gavel-land, gavelmen, 109, 112, 428 n.; holdings, 102 n., 203 n., 219, 288; labour services, 112, 223 n., 227 f., 231 n., 232, 303 n.;

Staines (Midd.) (*cont.*):
land transactions, 303, 305; manor, 27 n., 102, 124 (Table VII), 203 n., 226, 229, 240, 315, 349, 351, 353 ff.; meadow, 235 ff.; rectory, 48 ff., 349, 402, 409 f.; rents, 231 n., 237, 293, 440, 444; tenant-land, 112, 122 n., 128, 277 n., 428; tenants, 112, 240, 288; town, 112 f.; vicar, vicarage, 409; virgate, half-virgate, 102 n., 203 n., 208, 235
Staines and Yeoveney (Midd.), mills, 415 n.
Stanes, Gregory de, monk of Westminster, 392
Stanes, William, s. of Robert de, 118
Stanford-in-the-Vale (Berks.), 410
Stangraves manor, in Edenbridge (Kent), 348, 419
Stanley, Sir Humphrey (d. 1505), 385
Stanley, Sir John (d. 1528), 368, 385, 387; Anne, sister of, John, s. of, and Margaret, wife of, 387
Stanley, Thomas, earl of Derby (d. 1504), 387, 399
Stanway (Glos.), 201 f., 427
Stanwell (Midd.), 171
Stebbynge, Nicholas de, 174 n.
Stephen, king of England (1135–54), 78
Stephen, free tenant at Battersea, 115 n., 116
Sterling, Robert, 297
Stevenage (Herts.), 111, 120; contractual tenancies, 249 f., 253 f.; demesne, 129, 150, 157, 249 n., 346 n., 429; heriot, 308, 312; holdings, 207, 210, 432, 436; jointure, 281 n.; labour services, 216 f., 232, 234, 250, 259; manor, 27 n., 86, 104 f., 124 (Table VII), 127 n., 224 n., 240 ff., 346, 389; meadow and pasture, 429; rents, 217 f., 254, 264, 441, 446; tenant-land, 120, 122 n., 249 n., 259 n., 264 n., 429; virgate, 207 n., 434; woodland, 429
Stevens, John, 280 n.
Stevens, Richard, 280 n.
Steventon (Berks.), 154, 271, 338, 410
Stoke manor, 391
Stoke, Richard, Richard de, 422 f.
Stokenchurch (Bucks.), 339

Stonor, Sir William (d. 1494), 384; Anne, wife of (Anne Neville), 384 n.
Stourton manor, in Whichford (Warwicks.), 424
Stow, John (d. 1605), 368
Stowood (Oxon.), 288
Stowte, Richard and Thomas, 152
Stratford (Essex), 39 f., 169, 181, 189, 424
Stratton, Thomas, 387, 398
Streatley (Berks.), rectory, 410 f.
Stretford, Thomas de, 392
Style, Walter atte, 302
Sudborough (Northants.), 27 n., 83 n., 102 n., 124 (Table VII), 355 f.
Sudborough, Bartholomew de, 355 n.
Sudbury (Suff.), Benedictine priory of St. Bartholomew at, 400 n.
Sulby (Northants.), 356
Sulcard, monk of Westminster, 18, 20 ff., 24 f., 46, 372
Sumer, tenant in Wandsworth, 115 n., 116
Sumer, Henry, Ralph and Richard, 116
Summi Magistri (1336), 99
Sunbury (Midd.), 24 n., 113 n., 124 (Table VII), 354
Sutton-under-Brailes (Warwicks., formerly Glos.): contractual tenancies, 254; cotlands, 280 n.; *cotmanni*, 238, 440 n., 444 n.; customary leases, 280; demesne, 128, 149, 152, 267 n., 360 n., 429; heriots, 272; holdings, 267, 289, 290 n., 432, 437; labour services, 233, 237 f., 254; manor, 114 n., 133, 229 n., 238 n., 276, 280, 283, 286, 307 n., 310, 344 n., 360, 424; mill, 424; rents, 224, 233 n., 237 f., 440, 444; tallage, 224; tenant-land, 128, 275, 429; virgate, 434
Swaffham Market (Norf.), rectory, 200 n., 410
Swein, kinsman of Edward the Confessor, 359 n.
Swineshead (Lincs.), rectory, 405
Swyft, John, 288 n.

Takepenny, Walter, 235 n.
Tayleboys, Gregory, monk of Westminster, 390

Tayleboys, Robert, monk of Westminster, 392

Taylor, John, 261 n.

Teddington (Midd.): chapel, 409; church and rectory, 50 f., 354 n., 409 f.; contractual tenancies, 250, 444; demesne, 354 n., 410 n., 428 n., 430; glebe, 354 n., 410 n.; holdings, 205, 207, 267, 432, 435 f.; jointure, 267 n.; leases in villeinage, 256; manor, 104, 127 n., 220, 337, 354, 444; meadow and pasture, 221, 430; rents, 217 ff., 226 f., 232 n., 250, 441, 446; tallage, 222, 256 n.; tenant-land, 430; tenants, 115 n., 116 f., 241 f.; virgate, 434

Terry, Henry, of Brackley, 183, 186, 196, 417; Alice, wife of, 417

Testard, Ralph, 115 n.

Tetworth (Hunts.), 79

Tewin (Herts.), 124 (Table VII), 346

Tewkesbury (Glos.), abbot and convent of, 201, 427

Tey, Teye, Little (Essex), 47 n., 341 n.

Thecheham, Gilbert, and Alice, his wife, 400

þecthere, William de, 302

Thomas *de camera*, 115 n.

Thomas the martyr, St., 366 n.

Thornborough (Bucks.), 339, 355 n., 402 n., 405

Thorne (Surr.), 185 n.

Thorney Island (Midd.), 20

Thornle, John, 187

Thorpe manor (Lincs.), 124 (Table VII); *see also* Doddington and Thorpe

Throp, William de, snr., 108 f., 119; Matilda, wife of, 119

Throp, William de, jnr., 108, 119

Thurstan, housecarl, 349 n.

Thurston, John, 185 n., 424

Thwaytes, Sir Thomas, and Alice, his wife, 387

Tickhill (Yorks.), 412

Tilbury (Essex), 38 n.

Tirell, Sir Thomas, and Alice, his wife, 423

Titeberst, *see* Titeburst

Titeburst (Herts.), 24 n., 72, 124 (Table VII), 346

Todenham (Glos.): contractual tenancies, 250 f., 254, 444; cotlands, 262; *cotmanni*, 229, 254 n., 261, 262 n., 270 n., 432 n., 439 n.; customary leases, 280; demesne, 128, 134 f., 345 n., 428; holdings, 288 f., 432, 435; labour services, 229 ff., 254, 270; leases in villeinage, 251 n., 256; manor, 114 n., 173, 229 n., 230 n., 240, 276, 283, 345; reeve, 231; rents, 224, 261, 270, 292, 439, 444; tallage, 224, 251 n.; tenant-land, 428; tenants, 286, 241 f.; virgate, 434

Tolleshunt (Essex), 341 n.

Tonge (Hunts.), 79

Tooting (Surr.), 36 n., 72, 113 n., 125 (Table VII), 357 n., 359

Top, John, 265

Tostig, and Leofrun, his wife, 358

Tothill, in Westminster (Midd.), 73 n., 75, 354

Tottenham (Midd.), 388

Toundesle, Agnes de, 423

Toundesle, Robert de, 423; Katherine, widow of, 423; John, s. of, 191 f., 423; William, s. of, 423

Trafford, Edmund, 387 n.

Troffote, Arthur, 386

Trussell, Sir William (d. *c.* 1346/7), 377

Trute, Alice, 280 n.

Tudor, Edward, 382 n.

Turcas, J. (d. 1501/2), 385

Turweston (Bucks.), 31, 178 f., 183, 196, 287, 339, 416 f., 429

Tusculum, Nicholas of, *see* Nicholas de Romanis

Tyteburst, John, 417; Geoffrey, s. of, and Alice, his widow, 417; William, s. of, 417

Ugley (Essex), 200 n., 340, 425

Ulstan, a thegn, 338

Underwood, Philip, monk of the London Charterhouse, 387

Undirwode, tenant at Sutton-under-Brailes, 290 n.

unthankenbotecorne, 221

Uplambourn (Berks.), free chapel, 411

Uppingham (Rutl.), 400 n.

Upton Snodsbury (Worcs.), 364

Urse, sheriff of Worcs., 71 f., 74, 76, 362 ff.

Vacancies at Westminster Abbey, 59 n., 90; 1117/18–21, 80, 84, 140; 1173–5, 56 f.; 1190–1, 89; 1246, 87; 1258, 120; 1307–10, 59, 127 n., 137 f.; 1386, 60; 1420, 60

Valence, Aymer de, earl of Pembroke (d. 1324), 377, 396; Mary, wife of (Mary of St. Pol), 396

Valence, William de (d. 1296), 375; John, s. of (d. 1277), and Margaret, d. of (d. 1276), 375

Valor Ecclesiasticus (1535), 11, 52 ff., 59, 61 ff., 336

Vaughan, Sir Hugh (d. 1500), 367, 385; Anne, wife of (d. 1522), 385

Vaughan, Sir Thomas (d. 1483), 367, 384

Vere, Aubrey de, earl of Oxford (d. 1214), 341

Villani, 73, 101 ff., 106 f., 123 ff. (Table VII), 219

Virgate, virgates, 206 ff., 234 ff., 265, 286 ff., 296, 318, 434; *see also under individual manors*

Vitalis, abbot of Westminster (1076– c. 1085), 20, 36, 372, 387

Vypel, John, 252

Wadelowe, Elias, 225

Wakelin, a sub-tenant, 75 f.

Waldby, Robert de, archbishop of York (1396–8), 379

Walden, Thomas, apothecary of London, 395

Walkelin, a free tenant at Wandsworth, 115 n., 116

Walker, Mr. Laurence, Mr. Laurence de, 424, 434 n.

Walter *heres*, a tenant at Wandsworth, 115 n.

Walter, onetime knight, 115 n., 116

Walth', Richard, 382 n.

Waltham (Berks.), rectory of St. Lawrence, 410 f.

Waltham (Essex), collegiate church of the Holy Cross (later Waltham Abbey), 25, 37

Waltham, John, John de, bishop of Salisbury (1388–95), treasurer of the Exchequer (1391–5), 38, 380, 397

Wandsworth (Surr.), 121, 168, 193, 217, 357 n., 358, 418, 421; Allfarthing in, *see* Allfarthing; church and rectory, 48, 54, 388 n., 411 f.; Downe in, *see* Downe; Finches manor in, *see* Finches; free tenants, 115 n., 116; Frithe, Frythe in, *see* le Frithe; manor, 116 f., 133, 359; mills, 116, 169, 181, 359 n., 424; purchases of property in, 169, 179 n., 181, 184, 418, 421, 424; vicarage, 48, 412; *see also* Battersea and Wandsworth

Warde, Alice (Alice Shirforde), 396 n.

Ware, Nicholas de, monk of Westminster, 393

Ware, Richard de, abbot of Westminster (1258–83), 97, 119 f., 134, 176, 183, 191, 194, 196, 371, 375, 392, 415; anniversary, 347, 392

Ware, William de, 121

Warefold, Adam de, monk of Westminster, 174 n.

Wassingham (Surr.), 357 n.

Watere, William s. of William atte, of Ware, and Robert, his son, 192 n.

Watkynnes, John, 386 n.; Anne, wife of, 386

Watre, William atte, 419

Watton (Herts.), manor, 124 (Table VII), 346 n.; *see also* Datchworth with Watton

Wattun', William, 115 n.

Webbe, Richard, 261 n.

Webbe, William, 280

Welle, Nicholas atte, 289, 290 n., 310

Welles, Hugh de, bishop of Lincoln (1209–35), 390

Welles, John, viscount Welles (d. 1499), 367, 384; Cecily, wife of, 384 n.

Wellingborough (Northants.), 228 n.

Wenden, Wendene, Richard de, bishop of Rochester (1238–50), 375

Wenden, Wendene, Robert de, and Lucy, his wife, 393 f.

Wenden, Wendene, William de, 386, 393 f., 400

Wendlesworth, Laurence de, 170

Wenlock (Salop), 98

Wenlok, Walter de, abbot of Westminster (1283–1307), 32 f., 59, 89, 91, 100, 108 f., 118 n., 119, 133, 167 f., 173 f., 181, 196 f., 228 f., 233, 290 f., 377, 393, 416; anniversary, 197 n., 393; household, 88, 134 ff.; income, 59, 137 ff.; parents, 97 f., 174

Wennington manor (Essex), 102 n., 103, 123 (Table VII), 141, 344
West, Thomas, 424
West, Walter, 110 n., 115 n.
Westbourne (Midd.), 45, 105 n., 350, 353 nn.
Westbury Priory manor, in Westbury (Wilts.), 360
Westerham (Kent), 31 f., 148, 154, 179, 181, 293, 348, 419 f., 430
Western Parts, the, 10, 77, 133, 135, 168, 276, 281, 283
Westminster (Midd.), 41, 45, 55, 111, 155, 168, 185 n., 187, 189, 332, 337 n., 338, 339 n., 353 nn., 355 n., 390, 392 ff., 396 f., 399
  almshouse, 399
  church of St. Margaret of Antioch, 45 f., 48, 167 n., 192, 378 n.; curate, 408 n.; parish, 15, 45 f., 354; rectory and vicarage, 46, 54 f., 407 f.
  fair, 197 n., 393, 395
  hospital of St. James in, 14 n.
  knights in, 75, 124 (Table VII), 132, 203 n.
  manor, 24 n., 73 f., 113 n., 124 (Table VII), 350, 354 f.
  meadows, 221 f., 428 n., 430
  purchases of property in, 179, 184 n., 416 f., 422
  reeve of, 389
  see of, 55 n.
  Tothill in, *see* Tothill
Westminster Abbey (collegiate foundation), 151, 158 n., 333
Westminster Abbey (monastic foundations), 42, 46, 285 n., 333, and *passim*
  altars: high, 78 n., 339 n., 342, 365, 372 nn., 373 n., 375 n., 376 nn., 377 n., 381 n., 407; Holy Cross, 378 n., 393; Holy Trinity, 380 n., 396; St. Andrew, 379 n.; St. Benedict, 376 n., 378 n., 395; St. Blaise, 379 n.; St. John the Evangelist, 394; St. Mary the Virgin, 39; St. Nicholas, 392; St. Thomas the martyr, 366 n.
  cemetery, 368, 370, 372 n.
  chapels: Henry V's chantry, 381 nn.; Henry VII's, 29, 45, 365 f., 383 n., 384 nn.; Jesus, 385 n.; Lady Margaret, 384 n.; St. Andrew, 379 n., 383 n.; St. Benedict, 366, 374 n., 378 n., 380 n.; St. Blaise, 382 n.; St. Dunstan in the subhostelry, 393 n.; St. Edmund (i), 374 n.; St. Edmund (ii) (*see* St. Edmund and St. Thomas the martyr); St. Edmund and St. Thomas the martyr, 366 n., 374 n., 375 n., 376 nn., 378 n., 379 n., 380 nn., 382 nn.; St. Edward the Confessor, also known as the chapel of kings, 366, 368, 374 n., 375 nn., 376 nn., 377 n., 378 n., 379 n., 380 nn., 381 nn., 382 n., 383 nn., 384 n., 401 n.; St. Erasmus, 366, 368, 383 nn., 398; St. John the Baptist, 367, 376 n., 377 n., 381 n., 383 n., 384 nn., 385 nn.; St. John the Evangelist, 367 n., 378 n., 381 n., 383 n.; St. Mary Pew, 367, 396; St. Mary the Virgin (old), 44 n., 64 f., 92, 353, 365 ff., 369, 374 n., 381 nn., 383 n., 384 nn., 385 n., 387 n., 389, 400; St. Mary the Virgin (new) (*see* Henry VII's chapel); St. Michael, 367, 377 n., 385 n.; St. Nicholas, 369, 376 n., 381 n., 383 nn., 385 n.; St. Paul, 367, 374 n., 382 n., 384 n., 386 n.
  church, 42, 44, 46, 51, 95; ambulatory, 366, 369, 377 n., 378 n., 380 nn., 381 nn., 382 nn., 383 nn., 384 n., 385 n.; choir, 87, 400 n.; cloister door, 38, 379 n.; Corpus Christi lamp, 342; holy water stoup, 38, 379 n.; images, 44 n.; nave, 46, 374 n., 378 nn., 393; north door, 365 ff., 369, 374 n., 380 n.; presbytery, 366, 368, 372 n., 375 nn., 376 nn., 377 nn., 382 n.; transepts, 366, 377 n., 378 n., 379 n., 380 n.
  common seal, 90, 152 f.
  exempt status, 13 f., 24 f., 332
  martyrology, 39, 41, 370 f., 394 f., 400 n., 401 n.
  monastic buildings, 51, 66; abbot's house, 87, 133; chapter house, 51, 95, 366, 369, 372 nn., 373 n., 375 n., 376 nn., 377 n.; cloister, 51, 185, 366, 369, 370, 372 nn.,

Westminster Abbey (*cont.*):
  monastic buildings (*cont.*):
    373 nn., 375 n., 376 nn., 377 n.;
    infirmary, 170; misericord, 42,
    99, 400 n.; refectory, 42, 87,
    400 n.; sub-hostelry, 393 n.
  offices: almonry, 85, 141, 165, 340 f.,
    343 f., 353, 355, 358, 388, 408,
    415; cellar, 184, 338, 343, 350,
    353 f.; chamber, 85, 87, 143, 338,
    348, 354, 356, 359, 387; granary,
    144; hostelry, 409; infirmary, 354,
    359, 388 n., 389, 391, 409;
    kitchen, 80, 85 f., 141, 342 ff.,
    346, 350, 352, 356, 358 f.; monk
    bailiff's, 344, 350, 354 ff.; new
    work, 41 f., 353, 355, 379 n., 395,
    400, 412; refectory, 42, 349 n.,
    354; sacrist's, 354, 408, 410;
    treasury, appendix I *passim*, 404 f.,
    409, 412
  officials: lay and clerical, 141, 174 n.;
    forinsic bailiff, 179; janitor, 184;
    monastic: almoner, 15, 409; arch-
    deacon, 96; cellarer, 93 n.,
    142 f., 337 n.; chamberlain, 14,
    85 n., 141; granger, 61, 137,
    143 f., 146 f., 150 n.; keeper of
    the new work, also known as
    warden, 14, 93, 96, 353 n.,
    380 n.; kitchener, 85 f., 347;
    monk-bailiff, 344, 350, 354 ff.;
    pittancer, 58, 142, 404 f.; pre-
    centor, 337 n.; prior, 58 f., 62,
    97, 100, 132, 354, 357 n., 408;
    sacrist, 14, 38, 41 n., 44 n., 45,
    93, 337 n., 347, 358 n., 359 n.,
    369 f., 377 ff., 409; treasurers,
    11, 57 ff., 61 f., 96, 127, 143 f.,
    146 ff., 175, 179, 184, 231 f.,
    337 n., 347, 395 n., 420 ff.,
    424 f., 438 n., 440 f., 445 f.;
    warden of Henry V's manors,
    14; warden of Queen Eleanor's
    foundation, also known as treas-
    urer, 14, 183, 196, 416 f., 419 f.;
    warden of St. Mary's chapel,
    93 n., 337 n.; warden of the
    churches, 61 n., 357, 404, 409
  preaching in, 95
  precinct, 167, 178
  relics, 43 f.
  sanctuary in, 15

Westminster, abbot of:
  chamber, 132
  confirmation, 64, 89
  council, 291
  election, 94 f.
  itinerary, 132 ff.
  officials: chamberlain, 132; chap-
    lain, 132; marshal, 135; receiver,
    also known as treasurer, 10, 14,
    59; steward, 132; steward of the
    household, also known as clerk,
    10, 60, 134 ff., 139 n.; steward
    of the lands, 59 n., 290 n.; steward
    of the Western Parts, also known
    as receiver, 10, 60, 290
  retainers, 89, 90 n., 93, 174 n., 291;
    see also under individual abbots.
Westminster, Palace of, 15 f., 178,
  315, 376 n.
  chapel of St. Stephen in, 15, 38, 92;
    canon of, 396 n.; dean of, keeper
    of, 379 n.; prebendary of, 397 n.
  treasury of receipt in, 16
Weston, Richard de, goldsmith of
  London, 189, 192, 422
Wheathampstead (Herts.), 49, 84 n.,
  116, 118, 121, 285 n., 295, 347 n.;
  demesne and manor, *see* Wheathampstead and Harpenden; mill,
  157 n.; tithes, 49, 157 n., 347, 402,
  405
Wheathampstead and Harpenden
  manor, also known as Wheathampstead and Kinsbourne manor (Herts.),
  27 n., 86, 104 f., 121 n., 124 (Table
  VII), 127 n., 269 n., 283, 346 f., 416;
  contractual tenancies, 273 f., 276 f.;
  demesne, 129, 150, 261 n., 328 n.,
  347 n., 429, 446 n.; entry fines, 225,
  446 n.; heriots, 272; holdings, 207,
  209, 265, 432, 436; jointure, 272;
  land transactions, 279 n., 310, 314,
  320 f., 327 f.; leases in villeinage,
  256, 261 n.; meadow and pasture,
  429; rents, 216 f., 232 n., 234,
  260 f., 263 f., 271, 441, 446; tallage,
  224; tenant-land, 114, 122 n., 312,
  316, 429; villeinage, villeins, 241 f.,
  261, 312 f.; virgate, 434; woodland,
  114
Wheathampstead and Kinsbourne
  manor (Herts.), *see* Wheathampstead
  and Harpenden manor

Wheatley, South (Notts.), 356

Whichford (Warwicks.), 424

White Roding (Essex), 47 n.

Whitewell, John de, 184, 421

Whitham rectory (Essex), 403, 408, 410

Whittington, Richard, citizen of London (d. 1423), 42

Whittlebury (Northants.), 355 n.

Wick, by Pershore (Worcs.), 78, 125 (Table VII), 241, 256, 286 f., 363 n., 364

Wick, Peter de, 361, 364; Robert, s. of, 361

Wicken Bonant (Essex), 425

Wickford (Essex), 185, 418

Wickham (Essex), 200 n., 426

Wickham, East (Kent), 347, 348 n., 426

William I (1066–87), 25, 27, 39, 47, 49, 55, 75, 78, 338, 340 f., 343, 346, 359

William II (1087–1100), 339, 348

William, Mr., tenant at Ashwell, 104

William, chamberlain to William I, 39, 71 n., 343 n., 349, 386

William *de palacio*, 38, 379; John, *socius* of, 379 n.

William of Malmesbury, 22

William, priest and sub-tenant, 71 n.

William, priest, tenant of Besford, 126 n. 12

William, s. of Ansculf the sheriff, 190

Winchester (Hants), bishop of, 68; *see also* Fox, Richard; Ilchester, Richard of; Pontissara, John de

Winchester, diocese of, 48, 411 f.

Winchester, Franciscan friary at, 377 n.

Winchester, Walter of, abbot of Westminster (1175–90), 56, 81, 94 n., 164 n., 338 n., 373, 386 n., 388

Windsor (Berks.): Forest, 301, 338 n.; manor, 27, 338, 340 f., 343, 357, 359

Windsor, Sir John (d. 1414), 382

Windsor, William of, s. of Edward III (d. 1348), 376 n., 377

Winneledun', Richard, 110 n., 115 n.

Wode, William atte, of Feering, and Margery, his wife, 422

Woderove, Walter, 115 n.

Woking (Surr.), 307

Wolsey, Thomas, archbishop of York (d. 1530), 384 n.

Woodham (Surr.), 301, 302 n., 359 n.

Woodstock, Edmund of, earl of Kent (d. 1330), 377

Woodstock, Thomas of, duke of Gloucester (d. 1397), and Eleanor, his wife (d. 1399), 380, 397

Woodville, Elizabeth, wife of Edward IV (d. 1492), 362, 398

Wool, sales of, 137, 139 f., 148, 150

Worcester, bishop of, *see* Montacute, Simon; Orleton, Adam

Worcester, diocese of, 60, 412

Worcester, Roger of, 56 n.

Wroth, John, jnr., 423

Wroxhille, Hamo de, 375, 392

Wudegar, William de, and Robert, his son, 390

Wulnoth, abbot of Westminster (c. 1020–49), 17 f., 24 n.

Wulsin, abbot of Westminster (958–993/7), 17 f.

Wyfold, Nicholas, mayor of London (d. 1456), 385 n.

Wykebourne, John (i), 289 n., 310

Wykebourne, John (ii), 289

Wylcockes, John, 329

Wynbush, Alice, 288 n.

Yate, Alice, 280

Yeoveney (Midd.), 415; chapel, 349 n., 409; contractual tenancies, 249 n., 444; demesne, 128, 135, 138 n., 428; manor, 226, 228 f., 354 n., 355; meadows, 128, 235; rents, 231 n., 440, 444; tenant-land, 122 n., 128, 428; virgate, 235; *see also* Staines and Yeoveney

York, diocese, 412